CASES IN MARKETING MANAGEMENT

Sixth Edition

Kenneth L. Bernhardt
College of Business Administration
Georgia State University

Thomas C. Kinnear
School of Business Administration
University of Michigan

IRWIN

Burr Ridge, IL 60521
Boston, MA 02116

Executive editor: Rob Zwettler
Developmental editor: Heather McCammond-Watts
Marketing manager: Jim Lewis
Project editor: Waivah Clement
Production manager: Laurie Kersch
Designer: Mercedes Santos
Art studio: Benoit Associates
Compositor: Better Graphics, Inc.
Typeface: 10.5/12 Times Roman
Printer: R. R. Donnelley & Sons Company

Library of Congress Cataloging-in-Publication Data

Bernhardt, Kenneth L., 1944–
     Cases in marketing management / Kenneth L. Bernhardt, Thomas C.
Kinnear.—6th ed.
          p.   cm. -- (The Irwin series in marketing)
     Includes bibliographical references.
     ISBN 0-256-12246-6
     1. Marketing—Management—Case studies. 2. Marketing—Decision
making—Case studies. I. Kinnear, Thomas C., 1943–   . II. Title.
III. Series.
     HF5415.13.B448   1994
     658.8—dc20   93–5594

Printed in the United States of America
1 2 3 4 5 6 7 8 9 0 DO 0 9 8 7 6 5 4 3

To Kathy and Karen
To Connie, Maggie, and Jamie

THE IRWIN SERIES IN MARKETING

Gilbert A. Churchill, Jr., Consulting Editor
University of Wisconsin, Madison

Alreck & Settle
The Survey Research Handbook, 1/e

Arens & Bovee
Contemporary Advertising, 5/e

Belch & Belch
Introduction to Advertising and Promotion:
An Integrated Marketing Communications Approach, 2/e

Bernhardt & Kinnear
Cases in Marketing Management, 6/e

Bonoma & Kosnik
Marketing Management: Text & Cases, 1/e

Boyd & Walker
Marketing Management: A Strategic Approach, 1/e

Boyd, Westfall & Stasch
Marketing Research: Text and Cases, 7/e

Burstiner
Basic Retailing, 2/e

Cadotte
The Market Place: A Strategic Marketing Simulation, 1/e

Cateora
International Marketing, 8/e

Churchill, Ford & Walker
Sales Force Management, 4/e

Cole
Consumer and Commercial Credit Management, 9/e

Cravens
Strategic Marketing, 4/e

Cravens & Lamb
Strategic Marketing Management Cases, 4/e

Crawford
New Products Management, 4/e

Dillon, Madden & Firtle
Essentials of Marketing Research, 1/e

Dillon, Madden & Firtle
Marketing Research in a Marketing Environment, 3/e

Engel, Warshaw & Kinnear
Promotional Strategy, 8/e

Faria, Nulsen & Roussos
Compete, 4/e

Futrell
ABC's of Selling, 4/e

Futrell
Fundamentals of Selling, 4/e

Hawkins, Best & Coney
Consumer Behavior, 5/e

Kerin, Hartley, Rudelius & Berkowitz
Marketing, 4/e

Lambert & Stock
Strategic Logistics Management, 3/e

Lehmann
Market Research and Analysis, 3/e

Lehmann & Winer
Analysis for Marketing Planning, 3/e

Lehmann & Winer
Product Management, 1/e

Levy & Weitz
Retailing Management, 1/e

Mason, Mayer & Wilkinson
Modern Retailing, 6/e

Mason, Mayer & Ezell
Retailing, 5/e

Mason & Perreault
The Marketing Game!, 2/e

McCarthy & Perreault
Basic Marketing: A Global-Managerial Approach, 11/e

McCarthy & Perreault
Essentials of Marketing: A Global-Managerial Approach, 6/e

Patton
Sales Sim, 1/e

Peter & Donnelly
A Preface to Marketing Management, 6/e

Peter & Donnelly
Marketing Management: Knowledge and Skills, 3/e

Peter & Olson
Consumer Behavior and Marketing Strategy, 3/e

Peter & Olson
Understanding Consumer Behavior, 1/e

Quelch & Farris
Cases in Advertising and Promotion Management, 4/e

Quelch, Dolan & Kosnik
Marketing Management: Text & Cases, 1/e

Smith & Quelch
Ethics in Marketing, 1/e

Stanton, Buskirk & Spiro
Management of a Sales Force, 8/e

Thompson & Stappenbeck
The Marketing Strategy Game, 1/e

Walker, Boyd & Larréché
Marketing Strategy: Planning and Implementation, 1/e

Weitz, Castleberry & Tanner
Selling: Building Partnerships, 1/e

Preface

Marketing is an exciting and dynamic discipline. Unfortunately, much of the excitement is hidden among the definitions and descriptions of concepts that are a necessary part of basic marketing textbooks. We believe that one way to make the study of marketing exciting and dynamic is to use cases. Cases allow the student to work on real marketing problems, to develop an appreciation for the types of problems that exist in the real world of marketing, and to develop the skills of analysis and decision making so necessary for success in marketing and other areas of business. Cases represent as close an approximation of the realities of actually working in marketing as is possible without taking a job in the field.

Your task as a user of this casebook is to work hard to develop well-reasoned solutions to the problems confronting the decision maker in each of the cases. A framework to assist you in developing solutions is presented in Part 1 of this book. Basically, you will be using this, or some other framework suggested by your instructor, to analyze the cases in this book. By applying this framework to each case that you are assigned, you will develop your analytic skills. Like all skills, you will find this difficult at first. However, as you practice, you will get better, until it will become second nature to you. This is exactly the same way one develops athletic or musical skills.

The cases in this book represent a broad range of marketing problems. The book contains consumer and industrial cases, profit and nonprofit cases, social marketing cases, specific marketing area cases, and general cases, plus cases on marketing and public policy. Each case is designed to fit into a specific section of a course in marketing management. The cases are long and complex enough to require good analysis, but not so long and complex as to be overly burdensome. Within sections, cases do vary in terms of difficulty and complexity.

Users of the first five editions will note that the fundamental thrust and positioning remains the same in this edition. However, we do note the following changes. First, 15 new cases have been added. Second, a number of cases with greater complexity have been added to allow more in-depth work. Third, in order to reflect the trend toward the globalization of marketing activities, we have added a number of new cases that address significant international marketing issues.

This book contains 40 cases and 2 case-related exercises. Nineteen of the cases and both exercises were written by the authors of this book. In some instances we had a coauthor, and we have noted the names of the coauthors on the title pages of the cases concerned. We wish to thank these coauthors for their assistance and for allowing us to use the cases: Richard Aiken, Eric Andrew, Bruce Bassett, Stephen Becker, Danny Bellenger, Merle Crawford, Craig Ehrnst, Matthew Hausmann, Tom Ingram, Susan Johnstal, Constance Kinnear, Brian Murray, Joanne Novak, James Novo, Martin Schreiber, Jos Viehoff, and John Wright.

We would like to thank the executives of the organizations who allowed us to develop cases about their situations and who have released these cases for use in this book.

The remaining 21 cases were written by many distinguished marketing casewriters. We appreciate them allowing us to reproduce their cases here. The names of each of these persons are noted on the title page of the cases concerned. They are: Reinhard Angelmar, M. Edgar Barrett, Daniel C. Bello, Christopher D. Buehler, Helen Chase, Mort Ettinger, H. Michael Hayes, Shreekant G. Joag, Fred W. Kniffin, Zarrel V. Lambert, James M. Lattin, Daniel Lindley, Patrick Murphy, James E. Nelson, Michael Pearce, Christian Pinson, Adrian B. Ryans, James Scott, Ronald Stiff, and John Wright.

We were helped in selecting cases for this edition by the following people who responded to our survey: Wendy L. Acker, Avila College; Julian Andorka, DePaul University; Thomas J. Babb, West Liberty State College; Joseph A. Bellizzi, Arizona State University–West; Deirdre Bird, Northeastern University; Charles Born, Golden Gate University; Mary Lynn Buck, Ferris State University; Robert E. Burnkrant, The Ohio State University; Charles R. Canedy III, University of Hartford; W. Fred Chatman, Jr., Presbyterian College; Henry C.K. Chen, University of West Florida; Yusuf A. Choudhoy, University of Baltimore; Susan Cisco, Oakton Community College; Paul Cohen, Castleton State College; Richard Cooley, California State University–Chico; Jerry A. Cooper, Southern Oregon State College; Philip Cooper, Loyola College; Michael W. Couture, University of Missouri–Columbia; Melvin R. Crask, University of Georgia; Roger Davis, Baylor University; M. Wayne DeLozier, Nicholls State University; Peter R. Dickson, The Ohio State University; Robert A. Fischer, Northeastern University; Heidi Foreman, Columbia College; Irene R. Foster, Vanderbilt University; George Galiouridis, Webber College; Robert L. Goldman, Golden Gate University; John R. Grabner, The Ohio State University; Jim Hazeltine, Northeastern Illinois University; Tony L. Henthorne, University of Southern Mississippi; Susan Hibbins, John Carroll University; William G. Hines, Northeastern University; Thomas F. Hitzelberger, Southern Oregon State College; John W. Hummel, St. Michael's College; Don Jackson, Ferris State University; Keren Ami Johnson, Old Dominion University; Kissan Joseph, Purdue University; Norman Kangun, Clemson University; Debora A.

Kielcover, Calvin College; John A. Kuehn, University of Missouri–Columbia; Virginia Langrehr, Valparaiso University; Robert Brock Lawes, Chaminade University; Paul A. Lawhorne, Bowie State University; Robert Lawrence, South Carolina State University; David Lohmann, Hawaii Pacific University; Peter M. Lynagh, University of Baltimore; Terry A. Madoch, Elmhurst College; Ernest Maier, Lawrence Technological University; Jennifer Meoli, Elizabethtown College; Stephen J. Miller, Oklahoma State University; Anusree Mitra, American University; Janet B. Monroe, Wayne State University; Janet Y. Murray, University of Missouri–Columbia; Harold E. Oakley, Belleville Area College; Christie H. Paksoy, University of North Carolina–Charlotte; Yigang Pan, DePaul University; A. William Pollman, University of Wisconsin–LaCrosse; Jay E. Poutinen, University of Wisconsin–Stevens Point; Marco Protano, Northeastern University; Pradeep A. Rau, George Washington University; Nina M. Ray, Boise State University; Mary Anne Raymond, American University; Irving E. Richards, Cuyahoga Community College; Lee Richardson, University of Baltimore; Donald P. Robin, Southern Mississippi Univeristy; Robert S. Russell, Northeastern University; William J. Schmid, Northeastern University; Harold S. Sekiguchi, University of Nevada; William L. Shanklin, Kent State University; Alan Terrence Shao, University of North Carolina–Charlotte; Richard Siedlecki, Emory University and Georgia State University; Stanley F. Slater, University of Colorado–Colorado Springs; James V. Spiers, Arizona State University; Vlasis Stathakopoulos, University of Hartford; John E. Swan, University of Alabama–Birmingham; Fred Trawick, University of Alabama–Birmingham; Frances G. Tucker, Syracuse University; Jonn S. Wagle, Northern Illinois University; Jay C. Wayne, Golden Gate University; James E. Welch, Kentucky Wesleyan College; Richard Wilcox, Rockford College; Edward D. Wirth, Jr., Florida Institute of Technology; and George M. Zinkhan, University of Houston.

We would also like to thank our colleagues at Georgia State University, the University of Michigan, and the Case Research Association for their helpful comments and their classroom testing of cases. Finally, we want to acknowledge the help in the many tasks associated with the editing and production of the book we received from Heather McCammond-Watts and from Waivah Clement, Jim Lewis, and Rob Zwettler at Irwin.

Kenneth L. Bernhardt
Thomas C. Kinnear

Contents _____

Part 1

An Orientation to the Case Method

Chapter 1

Note to the Student on the Case Method

The case method is different from other methods of teaching, and it requires that students take an active role rather than a passive one. The case method places the student in a simulated business environment and substitutes the student in the place of the business manager required to make a set of decisions. To define it, a case is:

> typically a record of a business issue which actually has been faced by business executives, together with surrounding facts, opinions, and prejudices upon which the executives had to depend. These real and particularized cases are presented to students for considered analysis, open discussion, and final decision as to the type of action which should be taken.[1]

With the case method the process of arriving at an answer is what is important. The instructor's expectation is that the student will develop an ability to make decisions, to support those decisions with appropriate analysis, and to learn to communicate ideas both orally and in writing. The student is required to determine the problem as well as the solution. This method of teaching thus shifts much of the responsibility to the student, and a great deal of time is required on the part of the student.

The case method often causes a great deal of insecurity on the part of students who are required to make decisions often with very little information and limited time. There is no single right answer to any of the cases in this book, an additional source of insecurity. The goal is not to develop a set of right answers, but to learn to reason well with the data available. This process is truly learning by doing.

Studying under the case method will result in the development of skills in critical thinking. The student will learn how to effectively reason when dealing with specific problems. The development of communication skills is also

---

[1] Charles I. Gragg, "Because Wisdom Can't Be Told," *Harvard Alumni Bulletin*, October 19, 1940.

important, and students will learn to present their analysis in a cogent and convincing manner. They must defend their analysis and plan of action against the criticism of others in the class. In the class discussion, individual students may find that the opinions of other members of the class differ from their own. In some cases this will be because the individual has overlooked certain important points or that some factors have been weighted more heavily compared to the weighting used by other students. The process of presenting and defending conflicting points of view causes individual members of the class to reconsider the views they had of the case before the discussion began. This leads to a clearer perception of problems, a recognition of the many and often conflicting interpretations of the facts and events in the case, and a greater awareness of the complexities with which management decisions are reached.

In preparing for class using the case method, the student should first read the case quickly. The goal is to gain a feel for the type of problem presented in the case, the type of organization involved, and so on. Next, the student should read the case thoroughly to learn all the key facts in the case. The student should not blindly accept all the data presented, as not all information is equally reliable or relevant. As part of the process of mastering the facts, it frequently will be desirable to utilize the numerical data presented in the case to make any possible calculations and comparisons that will help analyze the problems involved in the case. The case will have to be read a number of times before the analysis is completed.

The student must add to the facts by making reasonable assumptions regarding many aspects of the situation. Business decision making is rarely based on perfect information. All of the cases in this book are actual business cases, and the student is provided with all the information that the executives involved had at their disposal. Often students cannot believe the low level of information available for decision making, but this is often the case. What is required in those situations is the making of reasonable assumptions and learning to make decisions under uncertainty. There is often a strong reluctance on the part of the student to do this, but the ability to make decisions based on well-reasoned assumptions is a skill that must be developed for a manager to be truly effective.

Once the student has mastered the facts in the case, the next step is to identify and specify the issues and problems toward which the executive involved should be directing his or her attention. The issues may be very obscure. Learning to separate problems from symptoms is an important skill to learn. Often there will be a number of subissues involved, and it will be necessary to break the problem down into component parts.

The next step in the student's case preparation is to identify alternative courses of action. Usually there are a number of possible solutions to the problems in the case, and the student should be careful not to lock in on only one alternative before several possible alternatives have been thoroughly evaluated.

The next step is to evaluate each of the alternative plans of action. It is at this stage of the analysis that the student is required to marshall and analyze all the facts for each alternative program. The assumptions the student is required to make are very important here, and the student must apply all the analytical skills possible, including both qualitative and quantitative.

After all the alternatives have been thoroughly analyzed, the student must make a decision concerning the specific course of action to take. It should be recognized that several of the alternatives may "work," and that there are a number of different ways of resolving the issues in the case. The important consideration is that the plan of action actually decided upon has been thoroughly analyzed from all angles, is internally consistent, and has a high probability of meeting the manager's objectives.

Once an overall strategy has been determined, it is important that consideration be given to the implementation of that strategy. At this stage, the student must determine who is to do what, when, and how. A professor may start out a class by asking the question, "What should Mr. Jones do tomorrow?" Unless the students have given some thought to the implementation of the strategy decided upon, they will be unprepared for such a question. Improper implementation of an excellent strategy may doom it to failure, so it is important to follow through with appropriate analysis at this stage.

During the class discussion the instructor will act more as a moderator than a lecturer, guiding the discussion and calling on students for their opinions. A significant amount of learning will take place by participating in the discussion. The goal is for the students to integrate all their ideas, relating them to the goals of the company, the strengths and weaknesses of the company and its competition, the way consumers buy, and the resources available. A suggested framework for the integration of these ideas is presented in the next chapter of this book in the appendix titled "Outline for case analysis."

The student's classroom discussion should avoid the rehashing, without analysis, of case facts. Students should recognize that the professor and all the other students in the class have thoroughly read the case and are familiar with the facts. The objective, therefore, is to interpret the facts and use them to support the proposed plan of action. The case method obviously requires a great deal of preparation time by the student. The payoff is that, after spending this time adequately preparing each of the steps described, the student will have developed the ability to make sound marketing management decisions.

Chapter 2

Introduction to Marketing Decision Making

In Chapter 1, you were introduced to your role in the execution of an effective case course in marketing. In summary, the primary task is to complete a competent analysis of the cases assigned to you. If you have never undertaken the analysis of a marketing case before, you are probably wondering just how you should go about doing this. Is there some framework that is appropriate for this task? Indeed, there are a number of such frameworks. The purpose of this chapter is to present one such framework to you. We think you will find it useful in analyzing the cases in this book.

An Outline for Case Analysis

The appendix to this chapter is the summary document for the approach we believe that you should use for case analysis. We suggest that you apply the types of questions listed there in your analysis. Figure 2–1 provides an overview of this outline. Basically, we are suggesting that you begin by doing a complete analysis of the *situation* facing the organization in the case. This *situation analysis* includes an assessment of (1) the nature of demand for the product, (2) the extent of demand, (3) the nature of competition, (4) the environmental climate, (5) the stage of the life cycle for the product, (6) the skills of the firm, (7) the financial resources of the firm, and (8) the distribution structure. In some cases legal aspects may also form part of a good situation analysis. The premise here is that one cannot begin to make decisions until a thorough understanding of the situation at hand is obtained.

Once a detailed situation analysis is prepared, one is in a position to summarize the *problems* and *opportunities* that arise out of the situation analysis. These problems and opportunities provide an organized summary of the situation analysis. This in turn should lead to the generation of a set of *alternatives* that are worthy of being considered as solutions to the problems and actualizers of the opportunities.

FIGURE 2-1   Overview of a framework for case analysis

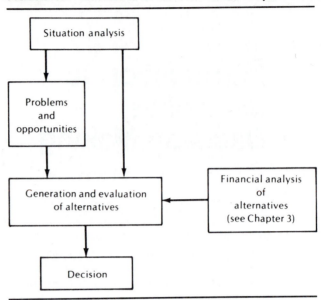

These alternatives are then *evaluated* using arguments generated from (1) the detailed situation analysis, (2) the summary statement of problems and opportunities, and (3) relevant financial analysis (break-even points, market shares, and so on). The use of financial analysis is discussed in Chapter 3. The point here is that we use the situation analysis to generate and evaluate alternative programs. The pros and cons of each alternative are weighed as part of this evaluation and a *decision* is then reached.

A Good Case Analysis

The question naturally arises: In applying the outline in the appendix to a case, how do I know when I have done a good analysis? The purpose of this section is to raise some points that are often used by instructors to evaluate either an oral or written analysis.

1. Be complete. It is imperative that the case analysis be complete. There are two dimensions to this issue. First is that each area of the situation analysis must be discussed, problems and opportunities must be identified, alternatives must be presented and evaluated using the situation analysis and relevant financial analysis, and a decision must be made. An analysis that omits parts of the situation analysis, or only recognizes one alternative, is not a good analysis. Second, each area above must be covered in good depth and with insight.

2. *Avoid rehashing case facts.* Every case has a lot of factual information. A good analysis uses facts that are relevant to the situation at hand to make summary points of analysis. A poor analysis just restates or rehashes these facts without making relevant summary comments. Consider the use of a set of financial facts that might appear in a case:

Rehash: The current ratio is 1.5:1, cash on hand is $15,000, retained earnings are $50,000.

Analysis: Because of a very weak financial position, as demonstrated by a poor cash position and current ratio, the firm will be constrained in the activities it can undertake to ones requiring little immediate cash outlay.

3. *Make reasonable assumptions.* Every case is incomplete in terms of some piece of information that you would like to have. We would, of course, like to have all the necessary information presented to us in each case. This is not possible for two reasons. First, it would make the cases far too long to be capable of being analyzed in a reasonable period of time. Second, and more important, incomplete information is an accurate reflection of the real world. All marketing decisions are made on the basis of incomplete information. Often, it just costs too much or takes too long to collect the desired information.

A good case analysis must make realistic assumptions to fill in the gaps of information in the case. For example, the case may not describe the purchase decision process for the product of interest. A poor analysis would either omit mentioning this or just state that no information is available. A good analysis would attempt to present this purchase decision process by classifying the product (a shopping good?) and drawing on the student's real-life experience. Could you not describe the purchase decision process for carpeting, even though you have never read a research report about it?

The reasonableness of your assumptions will be challenged by your fellow students and instructor. This is one of the things that makes case discussions exciting. The point is that it is better to make your assumptions explicit and incorporate them in your analysis than to use them implicitly or not make them at all. If we make explicit assumptions we can later come back and see if our assumptions were correct or not.

4. *Don't confuse symptoms with problems.* In summarizing a firm's problems a poor analysis confuses the symptoms with real problems. For example, one might list two problems as (1) sales are down and (2) sales force turnover is high. This would not be correct. These are symptoms. The real problem is identified by answering the question: Why are sales down or why is sales force turnover high? For example, sales force turnover may be high due to inadequate sales training. But this may not yet be the root problem. You still need to ask: Why is sales training inadequate? It may be that the sales manager has ignored this area through his or her lack of knowledge of how to train people. What you do is keep asking "why" until you are satisfied that you have identified the root problem.

5. *Don't confuse opportunities with taking action.* One can recognize an opportunity but not take any action related to it. For example, a large market for a product may exist. This is an opportunity. However, a firm may decide not to compete in this market due to lack of resources or skills or the existence of strong competition. Decisions involve the complex trading-off of many problems and opportunities. Thus, don't make statements that direct action—"target to . . . , promote as . . . ," and the like—as opportunity statements.

6. *Deal with objectives realistically.* Most cases present a statement from management about their objectives. For example, it might say they want a sales growth rate of 25 percent per year. Good analysis critically evaluates statements of objectives and revises them if necessary. Then it uses these revised objectives as part of the argument about which alternative to select. Poor analysis either ignores the stated objectives or accepts them at face value.

7. *Recognize alternatives.* A good analysis explicitly recognizes and discusses alternative action plans. In some cases, these alternatives are stated in the case. In other cases, the student must develop alternatives beyond those stated in the case. A poor analysis explicitly recognizes only one or two alternatives or only takes the ones explicitly stated in the case.

8. *Don't be assertive.* In some case analyses, the decision that was made is clear to the reader or listener in about the first sentence of the situation analysis. The whole rest of the analysis is then a justification of the desired solution. This type of analysis is very poor. It has asserted an answer before completing a situation analysis. Usually, other alternatives are ignored or treated as all bad, and the desired solution is treated as all good. You must do your situation analysis and recognize alternatives before evaluating them and reaching a decision.

9. *Discuss the pros and cons of each alternative.* Every alternative always has pros and cons. A good analysis explicitly discusses these. In a poor analysis there is no explicit discussion of the pros and cons of each alternative. Problem and opportunity statements serve as the basis of your pro (opportunities) and con (problems) discussion. Different ones relate to specific alternatives.

10. *Make effective use of financial and other quantitative information.* Financial data (break-even points and so on) and information derived from other quantitative analyses can add a great deal to a good case analysis. Totally ignoring these aspects or handling them improperly results in a poor case analysis. This analysis should be presented in detail in a written appendix or in class if asked for. However, in the body of a paper or in an oral discussion present only the summary conclusions out of the analysis. Say "The break-even point is 220,000 units," and be prepared to present the detail if asked.

11. *Reach a clear decision.* You must reach a clear decision. You might like to hedge your bets and say "maybe this, maybe that." However, part of the skill of decision making is to be forced to reach a decision under ambiguous circumstances and then be prepared to defend this decision. This does not mean that you do not recognize limitations of your position or positive aspects of other positions. It just means that despite all that, you have reached a particular decision.

12. *Make good use of evidence developed in your situation analysis.* In reaching a decision, a good analysis reaches a decision that is logically consistent with the situation analysis that was done. This is the ultimate test of an analysis. Other students may disagree with your situation analysis and thus your resultant conclusion, but they should not be able to fault the logical connection between your situation analysis and decision. If they can, you have a poor case analysis.

The "Outline for case analysis" contained in the appendix is designed to assist you in doing case analysis. You should keep the points stressed in this section in mind when you apply this outline.

Appendix

Outline for case analysis*

Overview of Analysis Structure

  I. Situation analysis
- A. Nature of demand.
- B. Extent of demand.
- C. Nature of competition.
- D. Environmental climate.
- E. Stage of product life cycle.
- F. Cost structure of the industry.
- G. Skills of the firm.
- H. Financial resources of the firm.
- I. Distribution structure.

 II. Problems and opportunities
- A. Key problem areas.
- B. Key opportunities.
- C. On balance, the situation is.

III. Generation and evaluation of alternative marketing programs
- A. Objectives defined.
- B. Marketing mix/program decisions.

IV. Decision

Details of Analysis Structure

  I. **SITUATION ANALYSIS**

    A. **Nature of demand**

The purpose of this section is to make *explicit* your beliefs and assumptions regarding the nature of the purchase decision process (consumer or industrial) for the goods or services under investigation. In case analysis we are concerned primarily with developing your *skills* of analysis to identify areas of problems and opportunities and in developing well-supported marketing program recommendations. Conflicting student beliefs and assumptions should lead to interesting and enlightening class discussion regarding the nature of the purchase decision process and its implication for marketing programs. We hope that through this type of class discussion, you will increase your sensitivity to, and understanding of, buyers and

---

* This outline is adapted from an unpublished note by Professor James R. Taylor of the University of Michigan. Used with permission.

their behavior. Again, the value of this type of analysis concerns its application to better *reasoned* and *supported* marketing program decisions. Hopefully, the development of your skills in this area has value in improving your *judgment capabilities* and in increasing your understanding of marketing decision making.

Analysis areas and questions
1. How do buyers (consumer and industrial) *currently* go about buying existing products or services? Describe the main types of behavior patterns and attitudes.
   a. Number of stores shopped or industrial sources considered.
   b. Degree of overt information seeking.
   c. Degree of brand awareness and loyalty.
   d. Location of product category decision—home or point of sale.
   e. Location of brand decision—home or point of sale.
   f. Sources of product information and current awareness and knowledge levels.
   g. Who makes the purchase decision—male, female, adult, child, purchasing agent, buying committee, so on?
   h. Who influences the decision maker?
   i. Individual or group decision (computers versus candy bar).
   j. Duration of the decision process (repeat, infrequent, or new purchase situation).
   k. Buyer's interest, personal involvement or excitement regarding the purchase (hairpins versus trip to Caribbean).
   l. Risk or uncertainty of negative purchase outcome—high, medium, or low (specialized machinery versus hacksaw blades) (pencil versus hair coloring).
   m. Functional versus psychosocial considerations (electric drill versus new dress).
   n. Time of consumption (gum versus dining room furniture).

   Basically, we are attempting to determine the *who, what, where, when, why,* and *how* of the purchase decision.

   Note: The key to using the above analysis is to ask what are the implications for marketing programs. For example, if the purchase (brand) decision is made in the store and branding is not important to the buyers, what implication does this have for national TV advertising versus in-store display? Do you see how you might *use* this information to support a recommendation for intensive distribution and point-of-purchase promotion and display?

2. Can the market be meaningfully segmented or broken into several homogeneous groups with respect to "what they want" and "how they buy"? Criteria:
   a. Age.

    b. Family life cycle.
    c. Geographic location.
    d. Heavy versus light users.
    e. Nature of the buying process.
    f. Product usage.

Note: For each case situation, you should determine whether a more effective marketing program could be developed for each segment versus having an overall program for all segments. The real issue is whether tailoring your program to a segment will give you a competitive advantage. Of course, there may be negatives to this strategy in terms of volume and cost considerations.

B. Extent of demand

The purpose of this section is to evaluate demand in an aggregate and quantitative sense. We are basically concerned with the actual or potential size of the overall market and developing sound estimates of company sales potential.

Analysis areas and questions
1. What is the size of the market (units and dollars) now and what will the future hold?
2. What are the current market shares, and what are the selective demand trends (units and dollars)?
3. Is it best to analyze the market on an aggregate or on a segmented basis?

Note: We are basically concerned with making *explicit* assumptions regarding primary and selective demand trends. These estimates are critical to determining the profit (loss) potential of alternative marketing programs.

C. Nature of competition

The purpose of this section is to evaluate the present and future structure of competition. The key is to understand how the buyer evaluates alternative products or services relative to his or her needs.

Analysis areas and questions
1. What is the present and future structure of competition?
    a. Number of competitors (5 versus 2,000).
    b. Market shares.
    c. Financial resources.
    d. Marketing resources and skills.
    e. Production resources and skills.
2. What are the current marketing programs of established competitors? Why are they successful or unsuccessful?
3. Is there an opportunity for another competitor? Why?

4. What are the anticipated retaliatory moves of competitors? Can they neutralize different marketing programs we might develop?

Note: Failure to correctly evaluate demand and competition is one common reason for unprofitable marketing programs. Also, Sections A, B, and C are analysis areas particularly important in making decisions concerning "positioning" your product and developing the marketing program to support your positioning strategy.

D. Environmental climate

It's not hard to identify current marketing programs that have been highly disrupted by a changing environmental climate. The energy crisis together with pollution, safety, and consumerism concerns, can bring many such examples to mind. We are sure you can identify firms who have benefited from the energy crisis. The point is that the environment is constantly changing and those organizations which can adapt to change are the ones which enjoy long-run success.

Analysis areas and questions
1. What are the relevant social, political, economic, and technological trends?
2. How do you evaluate these trends? Do they represent opportunities or problems?

E. Stage of product life cycle

The purpose of this section is to make explicit assumptions about where a product is in its life cycle. This is important because the effectiveness of particular marketing variables may vary by stages of the life cycle.

Analysis areas and questions
1. In what stage of the life cycle is the product category?
    a. What is the chronological age of the product category? (Younger more favorable than older?)
    b. What is the state of the consumers' knowledge of the product category? (More complete the knowledge—more unfavorable?)
2. What market characteristics support your stage of life-cycle evaluation?

F. Cost structure of the industry

Here we are concerned with the amount and composition of the marginal or additional cost of supplying increased output. It can be argued that the lower these costs, the easier it may be to cover the costs of developing an effective marketing program (see accompanying table). Basically, one is relating the level of fixed cost to variable cost.

	Marginal costs	
	High*	Low†
Selling price per unit	$1.00	$1.00
Variable costs per unit	0.80	0.10
Contribution per unit	$0.20	$0.90

* Such as the garment and auto industries.
† Such as the hotel and telephone industries.

G. Skills of the firm

The purpose of this section is to critically evaluate the organization making the decision. Here, we effectively place limits on what they are capable of accomplishing.

Analysis areas and questions
1. Do we have the skills and experience to perform the functions necessary to be in this business?
    a. Marketing skills.
    b. Production skills.
    c. Management skills.
    d. Financial skills.
    e. R&D skills.
2. How do our skills compare to competitors?
    a. Production fit.
    b. Marketing fit.
    c. Etc.

H. Financial resources of the firm

Analysis areas and questions
1. Do we have the funds to support an effective marketing program?
2. Where are the funds coming from, and when will they be available?

I. Distribution structure

The purpose of this area is to identify and evaluate the availability of channels of distribution.

Analysis areas and questions
1. What channels exist, and can we gain access to the channels?
2. Cost versus revenue from different channels?
3. Feasibility of using multiple channels?
4. Nature and degree of within and between channel competition?
5. Trends in channel structure?
6. Requirements of different channels for promotion and margin?
7. Will it be profitable for particular channels to handle my product?

II. PROBLEMS AND OPPORTUNITIES

Here we prepare a definite listing of *key* problems and opportunities identified from the situation analysis which relate to the specific issues or decision questions faced by management.

A. Key problem areas

B. Key opportunities

C. On balance, the situation is:
1. Very favorable.
2. Somewhat favorable.
3. Neutral.
4. Somewhat unfavorable.
5. Very unfavorable.

Note: At this point, the critical issue is whether a profitable marketing program can be formulated or whether a current marketing program needs to be changed in order to overcome the problem areas and/or take advantage of opportunities.

III. GENERATION AND EVALUATION OF ALTERNATIVE MARKETING PROGRAMS

A marketing program consists of a series of marketing mix decisions which represent an integrated and consistent "action plan" for achieving predetermined goals. Different marketing programs may be required for various target segments. For a given target segment, alternative programs should be formulated and evaluated as to the effectiveness of each in achieving predetermined goals.

A. Objectives defined
1. Target market segments identified.
2. Volume to be sold (dollars or units).
3. Profit analysis (contribution analysis, break-even analysis, ROI, etc.).

B. Marketing mix/program decisions
1. Product decisions
   a. Develop new product(s).
   b. Change current product(s).
   c. Add or drop product from line.
   d. Product positioning.
   e. Branding (national, private, secondary).
2. Distribution decisions
   a. Intensity of distribution (intensive to exclusive).
   b. Multiple channels.
   c. Types of wholesalers and retailers (discounters, etc.).
   d. Degree of channel directness.
3. Promotion decisions
   a. Mix of personal selling, advertising, dealer incentives, and sales promotion.

      b. Branding—family versus individual.
      c. Budget.
      d. Message.
      e. Media.
4. Price decisions
      a. Price level (above, same, or below).
      b. Price variation (discount structure, geographic).
      c. Margins.
      d. Administration of price level.
      e. Price leadership.

Note: The above four decision areas involve specific strategy issues which together form a marketing program.

The key to effective marketing decision making is to evaluate alternative marketing programs using information from the situation analysis. The pros and cons for each alternative should be presented and discussed.

IV. DECISION

The outcome of the evaluation of alternatives is a decision. You must make a decision. Case analysis is designed to develop your skills in making well-supported and reasoned marketing decisions. The quality of your reasoning is much more important than reaching any particular decision. Generally, if your situation analysis is different (you perceive the facts differently and have made different assumptions) from someone else's, you should reach different decisions.

Chapter 3

Financial Analysis for Marketing Decision Making

In Chapter 2, we laid out an approach to marketing decision making. The "Outline for case analysis" summarized this approach. There is, however, one more important aspect of a competent case analysis that was not presented in that outline. This is the financial analysis of the alternatives presented in a case.

The ultimate goals of all marketing activities are usually expressed in financial terms. The company has a particular return on investment in mind, or growth in earnings per share. Proposed marketing activities must thus be evaluated for their financial implications. Can you imagine asking your boss for $1 million for a new distribution center or an advertising program without having to present the financial implications of such a request? It does not happen in the real marketing world, nor should it happen in a good case analysis.

Financial analysis can be complex. Our purpose here is to present some simple financial calculations that can be useful in case analysis. More sophisticated financial techniques are left to courses in financial management. Basically, the advanced techniques add little to the understanding of the cases in this book and take too much time and effort for the reader to implement.

It should clearly be understood that financial considerations are only one aspect in the evaluation of marketing alternatives. Marketing alternatives cannot be reduced to a set of numbers. Qualitative aspects derived from the situation analysis are also relevant. Sometimes the qualitative aspects are consistent in terms of pointing to an alternative to select. In other cases, they may point to different alternatives. The task of the student is to formulate both types of arguments for each alternative, and to select an alternative based upon which arguments the student thinks should carry the most weight.

This chapter assumes that the student is familiar with elementary financial accounting concepts. What we will present here are some useful concepts not usually presented in basic accounting courses.

Contribution

Contribution per unit is defined as the difference between the selling price of an item and the variable costs of producing and selling that item. It is in essence the amount of money per unit available to the marketer to cover fixed production costs, corporate overhead and, having done that, to yield a profit. So, if a manufacturer sells an item for $12.00, and the variable costs are $8.40, then

$$\text{Contribution per unit} = \text{Selling price} - \text{Variable costs}$$
$$= \$12.00 \quad - \$8.40$$
$$= \$ \ 3.60$$

Each unit this company sells gives it $3.60 to cover fixed costs.

Total contribution is the contribution per unit times the number of units sold. So, if this firm sold 20,000 units:

$$\text{Total contribution} = \text{Contribution per unit} \times \text{Units sold}$$
$$= \$ \ 3.60 \times 20,000$$
$$= \$72,000$$

If the total relevant fixed costs of this product were $42,000, the *profit* earned by this product would be:

$$\text{Profit} = \text{Total contribution} - \text{Fixed costs}$$
$$= \$72,000 \quad - \$42,000$$
$$= \$30,000$$

Costs

In determining contributions and profit we used the terms *variable cost* and *fixed cost*. At this point we want to define them more formally. Variable costs are those costs that are fixed *per unit* and, therefore, vary in their total amount depending upon the number of units produced and sold. That is, it takes a certain amount of raw materials and labor to produce a unit of product. The more we produce, the more total variable costs are.

Fixed costs are costs that remain constant in *total amount* despite changes in the volume of production or sales. These costs would thus vary per unit depending upon the number of units produced or sold.

Sorting out which costs are variable and fixed is important in good case analysis. The rule to apply is: if it varies in *total* as volume changes, it is a variable cost. Thus, labor, raw materials, packaging, and salespersons' commissions would be variable costs. Note that all marketing costs except commissions would be considered fixed costs. Don't be fooled if a marketing cost or other fixed cost is presented in a per unit form. It may look like a variable cost, but it is not. It is only that much per unit at one given volume. For example, if we are told that advertising cost per unit will be $1, this means that at the end of the year when we divide total sales into advertising expenditures the result is expected to be $1 per unit. What we must be told is at what volume advertising is expected to be $1 per unit. If the expected volume level is 300,000 units, we then know that the firm intends to spend $300,000 ($1 × 300,000 units) on advertising. This $300,000 is a fixed cost. Note that if they sold less than 300,000 units, the cost per unit would exceed $1 and vice versa. So beware of fixed costs that are allocated to units and presented in a per unit form.

Break Even

A solid perspective on many marketing alternatives can often be obtained by determining the unit or dollar sales necessary to cover all relevant fixed costs. This sales level is called the break-even point. We define

1. Break-even point in units $= \dfrac{\text{Total fixed costs}}{\text{Contribution per unit}}$

2. Break-even point in dollars $= \dfrac{\text{Total fixed costs}}{1 - \dfrac{\text{Variable cost per unit}}{\text{Selling price per unit}}}$

or

$$= \begin{array}{c} \text{Break-even point} \\ \text{in units} \end{array} \times \begin{array}{c} \text{Selling price} \\ \text{per unit} \end{array}$$

Let's illustrate these definitions. Suppose that (1) direct labor is $7.50 per unit, (2) raw materials are $2 per unit, (3) selling price is $22 per unit, (4) advertising and sales force costs are $400,000, and (5) other relevant fixed costs are $100,000.

$$
\begin{aligned}
\text{Contribution per unit} &= \text{Selling price} - \text{Variable costs} \\
\text{Contribution per unit} &= \$22.00 - (\$7.50 + \$2.00) \\
&= \$22.00 - \$9.50 \\
&= \$12.50
\end{aligned}
$$

$$
\begin{aligned}
\text{Break-even point in units} &= \frac{\text{Total fixed costs}}{\text{Contribution per unit}} \\
&= \frac{\$400,000 + \$100,000}{\$12.50} \\
&= 40,000 \text{ units}
\end{aligned}
$$

$$
\begin{aligned}
\text{Break-even point in dollars} &= \frac{\$500,000}{1 - \dfrac{\$9.50}{\$22.00}} \\
&= \frac{\$500,000}{1 - 0.4318181} = \$880,000
\end{aligned}
$$

Alternatively

$$
\begin{aligned}
\text{Break-even point in dollars} &= 40,000 \times \$22.00 \text{ per unit} \\
&= \$880,000
\end{aligned}
$$

Profit Targets

Breaking even is not as much fun as making a profit. Thus, we often want to incorporate a profit target level into our calculations. Basically, we are answering the question: at what volume do we earn X profits? Covering a profit target is just like covering a fixed cost. So in the previous example, if we set $60,000 as our profit target we would have to sell an additional number of units equal to:

$$\text{Units to cover profit target} = \frac{\text{Profit target}}{\text{Contribution per unit}}$$
$$= \frac{\$60,000}{\$12.50} = 4,800 \text{ units}$$

Total units to reach this target is

$$40,000 + 4,800 = 44,800 \text{ or } \frac{\$500,000 + \$60,000}{\$12.50} = 44,800$$

Break-even analysis is a useful tool for comparing alternative marketing programs. It tells us how many units must be sold but does not help us with the critical question of how many units will be sold.

Market Share

$$\text{Market share} = \frac{\text{Company sales level}}{\text{Total market sales}}$$

This calculation adds perspective to proposed action plans. Suppose that the total market sales are 290,000 units and our sales level needed to break even is 40,000 units. Thus, the required market share to break even is:

$$\frac{40,000}{290,000} = 13.8\%$$

The question then to ask is whether this market share can be obtained with the proposed marketing program.

Capital Expenditures

Often a particular marketing program proposes expenditures for capital equipment. These would be fixed costs associated with the proposed program. Typically, they should not all be charged to the relevant fixed cost for that proposal. For example, suppose that $5 million are to be expended for equipment that will last 10 years. If we charge all this to the break-even calculation in year one, it will be very high. Further, for years 2 through 10, the break-even point will fall substantially. It is better to allocate this $5 million equally over the 10 years. Thus, $500,000 would be a relevant fixed cost in each year associated with the equipment. What one needs to do is to make some reasonable assumption about the useful life of capital assets and divide the total cost over this time period.

Relevant Costs

The issue often arises as to what fixed costs are relevant to a particular proposal. The rule to use is: A fixed cost is relevant if the expenditure varies due to the acceptance of that proposal. Thus, new equipment, new research and development, and so on, are relevant. Last year's advertising or previous research and development dollars, for example, do not vary with the current decision and thus are not a relevant cost of the proposed program. Past expenditures are referred to as *sunk costs*. They should not enter into current decisions. Decisions are future oriented.

Corporate overhead presents a special problem. Generally, it does not vary with a particular decision. We don't fire the president in selecting between marketing programs. However, in some instances, some overhead may be directly attributable to a particular decision. In this instance, it would be a relevant cost. We should recognize that to stay in business a firm must cover all its costs in the long run. Also, from a financial accounting point of view, all costs are relevant. This type of accounting is concerned with preparing income statements and balance sheets for reporting to investors. In marketing decision making we are interested in managerial, not financial, accounting. Managerial accounting is concerned with providing relevant information for decision making. It, therefore, only presents costs that are relevant to the decision being considered. Such things as allocated overhead or amortized research and development costs only serve to confuse future-oriented decisions.

Margins

Often a case will present us with a retail selling price, when what we really want to know is the manufacturer's selling price. To be able to work back to get the manufacturer's selling price, we must understand how channel margins work.

When firms buy a product at a particular price and attempt to sell it at a higher price, the difference between the cost price and the selling price is called margin or markup or mark-on. Thus,

$$\text{Selling price} = \text{Cost price} + \text{Margin}$$

An example could be:

$$\$1.00 = \$0.80 + \$0.20$$

So a company has bought a product for $0.80, added on a $0.20 margin, and is charging $1.00 for the product.

Margins are usually expressed as percentages. This raises the question as to the base on which the margin percentage should be expressed: the cost price or the selling price. Here, if the $0.20 margin is expressed as a percentage of selling price, the margin is $0.20/$1.00 = 20 percent. If it were expressed as a percentage of cost price, the margin is $0.20/$0.80 = 25 percent. The most common practice in marketing is to express margins as a percentage of selling price. Margins expressed in this fashion are easier to work with, especially in a multilevel channel situation. Unless explicitly stated otherwise, you may assume that all margins in the cases in this book use selling price as the relevant base.

A number of different types of margin-related problems arise. They include:

1. Determining the selling price, given you know the cost price and the percentage margin on selling price. Suppose that a retailer buys an appliance for $15 and wants to obtain a margin on selling price of 40 percent. What selling price must be charged? The answer $21 is not correct because this margin ($6 = $15 × 0.4) would be on cost price. To answer this question we must remember one fundamental relationship. This is that

$$Selling\ price\ =\ Cost\ price\ +\ Margin$$

Here we are taking selling price as the base equal to 100 percent, so we can write

$$100\% \ =\ \$15\ +\ 40\%$$

That is, the cost price plus the margin must add to 100 percent. Clearly the $15 must then be 60 percent of the desired selling price. Thus,

$$\begin{aligned} Derived\ selling\ price\ &=\ \$15/60\% \\ &=\ \$25 \end{aligned}$$

The dollar margin is then $10 which is $10/$25 = 40 percent of selling price.

The general rule then is to divide one minus the percentage margin expressed as a decimal on selling price, into the cost price. For example, if cost price is $105 and the margin on selling price is 22.5 percent, then the desired selling price is $105/(1 − 0.225) = $105/0.775 = $135.48.

2. Conversion of margin bases.   Sometimes a margin is given on a cost price basis, and we wish to convert it to a selling price base or vice versa. How do we make the conversion? Suppose that a product costs $4.50 and sells for $6.00. The margin is $1.50. On a selling price basis, the margin is $1.50/$6.00 = 25 percent. On a cost price basis, the margin is $1.50/$4.50 = 33.33 percent. The conversion from one percentage margin to the other is easy if we remember that selling price is composed of two parts: margin and cost.

For selling price base.

$$\begin{aligned} Selling\ price\ &=\ Margin\ +\ Cost \\ \$6.00\ &=\ \$1.50\ +\ \$4.50 \end{aligned}$$

or more important

$$100\% \ =\ 25\%\ +\ 75\%$$

For cost price base.

$$\begin{aligned} Selling\ price\ &=\ Margin\ +\ Cost \\ \$6.00\ &=\ \$1.50\ +\ \$4.50 \end{aligned}$$

but here the cost is the 100 percent base, so

$$\$6.00 = \$1.50 + 100\%$$

or

$$133.33\% = 33.33\% + 100\%$$

That is, the selling price should be thought of as 133.33 percent of the cost price.
Conversion from selling price to cost price base.

$$\text{Selling price} = \text{Margin} + \text{Cost}$$
$$100\% = 25\% + 75\%$$

So, if we want to convert the 25 percent margin to a cost price basis, the 75 percent that is the cost becomes the relevant base and

$$\text{Margin as a percentage of cost price} = \frac{25\%}{75\%} = 33.33\%$$

Note that this is exactly the same as dividing \$1.50 by \$4.50.
A simple formula for making this conversion is

$$\text{Percentage margin on cost price} = \frac{\text{Percentage margin on selling price}}{100\% - \text{Percentage margin on selling price}}$$

In our example, this is

$$\frac{25\%}{100\% - 25\%} = \frac{25\%}{75\%} = 33.33\%$$

Note that the only piece of information that we need to make this conversion is the margin percentage on selling price.
Conversion from cost price to selling price base.

$$\text{Selling price} = \text{Margin} + \text{Cost}$$
$$133.33\% = 33.33\% + 100\%$$

The margin is 33.33 percent and the relevant selling price base is 133.33 percent, so

$$\text{Margin as a percentage of selling price} = \frac{33.33\%}{133.33\%} = 25\%$$

Note that this is exactly the same as dividing \$1.50 by \$6.00.
A simple formula for making this conversion is

$$\frac{\text{Percentage margin on selling price}}{} = \frac{\text{Percentage margin on cost price}}{100\% + \text{Percentage margin on cost price}}$$

In our example, this is

$$\frac{33.33\%}{100\% + 33.33\%} = \frac{33.33\%}{133.33\%} = 25\%$$

Note that the only piece of information that we need to make this conversion is the margin percentage on cost price.

Multiple Margins

Often a manufacturer gives a suggested retail selling price and suggested retail and wholesale margins. For example, the suggested retail price may be $7.50 with a retail margin of 20 percent and a wholesale margin of 15 percent. To determine the manufacturer's selling price in this situation, we simply take the appropriate margins off one at a time. Thus,

Retail selling price	$7.50
Less retail margin (20% of $7.50)	1.50
Equals retail cost price or wholesale selling price	6.00
Less wholesale margin (15% of $6.00)	0.90
Equals wholesale cost price or manufacturer's selling price	$5.10

No matter how many levels there are in the channel, the approach is the same. We simply take the margins off one at a time. Note that we cannot just add up the margins and subtract this amount. Here 20% + 15% = 35%, and 35% of $7.50 is $2.63, making the manufacturer's selling price $7.50 − $2.63 = $4.87. This is not correct.

This chapter has outlined some financial concepts that add greatly to our abilities to make sound marketing decisions. These concepts should be applied where needed in the cases in this book.

Chapter 4

A Case with a Student Analysis

The fundamental premise of this book is that one learns by doing. However, one can also learn from example. The purpose of this chapter is to give an example of a case analysis. The framework of analysis presented in the previous two chapters will be used here in order to clarify how one can use the framework.

The case presented in this chapter, ''Crow, Pope, and Land Enterprises,'' is a broad issue marketing case that has no textbook or single ''correct'' answer. A student analysis of the case follows the case presentation, and in the last section of the chapter we present our commentary on the case analysis.

We suggest the following steps in using this chapter:

1. Read and prepare your analysis of ''Crow, Pope, and Land Enterprises.'' This will give you a better perspective on the case analyses presented in this chapter.
2. Read and evaluate the analysis presented here. You may wish to use the points that constitute a good case analysis as presented in Chapter 2.
3. Read our commentary on the case analysis. Compare our view with yours.

Case

Crow, Pope, and Land Enterprises*

In early August 1973, Mr. Dan Thatcher, vice president of CPL Condominium Enterprises, a subsidiary of Crow, Pope, and Land Enterprises, was planning his strategy for a new condominium project in Jacksonville, Florida. The project was an important one, since it was the company's first attempt to diversify out of the Atlanta area with nonresort condominiums. Earlier in the year, Mr. Thatcher had arranged the purchase of an option on a 40-acre tract just outside the city limits of Jacksonville, and the company had to renew the option in the next week or they would lose their earnest money. Before the senior officers of the firm would approve the final purchase of the land for approximately $700,000, Mr. Thatcher had to prepare a report discussing the proposed marketing strategy for the condominiums to be built there. His report was to include discussions of the target market, the specifications of the units to be built, the price range of the condominiums, and the promotional strategy to be used in marketing the units.

Company Background

Crow, Pope, and Land Enterprises, Inc., is a developer of residential, commercial, and motel/hotel real estate property, with projects located throughout the world. Headquartered in Atlanta, Georgia, the company was incorporated on January 14, 1967, under the name Lincoln Construction Company. Trammell Crow of Dallas, Ewell Pope of Atlanta, and Frank Carter of Atlanta were the shareholders of the company. Mr. Pope and Mr. Carter had been partners in the real estate brokerage firm, Pope and Carter Company, which had acted as the leasing agent for several of Trammell Crow's developments, namely, Chattahoochee Industrial Park and Greenbriar Shopping Center. These two ventures had proved so successful that the three men decided to strengthen their association and form Lincoln Construction Company.

---

* This case was written by Kenneth L. Bernhardt and John S. Wright, Professor of Marketing, Georgia State University. Copyright © 1975 by Kenneth L. Bernhardt.

In June 1972, Mr. Pope and Mr. Carter decided to establish separate organizations, both of which were formed in association with Mr. Crow. Crow and Carter started Crow, Carter, and Associates, Inc., and Crow and Pope, in association with A. J. Land, Jr., became owners of the continuing company, Crow, Pope, and Land Enterprises, Inc.

The company is organized on a project-management basis, with a managing partner who oversees and is responsible for every phase of the development assigned to each project. The manager of each project acts very much like the president of a small company, with the exception that he has the resources of a much larger corporation to draw upon when it is felt that added expertise would be of assistance. Most of the project managers, including Mr. Thatcher, are young, aggressive MBA graduates from leading schools of business administration.

The projects in which the company is involved range from the development of apartment complexes, condominium complexes, office parks, and shopping centers, to "total community" complexes complete with apartments, condominiums, single-family houses, retail outlets, parks, schools, office buildings, and recreational facilities. The firm has recently become active in the development of urban community centers containing a mixture of such features as commercial high-rise office buildings, luxury hotels, retail shopping facilities, and other pedestrian conveniences designed for high architectural impact in downtown environments. Examples of some of the company's projects include the $100 million Atlanta Center project (a large Hilton Hotel together with office buildings and shopping areas in downtown Atlanta), the $40 million Sheraton Hong Kong Hotel and shopping mall complex, and the Cumberland, Fairington, and Northlake total community complexes in Atlanta. Cumberland, a $65 million joint venture development with the Metropolitan Life Insurance Company, will, upon its completion in 1978, include a 1 million-square-foot enclosed shopping center, 750,000 square feet of office space, 1,800 apartments and condominiums situated around a 17-acre lake, an indoor tennis center, and hotel/motel facilities.

Crow, Pope, and Land has built a number of condominium and apartment complexes in Atlanta and has built more condominiums than any other developer in the area. Among the projects currently being sold in the Atlanta area are projects oriented toward retired couples, young swingers, sports-minded couples and families, and couples who want to own their own residence but cannot afford single-family detached housing. The company also has several resort projects in Florida.

Background on the Jacksonville Project

The original idea for the Jacksonville project came out of a meeting Mr. Thatcher had in early 1973 with Lindsay Freeman, another vice president of CPL Condominium Enterprises. In discussing the future goals and directions for the subsidiary, they decided that a high priority should be placed on reducing their dependence on the Atlanta condominium market where all nine of their projects were located. Since different geographic areas often were at different stages of the business cycle, they felt expansion into new geographical areas would provide a hedge against economic downturns as well as opening up profitable new markets for their products.

The first decision made was that they should concentrate on the Southeast, within a 400-mile radius of Atlanta, allowing greater control from the Atlanta headquarters. Also, projections of housing market demand indicated that this region of the country would experience rapid growth in the coming few years.

A number of cities, including Memphis, Louisville, Chattanooga, Mobile, and Birmingham, were investigated as possible sites for a condominium project. Several criteria were established. The area had to have several condominium projects already in existence since they did not want to be the first project in the area. Their experience had shown that the pioneers had to undertake a large educational effort, which usually took two years and a lot of money. The city should have a population of at least 250,000 so it would absorb a large number of condominiums if the company decided to add other projects at a later date. Lastly, the area should have a large number of residents in the target market for condominiums—young married couples and "empty nesters," couples whose children are grown and have moved out of the home.

Using census data, information obtained from Chambers of Commerce, and other real estate research sources, Thatcher narrowed the choice to Charlotte, North Carolina, and Jacksonville, Florida. In both places, condominiums had been marketed for two to three years, and a number of developments were being built. In Charlotte, however, the only land that was available for immediate development was not particularly well suited for multifamily building. It had been decided that land that had been zoned for condominium development, with utilities easily accessible, would be favored to avoid the normal two-year period to get undeveloped raw land ready for development. Therefore, it was without reservation that Thatcher made the decision to expand into the Jacksonville market.

Background on the Jacksonville Area

Jacksonville is the most populated city in Florida and ranks second in the Southeast and 23rd in the United States. In October of 1968, the city adopted a new charter which consolidated the city and county governments. All of Duval County is now operated as one government, and the consolidation made the new city of Jacksonville the largest city in the continental United States with 840 square miles (537,664 acres). To put the figures into comparative terms, the city is two thirds the size of the state of Rhode Island.

Recent growth has brought many young people to the Jacksonville area. In 1970, the median age of the population was 26 years, compared to 32.3 years for the state of Florida and 28.3 years for the total United States. Duval County has a large, rapidly growing economy, with a balanced employment profile and a rather diversified economic base. This diversification has produced a stable economy by minimizing its sensitivity to both industrial and national business cycles.

For a distance of approximately 100 miles in all directions, the area surrounding the city is predominantly rural in character. With over 500,000 residents, Jacksonville is the commercial and cultural center of northeast Florida and southeast Georgia. It is one of the principal distribution, insurance, and convention centers in the Southeast.

One of the major impacts on the city's economy is the presence of three large military installations in the area, particularly the Jacksonville Naval Air Station located in the southern part of the county on the St. Johns River just north of the city of Orange Park. This facility is one of the largest naval air bases in the United States. It is supported by a smaller air station, Cecil Field, located in the western part of the county, where several air squadrons operate in preparation for air carrier qualifications. The third facility, the Mayport Carrier Basin east of Jacksonville, has berthing capacity for three of the country's largest aircraft carriers. The military installations employ approximately 34,000 people including some 5,000 civilians, 9,000 shore-based military personnel, and 20,000 mobile/afloat military. Another 5,000 military employees are expected to be transferred to these facilities in the next year or two.

Extensive bedroom areas are forming just outside Duval County, reflecting lower tax rates, lower land prices, an absence of restrictive zoning ordinances, and a preference for suburban living. Also, the city of Jacksonville was busing children to achieve racial integration in the schools, and many residents were moving to Orange Park and other areas of Clay County (just south of Duval County) where there was no busing of students. The impact of all these factors made Clay County, and the Orange Park area in particular, a rapidly growing area.

The city of Orange Park lies adjacent to and south of the Duval County line, and is approximately 15 miles from the central business district of Jacksonville. Exhibit 1 presents a map of the area showing the location of Orange Park in relation to the naval air station, Cecil Field, and the business district of Jacksonville.

After talking with many real estate people in the area, and after reviewing the statistics presented in Exhibit 2, Mr. Thatcher decided to obtain an option on a 40-acre tract of land just west of the city limits of Orange Park. As shown in the exhibit, the residents of Orange Park had an above-average median family income for the area and were better educated than Duval County residents. Also, over half the population in the area worked outside the county (principally in Duval County). Thatcher thought the higher-income, better-educated people would be receptive to condominiums. Also, he felt that the close proximity to Duval County would be attractive to many potential purchasers.

Access to the site is off Blanding Boulevard (State Road 21 on the map), a heavily traveled two-lane thoroughfare with development, for the most part, consisting of commercial and single-family residential development. Within the

EXHIBIT 1
Map of Jacksonville and Orange Park area

EXHIBIT 2
Selected statistics for Orange Park, Clay County, and Duval County/Jacksonville

	City of Orange Park	Clay County	Duval County/ Jacksonville
Total population, 1970	7,677	32,059	528,865
Median family income, 1970	$10,021	$8,430	$8,671
Median school years completed— 1970, adults	12.5	12.1	12.0
Percent of residents who work outside the county	—	53.5%	2.6%
Percent of residents who have lived in the same area for five years or more, 1970	30.0%	45.6%	67.1%

past year a considerable amount of multifamily development had occurred, but it was mainly concentrated further northeast in the vicinity of U.S. Highway 17.

Within one mile of the site to the north is a minor shopping center with a Winn-Dixie supermarket as the cornerstone tenant. Two and one half miles north, a 1 million-square-foot regional shopping center is being developed and is scheduled to open in 1975. The school system in the area is rated excellent, and several elementary schools as well as junior and senior high schools are in close proximity to the site. Churches of all denominations and hospital and recreation facilities are all well represented in the area.

The current housing market in the Orange Park area is composed substantially of single-family houses, with prices of these units beginning at $32,000. Apartments in the vicinity of the site have achieved 100 percent occupancy, with many of the apartments renting for between $150 and $200 per month. There are a number of condominium projects in the area, as shown in Exhibit 3, although almost all of them are situated much farther north. The price range on these condominium projects typically begins in the low $30,000 range and goes up to almost $60,000.

Marketing Strategy

The first question Thatcher had to resolve concerned the target market for the condominiums. There were three basic strategies he had been considering: (*a*) a specialty type product with a large amenity package oriented toward active, young "swinging" couples; (*b*) a project oriented toward the retiree market; or (*c*) a project oriented toward families who wanted to purchase their residence but could not afford a single-family house. Crow, Pope, and Land had considerable experience in building all three types of condominiums in the Atlanta area, and Thatcher was reluctant to consider other types of condominiums that the company had not had experience with. He reasoned that taking a product that had worked elsewhere would reduce some of the risk of entering a new, relatively unknown market. Also, use of a product that the company had built in Atlanta would save the cost of architect's fees, and he would be in a better position to negotiate with a contractor to build the units because he would know in advance what the costs should be (building costs in the Jacksonville area were virtually the same as costs in Atlanta).

EXHIBIT 3
Condominium projects in the Orange Park area

Project	Rooms	Square feet	Price range
Bay Meadows	2BR,2B –3BR,3B	1,350–2,243	$34,850–$48,300
Solano Grove	1BR,1B –3BR,3B	874–2,006	26,100– 58,200
Regency Woods	2BR,2B –4BR,2½B	1,456–2,102	35,500– 45,900
Sutton Place	2BR,2½B–4BR,2½B	1,366–1,842	31,500– 38,000
Baytree	2BR,1½B–4BR,3½B	1,404–2,214	32,000– 46,750
The Lakes	2BR,2B –3BR,2½B	1,330–2,050	37,500– 59,400
Oxford Forest	2BR,1½B–3BR,2½B	1,282–1,622	28,500– 35,500

Thatcher had located a site along the St. Johns River that would be suitable for the specialty, high-amenity product. There might be some environmental problems with the Army Corps of Engineers, who had jurisdiction over the site, but he thought these could be worked out. The Orange Park site under option would not be suitable for this type of project, which Thatcher thought should be built around a body of water. With the high land cost for an appropriate site, and with the high cost for all the recreational amenities, the company would have to price the condominiums under this strategy at about $40,000 (the same price charged for the comparable Riverbend Condominiums in Atlanta).

The optioned site was also not acceptable for the second alternative, a project oriented toward the retirees' market. Experience in Atlanta had shown that retired couples preferred to purchase condominiums with a golf course on site, and the present site was not suited for development of a golf course. Thatcher had located several possible sites suitable for this alternative several miles south of the property under option. Because of the very large investment involved in building a golf course, he felt that a project oriented toward this market would have to be a large one to support the high fixed cost of the golf course.

If the company decided to purchase the property under option, about 12 units per acre could be constructed, or about 480 in total. As they did with almost all their projects, the units would be built in several phases, with phase I consisting of 50 units. Thatcher had determined that units built in the Fairgrounds project in Atlanta could be built and sold profitably in Orange Park for $24,900 for a 1,040-square-foot, two-bedroom unit, and $29,900 for a 1,265-square-foot, three-bedroom unit. The price per square foot was comparable to the other condominium projects in the area, and the total price was well below most of them because of the smaller size. In addition to the difference in square footage and price, the Fairgrounds models also had different exteriors than the typical ones sold in the Jacksonville area; the Fairgrounds units used brick and aluminum siding, whereas most of the others had a stucco exterior. Although he basically believed that the Jacksonville condominium prospect was very similar to the Atlanta prospect, he wondered whether he should incorporate some stucco treatment into the exterior of the units if he should decide to follow through with this strategy.

Another issue he had not resolved concerned the extent to which the strategy should be oriented toward the large (and growing) military market. If he did define his target market as the military market, what impact would this have on the physical product and on his promotional strategy, which was still to be determined? Close to half of the residents of Orange Park worked at one of the three military installations in the area, and both the naval air station and Cecil Field were within seven miles of the proposed site. He was aware of the large word of mouth influence in the Navy—an apartment project not far from the site which was just beginning to lease new units had gone from 5 percent Navy to 30 percent Navy in less than two months.

Another question which concerned Thatcher was the low sales rate of the other condominiums in the area. He thought the reason was the relatively high prices, which caused them to compete directly against single-family housing. Also, he had shopped all the projects and found the on-site salesmen to be very uninformed and uninterested in selling the condominiums. He felt certain that this was hurting sales but was still not sure that the consumers in the Jacksonville/Orange Park area would buy condominiums, even in the price range he was proposing.

The senior officers of Crow, Pope, and Land would also expect a detailed promotional strategy as part of his report. In working with budget figures, he had determined that he could afford to spend $22,000 for promotion (1.5 percent of sales) for the first 50 units, which would be about 12 months' projected sales. Brochures, signs, business cards for salesmen, and other miscellaneous items would cost about $2,000, leaving $20,000 for media and production costs.

Crow, Pope, and Land used a small local advertising agency for all their apartment and condominium advertising in Atlanta. Thatcher was uncertain about the role he wanted the agency to play in this project and was worried that the agency was not attuned to the Jacksonville market. He wondered whether he should try to hire a Jacksonville agency but was afraid that the account was too small for anyone to pay much attention to it. Also, he felt that the retainer that any decent agency would want to handle the account, about $3,000, could be better spent on media. He had studied advertising and promotion in courses in college and thought he should consider creating the advertising himself.

There were really only two alternatives for media strategy in the Jacksonville area—radio and newspaper. There were nine AM radio stations and four FM stations. The rates for the four largest stations were all about the same, between $25 and $30 for a one-minute spot during drive time (6–10 A.M. and 3–7 P.M.) and about 20 percent cheaper at other times, assuming 12 spots per week for 13 weeks. There were two daily newspapers in Jacksonville, a morning paper with 210,000 circulation and an evening paper with 148,000 circulation. As a result of common ownership, there was a combination rate available which was only 10 percent higher than the $13.16 per column inch rate for the morning paper alone. The morning paper had a Sunday edition, with a circulation of 182,000 and a cost per column inch of $13.72.

Mr. Thatcher was also concerned about what message to use in his promotional campaign. He was uncertain to what extent they should mention the fact that there was no busing to schools, an important advantage for many potential buyers. He was worried that other people might be upset with the implied racism in such a campaign. He was also concerned with the implications for the advertising creative strategy as a result of the target market decision concerning whether or not to concentrate on the military market. Another advertising issue was the extent to which the copy should promote the fact that Crow, Pope, and Land was a large Atlanta developer, and that this was their first North Florida project.

The one decision Thatcher had made was that there was much opportunity for the company in the Jacksonville market, and, therefore, much opportunity for him personally to expand his responsibilities in the company. As a result, he wanted to make a recommendation that the company definitely enter the market; the only uncertainty was the strategy to be followed. The company had paid $1,000 for the initial option on the Orange Park property. Next week they had to either pay $20,000 to renew the option for 90 days or lose their $1,000 investment. If they decided to renew the option, this would give them time to arrange for the financing of the project and to arrange a production schedule with the contractors. They had to begin this planning immediately since it usually took at least six months to build condominiums, and that meant that they would have to act fast if they wanted to be selling condominiums by the height of the selling season in June. As he sat down to write the report containing his recommendations, Thatcher realized that a decision to renew the option would be a commitment to actually build the units he recommended.

Example Situation Analysis of Crow, Pope, and Land Enterprises (CPL)

CPL Condominium Enterprises, a subsidiary of CPL Enterprises, Inc., a residential housing and commercial builder, had built a number of *condominium* complexes in Atlanta, designed for specific segments such as retired couples, young swingers, families, and low-middle-income couples. In addition, they had several resort projects in Florida.

In order to reduce their dependence on the Atlanta condominium market, a *goal* of expanding into new geographic areas where profitable markets were opening up was developed by two CPL Condominium Enterprises VPs. The *tactics* were to choose a city of at least 250,000 population within a 400-mile radius of Atlanta, since forecasts of the housing market projected rapid growth in this general region in the coming few years. Dan Thatcher was to put together a marketing *strategy* discussing product, price, place, and promotion to pursue in reaching this goal. Since this discussion is centered around Dan Thatcher's review of the Orange Park condominium market, it will be assumed here that the product is *condominiums*. In the larger context of the company, which will be touched on at the end of this paper, the product considered is *housing*.

A. NATURE OF DEMAND

1. How do buyers currently go about buying condos?

In the search for housing, buyers will generally define the neighborhood they are interested in, then select among the alternatives within their price range. The decision to buy a condominium, rather than a single-family detached dwelling, may be influenced by several factors—price, ease of maintenance, amenities, and the like—which are discussed more thoroughly in part 2. The buyer will seek information to a high degree through media, family, friends, co-workers, real estate brokers, and, if available, reports on developers of other condominium projects to ascertain their reputation and workmanship quality. After looking at a number of developments, the decision of which condo to buy will probably be made at home or after a second or third look at the property under consideration. Sources of information about condos in the Jacksonville/ Orange Park area are probably newspapers, some broadcast coverage, and word of mouth. Although condos have existed for more than two years in this area, awareness level seems low due to the slow sales of condos in the area. In 1973, condos were not in vogue, and hence buyer knowledge and acceptability were not particularly well developed. The decision to purchase is made by the adults; if a couple, by a joint decision. This is the most important major purchase decision in most people's lives, thus much time, thought, and effort goes into the decision process. The buyer is highly influenced by the salesperson, the physical plant itself, friends, the real estate broker, and possibly the bank loan officer. This is usually a new purchase situation, evoking high interest, personal involvement, and excitement by the buyer. All of these factors contribute to a high risk associated with a poor purchase decision—it's hard to get rid of a condo that no one else wants either! A number of functional considerations enter into the decision, such as location, utilities, and convenience (more on this in part 2). A number of psychosocial considerations also enter into the decision, such as aesthetics, social contact, safety, prestige, and self-esteem. This being a durable good, the consumption time is long term.

2. Can the market be meaningfully segmented?

Due to CPL Condominium Enterprises' expertise in building condo complexes geared toward specific segments, and since Dan Thatcher desires to use an existing set of plans for the new condo development, it seems best to segment the market into those areas CPL can build for— namely, singles, retired couples, and young (low-middle-income) families. In addition, due to the demographic composition of the area (50 percent employed by the Navy), a Navy/military segment is also relevant. Attributes important to each segment are ranked in Table 1. Table 2 then ranks these attributes together with the housing options in the area, limited here to condos, single-family homes, and rental apartments, since these are the housing types mentioned in the case. Since the median age of Jacksonville is 26, below both the Florida and national medians, we can probably safely assume that there are many young couples and singles associated with the large military labor base, perhaps a growing number of babies and children (helping to lower the median), and that the family life-cycle stage is generally early. Additional data on average household size, the age distribution, and income versus age would be helpful in this analysis. The high turnover rate of Orange Park residents suggests either a very mobile population or a very fast-growing area.

Comparing Tables 1 and 2, there is not a one-to-one correlation

TABLE 1 Attributes important to the Navy/military segment

	Segments			
Attributes	Singles	Retirees	Young families	Navy (families)
Price	++++	++++	++++	+++++
Size	+	+	++++	+++
Neighborhood	++	+++	++++	++
Convenience to shopping	++	+++	+++	+
Schools	+	+	++++	+++
Social acceptability	++++	++	++	++
Social interaction	++++	+++	++	++
Recreation/amenities	++++	++++	+++	+++
Safety	++	++++	++++	++
Low tax base	+	++	++	++
Accessibility to work	++	+	++	++++
Mass transportation	++	+++	++	++
Access to entertainment	+++	++	++	++
Maintenance	++++	++++	+++	+++
Financing convenience*	++++	++	+++	+++
Public works	+	+++	+	+
Land availability	++	++	++++	++

* Defined as renting versus down payment/monthly mortgage commitments.

between all the boxed attributes of option: condo and segment. Note, however, that there is a correlation between options: apartment and singles segment.

B. EXTENT OF DEMAND
1. Sufficient demand for more condo housing?

Although there is limited information, one can still make some estimate of the total demand in the Jacksonville market. It is well known that nationally about 20 percent of the population moves each year. We also know from Exhibit 2 in the case that 32.9 percent of the population of Duval County (and a much higher percentage of Clay County) have lived there five years or less. On the basis of this information, we might expect about 5 percent of the households to be looking for a house; and, with an average of about 2.5 children and 4.7 people per family, the number of houses shifting hands may equal about 1 to 1.5 percent of the population or in the neighborhood of 6,000 to 7,000 homes. Even if we recognize that a

TABLE 2 Ranking of various housing options

	Options		
Attributes	*Our condo*	*Rental apartment*	*Single-family home*
Price	+ + + +	+ + + +	+ +
Size	+	+ +	+ + + +
Neighborhood	+ + +	?	?
Convenience to shopping	+ + +	?	?
Schools	+	?	?
Social acceptability	+ +	+	+ + + +
Social interaction	+ + +	+ + +	+
Recreation/amenities	+ +	+ + +?	+
Safety	+ +	+	+ +
Low tax base	+ + +?	+?	+ + +?
Accessibility to work	+ + +?	+ +?	+ +?
Mass transportation	+	+	+
Maintenance	+ + + +	+ + + +	+
Financing convenience*	+	+ + + +	+
Land availability	+ +	+ +	+ + + +
Equity	+ + + +	+	+ + + +

* Defined as renting versus down payment/monthly mortgage commitments.

large proportion of the 20 percent of the population that move in a typical year consists of young people moving from one apartment to another, it would seem that this estimate of 6,000 to 7,000 homes is extremely conservative. Since Jacksonville is a very rapidly growing area full of economic activity, and since the "baby boomers" are just entering the age where they will be buying houses, we might raise this estimate to around 10,000 homes. With projected sales of 50 units the first year, Crow, Pope, and Land is trying to achieve around .5 percent of the market.

What part of this will be condos is the next issue to judge.

2. Current market shares

We have no information to judge this. It appears that single-family home purchases dominate the purchasing mode and that apartment rentals are 100 percent occupied. There may exist excess demand for apartments. This can raise apartment rents (if no new apartments will soon be built), making the price advantage of renting less of a factor over time. Selective demand trends suggest that consumer awareness of condo developments is increasing and, along with that, public acceptance. Since single-family homes start selling at $32,000, it could be that condos are not selling because people can just as easily afford single-family homes. Banks usually like housing to account for only 25 to 30 percent of one's gross income; hence these could be too high priced, even though they are less than the other alternatives. Purchasing the smaller condo at $24,000 would lead to the following results:

a.   12 percent, 20-year mortgage:

$$\frac{\$24,000}{7.469} = \$3,213.28 \text{ or } \$267.77/\text{month} = 32.1 \text{ percent of income.}$$

b.   8 percent, 20-year mortgage:

$$\frac{\$24,000}{9.818} = \$2,444.49 \text{ or } \$203.71/\text{month} = 24.4 \text{ percent of income.}$$

It would be difficult for the average person to finance anything but the lower-priced condo at the lower interest rate. Of course, when Thatcher needs to make his decision, he cannot foresee possible future increases in interest rates.

C.   NATURE OF COMPETITION
1.   Present and future structure of competition

Seven other condo projects in the general area as well as numerous single-family home developments exist. Market shares are unknown, although we know that rental apartments have 100 percent occupancy. Financial resources of competitors are unknown. Marketing resources and skills of condo competitors, judged by their salespeople, are poor. They lack interest, enthusiasm, and knowledge of the projects they are trying to sell. Production resources and skills of competitors are unknown.

2.   Current marketing programs of established competitors

We do not know much but, judging from the slow sales, it might be reasonable to suppose that consumer awareness is low, knowledge of market needs is poor, and the salesperson's role is a very critical part of the competition's marketing program, although it seems to be unsuccessful.

3.   Opportunity for another competitor?

The fact that the property Thatcher has an option to buy is *zoned* for condos indicates that the planning body of the county feels that condos will serve as one of the housing mixes for the area. Since the opportunity for CPL to drastically price cut the market exists, there does seem to be opportunity for another competitor. Whether buyer demand exists is another question, however.

4.   Retaliatory moves of competitors?

Competitors can probably drop their prices somewhat. The other developments appear to be a few miles away from this one, though, so perhaps another condo development may not greatly affect the competitors.

D. ENVIRONMENTAL CLIMATE

1. Relevant social, political, economic, and technological trends

Since this project is located in the South, busing is a hot issue. People opposed to busing (which is taking place in Jacksonville/Duval County) will want to live in an area with no forced busing. Condominiums are just hitting the market—they are in a young product life-cycle stage; thus social acceptability is currently in the developing stage.

The last lottery for the Vietnam War draft took place in 1973. The war is starting to wind down. In 1975, some military ships were moth-balled. Hence the lifeblood of Orange Park, which is over half military, will soon be in a transition stage. Basing a project on military personnel housing demand is probably very risky at this time.

Some of these factors may increase the attractiveness of condos. People will want to live closer to work but in an area with low land rates and a low tax base due to the ever-increasing squeeze on their pocket-books. A condo may be easier to keep cool; the accessibility to a pool, which a condo development in Florida is likely to have, may further increase its attractiveness.

E. STAGE OF PRODUCT LIFE CYCLE

The product category, condominiums, is at an early life-cycle point. Some people are aware of their existence, but the concept is not yet so well tested that people are rushing out to buy condos. As the product ages and more people begin purchasing condos, social acceptability will increase. The slow sales of the present condo developments in the area are indicative of this lack of social acceptability due to the product's early life-cycle stage. Of course, other factors that are perhaps more important (price, location, etc.) enter into this, too. The fact that one of CPL's development criteria was that other condo projects should have existed in the area for at least two years supports the argument that an educational and acceptability process must first take place before the product sells well. The more knowledge the consumer has, the more he/she will want to buy this product.

F. COST STRUCTURE OF THE INDUSTRY

Comparing our project to the other projects' $/square feet range, the CPL project is about average in $/square foot price, although lower in total price due to the low square footage of the units. A comparison with competitors is presented in Table 3. The highs and lows are boxed. We know that $22,000 of selling costs equals 1.5 percent of sales. Hence, the first 50 units will bring in an expected revenue of

$$\frac{\$22,000}{.015} = \$1,466,667.$$

For sale of 480 units, total revenues would equal

$$\frac{480}{50} \times \$1,466,667 = \$14,080,003.$$

TABLE 3 Comparison of cost by competitor

Project	Rooms	Sq. ft.	Price range	$/Sq. ft. range
Bay Meadows	2B2B/3B3B	1,350–2,243	$34,850–$48,300	$25.81–$21.53
Solana Grove	1B1B/3B3B	879–2,006	26,100– 58,200	29.86– 29.01
Regency Woods	2B2B/4B2½B	1,456–2,102	35,500– 45,900	24.38– 21.84
Sutton Place	2B2½B/4B2½B	1,366–1,842	31,500– 38,000	23.06– 20.63
Baytree	2B1½B/4B3½B	1,404–2,214	32,000– 46,150	22.79– 21.12
The Lakes	2B2B/3B2½B	1,330–2,050	37,500– 59,400	28.20– 28.98
Oxford Forest	2B1½B/3B2½B	1,282–1,622	28,500– 35,500	22.23– 21.89
CPL	2 Bdr	1,040	$24,900	23.94
	3 Bdr	1,265	$29,900	23.64
Single-family home		Assume 1,400	$32,000	$22.86

Other costs we know of:

Land = $721,000 (include $1,000 + $20,000 in option).
Selling costs = 1.5% = $210,000 ($14 million × .015).

Assume construction is approximately $20/square foot:

1,000 square feet × 480 condos × $20/square foot
= $9,600,000 per condo, approximately.

Sales	$14,080,000	100%
CGS	9,600,000	68%
Gross margin	$ 4,480,000	32%
Sales	210,000	
Land	721,000	8%
Other (guess)	100,000	
Net profit (pretax)	$ 3,449,000	24%

The project looks profitable at this point, if these assumptions are valid. If the company highly leverages the development, this would be a very attractive investment indeed.

G. SKILLS OF THE FIRM
1. Marketing

Apparently the firm as a whole has been quite successful, and much of this success for a real estate company must be attributed to marketing. A small Atlanta advertising agency is used for the Atlanta apartment and condominium advertising, but Thatcher is not sure the agency will be able to adequately and successfully come up with a Jacksonville marketing plan. To hire a local Jacksonville agency, about $3,000 would need to be spent on a retainer, which Thatcher thought could be better spent on media.

Since he had studied advertising and promotion in college courses, Thatcher thought he had the skills to create the advertising himself. If CPL commonly has its project managers create the advertising for projects, then

I would question whether the marketing skills of the firm were really very good. I do not think Thatcher is who we want promoting a $14 million condo complex!

We do not know how successful CPL has been with its condo developments, but we can only assume that continued existence and expansion in the business means that it has been successful thus far, and hence its marketing is good.

2. Production

Again, we don't have too much data to access this, but judging from the size of some of the projects, such as the Atlanta Center Project, the Sheraton Hong Kong Hotel, and the Cumberland, Fairington, and North-lake total community complexes, CPL must be able to "produce" build-ings or else it wouldn't be undertaking such large efforts. Thatcher says that CPL has experience building the three condominium types in Atlanta (swinging couples, retirees, and young families) and could thus negotiate well with the contractor in Jacksonville, since he would have a good idea of what the actual costs would be. He also mentioned that this "product had worked"; therefore, he thought it could work again. Also, perhaps the use of brick and aluminum siding exteriors is popular and well liked, thus helping the firm to sell a slightly different product better than the stucco exterior norm in Jacksonville.

3. Management

Apparently, the company has a lot of MBA types and, due to the project-management emphasis, fairly aggressive self-starters. Crow and Pope had a good record of success in the real estate brokerage business prior to their forming CPL. It looks like we can assume the company has good management skills and talented, although perhaps overly confident, people on staff.

4. Financial

Their financial skills are probably very good, since the owners have over five years of experience in the business and the project managers, similar to Thatcher, have business training backgrounds/education. Due to the size of the projects the parent company is undertaking, we can assume it has a good financial relationship with its bank and must be doing well to continue getting large sums of financing. The subsidiary, CPL Condomini-ums, is thus backed by a strong parent company. The parent company is probably making nice profits from its hotel operations, as high margins are typically the rule in this area.

5. R&D

R&D in terms of a popular product design appears to be good, since it sounds like a brick and aluminum siding exterior condo is an attractive and long-lasting exterior. Modifying their developments to meet the needs of particular market segments in terms of amenities shows good insight in producing a product to meet the needs of the consumer.

However, the background research Thatcher has performed for judg-ing the Jacksonville condo market is quite limited. He is basing his decision on very limited data. A much better decision could be reached with more research into demographic trends in the area, determining the mobility of the Navy personnel, and finding out how future road work will favorably or adversely affect this proposed condo development. The fact that apartments are 100 percent occupied but condo sales are slow should cause Thatcher to question whether condos are what is needed here. Perhaps apartments would be a better fit to community needs.

As far as comparing CPL's skills to the competitors, we do not know enough about the competitors, except that their marketing seems weak, to make a particularly valid comparison.

H.   FINANCIAL RESOURCES OF THE FIRM

As the calculations in part F show, the financial return on this investment looks very attractive. Since CPL Condominium Enterprises has the backing of the parent company, I think it is safe to assume that financing this project will pose no problem.

I.   DISTRIBUTION/PROMOTIONAL STRUCTURE AVAILABLE

Classic distribution institutions are not a directly relevant dimension here. However, the existence of an institutional structure for promotion is important.

This is where media advertising comes in: a number of types could be utilized, under the constraint of $20,000 for the first year's promotional activities after spending $2,000 for brochures, wages, and business cards. Advertising on commute time radio could take up most of this budget, if four radio stations are used, with 12 spots a week for 13 weeks (4 stations $\times$ $30/minute $\times$ 12 spots/week $\times$ 13 weeks = $18,700). Advertising in the newspaper only, using the Sunday rate of $13.72/column inch would allow $\frac{\$20,000}{13.72/\text{col. in.}} = 1,455$ inches over 26 weeks. This is 56 column inches per week, which seems like a lot of newspaper coverage. A combination of these two mixes would probably be good. The Atlanta advertising agency would be able to determine what would be best. In addition, the agency might try to find a Navy newsletter to advertise in because this market, if encouraged to investigate the condo alternative, might through word of mouth be a very helpful advertising method. Also, the use of coupons in the paper to be exchanged for a gift upon coming to look at the development may further increase buying traffic. These media institutions are available for CPL use.

Problems and Opportunities

A.   Problems
   1.   Dan Thatcher:
       a.   His inexperience in the Florida condominium market.
       b.   His ambitiousness, possibly causing him to miss opportunities as he sees the "success" of this project promoting his career.

   c. His shortsightedness in only considering condominiums rather than apartments also, which may be more suited to the community needs.

  2. Economic dependence of the areas on the three military installations.

  3. Availability of close substitutes to condos, namely, similarly priced single-family housing.

  4. The instability of the Orange Park housing market, symptomized by the high turnover/mobility.

  5. Advertising agency located in Atlanta, with no promotion experience in this Florida, highly military market.

  6. High prices of the projects.

  7. Low social acceptability, as shown by the low demand.

  8. Transportation:

   a. The project under consideration is located on a heavy use corridor. More development will cause traffic problems.

   b. New freeway allowing easy access to the navy base is under construction, thus easy accessibility to work is not yet present.

  9. If the young swingers or retirees are the chosen market segment, need more land to put in amenities. Army Corps of Engineers may not approve other option plot if that one is pursued.

 10. Need better demographic data to properly evaluate the market, demand, and supply.

 11. Public still needs educating about the product itself.

B. Opportunities

  1. Very attactive area to build, as there are low taxes, low land rates, and no busing.

  2. Military market is large.

  3. The aluminum siding and brick exterior condo can provide a new look and style to the Jacksonville condo market.

  4. Market for rental housing is excellent, due to low vacancy rates, a large influence of relatively mobile military personnel, and low median age of the area.

  5. Good reputation and experience of CPL. They know housing construction and costs. Financial strength of CPL.

  6. Market open to new competitor; fast-growing regions are the Southeast and Florida.

  7. The plot under option is zoned for condos.

C. On balance, the situation is:

  1. Very favorable for *housing*.

  2. Neutral for *condo*.

Commentary on the Case Analysis

  Table 4 presents our point-by-point summary evaluation of the case analysis. In our view, it is very well done, and our guess is you will agree. We should point out, however, that it is far easier to evaluate an analysis than to do one.

TABLE 4   Summary of the evaluation of the case analysis

Criteria	Analysis
1. Completeness	Very complete on all aspects of situation analysis structure Reasonable depth of analysis
2. Avoids rehash	Good Most points are made with an analysis purpose
3. Makes reasonable assumptions	Excellent
4. Proper problem statements	Excellent; has not confused them with symptoms Somewhat incomplete; e.g., competitors
5. Proper opportunity statements	Good; has not given action statements
6. Deals with objectives realistically	Very good; has questioned this issue Alternatives given and discussed
7. Recognizes alternatives	*
8. Is not assertive	Generally OK Some actions are implied in situation analysis, but not a big problem here
9. Discusses pros and cons of alternatives	*
10. Makes effective use of financial and other quantitative information	Excellent All options are given a good quantitative appraisal
11. Reaches a clear and logical decision	*
12. Makes good use of evidence developed in situation analysis	*
13. Overall appraisal	A very good situation analysis of a tough situation

* Not applicable as only situation analysis is presented.

Part 2

Introduction to Marketing Decision Making

In Part 1 of this book you have studied how marketing decisions should be made. The cases in this section are designed to let you begin to apply this approach in decision making. These cases should be viewed as an opportunity to practice your skills on some broad issue marketing cases before we go to other sections of this book, where we study cases that are more specifically tied to product or distribution, and so on.

Case 1

General Motors: Cadillac*

When Executive Vice President Lloyd Reuss took his job as the head of all North American car operations for General Motors (GM) in February 1986, he had a four-item list of goals. One of the four—clearly of the highest priority for GM—concerned a single division, Cadillac. The words were strong and simple: "Restore Cadillac products and image to where they are the standard of the world."[1] The task before Reuss was an ominous one. The U.S. auto market, General Motors, and Cadillac had all changed significantly since he joined GM in 1959. At that time, the U.S. market largely belonged to the "big three" domestic producers (GM 42 percent, Ford 28 percent, Chrysler 11 percent), and Cadillac *was* the "standard of the world." Now, 30 years later, things had changed. The three major domestic producers' market share has fallen to 67.8 percent, and Cadillac's share and reputation in the luxury market is being challenged not only by domestic competition but also by European and Asian competitors as well.

In order to analyze Cadillac's position in the market, Reuss must seek the answers to several questions. For example: Is it selling the right products? Are its products targeted at the right market? Does its image appeal to the buyers Cadillac seeks? Does Cadillac's advertising effectively reach the right market and convey Cadillac's desired image?

Current Environmental Factors

Throughout the 1950s and 1960s, while energy was plentiful and inexpensive, American car manufacturers enjoyed great success building cars that were large and powerful. During the 1970s, energy prices increased—the product of temporary shortages in the supply of oil. As a result, import manufacturers,

---

* This case was prepared from public sources by Eric P. Andrew, under the supervision of Thomas C. Kinnear. Copyright © 1989 by Thomas C. Kinnear.
[1] Jerry Flint, "Hold the Velveeta—Please Pass the Brie," *Forbes* 8 (September 1986), p. 30.

many of which were building small, fuel-efficient automobiles, were in prime position to take advantage of the situation. With the influx of these fuel-thrifty imports, the domestic portion of the U.S. automobile market began to shrink from approximately 96.5 percent in 1957 to 85 percent in 1973, to 77 percent in 1979, and finally to approximately 68 percent in 1987.[2] Most of these imports were coming from Japan (Toyota, Nissan, Honda, etc.), now the world's largest producer of motor vehicles.

Western European countries also have been major suppliers of automobiles to the U.S. market. Makers such as Volkswagen, Mercedes-Benz, and BMW from West Germany; Volvo and Saab from Sweden; to a lesser degree, Peugeot and Renault from France; and sporadically, Fiat, Lancia, and Alfa Romeo from Italy. Also, during the 1980s the Yugoslavians (Yugo) and the Koreans (Hyundai and partnerships through Ford and GM) began exporting cars to the United States. (See Exhibit 1 for 1987 import sales.)

Throughout the energy shortage and until the mid-1980s, the Japanese enjoyed favorable yen/dollar exchange rates and were, therefore, in large part able to offer vehicles that cost less than comparable U.S. or West European products. The Japanese manufacturers also had significant success in producing

EXHIBIT 1   Selected 1987 U.S. import sales

Manufacturer	Country	Sales
Acura	Japan	109,470
Alfa Romeo	Italy	6,320
Audi	West Germany	41,322
BMW	West Germany	87,839
Eagle/Renault	France	13,991
Ford/Kia	South Korea	26,750
Honda	Japan	312,218
Hyundai	South Korea	263,610
Isuzu	Japan	39,587
Jaguar	Great Britain	22,919
Mazda	Japan	206,354
Mercedes-Benz	West Germany	89,918
Merkur	West Germany	14,301
Mitsubishi	Japan	67,954
Nissan	Japan	405,996
Peugeot	France	9,422
Saab	Sweden	45,106
Subaru	Japan	175,864
Toyota	Japan	583,809
Volkswagen	West Germany	130,641
Volvo	Sweden	106,539
Yugo	Yugoslavia	48,812

Source: *Automotive News, 1988 Market Data Book.*

---

[2] Sales/Registrations, "Market Shares for 36 Years," *Automotive Industries—1988 Market Data Book Issue,* May 25, 1988, p. 32.

these small, fuel-efficient automobiles with high quality. However, the U.S. government, pressured by GM, Ford, and Chrysler, imposed a ''voluntary restraint,'' or quota, on the number of Japanese cars which could be exported to the United States. With this quota and with the appreciation of the yen, which occurred in the mid- to late-1980s, Japanese manufacturers began to lose their ability to sell large volumes of small cars and still make desirable profit margins. These factors began to force the Japanese to adjust their product mix to include a greater percentage of the more profitable larger, upscale, and specialty automobiles.

While the Japanese first concentrated on small, fuel-efficient cars, the European car manufacturers, with Volkswagen as the possible exception, have targeted distinct market niches. Mercedes-Benz, BMW, Audi, Saab, and Volvo have all, to varying degrees, concentrated on the upper segments of the market. The Koreans and Yugoslavians have targeted the low-end market and, due to the strength of the Japanese yen against the U.S. dollar and other currencies, have replaced Japan as the low-cost automotive exporters to the U.S. market.

In response to the high cost of fuel in the mid-1970s, the U.S. big three began to downsize their products and increase the number of small and fuel-efficient models. As a result, cars in the 1980s are generally smaller and more fuel efficient than earlier models. However, when fuel prices in the mid- to late-1980s stabilized, manufacturers began to build and consumers began to purchase the larger and more powerful models as they had in previous years. These cars were, however, still more efficient than the vehicles of the 1960s.

Car sales are a function of the economy. When work forces are employed and the economic outlook is favorable, sales will more than likely be healthy. If gasoline prices are perceived as high or not stable, sales of small, fuel-efficient vehicles will rise. In the mid-80s, during a period of high interest rates and a slow economy, domestic automobile manufacturers offered large cash rebates and attractive low-interest financing (as low as 0 percent on a 24-month term by American Motors) to spur sales. During this period, when customers shopped, they not only shopped for the best model but for the best sale incentive.

Developments in the Luxury Car Market

Traditional versus Functional Luxury

The U.S. luxury car market can be classified into two segments: traditional and functional. U.S. manufacturers have typically produced entries to the traditional segment, and the Europeans, the functional segment. Traditional luxury cars have been represented primarily by Cadillacs and Lincolns in the first tier and Oldsmobile, Buick, Mercury, and Chrysler in the second. The functional luxury cars of Europe were primarily made up of Germany's Mercedes-Benz, BMW, and Audi; Britain's Rolls-Royce and Jaguar; and certain models of Sweden's Saab and Volvo.

Traditional luxury cars strive to make the driving experience as effortless as possible. This has been accomplished by providing passengers with plush, living-room-style interiors and rides so smooth that Mercury commercials of the mid-1970s boasted that a Cartier jeweler could flawlessly cut a diamond while riding in the back seat of a Mercury luxury car. The functional luxury car, on the other hand, attempts to put the driver in touch with the road via steering and suspension systems that inform the driver of the immediate environment.

Throughout Cadillac's history, the division has had a variety of competitive products to contend with. In the 1930s, brands such as Packard, Pierce-Arrow, Auburn, Cord, Imperial, and Lincoln were vying for a piece of the luxury car market. By the early 1960s, most of these great marques had become memories with only Ford's Lincoln division and Chrysler's Imperial (until 1985) left to offer a measurable amount of domestic competition.

Domestic Competition

As Cadillac plotted its strategy for the luxury car market, Ford's Lincoln wasn't far behind. In 1979, the Town Car/Coupe, Lincoln's equivalent to the de Ville, was downsized to dimensions similar to the Cadillac. (See Exhibit 2 for a description of models.) In that same year, the Mark V, competitor to the Eldorado, was also downsized. The new Mark VI (each new design of the Mark series advances one Roman numeral) in fact shared the same platform as the

EXHIBIT 2 Descriptions of models, domestic comparison

	1978 target	*1988 target*
Cadillac		
de Ville/Fleetwood	Traditional large, 4-door, 6-passenger, rear wheel drive, V–8	New size traditional, 4-door, 6-passenger, front wheel drive, V–8
Brougham	N/A	Traditional large, 4-door, 6-passenger, rear wheel drive, V–8
Eldorado	Traditional large, 2-door, front wheel drive, V–8	International size, 2-door, front wheel drive, V–8
Seville	International size, 4-door, front wheel drive, V–8	International size, 4-door, front wheel drive, V–8
Allante	N/A	2-seat, coupe/convertible, functional
Lincoln		
Town Car	Traditional large, 4-door, 6-passenger, rear wheel drive, V–8	Traditional large, 4-door, 6-passenger, rear wheel drive, V–8
Mark V/VII	Traditional large, 2-door, rear wheel drive, V–8	Smaller, functional 2-door, rear wheel drive, V–8
Versailles/Continental	International size, 4-door, rear wheel drive, V–8, traditional market	International size, functional, 4-door, front wheel drive, V–6

Town Car; therefore, it shared similar overall dimensions and was now for the first time available with four doors. In 1982, Lincoln introduced the Continental, the replacement for the poor selling Versailles. Both cars were direct competition to Cadillac's Seville and attempted to emulate virtues of the Seville. The new Continental went so far as to borrow certain styling cues from the Seville, particularly the "bustle" style trunk.

In 1984, Lincoln's strategy began to change. This year Lincoln introduced the Mark VII. No longer built off the Town Car/Coupe chassis, the Mark VII was back to purely a two-door body style and offered two distinct versions: the traditional luxury model based on the Designer Series, and the functional luxury model—the LSC. The Mark VIIs used a newly developed air suspension system not found in any other car in the United States. The LSC version came with upgraded sport-oriented appointments such as European-style seats and a firmer version of the air suspension. Over the following years, a tachometer and a higher output engine were also added to the LSC to increase its functional appeal.

In 1988, Lincoln introduced an all new design for the Continental. (See Exhibit 3.) Borrowing heavily on the functional theme of the Mark VII LSC, the Continental now seemed as eager to differentiate itself from the Seville as it was earlier to emulate it. According to Maryann N. Keller, automotive industry analyst and vice president of the New York brokerage firm Furman, Selz, Mager, Deltz and Birney, ". . . Lincoln's new Continental, priced just under $30,000, is demonstrating that an American car maker can produce an automobile that combines appealing features from two continents [Europe and North America]. The body style and interior appointments have a definite European flavor. The size and generous complement of creature comforts are distinctly American. Though it could use a more powerful engine, the Continental signals Ford's arrival as a real challenger in the functional luxury car market."[3]

Foreign Competition—European

As Cadillac moved through the 1960s and 70s, the European luxury cars were emerging as serious alternative types of luxury automobiles. Rolls-Royce of England, long recognized as providing expensive, hand-built luxury cars, was never a Cadillac alternative. Mercedes-Benz, however, was a different kind of luxury car. If Cadillacs were as plush as fine living rooms, the Mercedes-Benz was as functional as a well-appointed study. The Mercedes-Benz mission was not to surround the driver or passengers in cushions of soft velour or provide them with a silky smooth ride, but to provide firm, supportive seating and a controlled ride in an automobile engineered for traveling at high speeds on the German autobahn.

---

[3] Maryann N. Keller, "Streetwise Showdown in the High-Priced Sector," *Motor Trend,* October 1988, p. 138.

EXHIBIT 3 1988 Continental

"The new Continental will change the way the world thinks of American cars." —*Car and Driver*

"Under the Continental's sleek sheetmetal lurks a suspension engineer's dream come true: computer-controlled air springs and dual-damping shocks at each wheel." —*Automobile*

"...it's a magic-carpet limo that shifts to tied-down sports sedan exactly when you want or need it to. Amazing!" —*Motor Trend*

"This car translates much of the European standard of luxury into the American idiom. In so doing it redefines automotive luxury in the U.S. We think it will be a hit." —*AutoWeek*

The new Lincoln Continental. It's the world's most advanced luxury car. And that's not an opinion. It's a fact. For more information, call 1 800 822-9292.

LINCOLN
What a luxury car should be.

The Europeans would prefer we keep these opinions to ourselves.

LINCOLN-MERCURY DIVISION *Ford*
Buckle up—together we can save lives.

C O N T I N E N T A L

The heritage of today's Mercedes-Benz can be traced back to 1885 and the streets of Mannheim, Germany. It was then that Carl Friedrich Benz produced the world's first motor car. While others had pioneered and patented the gas engine, Benz applied it to a passenger-carrying vehicle.

Since the very beginning, Mercedes-Benz has stood for solid engineering. All of the company's automobiles are targeted to various price points in the functional luxury segment. While a $30,980 entry-level 190–D 2.5 model may share components with the top of the line $79,840 560–SEC, there are no other "lesser" divisions that might require Mercedes-Benz components. This also affords Mercedes-Benz the luxury of maintaining a single automobile focus. However, the company is also one of the world's largest medium- and heavy-duty truck manufacturers.

As the 1970s progressed and the 1980s approached, additional European manufacturers began to market their products in the functional luxury segment. Bavarian Motor Works (BMW) of West Germany moved from importing primarily two-door sports coupes to vehicles similar to Mercedes-Benz. BMW's strategy differed from Mercedes in that BMW catered even more so to the sport-oriented functional luxury buyer. The BMW product offerings begin with the small two- and four-door 3 series, the four-door midsize 5 series, large four-door 7 series, and the two-door 6 series. Over the past few years, BMW has broadened its product offering by introducing the previously mentioned 3 series four-door. The all new 1987 BMW 7 series includes a replacement for the 1986 735i model as well as an all new model for 1988, the 750iL. The 750iL is the largest, and at $70,000 the most expensive, sedan BMW has ever sold in the United States. The 750iL is unique from the lesser 735i in its 4.5-inch-longer wheelbase, distinctive hood and grille treatment, and most notably its 12-cylinder engine. The 750iL is $13,000 more expensive than the 735i and is the only five-passenger sedan in the world to offer a 12-cylinder engine. (See Exhibit 4.)

As the functional luxury market has developed, Mercedes-Benz has also become considered by many to be the ultimate car in the luxury market. (However, it is recently being challenged by BMW.) According to the automotive research company, J. D. Powers and Associates, Mercedes-Benz owners rated their cars and dealer service higher than Cadillac owners did when asked to rate the level of satisfaction of vehicle ownership and dealer service.[4] The Mercedes-Benz line is similar to that of the BMW. The 190 Class is similar in size to the BMW 3 series, the 300 Class the 5 series, and the S Class the 7 series. Mercedes-Benz also offers various two-door coupe and convertible models. In 1987, the combined U.S. sales of Mercedes-Benz and BMW reached approximately 178,000 vehicles, over half of Cadillac's current volume. (See Exhibit 5 for complete market segment sales analysis.)

---

[4] J. D. Powers reports from various years.

EXHIBIT 4 1988 BMW 735i and 1987 Mercedes-Benz S-Class

THE LUXURY CAR AS ONLY BMW COULD ENVISION IT.

When most automakers speak of vision, it's usually to discuss the rake of a windshield.

When BMW employs the term, it's to expound a philosophy.

One of unremitting zeal for performance, for which there is no greater thesis than the new BMW 735i.

A car which emerged after seven years, three million test miles and over 400 prototypes as not just a new luxury car. But a new conception of the luxury car.

LUXURY RETHOUGHT FROM MACROCOSM TO MICROCOSM.

That the BMW 735i heralds a new vision of the luxury car is proclaimed in every feature, from its largest component to its minutest detail.

From a torque-rich new 208-horsepower engine whose catalytic converter paradoxically enhances both fuel economy and performance, to electronic variable assist power steering that provides something rare in ultra-luxury cars: a feel of the road.

From a veritable brain trust of technology that optimizes driver, engine and brake performance (the check control alone monitors 26 functions on a single readout), to 9-mph bumpers at a time when the industry standard has dropped to 2.5 mph.

From computer-perfected front and rear crush zones, to a seat belt that adjusts itself automatically to the size of the driver.

From an elegantly sensuous interior swathed in supple, hand-crafted leather, to a buffer between suspension and chassis that banishes road noise from an already serene interior.

From air-conditioning considered the world's "strongest and most automated" (Auto Motor und Sport), to an electronic automatic transmission that lets you choose sport, economy or manual shifting modes.

And, finally, from a wider, longer, lower, more feline and aerodynamic body, to seats that "remember" positions for three different drivers, including outside mirror settings.

A 3,800-POUND WATCH.

To manufacture such a total rethink of the luxury car mandates a rethink of the whole assembly process. Engine tolerances one-fifth the thickness of a human hair.

A rigorous 37-step rust-proofing and painting regimen.

Inquisition-like inspections, demanding not a hundred or even a thousand steps, but a torturous 7000-step process.

With a daily average of one quality control inspector for every car off the assembly line.

The result is the new BMW 735i. A luxury sedan more akin to a 3,800-lb. Swiss watch than an automobile.

A creation which could only be the handiwork of visionaries.

A group of whom invite you to relish in their vision. Which can be accomplished by a test drive of the new BMW 735i at your authorized BMW dealer.

THE ULTIMATE DRIVING MACHINE.

EXHIBIT 4   *(concluded)*

THE MERCEDES-BENZ S-CLASS: THE ONE THING MORE IMPORTANT THAN THE TECHNOLOGY INSIDE IT IS THE TRADITION BEHIND IT.

A "big Mercedes" has crowned the line for almost as long as there has been a Mercedes-Benz.

This is Mercedes-Benz engineering at its most ambitious. And at its most assertive. From the 540 K of 1936 pictured at left, to the S-Class sedan of 1987 shown above, every big Mercedes and its performance has seemed to scale slightly larger than life.

The 540K, for example, thundered into legend on the power of a supercharged eight-cylinder engine and the flamboyance of low-slung roadster coachwork. Half a century of technological progress later, the S-Class seems to glide rather than thunder over the road; in the case of the flagship 560 SEL Sedan on the roads of its native Europe, two tons of S-Class authority, capable of gliding along at 142 mph all day.

The Mercedes-Benz impulse to engineering masterstrokes marks the S-Class in other ways as well. In a body design that brilliantly combines large dimensions and low aerodynamic drag. In handling agility that large sedans have seldom aspired to, much less achieved. In vital technological innovations — an Anti-lock Braking System (ABS); and a Supplemental Restraint System (SRS) with driver's-side air bag and knee bolster, and emergency tensioning retractors at both front seat belts — that are gradually being emulated by other large sedans.

And laid over this bedrock of technical excellence, a thick layer of civilization and creature comfort. Experienced within a spacious cabin redolent of fine leathers, plush with velour carpeting, garnished with precious handworked woods.

Part limousine, part performance car — the uncommon versatility of the S-Class is reflected in its selection not only by connoisseurs of automotive luxury, but also by most of today's top-ranked Grand Prix motor racing fraternity.

The S-Class is available in three distinctive sedan models and as a two-plus-two closed coupe. You will find nothing to compare with them, in form or in function, wherever you look in the automotive world. They are unique, as is the tradition that spawned them.

Engineered like no other car in the world

EXHIBIT 5 Calendar year U.S. car sales

	1987	1986	1985	1984	1983
		Domestic luxury markets (units)			
Cadillac	261,284	304,057	298,762	320,017	300,337
Lincoln	166,037	177,584	165,138	151,475	101,574
Total domestic sales	7,081,262	8,214,897	8,204,542	7,951,523	6,795,295
		Luxury market (units)			
Domestic					
Cadillac (C)	261,284	304,057	298,762	320,017	300,337
Lincoln (L)	166,037	177,584	164,868	151,475	101,574
Import					
Acura (A)	109,470	52,869	*	*	*
Audi (AU)	41,322	59,797	74,061	71,237	47,936
BMW (B)	87,839	96,759	87,832	70,897	59,242
Jaguar (J)	22,919	24,464	20,528	18,044	15,815
Mercedes-Benz (M)	89,918	99,314	89,098	79,222	73,692
Total (C,L)	427,321	481,641	463,630	471,492	401,911
Total (A,AU,B,J,M)	351,468	333,203	271,519	239,400	196,685
Total luxury market	778,789	814,844	735,149	710,892	598,596
Total U.S. car sales	10,225,304	11,453,705	11,045,784	10,393,230	9,181,036

* Not in production.

Source: *Automotive News, 1988 Market Data Book. MYMA Motor Vehicle Facts & Figures '88*

The third German player in the luxury car market is Audi. Audi reached an all time high U.S. sales volume of over 74,000 units in 1985 due in large part to the sleekly styled 5000 series (48,057 units). The size of a mid-Mercedes and BMW offering, the 5000 was priced lower and could be purchased with one of the first applications of four-wheel drive in a passenger car. However, in 1986 under reports that 5000s equipped with automatic transmissions could unintentionally accelerate, sales began to slide. In 1987, sales were off 44.2 percent from just two years earlier.

For the 1988 model year, in an effort to restore Audi's presence in the luxury car market, the company introduced an all new replacement for the 4000 series, now dubbed the 80 (as it is in Europe). For the 1989 model year, the Audi 5000 has been relaunched as the Audi 100 and 200 (depending on engine size). The 100 and 200 models do not differ from the 5000 series before them in exterior appearance. However, the interior has been redesigned, and the Audi engineers are quick to point out the new engineering developments that differentiate the 100/200 Audis from the old 5000 series.

Foreign Competition—Japanese

The mid- to late-1980s have been accompanied by generally stable fuel costs. As a result, manufacturers are again offering larger models and more powerful engines. In addition, the late 1980s has also included a weaker dollar against other Western currencies such as the West German mark and the Japanese yen. A weak dollar makes buying West German or Japanese imports more expensive. In an effort to maintain acceptable margins on their automobiles, many of the foreign manufacturers have raised prices. This upscale movement in prices by these manufacturers is accompanied, in many cases, by efforts to market models that are also further upscale in class and content.

In the late 1980s, a strong Japanese yen helped create a situation in which the Japanese were no longer the low-cost producers. No longer were the Japanese able to build entry-level cars and price them as competitively against domestic, Korean, and Yugoslavian entries as they had in previous years. The Japanese, unable to make their desired profit margins on these vehicles, began to expand their product line upward to include a greater proportion of compact and midsize cars. These cars include larger models of Honda Accord, Toyota Camry and Cressida, and Nissan Maxima.

Watching the Germans move further upscale in image and in price, Honda saw an opportunity to provide European-style functional luxury cars, but at the price of traditional domestic luxury models. Acura also places emphasis on dealer service. In combination with product quality, dealer service accounted for the number one rating in the 1988 J. D. Powers Consumer Satisfaction Index.

Acura, and other soon-to-be-released Japanese luxury cars from Toyota (Lexus) and Nissan (Infiniti), hope to appeal to those import buyers that have bought nonluxury imports in the past and now want to move upscale but maintain certain import virtues. Acura models include the midsize Legend. The Legend comes well equipped with four-wheel power disc brakes, air conditioning, power door locks and windows, and stereo radio with cassette tape deck— all standard. Like the European functional luxury cars, Acura also pays special attention to the vehicle's handling and performance. To that end, the Legend carries a high-tech racing-bred multivalve V–6 engine and a suspension not found in any other Honda vehicle. Of the Acura Legend, automotive analyst Maryann N. Keller said, ''In less than three years, Honda's Acura division will surpass the magic 100,000-unit mark, which means it will outsell every high-priced European brand in the market.''[5] Hans Jordan, head of U.S. marketing for Mercedes-Benz says, ''Acura is a legitimate contender in the $20,000 to $30,000 price range.''[6] (See Exhibit 6.)

As Acura continues to establish itself in the U.S. luxury car market, Toyota and Nissan are in the process of launching their own luxury car divisions: Lexus and Infiniti, respectively. These new offerings will follow Acura's lead by initially introducing two products for each of the new divisions and selling them only in dealerships dedicated to that division. Acura, Lexus, and Infiniti will not share facilities with the lesser Hondas, Toyotas, or Nissans

---

[5] Maryann N. Keller, ''Streetwise Showdown in the High-Priced Sector,'' p. 138.
[6] Alex Taylor III, ''Detroit versus New Upscale Imports,'' *Fortune*, April 27, 1987, p. 78.

EXHIBIT 6   Acura Legend

MOST AUTOMAKERS WOULD CALL THIS A VERY GOOD YEAR. WE'D CALL IT A VERY GOOD START.

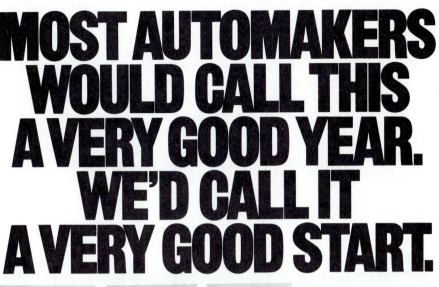

1988 J.D. POWER & ASSOCIATES

C·S·I
CUSTOMER SATISFACTION INDEX

1. Acura
2. Mercedes
3. Honda

DEALER SATISFACTION INDEX
AUTO AGE, 1988

① Acura
② Mercedes
③ Honda
④ Saab

1988 LUXURY IMPORT SALES
Automotive News

1. Acura
2. Volvo
3. Mercedes
4. BMW

Number one in the J.D. Power Customer Satisfaction Index. Number one in Auto Age's first annual Dealer Satisfaction Index. Number one in sales for all luxury imports.*

There's no two ways about it: Acura automobiles and their dealers were an overwhelming success in 1988. But to our way of thinking, last year's performance is only the beginning.

From the day the very first Acura rolled off the assembly line, we've had a reputation for being innovative. And we have every intention of keeping it that way. Not only by continuing to improve the technology and craftsmanship that give Acura automobiles their edge, but also by striving to provide the highest level of satisfaction to our customers as well as our dealers.

Maintaining that reputation won't be easy. But we feel we already have the keys.

Namely, strong dealers whose sales, service and parts departments have consistently made customer satisfaction their top priority. Not to mention products of uncompromising quality.

1988 was unquestionably a year to remember. But the fact is, even if we wanted to rest on our laurels, we couldn't.

We're too busy working on next year.

ACURA
Precision crafted performance.

as Lincoln does with Mercury or as Cadillac is allowed with other GM divisions. The Lexus and Infiniti models will also follow Acura by offering a high degree of Lexus/Infiniti ''only'' content and distinct styling not to be shared by Toyotas or Nissans.

Lexus' initial offering in 1990 will be an all new sedan with a modern multivalve V–8. (See Exhibit 7.) According to *Automobile Magazine,* the Lexus LS 400 ''is a large, roomy, rather conservatively styled four-door sedan that appears to be an amalgam of BMW and Mercedes-Benz design cues, given an American spin with a Cadillacesque egg-crate grille, Detroit-style wood trim, and wrinkled leather upholstery. Its drag coefficient makes it the slipperiest of production sedans, and its four-liter, four-cam, 250-horsepower V–8 engine will push that slippery shape through the air at speeds guaranteed to keep Mercedes-Benz, BMW, and Jaguar engineers working late for the next decade

EXHIBIT 7   1990 Lexus LS 400

or so.''[7] The LS 400 is expected to be priced at approximately $35,000, roughly half of a comparable-size Mercedes-Benz or BMW.

Lexus will also introduce a midsize sedan derived from an existing Toyota, the midsize Camry. The ES250 will be powered by a high-tech multivalve V–6 similar to the Acura Legend. A year later Lexus will debut a new coupe model.

Nissan's Infiniti brand will be introduced at roughly the same time as the Lexus. The introduction of the Infiniti brand will begin with a large sedan similar to the Lexus LS 400. The Infiniti Q45 will be powered by a 4.5 liter V–8 and sell for approximately $35,000. (See Exhibit 8.) Commenting on the image intentions of the sedan, Takashi Oka, senior project manager of the Q45 said, ''We want to create a new definition of luxury and establish an international image beyond that of BMW and Mercedes.'' The Q45 will be joined at introduction with a smaller, less expensive two-door model based on the Japanese market Nissan Leopard. The new coupe will be powered by a multi-valve V–6 and sell for around $25,000. A third model will join the Infiniti brand in 1991. A multivalve V–6 powered midsize sedan, based on the Nissan Maxima, will go head-to-head with the Lexus ES250 as well as the Acura Legend.

EXHIBIT 8   1990 Infiniti Q45

_____
[7] David E. Davis, Jr., ''First Look at Toyota's New Lexus,'' *Automobile Magazine,* January 1989, p. 74.

EXHIBIT 9 Comparison of key specifications

	Lexus LS 400	Infiniti Q-Series	BMW 735i	Mercedes 300-E	Cadillac de Ville	Cadillac Seville	1989 Lincoln Continental
Wheelbase	110.8	113.4	111.5	110.2	113.8	108	109
Length	197.6	199.8	193.3	187.2	205.3	190.8	205.1
Width	71.7	71.9	72.6	68.5	72.5	70.9	72.7
Height	55.1	56.3	55.6	56.9	55	53.5	55.6
Weight	3,800	3,860	3,835	3,195	3,470	3,449	3,626
Engine	V–8	V–8	I–6	I–6	V–8	V–8	V–6
Size (liters)	4	4.5	3.4	3	4.5	4.5	3.8
Horsepower	250	270	208	177	155	155	140

Source: *Automotive News,* December 5, 1988.

(See Exhibit 9 for a key specification comparison between the new Lexus/Infiniti models and selected competition.)

Both Lexus and Infiniti have targeted to sell approximately 100,000 units each when the full range of models is available. This contrasts to Acura's estimated sales of 300,000–400,000 by the mid-1990s.[8]

Cadillac

Cadillac Motor Car Division of General Motors got its start in 1899 as the Detroit Automobile Company and was renamed Cadillac in 1902. The car was named after the French adventurer who founded Detroit 200 years earlier. The force behind Cadillac's early years was Henry M. Leland, operator of Leland & Faulconer Mfg. Co., a precision manufacturer of automotive components. Unlike Henry Ford, who once worked for Leland, Leland was not interested in building an "everyman's" car. Leland and his company were devoted to building the best and "despite record production of 4,307 vehicles in 1906, Cadillac management disregarded the lure of volume sales and dedicated the company to making quality automobiles. This lost Cadillac its position as a high-volume producer, but led to engineering accomplishments that made Cadillac one of the leading fine-car manufacturers."[9]

In 1909, Cadillac was purchased by the young General Motors Corporation. The Lelands, Henry and son Wilfred, stayed on to run Cadillac exactly as if it were their own. They did so until 1917 when they left to begin the Lincoln Motor Co. which was later sold to the Ford Motor Company.

The Lelands had left their impression on Cadillac. Their commitment to quality and innovation propelled Cadillac's status as the "standard of the

---

[8] Jesse Snyder, "INFINITI: Nissan Screening Luxury-Line Dealers," *Automotive News,* July 27, 1987, p. 65.

[9] Frank Gawronski, "Detroit's Oldest Auto Manufacturer," *Automotive News,* September 16, 1983, p. 98.

world.'' Innovations that helped to build this reputation included the self-starter in 1912, America's first V–8 engine in 1914, synchromesh gear boxes, and safety glass as standard equipment in 1929–30. In those same years a V–12 and the world's first production V–16 automobile engine were offered. In the late 1930s, as traditional coach building died out, GM used the Fisher and Fleetwood names to maintain the quality image of its prestige models. In 1941 Cadillac was the second manufacturer to offer a fully automatic transmission. In the 1950s Cadillac styling reigned supreme in the art of tail fins. (See Exhibit 10.) The 1960s brought longer, even more powerful luxury cars, and in 1966 Cadillac introduced its first front wheel drive (FWD) vehicle, the Eldorado, years before FWD was offered by any of Cadillac's non-GM competitors.

EXHIBIT 10   1959 Cadillac

Through the ''longer, lower, wider'' years of the 1960s to late 1970s Cadillac remained a distinguished luxury automobile. The Cadillac de Ville of the day weighed over 5,000 pounds, measured over 230 inches long, and was powered by an 8.2 liter engine. In comparison, the 1988 de Ville weighs only 3,437 pounds, is 196.5 inches long, and is powered by a V–8 engine that is 45 percent smaller than the 1976 model it replaces.

The trend toward smaller Cadillacs began in 1977, in reaction to the first oil embargo of 1973. The new de Villes and Fleetwoods were 8 to 12 inches shorter and averaged 950 pounds lighter than their 1976 counterparts. These models represented the first of the downsized Cadillacs. In 1979, the Eldorado received similar treatment. For 1979, the Eldorados were 20 inches shorter and 1,150 pounds lighter than the 1978 models. In 1985 and 1986, respectively, the de Villes and Eldorados underwent yet another round of downsizing to approximately the size they are today.

Cadillac customers are those who have demanded the best in traditional luxury cars. These traditional Cadillac consumers were most often professionals, above average in income and education, and in recent years an average of 58 years of age. (See Exhibit 11 for a demographic profile of the luxury car market.) These Cadillac buyers had also been accustomed to buying the biggest and most powerful. This, however, had begun to change over the course of the 1970s and 80s.

EXHIBIT 11 Demographics

	Median Age	Age percent < 35	Median income ($000)	Percent college grad +
Industry				
Domestic				
Cadillac	62	2.5%	$61.1	38.4
Lincoln	59	4.4	66.3	39.9
Import				
Acura	35	50.4	55.5	74.6
Audi	41	27.7	78.4	70.8
BMW	42	24.0	98.4	68.3
Jaguar	50	7.9	>150.0	64.6
Mercedes-Benz	45	14.9	117.7	61.7
Saab	38	39.4	69.2	78.1
Volvo	38	36.0	61.7	67.5
Domestic				
Cadillac				
Sedan de Ville	62	6.9	61.0	40.3
Brougham	65	0.3	53.2	27.4
Eldorado	60	4.1	70.2	39.7
Seville	63	1.6	90.0	47.2
Allante	54	6.1	150.0	47.1
Cimarron	60	9.5	45.2	47.0
Lincoln				
Town Car	60	3.2	58.6	35.6
Mark VII	50	10.2	71.3	45.0
Continental	61	3.6	95.2	49.6

Source: *Meritz 1988 Second Quarter Buyers' Study*

In an effort to appeal to the younger upscale consumers who were not a part of the traditional Cadillac market, GM offered a new Cadillac in the 1970s. In May 1975, the Seville was a smaller, international-size Cadillac. Featuring a fuel injected 5.7 liter V–8 as standard equipment along with a long list of other features, the Seville was one of the most well-equipped cars in the world. In 1981, GM introduced the smallest Cadillac ever, the Cimarron. Built on the ''J'' chassis shared by the Chevy Cavalier and Pontiac 2000, the Cimarron was introduced to take on the small ''near luxury'' imports such as the BMW 320 and later 325i. In 1985, the standard Cadillac, the Sedan de Ville/Coupe de

Ville, was thoroughly redesigned. The de Ville series was shortened and placed on a front wheel drive chassis shared with the Buick Electra and the Oldsmobile 98. (Sharing the chassis, or platform, among car divisions is a common automotive industry practice, particularly among U.S. manufacturers. Henry M. Leland recognized that this sharing of parts, or what he referred to as the "true interchangeability of parts," was the key to a great future for the automotive industry.)[10] In 1986, in a further attempt to appeal to the younger and the more functional-demanding customers, Cadillac began offering a functional luxury version to its de Ville series, the Touring Sedan. The Touring Sedan came complete with front air dam, fog lamps, rear deck lid spoiler, blackwell performance tires on 15-inch aluminum alloy wheels, higher spring rates, and faster ratio steering.

In 1986, Cadillac downsized its Eldorado and Seville (the Seville had grown larger from the 1979 model to the 1980 model year) models back to the international size. These two Cadillacs continue to share common platforms with Oldsmobile and Buick models.

Speaking of the 1986 Eldorado/Seville (E/S) models, Braz Pryor, Cadillac's general sales manager says, "We [are] after a contemporary statement with international appeal for buyers young and old who want the luxury of a Cadillac in a more personal package."[11] GM's director of design, Chuck Jordan, calls the fourth-generation Eldorado "Cadillac's youthful sporty car," adding that "sporty elegance was the design theme."[12] Peter Levin, director of special marketing projects at Cadillac, offered some pertinent insights about the basic market philosophy behind the E/S models when he said, "Today, we're going through a revolution in customer expectations. We're after buyers of a certain mindset. . . . The challenge we gave our engineers was to create vehicles that were more responsive and refined but still retained outstanding comfort, because our buyers demand it."[13]

The 1987 model year Cadillac debuted one of its most unique automobiles, the Allante. The Allante, a two-seat, coupe/convertible, is built on a shortened Eldorado/Seville chassis that is assembled and matced in the United States to bodies and interiors that arrive twice weekly, via 747 cargo jets, from their designer/manufacturer, Pininfarina, in Italy. The Allante assumes the position as the flagship model in the Cadillac line. With a 1988 base price of $57,183 and limited to a supply of 6,000 units, it is the most expensive as well as one of the most exclusive Cadillacs ever produced.

Implementing this new strategy and striving to regain the aura of quality, technology, and exclusivity now associated with European luxury cars is not an

---

[10] Ibid.

[11] Mary Ann Angeli, "'86 Eldorado/Seville: Caddy's New Yuppie Lures?," *Automotive Industries,* November 1985, p. 40.

[12] Ibid.

[13] Bob Nagy, "Cadillacs across America," *Motor Trend,* June 1986, p. 91.

easy task. John Grettenberger, Cadillac's general manager states, "We have to be very careful that we offer the right balance. If you go too far in either direction, a manufacturer like Cadillac could lose on either end of the spectrum. If we go too far in the high-tech direction, we could turn off some of our traditional buyers, but if we stick where we are then we won't appeal to the younger ones."[14]

To help achieve Cadillac's strategy of maintaining the traditional, as well as capturing new customers, Cadillac's 1987 advertising emphasized the "Spirit of Cadillac." (See Exhibit 12 for Cadillac's 1987 model line.) All Cadillac models shared a number of common themes including: making an "eloquent design statement," providing customers "worldwide Cadillac exclusives" (e.g., transverse mounted V–8 engine), balanced performance, a commitment to security, and "the ultimate comfort: peace of mind" via "quality craftsmanship" and extensive warranties.[15]

From this common basis each Cadillac model has its own individual spirit. For example, the Allante is the "new spirit of Cadillac." The Allante was positioned to create a new class of performance that merges European road manners with Cadillac comfort and convenience.[16] The Sedan de Ville and Coupe de Ville are Cadillac's "contemporary spirits representing Cadillac's belief that today's luxury cars should reflect today's values."[17] The Fleetwood d'Elegance and Fleetwood Sixty Special are the "sophisticated spirits" of Cadillac. The d'Elegance's formal Cabriolet roof and opera lamps and the Sixty Special's five-inch extended wheelbase make these the most luxurious of the Cadillac "C-bodies" (chassis shared with the de Ville, Buick Electra, and Olds 98). Eldorado is the "driving spirit" while the Seville is the "elegant spirit." Sharing the same chassis, the Eldorado is a two-door coupe with a suspension system that delivers control with a minimum of body roll and sway, while the Seville is a four-door sedan that emphasizes supreme comfort and an exceptional array of standard luxury features. The Brougham d'Elegance is the "classic spirit" for this large, rear wheel drive Cadillac. It is a carryover from the model that the "C-body" cars were to have replaced. Because it and its competitor, the Lincoln Town Car, are in high demand, the Brougham has lived three years past its originally scheduled termination and will likely live on until the early 1990s. Last and certainly least in terms of size is the "sporty spirit" of Cadillac, the Cimarron. In 1988, the Cimarron was discontinued due to poor sales. In 1988, the spirit theme of Cadillac was also discontinued.

In all of 1987, Cadillac spent $35,334,300 on TV advertising to promote the "spirit of Cadillac," a 32.5 percent increase from the previous year.

---

[14] John McElroy, "Cadillac's Grettenberger: Resetting the Standard," *Automotive Industries*, November 1985, p. 36.

[15] *Cadillac 1987* (Detroit, Mich: Cadillac Motor Division, General Motors Corporation, 1986), pp. 2–3.

[16] Ibid.

[17] Ibid.

EXHIBIT 12   1987 Cadillac Line

Allanté shown at the Music Center of Los Angeles County, Los Angeles, California.

Sedan de Ville shown at the Detroit Institute of Arts, Detroit, Michigan.

EXHIBIT 12 1987 Cadillac Line *(continued)*

Fleetwood d'Elegance shown at the High Museum of Art, Atlanta, Georgia.

Eldorado shown at the Kitt Peak National Observatory, Kitt Peak, Arizona.

EXHIBIT 12 1987 Cadillac Line *(concluded)*

Seville shown at the Adler Planetarium, Chicago, Illinois.

Cimarron shown at the Laumeier Sculpture Park, St. Louis, Missouri.

However, BMW's TV total was $45,498,700, and start-up Acura was almost even with Cadillac at $34,478,500.[18] Cadillac's TV budget in 1988 increased to $54,126,200.[19]

Cadillac is GM's luxury market division. Where it actually fits among the other GM divisions can be seen in the market plots of Exhibit 13. In 1986, Cadillac was positioned as the highest-priced division, offering the consumer automobiles that are conservative but not far from an even split between conservative and aggressive, and family and personal orientations. GM's goals

EXHIBIT 13   GM plots its markets

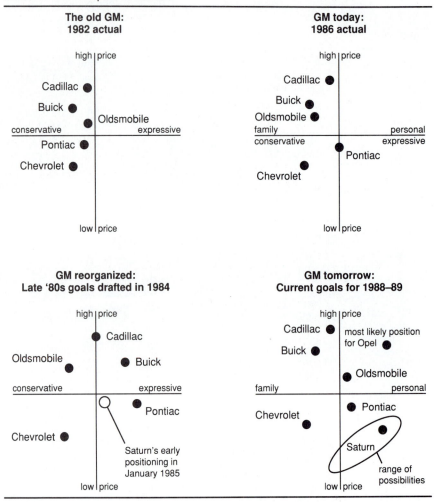

AUTOMOTIVE NEWS/CHARLOTTE WINTER

---

[18] "Et Cetera," *Automotive News, 1988 Market Data Book,* p. 208.
[19] Ibid.

for the 1988–89 model year show Cadillac maintaining its basic position except in terms of price, where it continues to move further upscale. According to General Manager Grettenberger, "Our vision is to move every Cadillac upscale in terms of its expressiveness, image, distinctiveness, and overall content. I don't see us having a sale-weighted average of $43,000–44,000 like Mercedes-Benz. But I would like to see Cadillacs move upscale."[20] Cadillac's 1989 model line ranges in price from approximately $25,000 for a Coupe de Ville, $26,000 for the Brougham, and $30,000–34,000 for the Fleetwood. The Eldorado begins at about $27,000 while the Seville begins at $30,000. The Allante is, of course, the high-price leader at $57,183.

The Problem

Throughout most of its existence, Cadillac has been synonymous with the finest in luxury automobiles. In the early years under the Lehland family's leadership, the company won the Dewar Trophy from the Royal Automobile Club. Cadillac not only won this coveted prize for engineering excellence and innovation once but also was the only car company to do it twice. After the Lehlands left, and for quite some time, Cadillac managed to keep its eye trained on building the best luxury cars possible.

By the 1978 model year, Cadillac sales had hit an all time record of 350,813 units. At that time and as recently as 1983, Cadillac accounted for over one third of all luxury car sales. In 1987 Cadillac made up less than one quarter of all such sales. Models that had been previously very popular were selling

EXHIBIT 14 Cadillac 15-year sales trend by model

Year	Cadillac	Eldorado	Seville	Cimarron	Allante
1987	203,487	21,470	24,266	12,295	2,517
1986	235,206	24,266	21,150	23,435	*
1985	187,664	58,310	29,034	23,754	*
1984	195,177	70,577	35,349	18,014	*
1983	176,003	71,624	33,522	19,188	*
1982	148,211	55,761	23,030	13,195	*
1981	134,765	53,233	23,054	13,406	*
1980	126,145	51,065	35,347	*	*
1979	202,681	61,000	44,216	*	*
1978	238,976	43,681	52,396	*	*
1977	238,066	45,206	42,452	*	*
1976	214,649	39,333	39,734	*	*
1975	189,034	44,363	22,738	*	*
1974	183,633	36,360	*	*	*
1973	235,504	50,205	*	*	*

Note: Sales for years 1973–1983 are represented by registrations.
* Not in production.
Source: *Automotive News Annual Almanac Issues/Market Data Books.*

---

[20] Dave Zoia, "Cadillac Eyes an Allante Sedan," *Automotive News* 16 (February 1987), p. 37.

poorly. In 1985 the Eldorado and Seville had sales of 66,863 and 32,986, respectively. During the following year, the smaller, redesigned models sold only 45 percent of the 1985 models they replaced; 1987 sales fared somewhat worse. Sales of the exclusive Allante have also been disappointing. The two-door coupe/convertible was expected to be a sellout its first year at 6,000 units, but by year's end the Allante tallied just over 2,500 units. (See Exhibit 14 for Cadillac's 1973–87 sales figures and Exhibit 15 for announced 1988 competitive car prices.)

EXHIBIT 15 1988 Luxury car manufacturers' suggested retail prices

U.S. domestic	4-door	2-door	European import	4-door	2-door
Cadillac			Audi		
Cimarron V-6	$16,071		80 Series 4	$18,600	
de Ville V-8	23,404	$23,049	80 Quattro 5	22,700	
Fleetwood d'Elegance V-8	28,024		90 Series 4	24,330	
Fleetwood Sixty Special V-8	34,750		90 Series 5	24,330	
Brougham V-8	23,846		90 Series Quattro 5	27,720	
Eldorado V-8		24,891	5000S 5	22,850	
Seville V-8	27,627		5000S Quattro 5	27,280	
Allante V-8		56,533	5000CS Turbo 5	30,910	
			5000CS Turbo Quattro 5	34,810	
Lincoln					
Town Car V-8	24,373		BMW		
Town Car Signature V-8	27,374		325 6	25,150	$24,350
Town Car Cartier V-8	28,520		325is6		28,950
Mark VII LSC V-8		26,380	325i6	28,950	
Mark VII Bill Blass V-8		26,380	325ix6		33,290
Continental V-6	26,078		M-3 4		34,800
Continental Signature V-6	27,944		528e6	31,950	
			535i6	36,700	
			535is6	37,800	
			M-5 6	47,500	
			635CSi6		46,000
			M-6 6		55,950
			735i6	54,000	
			750iL 12	69,000	
			Jaguar		
			XJ-6 6	43,500	
			Vanden Plas 6	47,500	
			XJ-S V-12		47,000
			XJ-SC V-12		50,450
			Mercedes Benz		
			190-E 2.3 4	29,190	
			190-D 2.5 5	29,960	
			190-E 2.6 6	33,500	
			260-E 6	37,845	
			300-E 6	43,365	
			300-CE 6		53,340
			300-SE 6	49,900	
			300-SEL 6	53,490	
			420-SEL V-8	59,080	
			560-SEL V-8	69,760	
			560-SL V-8		62,110
			560-SEC V-8		77,065

Source: *Automotive News, 1988 Market Data Book.*

What's more important to Cadillac and to Reuss, executive vice president of North American car operations, was the division's steadily declining reputation for luxury car excellence. On the surface the cause for the decline was multifaceted. First, Cadillac suffered from what the press called "look-alike cars." The Cadillac de Villes and Fleetwoods looked like Buick Electras and Oldsmobile Ninety Eights. This perception was even played up in a Lincoln Town Car television commercial where Cadillac, Buick, and Olds owners can't tell their cars apart at a restaurant when the valets bring the three cars forward. Concedes one GM man, "Cadillac, one could say, is selling 300,000 Buicks."[21]

Cadillac innovation in the late 1970s and early 1980s was also a cause for concern. The availability of a V–8 diesel engine, manufactured from a modified gasoline engine, was discontinued when its reliability proved disastrous. This same scenario played a second time, and in the same time period, with Cadillac's exclusive multidisplacement engine. The engine was programmed to run on 8, 6, or 4 cylinders depending on engine load demand. However, as with the diesel, lack of reliability killed the innovative engine.

On September 27, 1988, consumer activist Ralph Nader issued a report called "Cadillac—The Heartbreak of America."[22] According to Nader, "This report was written because of the large volume of mail we have received from indignant Cadillac purchasers who expect better quality from a $25,000 investment."[23] GM called the Nader document outdated, unfair, and inaccurate.

As Reuss looks over these problems and others, his task appears not to be an easy one. Could the quality and design of Cadillac's cars be the sole cause of the division's problems? Maybe advertising and imaging are being directed at the wrong customer, or perhaps the division has lost sight of just who the Cadillac customer is. Seeing the result of the problems may be easy, but finding solutions to their causes will be the real test to restoring Cadillac as the standard of the world.

---

[21] Flint, "Hold the Velveeta—Please Pass the Brie," p. 31.
[22] John E. Peterson, "The Heartbreak of America," *The Detroit News* 28 (September 1988), p. C1–2.
[23] Ibid.

Case 2 _____

Valley BancSystem, Inc.*

Chuck Smith walked briskly across the lobby of the Broadmoor bank to his office. It was 7:30 on a chilly morning in November 1992. He would have at least an hour before the rush of Friday customers would begin. Friday always meant a great deal of "public relations" for Smith in terms of exchanging greetings and small talk with customers. "Today I could do without it," Smith thought, "I'd rather work on what the marketing committee discussed yesterday." However, he knew that customers expected to see his door open and his face break into a smile whenever they voiced a greeting. The hour or so would be enough time to get his thoughts down on the Shop and Save proposal. The other topics that he had discussed with the committee would have to wait.

Valley BancSystem, Inc.

Valley Bank and Trust Company of Broadmoor was one of eight members of Valley BancSystem, Inc., a multibank holding company under the laws of the state of Illinois. Seven of the eight subsidiaries were located within 25 miles of each other in Polk and Madison counties. The sixth, Valley Bank and Trust Company of Columbus, was almost 80 miles south in Jackson County. Polk and Madison counties were due west of Chicago.

Valley BancSystem, Inc. was formed on April 30, 1982, about one year after enactment of an Illinois law permitting multibank holding companies. Earlier, the eight subsidiaries were considered "affiliated" in the sense that they shared several officers and directors. The holding company provided auditing, investment, and accounting services for its subsidiaries. It contracted with an outside organization for computer services and managed the ATM

---

* This case was written by Prof. James E. Nelson, University of Colorado. It is intended for use as a basis for class discussion rather than to illustrate either effective or ineffective decision making. Data and case location are disguised. © 1993 by Prof. James E. Nelson, College of Business and Administration, University of Colorado, Boulder, Colorado 80309. Used with permission.

service. The holding company had authority and responsibility for major financial and marketing decisions for all subsidiaries. As an example of financial decision making, senior management had decided in late 1991 to charge off about $4.7 million in loans (primarily agricultural). The action had produced a net loss of $25,000 (see Exhibit 1 for financial data).

EXHIBIT 1   Financial data*

	1989	1990	1991	1992†
Assets	$308,339	$321,067	$312,104	$318,093
Liabilities	283,268	295,415	289,872	294,312
Stockholders' equity	25,071	25,652	22,232	23,781
Interest income	32,687	33,399	30,807	26,871
Interest expense	20,300	21,460	18,871	16,051
Net interest income	12,387	11,939	11,936	10,820
Provision for possible loan losses	285	309	4,140	258
Net interest income after provision for possible loan losses	12,102	11,630	7,796	10,562
Other income	1,676	1,685	661	1,758
Other expenses	7,473	7,924	8,482	6,242
Income (loss) before income taxes and extraordinary item	6,305	5,391	(25)	6,078
Deposit growth, percentage	3.9%	6.2%	−2.0%	−1.5%
Return on assets, percentage	1.0	0.6	0.0	1.0
Return on equity, percentage	12.6	8.6	−0.1	14.4
Capital to assets, percentage	7.6	7.4	6.1	6.6

*All data are stated in thousands of dollars except data for deposit growth, return on assets, return on equity, and capital to assets.
†As of September.

Now that financial matters had been resolved, the attention of senior management turned to marketing. A marketing committee had been formed at the request of the new chairman of the board and president, James Kuhn. Kuhn had joined the holding company in late 1989, replacing John Charles, who had served as chairman and president since 1958. Kuhn's previous experience included positions as senior vice president of Essex County Bank and Trust, senior vice president of the Bank Marketing Association, and vice president of Beverly Bankcorporation. Kuhn held an MS in marketing and took a keen interest in the marketing issues facing Valley BancSystem.

Marketing Issues

Smith settled into his chair and read the five marketing issues he had summarized last night:

1. What should be our response to the Shop and Save proposal to put "four or five" full-service branch offices in their supermarkets in Polk and Madison counties?

2. How can we capitalize and build on the sales training program?
3. How should we organize for the marketing function—at the holding company and at each subsidiary? What should be the authority and responsibility at each level?
4. How do we translate corporate financial goals into marketing goals? How do we make marketing goals part of the management process?
5. What should be Valley's marketing strategy over the next five years?

Smith knew the senior management considered all issues to be high-priority items.

The Shop and Save Proposal

Early in October, the Broadmoor bank president had paid a call on the manager of a Shop and Save supermarket located in nearby Ridgeway, Illinois. The purpose of the call was to inquire into the possibility of placing a Valley branch facility in the store. The timing could not have been better—the store was soon to begin a remodeling project and could easily accommodate the facility. Further discussion between Valley officers and Shop and Save's executive committee had led to the latter group's offer last month of leases at four stores.

Smith and the marketing committee had discussed the proposal at length. Branches would occupy about 500 square feet at each location (sites to be identified later and to be mutually acceptable to both parties). Costs to Valley for the space would be $15 per square foot. Other costs would include wages and benefits for the two tellers expected to staff the branch and the manager (who might be responsible for all four locations). If branches proved popular with Shop and Save customers, Smith thought that each might generate some $2 to $4 million in deposits in a year. As much as $1 or $2 million in loans per branch should also be possible.

The entire matter deserved much analysis, but Smith and the committee were unsure about how to proceed. What they needed most was a framework for their analysis—what to examine, what to forecast, what to summarize and present to the board. Each member had promised to spend some time on this issue before the next meeting. Once they had a good framework for the decision, data collection and analysis would be much easier.

The Sales Training Program

Early in 1992 Kuhn and the marketing committee had seen the need for a comprehensive sales training program for all 250 Valley employees. Actually, Valley preferred to call its employees "associates" to highlight the common interest that all had in the success of the organization. All associates were to receive 20 hours of sales training.

The training was intended to improve Valley's performance by developing associates' customer relations and customer development skills. Training for customer relations skills included lectures, discussion, and exercises on such topics as what customers expect from a bank and its employees, how to deal effectively with customers, and what to avoid as customer service mistakes. Training for customer development skills covered the seeking of new business both on and off bank premises. While the training would show direct effects on performance, Kuhn and the marketing committee felt that an equal if not more important benefit was that the training would raise an awareness that selling was an important part of *everyone's* job description.

Presidents, other officers, and some selected associates would receive advanced training on customer relations and customer development in 20 hours of sessions held separately from those for most associates. Presidents and selected officers were also to receive eight more hours of training on sales management and planning. All sessions would be held at Valley facilities. A Chicago consultant who specialized in sales training would conduct the sessions, during late afternoon hours, from October 1992 through March 1993. The consultant's fee was $45,000.

Already Smith thought he could see some effects of the first two-and-one-half hour session. For example, many tellers and new accounts people had worn costumes on Halloween to represent bank products. The best, in his mind, was a teller dressed as a house with dollar bills protruding from her doors and windows. A sign by the house urged customers to get money from their houses by signing up for an Equity Plus loan. The teller had gotten seven referrals—if all resulted in a booked loan, the teller would receive $350 from Valley for her efforts. Apart from Halloween costumes, Smith had noticed a general improvement in associates' attitudes and behavior toward customers. However, a few associates thought that acquiring customer development skills was a bit distasteful and probably unnecessary. Some officers at one or two banks felt the same way.

The marketing committee wanted to change this attitude and keep the momentum begun by the training. Several things seemed to be needed. One consisted of motivational mechanisms or systems to encourage selling activity by associates and officers. Kuhn had told the committee that he could support most any type of reward, including money, recognition, and career advancement. All he wanted was an effective, ethical, and simple approach. Another need was for control procedures to make sure associates and officers performed as expected. Kuhn's expectations here were for a system that allowed for a great deal of individuality—he wanted no associate or officer to feel that someone was constantly looking over his or her shoulder. Another need was for networking or communication systems to facilitate the sharing of sales problems and opportunities.

Smith's thoughts went back to his conversation yesterday with Kuhn. The two had compared their impressions of the early effects of the sales training. Kuhn had ended the exchange stating that "The way banking is going, the only potential advantages a bank can have over its competitors are its location and its people. I want you and the marketing committee to recommend everything we need to do to make sure our people are effective salespeople."

Organizing for the Marketing Function

The third major issue facing the committee was how to organize for marketing at Valley. Right now the marketing organization consisted of the three-member committee that reported directly to Kuhn. Members of the committee were: Chuck Smith, executive vice president of the Broadmoor bank; R. J. Day, president and director of the New Richmond bank; and Thomas Charles, president and director of the Alden bank. Smith chaired the committee because of his greater interest in marketing and his experience as a correspondent banker for a St. Louis bank before joining Valley some eight years ago. Day had the most banking experience of the three (23 years with Valley), primarily in commercial and mortgage lending. Charles had about the same number of years of banking experience as Smith, again with an emphasis on lending. The committee had been meeting about once a month since its beginning in early 1991. However, Smith and Day usually met with Kuhn about once a week to discuss marketing topics.

The committee's accomplishments to date included implementation of the training program and formulation of the first-ever promotion budget. The promotion budget planned for 1992 currently stood at $420,000. All but $50,000 of this amount had been carefully allocated by the committee and an advertising agency to various advertising and promotion activities. Each month in 1992 was scheduled for a major promotion (e.g., IRA, home improvement loan, ATM), a statement stuffer coordinated with the promotion, a newsletter, and several news releases. Major promotions always included newspaper advertising, lobby posters, teller cards (drive-up and counter), and brochures. Radio advertising would be added for June and October. The remaining $50,000 was available to satisfy requests by subsidiaries for local market promotions.

Accomplishments illustrated the committee's responsibilities. That is, the committee managed existing services and recommended, developed, and priced new services. It ensured that appropriate personnel were trained to sell all services. It budgeted and coordinated most of the advertising and promotion efforts. In short, the marketing committee was charged with setting marketing objectives; investigating, recommending, and implementing marketing strategies; and monitoring marketing results.

To do all of this took a great deal of time and effort. Each committee member spent several hours per week on marketing matters, yet each felt it was not enough. The investment of time and effort was doubly frustrating because it took away from each member's ability to do his primary job. However, the committee seemed a good way to organize for marketing because it made the acceptance of marketing activities relatively easy at each subsidiary.

An alternative to the committee organization would be to employ a full-time marketing director at the holding company. One committee member had noted that a marketing director could provide leadership and needed expertise on marketing matters. "A director would also have more credibility," Smith thought, "even though some subsidiaries might not like the idea of yet another

staff person at the holding company.'' A good marketing director with experience would probably cost around $80,000 per year in salary and benefits.

The committee had discussed marketing organization for several minutes
in yesterday's meeting. Members finally decided to give the matter more
thought before they met again, concluding that there probably were other
advantages and disadvantages of either type of organization. ''There might even
be some other ways of organizing,'' one of the members had said, ''ways that
would combine the best features of a committee and a director.''

The committee also had discussed the organization for marketing at each
subsidiary bank. No subsidiary could justify hiring a full-time marketing officer
given its size and the marketing efforts planned at the holding company. Yet it
seemed unwise to have no formal marketing authority and responsibility at each
subsidiary. Committee members had agreed that a marketing orientation at the
subsidiary was crucial to the success of a subsidiary. The problem was how to
achieve this orientation, because subsidiary officers generally lacked marketing
backgrounds.

Marketing Goals

The lack of marketing backgrounds made marketing goal setting difficult at both
the holding company and subsidiary levels. However, Kuhn and the committee
felt it important that the holding company and each subsidiary have marketing
goals. Marketing goals would encourage marketing thinking and focus marketing efforts. Marketing goals would also form a standard against which performance could be measured.

This was the first time that the holding company and subsidiaries had ever
set marketing goals. Most officers were familiar with financial goal setting and
the holding company's financial goals for 1992: 8 percent growth in deposits,
1.2 percent return on assets; 16 percent return on equity; and a 7 percent capital
to assets ratio. Each subsidiary's financial goals departed somewhat from these
figures, dependent on local market conditions and forecasts.

Neither the holding company nor the subsidiaries had translated financial
goals into marketing goals. The committee had discussed some criteria for the
translation, concluding that marketing goals should be consistent with financial
goals and be stated in specific and measurable terms at realistic levels. The
committee had even tried to write some marketing goals:

Obtain 200 Vacation Club accounts by October 1993.

Increase IRA deposits by 15 percent.

Book 350 Equity Plus loans by the end of 1993.

Each member had promised to spend more time thinking about marketing
goals after yesterday's meeting. Each was also to produce a more complete list
of goals by the end of next week, send it to the other committee members, and
be ready for a discussion at the next meeting. It would be important to get some

marketing goals approved at the holding company level before expecting each subsidiary to write its own.

Marketing Strategy

The last major issue discussed by the marketing committee was Valley's marketing strategy over the next five years. Kuhn had requested that the committee study this topic and propose two options, each with clearly identified strengths and weaknesses. He had also asked for the committee's choice between the options.

The first strategic option was growth via market development. This strategy would emphasize the marketing of existing financial services to new markets defined in terms of either geographic areas or market segments. Growth via new geographic areas could be done three ways. The first would be to stay in Polk and Madison counties and locate in one or more of several growing communities. The second would be to expand westward and southward to other Illinois counties. The third would be to cross the state line and enter the Wisconsin market, about 20 miles north of Alden. Valley could move into Wisconsin by its directors establishing a Wisconsin corporation in the banking industry. Alternatively, it could enter Wisconsin by offering a limited-service bank that would provide all of Valley's services except commercial loans.

Kuhn and the directors wanted any new market area chosen to show a deposit growth potential in excess of 8 percent per year; any new facility should show an operating profit within the first five years. Committee members thought that careful selection of new market areas could meet these criteria. However, the consequences of a mistake in their judgment could be substantial.

Less risky was a market development strategy based not on new geographic areas but on new market segments. These new segments would be in the local community where Valley's reputation was strongest. Examples of possible new segments were professionals, commercial accounts (mostly retailing and light industry), and young marrieds. Potential here was probably not as great as with geographic expansion.

The second strategic option was growth via service development. This strategy would emphasize the marketing of new financial services to existing markets. New services could be aimed at either consumer or commercial accounts with the goal of increasing deposits, loans, or service fees. There were literally hundreds of new services that Valley could add. Some of the more promising ones had been mentioned in yesterday's meeting. In-home banking would allow customers to link their home computers with the bank's system and pay bills, transfer funds, and check on account balances. Optimistic forecasts here called for about 10 percent of U.S. households to use some form of home banking by the mid 1990s. Auto leasing would have Valley as lessor to individual customers. Experts forecasted a 6 to 10 percent annual growth rate for the service, reaching a level of about 40 percent of all new car deliveries in the late 1990s. Personal financial planning would use financial advisers at the bank to investigate middle-aged customers' financial objectives and resources and then recommend a financial program. A "prestige" credit card would provide increased services and higher loan limits to upscale customers. The committee recognized the need for careful research before recommending one new service over another.

The committee also recognized that a recommendation to market any new service would subject Valley to the chance of failure. Costs associated with failure depended on the new service. However, in no case did the committee think that a major new service could be introduced for less than $100,000 in training, marketing, and other start-up costs.

Finally, the committee recognized that growth objectives could be met by either strategy and that Valley almost certainly would not pursue one strategy to the exclusion of the other. A mix between the two would be best; the issue really was which of the two strategies should be emphasized. Further, adoption of either strategy would not mean abandonment of existing customer segments. All Valley subsidiaries would be expected to continue to show growth via penetrating existing segments through the offering of present services.

Holding Company Strategy

Choosing between a market development and a product development strategy was the final decision in formulating the holding company's strategy. Earlier in the year, Kuhn and the directors had agreed on other strategic components: profitable growth, liquidity, active asset/liability management, financial and marketing control over subsidiaries, capable personnel, and market leadership. All components were tied to a community bank orientation: suburban locations, a high profile in local community affairs, personal relationships with customers, and deposits and loans generated in the local community.

"For the next few years, our strategy could also be described as 'conservative,'" Kuhn had told the committee. He had gone on to explain that a conservative approach was called for because it would avoid risks and produce profits (important because of last year's loss), allow Valley time to train and develop its associates and officers, and minimize the risk of any costly mistakes. The net effect of a conservative approach should be intermediate- and long-term profitability. However, Kuhn noted that in the short term the approach might mean some missed opportunities and some stronger competitors.

Atlanta Cyclorama*

The director of the Atlanta Cyclorama was sitting in his Grant Park office speculating over his greatest challenge, namely, devising the 1987 promotional plan for the Cyclorama and long-range strategies for the attraction for future years. Attendance will have to be increased from an estimated 342,000 in 1986 to 500,000 in 1989, and sales will have to exceed $1 million per year by 1990. Attendance in 1982 was 195,000 and in 1983 it reached 300,000. Attendance figures for 1984 through 1986, broken down by ticket class, are shown in Table I.

TABLE I Breakdown of Cyclorama attendance and revenue by ticket class

	1984		1985		1986	
Ticket class	Attendance	Revenue	Attendance	Revenue	Attendance	Revenue
Adult ($3.00)	117,000	$351,000	129,005	$387,015	146,789	$440,367
Adult group and senior citizens ($2.50)	82,463	206,158	77,030	192,575	82,325	205,813
Children ($1.50)	20,446	30,669	22,465	33,698	25,840	38,760
Child group ($1)	7,096	7,096	6,637	6,637	6,122	6,122
Free	41,217	—	37,578	—	42,120	—
Tour groups	30,000	57,483	29,315	67,891	38,900	90,098
Total	298,222	$652,406	279,000	$687,816	342,096	$781,160

The Atlanta Cyclorama

Before the invention of motion pictures, opportunities for the general public to view past events were definitely limited. One vehicle for accomplishing this desire was the cyclorama, which is defined as "a 360° circular painting which when viewed from its interior gives the illusion that the viewer is in the scene."

---

* This case was prepared at Georgia State University as a basis for class discussion rather than to illustrate either effective or ineffective handling of an administrative situation. All publication rights reserved; copyright © 1987, by John Wright and Daniel C. Bello. Used with permission.

A cyclorama is also sometimes referred to as a panorama. Hundreds of these cycloramas were painted and shown in American cities in the latter half of the 19th century; however, today only 14 survive throughout the world. In the United States, in addition to the Atlanta Cyclorama, a panorama is on exhibit at the Gettysburg Battlefield in Pennsylvania, and another is in the Metropolitan Museum of Art in New York.

The Atlanta Cyclorama was created in 1885 and depicts the 1864 Battle of Atlanta which is familiar to all who have seen the movie *Gone with the Wind*. The masterpiece is a 50-foot-high, 400-foot circumference painting in the round, with a three-dimensional diorama complete with figures added by the WPA in the 1930s. The cyclorama was first displayed in a frame building in Grant Park in 1912. In 1921, the painting was moved to its present building. After years of use and limited maintenance, the attraction had fallen into an advanced state of disrepair so serious that by 1979 the cyclorama had to be closed. Extensive restoration ensued at a cost of $11 million. For two and a half years, workers repaired the tears and flaws in the painting and revamped the three-dimensional diorama that serves as the painting's foreground. The restoration effort also included the installation of a revolving viewing platform as well as the refurbishing of the building that houses the painting. The exhibit reopened to the public in 1982. In addition to the famous painting, visitors can also admire other exhibits related to the Civil War: for instance, the famous locomotive Texas, winner of the "great locomotive chase." It is the same train that a group of Confederates drove to Ringgold to chase Union raiders who had stolen the locomotive General. Thus, the Atlanta Cyclorama is part historical museum, part artwork, and part Confederate memorial. The cyclorama shares its Grant Park location with the Atlanta Zoo, thus providing a combination sightseeing opportunity.

Grant Park is located three miles south of the downtown hotel district. In past years, the zoo had exerted a negative influence on attendance at the cyclorama because local media stories highlighted the fact that the zoo had fallen into a state of disrepair and that animals had been poorly treated. Fortunately, civic pride had lead to a revitalization program for the zoo in 1985, and a major renovation similar to that experienced by the cyclorama had been completed by late 1986. Attendance figures for the zoo are shown in Table II.

TABLE II   Attendance figures for the Atlanta Zoo

Year	Attendance
1978	452,051
1979	388,832
1980	363,433
1981	347,828
1982	402,118
1983	448,397
1984	279,805
1985	344,087
1986	567,269

Zoo attendance had increased steadily with the renovation efforts, growing from 280,000 in 1984 to almost 570,000 in 1986.

The cyclorama is owned and operated by the Atlanta city government. Exhibit 1 is an organization chart for this operation. In addition to a director and an associate director, there is a staff of 17 persons. The director is a professional, chosen by civil service procedures. The city council authorizes the budget and exercises control over other activities.

EXHIBIT 1   Organization chart—Atlanta Cyclorama

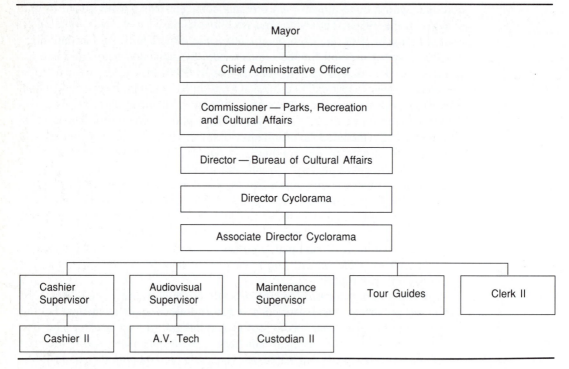

The Product and its Market

Every year, a very diversified crowd visits the cyclorama. The admission price is very reasonable: $3.00 for adults ($2.50 if in groups of 10 or more), $2.50 for senior citizens, $1.50 for children ($1 if in groups of 10 or more), and children under six are admitted free. School groups are also admitted free. Furthermore, there is no charge for parking.

Different groups of people flock to this attraction. The attendance can be segmented into four categories: tour groups (consisting mainly of senior citizens and school groups), conventioneers, visitors and tourists, and finally local residents. These market segments all exhibit particular characteristics.

Tour groups. This segment tends to visit the cyclorama on weekdays. For both segments (school children and senior citizens), the visit usually occurs once a year.

Conventioneers. Atlanta is the third largest convention city in the United States in terms of numbers of conventions hosted. In 1985, 1.5 million conventioneers came to Atlanta. Mostly, they stayed in the downtown area and remained in Atlanta about 3.0 days. Tables III and IV present the conventioneers' attendance growth and their average daily expenditure and length of stay from 1976 to 1985. The main problem they encounter is the lack of activity and entertainment close to downtown. At the heart of the convention world in Atlanta is the Georgia World Congress Center. The Georgia World Congress Center started its operations in Atlanta in September 1976. At that time, it offered 350,000 square feet of exhibition space. But with the convention market booming, it soon proved to be insufficient. In April 1985, the Georgia World Congress Center officially celebrated its expanded opening: 650,000 square feet of exhibition space, and over 1 million square feet of floor space. The center is one of the world's top meeting/exhibit facilities, with its ballroom, auditorium, corporate conference center, and 70 meeting rooms.

TABLE III   Atlanta conventioneers' attendance, per year

Year	Conventions Hosted	Attendance
1976	725	635,000
1977	760	760,000
1978	800	850,000
1979	970	876,800
1980	1,090	1,002,900
1981	1,150	1,128,000
1982	1,000	1,150,000
1983	1,100	1,300,000
1984	1,200	1,110,000
1985	1,400	1,500,000

TABLE IV   Atlanta conventioneers' daily expenditure and length of stay, per year

Year	Average Daily Expenditure	Length of Stay
1976	$ 70.00	3.2 days
1977	73.50	3.5 days
1978	77.00	3.5 days
1979	81.00	4.0 days
1980	99.00	4.0 days
1981	110.00	4.0 days
1982	126.00	3.5 days
1983	135.00	3.0 days
1984	141.00	3.0 days
1985	141.00	3.0 days

Expanded exhibition space is, of course, only one dimension of the convention business opportunity. To host large meetings requires a sufficient quantity of convenient hotel facilities. Atlanta has also experienced a dramatic increase in the number of downtown hotel rooms, from 9,065 in 1979 to 12,596 in 1985.

The combination of exhibition space and large number of hotel rooms has placed a marketing challenge before the Atlanta Convention and Visitors Bureau. This organization has spearheaded an aggressive program designed to persuade groups to hold their conventions in the city. Atlanta is expected to host even more conventions, thus endowing this market segment with a growth potential.

Tourists and sightseers. This market is more than twice the size of the conventioneer market. Summer is the favorite season to visit Atlanta, since 43 percent of the yearly tourists come to visit during June, July, and August. Table V presents cyclorama attendance figures month by month. Many Atlanta visitors come to meet with family (45 percent); others (39 percent) come to sightsee, with 14 percent specifically mentioning tourist sites and 3.5 percent mentioning cultural sites. Their stay is shorter: one or two days, but many of them enjoy two or three attractions during their visit.

TABLE V Average attendance by month, Atlanta Cyclorama

	Percent of total
January	5%
February	5
March	7
April	7
May	6
June	13
July	14
August	16
September	10
October	8
November	6
December	3

Mention should be made of another tourist group, namely the people who flow through Atlanta as they travel to and from the state of Florida. Atlanta is located on two interstate highways, I–75 and I–85, which provide corridors for traffic to and from the northeast and midwest sections of the United States. Large numbers of tourists living in these regions spend their vacations in Florida, and the State of Georgia has tried for many years to convince these persons to "Stay and See" Georgia. For example, a number of welcome centers were set up at the state borders where information about tourist attractions in the state is distributed. Table VI gives some indication of the magnitude of this opportunity. Sporadically, the state has done media advertising in such areas of

TABLE VI Number of visitors to the Atlanta Welcome Center

Year	Number of visitors
1976	6,605
1977	6,219
1978	5,229
1979	3,498
1980	14,763
1981	5,119
1982	2,035
1983	7,638
1984	10,995
1985	11,600

origin as Ohio and Michigan. In 1985, the state of Georgia tripled its tourist advertising budget to $2.1 million, using "Adventures in the great unknown—Georgia" as a campaign theme.

Local residents and their out-of-town guests. Atlanta and its metropolitan area, encompassing 18 counties, contained an estimated population of 2,326,000 at the end of 1984. This figure can be contrasted with the 1980 population figure of 2,138,231 people, and the 1970 and 1960 figures of 1,684,200 and 1,247,649, respectively. The city is growing rapidly, but the expansion is taking place mostly at the northern perimeter of the city, far from downtown. However, the population in Atlanta is very mobile: Most Atlantans are from other states, and many have been in Atlanta for only a short period of time.

Consumption Patterns and Attitudes

Visitors to the cyclorama seek to fulfill four different types of needs: education, enjoyment of art, history, and entertainment. But each segment exhibits specific trends which affect the attractiveness of the cyclorama.

Conventioneers. One major pattern observed is that Atlanta conventioneers very seldom bring their spouses with them, and only 18 percent bring their children. When planning tours, convention planners seek attractions with overall appeal, uniqueness, ability to accommodate large groups, and accessible parking. The cyclorama fits all these needs remarkably well, plus it has that Old South charm that is so appealing to conventioneers. Furthermore, the cyclorama can be rented to a private group. It will accommodate up to 180 people at a time on its rotating platform.

Tourists and sightseers. Tourists almost always have access to a car, and they are looking for a day-long entertainment schedule. Attributes that are solvent in their choice of attractions are: accessible from freeway, parking, fun for the whole family, near other attractions, and uniqueness. Once again, the cyclorama fares well on all.

Residents and guests. This segment is looking for a full-day experience offering a good time/value ratio. The closeness to the zoo and the low admission price play in the cyclorama's favor. However, it should be remembered that the guests' host will likely influence their choice. Thus, since the cyclorama is visited at most once a year by local residents, this can have a negative impact on the cyclorama.

The cyclorama is a product that is unique. But, it also has many competitors because it belongs in the generic category of tourist and cultural attractions. In the past, the cyclorama had cooperated with other historical/cultural attractions by the use of cross-promotion techniques such as distributing each others' brochures. Additional Atlanta attractions include: (1) Stone Mountain Park, with over 5.6 million visitors; (2) Six Flags Over Georgia, an amusement park that admitted over 2.5 million visitors; (3) Fernbank Science Center which attracted 700,000 visitors; and (4) the Martin Luther King, Jr. Center with its 500,000 visitors. In 1986, the Carter Presidential Library opened to the public and proved to be a popular attraction. Other competing activities in which visitors can participate are shopping, theater, and nightlife.

Trade

The cyclorama is a product that does not lend itself easily to trade activities. However, the cyclorama is a stop on the tour lists of six different Atlanta operators: Atlanta Tours, Arnell Tours, Brewster Motor Coach, Gray Line of Atlanta (a picture of the diorama is featured in their promotional brochure), Metro Tours, and Southeastern Stages. Furthermore, many school groups and senior citizen groups visit the cyclorama.

Past Experience with Communications Elements

Advertising

In 1986, most of the cyclorama's promotional budget was allocated to advertising. Ads were run for three months in *Southern Living* and for seven months in the weekly *Saturday Leisure Guide* of the *Atlanta Journal/Constitution*. In addition, special advertising in connection with special events was scheduled. In total, in 1986 $40,000 was budgeted for routine advertising plus $6,000 for special advertising. Advertising for the cyclorama tends to be simple, staid, and dignified. Print ads are of the reminder type, treating it as a presold product. Exhibit 2 is an example of the print ad run in the local newspaper.

EXHIBIT 2   Sample newspaper ad, 1984

EXPERIENCE THE EVENT
THAT FORGED THE REBIRTH OF

"OUR BRAVE AND BEAUTIFUL CITY"

16 SHOWS DAILY
MONDAY — SUNDAY
9:30 a.m. — 4:30 p.m.

IN HISTORIC GRANT PARK

800 CHEROKEE AVE, S.E.
ATLANTA. GA.

COUPON
ADMIT PARTY AT GROUP RATE
$2.50 – Adults
$1.00 – Child (6 – 13)

Personal Selling

Up to now, the product iself and the budgetary restrictions have prevented the use of this communication tool for the cyclorama.

Sales Promotion

Sales promotion tools used in 1986 were information brochures and cents-off coupons. The brochures are mostly distributed at welcome centers and at Atlanta Convention and Visitors Bureau booths.

The brochures are factual and focus on the historical appeal. They, too, possess the dignity and seriousness of tone generally associated with cultural and historical attractions. Couponing has been directed primarily at conventioneers, and $2,000 of the 1986 budget was spent on media for this purpose. Effectiveness studies have yet to be undertaken.

Publicity/Public Relations

The cyclorama has been the subject of many articles in local magazines and newspapers. It has also been featured in public service announcements on radio and television. The cyclorama is also doing cross-publicity with other national attractions such as the Gettysburg Cyclorama, the Boston Fine Arts Building, the Milwaukee Historical Society, and the Atlanta Historical Society.

Media Cost and Audience Information

The Atlanta area is served by a variety of print and broadcast media. Table VII shows some cost and audience data for the major print vehicles in the Atlanta area. The major newspaper is the *Atlanta Journal/Constitution* which publishes a morning and evening edition. A single three-inch ad costs $277 and runs in both the morning and evening papers. In terms of magazines, *Southern Living* is very popular, containing articles on travel, cooking, and history. An advertiser can place a full or fractional page ad in a statewide edition or a full page ad in a metro Atlanta edition. The three magazines, *Atlanta Magazine, Business Atlanta*, and *Georgia Trends*, are slick periodicals that reach an upscale suburban family or business audience. The two magazines *Where* and *Key* are "What to do in Atlanta" periodicals and are distributed free to hotel guests.

TABLE VII Atlanta area print media cost and audience data for black and white print ads

Newspaper; 3-inch ad	Costs		Number of Readers (000's)		
	1 time	52 times	All Adults	Women	Men
1. *Atlanta Journal/Constitution*	$277	$14,404	963	475	488
Magazines; 1/3-page ad	1 time	6 times	All Adults	Women	Men
1. *Southern Living* Georgia edition	$2,090	$12,540	190	133	57
Atlanta edition, full-page ad only	3,930	21,240	100	70	30
2. *Atlanta* magazine	1,025	5,670	33	—	—
3. *Business Atlanta*	755	4,110	24	3	21
4. *Georgia Trends*	850	4,530	27	—	—
5. *Where/Atlanta*	850	4,260	60	—	—
6. *Key/Atlanta*	115	690	10	—	—

Table VIII shows the cost and audience data for broadcast media. The data for a 30-second television spot on the networks' morning news programs are shown. Also, data for Atlanta's five biggest radio stations are shown for the

TABLE VIII Atlanta area broadcast media cost and audience data for 7:00 A.M. to 9:00 A.M., weekdays

			Number of Viewers/Listeners (000's)		
Television: 30-Second Spot	Cost	Rating*	All Adults	Women	Men
1. WSB (ABC, "Good Morning America")	$350	4.0	108	64	44
2. WAGA (CBS, "Morning News")	125	1.3	36	22	14
3. WXIA (NBC, "Today Show")	375	3.4	92	56	36
Radio: 60-Second Spot					
1. WZGC (Top 40)	$250	1.3	36	19	17
2. WQXI (Adult rock)	350	1.9	51	27	24
3. WSB (Contemporary)	200	1.4	38	20	18
4. WFOX (Rock oldies)	150	0.9	24	13	11
5. WKHX (Country)	250	1.9	51	26	25

* Rating is a measure of audience size expressed as a percentage of 2,699,800 adults which is the survey area's population base for 1987.

morning drive-time period. The radio stations have different creative formats in addition to different costs and audiences.

A serious constraint facing the director of the cyclorama as he sets about designing the 1987 promotional plan for the cyclorama is in the area of budget. The Atlanta City Council has authorized an expenditure of $50,000 for a publicity fund. The amount is available for media advertising and sales promotion efforts. Personal selling and publicity activities are carried out by the director and associate director as part of their overall duties. A separate printing budget of $25,000 pays for brochures and similar forms of direct advertising.

The director realizes that the budget allocated to the cyclorama is not sufficient given the task of generating an appreciable increase in attendance. Therefore, he is fully aware of the importance of making the right decisions as he designs the cyclorama's 1987 promotional plan.

Case 4

Exercise on Financial Analysis for Marketing Decision Making*

An important part of the analysis of alternatives facing marketing decision makers is the financial analysis of these alternatives. This exercise is designed to give students experience in handling the types of financial calculations that arise in marketing cases. If you can do the calculations in this exercise, you should be able to handle the financial calculations necessary to properly do the cases in this book.

1. You have just been appointed the product manager for the "Flexo" brand of electric razors in a large consumer products company. As part of your new job, you want to develop an understanding of the financial situation for your product. Your brand assistant has provided you with the following facts:

a.	Retail selling price	$30 per unit
b.	Retailer's margin	*less (20% of 30)* 20%
c.	Jobber's margin	20%
d.	Wholesaler's* margin	15%
e.	Direct factory labor	$2 per unit
f.	Raw materials	$1 per unit
g.	All factory and administrative overheads	$1 per unit (at a 100,000 unit volume level)
h.	Salespersons' commissions	10% of manufacturer's selling price
i.	Sales force travel costs	$200,000
j.	Advertising	$500,000
k.	Total market for razors	1 million units
l.	Current yearly sales of Flexo	210,000 units

* An agent who sells to the jobbers, who in turn sell to the retailers.

* Copyright © 1993 by Thomas C. Kinnear.

Questions

1. What is the contribution per unit for the Flexo brand?
2. What is the break-even volume in units and in dollars?
3. What market share does the Flexo brand need to break even?
4. What is the current total contribution?
5. What is the current before-tax profit of the Flexo brand?
6. What market share must Flexo obtain to contribute a before-tax profit of $4 million?

2. One of the first decisions you have to make as the brand manager for Flexo is whether or not to add a new line of razors, the "Super Flexo" line. This line would be marketed in addition to the original Flexo line. Your brand assistant has provided you with the following facts:

a.	Retail selling price	$40 per unit
b.	All margins the same as before	
c.	Direct factory labor	$ 3 per unit
d.	Raw materials	$ 2 per unit
e.	Additional factory and administrative overheads	$ 2 per unit (at a 50,000 unit volume level)
f.	Salespersons' commissions the same percent as before	
g.	Incremental sales force travel cost	$ 50,000
h.	Advertising for Super Flexo	$600,000
i.	New equipment needed	$500,000 (to be depreciated over 10 years)
j.	Research and development spent up to now	$200,000
k.	Research and development to be spent this year to commercialize the product	$500,000 (to be amortized over five years)

Questions

1. What is the contribution per unit for the Super Flexo brand?
2. What is the break-even volume in units and in dollars?
3. What is the sales volume in units necessary for Super Flexo to yield, in the first year, a 20 percent return on the equipment to be invested in the project?

3. The $40 per unit selling price for Super Flexo seems high to you. You thought you might lower the price to $37 per unit and raise retail margin to 25 percent.

Question

What is the break-even volume in units?

Part 3

Marketing Information and Forecasting

Good information is essential for all marketing decision making. Most cases in this book present some information provided by marketing research. However, they also leave many points of uncertainty. The skill of marketing decision making is the use of the information that is available, along with explicit assumptions about uncertain points to make good decisions. The suggestion that we do marketing research has usually not been allowed in other parts of this text. In this section we turn to the undertaking of marketing research activity.

First, let us define marketing research. It is the systematic gathering, recording, and analyzing of data about problems relating to the marketing of goods and services. There are three kinds of marketing research: (1) exploratory, (2) conclusive, and (3) performance monitoring. Exploratory research is useful for identifying situations calling for a decision and for identifying alternative courses of action. Conclusive research is useful for evaluating alternative courses of action and selecting a course of action. Performance monitoring research is designed to provide the control function over marketing programs.

The marketing research process may be thought of as being composed of the following steps:

1. Establish the need for information.
2. Specify the research objectives and information needs.
3. Determine the sources of data.
4. Develop data collection forms.
5. Design a sample.
6. Collect the data.
7. Process the data.

8.   Analyze the data.
9.   Present research findings.

The responsibility for the execution of these stages is shared by the marketing manager and the marketing researcher. They both must be sure that the problem has been defined properly, that the objectives make sense, and so on. The researcher holds primary responsibility for the technical details of the study. However, he or she must always be prepared to explain these aspects to the manager in nontechnical terms.

Marketing research costs money. Before it is undertaken, it must be ascertained that the value of the information provided justifies the cost. Also, before research is undertaken, the use to which that research will be made should be clearly understood. A specific decision should be the target of the research, and the way the new information will be used in helping make the decision should be clearly understood.

This note and the cases in this section focus on the managerial aspects of marketing research. The technical details are mostly left for more advanced texts.

Case 5

MacTec Control AB*

"The choices themselves seem simple enough," thought Georg Carlsson, "either we enter the U.S. market in Pennsylvania and New York, we forget about the U.S. for the time being, or we do some more marketing research." The difficult part was the decision.

Georg was president of MacTec Control AB, a Swedish firm located in Kristianstad. Georg had begun MacTec in 1980 along with his wife Jessie. MacTec had grown rapidly and now boasted some 30 employees and annual revenues of about $2.8 million. Since 1985, MacTec had been partly owned by The Perstorp Corporation, whose headquarters were located nearby. Perstorp was a large manufacturer of chemicals and chemical products, with operations in 18 countries and annual revenues of about $600 million. Perstorp had provided MacTec with capital and managerial advice, as well as chemical analysis technology.

MacTec's Aqualex System

MacTec's product line centered about its Aqualex System, a design of computer hardware and software for the monitoring and control of pressurized water flows. Most often these water flows consisted of either potable water or sewage effluent as these liquids were stored, moved, or treated by municipal water departments.

The Aqualex System employed MacTec's MPDII microcomputer (see Exhibits 1 and 2) installed at individual pumping stations where liquids are stored and moved. Often these stations were located quite far apart, linking geographically dispersed water users (households, businesses, etc.) to water and

* This case was written by Professor James E. Nelson, University of Colorado. This case is intended for use as a basis for class discussion rather than to illustrate either effective or ineffective administrative decision making. Some data are disguised. © 1989 by the Business Research Division, College of Business and Administration and the Graduate School of Business Administration, University of Colorado, Boulder, Colorado, 80309-0419. Used with permission.

EXHIBIT 1

MPDII which controls and monitors pumping stations

An MPDII microcomputer is installed at a pumping station and then works as an independent, intelligent computer. When required, it can go on-line with the central computer and report its readings there.

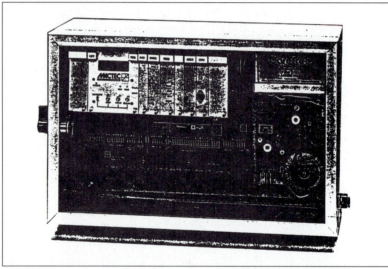

Here are some of the functions of the MPDII

- It governs the starts, stops and alarms of up to four pumps, controlled by an integrated, piezo-resistive pressure-level sensor.

- It checks the sump level.

- It checks pump capacity and changes therein.

- It activates an alarm when readings reach preset deviation limits.

- It registers precipitation and activates an alarm in case of heavy rain.

- It constantly monitors pump power consumption and activates an alarm in case of unacceptable deviation.

- It registers current pump flow by means of advanced calculations of inflow and outfeed from the sump.

- It can register accumulated time for overflow.

- It switches to forward and reverse action, even by remote command.

- It stores locally the last nine alarm instances with time indications.

- These may be read directly on an LCD display.

- It can be remotely programmed from the central computer.

EXHIBIT 2 Computerized monitoring and control of water treatment plants

The Aqualex System cuts operating and maintenance costs for water treatment plants.

The System takes over most of the monitoring and control of the plant by means of computerized controls. This frees resources for use in planned and efficient maintenance work, type of work that cannot be automated.

The Aqualex System is based on a number of intelligent computer sub-stations. These are placed at the pumping stations, sewage treatment plant, waterworks, etc. and are on-line to the central computer.

The computer sub-stations can independently handle local process control, store readings and analyze trends. They carry on advanced communication with the central computer to transmit readings and alarms and receive remote commands.

The central computer has the capacity to process the readings received from the sub-stations and present them in the form of reports and trends. Alarms can also be transmitted to one or more pocket-sized receivers with alarm code displays.

The operator on call can monitor the entire system at home by means of a portable home terminal. This terminal also has the capacity for remote commands, which saves many costly service calls.

The Aqualex System does the job of many people with high precision and reliability.

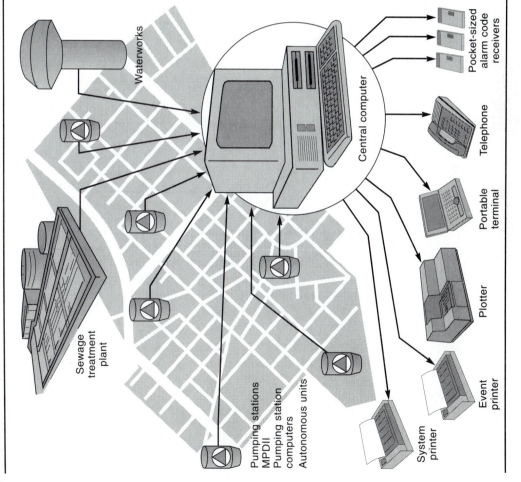

Waterworks

Sewage treatment plant

Pumping stations
MPDII
Pumping station computers
Autonomous units

Central computer

Pocket-sized alarm code receivers

Telephone

Portable terminal

Plotter

Event printer

System printer

sewer systems. The microcomputer performed a number of important functions —it controlled the starts, stops, and alarms of up to four pumps; monitored levels and available capacities of storage reservoirs; checked pump capacities and power consumptions; and recorded pump flows. It could even measure amounts of rainfall entering reservoirs and adjust pump operations or activate an alarm as needed. Each microcomputer could also be easily connected to a main computer to allow remote control of pumping stations and produce a variety of charts and graphs useful in evaluating pump performance and scheduling needed maintenance.

The Aqualex System provided a monitoring function that human operators could not match in terms of sophistication, immediacy, and cost. The system permitted each individual substation to control its own pumping operations; collect, analyze, and store data; forecast trends; transmit data and alarms to a central computer; and receive remote commands. Alarms could also be transmitted directly to a pocket-sized receiver carried by one or more operators on call. A supervisor could continually monitor pumping operations in a large system entirely via a computer terminal at a central location and send commands to individual pumps, thereby saving costly service calls and time. The system also reduced the possibility of overflows that could produce disastrous flooding of nearby communities.

MacTec personnel would work with water and sewage engineers to design and install the desired Aqualex System. Personnel would also train engineers and operators to work with the system and would be available 24 hours a day for consultation. If needed, a MacTec engineer could be physically present to assist engineers and operators whenever major problems arose. MacTec also offered its clients the option of purchasing a complete service contract whereby MacTec personnel would provide periodic testing and maintenance of installed systems.

An Aqualex System could be configured a number of ways. In its most basic form, the system would be little more than a small "black box" that monitored two or three lift station activities and, when necessary, transmitted an alarm to one or more remote receivers. An intermediate system would monitor additional activities, send data to a central computer via telephone lines, and receive remote commands. An advanced system would provide the same monitoring capabilities but add forecasting features, maintenance management, auxiliary power backup, and data transmission and reception via radio. Prices to customers for the three configurations in early 1989 were about $1,200, $2,400, and $4,200.

Aqualex Customers

Aqualex customers could be divided into two groups—governmental units and industrial companies. The typical application in the first group was a sewage treatment plant having some 4 to 12 pumping stations, each station containing one or more pumps. Pumps would operate intermittently and—unless an Aqualex or similar system were in place—be monitored by one or more operators who would visit each station once or perhaps twice each day for about a half hour. Operators would take reservoir measurements, record running times of pumps, and sometimes perform limited maintenance and repairs. The sewage plant and stations typically were located in flat or rolling terrain, where gravity could not be used in lieu of pumping. If any monitoring equipment were present at all, it typically would consist of a crude, on-site alarm that would activate whenever fluid levels rose or fell beyond a preset level. Sometimes the alarm would activate a telephone dialing function that alerted an operator some distance from the station.

Numerous industrial companies also stored, moved, and processed large quantities of water or sewage. These applications usually differed little from those in governmental plants except for their smaller size. On the other hand, there were a considerably larger number of industrial companies having pumping stations and so, Georg thought, the two markets often offered about identical market potentials in many countries.

The two markets desired essentially the same products, although industrial applications often used smaller, simpler equipment. Both markets wanted their monitoring equipment to be accurate and reliable, the two dominant concerns. Equipment should also be easy to use, economical to operate, and require little regular service or maintenance. Purchase price often was not a major consideration—as long as the price was in some appropriate range, customers seemed more interested in actual product performance than in initial outlays.

Georg thought that worldwide demand for Aqualex Systems and competing products would continue to be strong for at least the next 10 years. While some of this demand represented construction of new pumping stations, many applications were replacements of crude monitoring and alarm systems at existing sites. These existing systems depended greatly on regular visits by operators, visits that often continued even after new equipment was installed. Most such trips were probably not necessary. However, many managers found it difficult to dismiss or reassign monitoring personnel that were no longer needed; many were also quite cautious and conservative, desiring some human monitoring of the new equipment "just in case." Once replacements of existing systems were complete, market growth would be limited to new construction and, of course, replacements of more sophisticated systems.

Most customers (as well as noncustomers) considered the Aqualex System to be the best on the market. Those knowledgeable in the industry felt that competing products seldom matched Aqualex's reliability and accuracy. Experts also believed that many competing products lacked the sophistication and flexibility present in Aqualex's design. Beyond these product features, customers also appreciated MacTec's knowledge about water and sanitation engineering. Competing firms often lacked this expertise, offering their products somewhat as a sideline and considering the market too small for an intensive marketing effort.

The market was clearly not too small for MacTec. While Georg had no hard data on market potential for Western Europe, he thought that annual demand here could be as much as $9 million. About 40 percent of this came from new construction, while the rest represented demand from replacing existing systems. Industry sales in the latter category could be increased by more aggressive marketing efforts on the part of MacTec and its competitors. Eastern European economies represented additional, new potential. However, the water and sewer industries in these countries seemed less interested than their Western counterparts in high-technology equipment to monitor pumping operations. Additionally, business was often more difficult to conduct in these countries. In contrast, the U.S. market looked very attractive.

MacTec Strategy

MacTec currently marketed its Aqualex System primarily to sewage treatment plants in Scandinavia and other countries in Northern and Central Europe. The company's strategy could be described as providing technologically superior equipment to monitor pumping operations at these plants. The strategy stressed frequent contacts with customers and potential customers to design, supply, and service Aqualex Systems. The strategy also stressed superior knowledge of water and sanitation engineering along with up-to-date electronics and computer technology. The result was a line of highly specialized sensors, computers, and methods for process controls in water treatment plants.

This was the essence of MacTec's strategy, having a special competence that no firm in the world could easily match. MacTec also prided itself on being a young, creative company without an entrenched bureaucracy. Company employees generally worked with enthusiasm and dedication; they talked with each other, regularly, openly, and with a great deal of give and take. Most importantly, customers—as well as technology—seemed to drive all areas in the company.

MacTec's strategy in its European markets seemed to be fairly well decided. That is, Georg thought that a continuation of present strategies and tactics should continue to produce good results. However, an aspect that would likely change would be to locate a branch office having both sales and manufacturing activities somewhere in the European Community (EC), most likely the Netherlands. The plan was to have such an office in operation well before 1992, when the 12 countries in the EC (Belgium, Denmark, France, Greece, Ireland, Italy, Luxembourg, the Netherlands, Portugal, Spain, United Kingdom, Germany) would mutually eliminate national barriers to the flow of capital, goods, and services. Having a MacTec office located in the EC would greatly simplify sales to these member countries. Moreover, MacTec's presence should also avoid problems with any protective barriers the EC itself might raise to limit or discourage market access by outsiders.

Notwithstanding activities related to this branch office, Georg was considering a major strategic decision to enter the U.S. market. His two recent visits to the United States had led him to conclude that the market represented potential beyond that for Western Europe, and that the United States seemed perfect for expansion. Industry experts in the United States agreed with Georg that the

Aqualex System outperformed anything used in the U.S. market. Experts thought that many water and sewage engineers would welcome MacTec's products and knowledge. Moreover, Georg thought that U.S. transportation systems and payment arrangements would present few problems. The system would be imported under U.S. Tariff Regulation 71249 and pay a duty of 4.9 percent.

Entry would most likely be in the form of a sales and service office located in Philadelphia. The Pennsylvania and New York state markets seemed representative of the United States and appeared to offer a good test of the Aqualex System. The two states together probably represented about 18 percent of total U.S. market potential for the system. The office would require an investment of some $200,000 for inventory and other balance sheet items. Annual fixed costs would total upwards of $250,000 for salaries and other operating expenses— Georg thought that the office would employ only a general manager, two sales technicians, and secretary for at least the first year or two. Each Aqualex System sold in the United States would be priced to provide a contribution of about 30 percent. Georg wanted a 35 percent annual return before taxes on any MacTec investment, to begin no later than the second year. At issue was whether Georg could realistically expect to achieve this goal in the United States.

Marketing Research

To this end, Georg had commissioned the Browning Group in Philadelphia to conduct some limited marketing research with selected personnel from the water and sewage industries in the city and surrounding areas. The research had two purposes: to obtain a sense of market needs and market reactions to MacTec's products and to calculate a rough estimate of market potential in Pennsylvania and New York. Results were intended to help Georg interpret his earlier conversations with industry experts and perhaps allow a decision on market entry.

The research design itself employed two phases of data collection. The first consisted of five one-hour interviews with water and sewage engineers employed by local city and municipal governments. For each interview, an experienced Browning Group interviewer scheduled an appointment with the engineer and then visited his office, armed with a set of questions and a tape recorder. Questions included:

1. What procedures do you use to monitor your pumping stations?
2. Is your current monitoring system effective? Costly?
3. What are the costs of a monitoring malfunction?
4. What features would you like to see in a monitoring system?
5. Who decides on the selection of a monitoring system?
6. What is your reaction to the Aqualex System?

Interviewers were careful to listen closely to the engineers' responses and to probe for additional detail and clarification.

Tapes of the personal interviews were transcribed and then analyzed by the project manager at Browning. The report noted that these results were interesting in that they described typical industry practices and viewpoints. A partial summary from the report appears below:

> The picture that emerges is one of fairly sophisticated personnel making decisions about monitoring equipment that is relatively simple in design. Still, some engineers would appear distrustful of this equipment because they persist in sending operators to pumping stations on a daily basis. The distrust may be justified because potential costs of a malfunction were identified as expensive repairs and cleanups, fines of $10,000 per day of violation, lawsuits, harassment by the Health Department, and public embarrassment. The five engineers identified themselves as key individuals in the decision to purchase new equipment. Without exception, they considered MacTec features innovative, highly desirable, and worth the price.

The summary noted also that the primary use of the interview results was to construct a questionnaire that could be administered over the telephone.

The questionnaire was used in the second phase of data collection, as part of a telephone survey that had contacted 65 utility managers, water and sewage engineers, and pumping station operators in Philadelphia and surrounding areas. All respondents were employed by governmental units. Each interview took about 10 minutes to complete, covering topics identified in questions 1, 2, and 4 above. The Browning Group's research report stated that most interviews found respondents to be quite cooperative, although 15 people refused to participate at all.

The telephone interviews had produced results that could be considered more representative of the market because of the larger sample size. The report had organized these results about the topics of monitoring procedures, system effectiveness and costs, and features desired in a monitoring system:

> All monitoring systems under the responsibility of the 50 respondents were considered to require manual checking. The frequency of operator visits to pumping stations ranged from monthly to twice daily, depending on flow rates, pumping station history, proximity of nearby communities, monitoring equipment in operation, and other factors. Even the most sophisticated automatic systems were checked because respondents "just don't trust the machine." Each operator was responsible for some 10 to 20 stations.
>
> Despite the perceived need for double-checking, all respondents considered their current monitoring system to be quite effective. Not one reported a serious pumping malfunction in the past three years that had escaped detection. However, this reliability came at considerable cost—the annual wages and other expenses associated with each monitoring operator averaged about $40,000.
>
> Respondents were about evenly divided between those wishing a simple alarm system and those desiring a sophisticated, versatile microprocessor. Managers and engineers in the former category often said that the only feature they really needed was an emergency signal such as a siren, horn, or light. Sometimes they would

add a telephone dialer that would be automatically activated at the same time as the signal. Most agreed that a price of around $2,000 would be reasonable for such a system. The latter category of individuals contained engineers desiring many of the Aqualex System's features, once they knew such equipment was available. A price of $4,000 per system seemed acceptable. Some of these respondents were quite knowledgeable about computers and computer programming while others were not. Only four respondents voiced any strong concerns about the cost to purchase and install more sophisticated monitoring equipment. Everyone demanded that the equipment be reliable and accurate.

Georg found the report quite helpful. Much of the information, of course, simply confirmed his own view of the U.S. market. However, it was good to have this knowledge from an independent, objective organization. In addition, to learn that the market consisted of two, apparently equal-sized segments of simple and sophisticated applications was quite worthwhile. In particular, knowledge of system prices considered acceptable by each segment would make the entry decision easier. Meeting these prices would not be a major problem.

A most important section of the report contained an estimate of market potential for Pennsylvania and New York. The estimate was based on an analysis of discharge permits on file in governmental offices in the two states. These permits were required before any city, municipality, water or sewage district, or industrial company could release sewage or other contaminated water to another system or to a lake or river. Each permit showed the number of pumping stations in operation. Based on a 10 percent sample of permits, the report had estimated that governmental units in Pennsylvania and New York contained approximately 3,000 and 5,000 pumping stations for waste water, respectively. Industrial companies in the two states were estimated to add some 3,000 and 9,000 more pumping stations, respectively. The total number of pumping stations in the two states—20,000—seemed to be growing at about 2 percent per year.

Finally, a brief section of the report dealt with the study's limitations. Georg agreed that sample was quite small, that it contained no utility managers or engineers from New York, and that it probably concentrated too heavily on individuals in larger urban areas. In addition, the research told him nothing about competitors and their marketing strategies and tactics. Nor did he learn anything about any state regulations for monitoring equipment, if indeed any existed. However, these shortcomings came as no surprise, representing a consequence of the research design proposed to Georg by the Browning Group some six weeks ago, before the study began.

The Decision

Georg's decision seemed a difficult one. The most risky option was to enter the U.S. market as soon as possible; the most conservative was to stay in Europe. In between was the option of conducting some additional marketing research.

Discussion with the Browning Group had identified the objectives of this research as to rectify limitations of the first study as well as to provide more accurate estimates of market potential. (The estimates of the numbers of pumping stations in Pennsylvania and New York were accurate to around plus or minus 20 percent.) This research was estimated to cost $40,000 and take another three months to complete.

Case 6

*The Atlanta Journal and Constitution (A)**

Mr. Ferguson Rood, research and marketing director for *The Atlanta Journal* and the *Atlanta Constitution,* was still perspiring from the three-block walk in the hot August sun back to his office from the meeting he had just been to at Rich's Department Store. At the meeting, he had been told that Rich's, the newspaper's largest advertiser, wanted to test the effectiveness of TV and radio advertising versus newspaper advertising for its upcoming Harvest Sale. He had promised to make his suggestions for the research plan in 48 hours and felt he had much work to do in that short time. He wondered what recommendations he should make for the study and was concerned that the research design and questionnaire be developed so the study would represent fairly the effectiveness of *The Atlanta Journal* and the *Atlanta Constitution.* As he began to review his notes from the meeting, he picked up the phone to call his wife and tell her he would be home very late that evening.

Background

The Atlanta Journal and the *Atlanta Constitution* are a union of two of the largest circulation newspapers in the South. The *Atlanta Constitution,* winner of four Pulitzer Prizes for its efforts in the area of social reform, was founded June 16, 1868. *The Atlanta Journal,* founded February 24, 1883, became the largest daily newspaper in Georgia by 1889. Also a winner of the Pulitzer Prize, *The Journal* is the Southeast's largest afternoon newspaper.

In 1950, *The Atlanta Journal* and the *Atlanta Constitution* were combined into Atlanta Newspapers, Inc., a privately held company. The two newspapers maintained independent editorial staffs, and there was very little overlap of readers. Exhibits 1 through 4 present data concerning the adult readership of the newspapers, the gross reader impressions, reach and frequency, and readership over five weekdays and four Sundays.

---

* This case was written by Kenneth L. Bernhardt. Copyright © 1993 by Kenneth L. Bernhardt.

EXHIBIT 1 Gross readership impressions, reach, and frequency of *The Atlanta Journal* and *Constitution*

Gross reader impressions

The Atlanta Journal and *Constitution* in 15-county metro Atlanta:

During any five weekdays, 864,500 adults read *The Atlanta Journal* or *Constitution* an average of 3.5 times for a total of 3,025,800 weekday gross reader impressions.

During any four Sundays, 907,600 adults read *The Atlanta Journal* and *Constitution* for an average of 3.4 times for a total of 3,085,800 Sunday gross reader impressions.

These newspapers deliver 3,933,400 adult gross reader impressions when one Sunday is added to five weekdays.

Reach and frequency of newspaper reading

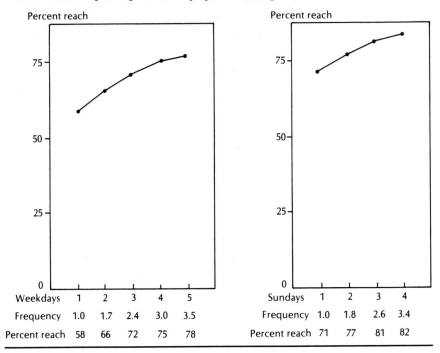

Weekdays	1	2	3	4	5
Frequency	1.0	1.7	2.4	3.0	3.5
Percent reach	58	66	72	75	78

Sundays	1	2	3	4
Frequency	1.0	1.8	2.6	3.4
Percent reach	71	77	81	82

EXHIBIT 2 *The Atlanta Journal* and *Constitution* readership information

78 percent of all daily circulation and 66 percent of all Sunday circulation is within 15-county metro Atlanta.

Of all metro Atlanta adults, 644,400 read *The Atlanta Journal* or *Constitution* on the average week-day. Of this total, 412,700 read *The Journal* and 366,100 read the *Constitution*. 134,400 adults read both. On the average Sunday 782,200 metro Atlanta adults read *The Atlanta Journal* and *Constitution*.

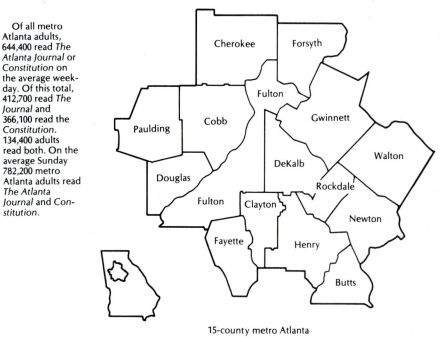

15-county metro Atlanta

Adult readers of *The Atlanta Journal* and *Constitution* in 15-county metro Atlanta

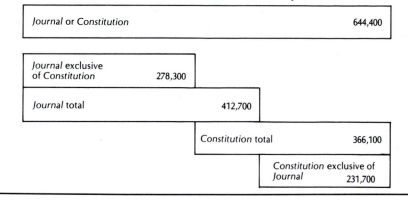

Journal or *Constitution*	644,400
Journal exclusive of *Constitution*	278,300
Journal total	412,700
Constitution total	366,100
Constitution exclusive of *Journal*	231,700

EXHIBIT 3 Readership of *The Atlanta Journal* and *Constitution* over five weekdays

644,400, or 58 percent, of all metro Atlanta adults read *The Atlanta Journal* or *Constitution* on the average weekday. Over five weekdays these newspapers deliver 864,900, or 78 percent, of all metro-area adults with an average frequency of 3.5 days.

	Total metro area adults	Average 1-day readership		Cumulative 5-weekday readership		Frequency
		Number	Percent	Number	Percent	
Total adults	1,105,500	644,400	58%	864,900	78%	3.5
Sex						
Female	588,500	331,700	56	447,600	76	3.5
Male	517,000	312,700	61	416,800	81	3.5
Household income						
$25,000 and over	104,200	85,900	82	102,700	99	4.2
$15,000–24,999	195,300	146,400	75	181,900	93	4.0
$10,000–14,999	241,900	152,800	63	203,900	84	3.7
$5,000–9,999	334,200	170,600	51	241,800	72	3.5
Under $5,000	229,900	88,500	39	133,000	58	3.3
Age						
18–34	470,500	234,500	50	345,200	73	3.4
35–49	305,600	197,200	65	250,300	82	3.9
50–64	211,900	145,800	69	184,600	87	3.9
65 and over	116,500	66,700	57	84,700	73	3.9
Race						
White	872,800	528,800	61	685,100	78	3.9
Nonwhite	232,700	115,600	50	180,100	77	3.2
Education						
College graduate	173,500	138,000	80	172,600	99	4.0
Part college	194,700	137,600	71	174,100	89	4.0
High school graduate	360,500	225,000	62	302,900	84	3.7
Part high school or less	365,600	137,000	38	202,200	55	3.4

To provide the advertisers and potential advertisers with information necessary to help them make their advertising media decisions, the newspaper does a considerable amount of research, often approaching $25,000 in a year. Most of the research is designed to be used in selling advertising to a wide range of advertisers, and includes data on retail trading areas, shopping patterns, product usage, and newspaper coverage patterns. In addition to Mr. Rood, the research department had two other trained market researchers and one secretary.

Although there are nine daily newspapers in the Atlanta trading area, all but *The Journal* and the *Constitution* have very small circulations. The principal competition for large advertisers is with radio and TV stations. Exhibit 5 presents information on the circulation of the print media in the Atlanta area. Exhibit 6 contains information on the broadcast media in Atlanta. Although there were 40 radio stations, 28 AM and 12 FM, and 6 TV stations, WSB Radio

EXHIBIT 4 Readership of *The Atlanta Journal* and *Constitution* over four Sundays

782,200, or 71 percent, of all metro Atlanta adults read *The Atlanta Journal* and *Constitution* on the average Sunday. Over four Sundays these newspapers deliver 907,300, or 82 percent, of all metro-area adults with an average frequency of 3.4 Sundays.

	Total metro area adults	Average 1-Sunday readership	Cumulative 4-Sunday readership	Number of Sundays frequency
Total adults	1,105,500	782,200	907,300	3.4
Sex				
Female	588,500	418,800	477,800	3.5
Male	517,000	363,400	429,500	3.4
Household income				
$25,000 and over	104,200	89,100	97,200	3.7
$15,000–24,999	195,300	168,800	180,700	3.7
$10,000–14,999	241,900	190,100	216,400	3.5
$5,000–9,999	334,400	215,600	267,300	3.2
Under $5,000	229,900	118,500	145,600	3.3
Age				
18–34	470,500	313,000	390,000	3.2
35–49	305,600	221,300	248,500	3.6
50–64	211,900	167,000	179,900	3.7
65 and over	116,500	80,600	88,500	3.6
Race				
White	872,800	633,100	727,900	3.5
Nonwhite	232,700	149,100	179,100	3.3
Education				
College graduate	173,500	150,200	163,700	3.7
Part college	194,700	157,300	180,200	3.5
High school graduate	360,500	273,900	313,500	3.5
Part high school or less	365,600	192,300	240,000	3.2

and TV dominated the market. WSB Radio, for example, was consistently rated among the top six stations in the nation and had a greater Atlanta audience than the next four stations combined. WSB-TV and WSB Radio, both affiliated with the NBC Network, were owned by Cox Broadcasting Corporation, which also owns television stations in Charlotte, Dayton, Pittsburgh, and San Francisco and radio stations in Charlotte, Dayton, and Miami. Cox Broadcasting and WSB-TV and Radio stations shared corporate headquarters in Atlanta.

WSB Radio was founded in 1922 by *The Atlanta Journal* newspaper. In 1939, former Democratic presidential nominee and Governor of Ohio James M. Cox acquired the newspaper-radio combine. In 1948, WSB-TV was founded, and two years later the newspapers and broadcast media were separated when Atlanta Newspapers, Inc., was established. Today, there is no relationship between the newspapers and WSB Radio and TV.

Rich's Department Store was the largest advertiser for *The Journal* and the *Constitution,* accounting for almost 5 percent of their advertising revenue, and was WSB's largest local advertiser. Founded in 1867, Rich's by 1970 had

EXHIBIT 5 Circulation of print media in Atlanta

Metro Atlanta newspapers	Edition	Total circulation
Dailies		
Atlanta Constitution	Morning	216,624
Atlanta Journal	Evening	259,721
Journal-Constitution	Sunday	585,532
Gwinnett Daily News	Evening (except Sat.)	10,111
Gwinnett Daily News	Sunday	10,100
Marietta Daily Journal	Evening (except Sat.)	24,750
Marietta Daily Journal	Sunday	25,456
Fulton County Daily Report	Evening (Mon.–Fri.)	1,600
Atlanta Daily World	Morning	19,000
Atlanta Daily World	Sunday	22,000
The Wall Street Journal	Morning (Mon.–Fri.)	16,180
Jonesboro News Daily	Evening (Mon.–Fri.)	9,100
North Fulton Today	Evening (Mon.–Fri.)	2,300
South Cobb Today	Evening (Mon.–Fri.)	2,400
New York Times	Morning (Mon.–Sat.)	500
New York Times	Sunday	3,100
Weekly newspapers		
Atlanta Inquirer		30,000
Atlanta Voice		37,500
DeKalb New Era		16,400
Atlanta's Suburban Reporter		3,900
Lithonia Observer		2,765
Northside News		8,000
Georgia Business News		4,900
Southern Israelite		4,300
Decatur-DeKalb News		73,000
Southside Sun (East Point)		37,700
Tucker Star		10,000
Alpharetta, Roswell Neighbor		6,800
Austell, Mableton, Powder Springs Neighbor		12,123
Acworth, Kennesaw-Woodstock Neighbor		3,242
Northside, Sandy Springs, Vinings Neighbor		20,836
Smyrna Neighbor		6,872
College Park, East Point, Hapeville, South Side, West End Neighbor		18,813
Chamblee, Doraville, Dunwoody, North Atlanta Neighbor		14,963
Clarkston, Stone Mountain, Tucker Neighbor		15,074
The Journal of Labor (Atlanta)		17,500
Austell Enterprise		1,911
The Cherokee Tribune (Canton)		7,100
Rockdale Citizen		6,031
The Covington News		6,000
The Forsyth County News		4,800
Dallas New Era		4,075
Douglas County Sentinel		7,350
South Fulton Recorder (Fairburn)		4,000
Fayette County News		4,500
Jackson Progress Argus		2,635
The Weekly Advertiser (McDonough)		5,650
The Walton Tribune (Monroe)		5,102
Lilburn Recorder		5,000
Lawrenceville Home Weekly		2,000
The Great Speckled Bird (Atlanta)		7,925
The Georgia Bulletin		14,000
The Covington News (Tues. & Thurs.)		6,200
Creative Loafing in Atlanta		30,000

EXHIBIT 5 (concluded)

Metro Atlanta newspapers	Total circulation
Atlanta area newspapers*	
Cobb	28,000
North Fulton	36,000
North DeKalb-Gwinnett	45,000
South DeKalb	44,000
South Fulton-Clayton	53,000
Major magazines in Georgia	
American Home	70,485
Better Homes and Gardens	145,962
Good Housekeeping	114,045
McCall's	139,728
Ladies' Home Journal	128,331
Family Circle	106,245
Woman's Day	100,566
Redbook	86,354
National Geographic	103,941
Reader's Digest	331,240
Newsweek	41,070
Time	60,438
U.S. News & World Report	40,417
TV Guide	345,871
Playboy	98,389
Sports Illustrated	38,263
Outdoor Life	25,918
True	18,244
Southern Living	95,000
Progressive Farmer	70,000
Cosmopolitan	25,075
Calendar Atlanta	50,000

* These are supplements to The Atlanta Journal, and circulation is to The Atlanta Journal subscribers only.
Source: WSB Research Department.

grown to a company with seven stores distributed throughout Atlanta, as shown in Exhibit 7. Sales were approximately $200 million per year with earnings after taxes of almost 5 percent of sales. The company was classified as a general merchandise retailer, and carried a very wide line of products including clothing, furniture, appliances, housewares, and items for the home. Rich's dominated the Atlanta market, with close to 40 percent of department store sales and approximately 25 percent of all the sales of general merchandise. The merchandising highlight of the year was the annual Harvest Sale, first held in October 1925. The sale typically ran for two weeks and had become a yearly tradition at Rich's.

Background on the Media Effectiveness Study

Before preparing his proposal to Rich's for the media effectiveness study, Mr. Rood reflected upon the events of the past 24 hours. The day before, he had

EXHIBIT 6 Broadcast media in Atlanta

Location	Station/ network	Established	Frequency	Power	Channel	Network
Metro Atlanta AM radio stations						
Atlanta	WSB (NBC)	1922	750 khz	50 kw		
	WAOK	1954	1380 khz	5 kw		
	WGKA (ABC)	1955	1190 khz	1 kw day		
	WGST (ABC-E)	1922	920 khz	5 kw day 1 kw night		
	WIGO (ABC-C)	1946	1340 khz	1 kw day 250 w night		
	WIIN (MBS)	1949	970 khz	5 kw day		
	WPLO	1937	590 khz	5 kw		
	WQXI	1948	790 khz	5 kw day 1 kw night		
	WXAP	1948	860 khz	1 kw		
	WYZE (MBS)	1956	1480 khz	5 kw day		
Decatur	WAVO	1958	1420 khz	1 kw day		
	WGUN	1947	1010 khz	50 kw day		
	WQAK	1964	1310 khz	500 w		
N. Atlanta	WRNG (CBS)	1967	680 khz	25 kw day		
Morrow	WSSA	1959	1570 khz	1 kw day		
East Point	WTJH	1949	1260 khz	5 kw day		
Smyrna	WYNX	1962	1550 khz	10 kw day		
Buford	WDYX	1956	1460 khz	5 kw day		
Austell	WACX	1968	1600 khz	1 kw		
Lawrenceville	WLAW	1959	1360 khz	1 kw		
Marietta	WCOB	1955	1080 khz	10 kw day		
	WFOM	1946	1230 khz	1 kw day 250 w night		
Canton	WCHK (GA)	1957	1290 khz	1 kw day		
Covington	WGFS	1953	1430 khz	1 kw day		
Cumming	WSNE	1961	1170 khz	1 kw		
Douglasville	WDGL	1964	1527 khz	1 kw		
Jackson	WJGA	1967	1540 khz	1 kw day		
Monroe	WMRE	1954	1490 khz	1 kw		
Metro Atlanta FM radio stations						
	WSB-FM	1934	98.5 mhz	100 kw		
	WPLO-FM	1948	103.3 mhz	50 kw		
	WZGC-FM	1955	92.9 mhz	100 kw		
	WKLS-FM	1960	96.1 mhz	100 kw		
	WQXI-FM	1962	94.1 mhz	100 kw		
	WBIE-FM	1959	101.5 mhz	100 kw		
	WLTA-FM	1963	99.7 mhz	100 kw		
	WJGA-FM	1968	92.1 mhz	3 kw		
	WCHK-FM	1964	105.5 mhz	3 kw		
	WGCO-FM	1969	102.3 mhz	100 kw		
	WABE-FM	1948	90.0 mhz	10.5 kw		
	WREK-FM	1968	91.1 mhz	40 kw		
Metro Atlanta television stations						
	WSB-TV	9/29/48			2	NBC
	WAGA-TV	3/8/49			5	CBS
	WXIA-TV	9/30/51			11	ABC
	WTCG-TV	9/1/67			17	IND
	WETV	1958			30	NET
	WGTV	1960			8	NET

Source: WSB Research Department.

EXHIBIT 7 Map of Atlanta and seven Rich's stores

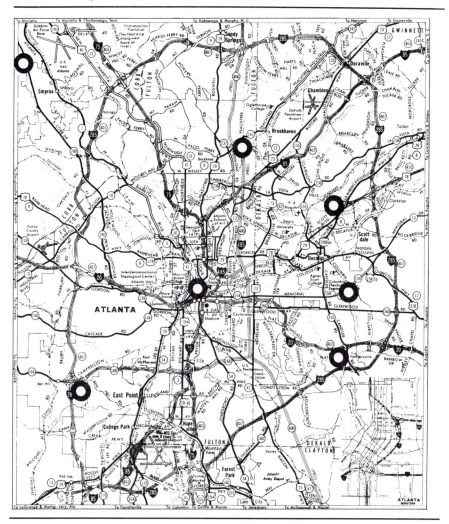

received a phone call from the vice president and sales promotion director from Rich's, inviting him to the meeting at Rich's the next day. Having been told that Rich's research director and the research director of WSB-TV and Radio would also be there, Mr. Rood had been a little apprehensive before going. At the start of the meeting he was asked if the Atlanta newspapers would be interested in participating in a cooperative research study aimed at measuring the effectiveness of various advertising media during Rich's September Harvest Sale, their largest annual sales event. It became immediately apparent that the research director from WSB, Jim Landon, had met with the Rich's people the week before, and was undoubtedly the source of the idea to conduct the study. A document was then passed out that had been prepared by WSB and was entitled "Suggestions for Rich's Media Research." This document is included in the appendix, and outlines the objectives of the study, a suggested methodology, together with a questionnaire.

The suggested objectives for the project were: (1) to measure the ability of TV, radio, and newspapers to sell specific items of merchandise in Rich's seven Atlanta stores; (2) to determine how each advertising medium complements the others in terms of additional units sold to various segments of the customer population (age, sex, charge account ownership, and so on); (3) to determine what each advertising medium contributed in regard to additional store traffic. Mr. Rood's broadcasting counterpart stated at the meeting that "If Rich's is interested in conducting research to measure the effectiveness of various advertising media, WSB-TV and WSB Radio will be happy to assist." Rood had no choice, so he volunteered the support of the newspapers to the study.

The Rich's research manager then asked if the media would participate financially in the study. Mr. Rood suggested that each of the three media participate equally and committed the newspapers to $500 for a study that he figured should cost between $2,500 and $3,000 for interviewing. Mr. Landon indicated that Cox Broadcasting would be willing to put in $500 each for TV and radio.

They then discussed how the research could be conducted. The WSB proposal suggested in-store surveys, with a separate survey conducted for each item of merchandise tested. The survey would be conducted by Rich's employees working overtime in appropriate store locations during the peak shopping hours. The tabulation of the results could be handled by the broadcast station's computer. Care was to be taken to ensure that the TV, radio, or newspaper advertising for the individual items not be "stacked" in favor of one particular medium. The questions in the proposed questionnaire (see the appendix) included questions on how the respondents happened to buy the merchandise at Rich's, if they recalled seeing TV, newspaper or radio advertising, and if they bought anything else. Questions were also asked concerning age and ownership of a Rich's charge account.

Mr. Landon stated that WSB was not trying to take business away from the newspapers and that Rood had nothing to fear. His recommendation was that Rich's not take anything away from the newspaper advertising budget. He suggested that the amount of space purchased in the newspapers be the same as the previous year, with additional monies being committed to the broadcast media. The Rich's sales promotion director then discussed some of his thoughts concerning the study. He indicated that Rich's had been sending 400,000 direct mail pieces to announce the Harvest Sale; this year they would send 200,000, diverting the other money to broadcast. This would make $7,600 available for broadcast, and another $12,000 to $15,000 would be made available to purchase broadcast time.

The Harvest Sale was to open with courtesy days on Monday and Tuesday, September 21–22, with the sale beginning the evening of the 22nd and running for 13 days. While decisions concerning which sales items were to be included in the study and the media schedules to be used were not yet available, some progress had been made. Approximately 10 items were to be researched, and the newspaper ads on Sunday, September 20, would include all or most of the 10 items. Newspaper ads for the items would be repeated Monday and Tuesday with emphasis on *The Journal*. The interviews were to be conducted Monday through Wednesday.

On Sunday and Monday, with a possible spillover to Tuesday due to availability, Rich's would run 120, 30-second TV commercials on all commercial stations except Channel 17. During the same time they would run 120 radio 30-second commercials on a list of stations which had not yet been determined. With both TV and radio, WSB was to get the lion's share if availability could be arranged. Mr. Rood felt certain in view of the client and the research that WSB would manage to come up with several prime-time commercial openings even if it meant bumping some high-paying national advertisers.

Eleven items were mentioned as possible subjects for the research. The 10 final items selected would come mostly from this list, although one or two other items might be chosen. The items mentioned included (1) color TV console at $499; (2) custom-made draperies; (3) Sterns & Foster mattress at $44; (4) carpeting at $6.99 per square yard; (5) Gant shirts at $5; (6) Van Heusen shirts and Arrow shirts at two for $11; (7) women's handbags at $9.99; (8) Johannsen's shoes; (9) pants suits; (10) Hoover upright vacuum cleaner; and (11) GE refrigerator.

Mr. Rood, who had not said very much at the meeting, then asked for 48 hours to review the proposal. Everyone agreed to this, and Mr. Rood promised to present a counterproposal at that time.

Even though it had been rather obvious who initiated the idea for the study and that he at first felt that newspapers were being "set up" by WSB, it had been basically a friendly and relaxed meeting among friends. Mr. Landon and Mr. Rood had worked together in the Atlanta Chapter of the American Marketing Association and had a great deal of mutual respect. Mr. Rood thought Landon was a tough competitor, and understood that he had been successful using awareness-type studies in Cox Broadcastings' other markets to gain additional advertising for broadcast.

When he returned to his office, Rood pulled out some of his files on Rich's. He noticed that the amount of advertising had been fairly constant, approximately 40 pages over the two-week period, during the past three Harvest Sales, and that basically the same products had been promoted. A typical Harvest Sale ad is included in Exhibit 8. He also pulled from the files rate schedules for *The Atlanta Journal* and *Constitution* and WSB (see Exhibits 9 and 10), even though he realized that the exact media schedule would be developed by Rich's advertising agency. Approximately $100,000 would be spent promoting the Harvest Sale, with perhaps a third of this amount being devoted to the sale items.

EXHIBIT 8 Typical Rich's Harvest ad

EXHIBIT 9 *The Atlanta Journal* and the *Atlanta Constitution* retail display rates

Open rate per column inch:*
Constitution	$8.15
Journal	$11.27
Combination	$14.83
Sunday	$15.56

Yearly bulk space rates:

Inches per year	Cost per inch			
	Constitution	Journal	Combined	Sunday
100	$6.21	$8.43	$11.09	$11.65
250	6.16	8.35	11.00	11.55
500	6.10	8.28	10.90	11.45
1,000	6.05	8.21	10.81	11.35
2,500	5.99	8.13	10.70	11.24
5,000	5.93	8.05	10.59	11.12
7,500	5.90	8.01	10.54	11.07
10,000	5.87	7.97	10.48	11.01
12,500	5.85	7.93	10.43	10.96
15,000	5.82	7.89	10.38	10.90
25,000	5.70	7.73	10.17	10.68
50,000	5.61	7.69	10.05	10.61
75,000	5.51	7.65	9.93	10.53
100,000	5.41	7.61	9.81	10.46
150,000	5.21	7.51	9.56	10.31
200,000	5.01	7.41	9.32	10.15
250,000	4.81	7.31	9.08	9.99

* There are 8 columns by 21 inches or 168 column inches on a full page.

EXHIBIT 10 WSB radio and TV advertising rates

	One minute	20/30 seconds	10 seconds
WSB-AM radio: Spot announcements—package plans*			
12 per week	$40.00	$34.00	$24.00
18 per week	38.00	30.00	21.00
24 per week	32.00	26.00	19.00
30 per week	28.00	24.00	17.00
48 per week	26.00	20.00	15.00
WSB-FM radio: Package plan—52 weeks†	16.00	14.00	

WSB-TV
Daytime rates
60 seconds	$ 75–235 depending on program
30 seconds	40–140 depending on program

Prime-time rates
60 seconds‡	$540–660 depending on program
30 seconds	390–725 depending on program

* Available 5:00–6:00 A.M., 10:00 A.M.–3:30 P.M., and 7:30 P.M.–midnight, Monday–Saturday; and 5:00 A.M.–midnight, Sunday. Best available positions in applicable times—no guaranteed placement.

† Quantity discounts available. For example, 18 times per week for 52 weeks is one half the above rates.

‡ Very few available.

Mr. Rood decided that he would have to assume confidence in the effectiveness of the newspapers. He felt if the study were done right he would get his share of media exposure and influence. The other decision he quickly made was that in preparing his comments on the proposed research, he would take Rich's point of view rather than that of *The Atlanta Journal* and *Constitution*. He then began to review the events of the day and the WSB proposal in light of what he felt Rich's needed to know. He also knew that whatever he proposed would have to be acceptable to Mr. Landon. Noting the lateness in the day, he began work on the counterproposal.

Appendix   Suggestions for Rich's Media Research

Objectives

If Rich's is interested in conducting research to measure the effectiveness of various advertising media, WSB-TV and WSB-Radio will be happy to assist. As a basis for discussion, here are suggested objectives for this project:

1. Measure the ability of TV, radio, and newspapers to sell specific items of merchandise in Rich's seven Atlanta metro stores.
2. Determine how each advertising medium complements the others in terms of additional units sold to various segments of the customer population (age, sex, charge account ownership, etc.).
3. Determine what each advertising medium contributes in regard to additional store traffic.

How the Research Could Be Conducted

The project could consist of a series of in-store surveys. A separate survey would be conducted for each item of merchandise tested. The more items tested, the more reliable the results of the overall research project.

If possible, all seven Rich's stores in the Atlanta metro area should participate in the research.

Each survey could be conducted by placing interviewers (Rich's personnel working overtime) in appropriate store locations during "peak" shopping hours with instructions to complete *brief* questionnaires with customers purchasing the item being tested. (See accompanying questionnaire.)

The interview could cover how the customer got the idea to buy the item, other planned purchases in the store during the same visit, charge account ownership, and any other pertinent data. Each interview would last less than a minute and would not bother the customers.

The sample size would vary, depending upon the number of stores participating, the type of merchandise and the sales volume. Interviewers would strive to include all customers purchasing the items during peak hours. Tabulation of the results could be handled by the WSB computer.

Careful Attention to Items and Media Schedules

In order to make the research valid and meaningful, the items to be tested must be selected carefully. In addition, care should be taken to ensure that the TV, radio, or newspaper advertising for these items is not "stacked" in favor of one particular medium. Close attention to the items being tested and the media schedule for each is necessary.

Questionnaire

The proposed questionnaire follows:

(All customers purchasing the item advertised are interviewed.)

1. *How* did you happen to buy this merchandise at Rich's?

Saw on TV	( )
Heard on radio	( )
Saw in newspaper	( )
TV and radio	( )
TV and newspaper	( )
TV, radio, and newspaper	( )
Saw on display	( )
Other: _____	( )

ASKED OF CUSTOMERS NOT MENTIONING A MEDIUM: (2, 3, 4)

2. Do you recall seeing this merchandise advertised on the TV?
   Yes   ( )
   No   ( )

3. Do you recall seeing this merchandise advertised in the newspaper?
   Yes   ( )
   No   ( )

4. Do you recall hearing this merchandise advertised on the radio?
   Yes   ( )
   No   ( )

5. Are you buying *anything* else at Rich's today?
   Yes   ( )
   No   ( )
   Maybe   ( )
   Don't know   ( )

6. Do you have a charge account at *Rich's*?
   Yes   ( )
   No   ( )

---

7. In which group does your age fall?
    Under 25   (   )
    25–34   (   )
    35–49   (   )
    50 and over   (   )

Store _____

Time of Interview _____

Case 7 _____

Greenwood Federal
Savings and Loan*

In early October 1986, Ms. Jenny Harris was reviewing the results of the latest research that had been conducted by Greenwood Federal Savings and its advertising agency. Ms. Harris had been asked by the chairman of the board, Paul Robinson, to prepare a strategic marketing plan for Greenwood Federal. Annual marketing plans had been prepared in previous years, but these tended to be tactical in nature. Many changes had taken place in the previous year, necessitating a longer-term look at the organization's marketing planning. Ms. Harris grabbed several items off her bookshelf, including new research study results, last year's marketing plan, and the latest financial reports available documenting Greenwood's recent performance. She then reached for the phone to call her husband to tell him that she would be home very late that evening.

Background

Greenwood Federal Savings (GFS) is one of the nation's larger savings and loan associations. It was founded in 1927 in the largest milk-producing county south of Wisconsin. At the time, the county was beginning to emerge from an agricultural economy into a semi-urban economy oriented toward a major fast-growing city, Sunbelt City, located six miles to the west. The founder was an attorney, state legislator, and business and community leader who was president of the Chamber of Commerce and many civic and charitable groups. The board of directors consisted of a number of leading citizens in the community, and their goal was to make the city the finest residential city in the region. To ease unemployment and provide some new homes during the Depression, the Association pioneered in making construction loans. To ensure the quality of the homes built, the officers of Greenwood developed a code of minimum specifications and named an inspector to see that the homes complied with it.

---

* This case was prepared by Kenneth L. Bernhardt for the purpose of class discussion. Names and selected data have been disguised. Copyright © 1986 by Kenneth L. Bernhardt.

From the beginning, those who directed the policies of Greenwood Federal were concerned with people and the environment in which members of the Association lived. A commitment was made to serve all citizens without prejudice. The first loan to a black citizen was made in 1928. A close relationship with builders and developers was established and has been maintained throughout the years. In the early years, movies and slide presentations of land developments in other parts of the country kept the community's builders abreast of the latest developments. The first branch was established in 1952, when assets had grown to more than $25 million. During the 1960s the Association expanded its services, adding college education loans, home improvement loans, and FHA and VA loans. The officers were concerned that people in moderate and low-income categories should have adequate housing.

Greenwood was seeking to help the people of the community achieve "the good life," including the privilege of home ownership. Over the years, Greenwood was always on the forefront as an ethical, caring organization. For example, it was the last financial institution in the area to raise rates on loan assumptions. All employees were trained and continually reminded that their role was to satisfy customers. Greenwood had a strong corporate creed outlining its commitment to excellence. The officers and employees of Greenwood believed in the creed, which is reproduced in Exhibit 1.

Greenwood Federal Savings grew rapidly during the 1970s and 1980s, mirroring the growth of the city of Greenwood and the metropolis of Sunbelt City. In 1972 the first branch outside the city of Greenwood was opened, representing the Association's 10th office. During the mid- and late 1970s savings offices were opened in four regional malls, and by the end of the decade Greenwood had offices in five counties throughout the metropolitan area. In the early 1980s Greenwood moved statewide through a series of mergers. In 1984, faced with severe losses, the board of directors decided to concentrate on the Sunbelt City metropolitan area and the northern part of the state and sold off some of the offices purchased earlier.

An organization chart is shown in Exhibit 2. Jenny Harris reported directly to the chairman of the board and CEO and was responsible for all aspects of marketing, advertising, and product management. Since her arrival from a major packaged goods company several years earlier, Greenwood had introduced automated teller machines, discount brokerage services, homeowner's and personal lines of credit, automobile loans, credit cards, and checking accounts.

Competitive Environment

Many changes took place in the competitive environment for GFS in 1985. On June 10, 1985, the U.S. Supreme Court handed down a decision upholding regional banking. During the next several months, the major banks in Sunbelt City all merged with or acquired other large banks in surrounding states,

EXHIBIT 1 Corporate Creed

GREENWOOD FEDERAL
SAVINGS & LOAN ASSOCIATION

Commitment to Excellence: A Corporate Creed

Greenwood Federal Is Committed:

To the pursuit of a leadership position in the delivery of financial services and to the belief that quality is more important than size.

To be innovative in all that we do, including products we design and support services we render.

To understanding the value of customer confidence and realizing that achieving this goal is only outweighed by the need to maintain it.

To the setting of sound financial policies that protect the future while enhancing the present.

To be human, open, friendly, and sincere and to recognize that results should never be achieved at the expense of human dignity.

To specialize in product areas where the future appears strongest and the Association is best able to excel.

To our employees by rewarding merit, by providing an environment for growth, by creating a team spirit by encouraging open, two-way communications, and by enabling them to feel pride in the products and services we provide.

To honest, fair, and enduring relationships with suppliers and associates.

To the concept of corporate social responsibility to our local communities through individual and company participation.

To all of these precepts because they are not only intrinsically right but also happen to be good business.

---

resulting in the creation of "super banks." Other regulations resulted in a blurring of the distinction between banks and savings and loan institutions. In addition, large national organizations such as Sears, CitiCorp, Merrill Lynch, and several major insurance companies all expanded their financial service offerings and entered the Sunbelt City market in a big way.

Like most savings and loan associations, GFS concentrated on the "middle market," which comprised the bulk of its deposits and loans. GFS did not get much patronage from very high-income consumers or from low-income consumers. Competition for this retail middle market had become intense in recent years. There were 20 S&Ls in the Sunbelt City metropolitan area, and most of these, especially the major competitors, concentrated on the middle market. In addition, two of the three largest banks in town concentrated on

EXHIBIT 2 Greenwood's organization chart, 1986

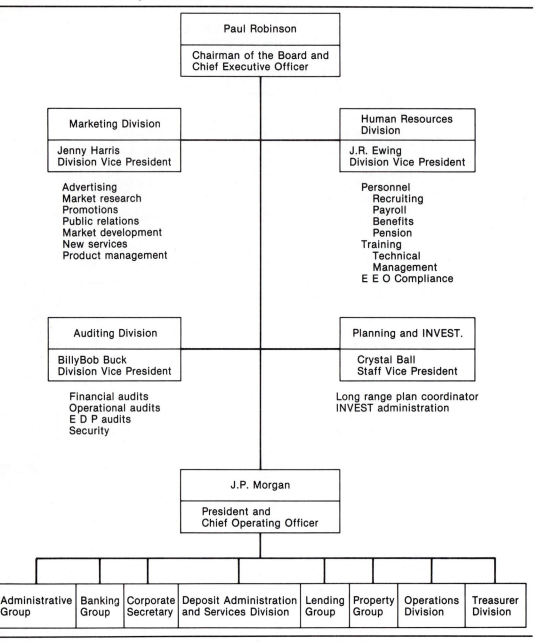

Paul Robinson

Chairman of the Board and
Chief Executive Officer

Marketing Division

Jenny Harris
Division Vice President

Advertising
Market research
Promotions
Public relations
Market development
New services
Product management

Human Resources
Division

J.R. Ewing
Division Vice President

Personnel
    Recruiting
    Payroll
    Benefits
    Pension
Training
    Technical
    Management
E E O Compliance

Auditing Division

BillyBob Buck
Division Vice President

Financial audits
Operational audits
E D P audits
Security

Planning and INVEST.

Crystal Ball
Staff Vice President

Long range plan coordinator
INVEST administration

J.P. Morgan

President and
Chief Operating Officer

| Administrative Group | Banking Group | Corporate Secretary | Deposit Administration and Services Division | Lending Group | Property Group | Operations Division | Treasurer Division |

this market, as did many of the national organizations that had recently entered the market. Jenny Harris recognized the problems created by the intense competition for this middle market and knew that it would be important for GFS to segment the market even more finely than it had in the past. The key, she thought, was to identify target markets where GFS could do a better job than competitors in meeting consumer needs.

Exhibit 3 shows GFS's market share and the shares for each of the major competitors. The data in Exhibit 3 comes from a study that GFS had conducted among residents living within three miles of each of its branches. The results show that about one quarter of the people living near its branches have one or more accounts with GFS. Only 9 percent of the residents, however, indicate that GFS is their primary financial institution. Information on each of the major competitors is presented in Exhibit 4. GFS's growth in assets, advertising expenditures, and number of branches are all below those of the major competitors, with the exception of Home Federal.

GFS was a major factor in construction lending due to its long-term strong relationship with builders and its excellent image in the construction community. GFS did not have the lowest interest rates, and over the years had been very conservative in its appraisals and the amount of its loans. It worked with the cream of the builders, catering to them and to the realtors in the community, who recognized that there would be fewer hassles in working with GFS. The organization was very "loan oriented," and almost all the senior management had come from the loan side of the Association.

In 1985 GFS became profitable again, following four straight years of losses. The reserve ratio (net worth/total assets) had deteriorated from 6.3 percent in 1980 to 2.7 percent in 1984. It had increased to 3 percent by the end

EXHIBIT 3 Market share analysis by competitor

	Percent who have relation- ship with institution	Percent Indicating primary institution	"Primary" as a percent of "have relationship"
City National Bank	32%	19%	59%
First National Bank	28	10	36
Greenwood Federal	24	9	38
Heritage Trust	24	15	63
Sunbelt Federal	13	5	38
Home Federal	8	3	38
Credit unions	24	7	29
All others	NA*	32	NA*
		100%	

Note: Table is interpreted as follows: 32 percent of the population living within three miles of Greenwood branches have a relationship with City National Bank; 59 percent of those with a relationship with City National (19 percent of the population) indicate City National is their primary financial institution.

*NA = not available.

EXHIBIT 4 Information on major competitors ($ in billions)

	Greenwood Federal Savings & Loan	Sunbelt Federal Savings & Loan	First National Bank	Heritage Trust Bank	City National Bank	Home Federal Savings & Loan
Total assets, 12/31/85	$1.3	$2.0	$12.7	$13.9	$ 9.8	$ 1.4
Percent growth in assets 1985 versus 1984	4.0%	20.6%	12.7%	22.9%	15.3%	5.4%
Total deposits, 12/31/85	$ 1.1	$ 1.5	$ 9.1	$10.6	$ 6.9	$ 1.3
Percent growth in deposits 1985 versus 1984	6.9%	4.0%	13.2%	15.1%	9.3%	4.6%
Net worth/assets, 12/31/85	3.0%	6.2%	5.8%	5.6%	5.9%	1.9%
Return on assets, 1985	.6%	1.0%	1.2%	1.0%	1.0%	(loss)
1985 advertising expenditures ($ millions)	$ 0.7	$ 1.4	$ 1.5	$ 1.6	$ 1.4	*
Number of branches in Sunbelt City area	19	30	55	41	63	15

* Figure not available.

of 1985. Most of GFS's savings and loan competitors had converted to stock organizations or were in the process of converting as a result of the 1985 Federal Home Loan Bank Board Regulations raising the required reserve ratio from 3 percent to 6 percent over the next five years. The easiest way to comply with this regulation would be to sell stock, thus raising a substantial amount of equity. GFS management believed that they could achieve the required ratio if they concentrated on increasing the profitability of the organization. Top management was concerned that if they converted to stock ownership it would not be clear how stockholders would fit in versus employees and customers. They feared they would lose flexibility in marketing and would need to direct a great deal of attention to investor relations and the stockbroker community.

Detailed financial information for Greenwood Federal, its number of accounts, and the structure for its savings and its loans are presented in Exhibit 5. Comments on the competitive situation for each of the major product categories follow.

Savings Certificates

The primary competitors for savings certificates are local banks, savings and loans, and credit unions. In the last year, First National Bank and several of the smaller banks and savings and loans have been particularly aggressive in their pricing. Banks especially are able to pay higher rates on certificates because of their greater ability to match assets and liabilities. Brokerage firms and insurance companies must also be considered competitors for these savings dollars.

EXHIBIT 5   GFS financial data and savings structure, July 31, 1986 (year to date)

Total assets .... $1.34 billion
Total savings deposits .... $1.18 billion
Number of savings accounts 140,144
Total loans... $1.14 billion
  Number of first mortgage loans 27,387
  First mortgage loans (average yield 10.0 percent) .... $1.07 billion
  Second mortgage loans, including home equity loans (home equity yield 10.5
    percent) .... $24.5 million
  Education loans (average yield 10.1 percent) .... $11.1 million
  Consumer loans (average yield 13.0 percent on unsecured and 11.6 percent
    on secured) .... $19.7 million
  Savings account loans .... $8.4 million
  Other loans .... $10.0 million
Operating income as percent of assets 11.75%
Average cost of all funds—July 8.2%
Average cost of new funds acquired—July 6.4%
Operating expenses 2.6%
Return on assets 6%

Savings structure	Dollars (millions)	Percent of total
Passbook savings	$ 61.2	5.2%
NOW accounts	37.9	3.3
Super NOW accounts	112.0	9.5
Money market accounts	202.7	17.0
Certificates:		
Jumbo	12.8	1.1
3-month	12.6	1.1
6-month	108.2	9.2
12–24-month	145.9	12.5
25–36-month	170.0	14.4
Greater than 36-month	234.7	20.0
Retirement accounts	78.6	6.7
	$1,176.6	100.0%

GFS has always been a leader in the savings certificate product area with high awareness levels. Recent strategy has been to replace 91-day and six-month certificates with long-term certificates in the portfolio.

Checking Accounts

Commercial banks, savings and loans, and credit unions are also direct competitors for both regular checking and NOW accounts. The source of business for checking accounts has been commercial banks, and Sunbelt Federal has been particularly aggressive in its marketing of checking accounts. The banks have a definite convenience advantage, and they possess the majority of checking accounts. Many, however, are demarketing the smaller-deposit checking accounts through the use of high service fees. Ms. Harris felt there was opportunity to attract new checking accounts, with pricing as an important part of the strategy.

Money Market Accounts

Competitors for money market deposit accounts (MMDA) include commercial banks, savings and loans, money market funds, and bond and equity funds. For a large number of consumers the MMDA has actually replaced the passbook as the primary savings relationship. Ms. Harris thought that with its large base of savings customers, GFS had some competitive advantage here, but marketing of the MMDA had not been very aggressive since its introduction in late 1982. Competitors in the Sunbelt City market were not actively marketing these accounts.

Credit Lines

Commercial banks, savings and loans, mortgage bankers, and brokerage firms have all marketed home equity and personal credit lines aggressively during the past two years. GFS introduced its homeowners line of credit (HOLOC) in 1984, and a personal line of credit product was introduced in 1985. Jenny Harris felt that GFS had a tremendous marketing opportunity with the home equity product because of GFS's large pool of mortgage loan customers and because of changes in the federal tax laws expected to occur in 1987.

Residential Mortgage Loans

GFS is the leader among mortgage bankers, savings and loans, and commercial banks in the mortgage loan market. The market has changed dramatically in the past few years, with a large number of new competitors in the local market. Ms. Harris believed the tradition of good service and market leadership at GFS, together with its entrenched position with the real estate professional target market, provided excellent opportunities for continued success for GFS.

Consumer Loans

GFS has a weak competitive position in the consumer loan product area. Commercial banks have much greater experience with consumer loans and higher awareness. Finance companies, credit unions, and other savings and loans also compete for loan volume. GFS has tried in a modest way to build awareness of the availability of the consumer loan product. Ms. Harris thought there were opportunities to build this volume by differentiation based on product features rather than on the interest rate. None of the major competitors had developed an aggressive, innovative way to market consumer loans.

Brokerage Services

GFS was an equity partner in INVEST, a discount brokerage service. The service became profitable for GFS in 1985, with over 2,000 new accounts and $43 million in sales. INVEST was not an exclusive service, and several savings and loans in the area, including Sunbelt Federal, offered the service. The competition for this service included traditional brokerage firms, discount brokers, insurance companies, and depository institutions.

Strategies of Major Competitors

The major competitors employed different strategies and tactics, depending on the product involved. Ms. Harris's perceptions of some selected competitors are discussed below.

Sunbelt Federal Savings operated almost 60 offices in 20 communities, with 30 of the offices in the Sunbelt City metropolitan area. Most of its recent marketing effort focused on checking accounts and consumer loans. It has priced its checking account lower than most competitors and is actively seeking younger checking account customers. Focus groups conducted by GFS showed that consumers perceived Sunbelt Federal as dynamic, progressive, friendly, having low service charges, and a good place for savings.

Ms. Harris felt that First National Bank had earned the reputation as an innovative retail bank and had begun in earnest to cultivate a position as a rate leader. The bank has experienced dramatic growth in consumer deposits during the past year, at the expense of lower interest margins. A major strength is its extensive branching network, with over 75 offices (55 in the Sunbelt City metropolitan area). Its current advertising campaign, "If your bank isn't First, you should have second thoughts," is more aggressive than previous campaigns. In two television commercials First National Bank compares its performance on investment products with that of Heritage Trust and City National Bank. First National aggressively markets VISA cards throughout the South and is among the top 10 VISA banks in the country. Key image attributes for First National Bank mentioned by the participants in the focus groups include efficient, innovative, flashy, colorful, and convenient.

Heritage Trust had successfully positioned itself as the bank for upwardly mobile people, according to Ms. Harris. Its advertising had enjoyed high awareness levels and had served as an umbrella for product advertising, stressing how well the bank suits the needs of its customers. Heritage Trust had aggressively attracted newcomers to the market through strong corporate relationships. Its upscale banking program had been in operation for years and was considered by Ms. Harris as one of the best in the region. Attributes for Heritage Trust identified by the focus group respondents included "pin-striped," educated, professional, confident, successful, convenient, and smart.

City National Bank is the largest commercial bank in the state and has a very strong retail presence through over 75 offices (63 in the Sunbelt City metropolitan area). City National had traditionally been a strong consumer lender and had recently been directing its advertising at the baby boom generation with its campaign, "Think of your future with City National." Product advertising had stressed simple interest loans, discount brokerage services, and Ready Equity (their equity-based credit line). City National's image as profiled by focus group respondents included convenience but also some negative attributes, such as "bully," impersonal, and greedy.

The image of GFS, as perceived by the attendees at the focus group sessions, is "established," conservative, friendly, and older. GFS had, in fact, attracted a market somewhat older than that of the banks.

Exhibit 6 presents data on the importance of various features to consumers, together with the ratings of GFS and four competitors on each of the features. The consumers in the study were asked to rate the importance of each of the features using a scale of 0–10. They were then asked to give a rating to each financial institution on each feature, again using a scale of 0–10 (with 0 being poor and 10 extremely good). Overall, the most important features for a financial institution include:

Seldom make mistakes.

Do a good job overall.

Statements are clear and easy to understand.

Open at convenient hours during the week.

Personnel are polite and courteous.

Long history of financial stability.

Offer all the services I need.

Sufficient tellers to avoid long lines.

GFS is not rated the best on any of these factors, although it is rated better than Sunbelt Federal Savings on six of the eight. It is also rated higher than City National Bank on four of the eight. GFS is rated lower than First National Bank on all eight and lower than Heritage on six of the eight. The biggest "gap" for GFS is in providing consumers with all the services they need. Ms. Harris wondered whether this perception could be changed by increasing the promotion of many of the services currently available at GFS.

Consumer Research

To learn more about what consumers wanted in financial services and how the overall market could be segmented better, Ms. Harris had commissioned, in cooperation with the GFS advertising agency, a major consumer segmentation study. The research was designed to provide several clusters of consumers (segments) based on activities, interests, and opinions rather than on conventional demographic characteristics such as age, sex, or income. Ms. Harris wanted to use the results of the study to help develop a market niche for GFS, to identify appropriate target markets, to evaluate existing and new products, and to improve marketing communications for GFS.

National Family Opinion (NFO), one of the nation's largest marketing research firms, was used to conduct the study. NFO maintains a nationally representative consumer panel of 150,000 households, with over 3,000 in the Sunbelt City metropolitan area. NFO mailed out 1,250 questionnaires, and 57 percent, 712, were returned. In addition, a supplemental sample of 122 GFS

EXHIBIT 6   Importance of features and comparative ratings

	Q10: Importance, scale of 0 to 10:	Ratings of Institutions (poor to extremely good, scale of 0 to 10)				
Q:10	Rank	GFS	CNB	FNB	HTB	SFS
Seldom make mistakes	1 — 8.9	6.8	6.1	6.9	7.0	6.6
Good job overall	2 — 8.8	7.0	6.4	7.1	7.0	6.8
Clear statements	3 — 8.4	6.5	6.7	7.0	6.8	6.5
Convenient weekday hours	4 — 8.4	6.9	6.9	7.1	6.9	6.8
Polite and courteous	5 — 8.3	6.9	6.4	7.1	7.0	6.8
History of stability	6 — 8.2	7.4	7.7	8.0	7.9	7.1
All services I need	7 — 8.1	6.6	7.2	7.5	7.2	6.6
Rarely long lines	8 — 8.1	6.0	5.8	6.2	6.3	5.8
Pay highest rate	9 — 7.9	6.4	5.4	6.0	5.9	6.4
Conveniently located branches	10 — 7.9	5.8	7.9	7.4	7.4	6.3
Convenient to live	11 — 7.9	5.3	7.3	6.9	7.0	6.1
Lowest charges, fees	12 — 7.7	5.9	4.8	5.4	5.4	6.1
Easily qualify for free checking	13 — 7.7	5.8	5.2	5.7	5.6	5.9
Tailor services to fit needs	14 — 7.0	5.4	5.0	5.6	5.5	5.3
Convenient to work	15 — 7.0	5.0	7.3	6.5	6.5	6.0
Offer consumer loans	16 — 6.8	6.8	7.6	7.4	7.3	6.8
Convenient Saturday hours	17 — 6.6	5.4	5.6	5.5	5.5	5.4
Interested in my financial position	18 — 6.2	5.2	4.8	5.3	5.1	5.0
Interest in me as a person	19 — 6.2	4.9	4.4	5.0	4.9	4.8
Work with me to achieve goals	20 — 6.1	5.1	4.8	5.3	5.1	5.0
Offer sound advice	21 — 6.1	5.7	5.4	5.8	5.7	5.6
Leader among institutions	22 — 6.0	6.7	7.4	7.5	7.5	6.6
Convenient to shop	23 — 6.0	5.3	7.0	6.5	6.5	5.6
Develop new products and services	24 — 5.0	5.5	5.3	5.9	5.8	5.2
Provide non-bank financial services	25 — 3.3	4.8	5.2	5.1	5.0	4.6

Key: GFS = Greenwood Federal   CNB = City National Bank   FNB = First National Bank
HTB = Heritage Trust Bank   SFS = Sunbelt Federal Savings

customers also completed the questionnaire. The study included results only from persons primarily responsible for household financial decisions (approximately half male and half female). The median age was just under 45 years old. The proportion classified as "working preferred," that is, employed and reporting a minimum of $5,000 savings, was 40 percent, a level considered normal based on previous studies conducted by GFS.

Slightly over half, 57 percent, used a commercial bank as the main financial institution, 23 percent used a savings and loan, 12 percent used a credit union, and 18 percent listed all other types of institutions. GFS's market share for the main study was 15 percent (having any account, not "primary" institution).

The questionnaire presented 100 opportunities for each respondent to record his or her attitudes or opinions about financial matters and about his or her banking habits and preferences. Examples of questions include "I like to pay cash for almost everything I buy," "I'm always looking for a way to make more interest on my money," and "I need very little advice when making decisions about the types of financial services I should use." In addition, each person was presented with 25 questions concerning the importance to them of individual banking practices and services, together with questions concerning the rating of the individual financial institutions.

A large mainframe computer then was used to perform advanced statistical analysis of the questionnaire data. The objective was to cluster or group the 712 respondents into meaningful segments based on commonality of their attitudes rather than into groups based on age, income, or other demographic characteristics. The computer program identified five clusters or segments similar enough in their attitudes to be classified as distinct survey segments. These segments were then given names to help describe them. Most segmentation studies of this type attempt to group people according to lifestyles, thus ending up with such groupings as "yuppies," "young suburbia," or "gray power." Here the groupings were based on the way the respondents think and act about money, credit, banking, and financial services. Five clusters were identified and named:

Secure Steve (self-confident and self-assured).

Retiring Richard (72 percent employed, but the highest proportion of retirees).

Fast Lane Phil (overspending, undersaving youth).

Minimal Martha (highest proportion of females, but not necessarily female; users of a minimum of products and services).

Single-Minded Sam (desire for one-stop banking at a full-service convenient institution).

Exhibits 7 through 10 present data from the two samples concerning the five segments, including size of the segments, demographics, amount of savings, and financial attitudes. Exhibits 11 through 13 present data from the study

EXHIBIT 7   Descriptions and size of each segment

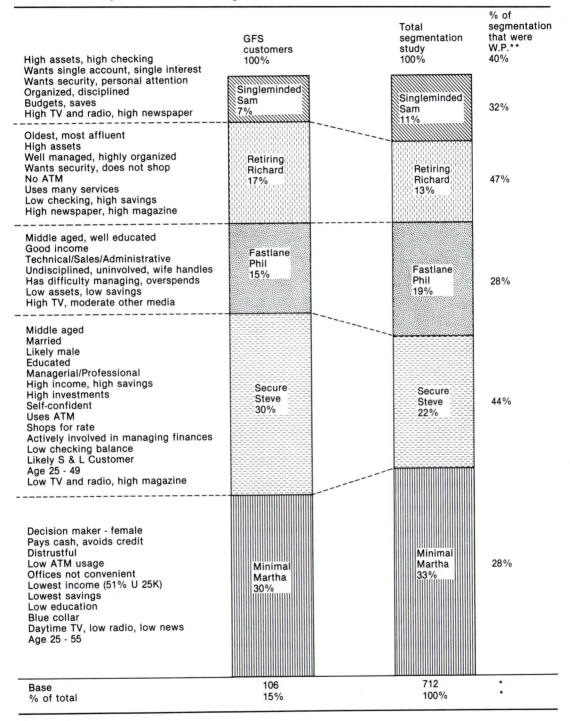

	GFS customers 100%	Total segmentation study 100%	% of segmentation that were W.P.** 40%
High assets, high checking Wants single account, single interest Wants security, personal attention Organized, disciplined Budgets, saves High TV and radio, high newspaper	Singleminded Sam 7%	Singleminded Sam 11%	32%
Oldest, most affluent High assets Well managed, highly organized Wants security, does not shop No ATM Uses many services Low checking, high savings High newspaper, high magazine	Retiring Richard 17%	Retiring Richard 13%	47%
Middle aged, well educated Good income Technical/Sales/Administrative Undisciplined, uninvolved, wife handles Has difficulty managing, overspends Low assets, low savings High TV, moderate other media	Fastlane Phil 15%	Fastlane Phil 19%	28%
Middle aged Married Likely male Educated Managerial/Professional High income, high savings High investments Self-confident Uses ATM Shops for rate Actively involved in managing finances Low checking balance Likely S & L Customer Age 25 - 49 Low TV and radio, high magazine	Secure Steve 30%	Secure Steve 22%	44%
Decision maker - female Pays cash, avoids credit Distrustful Low ATM usage Offices not convenient Lowest income (51% U 25K) Lowest savings Low education Blue collar Daytime TV, low radio, low news Age 25 - 55	Minimal Martha 30%	Minimal Martha 33%	28%
Base	106	712	*
% of total	15%	100%	*

*Each segment total

**Note: W.P. means working preferred, those employed with
      at least $5000 in savings.

EXHIBIT 8 Demographics of the segmentation study

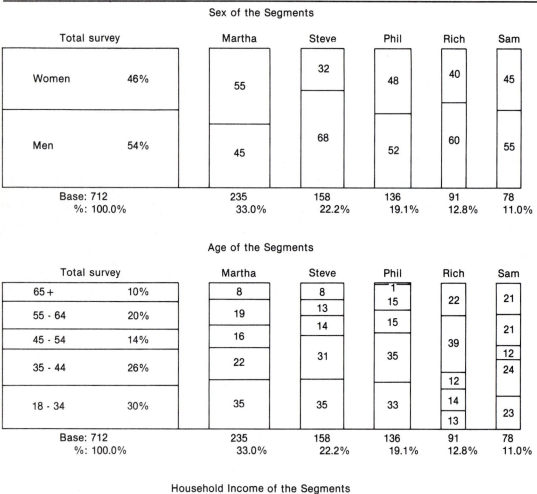

Sex of the Segments

	Total survey	Martha	Steve	Phil	Rich	Sam
Women	46%	55	32	48	40	45
Men	54%	45	68	52	60	55
Base: 712		235	158	136	91	78
%: 100.0%		33.0%	22.2%	19.1%	12.8%	11.0%

Age of the Segments

	Total survey	Martha	Steve	Phil	Rich	Sam
65 +	10%	8	8	1 / 15	22	21
55 - 64	20%	19	13	15	39	21
45 - 54	14%	16	14			12
35 - 44	26%	22	31	35	12	24
18 - 34	30%	35	35	33	14 / 13	23
Base: 712		235	158	136	91	78
%: 100.0%		33.0%	22.2%	19.1%	12.8%	11.0%

Household Income of the Segments

	Total survey	Martha	Steve	Phil	Rich	Sam
$50 +	15%	7	25	12	17	18
$35 - 49.9	23%	22	22	23	31	18
$25 - 34.9	21%	20	26	23	21	12
$10 - 24.9	41%	51	27	42	31	53
Base: 712		235	158	136	91	78
%: 100.0%		33.0%	22.2%	19.1%	12.8%	11.0%

EXHIBIT 8 *(concluded)*

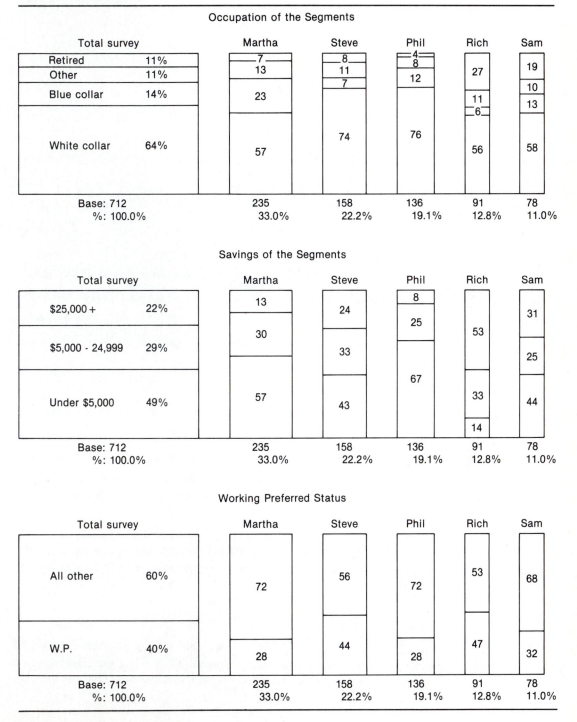

Occupation of the Segments

Total survey			Martha	Steve	Phil	Rich	Sam
Retired	11%		7	8	4	27	19
Other	11%		13	11	8		10
Blue collar	14%		23	7	12	11	13
						6	
White collar	64%		57	74	76	56	58
Base: 712			235	158	136	91	78
%: 100.0%			33.0%	22.2%	19.1%	12.8%	11.0%

Savings of the Segments

Total survey			Martha	Steve	Phil	Rich	Sam
$25,000 +	22%		13	24	8	53	31
			30		25		
$5,000 - 24,999	29%			33			25
					67	33	
Under $5,000	49%		57	43		14	44
Base: 712			235	158	136	91	78
%: 100.0%			33.0%	22.2%	19.1%	12.8%	11.0%

Working Preferred Status

Total survey			Martha	Steve	Phil	Rich	Sam
All other	60%		72	56	72	53	68
W.P.	40%		28	44	28	47	32
Base: 712			235	158	136	91	78
%: 100.0%			33.0%	22.2%	19.1%	12.8%	11.0%

EXHIBIT 9   Average amount of savings (by study segments)

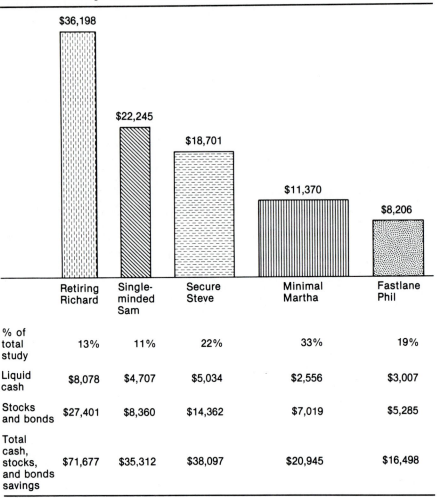

	Retiring Richard	Single-minded Sam	Secure Steve	Minimal Martha	Fastlane Phil
% of total study	13%	11%	22%	33%	19%
Liquid cash	$8,078	$4,707	$5,034	$2,556	$3,007
Stocks and bonds	$27,401	$8,360	$14,362	$7,019	$5,285
Total cash, stocks, and bonds savings	$71,677	$35,312	$38,097	$20,945	$16,498

concerning each segment's rating of Greenwood Federal and usage of various products and services. The share of market for GFS and its major competitors by segment is included in Exhibit 14. Selected findings for each segment are discussed below.

Minimal Martha

This segment was the largest identified, with one third of all consumers and 30 percent of GFS customers included. Minimal Martha had the least usage of financial products and institutions among the five segments. This was the only

EXHIBIT 10 Agreement with various attitudinal statements

		25	50	75	100%	Mean, Scale 1 - 7
When it comes to services such as checking accounts, I shop around to find the least expensive provider.	Total			49 GFS = 57		4.3
	Martha			56		4.7
	Steve			73		5.1
	Phil		35			3.9
	Richard	24				3.3
	Sam	31				3.3
I like to try new and different things.	Total			62 GFS = 65		4.9
	Martha			63		4.9
	Steve			77		5.4
	Phil			59		4.7
	Richard		45			4.2
	Sam			59		4.7
I would rather have one place for all my financial needs.	Total			59 GFS = 49		4.9
	Martha			67		5.2
	Steve		50			4.5
	Phil			67		5.1
	Richard	26				3.6
	Sam			78		5.8
It's more important to live well now than to save money for the future.	Total	13 GFS = 10				2.4
	Martha	11				2.3
	Steve	15				2.5
	Phil	11				2.6
	Richard	11				2.3
	Sam	24				2.7
It's important that my financial institution is conveniently located near home.	Total			80 GFS = 84		5.6
	Martha			86		5.9
	Steve			74		5.3
	Phil			83		5.7
	Richard			70		5.2
	Sam			86		5.8

segment where the financial decision maker was most often female and the banking chores were also handled most often by the female head of household. Minimal Martha generally manages her personal finances by paying cash, keeping funds in separate accounts, and avoiding credit. She is less comfortable and trusting of financial institutions. The convenience of a financial institution is probably the major determinant in its selection. Martha has a low income, less education, and is more likely to be married with a larger household and a blue-collar husband than other segments.

EXHIBIT 10 *(concluded)*

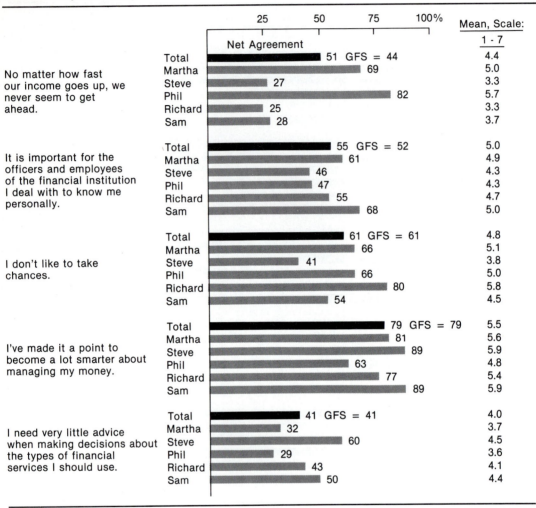

		Net Agreement	Mean, Scale: 1 - 7
No matter how fast our income goes up, we never seem to get ahead.	Total	51 GFS = 44	4.4
	Martha	69	5.0
	Steve	27	3.3
	Phil	82	5.7
	Richard	25	3.3
	Sam	28	3.7
It is important for the officers and employees of the financial institution I deal with to know me personally.	Total	55 GFS = 52	5.0
	Martha	61	4.9
	Steve	46	4.3
	Phil	47	4.3
	Richard	55	4.7
	Sam	68	5.0
I don't like to take chances.	Total	61 GFS = 61	4.8
	Martha	66	5.1
	Steve	41	3.8
	Phil	66	5.0
	Richard	80	5.8
	Sam	54	4.5
I've made it a point to become a lot smarter about managing my money.	Total	79 GFS = 79	5.5
	Martha	81	5.6
	Steve	89	5.9
	Phil	63	4.8
	Richard	77	5.4
	Sam	89	5.9
I need very little advice when making decisions about the types of financial services I should use.	Total	41 GFS = 41	4.0
	Martha	32	3.7
	Steve	60	4.5
	Phil	29	3.6
	Richard	43	4.1
	Sam	50	4.4

Secure Steve

The second largest segment is Secure Steve, who is upscale (managerial, professional, well educated, high income, high savings, high investment) and innovative. Secure Steve shops for low charges and high interest with self-confidence. He rejects frills and is unwilling to pay to get personal attention. Typically, Secure Steve is in the prime of his career, aged 25–49, married, with a confident, ambitious outlook. He maintains the minimum in checking, shops for the best terms, and is willing to try new products. He actively shops around

EXHIBIT 11   Rating of Greenwood Federal Savings (poor to extremely good; scale of zero to ten)

Attribute	Rank (importance)	GFS Rating: Total Study	Minimal Martha	Secure Steve	Fastlane Phil	Retirng Richard	Single Sam
Seldom make mistakes	1	6.8	6.3	7.2	6.7	7.2	6.6
Good job overall	2	7.0	7.0	7.0	6.8	7.5	7.1
Clear statements	3	6.5	6.4	6.5	6.3	6.9	6.7
Convenient weekday hours	4	6.9	7.1	6.6	6.6	7.5	7.1
Polite and courteous	5	6.9	6.6	7.3	6.5	7.2	6.9
History of stability	6	7.4	7.5	7.2	6.9	8.3	7.8
All services I need	7	6.6	6.8	6.9	6.2	6.5	6.4
Rarely long lines	8	6.0	5.7	6.1	6.0	6.3	6.0
Pay highest rate	9	6.4	6.4	6.5	6.1	6.5	6.8
Conveniently located branches	10	5.8	5.7	5.8	5.5	6.5	5.8
Convenient to live	11	5.3	5.0	5.6	5.2	6.1	5.1
Lowest charges, fees	12	5.9	5.9	6.0	5.6	5.8	5.9
Easily qualify for free checking	13	5.8	5.4	6.3	5.3	6.3	6.2
Tailor services to fit needs	14	5.4	5.6	5.2	5.3	5.4	5.4
Convenient to work	15	5.0	5.1	4.8	4.7	5.8	4.6
Offer consumer loans	16	6.8	6.9	6.9	6.6	6.6	7.1
Convenient Saturday hours	17	5.4	5.3	5.8	4.9	5.3	5.8
Interested in my financial position	18	5.2	5.3	4.8	5.2	5.4	5.3
Interest in me as a person	19	4.9	4.9	4.5	4.9	5.1	5.5
Work with me to achieve goals	20	5.1	5.2	4.9	4.9	5.1	5.5
Offer sound advice	21	5.7	5.8	5.5	5.7	5.5	5.8
Leader among institutions	22	6.7	6.7	6.4	6.3	7.3	7.2
Convenient to shop	23	5.3	5.1	5.4	5.1	5.7	5.4
Develop new products and services	24	5.5	5.6	5.5	5.1	5.9	5.6
Provide non-bank financial services	25	4.8	4.9	4.9	4.3	5.0	5.2

EXHIBIT 12 Product usage: Segmentation study: January 25—March 18, 1985

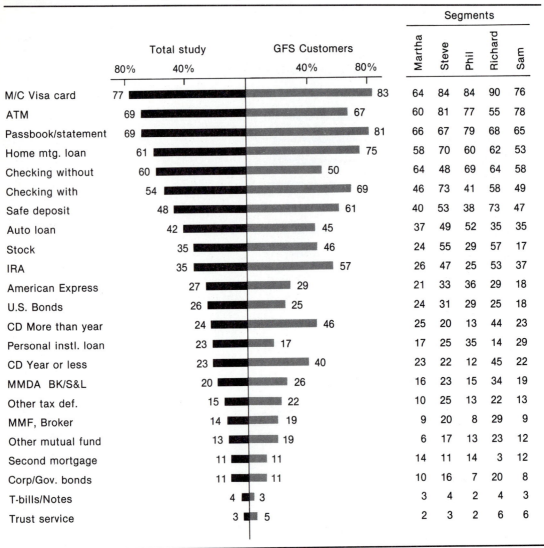

	Total study	GFS Customers	Martha	Steve	Phil	Richard	Sam
M/C Visa card	77	83	64	84	84	90	76
ATM	69	67	60	81	77	55	78
Passbook/statement	69	81	66	67	79	68	65
Home mtg. loan	61	75	58	70	60	62	53
Checking without	60	50	64	48	69	64	58
Checking with	54	69	46	73	41	58	49
Safe deposit	48	61	40	53	38	73	47
Auto loan	42	45	37	49	52	35	35
Stock	35	46	24	55	29	57	17
IRA	35	57	26	47	25	53	37
American Express	27	29	21	33	36	29	18
U.S. Bonds	26	25	24	31	29	25	18
CD More than year	24	46	25	20	13	44	23
Personal instl. loan	23	17	17	25	35	14	29
CD Year or less	23	40	23	22	12	45	22
MMDA BK/S&L	20	26	16	23	15	34	19
Other tax def.	15	22	10	25	13	22	13
MMF, Broker	14	19	9	20	8	29	9
Other mutual fund	13	19	6	17	13	23	12
Second mortgage	11	11	14	11	14	3	12
Corp/Gov. bonds	11	11	10	16	7	20	8
T-bills/Notes	4	3	3	4	2	4	3
Trust service	3	5	2	3	2	6	6

for the "best" financial products and is more willing to change institutions to get the best deal. He represents 22 percent of the sample and 30 percent of GFS customers.

Fast Lane Phil

Phil likely can be found in the fast lane at Household Finance Corporation, but is not found among the jet set in the fast lane at the airport. The segment is

EXHIBIT 13   Service usage

	Total study		GFS customers	Martha	Steve	Phil	Richard	Sam
							Segments	
Automatic deduction from checking	35		34	30	41	45	26	37
Direct deposit of payroll	29		23	7	51	40	31	33
Overdraft protection	29		32	23	35	34	23	39
Unsecured line of credit	19		15	11	27	21	21	25
Stock brokerage other than Bk/S&L	12		14	8	20	9	22	5
Automatic transfer saving to checking	11		6	8	13	12	7	20
Card that automatically deducts purchases	7		4	6	9	7	4	14
Secured line of credit	5		5	4	4	7	1	6
Telephone bill paying	5		2	4	4	4	4	5
Automobile leasing	3		4	3	3	5	2	4
Financial advice and counseling	3		4	2	6	1	3	3
Stockbrokerage at bank or S&L	1		3	1	1	2	2	1

undisciplined, and they are poor managers of financial affairs. Three out of four in this segment report less than $5,000 in savings. Phil frequently overspends with credit cards and often makes purchases with personal installment loans. He has the highest usage of checking accounts *without* interest and passbook accounts, but the lowest usage of other savings or investment products. This segment represents 19 percent of the total sample and 15 percent of GFS customers.

Retiring Richard

This segment has by far the highest savings. They prefer low risk to high interest and like personal attention. The Richard segment contains the highest

EXHIBIT 14 Share of market (by study segments)

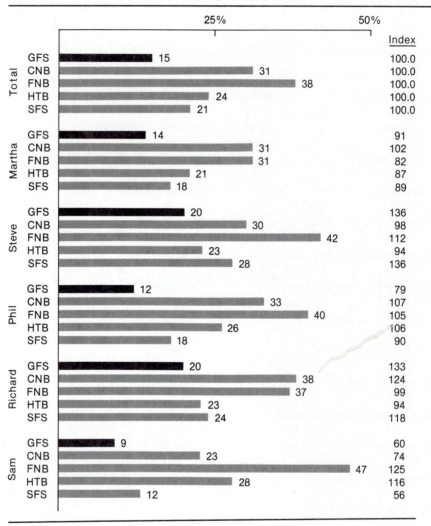

proportion of retirees, 28 percent, more than double the average for the total sample. His financial affairs are well established, and he is somewhat resistant to changing them. Retiring Richard has the highest usage of most financial products and is the oldest and most married of the five segments. The segment represents 13 percent of the total sample and 17 percent of GFS customers.

Single-Minded Sam

This segment, representing 11 percent of the sample and 7 percent of GFS customers, has the strongest preference for a single integrated account with one financial institution. This segment likes the security of a big institution, especially banks, and personal attention is very important. One-stop banking is more important than low fees or a high interest rate on savings. Sam is the second oldest and the most divorced, widowed, or separated of the segments.

Ms. Harris felt that the key to finding a niche for GFS and for differentiating it from the competition could be found in Exhibits 7 through 14. She planned to spend considerable time interpreting the meaning of this data.

Marketing Strategy Considerations

The senior management of Greenwood Federal had recently developed a mission statement. It read, "The mission of Greenwood Federal is to discover and provide needed financial services to consumers in a manner consistent with their reasonable expectations and consistent with the achievement of reasonable earnings." Given the change in regulations that had taken place in the past year and the mission statement, Ms. Harris felt that she should develop a strategic marketing plan to provide "controlled growth orchestrated to the beat of profitability, protecting assets and net worth while directing a positive course of profits." The Association had always used conservative policies, and loan delinquencies over the years had been consistently low because of the relatively strict loan underwriting standards. She felt it was important to maintain a conservative posture but still felt there was considerable opportunity to increase consumer lending with new products, such as the homeowners line of credit, the personal credit line, and a new type of auto loan, the "Payment Shrinker." Exhibit 15 contains copy the ad agency had developed for a brochure to explain how the Payment Shrinker auto loan works.

EXHIBIT 15 Payment Shrinker ad copy

Payment Shrinker Auto Financing Cuts Monthly Payments up to 49 Percent

Now you can afford to drive the automobile you really want. GFS Federal makes it possible with Payment Shrinker, the auto loan that can reduce your monthly payments by 25 to 49 percent.

Here's How Payment Shrinker Reduces Monthly Payments

GFS Federal Payment Shrinker combines the lower monthly payment advantages of auto leasing with the ownership and tax benefits offered by conventional car loans.

Depending on your choice of terms, your monthly payments will extend over 24, 36, or 48 months. The final payment amount will be determined at the time you make the loan and will be based on the residual value of the car* at the end of the loan.

Interest is computed on the full amount of the loan, but your monthly payments are lower because the residual car value is subtracted from the purchase price. The monthly principal payments are based upon the difference.

* The residual value of the automobile is determined by *Automotive Lease Guide*, a published residual value book, in effect at the time the loan is originated. The residual value represents the estimated value of the vehicle after the 24- to 48-month loan is completed.

EXHIBIT 15 *(concluded)*

The interest that is charged on the full amount of the loan is tax deductible, as well as any sales tax you pay. This tax benefit is not available for personal automobile leases.

Four Options at End of Loan Term

At the end of the loan term, you'll have a choice of four options regarding your final payment: If you wish to keep your car, you may (1) pay off the residual car value amount figured in with the last monthly payment or (2) refinance the residual. If you would like another car, you may (3) sell or trade your car and keep the profit you make over and above the residual value or (4) return the car in good working condition (subject to condition and mileage requirements) to GFS Federal with no further obligation except to pay a nominal return fee.

Example of How Payment Shrinker Auto Loan Works

Purchase price of the car you want	$13,528
Less: Down payment (10%)	1,353
Amount to be financed over 36 months at	
13¾%† **annual percentage rate**	$12,175
Residual value of car at end of 36 month loan term	$ 6,935

Monthly payments are composed of two parts:
1. Principal and interest payable on $5,240
   ($12,175 minus the $6,935 residual value) $178.44
2. Interest payments on the $6,935 residual car value .... $ 79.46

Total monthly payment $257.90

Monthly payment with conventional auto loan at
  12¼%† **annual percentage rate** $405.86
Monthly payment with Payment Shrinker $257.90
Amount saved per month $147.96

† This is an example. Actual rate may vary.

Compare Monthly Payments—
Payment Shrinker versus Conventional Financing

Amount financed	Conventional auto loan (monthly)	Payment Shrinker auto loan (monthly)
$24,000		
24 months	$1,132.57	$712.24
36 months	$ 800.01	$573.31
48 months	$ 634.96	$501.72
$16,000	—	—
24 months	$ 755.05	$474.82
36 months	$ 533.34	$382.21
48 months	$ 423.31	$334.48
$8,000	—	—
24 months	$ 377.52	$237.41
36 months	$ 266.67	$191.11
48 months	$ 211.65	$167.24

Note: The monthly payment chart shown is based on the following assumptions: Payment Shrinker auto loan: **13.75% annual percentage rate;** Conventional auto loan: **12.25% annual percentage rate.** Assume residual value is 50% of sticker price for 24 months, 45% of sticker price for 36 months, 40% of sticker price for 48 months. Amount financed is 90% of purchase price.

To help determine the relative importance of the various products offered by GFS, Ms. Harris had developed a product hierarchy ranking matrix. This is presented in Exhibit 16, together with the key used to give the ratings. According to her analysis, money market deposit accounts, certificates of deposit, IRAs, mortgage loans, and regular savings accounts were the products that should receive the highest priority. Ms. Harris was very uncomfortable with what she had done and wondered whether the results were accurate. For example, she had weighted each of the factors equally and was now having

EXHIBIT 16   Product hierarchy

	WP* usage	WP hot button	Comp. opp.†	GFS position	Profit	Commitment	Total
MMDA	3	3	3	2	3	2	16
CDs	3	3	2	2	3	3	16
IRA	3	3	1	2	2	3	14
Mortgage loans	3	2	1	3	2	3	14
Regular savings	3	1	3	2	3	2	14
Checking	3	2	2	1	1	3	13
HOLOC	1	3	1	3	3	1	12
INVEST	3	3	1	2	1	2	12
Consumer loans	2	3	2	1	1	3	12
Super NOW	1	2	3	2	2	1	11
Safe deposit	3	2	3	1	2	1	11
Credit card	3	2	1	1	2	1	10
Travel company	1	1	3	1	1	2	9

Product Hierarchy Key

Working Preferred Usage:
   1 = Less than 30 percent use the product.
   2 = 30–50 percent use the product.
   3 = More than 50 percent use the product.

Working Preferred Hot Button:
   1 = Low priority—not likely to move or open account.
   2 = Medium priority—might move or open if offer is strong.
   3 = High priority—will move or open if offer is strong.

Competitive Opportunity:
   1 = Competitors are actively marketing the product.
   2 = Some competitive activity.
   3 = No competitive activity.

Greenwood Federal's Position:
   1 = Weak position.
   2 = Potential for unique position.
   3 = Strong position.

Profitability:
   1 = Significant losses on product.
   2 = Product is losing money but has potential.
   3 = Product is profitable.

Commitment:
   1 = Little or no resources have been committed in the past.
   2 = Some resources have been committed in the past.
   3 = Major resources have been committed in the past.

* WP = Working preferred (employed and savings of $5,000 and up).
† Comp. Opp. = Competitive opportunity.

EXHIBIT 17 Proposed campaign for 25K Account

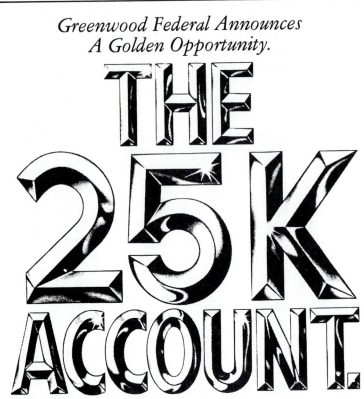

Greenwood Federal Announces
A Golden Opportunity.

THE 25K ACCOUNT.

Take a moment to review your investments. If you aren't currently earning a preferred rate on any amount of $25,000 or more, you should consider investing in Greenwood Federal's 25K Account. With 25K you'll earn our highest money market account rate. A fiercely competitive figure you'll rarely find bested. One that changes with market conditions to keep you head and shoulders above the crowd.

Your 25K Account is easily accessible every seven days. And federal insurance makes it as safe as, well, money in the bank.

The 25K Account. It's designed for those who are already experienced in recognizing golden opportunities. And for those interested in smaller investments, we offer competitive rates on a regular money market account with a minimum balance of $2,500. We invite you to come in to any Greenwood Federal office and seize the opportunity today.

your partner
GREENWOOD FEDERAL

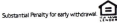

Substantial Penalty for early withdrawal.

EXHIBIT 18   Ad designed to attract more loans

AFFORDABLE LOANS.
ACADILLACABLE LOANS.
APONTIACABLE LOANS.
APOOLABLE LOANS.
ANEWPORCHABLE LOANS.
AVACATIONABLE LOANS.
ACOLLEGEABLE LOANS.
ASPEEDBOATABLE LOANS.

Available loans. We've got plenty. Everything from auto loans, boat loans, home improvement loans, lines of credit, and of course, mortgage loans. In fact, we've always been a leader in mortgage lending. And that leadership carries over into all the other loans you need.

Agreeable loans. We're there to make it easier for you. With convenient terms, a variety of services, quick responses, simple interest, no prepayment penalties and service with a smile.

Affordable loans. Don't worry. We'll make sure your monthly payments are well within your reach.

A whatever-you-wantable loans. You'll find all you need at Greenwood Federal.

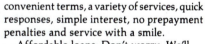

GREENWOOD FEDERAL

Experience The Partnership.

Member F.S.L.I.C.

some second thoughts about this decision. She vowed to take another look at the product hierarchy rankings as she started to develop the strategic marketing plan.

The advertising agency had recommended several new campaigns for her consideration. The "25K Account" proposal is included in Exhibit 17. The goal of this ad is to attract larger accounts, and the campaign would use the tag line "your partner."

Exhibit 18 contains an ad the agency had developed to attract more consumer loans. This ad made use of the proposed alternative tag line "Experience the Partnership." Finally, Exhibit 19 contains the third proposal from the ad agency, "For the Good Life." This ad was designed to attract high dollar volumes for longer periods of time through the use of attractive premiums. These new certificates of deposit were to be priced 35 basis points below comparable three-, five-, and six-year certificates, with interest to be paid and compounded annually rather than quarterly. The agency proposed that advertising previously scheduled for high-interest checking be switched to this premium promotion and that newspaper ads and radio also be used.

As shown in Exhibit 20, the majority of GFS customers used only one type of product from among the offerings available, although a number of households had more than one account within the type (two or more savings accounts in the household, for example). Ms. Harris thought that there was great opportunity to "cross sell more services to more households." GFS had recently established a small telemarketing operation and she wondered if this might be used for this purpose. She wondered how to direct mail to customers or prospects and if advertising might work to increase cross-selling opportunities. To determine what had happened recently with some of the newer products, she pulled out the report in Exhibit 21 which contained information on new loan production and consumer loans outstanding as of July 1986 (the latest report available).

Lots of things were popping into Ms. Harris's mind. She was concerned about how much attention she should pay to the short run versus the long run. For example, she knew that for GFS to devote strong emphasis to increase its penetration in the small business market would take a long time, given the lack of history in marketing to this segment. Likewise, a strong commitment to home banking using personal computers would be a long-run effort. On the other hand, increasing the emphasis on the Payment Shrinker auto loan, the homeowners line of credit (HOLOC), personal line of credit, or consumer loans would be easy to accomplish in the short run, given that the products had already been developed.

She wondered how much emphasis to put on INVEST, the discount brokerage service. A recent study GFS had conducted showed that 77 percent of the money invested through INVEST came out of other sources and that 23 percent came from GFS accounts. Some of the management at GFS felt that the money pulled out of the accounts would have been invested in stock or bonds

EXHIBIT 19 "For the Good Life" ad proposal

anyway, so that at least with INVEST some fees were generated. Also, heavy promotion of INVEST, which had just recently become profitable, could reduce the asset base for the Association while generating some fees, enabling a rise in the reserve ratio. Other GFS managers were more skeptical about this happening.

EXHIBIT 20 Types of accounts held by GFS customers

Account type	Percent of GFS households	Average number of GFS products per household
Savings only	28	
Mortgage only	18	
Checking only	7	
Consumer loan only	3	
Total one product type	56	1.4*
Checking and savings	16	
Mortgage and savings	5	
Consumer loan and savings	3	
Consumer loan and checking	2	
Consumer loan and mortgage	2	
Checking and mortgage	0	
Total two product types	28	3.1
Checking, savings, and mortgage	5	
Checking, savings, and consumer loan	3	
Savings, mortgage, and consumer loan	3	
Checking, mortgage, and consumer loan	1	
Total three product types	12	4.6
All four types	4	6.8
	100	2.5
Any savings	67	
Any checking	39	
Any mortgage	38	
Any consumer loan	21	
Any deposit	83	
Any loan	46	

* This number is greater than 1.0 because many households had more than one account (although all were the same type of account).

Ms. Harris had seen potential in the segmentation study for high-interest checking products with several of the segments. She also thought that the proposed tax law, which would remove deductions for consumer loans, could have a big impact on her strategic planning. Did it mean, for example, that emphasis should not be put on automobile loans (even the Payment Shrinker) and other consumer loans? Did it mean that homeowner equity loans were the wave of the future? She had seen Internal Revenue Service data indicating that only 38 percent of all taxpayers itemized deductions on their 1984 returns. Did this suggest that consumers simply will not care enough about tax savings to establish a home equity credit line when they are ready to buy a car? Home-owner equity lines typically cost $500–$700 in closing cost alone. She had heard rumors that several of the Sunbelt City banks were considering waiving the fees, and wondered how GFS should respond if this in fact happened in the near future. She also had heard rumors that one or more of the banks might lower the rates, currently two percentage points above prime, to prime or even below for several months to attract new accounts with home equity loans.

EXHIBIT 21   Banking group monthly report for July 1986

Consumer loans production:

Real estate loans	Number			Total dollar amount
Second mortgages	19			$ 358,800.00
Equity line	39			1,145,100.00
Total	58			$ 1,503,900.00
Installment and single pay loans				
Payment Shrinker	10			118,763.86
Auto	184			1,239,500.10
Personal, secured and unsecured	291			2,145,839.73
Personal LOC	80			760,100.00
Total	565			4,264,203.69
Total production for July	623			$ 5,768,103.69

Consumer loans outstanding:	Total available credit	Number	Total dollar amount
Unsecured		1,234	$ 3,280,607.34
Secured other		704	3,718,010.66
Auto		3,106	15,147,248.45
Payment Shrinker		106	1,409,657.19
Subtotal		5,150	23,555,523.64
Equity line	12,493,481.68	1,086	17,383,580.59
Personal LOC	5,348,844.40	760	2,552,124.24
Total		6,996	43,491,228.47

	Number	Total	
2nd mortgages	795	9,219,720.55	
Less participated 2nds	419	−4,956,014.39	
Total 2nd mortgages	376	4,263,706.16	
Grand total	7,372		$47,754,934.63
Second mortgages maintained on mortgage loan system	726	$12,488,112.80	

Credit life insurance − Net income for July: $8,374.52.

Delinquencies:	Over 30 days	Over 60 days	
Real estate	11	4	
Other	60	27	
Total	71 .8%	31 .3%	

Charge-offs in July—$11,382.62.   Recoveries—$198.00.

Finally, Ms. Harris thought about the advertising agency. It had been bugging her for some time to give it more direction. Did GFS intend to become a full-service financial institution in the mold of a traditional commercial bank, or did it plan to continue to specialize in the consumer savings and mortgage lending areas? Which niche would be appropriate for GFS to seek relative to other financial institutions? What competitive differences could be used to set GFS apart from the competition? She wondered whether it might just be simpler to become a stock company, which would be the quickest and easiest way to raise the net worth/total assets ratio to 6 percent.

Case 8

Modern Plastics (A)*

Institutional sales manager Jim Clayton had spent most of Monday morning planning for the rest of the month. It was early July and Jim knew that an extremely busy time was coming with the preparation of the following year's sales plan.

Since starting his current job less than a month ago, Jim had been involved in learning the requirements of the job and making his initial territory visits. Now that he was getting settled, Jim was trying to plan his activities according to priorities. The need for planning had been instilled in him during his college days. As a result of his three years' field sales experience and development of time management skills, he felt prepared for the challenge of the sales manager's job.

While sitting at his desk, Jim recalled a conversation that he had a week ago with Bill Hanson, the former manager, who had been promoted to another division. Bill told him that the sales forecast (annual and monthly) for plastic trash bags in the Southeast region would be due soon as an initial step toward developing the sales plan for the next year. Bill had laughed as he told Jim, "Boy, you ought to have a ball doing the forecast, being a rookie sales manager!"

When Jim had asked what Bill meant, he explained by saying that the forecast was often "winged" because the headquarters in New York already knew what they wanted and would change the forecast to meet their figures, particularly if the forecast was for an increase of less than 10 percent. The experienced sales manager could throw numbers together in a short time that would pass as a serious forecast and ultimately be adjusted to fit the plans of headquarters. However, an inexperienced manager would have a difficult time "winging" a credible forecast.

Bill had also told Jim that the other alternative meant gathering mountains of data and putting together a forecast that could be sold to the various levels of

* This case was written by Kenneth L. Bernhardt, Professor Tom Ingram, University of Kentucky, and Professor Danny N. Bellenger, Texas Tech University. Copyright © 1990 the authors.

EXHIBIT 19 "For the Good Life" ad proposal

Gifts for the Good Life.

Get a special bonus now with your new Greenwood Federal savings certificate ... you'll still get interest later.

RCA 20" ColorTrak TV w/Remote.

Sony 8mm Camera w/Recorder.

Pearl Grandfather Clock w/Chimes.

Apple Macintosh Personal Computer.

Litton Space Saving Microwave.

Fisher Deluxe VCR.

Cannon Typewriter.

Lawn-Boy Self-Propelled Mower.

GIFT DESCRIPTION	7 : Years	5 : Years	3 : Years
CERTIFICATE TERMS AND DEPOSIT LEVELS			
Toshiba Gourmet Coffee Maker, OR Pulsar Quartz Watch—Men's/Ladies	$2 500	$3 500	$5 000
Cannon Typewriter w/Adaptor, OR Litton Space-Saving Microwave	$4 000	$5 000	$8 000
GE 13" Portable Color TV	$5 000	$6 500	$10 000
Zenith 13" Color TV w/Remote, OR Magic Chef Deluxe Microwave w/Turntable	$7 000	$9 500	$15 000
RCA 20" ColorTrak TV w/Remote, OR GE VCR w/Wireless Remote	$9 500	$13 000	$20 000
Lawn-Boy Deluxe Self-Propelled Mower, OR Fisher Deluxe VCR w/MTS Stereo	$11 500	$16 000	$25 000
RCA 26" ColorTrak Console TV w/Remote	$14 500	$20 000	$30 000
Pearl Grandfather Clock w/Westminster Chimes	$19 000	$25 500	$40 000
Fisher Stereo Home Entertainment Center	$23 000	$32 500	$50 000
Sony 27" Console TV w/Stereo	$28 000	$38 000	$60 000
Sony 8mm Handycam Camera/Recorder	$32 500	$45 000	$70 000
Apple Macintosh Personal Computer	$35 000	$50 000	$80 000

Greenwood Federal announces a new, special kind of savings certificate. It pays you part of your interest income now, in the form of a luxury gift. You'll receive one or more of the gifts listed here, for yourself or to give as a gift. And your money will still earn interest compounded annually. For current rates, call 373-SAVE. So if you have money to invest, come to Greenwood Federal where your investment is rewarded handsomely ... and immediately.

Offer limited. Interest rates, qualifying deposit levels, and items of merchandise subject to change without notice. • Items of merchandise represent interest, therefore, the value of the merchandise will be reported as interest earned in the year received. • Allow minimum of 4 weeks for delivery. • This offer not applicable to IRA or KEOGH accounts • A substantial penalty, which will include the value of merchandise received, may be imposed for early withdrawal of certificate funds.

GREENWOOD FEDERAL

FOR THE GOOD LIFE

"Why don't you get your grandson a TV set?"   *"I'm giving him the Apple computer."*

anyway, so that at least with INVEST some fees were generated. Also, heavy promotion of INVEST, which had just recently become profitable, could reduce the asset base for the Association while generating some fees, enabling a rise in the reserve ratio. Other GFS managers were more skeptical about this happening.

EXHIBIT 20 Types of accounts held by GFS customers

Account type	Percent of GFS households	Average number of GFS products per household
Savings only	28	
Mortgage only	18	
Checking only	7	
Consumer loan only	3	
Total one product type	56	1.4*
Checking and savings	16	
Mortgage and savings	5	
Consumer loan and savings	3	
Consumer loan and checking	2	
Consumer loan and mortgage	2	
Checking and mortgage	0	
Total two product types	28	3.1
Checking, savings, and mortgage	5	
Checking, savings, and consumer loan	3	
Savings, mortgage, and consumer loan	3	
Checking, mortgage, and consumer loan	1	
Total three product types	12	4.6
All four types	4	6.8
	100	2.5
Any savings	67	
Any checking	39	
Any mortgage	38	
Any consumer loan	21	
Any deposit	83	
Any loan	46	

* This number is greater than 1.0 because many households had more than one account (although all were the same type of account).

Ms. Harris had seen potential in the segmentation study for high-interest checking products with several of the segments. She also thought that the proposed tax law, which would remove deductions for consumer loans, could have a big impact on her strategic planning. Did it mean, for example, that emphasis should not be put on automobile loans (even the Payment Shrinker) and other consumer loans? Did it mean that homeowner equity loans were the wave of the future? She had seen Internal Revenue Service data indicating that only 38 percent of all taxpayers itemized deductions on their 1984 returns. Did this suggest that consumers simply will not care enough about tax savings to establish a home equity credit line when they are ready to buy a car? Homeowner equity lines typically cost $500–$700 in closing cost alone. She had heard rumors that several of the Sunbelt City banks were considering waiving the fees, and wondered how GFS should respond if this in fact happened in the near future. She also had heard rumors that one or more of the banks might lower the rates, currently two percentage points above prime, to prime or even below for several months to attract new accounts with home equity loans.

Modern Plastics management. This alternative would prove to be time-consuming and could still be changed anywhere along the chain of command before final approval.

Clayton started reviewing pricing and sales volume history (see Exhibit 1). He also looked at the key account performance for the past two and a half years (see Exhibit 2). During the past month Clayton had visited many of the

EXHIBIT 1 Plastic trashbags—sales and pricing history, 1987–1989

	Pricing dollars per case			Sales volume in cases			Sales volume in dollars		
	1987	1988	1989	1987	1988	1989	1987	1988	1989
January	$6.88	$ 7.70	$15.40	33,000	46,500	36,500	$ 227,000	$ 358,000	$ 562,000
February	6.82	7.70	14.30	32,500	52,500	23,000	221,500	404,000	329,000
March	6.90	8.39	13.48	32,000	42,000	22,000	221,000	353,000	296,500
April	6.88	10.18	12.24	45,500	42,500	46,500	313,000	432,500	569,000
May	6.85	12.38	11.58	49,000	41,500	45,500	335,500	514,000	527,000
June	6.85	12.65	10.31	47,500	47,000	42,000	325,500	594,500	433,000
July	7.42	13.48	9.90*	40,000	43,500	47,500*	297,000	586,500	470,000*
August	6.90	13.48	10.18	48,500	63,500	43,500	334,500	856,000	443,000
September	7.70	14.30	10.31	43,000	49,000	47,500	331,000	700,500	489,500
October	7.56	15.12	10.31	52,500	50,000	51,000	397,000	756,000	526,000
November	7.15	15.68	10.72	62,000	61,500	47,500	443,500	964,500	509,000
December	7.42	15.43	10.59	49,000	29,000	51,000	363,500	447,500	540,000
Total	$7.13	$12.25	$11.30	534,500	568,500	503,500	$3,810,000	$6,967,000	$5,694,000

* July–December 1989 figures are forecast of sales manager J. A. Clayton, and other data comes from historical sales information.

EXHIBIT 2 1989 key account sales history (in cases)

Customer	1987	1988	First six months 1989	1987 monthly average	1988 monthly average	First half 1989 monthly average	First quarter 1989 monthly average
Transco Paper Company	125,774	134,217	44,970	10,481	11,185	7,495	5,823
Callaway Paper	44,509	46,049	12,114	3,709	3,837	2,019	472
Florida Janitorial Supply	34,746	36,609	20,076	2,896	3,051	3,346	2,359
Jefferson	30,698	34,692	25,044	2,558	2,891	4,174	1,919
Cobb Paper	13,259	23,343	6,414	1,105	1,945	1,069	611
Miami Paper	10,779	22,287	10,938	900	1,857	1,823	745
Milne Surgical Company	23,399	21,930	—	1,950	1,828	—	—
Graham	8,792	15,331	1,691	733	1,278	281	267
Crawford Paper	7,776	14,132	6,102	648	1,178	1,017	1,322
John Steele	8,634	13,277	6,663	720	1,106	1,110	1,517
Henderson Paper	9,185	8,850	2,574	765	738	429	275
Durant Surgical	—	7,766	4,356	—	647	726	953
Master Paper	4,221	5,634	600	352	470	100	—
D.T.A.	—	—	2,895	—	—	482	—
Crane Paper	4,520	5,524	3,400	377	460	566	565
Janitorial Service	3,292	5,361	2,722	274	447	453	117
Georgia Paper	5,466	5,053	2,917	456	421	486	297
Paper Supplies, Inc.	5,117	5,119	1,509	426	427	251	97
Southern Supply	1,649	3,932	531	137	328	88	78
Horizon Hospital Supply	4,181	4,101	618	348	342	103	206
Total cases	346,007	413,217	156,134	28,835	34,436	26,018	17,623

key accounts, and on the average they had indicated that their purchases from Modern would probably increase about 15–20 percent in the coming year.

Schedule for Preparing the Forecast

Jim had received a memo recently from Robert Baxter, the regional marketing manager, detailing the plans for completing the 1990 forecast. The key dates in the memo began in only three weeks:

August 1	Presentation of forecast to regional marketing manager.
August 10	Joint presentation with marketing manager to regional general manager.
September 1	Regional general manager presents forecast to division vice president.
September 1–September 30	Review of forecast by staff of division vice president.
October 1	Review forecast with corporate staff.
October 1–October 15	Revision as necessary.
October 15	Final forecast forwarded to division vice president from regional general manager.

Company Background

The plastics division of Modern Chemical Company was founded in 1965 when Modern Chemical purchased Cordco, a small plastics manufacturer with national sales of $15 million. At that time the key products of the plastics division were sandwich bags, plastic tablecloths, trash cans, and plastic-coated clothesline.

Since 1965 the plastics division has grown to a sales level exceeding $200 million with five regional profit centers covering the United States. Each regional center has manufacturing facilities and a regional sales force. There are four product groups in each region:

1. Food packaging: Styrofoam meat and produce trays; plastic bags for various food products.
2. Egg cartons: Styrofoam egg cartons sold to egg packers and supermarket chains.
3. Institutional: Plastic trash bags and disposable tableware (plates bowls, etc.).
4. Industrial: Plastic packaging for the laundry and dry cleaning market; plastic film for use in pallet overwrap systems.

Each product group is supervised jointly by a product manager and a district sales manager, both of whom report to the regional marketing manager. The sales representatives report directly to the district sales manager but also work closely with the product manager on matters concerning pricing and product specifications.

The five regional general managers report to J. R. Hughes, vice president of the plastics division. Hughes is located in New York. Although Modern Chemical is owned by a multinational oil company, the plastics division has been able to operate in a virtually independent manner since its establishment in 1965. The reasons for this include:

1. Limited knowledge of the plastic industry on the part of the oil company management.
2. Excellent growth by the plastics division has been possible without management supervision from the oil company.
3. Profitability of the plastics division has consistently been higher than that of other divisions of the chemical company.

The Institutional Trash Bag Market

The institutional trash bag is a polyethylene bag used to collect and transfer refuse to its final disposition point. There are different sizes and colors available to fit the various uses of the bag. For example, a small bag for desk wastebaskets is available as well as a heavier bag for large containers such as a 55-gallon drum. There are 25 sizes in the Modern line with 13 of those sizes being available in 3 colors—white, buff, and clear. Customers typically buy several different items on an order to cover all their needs.

The institutional trash bag is a separate product from the consumer-grade trash bag, which is typically sold to homeowners through retail outlets. The institutional trash bag is sold primarily through paper wholesalers, hospital supply companies, and janitorial supply companies to a variety of end users. Since trash bags are used on such a wide scale, the list of end users could include almost any business or institution. The segments include hospitals, hotels, schools, office buildings, transportation facilities, and restaurants.

Based on historical data and a current survey of key wholesalers and end users in the Southeast, the annual market of institutional trash bags in the region was estimated to be 55 million pounds. Translated into cases, the market potential was close to 2 million cases. During the past five years, the market for trash bags has grown at an average rate of 8.9 percent per year. Now a mature product, future market growth is expected to parallel overall growth in the economy. The 1990 real growth in GNP is forecast to be 4.5 percent.

General Market Conditions

The current market is characterized by a distressing trend. The market is in a position of oversupply with approximately 20 manufacturers competing for the business in the Southeast. Prices have been on the decline for several months but are expected to level out during the last six months of the year.

This problem arose after a record year in 1988 for Modern Plastics. During 1988, supply was very tight due to raw material shortages. Unlike many of its competitors, Modern had only minor problems securing adequate raw material supplies. As a result the competitors were few in 1988, and all who remained in business were prosperous. By early 1989 raw materials were plentiful, and prices began to drop as new competitors tried to buy their way into the market. During the first quarter of 1985, Modern Plastics learned the hard way that a competitive price was a necessity in the current market. Volume fell off drastically in February and March as customers shifted orders to new suppliers when Modern chose to maintain a slightly higher than market price on trash bags.

With the market becoming extremely price competitive and profits declining, the overall quality has dropped to a point of minimum standard. Most suppliers now make a bag "barely good enough to get the job done." This quality level is acceptable to most buyers who do not demand high quality for this type of product.

Modern Plastics versus Competition

A recent study of Modern versus competition had been conducted by an outside consultant to see how well Modern measured up in several key areas. Each area was weighted according to its importance in the purchase decision, and Modern was compared to its key competitors in each area and on an overall basis. The key factors and their weights are shown below:

		Weight
1.	Pricing	.50
2.	Quality	.15
3.	Breadth of line	.10
4.	Sales coverage	.10
5.	Packaging	.05
6.	Service	.10
Total		1.00

As shown in Exhibit 3, Modern compared favorably with its key competitors on an overall basis. None of the other suppliers were as strong as Modern in breadth of line nor did any competitor offer as good sales coverage as that provided by Modern. Clayton knew that sales coverage would be even better next year since the Florida and North Carolina territories had grown enough to add two salespeople to the institutional group by January 1, 1990.

Pricing, quality, and packaging seemed to be neither an advantage nor a disadvantage. However, service was a problem area. The main cause for this, Clayton was told, was temporary out-of-stock situations which occurred occasionally, primarily due to the wide variety of trash bags offered by Modern.

During the past two years, Modern Plastics had maintained its market share at approximately 27 percent of the market. Some new competitors had entered the market since 1987 while others had left the market (see Exhibit 4).

EXHIBIT 3 Competitive factors ratings (by competitor*)

Weight	Factor	Modern	National Film	Bonanza	South-eastern	PBI	BAGCO	South-west Bag	Sun Plastics	East Coast Bag Co.
.50	Price	2	3	2	2	2	2	2	2	3
.15	Quality	3	2	3	4	3	2	3	3	4
.10	Breadth	1	2	2	3	3	3	3	3	3
.10	Sales coverage	1	3	3	3	4	3	3	4	3
.05	Packaging	3	3	2	3	3	1	3	3	3
.10	Service	4	3	3	2	2	2	3	4	3

Overall weighted ranking†

1.	BAGCO	2.15	6.	Southeastern	2.55
2.	Modern	2.20	7.	Florida Plastics	2.60
3.	Bonanza	2.25	8.	National Film	2.65
4.	Southwest Bag (Tie)	2.50	9.	East Coast Bag Co.	3.15
5.	PBI (Tie)	2.50			

* Ratings on a 1-to-5 scale with 1 being the best rating and 5 the worst.

† The weighted ranking is the sum of each rank times its weight. The lower the number, the better the overall rating.

EXHIBIT 4 Market share by supplier, 1987 and 1989

Supplier	Percent of market 1987	Percent of market 1989
National Film	11	12
Bertram	16	0*
Bonanza	11	12
Southeastern	5	6
Bay	9	0*
Johnson Graham	8	0*
PBI	2	5
Lewis	2	0*
BAGCO	—	6
Southwest Bag	—	2
Florida Plastics	—	4
East Coast Bag Co.	—	4
Miscellaneous and unknown	8	22
Modern	28	27
	100	100

* Out of business in 1989.

Source: This information was developed from a field survey conducted by Modern Plastics.

EXHIBIT 5 Characteristics of competitors

National Film	Broadest product line in the industry. Quality a definite advantage. Good service. Sales coverage adequate, but not an advantage. Not as aggressive as most suppliers on price. Strong competitor.
Bonanza	Well-established tough competitor. Very aggressive on pricing. Good packaging, quality okay.
Southeastern	Extremely price competitive in southern Florida. Dominates Miami market. Limited product line. Not a threat outside of Florida.
PBI	Extremely aggressive on price. Have made inroads into Transco Paper Company. Good service but poor sales coverage.
BAGCO	New competitor. Very impressive with a high-quality product, excellent service, and strong sales coverage. A real threat, particularly in Florida.
Southwest Bag	A factor in Louisiana and Mississippi. Their strategy is simple—an acceptable product at a rock bottom price.
Sun Plastics	Active when market is at a profitable level with price cutting. When market declines to a low profit range, Sun manufactures other types of plastic packaging and stays out of the trash bag market. Poor reputation as a reliable supplier, but can still "spot-sell" at low prices.
East Coast Bag Co.	Most of their business is from a state bid which began in January 1984 for a two-year period. Not much of a threat to Modern's business in the Southeast as most of their volume is north of Washington, D.C.

The previous district sales manager, Bill Hanson, had left Clayton some comments regarding the major competitors. These are reproduced in Exhibit 5.

Developing the Sales Forecast

After a careful study of trade journals, government statistics, and surveys conducted by Modern marketing research personnel, projections for growth potential were formulated by segment and are shown in Exhibit 6. This data was compiled by Bill Hanson just before he had been promoted.

Jim looked back at Baxter's memo giving the time schedule for the forecast and knew he had to get started. As he left the office at 7:15, he wrote himself a large note and pinned it on his wall—"Get Started on the Sales Forecast!"

EXHIBIT 6 1990 real growth projections by segment

Total industry	+5.0%
Commercial	+5.4%
Restaurant	+6.8%
Hotel/motel	+2.0%
Transportation	+1.9%
Office users	+5.0%
Other	+4.2%
Noncommercial	+4.1%
Hospitals	+3.9%
Nursing homes	+4.8%
Colleges/universities	+2.4%
Schools	+7.8%
Employee feeding	+4.3%
Other	+3.9%

Source: Developed from several trade journals.

Part 4

Product and Brand Management Decisions

The six cases concerned with product strategy decisions in this section involve a number of different kinds of decisions. Many marketers believe that product decisions are the most critical of the marketing mix variables because of their importance to consumers in their decision-making process, and because product decisions, once made, are not quickly or easily reversed or changed. Promotion and pricing changes, for example, can be made much more quickly and with greater ease. Furthermore, most product changes usually require changes in the rest of the marketing strategy—changes in promotion, pricing, and sometimes distribution.

Before examining the various issues in the product strategy area, the concept of what a product is should first be understood. A product is "anything that can be offered to a market for attention, acquisition, or consumption; it includes physical objects, services, personalities, places, organizations, and ideas."[1] A product is thus much more than its physical properties and is everything a consumer buys when he or she makes a purchase. It is a set of want-satisfying attributes. It is important to understand this definition because what the consumer is buying is not necessarily what the company thought it was marketing. So marketers must be aware of consumer attitudes, values, needs, and wants with respect to their products.

The major decisions related to product strategy are:

1. What new products should be developed?
2. What changes are needed in current products?
3. What products should be added or dropped?

---

[1] Philip Kotler, *Marketing Management: Analysis, Planning and Control*, 3rd ed. (Englewood Cliffs, N.J.: Prentice-Hall, 1976), p. 183.

4. What positioning should the product occupy?
5. What should the branding strategy be?

A brief discussion of some of the concepts related to each of these decisions follows.

New Product Development

The sales and profits of a product category tend to change over time. The pattern a product category typically follows is called the product life cycle. It is defined to have the introductory, growth, maturity, and decline stages. Because most products reach the maturity and decline stages eventually, a marketer must continually seek out new products which can go through the introductory and growth stages in order to maintain and increase the total profits of the firm. But what new products should be introduced?

To answer this question, a marketer must consider the objectives of the firm, the resources available, the target markets the firm is trying to satisfy, and how the new product would fit in with other products offered by the company and the competition.

To successfully develop new products, the organization will have to set up formalized strategies for generating new product ideas, means for screening these ideas, product and market testing procedures, and finally commercialization. The objective is to obtain products which are differentiated from those of its competitors and which meet the needs of a large enough segment of the market to be profitable.

Changes in Current Products

The needs, wants, attitudes, and behavior of consumers change over time, and a company must change its products also or risk losing these consumers to a competitor who more quickly responds to these changes in the marketplace.

Should new features be added to the product? Should the warranty be extended? Should the packaging be changed? Should new services be offered? The marketer must continually monitor its target market and the competition to be able to answer such questions.

What Products Should Be Added or Dropped

A marketer must make decisions concerning the product mix or composite of products the firm will offer for sale. This requires decisions concerning the width and depth of products. Width refers to the number of product lines marketed by the firm. For example, General Electric has many lines while Kellogg's has concentrated on breakfast foods. The depth of the product mix is the number of items offered for sale within each product line. Kellogg's, for example, would have a very deep product line with many different alternatives offered for sale.

Whether a product line should be extended or reduced depends on a number of factors, including financial criteria, market factors, production considerations, and organizational factors. The marketer in making these decisions must examine the potential profit contributions, return on investment, impact on market share, fit with consumers' needs, fit with the needs of the channels of distribution, and the expected reactions of competitors. The production and organizational considerations include impact on capacity for other products, and on the goals and objectives of the firm, both in the short and long run.

Product Positioning

Product positioning is defined as that idea that is put into the consumers' minds by telling them how our product differs from its competitors. The position we strive to occupy will depend on the different market segments available, the attributes of our product compared to the needs of each segment, and the positions occupied by our competitors against each market segment.

Branding Strategy

The basic decisions here are whether or not to put brand names on the organization's products, whether the brands should be manufacturers' or distributors' brands, and whether individual or family brands should be used.

These decisions depend on the company's resources, objectives, the competition, and consumer choice behavior. For example, a small firm with few resources and much competition in a product category where consumers perceived small differences in the brands available would probably choose to market its product using private distributors' brands. Family brands such as General Electric and Campbell's are used when the marketer wants the consumer to generalize to the new products all those attributes he associates with the family brand name. The time and money required to establish the brand's name is much lower with this strategy but it does not allow the marketer to establish a separate image for the new product.

Case 9

Lotus Development Corporation: Project 3*

The meeting was over, and Steve Jobs, the founder of NeXT, Incorporated, returned to California. Steve Jobs had once again attempted to persuade the management of Lotus Development Corporation to develop a software package for his new NeXT computer. Lotus was presently involved in creating two new spreadsheet products on the OS/2 operating system for the IBM PS/2 personal computer. The first product was a graphical version of its popular 1–2–3 spreadsheet. This product was being developed to take advantage of the OS/2 operating system, which many industry analysts believe will be the most commonly used system in the 1990s. Management was billing the second product, Project 3, as "the next generation in spreadsheets." It is Project 3 that Steve Jobs wants Lotus to develop for his NeXT computer.

Lotus management was now faced with three alternatives. First, Lotus could create a new team to develop a product for the NeXT computer while at the same time continuing development of Project 3 on the OS/2 operating system. Second, Lotus could port Project 3 to the NeXT system and finish the product on that platform. Finally, the firm could ignore the wishes of Steve Jobs and not develop a product on the NeXT system.

Company History

Lotus Development Corporation was founded in 1982 by Mitchell D. Kapor. Its first product was Lotus 1–2–3, a spreadsheet software package designed for the IBM personal computer (PC). Lotus 1–2–3 was well received and helped propel sales of the personal computer. Since 1982, the firm has grown to reach $468,547,000 in sales in 1988.[1] Exhibit 1 provides a five-year summary of sales data, while Exhibit 2 provides the firm's balance sheet for the last three

---

* This case was written from public sources and from interviews with people knowledgeable about this industry by Matthew J. Hausmann under the supervision of Thomas C. Kinnear. Copyright © 1990 by Thomas C. Kinnear.
[1] *Compact Disclosure.* February 1990.

EXHIBIT 1   Lotus Development Corporation five year
summary (in thousands)

Date	Sales	Net income	EPS
1988	468,547	58,925	1.29
1987	395,595	72,043	1.58
1986	282,864	48,300	1.03
1985	225,526	38,150	0.77
1984	156,978	36,046	0.75

Source: *Compact Disclosure.*

EXHIBIT 2   Lotus Development Corporation balance sheet (in $thousands)

Fiscal year ending	12/31/88	12/31/87	12/31/86
Cash	192,433	164,909	93,157
Receivables	92,035	45,541	37,844
Inventories	18,088	9,210	6,794
Other current assets	7,430	5,665	6,396
Total current assets	309,986	225,325	144,191
Property, plant, and equipment, net	86,953	51,920	40,964
Intangibles	16,026	32,297	23,270
Deposits and other assets	9,157	8,111	584
Total assets	422,122	317,653	209,009
Notes payable	9,441	7,736	N/A
Accounts payable	45,491	31,685	20,147
Accrued expenses	11,771	15,287	23,883
Income taxes	1,231	19,165	12,055
Other current liabilities	16,592	11,734	6,775
Total current liabilities	84,526	85,607	62,860
Deferred charges/income	10,400	N/A	1,556
Long-term debt	95,000	30,000	N/A
Other long-term liabilities	N/A	N/A	30,000
Total liabilities	189,926	115,607	94,416
Common stock, net	556	546	526
Capital surplus	109,429	83,274	66,624
Retained earnings	266,285	207,360	135,317
Treasury stock	144,030	87,743	83,135
Other liabilities	(43)	(1,390)	(4,783)
Shareholders' equity	232,196	202,046	114,593
Total liabilities and net worth	422,122	317,653	209,009

Source: *Compact Disclosure.*

years. The firm's remarkable growth has been fueled by the popularity of 1–2–3 and its subsequent upgrades. In addition, the firm has developed other product lines including word processing packages, CD–ROM disks, and personal information management packages. These products were developed to change Lotus's one-product dependence. During 1989, however, the firm once again began to focus on its core product: spreadsheets.

Strengths and Weaknesses of Lotus

Lotus has a strong reputation in the industry for the conception and design of products. Many of the firm's latest projects, such as Magellan (a utility program that provides quick and easy access to all the information stored on a PC hard disk) and Notes (an application platform that allows groups to share textual and graphical information across local area networks) are considered to be excellent technical accomplishments. The firm, however, is not considered a technical leader in spreadsheets. A number of software industry observers have been critical of Lotus 1–2–3 upgrades. These critics suggest that 1–2–3 offers poor output and is not user friendly. Many point to Microsoft Corporation's Excel as an example of a product which has been created with an ear to the customer. Yet, Lotus 1–2–3 has an installed base of approximately 4 million users, controls 71 percent of the market in terms of revenues, and boasts 53 percent of units sold. Meanwhile, Microsoft Excel has been able to garner only a 10 percent share of the DOS operating system-based PC spreadsheet market.[2]

Lotus has very strong marketing skills and has been working to make Lotus's customer service the best in the industry. A toll-free number has been instituted, and the service department is carefully monitoring how long customers wait until they speak with a consultant. The goal is to keep waiting time to a minimum and improve customer satisfaction. The firm also has a large, well-trained sales force. The sales force has been extremely effective in pushing Lotus products.

Lotus insiders believe the firm has begun to focus on the customers. As evidence of this, insiders point to the design partner program in which the firm involves select customers in the selection of product features. Lotus is also trying to keep its largest customers abreast of its moves. According to the firm's 1988 annual report, the firm is sharing its product direction and strategy with its biggest customers (under confidential disclosure).[3] Industry analysts believe that this new posture is designed to reverse Lotus's reputation as a brash company that is unresponsive to its customers.

Lotus has had a large problem with product announcements and shipping products. Lotus announced that it was creating 1–2–3 Release 3.0 in 1987 and stated that it would ship this upgrade in the second quarter of 1988. However, the firm experienced major problems with the development process and repeatedly delayed the shipment. (In the industry, this is referred to as vaporware.) Release 3 is now scheduled to be shipped in the second quarter of 1989. Many customers have become angry at the delay and have begun looking at other spreadsheet products. Industry experts, however, say that Lotus has retained most of its user base. According to industry analyst Lincoln Spector, ''It is a

---

[2] Ed Scannell. ''The Once and Future King?'' *Infoworld* (January 23, 1989), p. 41.
[3] Lotus Development Corporation, 1989 Annual Report.

sign of Lotus's hold on the market that one of the major selling points of every new PC spreadsheet is still 1–2–3 compatibility.''[4]

In 1988, Lotus hired Frank King from IBM. King has been responsible for instituting stricter developer and development scheduling guidelines. Now, when project teams declare a date by which they plan to ship, they must show Frank King that they have planned out what they must accomplish to meet the date. That is, they start with the ship date and work back to the present to show they can meet the target ship date. This practice has forced project managers to be realistic in their expected ship dates rather than choosing a date they believe will please management. In addition, the firm has instituted cost controls to keep expenses in line. According to Lotus employees, even with all of this control, the firm is continuing to encourage creativity and a relaxed, entrepreneurial atmosphere.

The Project 3 Product

In 1989, Lotus is developing a new product, Project 3, which is billed as the next generation in spreadsheets. According to *Fortune* magazine, the supercharged spreadsheet will ''allow users to redesign spreadsheets instantly with new formulas and categories without having to reenter data or rebuild financial models. It will also produce a variety of attractive charts and graphs rather than the simpler graphics most PC spreadsheets offer.''[5]

As mentioned earlier, the decision facing management is whether to continue developing the product on OS/2, begin development on the NeXT computer, or develop a product on both platforms. Some insiders argue that Project 3 will cannibalize the sales of 1–2–3 on OS/2 and, thus, should be developed on the NeXT computer. They also argue that Project 3 should be on a new platform that will expand the limits of present spreadsheets. Also of concern are the slow sales of the OS/2 system. On the other side of the coin, some managers feel that the NeXT computer is simply too risky. They feel that the market is crowded with competing platforms and that the NeXT computer is going to be too expensive to be a commercial success. Both platforms are discussed in detail in the following sections.

OS/2

OS/2 is an operating system designed to run on PCs. The system was developed by Microsoft Corporation and IBM. IBM first announced OS/2 on April 2,

---

[4] Lincoln Spector, ''Dynamic Linking, 3-D Move Contest to Next Level,'' *Infoworld*, January 23, 1989, p. 42.

[5] Brenton R. Schlender, ''How Steve Jobs Linked Up with IBM,'' *Fortune*, October 9, 1989, p. 54.

1987, amid a laser light show and blaring pop music. At the time of the announcement of OS/2, the company spoke of the many advantages of OS/2, including the capability to multitask DOS and OS/2-compatible applications simultaneously, while communicating with large host systems. Another advantage was an interface that would allow developers to create applications that would all have the same appearance. All applications would have a graphical user interface (GUI), with pull-down menus and icons to enhance user friendliness.[6]

The first version of OS/2 was shipped eight months later in early 1988. The more sophisticated version, which included Presentation Manager, was shipped four months after this in the middle of 1988.

OS/2 is designed to run on PCs with either a 286 or 386 processor. According to Nancy McSharry, a senior PC analyst at International Data Corporation, "OS/2 does not run well on a 286 machine. At least a 16 MHz 386 system is needed in order to run OS/2 applications at an acceptable speed."[7]

By 1989, OS/2 had an installed base of only 300,000.[8] This slow acceptance was thought to result from a lack of applications developed for OS/2. Julian Horwich, executive director of the Chicago Area Microcomputer Managers Association and a Fortune 100 company microcomputer manager, says, "Simply having a DOS application run faster under OS/2 does not justify the hardware upgrades and the expenses necessary to retrain users and information-center staffers. OS/2 needs a breakthrough product—similar to what VisiCalc did for the Apple II and what Lotus 1–2–3 did for the IBM PC—before there will be enough business benefits to switch to a new operating system."[9]

Forecasts for the future installed base of OS/2 vary greatly. According to International Data Corporation, there will be about 5.7 million copies of OS/2 sold worldwide by the end of 1992, which would constitute approximately 8 percent of the installed microcomputer base. Forrester Research Incorporated estimates that there will be 11 million units installed by the end of 1992, which would make up 25 percent of the installed base.[10]

The cost of the hardware necessary to run OS/2 also varies. The cost of completely new hardware runs from $4,000 to almost $11,000. The cost to upgrade a computer so that it meets OS/2's memory and disk requirements is dependent upon the present computer.

[6] Ed Scannell, "OS/2: Waiting for the Killer Applications," *Infoworld,* February 20, 1989, p. 41.

[7] Ed Scannell, "True Believer," *Infoworld,* January 29, 1990; p. 41.

[8] Ed Scannell, "OS/2: Waiting for the Killer Applications," p. 44.

[9] Craig Zarley, "OS/2 vs. DOS: The Decision's on Hold," *PC Week*, November 14, 1988, p. S/17.

[10] Ed Scannell, "OS/2: Waiting for the Killer Applications," p. 42.

NeXT

In October 1988, Steve Jobs, ex-chairman of Apple Computer, announced the NeXT Computer System. The NeXT computer was designed to be the definitive future workstation with emphasis placed on high throughput, multiprocessor support, and an object-oriented environment. The development also anticipates emerging trends by including support for UNIX, work-group computing, and audio/video integration. The goal for the NeXT computer is to combine the ease of use and functionality of a Macintosh with the power and configurability of a Sun Microsystems Unix workstation.[11]

The NeXT computer's Workspace Manager has a graphical user interface which echoes interfaces used by the Apple Macintosh and IBM's Presentation Manager. Features include use of a mouse, pull-down windows, and scroll bars. In addition, the Workspace Manager supports Display Postscript resulting in a WYSIWYG ("What you see is what you get") screen display.[12] (WYSIWYG means that what the user sees on the computer screen is exactly what the output will look like.)

The NeXT system combines optical storage, which provides massive capacity, and a multitasking operating system called Mach, which allows users to access and run many applications at once. (An explanation of computer-selected computer terminology is provided in the appendix.) NeXT is the first computer maker to choose an erasable optical drive as its primary storage vehicle.[13] Though a number of industry experts have expressed doubts about this choice, Steve Jobs insists that it is the wave of the future.

The NeXT computer's central processing unit (CPU) uses Motorola Inc.'s top-of-the-line 68030 chip, rated at 26 MHz. The machine also includes Motorola's 25 MHz 68882 coprocessor for floating-point operations. NeXT has added two custom chips to that foundation to provide greater throughput and storage capacity than is available for most workstations.[14]

The NeXT computer is designed for use at institutions of higher education. There has been talk in the industry, however, that NeXT is trying to line up software developers to create business software for the machine.

Sales of the NeXT computer have been slow. *Business Week* magazine estimates that less than 1,000 machines have been sold to software writers and universities.[15] Sales are expected to increase when software for the machine hits the market. Many industry analysts, however, believe that NeXT will have to reduce the $10,000 price tag on its computer before sales increase substantially.

NeXT recently licensed the NeXT user interface and its object-oriented programming environment to IBM. It is believed that this will help legitimize

---

[11] Barbara Francett, Lee Keough, Byron Belitsos, and John Soat, "What's NeXT?" *Computer Decisions*, January 1989, p. 63.

[12] Ibid.

[13] Ibid.

[14] Ibid.

[15] Richard Brandt and Maria Shao, "Steve Jobs Gets the Keys to the Office PC Market," *Business Week,* April 10, 1989, p. 80.

the NeXT system while simultaneously promoting an army of Unix programmers prepared to support the IBM mainframe.

Competitors

In addition to Lotus Development, there are five major players in the spreadsheet market: Informix Corporation, Ashton-Tate Corporation, Computer Associates International Incorporated, Borland International, and Microsoft Corporation. A listing of the spreadsheet products' features for selected companies is included in Exhibit 3. Each of the five competing companies is briefly discussed in the following sections.

EXHIBIT 3 Comparison of spreadsheets' features

	Wingz	Full Impact	Excel	Lotus 1–2–3
Numerical Analysis Features				
Financial	17	11	14	12
Logical	10	8	14	9
Mathematical	33	19	24	17
Statistical	10	9	14	14
Date/time	17	12	11	13
Database	10	7	10	11
Text/string	23	5	18	18
User-defined functions	Yes	Yes	Yes	Yes
Regression/analysis	No	No	No	Yes
Charting Features				
Types	11	12	12	12
Quick graph	Yes	Yes	Yes	Yes
Data Presentation				
Data formatting	Yes	Yes	Yes	Yes
Special output formatting	Yes	No	Yes	No
Notation	Yes	No	Yes	Yes
Printing				
Print preview	Yes	Yes	Yes	No
Dot matrix support	Yes	Yes	Yes	Yes
Plotter support	No	No	Yes	Yes
Color support	Yes	Yes	Yes	Yes

Informix Corporation

Informix Corporation of Menlo Park, California, is the 10th largest publicly owned company in the packaged software industry. Informix designs, develops, manufactures, markets, and supports computer software systems to perform general purpose data management functions on various computer systems. The firm had 1988 sales of $103,505,000 and net income of $1,458,000. Informix has enjoyed eight consecutive annual increases in net income.[16]

---

[16] *Compact Disclosure.* February 1990.

Informix is scheduled to ship Wingz for the NeXT computer in the first quarter of 1990. The product is expected to be exactly like Wingz on the Macintosh, which means that users can expect numerous functions and excellent output capabilities. Specifically, Wingz will offer users a tremendous number of functions (statistical, logical, financial, etc.), database capability, and a vast array of graphs. However, the product will most likely be weak in ease of use. For example, Wingz does not offer context-sensitive help, usable sample files, or formula advice/syntax prompting. Informix's strength is the ability to roll products out quickly and with relatively few bugs. Also, the firm appears to offer what customers demand. On the downside, the firm's weaknesses include poor relations with distributors and poor customer service. In the past three years, however, the firm has been concentrating its efforts on the expansion of its network of regional, domestic, and international sales offices.

Finally, in January 1989, the firm reduced its work force by 15 percent and reorganized product development and marketing into two divisions.[17] It is believed the new structure will further assist the firm in its efforts to focus its energies.

Ashton-Tate

Ashton-Tate is in the business of acquiring, developing, marketing, and supporting microcomputer software. It also publishes books and combination book/disk packages relating to hardware and software. In fiscal year 1989, the firm had sales of $307,283,000 and net income of $47,755,000. Both its sales and net income have been growing since 1985.[18]

Ashton-Tate is the developer and marketer of Full Impact for the Macintosh. It has not announced a product for the NeXT computer and is not believed to be developing for the NeXT platform. The firm, however, recently consolidated all of their non-database applications development and product management activities in a newly acquired product center in northern California. According to Ashton-Tate President Luther Nussbaum, this action will facilitate the development of more product commonality across hardware platforms and operating systems.[19]

In 1988, Ashton-Tate had a tremendous problem with repeated shipment delays of dBase IV, a database product. When it was finally shipped, the product was laden with bugs. The situation hurt their sales and forced Ashton-Tate to lay off 20 percent of their work force.

Finally, Ashton-Tate is believed to have poor customer service and a poor reputation with dealers. In an effort to combat this problem, the firm has declared, ''We are committed to expanding our sales and training staffs, and to

---

[17] Informix Corporation, 1988 Annual Report.
[18] *Compact Disclosure*. February 1990.
[19] Ashton-Tate, 1989 Annual Report.

increasing the level of our advertising and promotion activities. We intend to double our field sales force in the coming year and to add the field technical support and consulting services demanded by the increased sophistication of our products.''[20]

Computer Associates

Computer Associates International (CA) designs, develops, markets, and supports standardized computer software products for use primarily with IBM and IBM-compatible computers as well as for mini- and microcomputers. According to Anthony W. Wang, president and chief operating officer of CA, the firm's strategic direction is ''to integrate our various software systems where that provides additional value, even across diverse hardware platforms and operating environments.''[21]

CA makes a spreadsheet called SuperCalc 5 which runs on DOS machines. It is considered to be a good product on an operating system dominated by 1–2–3. The firm itself is the largest software firm in the nation, achieving this via the acquisition of other firms. CA's president has announced that the firm will not develop any products for the NeXT computer. It is rumored, however, that the firm is taking a second look at the NeXT computer.

Computer Associates had sales of $1,030,235,000 in fiscal year 1989 and a net income of $163,546,000.[22]

Borland International

Borland International is a California-based firm in the business of designing, developing, and marketing software and software-related products for personal computers. In fiscal year 1989, Borland had sales of $90,555,000 and a net loss of $2,844,000.[23]

Borland's spreadsheet software is called Quattro. It runs on the IBM PC and is noted for its ability to run using only small amounts of memory. Borland is currently developing a new version of this software. Termed Quattro Pro, it is expected to be released in fiscal year 1990. According to Philippine Kahn, president and CEO of Borland, Quattro Pro ''will incorporate unprecedented advances in spreadsheet technology, strengthening our competitive position.''[24]

After losing money in fiscal year 1989, Borland management believes that the firm has turned the corner.

---

[20] Ibid.
[21] Computer Associates, 1989 Annual Report.
[22] *Compact Disclosure*. February 1990.
[23] Ibid.
[24] Borland International, 1989 Annual Report.

The challenges were met, and they have made us stronger than ever. We streamlined our operations, focused our efforts, managed our growth and expenditures, and laid the foundation for a profitable future as evidenced by the three following profitable quarters. We emerged from the transition with our driving entrepreneurial spirit intact, and we have gained the maturity of an industry leader positioned for sustained profitability in the next decade."[25]

Industry analysts question whether Borland has completed this transition or is still in for more tough times.

Microsoft

Microsoft Corporation is the second largest software firm in the United States. The firm is engaged in the design, development, marketing, and support of a line of systems and applications microcomputer software for business and professional use. In fiscal year 1989, the firm had a net income of $170,538,000 on sales of $803,530,000.[26]

Microsoft is a large and powerful firm. Much of its power is derived from the fact that it controls a number of the operating systems. Also, Microsoft is thought to be in touch with the market and has shown remarkable ability to correctly interpret industry trends.

Microsoft's Excel spreadsheet is the number one spreadsheet on the Macintosh and the number two spreadsheet on DOS systems after 1–2–3. Many industry observers and trade journals, including *Infoworld,* consider Excel to be superior to Lotus 1–2–3 (Release 2.01). Excel set new standards for graphing and database capabilities and is believed to have gained market share at the expense of 1–2–3. In addition, as the Macintosh garners more of the business computing market, Excel will continue to grow in importance.

Microsoft has led the public to believe that it will not be developing a product for the NeXT computer. In fact CEO Bill Gates has pronounced that the NeXT computer will be a miserable failure. Also, Bill Gates and Steve Jobs are publicly warring with each other. Regardless, the NeXT system is believed to fit in well with Microsoft's announced push toward multimedia as it can reproduce sound and has excellent graphic capabilities. (According to Stuart J. Johnston of *Infoworld* magazine, multimedia "combines the capabilities of a variety of media, including extremely large data storage, CD-quality audio, photographic special effects, and text overlays.")[27] In addition, Steve Jobs has declared that he believes that consumers desire computers with multimedia capabilities and the NeXT computer was designed with this in mind.

---

[25] Ibid.

[26] *Compact Disclosure.* February 1990.

[27] Stuart J. Johnston. "Microsoft Looks to Establish a Hold on the Emerging Multimedia Market," *Infoworld,* August 7, 1989, p. 44.

Buyer Behavior

There are three decisions which must be considered when looking at buyer behavior for Product 3.

OS/2 versus NeXT

The first question is what criteria will be used when considering whether to buy a NeXT computer or a computer that runs an OS/2 operating system. One criterion is the cost of the hardware necessary to run the system. Currently, the cost of a NeXT system is $10,000, while the cost of a computer capable of running OS/2 is between $4,000 and $11,000. Another criterion is the ease of use. Training personnel to use new systems is expensive, so when all other factors are equal, corporations will choose the platform that requires the least training. A final criterion is the number, quality, and usefulness of the software packages available on the platform. Users will choose platforms which have software meeting their individual needs.

Switching from 1-2-3 to Project 3

If Lotus chooses to continue developing Project 3 on OS/2, it needs to consider factors which would induce a user to switch from 1-2-3 to Project 3. Users will make this switch for two reasons. The first reason is a need for more advanced output. Lotus 1-2-3 is limited in its graphing capabilities, so Project 3 would be a better choice. The second reason for switching is the need for a product which facilitates building large, complicated models. Project 3 is designed to handle such models and would be the preferred software package.

Why Buy Project 3 on the NeXT Computer

Once a user has chosen to use the NeXT computer, one must question why Project 3 would be the preferred spreadsheet over any available competitor. If the user will be creating large models, Project 3 would be selected because it was specifically designed for such projects. Project 3 would also be selected if it offered higher-quality output relative to the competition. The final criterion for choosing a spreadsheet is whether it is easy to learn. High costs associated with training personnel on new software products dictate that the spreadsheet that is the easiest to learn will be the one that is bought.

The Decision

Lotus management has recognized a number of relevant factors to consider while deciding what, if any, products they should develop for the NeXT computer. Management is concerned about the uncertainty of the NeXT computer's future. Will sales materialize? Will corporations accept it as a business computer? Also of concern is Lotus' own development efforts. What will be the effect of Project 3 on the sales of 1–2–3 on OS/2? These are issues Lotus management is facing.

Appendix

An *erasable optical drive* is a drive that uses an optical disk for storage. (This is much like a compact disk.) Information is stored digitally and is read by a laser. Erasable refers to the fact that information that is stored on the disk can be erased.[1]

MHz, or megahertz, is defined as one million cycles per second. A cycle, in turn, is a self-contained series of instructions in which the last instruction can modify and repeat itself until a terminal condition is reached. To the user, this means that the greater the number of megahertz, the faster the computer will operate on instructions.[2]

A *multitasking operating system* is a system that allows a user to run multiple operations in the background while concentrating on a single operation in the foreground.[3]

---

[1] Computer Definitions Book.

[2] Ibid.

[3] David Strom and Mike Edelhart, "Within OS/2 Beats a Tough, Multitasking Heart," *PC Week,* March 20, 1989, p. S/3.

Case 10

Machine Vision International®*

Our industry is very much like a newly found gold mine. Each vein in the mine is a different market opportunity. We're entering the main mine shaft, digging first in the directions our research shows will contain the largest ore deposits, those in the automotive and electronics industries. We'll use the knowledge we gain in those shafts of the mine to tunnel to other veins, finding gold deposits in other markets. This is our approach.

Richard P. Eidswick
Chairman and CEO, MVI

As 1985 came to a close, Machine Vision International (MVI) was completing its third year of operations. Only two years earlier, MVI had had only 37 employees. By the end of 1985, MVI had expanded greatly. The company now had three sales divisions and was selling products for very diverse applications in many varied industries. However, the financial results for 1985 showed that MVI was not yet making a profit. The question being asked was whether MVI had expanded into too many markets too quickly for a company in a fast-growing, quickly changing industry.

The Machine Vision Industry—a Definition

A machine vision product is a high-technology, computer-based image processing system enabling a machine or other device to "see." The use of this technology permits automation of industrial tasks involving the interpretation of the work scene or the controlling of work activity.

---

* This case was prepared by Constance M. Kinnear, Research Associate, with the assistance of Thomas C. Kinnear, Professor of Marketing, both at the Graduate School of Business Administration, The University of Michigan. Copyright © 1986 by the authors. This abridged version was prepared, with permission of the authors, by Adrian B. Ryans and Terry Deutscher, faculty at Western Business School, University of Western Ontario.

Machine vision may be understood by way of analogy to human vision. A human eye captures an image, which is then transmitted to the brain via the optic nerve. The brain processes those parts of the image most important to the situation; it ignores parts of the image which are irrelevant. The brain then tells other parts of the body what actions to take. In machine vision, the camera (eye) captures an image and transmits it to the controller (brain) via a coaxial cable (optic nerve). The controller sorts relevant from irrelevant data and instructs the machine tool, conveyor, or robot what action to take.

MVI's Prospectus
September 18, 1985

There were many potential application areas for machine vision in the industrial workplace. Data received by a computer from television cameras viewing an assembly area could be almost instantaneously analyzed so that task performance guidance commands could be sent to a robot. Vision systems could be used in quality control processes to check work in process against required product parameters, which were stored in the system's computer. A vision system could, therefore, check during production for the proper dimensions and shape of the product, for the presence of all features or parts, and for its general condition including surface flaws. Deviations from acceptable parameters could be brought to the attention of supervisory staff before they caused a substandard product to be produced. Because vision systems could recognize different shapes or identifying markings, production parts could be sorted, facilitating the movement, processing, or assembly of parts. The goals in the use of vision systems were to increase product quality, increase product rates and industrial efficiency, and provide labour savings.

The Market for Machine Vision Products

The machine vision industry did not exist in 1980. In 1981, total industry sales were $7 million. Between 1981 and 1984, sales more than doubled each year, so that by 1984 industry sales totalled $80 million. A compound average growth rate of 60 percent per year had been estimated for the industry as a whole for the period from 1984 to 1990. Estimated sales for 1985 were $125 million. For 1990, the total market was estimated to reach between $750 and $800 million.

Despite all the optimistic estimates for growth in the market, not one competitor in machine vision had consistently made a profit by 1985. Between 70 and 100 competitors were vying for the industry's total sales of $125 million in that year, in literally thousand of different applications. The bulk of this revenue was shared among 20 companies. The major competitors in the industry and their sales for the period 1983–85 are shown in Exhibit 1. In 1984, none of these competitors made a profit in this industry.

Analysts of the machine vision industry were hard pressed to pick which companies would survive the early growth years. For one thing, the technologies in the industry were not yet perfected. There were many technologies applicable to vision applications, and these technologies were still very much in

EXHIBIT 1 Competitive sales figures (millions)—1983–85

Company	1983 Sales	1984 Sales	Expected 1985 sales	Type of financing
Applied Intelligent Systems, Inc. (1976)	$ 0.4	$ 1.4	$ 5.0	Private
Automatix	6.3	17.3	27.0	Public
Cognex Corp.	2.0	5.0	6.0	Private
Diffracto Ltd. (1973)	3.7	5.1	7.3	Private
International Robomation/ Intelligence	1.0	2.3	8.0	Public
Itran Corp. (1982)	0.2	1.1	2.2	Private
Machine Vision International	0.5	4.0	10.0	Public
Perceptron, Inc. (1981)	1.0	5.5	15.0	Private
Robotic Vision Systems, Inc. (1977)	1.0	5.1	10.0	Public
View Engineering (1976)	7.5	15.0	19.0	Private
All others	11.4	18.2	15.5	
Total market	$35.0	$80.0	$125.0	

the developmental stage. Possible applications of machine vision could be found in almost any industrial setting where part inspection, part identification, or automated assembly processes were used. These usually came from large-volume sales or repeatably manufacturable products. The market was often uneducated or unrealistic about the true capabilities of machine vision. Competitors were finding it very difficult to determine all the variables that had to be satisfied and solved to make the products work in an actual, operating industrial environment.

One development with great potential impact on the machine vision industry was the involvement of General Motors. GM became very interested in production automation. This interest was spurred by the results of several automobile industry studies, which found that the Japanese had a sizable cost advantage, ranging between $1,500 and $1,800 per car, over U.S. producers in 1985. Also, it was estimated that it took approximately three times as many labour-hours for U.S. automobile manufacturers to produce a car than it did their Japanese competitors. Studies predicted that U.S. car manufacturers would have to reduce their costs by about 25 percent between 1985 and 1990 to remain competitive in the industry. Of possible automation alternatives, it was determined that the use of robotics and machine vision was key strategy to solve the problem. Forty-four thousand machine vision applications were identified within GM alone by GM analysts.

Taking action on these findings, GM entered into a joint venture with Fanuc Ltd. of Japan, forming GMF, a highly respected robotics firm. To back its belief that vision was also key to automation, GM invested in five machine vision companies in 1983 and 1984. These were Applied Intelligent Systems (AIS), Automatix, Diffracto Ltd., Robotic Vision Systems (RVS), and View Engineering. The full impact of these investments on the machine vision industry was yet unknown.

The Customers for Machine Vision Products

Though the machine vision market was very fragmented and very new, some information about the buyers of these products was provided by a study entitled *Vision Systems Survey of End Users,* conducted by Prudential-Bache Securities and published on February 6, 1985.

The report showed several interesting characteristics of present and potential machine vision customers. Sixty-seven percent of the companies surveyed achieved annual gross revenues of greater than $1 billion. Eighty-four percent of the companies had annual gross revenues of greater than $100 million. Fifty-seven percent of the companies interested in vision were located in the Midwest. Another 19 percent were located in the Northeast, with 9 percent on the West Coast. The end users surveyed were in the following industries:

Industry	Percentage of study
Automotive	35%
Electrical/electronics	35
Aerospace	12
Construction	3
Pharmaceutical	1
Other*	14

* Ranges from paper products to metal fabricators.

Ninety-seven percent of the end users surveyed indicated that vision was an important factor in the overall manufacturing process. Sixty-four percent had an actual capital budget for vision system purchases.

Decision makers in the purchasing of vision systems were located in many different levels of the companies surveyed. Sixteen percent responded that the purchase decision was made at the corporate level only, while 29 percent said that the decision was made at the division level. Another 37 percent responded that vision system purchase decisions were made at the department level, with the remaining 17 percent of those surveyed answering that the decision involved more than one level within the company.

The lengths of present and anticipated future buying cycles for vision systems were as follows:

Buying cycles	Present	Future
Less than 3 months	13%	31%
6–9 months	47	41
9–12 months	23	18
Over a year	8	6

Many customers believed that machine vision systems would not only be installed for production work applications but also for internal development work on automation processes. Nineteen percent of respondents had installed vision systems for development work only, while 54 percent said that they had or planned to install vision systems for both production work and development work.

Fifty-nine percent of survey respondents purchased their vision systems through the direct salesforces of the suppliers. Twenty percent used only OEMs, while 8 percent purchased through distributors. The remaining 13 percent used more than one channel for their purchases.

Vision companies most often mentioned as possible suppliers were Automatix, View Engineering, Machine Vision International, and Perception. The factors most important to purchasers of vision systems, in their order to importance, were technology, service and support, applications engineering, user friendliness, reputation or vendor, expendability, and price.

The end users were also asked to list areas of application or vision systems in both the present and the future. The responses were:

Applications	Present	Future
Inspection	84%	93%
Gauging	44	60
Sorting	21	35
Process control	37	63
Robot guidance	40	45

The Technologies Employed in Machine Vision

There were four main technologies employed in machine vision systems. These were signal processing, mathematical morphology, statistical pattern recognition, and artificial intelligence. These four and the significant characteristics of each are displayed in Exhibit 2.

EXHIBIT 2   Vision systems technologies and their characteristics

How is the processing done?	Image based	Object based	
	Signal processing High speed Simple discrimination Requires special hardware	**Statistical pattern recognition** Low speed Simple discrimination No special hardware required	Arithmetic computations
	Mathematical morphology High speed Complex discrimination High hardware requirements	**Artificial intelligence** Low speed Very complex discrimination Can require special hardware	Logical computations

What is being processed?

To more fully understand these technologies, it is useful to see how each is used in a given application. MVI had a 3-D robot guidance product in which vision was used to direct the robot's placement of windshields in a car moving along an assembly line at the pace of 60 cars per hour. All four technologies were employed in this application. Lighting was used to produce a very sharp, mirrorlike image of the car as it came into the work area. The bouncing of the light off the car surface to produce this image employed signal processing, a technology developed from radar technology. However, this light reflected off more than just the edge of the car body needed to be seen to perform the window insertion task; mathematical morphology allowed the computer control to extract from the image reflected only the part of the image needed for the task, and eliminated the rest from consideration. That was done through complex computer programs that directed the computer to search the image for the exact shape needed for analysis. Statistical pattern recognition was used to take measurements of window position and orientation, since the actual opening size and the position of the car body on the assembly line could vary slightly from car to car. Thus, this technology made use of another set of computer algorithms to take statistical measurements of the pertinent areas of the problem in question. Artificial intelligence software was used to answer such questions as "Is the window opening the right shape for the windshield that is here?" and "Can the robot reach the opening from its present position?" These questions could all be answered logically; they were either true or false. If corrections were necessary, the computer controls could command the robot to move and change position before actual insertion commands were given.

Exhibit 3, p. 183, takes the example given above one step further, showing which technologies were necessary to perform the most common applications of vision systems currently on the market. Many applications required the use of only one of the technologies available, while others required multiple technologies. It was estimated that between 50 percent and 60 percent of the applications in the market in 1985 used signal processing. Between 20 percent and 30 percent of applications made use of statistical pattern recognition. The remaining 15 percent of the applications relied on mathematical morphology to perform the desired task.

Exhibit 4, p. 182, shows how many of the current competitors in the vision systems market were positioned along technology lines. Most competitors used only one technology. MVI was unique in the employment of all four technologies. MVI began as a mathematical morphology company; then it consciously developed the use of the other three technologies in order to be able to handle more difficult industrial problems and to give itself a technology edge over its competition. This was explained in the company's prospectus, as follows:

> The company specializes in mathematical morphology, which it believes is the most suitable technology for application in machine vision. Moreover, the company is complementing its capabilities in mathematical morphology by establishing capabilities in pattern recognition, signal processing, and artificial intelligence, and believes that the combination of these technologies will enhance

EXHIBIT 3 Technologies used in machine vision applications

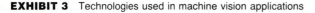

Two-dimensional
signal processing

Statistical
pattern recognition

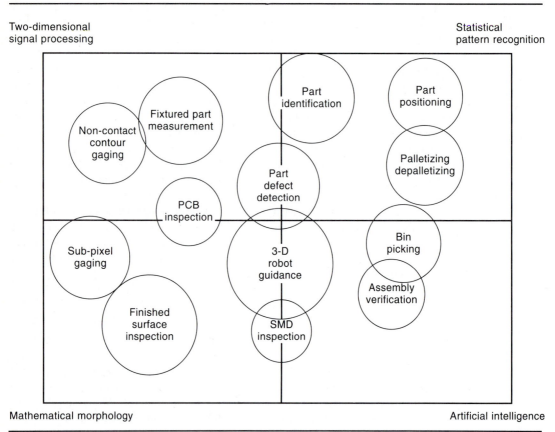

Mathematical morphology

Artificial intelligence

the applications of the company's systems. It is the advanced application of mathematical morphology and the move toward a combination of technologies to complement mathematical morphology that the company believes differentiates it significantly from its competitors.

Dr. Sternberg explained why it is important to use all the available technologies. He said:

> You can force a solution using just one tool, but you end up working 10 times harder than if you use the right tool for the right part of the job. You can find a way to change the spark plugs on your car with just a hammer, but it will take you a lot longer to do it this way than if you had all the right tools for the job.

Machine Vision International—History

MVI was founded in June 1981 by Dr. Stanley R. Sternberg. Dr. Sternberg had previously worked at the Environmental Research Institute of Michigan, where he was instrumental in the development of the technology of mathematical

EXHIBIT 4 Industry competitors' technology positions

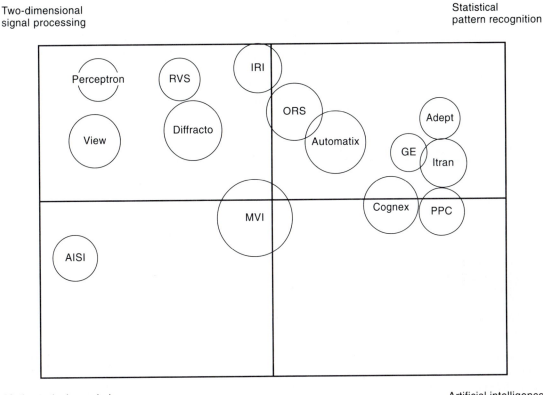

Two-dimensional
signal processing

Statistical
pattern recognition

Mathematical morphology

Artificial intelligence

morphology. Dr. Sternberg's idea was to develop products based on this technology that could be used for measurement, inspection, and control in manufacturing processes. In the fall of 1982, Dr. Sternberg joined with Richard P. Eidswick to develop strategy to bring this technology to market. Prior to joining MVI, Mr. Eidswick was senior vice president and director of Comshare, Inc., an international computer services company.

To fund the company, nearly $9.5 million of equity capital was raised through private offerings of MVI securities. Approximately $5 million of these funds were raised through the sales of common stock to Safeguard Scientifics, Inc. As of November 5, 1985, MVI was a public company, with its shares traded in the over-the-counter market.

As its strategy in the vision industry, MVI chose to focus on three business areas and three specific applications of machine vision. The business areas were automotive, electronics, and general industrial. The applications were three-dimensional robot guidance, surface inspection, and surface-mounted electronic component inspection. The principal component of all systems sold by MVI was the image flow computer (IFC), an image processing computer that used MVI's proprietary operating software, BLIX, to perform the mathematical calculations necessary for image analysis.

MVI marketed its products primarily through direct sales groups dedicated to end users in the three business areas. It also marketed its products to original equipment manufacturers (OEMs) who specified MVI products in their systems, and through certain specialized sales representatives. Through September 1985, MVI had manufactured and sold approximately 100 machine vision systems for an aggregate sales price of nearly $12 million. Financial statements for MVI are presented in Exhibit 5 and 6.

EXHIBIT 5 Machine Vision International Corporation—statements of operations

	June. 25. 1981– Dec. 31, 1983	Jan. 1– Dec. 31, 1984	First six months	
			1984	*1985*
Net sales	$ 541,058	$ 4,011,730	$ 760,807	$ 4,481,476
Cost of sales	338,921	2,536,398	555,891	2,021,068
Gross profit	$ 202,137	$ 1,475,332	$ 204,916	$ 2,460,408
Operating expenses:				
Product development	$ 318,961	$ 1,733,667	$ 610,836	1,354,943
Selling	360,601	1,979,102	652,364	2,011,329
General and administration	542,101	904,272	420,356	365,184
Total operating expenses	$ 1,221,663	$ 4,617,041	$ 1,683,556	$ 3,731,456
Loss from operations	$(1,019,526)	$(3,141,709)	$(1,478,640)	$(1,271,048)
Other income (expense):				
Interest expense	$ (5,076)	$ (105,089)	$ (15,697)	$ (116,207)
Other	23,342	67,895	64,858	19,410
Total other income (expense)	$ 18,266	$ (37,194)	$ 49,161	$ (96,797)
Net loss	$(1,001,260)	$(3,178,903)	$(1,429,479)	$(1,367,845)
Loss per share	$(.41)	$(.56)	$(.28)	$(.18)
Weighted average number of shares	2,458,495	5,714,391	5,164,775	7,457,460

Market Approach

An organizational chart for MVI is shown in Exhibit 7. The sales function within MVI was divided along market segment lines. The three current sales divisions—automated systems, electronic systems, and manufacturing technology—mirrored those markets pointed out by the Prudential-Bache survey as the major customers interested in machine vision products.

The Automated Systems Division (ASD)

MVI began its search for applications in the automotive industry, where executives were already talking about putting resources into finding vision solutions to solve automation problems. Mr. Jake Jeppesen, who joined MVI in June

EXHIBIT 6 Machine Vision International Corporation—balance sheet

| | December 31, | | June 30, 1985 |
	1983	1984	(unaudited)
Assets			
Current assets:			
Cash and cash equivalents	$ 104,117	$ 191,361	$ 151,601
Receivables	272,945	2,095,875	3,255,081
Inventories	238,772	1,964,951	3,749,191
Prepaid expenses and deposits	8,689	34,961	34,228
Total current assets	$ 624,523	$4,287,148	$7,190,101
Property and equipment			
Computer and other equipment	$ 221,274	$ 972,614	$1,213,574
Office furniture and equipment	91,436	171,737	249,738
Leasehold improvements	6,520	91,665	102,232
	$ 319,230	$1,236,016	$1,565,544
Less: accumulated depreciation	31,154	275,087	470,087
Net property and equipment	$ 288,076	$ 960,929	$1,095,457
	$ 912,599	$5,248,077	$8,285,558
Liabilities and shareholders' equity			
Current liabilities:			
Current portion of long-term debt	$ 42,500	$ 74,823	$ 118,000
Note payable	—	675,000	500,000
Accounts payable	246,058	993,292	1,887,677
Accrued liabilities	104,540	407,842	633,709
Total current liabilities	$393,098	$2,150,957	$3,139,386
Long-term debt, less current portion above	$118,365	$1,671,775	1,205,073
Shareholders' equity			
Common stock, no par value, stated value $.001	4,018	6,509	8,214
Paid-in capital	1,398,378	5,598,999	9,480,893
Accumulated deficit	(1,001,260)	(4,180,163)	(5,548,008)
Total shareholders' equity	$401,136	$1,425,345	$3,941,099
	$912,599	$5,248,077	$8,285,558

1983 to head the Automated Systems Division, found a group at GM that had been talking for two years to various vision companies about the possibility of using vision to automate auto glass insertion. The other companies had failed to develop a product that worked. Mr. Jeppesen convinced them to try again with the mathematical morphology technology that MVI offered. The first order for the window insertion product was received by MVI in December 1983. A prototype was working in a GM lab in March 1984, and the first plant installation was made in June 1984. See Exhibit 8 for a representation of how this product worked.

Even through the first vision applications taken on by MVI showed themselves to be successfully working projects within the automotive industry, the sales process for ASD remained a very complicated one. The division

EXHIBIT 7 Corporate organization chart

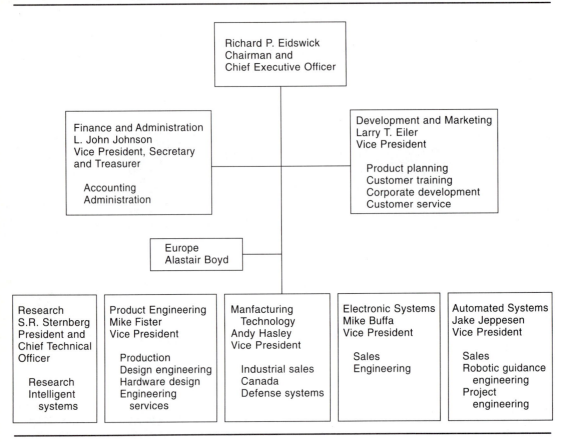

maintained an ongoing educational sales effort, selling everyone from the executive level to plant production people on who MVI was and what the company and machine vision were capable of doing. Automotive executives and manufacturing research staff personnel were interested in the technology involved and its advantages over existing or alternative assembly automation techniques. However, manufacturing staff were interested in finding ways in which higher-quality cars could be built better, cheaper, and faster. Plant production staff were generally interested in improvements in product quality, but were mainly concerned with production speed so that their quotas could be met. To this group, a product's reliability on the assembly line was of the utmost importance. Since orders within automotive companies came most often from the manufacturing staff or the plant production people, it was the goal of the sales process to give these people confidence that MVI's product "will do what we say it's going to do forever, first time every time, and never fail," as

EXHIBIT 8   Representation of MVI's window insertion system

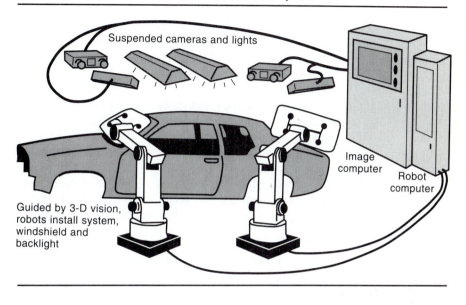

Suspended cameras and lights

Image computer

Robot computer

Guided by 3-D vision, robots install system, windshield and backlight

Mr. Jeppesen put it. These groups were not interested in machine vision for its technology; they wanted their task performed in the most reliable, fastest way possible.

Since this sales effort was so educational in nature, the decision was made to approach the market on a direct basis; MVI did not want to entrust this type of basic technology and company-image selling to a third party. The ASD was currently selling products for two applications in the automotive industry. These were 3-D robot guidance for window insertion and other applications, and surface paint inspection.

The window insertion product had a selling price of approximately $450,000 per installation. It was only a part of an entire window insertion system that included robots, body handling equipment, material handling equipment, and controls supplied by other vendors. This total system cost in the neighborhood of $5 million. The surface paint inspection product was currently used only to inspect finished paint surfaces; it sold for approximately $500,000 per system. MVI had received seven orders for window insertion systems and one for a paint inspection system.

Though relatively few orders for these products had been received to date, the markets for these products were very large. Mr. Jeppesen saw many potential application areas for both MVI's 3-D robot guidance and paint surface inspection products. 3-D robot guidance could also be employed to automate such tasks as automobile wheel and cockpit loading, to apply paint stripes, and to control many fluid fill operations. Although paint inspection systems were currently used only for finished product inspection, the market could be expanded to include inspection of bare metal after frameup, phosphate coating before priming, primer coats, and other checkpoints during automobile production. In total, Mr. Jeppesen currently foresaw 10 application possibilities for 3-D robot guidance and 6 application areas for surface inspection in each automobile plant. In 1985, there were 73 automobile assembly plants operating in the United States, and many of these operated with more than one assembly line per plant.

At the time, no other vision company even claimed to be able to supply a product that could perform surface inspection. Mr. Jeppesen listed three companies as major competitors in the 3-D robotics business: GMF Robotics, ASEA Robotics, and Automatix. In this area, Mr. Jeppesen said that many companies claimed to be able to perform this task, but they really did not have the necessary capabilities. As a result, there was a great amount of confusion in the marketplace, but Mr. Jeppesen believed that this confusion would soon be dispelled as competitors tried to supply the market and failed.

The Electronics Sales Division (ESD)

The electronics market was very different from the automotive area. Therefore, the sales strategy and marketing positioning employed in the electronics market were unique to it. The sales process for the ESD began with marketing research to find out the vision needs in the electronics industry and was subsequently combined with a concerted effort to get to know the decision makers within that industry. In this effort, MVI marketing personnel attended electronics industry meetings, where they got to know the technology leaders within the industry. Thus they gained firsthand knowledge of the industry's technology trends as well as the strategies of the major electronics firms.

In 1985, the U.S. electronics industry was currently undergoing a great change in production procedures. Ninety percent of electronics assembly was being done on lead-through boards. However, overseas, and especially in Japan, nearly 95 percent of electronics assembly was being done on higher-quality, more reliable surface-mounted boards. It was believed that U.S. production would shift to surface-mounted boards very rapidly. This type of production would be highly compatible with automated assembly techniques since the components on surface-mounted boards were much smaller and required greater production sensitivity than lead-through boards.[1]

The total market for surface-mounted inspection systems was divided into three segments by MVI's market researchers. The two in which MVI thought it could successfully compete were: (1) low-speed, high-precision inspection of a

---

[1] Surface mount technology (SMT) was an electronic manufacturing method in which miniaturized, prepackaged components were assembled on the top (hence surface) of a circuit. In lead-through assembly, the components had conductors or leads that were inserted through holes that are drilled or punched through the board. These leads were folded or clinched on the back of the board to provide mechanical component attachment. In SMT manufacturing, the components were placed on the board by an automatic mechanism and then soldered in place.

broad range of components, and (2) high-volume, low-precision inspection of a limited range of components. For these areas, MVI made the following total market size projections.

Year	Segment 1 total number of vision systems	Segment 1 total dollar market (in millions)	Segment 2 total number of vision systems	Segment 2 total dollar market (in millions)
1984	30	$ 3.6	7	$ 1.05
1985	65	7.8	20	3.0
1986	90	10.8	130	19.5
1987	125	15.0	340	51.0
1988	350	42.0	525	78.75

MVI had spent two years developing a product that could use vision to control the assembly process and provide inspection for this automated production. MVI believed that the contrast and complexity of the components used in this process required the capabilities of the company's mathematical morphology technology. An effective product for this market had to be able to perform three tasks: (1) determine if the correct component (chip, diode, resistor, or capacitor) was present; (2) determine if each part was in the correct position relative to the other components; and (3) check the solder used to attach parts to the board for voids and excess solder material. MVI's vision technology was capable of solving the first two tasks. The third task required a low-level X-ray capability, which MVI did not currently have but was working to achieve.

Unlike ASD sales, ESD sales were technology sales. ESD's personnel talked to technical processing engineers, not the traditional purchasing departments within the electronics firms. MVI people talked to these technical people to determine their automation needs and to educate them as to the capabilities of MVI's product. The goal was to get to know the people who would use the system and get their support before there was a quotation request made on the part of the electronics firm.

By the end of the third quarter of 1985, MVI had three working surface-mounted inspection systems in the field. The company expected to make deliveries on nine or ten more orders before the end of the year. Prices on these systems ranged from $80,000 to $200,000. The hardware used in these systems was priced to match closely the prices of MVI's competition. The software used was specific to each application and, therefore, was priced to be the profit margin producer for the company.

Competitors in this market were View Engineering, International Robomation/Intelligence (IRI), and Automatix. IRI was specifically mentioned as an aggressive price competitor. IRI's system that competed with MVI was priced between $75,000 and $125,000.

The Manufacturing Technology Division (MTD)

MVI's Manufacturing Technology Division comprised two sales groups, the Industrial Sales Group (ISG) and the Aerospace Sales Group (ASG). This division had as its goal finding new markets for the products developed by the other sales divisions. Manufacturing technology sales groups were to take on applications that required extensions of existing technology or new combinations of what had already been developed by MVI's R&D and engineering personnel. The MTD was headed by Mr. Andrew Hasley.

Industrial sales group.   MVI received between 250 and 300 inquiries each month through its marketing work, by its presence in several vision shows, and through references from its present customers. Many of these inquiries did not come from people within the automotive or electronics industries. Leads from these other nonspecialized industries were turned over to the Industrial Sales Group, which was under the direction of Mr. John Kufchock.

Mr. Kufchock used three initial criteria to determine whether MVI would pursue these inquiries. The lead had to come from a Fortune 500 company; thus, the company would have considerable funds to spend on capital investments. The application being pursued had to involve the use of technology already developed by MVI; thus, sales of the ISG were meant to produce a multiplier effect on sales for MVI. Furthermore, the inquiry had to come from a company that had an established engineering group capable of understanding both the technology involved and the advantages of MVI's technology over competitors.

The ISG had made sales in many industries, all of surface inspection products that performed very diversified tasks. For example, in the food industry, surface inspection was used to identify foreign objects in produce coming from the fields as well as produce of less than acceptable grade, so that these could be eliminated from further processing. In the lumber industry, surface inspection was used to check plywood as it was produced so that its grade and sales quality could be determined. In the rubber industry, tires were checked for flaws. By the end of 1985, the ISG had placed more than 20 systems in the industrial workplace. Mr. Kufchock expected to have nearly 50 more systems on the market in the first six months of 1986. He predicted that ISG could sell over 100 systems per year from a total of only 20 different customer corporations.

The sales process for the ISG usually began with an inquiry from a prospective customer. Qualified leads were turned over to one of Mr. Kufchock's two sales-oriented application engineers. Through talking with and visiting the prospect, the application engineer studied the customer's vision needs to determine whether MVI's technology could meet the requirements of the task. The application engineer also identified the right people to deal with in the customer's organization. These included those who would understand the technology, those who would use the product, and those who would actually make the purchase decision. All those involved in the decision process had to be "put on the team" if the sales process was to be successful. When this had been completed, a test of MVI's product on the prospect's material would be made at ISG's own lab. When the test was successful, the application engineer contacted the customer, asking that they send people to see the test results. Then, a trip was made to the customer's business to determine the actual conditions under which the system had to perform and to talk to all the decision makers involved, getting their input on a preliminary sales proposal. Then a final proposal was drawn up and sent to the purchasing department of the customer. This entire selling process took between three and nine months.

The ISG also sold its products to other firms that needed vision to make their large automation systems work for their customers. MVI called these firms strategic partners because often significant development work had been done by MVI's engineering staff to make the vision products work successfully for this partner. These strategic partners had market knowledge that MVI did not possess. Often, the vision portion of the systems sold by these partners comprised less than 20 percent of the entire system's selling price.

Prices on vision systems sold through the ISG ranged from $45,000 to $75,000 each. These prices included the hardware and software necessary for the application plus training. Fees for engineering services at the customer's plant to get the system up and running were charged separately at an established per diem rate. In the first applications, it was common for MVI to find this engineering support taking more time than expected. This resulted in profit margins less than what had been predicted.

Aerospace Sales Group (ASG). The Aerospace Sales Group was established in mid-1985. It was spun off from the ISG when it was believed that there was enough business in this area alone to support a dedicated sales effort. The first sales made in the aerospace industry were made by the ISG group.

This group sold products for many different applications involving the different technologies developed by the ASD and ESD. These included 3-D robot guidance systems, small parts inspection systems, surface inspection products, and combinations of small parts inspection and 3-D robot guidance in which the system would recognize, inspect, and control the handling of parts. Current applications included turbine blade inspection, surface-coating inspections on space shuttle booster rockets, and 3-D robot guidance used for assembling wiring harnesses in aircraft.

The defense supply industry had different requirements for vision products than did the other industries MVI sold to. Here speed was of less concern than it was in other industrial environments. What was important here was the complexity of the parts to be inspected or assembled. As a result, the systems sold by the ASG were complicated and averaged in price from $400,000 to $500,000.

Major competitors were Robotic Vision Systems, IRI, and View Engineering. As in the automotive industry, no other competitor even claimed to be able to perform surface inspection. Also, MVI believed there was little competition in the area of parts inspection. In discussing the competitive environment, Mr. Hasley, director of the Manufacturing Technology Division, said,

In a lot of cases, we don't find we're competing directly with anybody. We still make a lot of cold calls. Selling here is a market development problem really. It's just getting the application defined. Can you do this? Can you do that? It involves a lot of education on what vision can do.

Commonalities of Sales Approach

Though each of MVI's three divisions sold to different markets and to different groups of people within customer firms, each application's real bottom-line sales approach was similar. What MVI was really selling was improved return on investment (ROI). In some sales, MVI's salespeople were showing how their product could reduce warranty claim costs. This was especially true in automobile paint inspection, since paint flaws were the industry's fourth-largest warranty claim cost. Thus, improving paint finish quality was a paramount goal for these firms. In others, it was improved product quality that resulted from the use of vision equipment. For yet other applications, the main purpose of the vision equipment was to reduce the costs of inspection. For example, Mr. Kufchock pointed out that the plywood inspection system in one facility replaced the use of eight inspectors each earning $21 per hour.

Production

For each first-time application, MVI built whatever hardware and software were needed to make the project work for the customer. For further similar applications, MVI looked for a supplier for the necessary components of the system. Thus, for all of MVI's multiple applications, it purchased the optics, hardware, circuit boards, cables, communications devices, and other material handling equipment from outside suppliers. The role of production then became that of packaging the optical equipment, the hardware, the software, and the communications materials so that the application worked for the customer.

The Future Goals for MVI

Mr. Eidswick, MVI's chairman and CEO, established the company's goal of being a dominant supplier in the machine vision industry. This goal translated into obtaining a 15 percent share of this market within five years and then sustaining that 15 percent share.

Mr. Eidswick also set achievement goals for each sales division. The ASD and the ESD were to be specialized divisions and, as such, technology and market share leaders within their industries. Here, there would be a continuing effort to take on new projects that had a strategic purpose. The groups within the Manufacturing Technology Division were to have multiplier strategies; their sales were to come from extensions of products developed by the ASD and ESD. The MTD groups were also to seek out strategic partners, finding companies who needed vision in their products and who already had market knowledge and a strong customer base. For this type of customer, MVI would sell its products at a discount from the prices quoted to direct end users since the strategic partners would take over much of the selling process for MVI.

Mr. Eidswick prepared sales expense breakdowns for the company's two types of sales, those direct to end users and those made through strategic partners. These expense breakdowns, expressed as percentages of sales revenue, are shown below. The third column shows the breakdown of expenses as percentages of sales for MVI's sales for the first half of 1985.

	End user	Strategic partner	First six months of 1985
Revenue	100%	100%	100%
Cost of goods sold	35	55	45
Gross margin	65%	45%	55%
Selling expense	25	9	45
R&D and engineering	10	10	30
Corporate expenses	10	6	8
Total expenses	45%	25%	83%
Profit before taxes	20%	20%	(28%)

MVI had not made a profit to date; however, no competitor in the vision industry had been consistently profitable. MVI had bid each project, even the first one for each of its applications, at a price that the company thought would be profitable. However, the number of engineering, selling, and application development hours that these early applications needed to achieve systems capable or working in real industrial environments and to educate customers on the use of the products had been hard to estimate. These problems led to the higher than desired selling, R&D, and engineering expenses to date. Mr. Eidswick was most concerned about the high selling-expense figure. He was not so concerned about the R&D and engineering expense, since this was to be expected in a new, high-technology industry. MVI needed, as Mr. Eidswick saw it, to find ways to reduce its selling expense.

The Question of Focus

Some vision companies have chosen to be very specialized. They believe that an emerging company cannot afford to spread itself too thin. It must establish a market niche, exploit that niche, make some money, and then go out and spread itself. Others say that this is a new market. No one understands it. What may be a niche one day might just disappear. Some competitors are very specialized. Others are all over the place. Some of each have failed. Why? For the specialized firms, perhaps the market never appeared or the task they chose proved too difficult. For those who were in all markets, each project was different and they had no repeat sales.

Dr. Sternberg

Multiple orders of the same kind of things, that's the kind of result we want to have. We want more repeat orders for the same product, the same application . . . less customization. That way we don't have to keep reinventing the wheel, inventing new technology and engineering new software for every order that we get.

Mr. Eiler

Mr. Eidswick believed that the fact that MVI had "so much going on, in so many markets, with so many different applications" was the company's biggest problem. But he explained that "we have to do this if we want to find the applications that will provide repeat business, applications that will establish us as an industry leader."

Mr. Eiler pointed out that the company had purposefully chosen only very difficult applications, a strategic approach he called "a tough jobs positioning." That product positioning, along with what Mr. Kufchock called the company's credo that "There is no unhappy customer," was designed to build a strong company image for MVI as "the company that makes products that work," as Mr. Eiler put it.

MVI had not found that it was easy to get a vision application job even after another competitor had failed to provide a product that worked. Often customers who had spent thousands and thousands of dollars on vision equipment wanted to protect that investment by giving their supplier another chance to succeed. Other customers turned away from vision after initial system failures, waiting for the technology to mature and for the market winners to appear rather than give another company a chance at that time.

The prospectus published by MVI at the time of its stock offering to Safeguard Scientics shareholders stated that MVI focused on three applications. These were three-dimensional robot guidance, surface inspection, and surface-mounted electronic component inspection. Dr. Sternberg believed that, in looking at the company, one should be careful not to confuse its technological diversity with its market position. He said, "MVI is focused; we are working toward three standardized products."

Case 11

Logitech*

Early in the spring of 1990, Pierluigi Zappacosta, CEO of Logitech, reflected on the changing market conditions in North America and Europe and wondered what would be required to maintain and expand Logitech's position in the computer peripherals marketplace. Logitech had become one of three companies that dominated the global market for pointing devices for computers. While Logitech had captured a large unit share of the OEM (original equipment manufacturer) mouse market, Microsoft was the clear leader in terms of industry standards and dollar share of the retail market, and KYE (Genius), having a strong retail presence in Europe, was poised to compete aggressively in North America.

Pierluigi recognized that Logitech had been slow to react to changes in market conditions, such as the 1987 introduction of Microsoft's ''white mouse,'' a shapely design that had developed considerable consumer appeal. This, combined with eroding margins on the OEM mouse business, had left Pierluigi wondering whether Logitech could maintain a leadership position in the pointing device market. Logitech had been successful in developing leadership positions in other niches, such as scanners, and other opportunities existed. Committed to their mission of ''connecting the computer to the world'' by giving it ''senses,'' Pierluigi wondered what direction(s) the company should take and what the priorities should be.

Company Background

Logitech SA was founded in October 1981 by Mr. Zappacosta and Daniel Borel in Switzerland after Bobst Graphics, the company with which the two had been

* This case was prepared by Brock Smith under the supervision of Professor Adrian B. Ryans for the sole purpose of providing material for class discussion at the Western Business School. Certain names and other identifying information may have been disguised to protect confidentiality. It is not intended to illustrate either effective or ineffective handling of a managerial situation. Any reproduction, in any form, of the material in this case is prohibited except with the written consent of the School. Copyright 1992 © The University of Western Ontario.

developing a European word processing/DTP package, was sold and the new owners did not want to continue the project. Pierluigi had met Daniel at Stanford University, while they were completing their MS (in computer science) degrees. After an initial attempt to bring U.S. technology to Europe with their own software company, Daniel, and then Pierluigi, had joined Bobst to gain industry contacts. They had then formed their own software company with Bobst as the major client. Giacomo Marini, a software manager at Olivetti and a friend of Pierluigi's from the time when they had both worked in Pisa, Italy, joined in founding Logitech together with a group of young engineers.

Two contracts set the stage for the initial growth and development of the organization. First, they won a $1 million contract with Ricoh to develop hardware and software for use with Ricoh printers and scanners. Shortly thereafter, Logitech won a contract with Swiss Timing to develop hardware and software for use at the Olympic Games. Wanting to be close to Ricoh and developments in Silicon Valley, Pierluigi, and later Daniel, and then Giacomo, moved to Palo Alto, California, and created Logitech Inc. In March 1982, Logitech Inc. learned of a Swiss watch company, Depraz, that had developed a mouse. Recognizing the advantages of the mouse relative to other pointing devices such as cursor keys, light pens, and touch screens, Logitech secured the rights to market the Depraz mouse in the United States and packaged it with software for the operation of text and graphics programs.

A major turning point in the strategic direction of the organization came after Logitech secured a contract with Hewlett-Packard to supply 25,000 mice under an OEM contract. It quickly became evident that Hewlett-Packard's price and quality requirements could not be met by Logitech's initial strategy of contracting out manufacturing to Depraz. Adhering to a philosophy of having direct control of the critical elements of the business, Logitech bought the rights to manufacture and market a mouse designed by CC Corp. With help from Hewlett-Packard, Logitech redesigned the mouse for mass production and set up a manufacturing operation in Redwood City, California, in 1984. Production was moved to Fremont, California, in 1987 in a facility across the street from Logitech's U.S. headquarters.

Control over manufacturing and a commitment to quality led to rapid growth in the OEM mouse market with contracts from Apollo, Olivetti, AT&T, and other key computer manufacturers. However, Apple and IBM were wary of Logitech's manufacturing expertise and continued to buy most of their mice from Alps, a Japanese company operating in California, which had purchased Apple's keyboard and mouse facility and was the exclusive supplier to Microsoft.

In 1986 two events took place that would help solidify Logitech's future in the mouse market. First, due to slow growth in OEM sales, Logitech entered the retail market with the Series 7 mouse, a product that had been successful in the OEM market. Then, to win a piece of the Apple business and to satisfy the demands of OEM customers for Logitech to lower the cost of mice, Logitech set up a manufacturing base in Hsinchu, Taiwan, with an initial production capacity of 1 million mice per year, but potentially expandable to 10 times that volume. In retrospect, Pierluigi thought they had been a bit lucky. For a $300,000 investment, they had secured a high-volume, state-of-the-art manufacturing plant in Taiwan's "Silicon Valley" just before Taiwan became a leader in manufacturing technology and a hot-bed of design creativity, and just as the mouse industry took off under the combined forces of Apple's Macintosh, desktop publishing, Microsoft's Windows, and other applications using graphical user interfaces.

In 1988, anticipating a unified Europe in 1992, and wanting to be close to Apple and potential customers such as IBM and Compaq in Europe, Logitech opened another manufacturing facility in Cork, Ireland, which had a capacity, similar to that of the Fremont plant, of about 1.5 million mice per year. At the same time, they broadened their product line with the introduction of a hand-held scanner, a product that shared some technological features with the mouse, that capitalized on Logitech's experience in software development, and that could be marketed through established retail channels.

By the end of 1989, Logitech had reached sales of over $100 million, employed about 1,000 people, had manufacturing facilities on three continents, and had sales offices in England, Germany, Italy, France, Japan, Sweden, Switzerland, the United States, and Taiwan.

Culture

The culture at Logitech reflected the global nature and operations of the organization. Because employees had varied life and educational experiences from around the globe, they were appreciative and accepting of differences in backgrounds, perspectives, and styles. As Fabio Righi, vice president sales and marketing, put it: "Our greatest strength as well as our biggest challenge is that Logitech is an international company. It is difficult to be international and local at the same time. Local flavor affects/impacts everything."

Deeply rooted in the Logitech culture was a strong product/technical orientation. Employees gained considerable job satisfaction from being on the leading edge and working on bold, exciting projects. Fabio, for example, talked of the elusive "atomic mouse" like a Grail that helps define the common purpose of the employees. As senior executives admitted, employees tended to be quite internally focused and did not make a great effort to have their beliefs validated before launching a new product into the marketplace. As Ron McClure, vice president strategic marketing, put it: "We are the most critical users of our products. Customer-need recognition is limited by their understanding of technology—they don't know what is possible!"

Related to this technical orientation was a strong design and production orientation. According to Chip Smith, production manager in Fremont, "Everything revolves around production. The floor, receiving and shipping, traffic, and order processing are key processes by which we satisfy consumers." Therefore, manufacturing was seen as a key marketing success factor.

There was also a strong spiritual component to the culture at Logitech. This was supported in part by the personal philosophies of the founders, but also by the shared vision that employees had for shaping the future. For example, aesthetics were a high priority, not only in the products, but also in the workplace itself. One might infer that if there was a Logitech company handbook, it would probably be *Zen and the Art of Motorcycle Maintenance.*

Working relationships at Logitech tended to be very informal, flexible, open, and close. Employees were genuinely excited to be on the leading edge and found their jobs and the ''family'' atmosphere fun. This ''family'' atmosphere was reinforced by Logitech's policy of hiring talented young professionals from around the world and relocating them to enrich their own and others' perspectives. Dislocated from their own families and culture, employees often relied on each other for social, emotional, and cultural support.

Consistent with the informal, close working relationships, there were few formal procedures and structures within Logitech. Executive decisions were generally made by consensus after seeking employee input. Worldwide interaction of management and staff was maintained on a daily basis by an electronic mail system.

Business Strategy

Pierluigi explained the long-term Logitech vision by saying: ''Only if the computer becomes a little more human will it become an effective tool for the mind. And evolution of our own brain through computers is our long-term vision. Our more immediate mission is to connect the computer with the world by giving it 'senses,' humanize the interface to the computer, and help people turn data into meaningful information. Our goals are to maintain/attain the number one position in whatever markets we play in by redefining and continually changing the products and markets we compete in. We want to have a Logitech product on every computer desk.''

To achieve their mission and objectives, Logitech's business strategy was to recognize major trends and technologies early, move fast in bringing quality products to market (forming alliances if necessary), develop in-house expertise for product extensions, become effective and efficient manufacturers, have the best salesforce and channels to sell the products, and keep ahead of the competition by an accelerated pace of innovation.

Logitech competed aggressively in both the OEM and retail sides of the personal computer accessory business. On the OEM side of the business, they competed using innovation and skill in manufacturing and design that allowed them to bring new technology to market at very competitive prices (see estimated manufacturing costs in Exhibit 1). Toward this end, Logitech had achieved an experience curve in mouse manufacturing of about 70 percent. On the retail side of the business, Logitech focused on image management. They wanted to be perceived in the marketplace as innovators that developed neat products that were fun to use and were easy to sell.

EXHIBIT 1 Estimated manufacturing costs and selling prices

Mouse	Estimated manufacturing cost (January 1990)	Estimated average selling price to channel
Logitech S9	$25.00	$60.00
Microsoft mouse	27.00	75.00
Pilot mouse	17.40	33.00
Dexxa	16.30	19.50
Logitech OEM	15.20	22.00
Taiwanese OEM	13.10	16.50
Ergonomic (corded)	19.60	Not on the market
Ergonomic (cordless)	64.30	Not on the market

Source: Company records.

About 60 percent of Logitech's unit sales were in the OEM segment, but more than 60 percent of their revenue came from the retail segment. In both the OEM and retail markets, Logitech's financial success (see Exhibit 2) had been, and would continue to be, tied to the development and growth of the PC marketplace and recognition of the need to ''humanize'' the computer.

EXHIBIT 2 Selected financial data for Logitech SA (in Swiss francs)

	Full year ending			
	3/31/87	3/31/88	3/31/89	3/31/90 (projected)
Consolidated revenue	$ 33,543,351	$ 62,806,740	$ 124,110,684	$ 180,000,000
Net income after tax	$ 1,459,888	$ 7,032,066	11,206,922	$ 14,000,000
Percentage of revenues	4.35%	11.20%	9.03%	7.78%
Cash flow	$ 2,136,959	$ 9,413,623	$ 14,290,273	$ 17,500,000
Percentage of revenues	6.37%	14.99%	11.51%	9.72%
Earnings per bearer share	—	$ 54	$ 76	$ 96
Dividend per bearer share	—	—	$ 12	$ 16
Engineering, research & development expenses	$ 2,579,023	$ 4,663,430	$ 8,396,799	$ 13,700,000
Percentage of revenues	7.69%	7.43%	6.77%	7.61%
Number of personnel	240	442	731	1,000
Current assets	$ 12,117,422	$ 27,026,936	$ 75,526,814	$ 108,000,000
Property, plant, & equipment gross	6,212,338	8,843,297	22,421,727	30,600,000
less accumulated depreciation	(1,412,316)	(2,139,330)	(5,222,681)	(8,500,000)
Property, plant & equipment net	4,800,022	6,703,967	17,199,046	22,100,000
Other noncurrent assets	328,775	2,273,945	1,184,542	3,900,000
Goodwill	0	14,214,241	13,093,605	11,200,000
Total assets	$ 17,246,219	$ 50,219,089	$ 107,004,007	$ 145,200,000
Current liabilities	8,945,618	18,701,970	36,775,490	37,200,000
Long-term debt & deferred taxes	3,858,044	5,517,119	10,541,326	43,500,000
Stockholders' equity	4,442,557	26,000,000	59,687,191	69,500,000
Total liabilities & stockholders' equity	$ 17,246,219	$ 50,219,089	$ 107,004,007	$ 145,200,000

EXHIBIT 2   *(concluded)*

	1988	*1989*
Net sales	$ 62,806,740	$ 124,110,684
Cost of goods sold	30,921,004	71,493,833
Gross profit	$ 31,885,736	$ 52,616,851
Operating expenses		
Marketing, sales, and support	10,070,523	21,081,432
General and administration	5,553,719	10,276,622
Research, development, and engineering	4,663,430	8,396,799
	$ 20,287,672	$ 39,754,853
Income from operations	$ 11,598,064	$ 12,861,998
Other expenses, net	191,569	59,656
Income before income taxes	11,406,495	12,802,342
Provision for taxes on income	4,374,429	1,595,420
Net income	$ 7,032,066	$ 11,206,922

Product Development

Product development at Logitech involved finding or developing technologies that required Logitech's skills in design, mass manufacturing, and distribution to bring them to market. Logitech had three basic development strategies: start from scratch, evolve current in-house technology, or buy required technology at an advanced development stage from others. Starting from scratch added about a year to the product development process since employees had to learn about a technology, decide what to develop, and test product concepts. Building on current expertise to extend or develop new generations of products was the most common approach taken. If required technology was not available internally, then Logitech would buy it, make minor adjustments to bring it to market, then develop internally the skills required for product evolution.

Decisions on product development were usually based on consensus among senior managers and tended to be emotional and based on "gut feel" rather than extensive analysis and research. Some of the decision criteria that were considered, however, included licensing or development costs, manufacturing cost, margins, a six-month payback, whether it was going to be fun to work on, and whether the product could gain a 40 percent share of its market. Focus groups were sometimes used late in the process to validate the "gut feelings." However, Pierluigi recognized that more effort was needed to get qualitative feedback at earlier stages of the product development cycle.

At any given time there were 20–30 official projects in various stages of development, as well as others that were "unofficial." The major projects were managed by multifunctional new product teams. Currently, there was no central authority on any particular project, but Pierluigi recognized the need to have someone who knew how the whole picture was coming together. Logitech was spending over 7 percent of sales on R&D and money could be found for important projects. Pierluigi thought the biggest problem that Logitech faced in new product development was not getting caught up in ''the fun of it.''

Personal Computer Industry

After five years of rapid growth, the PC industry was in turmoil in early 1990. The initial standards established by IBM and Apple had given way to a confusing array of technologies, including IBM's Micro-Channel, EISA (the Micro-Channel alternative offered by Compaq and six other major vendors), RISC (various versions of reduced instruction set computing used primarily by engineering/scientific workstations running under the Unix operating system), and Apple's Macintosh. Confusing matters even more were competing operating systems such as DOS, OS/2, and Unix and competing graphical user interfaces such as Microsoft's Windows (version 2), IBM's Presentation Manager, the Open Systems Foundation's ''X,'' AT&T's Unix System 5, and NeXT's ''NeXtStep.'' All of these competing operating system and user interfaces, however, used mice or another pointing device to control the operating environment. While it was expected that graphical user interfaces would be adopted on most, if not all, systems, the rate of adoption would depend heavily on the success of Microsoft's newly announced Windows 3.0 for DOS and IBM's OS/2.

The industry itself exhibited characteristics of the maturity phase of the product life cycle. Competition was intense and a shakeout of the market was underway, which affected even some relatively large companies. Consumers were generally even more sophisticated and knowledgeable and did not require the same level of support and sales assistance that they had a few years earlier. Consequently, manufacturers were beginning to make inroads through alternative channels such as mail order, price clubs, and superstores, while traditional full-service retailers such as ComputerLand and Business Land were refocusing their efforts on organizations using outbound direct salesforces. Personal computers themselves were quickly becoming commodity items as limited product differentiation, short technology life cycles, and steep experience curves combined to put substantial downward pressure on prices. With the early mystique of computers wearing off, users, and in particular corporations, were beginning to question and evaluate the impact of computer technology on employee productivity, health, and other aspects of organizational life. Stress injuries, for example, were gaining prominence and were being linked to workplace computer operation. One of these was carpal tunnel syndrome, which involved painful damage to the nerve that runs through the arm as a result of repetitive strain from the use of typewriters, computers, and other arm- or hand-operated equipment. Carpal tunnel syndrome had received considerable media attention (see example in Exhibit 3) and a recent ordinance in California required corporations to take measures to reduce this type of workplace injury. Other concerns were also being raised about cathode ray tubes in terms of possible

EXHIBIT 3 Carpal tunnel syndrome

Repetitive Strain Repetitive Pain: Carpal Tunnel Becomes Major Workplace Hazard

By Himanee Gupta

. . . Throughout the country and in Puget Sound, companies are realizing the painful, often crippling condition [carpal tunnel syndrome] has grown into a major workplace hazard. No one's sure just when and how hard it will hit, but any worker who types at computers, works with electronic scanners or regularly performs other repetitive tasks on automated equipment is at risk.

Carpal tunnel syndrome, one of several ailments known as repetitive strain injuries, occurs when constant bending of the hands, wrists and arms inflames tendons that squeeze the main nerve that runs through the arm . . . The problems start with swelling, tingling and discomfort, and can wind up causing numbness, severe pain and paralysis. Treatment often means slow, painful therapy or surgery followed by therapy. And in terms of treatment, therapy and disability claims, the costs for employers can be enormous . . .

In 1988, the state Department of Labor and Industries paid $6.5 million for 1,910 workers' compensation claims filed for carpal tunnel syndrome. That compares with 1,228 claims in 1986 and 123 in 1979.

Source: *The Seattle Times,* 112, Iss: 223, September 18, 1989, Section F, p. 1.

harmful emissions from computer screens and in terms of eye strain. Thus, while unit growth in the PC industry was expected to be in the 10–15 percent range, profits were eroding and consumers were becoming more critical and discerning.

The Mouse Marketplace

In the computer sense, "mice" are handheld mobile devices that use a combination of hardware and software to translate physical movement into digital signals that control cursor movement on a computer screen and execute com-

EXHIBIT 3 *(concluded)*

Pressing for New Ways to Type

By Ronald Roel

. . . Hodges is one of a handful of iconoclasts promoting radical alternatives to today's conventional keyboard designs. Their devices, which so far have been roundly rejected by the big U.S. keyboard makers, range from variations on Hodges' split keyboard to keys that are moved much like a computer mouse. Like Hodges, most keyboard inventors say their passion for change has been spurred, in part, by an interest in reducing hand and wrist injuries, known as repetitive strain injuries, or RSI, experienced by thousands of computer users each year. Some medical experts believe that conventional flat keyboard designs may contribute to RSI . . .

IBM and other major manufacturers say they have no plans to radically change the keyboards used by 25 million office workers. If big changes are made within the next decade, it will probably be to eliminate the keyboard altogether, substituting them with other inputting devices that convert handwriting or human speech directly to computer print, says Maryann Karinch, a spokeswomen for the Computer and Business Equipment Manufacturers' Association, a Washington D.C.-based trade group.

Source: *Newsday*, v. 50 no. 50, October 22, 1989, Section 1, p. 71.

mands. Named for their basic shape, mice (and trackballs) were more precise and flexible than other pointing devices such as light pens, touch screens, and cursor keys and were generally more intuitive and easier to use. While the first mice developed in the 1960s were mechanical in design and were used predominantly by engineers, mice were now mostly opto-mechanical in technology and were used by a wide variety of users, including children, for a variety of applications ranging from drawing to interacting with most business software.

Market Development

In December 1985, Logitech entered the retail mouse market, first in North America and then in Europe, with the Logitech mouse, a retail version of their successful Series 7 OEM mouse. Adopting a penetration strategy for the more knowledgeable and price-sensitive North American market, Logitech priced the

Logitech mouse at $99 (U.S. currency), about half the suggested price of both the Microsoft mouse and the mouse offered by Mouse Systems Corporation (the first into the U.S. market). Targeting the computer "techies," Logitech initially sold the Logitech mouse directly to consumers by soliciting phone and mail orders in trade publications. Initial success generated sufficient market pull to enable Logitech to establish a dealer network and increase the price of their mouse by 10–20 percent. In the less-sophisticated European market, Logitech followed Microsoft's lead and used a skimming price strategy, charging about 30 percent more than it did in the United States. Instead of using mail-order for distribution, Logitech developed relationships with a strong dealer network in Europe, who were able to support higher prices and margins by meeting the full-service needs of customers with high quality and prestige image products. In 1987, Microsoft launched their new ergonomic "white mouse," for $200 in the United States but $350 in Europe. Logitech were slow to react and did not bring out their Microsoft-compatible Series 9 mouse until 1988. This new mouse was priced about 20 percent below Microsoft in North America and Europe. At this time, Logitech also introduced a "low-end" mouse under the Dexxa brand name to compete against the more than 20 Taiwanese manufacturers, who were pricing their mice in the $20–$35 range. These Taiwanese manufacturers had captured about 40 percent unit market share, compared to the 30 percent unit share of both Logitech and Microsoft in the United States and Europe.

Supporting their R&D efforts from their high margins in Europe, both Logitech and Microsoft were slow to react to changes in the increasingly sophisticated and price-conscious European market. KYE (Genius), the largest of the Taiwanese manufacturers, had introduced a high-quality mouse at $50 in mid-1988 and had captured a major share of the European market. In response, Microsoft and Logitech lowered their prices to $200 and $180, respectively, and Logitech began developing a new mouse at a price of $50–$60. This new "Pilot Mouse" was introduced in Europe at the end of 1989. Microsoft had unbundled their "paint" software from their mouse in the United States, and had lowered the price to within 20 percent of Logitech's. KYE (Genius) had just bought Mouse Systems Corporation and were poised to bring their "Genius" product into the United States under the Mouse Systems brand name, which had a strong user recognition despite its decreasing market share.

The positioning of the major mouse vendors in Europe and North America in early 1990 is shown in Exhibit 4. Worldwide dollar market shares were approximately 40–45 percent for Microsoft, 30 percent for Logitech, and 20 percent for KYE/Mouse Systems. Demand for mice was expected to grow about 50 percent in 1990 and only slightly less in the foreseeable future due to trends towards graphic user interfaces. Sales of portables and laptops were expected to grow 22 percent in 1990 to 1.2 million units (14 percent of the PC market) and were expected to account for almost half of PC sales within a few years.

EXHIBIT 4   Positioning of products in the retail market in January 1990

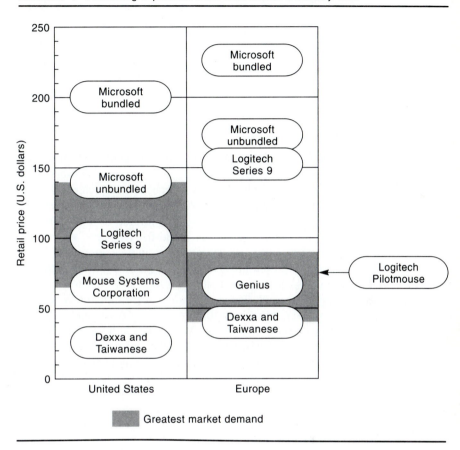

Manufacturers of these computers would have to offer a built-in pointing device. Mice or trackballs seemed to be the logical choice for these pointing devices, but other technologies involving track pens and pen-based computing would likely play an increased role. Moreover, there would be increasing retail demand for replacement products and upgrades. Industry observers expected KYE (Genius) to experience unit sales growth of 60 percent in 1990. Microsoft was expected to experience 50 percent growth and Logitech was expected to experience slightly lower growth. Logitech's retail sales were expected to remain at 40 percent of total unit sales in 1990. Previous years' unit sales are presented in Exhibit 5.

EXHIBIT 5 Estimated world retail sales (in thousands of units)

Calendar year	Logitech	Microsoft	Mouse Systems	Other	Total retail	Percentage of total market
1988	577	803	630	361	2,371	35%
1989	883	1,321	554	400	3,158	40

Source: Company records.

Buyer Behavior

The mouse marketplace could be segmented into home/personal users, home/business users, and corporate and educational users. Home/personal buyers, who accounted for about 48 percent of Logitech retail sales, were thought to be more price-sensitive than other segments and were less concerned about compatibility with software that they did not yet own. These consumers tended to buy from discount houses or no-frills dealers and would choose among the alternative mice available at the most convenient location. Home/business buyers, representing about 26 percent of Logitech's retail sales, were thought to be value- and brand-conscious, but less concerned about compatibility than corporate users. These consumers were thought to be influenced by articles in *PC World, Byte,* and other trade magazines, and to a lesser extent, advertisements in those magazines. Word-of-mouth and sales representative recommendations were thought to have the most influence of all. Finally, corporate buyers, representing 25 percent of Logitech's retail sales but 50 percent of Microsoft's, were thought to be more concerned with the brand name of a mouse and its likely compatibility with future hardware and software products. If use of the mouse was "mission critical" in the sense of being tied to productivity or used extensively, corporate buyers tended to play it safe and bought Microsoft.

While the profile of the Logitech mouse buyer was not completely understood, Logitech did keep track of who their retail customers were. Some 82 percent were desktop users and 48 percent of buyers were also the users. For 60 percent, the Logitech mouse was the second mouse they had purchased and 27 percent bought the mouse "bundled" with a paint program. Some 50 percent purchased the product at a retail store, 26 percent at a superstore, and 13 percent through mail order. Forty percent made the brand decision at the store. In terms of demographics, 80 percent were male, 55 percent were aged 30–45, and over 60 percent had five or more years of computer experience.

Competition

On the retail end of the business, the major competitors were Microsoft, Logitech, and Mouse Systems/Genius. Microsoft was positioned as the compatibility leader for both hardware and software and marketed its product to the premium, brand-conscious segment. It used its software reputation to help sell mice, and often bundled its mouse with Microsoft programs that required one. The second major competitor, Mouse Systems, was a bit of an enigma. It traditionally competed aggressively on price and promotions, but had limited resources and product quality was not believed to be as high as Logitech's or Microsoft's. However, with KYE's purchase of Mouse Systems, KYE was now claiming to be the largest mouse producer in the world (in terms of units) and was expected to become a force in North America.

On the OEM end of the business, Logitech's main competitors were Alps and Mitsumi, (the two Japanese companies that supplied Microsoft), KYE/ Mouse Systems, Z-nix, Truedox, and Primax and Silitec (Taiwanese manufacturers). Primax and Silitec were suppliers to Packard Bell, the fourth-largest PC vendor. All these competitors competed aggressively on price, resulting in low margins and profits. While Logitech felt it had a superior product both technically and in terms of quality, new users often could not tell the difference and most products met their basic needs.

Logitech's Positioning and Marketing Strategy

Logitech's overall mouse strategy was to compress technology life cycles and give consumers more options for increasing productivity. They competed by developing innovative designs and technologies, producing high-quality products, and pricing the products to deliver good customer value. They aggressively managed their costs and tried to maintain strong relationships with their distributors. Traditionally, their products had been positioned to attract the serious and technically oriented user, but were now also attracting creative and aesthetically oriented users looking for fun, form, and function. This overall strategy had led to an increase in unit sales of over 74 percent in 1989, but because the average selling price had decreased 22 percent, revenues increased at only about half the rate of unit sales.

Product Strategy

Logitech's product strategy was to develop products that were consistent with, but not obvious extensions of, current offerings. The image they were attempting to develop was that Logitech offered neat products that were fun to use. Marketed under the theme ''tools for the imagination,'' Logitech's current retail product offering included the Logitech (Series 9) mouse, the Pilot (Series 15) mouse (in Europe only), the Dexxa brand mouse, Trackman (a trackball pointing device), ScanMan (a handheld scanner), and utility software (desktop publishing, a DOS management shell, a paint program, and character recognition). The mice were sold unbundled or bundled with popular software such as Microsoft's Windows (Exhibit 6). On the OEM side, they offered the Series 9 mouse (a three-button, Microsoft-compatible mouse), the Series 14 mouse (a uniquely shaped two-button, Microsoft-compatible mouse that was expected to be very popular), and the new Series 15 mouse.

EXHIBIT 6 Illustrative product literature

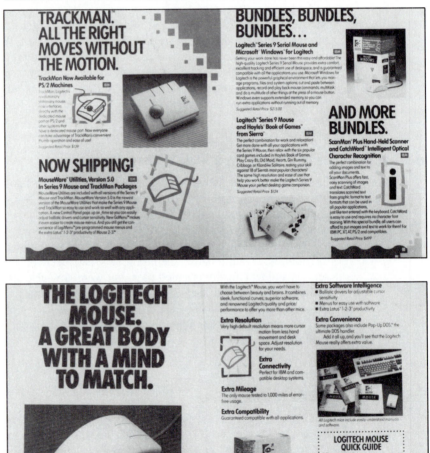

Pricing Strategy

Logitech's pricing strategy was to support a street price $10–$20 below Microsoft by differential channel pricing. This involved starting with a target street price and working back to the manufacturer's selling price using the margins expected by different channels. This was particularly tricky since different channels had very different expectations. Electronic superstores and price clubs worked with 8–25 percent margins, while traditional dealers and department stores worked with 30–40 percent margins, and stores would carry the Logitech product only if they could get their margin. Pricing was further complicated by grey marketing and cross-channel ownership. The former would arise if differential pricing in different countries created opportunities for the product to be bought by distributors in one market to be sold at a profit in another. The latter arose if a holding company owned more than one type of Logitech distributor and was able to supply a superstore, for example, with a product bought for a full-service dealer. Estimated average wholesale prices for Logitech's and Microsoft's mice products are presented in Exhibit 1.

Distribution and Sales Strategy

Logitech used a mix of direct sales, telemarketing, and distributors to achieve their objective of intensive distribution. Six OEM sales reps backed by 11 support staff managed ongoing relationships with key customers. On the retail side, Logitech had four retail channel groups: major retail and corporate accounts, education/government, international corporate accounts, and other retail chains or independents. While traditionally Logitech's salesforce had focused on developing channel relationships, management had increasing concerns about the lack of inroads made into corporate markets. Where Microsoft marketed directly to major corporations, Logitech had tried to reach the corporations through dealers.

Logitech's distribution goals were to be everywhere they could be, to have as many stock-keeping units (skus) as possible in each store to maximize their shelf space, and to maintain strong distributor relationships. This required utilizing a mix of wholesaling intermediaries and retailers ranging from small independent computer stores to major international chains. Logitech believed they had successfully covered 98 percent of the market with their distribution strategy and led the industry with 50 percent coverage in the rapidly growing channel of consumer electronic superstores. However, they actively sought alternative channels of distribution, such as mail-order and telemarketing, as the industry matured and evolved towards commodity products.

Communication Strategy

Logitech's communication strategy had traditionally been a no-nonsense cognitive feature-function-benefit approach designed to present solutions to customer needs. Wanting to develop an upscale image and develop greater affective appeal, Logitech created a new avant-garde visual identity and logo in January 1989. Although Logitech wanted to create an image of being a market leader in design and quality, and to communicate core product benefits of fun, creative freedom, and solution uniqueness, change was not achieved overnight. By the spring of 1990, some Logitech executives were concerned that they had not yet achieved a consistent feeling with their communication strategy. They had used a wide variety of communication media to spread their messages, but relied heavily on print advertising in trade magazines as well as point of purchase materials and packaging. Logitech also paid particular attention to cooperative advertising and special channel programs to motivate and support distributors.

The Situation in Early 1990

While Pierluigi was happy with the performance of Logitech, he was concerned with Logitech's ability to maintain margins in the mouse marketplace and wondered how he could maintain the current rate of growth and profitability into the 1990s. The Series 9 mouse had been a success, but it had been a quick response to Microsoft's sleek redesign and was not perceived internally as leading edge. As most mice now provided the same level of productivity, Pierluigi felt that a move towards ergonomic differentiation might be appropriate. Shortly after the launch of the Series 9 mouse, Logitech had begun developing two versions of a new ergonomic mouse based on the technology of the Series 9. One of these was designed specifically for right-handed users and the other for left-handed users. These new designs were shaped to fit the curve of the hand at rest and would help reduce repetitive stress problems, such as carpel tunnel syndrome. Prototypes of the ergonomic mouse had been completed (Exhibit 7) and had been received well in focus groups. In a second mouse

EXHIBIT 7 Mouse prototypes

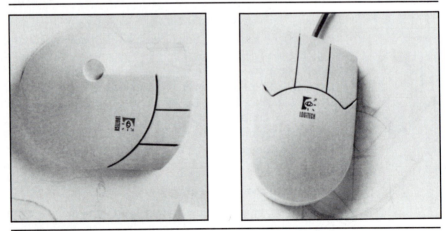

development, Logitech engineers had developed a radio "cordless" mouse that could be used to control a computer without the impediment of a cord and without the line-of-sight requirement of an infrared mouse. This technology could be packaged in the Series 9 mouse shape or the new ergonomic mouse shape at a price about $100 higher than a corded mouse. Finally, Logitech had developed technology for a three-dimensional mouse that showed promise for high-end CAD/CAM and design applications.

Pierluigi had to decide whether to launch one, two, or all of these new products, and if so, how. The cordless mouse and the 3-D mouse were "neat" from a technological perspective and had generated some excitement among the engineers. The ergonomic mouse was not particularly exciting from a technological perspective, but it might help differentiate the Logitech product in the marketplace. In addition, it might provide a "foot in the door" for attracting corporate business. However, from a strategic perspective, not everyone was comfortable with the right- and left-handed approach. Ron McClure, vice president strategic marketing, had expressed concerns about the potential reception for the product among corporate customers and resellers. Corporate buyers would probably not know whether the user would be left-handed or right-handed and many mice would be shared by multiple users. It was not clear, for example, how a purchaser for a school lab would decide how many right-handed versions and how many left-handed versions to buy. Corporate users also might not have much input into the purchase decision to specify brand preference. The "safe" corporate strategy would be to buy a generic "one type fits all" mouse. Ron had a similar concern about OEM customers. An OEM usually bundled the Logitech mouse with the OEM's software or hardware and would probably not want to package left-handed and right-handed versions. Resistance to the new ergonomic mouse was also based on three other factors. Distributor representatives said it could be a sku nightmare for resellers if they had to carry left- and right-handed, corded and cordless mice as well as the current bus, serial port, mouseport, serial and mouseport, IBM and Apple versions, bundled or unbundled. Many employees were concerned that it would be the first Logitech product launched that was not based purely on a technological innovation/advantage. Finally, for many of the reasons outlined above, Logitech SA did not think they would want to launch the product in Europe.

While Logitech had been built on mouse technology, there were other directions that seemed to have great long-term potential. Scanner technology was similar to mouse technology and Logitech's handheld ScanMan had been a great success in terms of market share, margins, and product image. Driven by increased demand for desktop publishing and multimedia solutions, the scanner market was expected to grow 25–30 percent per year and opportunities existed to produce better grey-scale or even color scanners. Another opportunity related to scanners would be to develop a digital camera that captured black and white images and downloaded them to a computer. Finally, the interactive gloves developed for computer games might be improved on to use with computers.

There were lots of neat products to develop, but Pierluigi knew he needed to act strategically. Personally, he was a strong champion of the new ergonomic mouse, but he recognized that it might be risky. The product was ready to launch and he could not put off the decision much longer. He wondered, if they did launch, how it should be done. Would this be an addition to the line or a replacement? How could Europe be convinced to carry the product? Should the cordless mouse be launched as part of the new ergonomic product line, or separately, or not at all? How should the products be priced? How would Microsoft react? Would pursuit of other opportunities be a better use of resources? Pierluigi thought the best place to start looking for answers and directions was in their mission statement and long-term vision. He wondered whether ''humanizing the computer'' by giving senses to the computer adequately reflected their current and potential operation.

Case 12

Schweppes Raspberry Ginger Ale*

As Sam Johnson stood looking out from the window of his luxurious office, he wondered how he should go about evaluating the performance of his division's new product—Schweppes Raspberry Ginger Ale—during the first half of 1991, as compared to his expectations at the beginning of the year when the product was first introduced to the market. Further, he wondered if in fact, the product would take his division into the mainstream soft drink market as he had hoped.

Company Background

Cadbury Schweppes Public Limited Company was one of the largest British-owned confectionery and soft drink companies, with marketing operations in more than 100 countries around the world. In 1989, the company recorded total sales of £2,843.2 million and a before-tax profit of £251 million.[1] The company managed its beverage operations in North America through Cadbury Beverages North America (CBNA). CBNA was organized into several subdivisions each handling projects under a specific brand, namely, Schweppes, Canada Dry, Sunkist, Crush, Hires, and Mott's. Although divisions of one company, they operated independently and competed freely in the market. A product director and an associate product manager, Sam Johnson, managed the Schweppes subdivision for the whole of North America. Exhibit 1 presents the organization structure of Cadbury Schweppes Public Limited Company.

---

* This case was prepared by Shreekant G. Joag as a basis for class discussion rather than to illustrate either effective or ineffective handling of an administrative situation. Used with permission from Shreekant G. Joag.

[1] £ 1 = U.S. $1.70.

EXHIBIT 1 Organization structure of Cadbury Schweppes Public Limited Company

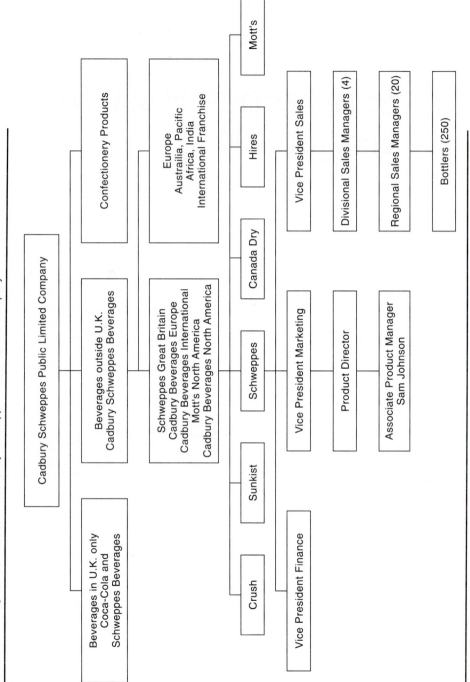

The Adult Soft Drink Business

Of the several subdivisions of CBNA, both Schweppes and Canada Dry divisions marketed products that came under the broad category of adult soft drinks. These included beverages that were used as mixers with alcoholic beverages as well as others that were consumed as general soft drinks. Adult soft drinks consisted primarily of ginger ale, club soda, tonic water, bitter lemon, unsweetened manufactured and natural sparkling waters, and sweetened sparkling waters. By composition, the sweetened sparkling waters were in fact identical to regular soft drinks even though they were marketed as waters. Exhibit 2

EXHIBIT 2 Basic information about adult soft drinks

			Percentage consumed as a	
Soft Drink	Composition	Used as a mixer with	Mixer	Soft drink
Ginger ale	Carbonated water, sugar syrup, ginger flavor	Bourbon, rye	5%	95%
Club soda	Carbonated water, sodium carbonate (soda), common salt (sodium)	Whiskey	50	50
Tonic water	Carbonated water, quinine, sugar	Gin, vodka, rum	85	15
Bitter lemon	Carbonated water, quinine, sugar, lemon flavor	Gin, vodka	95	5
Unsweetened sparkling manufactured/ seltzer/seltzer water	Purified water, carbonation	Used by itself for digestion	5	95
Natural	Carbonated water from natural springs	Used by itself for digestion	5	95
Sweetened sparkling waters	Soft drinks marketed as waters	Used by itself	5	95
Bottled still waters manufactured	Purified natural lake or spring water	Used by itself for drinking	0	100
Natural	Lake or spring water as available in nature	Used by itself for drinking	0	100

Source: Schweppes, CBNA.

presents some basic information about adult soft drinks and the alcoholic beverages with which they are mixed. There were four leading brands in the adult soft drink market: Schweppes, Canada Dry, Seagrams, and Polar. Many brands sold flavored and unflavored versions of sparkling water. Exhibit 3 presents the adult soft drinks marketed by Schweppes and major competing brands.

Although these four brands dominated the adult soft drink market, numerous small local brands together contributed a large portion of sales. Exhibit 4 presents the sales of the leading brands, collective sales of all other small brands, and total industry sales of each type of adult soft drink in 1990. In the soft drink industry, general soft drinks constituted the bulk of the market. The

EXHIBIT 3 Competing brands of adult soft drinks

Adult soft drink	Schweppes (SP)	Canada Dry (CD)	Seagrams (SG)	Polar (PR)
Ginger ale	SP ginger ale	CD ginger ale	SG ginger ale	PR ginger ale
	SP diet ginger ale	CD diet ginger ale	SG diet ginger ale	PR diet ginger ale
Club soda	SP club soda,	CD club soda	SG club soda	PR club soda
	SP sodium free club soda			
Tonic water	SP tonic water,	CD tonic water,	SG tonic water,	PR tonic water,
	SP diet tonic water	CD diet tonic water	SG diet tonic water	PR diet tonic water
Bitter lemon	SP bitter lemon	CD bitter lemon		
Unsweetened sparkling waters				
Manufactured—unflavored	SP unsweetened unflavored sparkling water	CD unsweetened unflavored sparkling water	SG unsweetened unflavored sparkling water	PR unsweetened unflavored sparkling water
Manufactured—flavored	SP unsweetened flavored sparkling water	CD unsweetened flavored sparkling water	SG unsweetened flavored sparkling water	PR unsweetened flavored sparkling water

Source: Schweppes, CBNA.

EXHIBIT 4 Sales and market shares of major brands of adult soft drinks in 1990 (in thousands of cases)

						Industry total	
Adult soft drink	Schweppes	Canada Dry	Seagrams	Polar	Others	Cases	Percentage of Industry
Ginger ale	23,820	55,580	9,600	700	69,100	158,800	2.0%
Club soda	6,350	23,820	1,400	100	90	31,760	0.4
Tonic water	19,850	15,880	2,500	450	8,960	47,640	0.6
Sparkling waters	1,240	—	—	—	316,360	317,600	4.0
Others	—	17,845	2,980	—	177,675	198,500	2.5
Total adult soft drinks	51,260	113,125	16,480	1,250	572,185	754,300	9.5
Other CBNA products							
Sunkist		56,000					
Diet Sunkist		3,500					
Total soft drinks	51,260	172,625	16,480	1,250		7,940,000	100.0

Source: Estimates based on *Beverage Industry Annual Manual 90–91* (New York: Edgell Communications Inc., 1990); Scanner Data, Schweppes, CBNA.

share of adult drinks in the total soft drink market had increased modestly from 6 percent in 1980 to 7 percent in 1990. Exhibit 5 presents the trends in market shares of various soft drink flavors and the leading marketers within each flavor for the period 1980 to 1990.

The soft drink industry as a whole competed with all other hot and cold beverages and liquids for a share of the consumer's stomach. In the period between 1965 and 1990, the soft drink share of the average per capita consumption of all liquids increased from 17.8 gallons to 48.0 gallons per year. The total U.S. population increased from 194 million to 250 million in the same period resulting in the increase in total soft drink sales/consumption from 2,490 million

EXHIBIT 5 Soft drink market trends in the United States by flavor

	1980	1985	1990
Cola	63.0%	67.5%	70.0%
Coca-Cola Company	30.0	33.0	33.0
PepsiCo	25.0	25.0	26.0
Royal Crown Company	3.0	3.0	3.0
Others	5.0	6.5	8.0
Lemon-lime	13.0	12.2	10.0
Coca-Cola Company	4.0	4.0	5.0
Seven-Up Company	5.0	5.0	4.0
Others	4.0	3.2	1.0
Pepper	6.0	4.9	5.0
Juice added	—	3.9	—
Root beer	3.0	2.7	3.0
Orange	6.0	4.7	2.5
Sunkist			0.8
Others			1.7
*All other flavors**	9.0	8.0	9.5
Total all flavors together	100.0	100.0	100.0

All other flavors in 1990	9.5 %
Ginger ale	2.0
Schweppes	0.3
Canada Dry	0.7
Other	1.0
Club soda	0.4
Schweppes	0.08
Canada Dry	0.3
Other	0.02
Tonic water	0.6
Schweppes	0.25
Canada Dry	0.20
Other	0.15
Sparkling waters	4.0
All remaining flavors	2.5

* All figures are rounded up.

Source: Estimates based on *Beverage Industry Annual Manual 90–91* (New York: Edgell Communications, Inc., 1990).

cases per year to 7,940 per million cases per year. Exhibit 6 presents the market trends in terms of per capita consumption of various liquids in the United States from 1965 to 1990. The exhibit reports all liquid consumption figures based on the assumption that the consumer, on average, consumes 182.5 gallons of liquids in a year. The exhibit also presents the U.S. population figures and actual total sales of all soft drinks for comparison.

Because of their popular image and use as mixers, adult soft drinks were primarily sold in 1-liter polyethylene (PET) bottles rather than 12-ounce cans and 2-liter PET bottles, which were popular packages for all other soft drinks. Exhibit 7 presents U.S. market trends in packaging for the industry. Exhibit 8 presents similar market trends in the diet versus regular versions.

EXHIBIT 6 Liquid market trends in the United States

	U.S. per capita liquids consumption, in gallons						
	1965	1970	1975	1980	1985	1989	1990
Soft drinks	17.8	22.7	26.3	34.2	40.8	46.6	48.0
Coffee	37.8	35.7	33.0	27.4	25.8	24.7	23.6
Beer	15.9	18.5	21.6	24.3	23.8	23.3	23.0
Milk	24.0	23.1	22.5	20.8	20.2	20.9	20.5
Tea	3.8	5.2	7.3	7.3	7.3	7.3	7.3
Bottled water	—	—	1.2	2.7	4.5	7.1	12.0
Juices	3.8	5.2	6.7	6.8	7.0	6.8	7.0
Powdered drinks	—	—	4.8	6.0	6.2	4.8	5.0
Wine	1.0	1.9	1.7	2.1	2.4	2.2	2.4
Distilled spirits	1.5	1.8	2.0	2.0	1.8	1.4	1.3
Subtotal	105.6	113.5	127.1	133.6	139.8	145.2	150.0
Imported tap water	76.9	69.0	55.4	48.9	42.7	37.3	32.5
Total	182.5	182.5	182.5	182.5	182.5	182.5	182.5
U.S. population (in millions)	194.0	205.0	216.0	223.0	238.0	247.0	250.0
Soft drink consumption (192-oz cases, in millions)	2,490	3,090	3,780	5,180	6,500	7,710	7,940

Source: *Beverage Industry Annual Manual 90—91* (New York: Edgell Communications, Inc., 1990); figures estimated by extrapolation and *Current Population Reports: Population Estimates and Projections* (Washington, D.C.: U.S. Bureau of the Census, various years).

EXHIBIT 7 Soft drink packaging trends in the United States—percentage of soft drinks using each

Packaging	1980	1985	1990
Cans	40.0%	40.8%	50.0%
Polyethylene (PET) bottles	30.0	30.6	30.0
Nonrecycled glass	14.0	13.0	12.0
Recycled glass	16.0	15.6	8.9
Total	100.0%	100.0%	100.0%

EXHIBIT 8 Soft drink market trends in the United States—diet versus regular

		1980	1985	1990
Diet	M Cases	770.0	1,500.2	2,223.0
	%	15.0	23.1	28.0
Regular	M Cases	4,403.0	4,999.8	5,717.0
	%	85.0	76.9	72.0
Total	M Cases	5,180.0	6,500.0	7,940.0
	%	100.0	100.0	100.0

Manufacturing of Schweppes Adult Soft Drinks

Both Schweppes and Canada Dry were primarily marketing companies. They imported the concentrate for tonic water from Great Britain. Concentrates for all other Schweppes soft drinks and most Canada Dry soft drinks were manufactured by the Dr Pepper Company in the United States. Both Schweppes and Canada Dry sold the concentrate to their separate bottlers under a licensing agreement. Each bottler was assigned a territory on an exclusive basis.

Historically, colas dominated the U.S. soft drink market (70 percent market share in 1990), as did, to a much lesser extent, lemon-limes (10 percent market share in 1990). Further, the cola market was dominated by Coca-Cola or PepsiCo brands. Therefore, most major bottlers had exclusive agreements with either Coca-Cola or PepsiCo to market their colas as the primary product line.

Because of their heavy dependence on the cola giants, the bottlers were under great pressure to bottle and market the other soft drink products produced by the cola companies. Many medium-sized bottlers had exclusive agreements with the Seven-Up Company and depended on 7-Up as their principal product. The remaining bottlers were mostly small local companies dependent on other smaller soft drink brands. Once the principal product line was established by an exclusive agreement, the bottlers widened their product assortment by marketing other noncompeting adult soft drinks such as ginger ale, tonic water, sodas, and bottled waters and general soft drinks such as the peppers, oranges, and root beers. Thus a typical product line of a medium- to large-sized bottler would consist of one of the following three combinations:

1. Coca-Cola, Fanta, Sprite, and Schweppes or Canada Dry (but not both)
2. Pepsi Cola, Slice, Mountain Dew, and Schweppes or Canada Dry (but not both)
3. 7-Up, 7-Up Gold, a noncompeting cola, and Schweppes or Canada Dry (but not both)

Fortunately for Schweppes and Canada Dry, Coca-Cola, Pepsi, and Seven-Up did not have their own brands of adult soft drinks. Therefore, the products marketed by Schweppes and Canada Dry complemented the general soft drinks of the cola and the lemon-lime giants. This made it relatively easy for them to convince major bottlers to accept adult soft drinks as complementary to their main product lines. Thus, though rigidly defined by factors beyond their control, Schweppes and Canada Dry found the market structure to be excellent. In some territories Schweppes had exclusive agreements with Coca-Cola bottlers to market its adult soft drinks and Canada Dry had exclusive agreements with Pepsi bottlers. In some other territories, Schweppes went with Pepsi bottlers while Canada Dry went with Coca-Cola bottlers. Thus, Schweppes and Canada Dry both marketed their products through Coca-Cola as well as PepsiCo bottlers. However, in no territory did Schweppes and Canada Dry use a common bottler. The competition between Schweppes and Canada Dry was carried out in earnest in every aspect of the business.

In addition, historically, Canada Dry had developed a network of exclusive Canada Dry bottlers. Though totally committed to Canada Dry, their strength and importance in the market as well as to Canada Dry had gradually been reduced because of their limited product line. The total volume of soft drink business handled by each bottler ranged from 500 thousand cases to 50 million cases per year, with 3 million cases per year as the typical size.

Distribution of Adult Soft Drinks

The exclusive agreements made the bottlers solely responsible for distributing the soft drinks of their principals in the assigned territories. Armed with the exclusive distributorship of a full range of products, each bottler competed with the others to market its products through the various channels available. Depending on its relative influence, each bottler obtained its share of the space in supermarkets, drug stores, retail chains, convenience stores, gas stations, vending machines, and other outlets for soft drinks.

Marketers commonly classified store space as shelf space or display space. Shelf space was the regular space allocated to a product on the shelves in the aisles. Display space was the space on the shelves located at the end of the aisles that faced outward toward the periphery of the store. Over half of all shoppers invariably circled the store to buy daily necessities such as meats, vegetables, dairy products, and bakery products, which the stores positioned along the periphery. The customers entered the aisles only when they needed specific items located there. As such, the end-of-aisle displays received the maximum consumer exposure and served to remind consumers of the items they might need. Thus, the shelf space and the display space each had its unique role in generating sales. Both were very precious to retailers, bottlers, and the soft drink companies alike. Naturally, there was great competition to acquire an adequate share of the limited store space.

Once a bottler had negotiated the store space with the retailers, management had to determine how to allocate it optimally among the various soft drink brands so as to offer a complete assortment to the consumers and maximize sales and profits. Conventionally, the bottlers displayed the general soft drinks, adult soft drinks, and the bottled waters in separate groups, though in close proximity to one another. Typically the colas and the lemon-limes accounted for most of the business of a bottler with the adult soft drinks constituting an important but very small portion of the business. Invariably the cola and the lemon-lime companies were able to dictate their terms in deciding the allocation of the total store space available to a bottler. As such, the colas and the lemon-limes dominated all prime display space and a large portion of the shelf space as well. In comparison, adult soft drinks had to fight hard for adequate shelf space. Fortunately, the dominant position of Canada Dry and Schweppes in the adult soft drink group and the noncompeting nature of their product lines made the task of obtaining shelf space slightly less difficult. Adult soft drinks accounted for 1 to 15 percent of the total business of Schweppes' bottlers, with 3.3 percent as the typical proportion. Generally a store carried an average inventory of six cases of each soft drink product that turned over 25 times in a year. The relatively low bargaining power of even large bottlers of adult soft drinks made the marketing of adult soft drinks one of the toughest and most challenging tasks. Convincing the bottlers to allocate adequate space to adult soft drink brands became the primary focus of Schweppes' marketing efforts. Johnson described the task: "Our bottlers spill more Coke or Pepsi than the ginger ale they sell. We have no illusions here. Although we make an important contribution to their profits, it is only a small contribution. They do not really depend on us. We need them far more than they need us."

Schweppes's Ginger Ale Product Line

Ginger ale consists of carbonated water, sugar syrup, and ginger flavor. Both Schweppes and Canada Dry marketed their own brands of ginger ale in regular and diet varieties. A much larger quantity of ginger ale was consumed when used as a soft drink than as a mixer. Therefore, in regions where both applications were popular, the consumption as a soft drink invariably generated the bulk of the sales volume. The relative consumption of the product for these two purposes varied in different regions of the United States. In the Northeast, ginger ale was equally popular as a soft drink or as a mixer. In the West, it was primarily consumed as a mixer with alcohol. Because the sales of both Schweppes and Canada Dry were heavily concentrated in the Northeast, a very large proportion of the total ginger ale marketed by the two divisions was consumed as a soft drink.

It was fair to assume that the various brands of ginger ale competed among themselves for the market segment preferring ginger ale flavor. However, in a general sense, they also competed with all other adult soft drinks as well as all general soft drinks, and even all hot and cold beverages. Canada Dry was the largest marketer of ginger ale in North America, controlling 33.5 percent of the U.S. ginger ale market. Schweppes was the second-largest marketer with 16.6 percent share of the market. The third competitor, Seagrams, had only 3.1 percent of the market.

Consumer Image of Ginger Ale

Despite the predominant use of ginger ale as a soft drink, most consumers did not think of ginger ale as a soft drink. Several unaided recall tests among users and nonusers of ginger ale had shown that very few people remembered or considered ginger ale to be a general soft drink. Most people primarily considered it either as a mixer or as a soft drink for special occasions such as adult social gatherings when alcohol was being consumed. There were many possible explanations for this phenomenon.

As mentioned previously, a person tended to consume a much larger quantity of ginger ale as a soft drink as compared to the quantity consumed as a mixer. Although the bulk of the ginger ale was consumed as a soft drink, only a small number of consumers were involved in generating that volume with each person consuming a relatively large quantity. In contrast, a relatively larger number of consumers were involved in generating a relatively smaller sales volume of ginger ale as a mixer, with each person consuming a small quantity of the soft drink. Such consumption was often in an adult setting where at least some people were consuming alcohol. This further confirmed the association of ginger ale with alcohol in the consumers' perceptions.

In addition, the small market share of ginger ale compared to all soft drinks suggested that a large proportion of individuals were nonusers of the product. The image of ginger ale in the minds of such consumers was based on where they saw it being consumed and what they heard about it. On both these accounts, the probability was far greater that the nonusers encountered the ginger ale as a mixer rather than as a soft drink.

The bottlers also perceived ginger ale primarily as a mixer; therefore, they distributed it mainly in 1-liter PET bottles and promoted it as a mixer. This further confirmed and perpetuated the consumer image of ginger ale as a mixer. The only exception was in the Northeast, where the product was widely available in popular soft drink packaging of 12-ounce cans and 2-liter PET bottles.

Interestingly, surveys showed that even those who consumed ginger ale as a soft drink considered it primarily a mixer. Johnson was always puzzled by this apparent contradiction in the use of the product and its image. Further, he often felt that such a distorted image prevented ginger ale from exploiting its full potential as a tasty, refreshing general-purpose soft drink for all occasions. He wondered what he could possibly do to change the image of the product and reposition it in the consumer's mind as a mainstream general soft drink.

Schweppes Raspberry Ginger Ale

In May 1988, one of the Schweppes's leading bottlers conceived the idea of marketing raspberry-flavored ginger ale as a general soft drink for all occasions. After obtaining initial clearance to explore the concept further, Johnson spent considerable time perfecting the product ingredients and conducting laboratory and field tests. The tests indicated that the product had a unique, appealing taste, and many of those who tried it felt that it was a fascinating new soft drink. By October 1990, the product was fully developed and Schweppes had to make the final decision about its commercial introduction. Johnson realized that product development was perhaps the easiest part of the whole process. The real challenge was to analyze the feasibility of the idea and prepare a new product proposal to convince top management to proceed with the product's introduction. Once that decision was made, Johnson would have to convince the bottlers to adopt the product and obtain their commitment to make it available in retail outlets by January 1991.

Johnson was really excited about Schweppes Raspberry Ginger Ale (SRGA). He had always felt that for some unknown reason all Schweppes adult soft drinks and especially ginger ale had been locked in the upscale mixer image that limited their growth potential and isolated them from the volume business of the mainstream general soft drinks. However, he was confident that the SRGA had a unique and distinct personality that was powerful enough to make a clear break from the ginger ale's traditional image and present itself as a legitimate general soft drink before the bottlers as well as the ultimate consumers. He felt that this product could launch the company on a totally new course to become a major player in the soft drink industry in time to come. This was an ideal way to bridge the gap between the company's image as a marketer of mixers and its desire to be a mainstream soft drink company.

In principle, the idea of creating new flavored versions of established soft drinks was not totally new. Other leading soft drink manufacturers had introduced different flavored soft drinks. Some of these products, such as Cherry Coke and Cherry 7-Up, had achieved limited success in the market, whereas others, such as 7-Up Gold, had failed and had to be withdrawn. Although the moderately successful products had created small segments of loyal consumers, they had been tried and rejected by many others. These consumers may be less enthusiastic about trying such new product versions the next time. Thus, despite the support of a major bottler, the product's unique refreshing taste, and strong consumer appeal, the company feared that it might face strong consumer resistance or disinterest. Moreover, Schweppes had always taken pride in its upscale image, if not its snob appeal. The new product concept aimed at the mass market might not fit this image as well.

Another area of uncertainty was the effect SRGA would have on other Schweppes products, as well as on Canada Dry and other CBNA divisions. Johnson felt that his immediate concern was to estimate the extent to which SRGA would cannibalize Schweppes's own ginger ale business. As a conservative estimate, he felt that initially about 20 percent of all SRGA sales would come from ginger ale. The cannibalized volume of Schweppes ginger ale would peak at 2 million cases per year and level off. However, he had no idea how the new product would impact various other brands of CBNA and other competitors in the market.

Johnson realized that he would have to modify the strategy he developed to convince his top management for them to convince the bottlers. In turn, he would have to help the bottlers convince the retailers to adopt the product. His major thrust would have to be on the new business generated by SRGA and the increase in total profits earned by each channel member.

In order to analyze the feasibility of SRGA, Johnson had compiled all relevant information. He estimated that ginger ale sold at an average price of

$10 per 192-ounce case to the ultimate consumer. SRGA would be sold at about the same price. The retailers expected a margin of 20 percent on their sales revenue. Similarly, bottlers expected a margin of 25 percent on their sales to the retailers. The cost of each case to the bottler was $1 for the ginger ale concentrate paid to Schweppes, $2 for other variable materials, and $3 for all other variable costs. In Johnson's opinion, the channel members earned similar margins on all other major competing brands. Schweppes would have to sell SRGA concentrate to the bottlers at the same price as that of ginger ale concentrate.

For Schweppes, the cost of buying the ginger ale concentrate from its supplier was 15 percent of its sales revenue. In addition, Schweppes spent 45 percent of its sales revenue for marketing expenses. The SRGA concentrate would cost Schweppes 20 percent of sales and its marketing costs would be 50 percent of sales. In addition, $990,000 would have to be spent on introductory promotions.

Johnson realized that his first task would be to analyze how consumers were likely to perceive the new product in comparison with Schweppes ginger ale. Such an analysis would help him to understand what efforts he had to make to successfully position SRGA as a main stream soft drink. On the basis of his previous experience with new products and considering the fact that SRGA was to be introduced as a mainstream soft drink, Johnson's conservative forecast of SRGA sales in the first five years was 2, 5, 8, 10 and 14 million cases. Using these figures as the basis, Johnson now had to establish SRGA's feasibility for Schweppes, its bottlers, and its retailers. He would also have to estimate the likely consumer response to the new product. He realized that he would have to prepare his new product proposal shortly so that there was sufficient time to approach the bottlers and actually introduce the product by January 1991.

Market Introduction of Schweppes Raspberry Ginger Ale

In January 1991, Schweppes Raspberry Ginger Ale was introduced nationally in the United States with full fanfare, spending a total of $1 million on introductory promotions. By the end of June, the company had surpassed all sales forecasts and sold 2 million cases of SRGA. When management compared the performance of various Schweppes product lines in the first six months of 1991 with the same period of 1990, they observed that Schweppes ginger ale sales had stayed at 15.6 million cases, although all other Schweppes products had recorded an increase of 4 percent, the same as the growth rate of the soft drink industry.

In an attempt to understand what impact SRGA had made on the other brands, the company conducted a consumer survey. Using a consumer panel the study compared actual purchases of various brands during the first six months of 1990 compared to the first six months of 1991. The data were analyzed to determine what percentage of total SRGA sales had been generated at the cost of various other brands. The results of the study are summarized in Exhibit 9.

EXHIBIT 9 Percentage of SRGA sales sourced from various competing brands

Soft drink types	Schweppes	Canada Dry	Other CBNA	Total CBNA	Other competitors	Total
Colas					22%	22%
Lemon-lime					10	10
Peppers					1	1
Root beer					5	5
Orange			3%	3%	11	14
All other flavors	4%	23%	_	27	21	48
Total	4	23	3	30	70	100
All other flavors						
Ginger ales	3	23		26	10	36
Club Soda + Tonic Water	1	0		1	0	1
Bottled Waters					1	1
Other					10	10

Source: Schweppes, CBNA Consumer Study, January–June 1991.

Johnson realized that he had only a few days to analyze the SRGA's sales performance and the results of the survey. By the following week, he would have to present his findings before CBNA's top management and recommend a future course of action.

Case 13

K mart Corporation*

> Rising in the early 1960s from a mundane variety store chain, K mart set the retail industry on its ear by stamping out enough prototype stores, like so many apple pies, to become the largest discount store chain. It elbowed J. C. Penney aside as the nation's number two, nonfoods retailer. In the first transformation year of 1962, the former S.S. Kresge Co. had sales of $450.5 million and net profits of $9 million. By 1984's end, those numbers had mushroomed to $21 billion in sales . . . and profits rolled in at $499 million.
>
> *Marketing & Media Decisions*
> Spring 1985 Special Edition

The story of K mart Corporation's rise is one of the truly great success stories in the retailing business. The first K mart was opened in 1962. By 1973, there were 745 K mart stores in 47 states. Total sales in that year were $4.6 billion, with $138 million in net income. Stores were added to the chain at a very rapid rate through the 1970s. One hundred and ninety-three new K marts were opened both in 1979 and 1980, with 171 new stores added in 1981. By 1984, there were 2,041 K mart stores throughout the country. The chain enjoyed a compound growth rate in sales of 16.6 percent from 1974 to 1984. Its share of the total mass merchandising market in the United States grew from 1.8 percent in 1972 to 3.7 percent in 1982.

In the company's 1974 annual report, Mr. Robert E. Dewar, chairman of the board and chief executive officer, defined K mart's market position as that of a mass merchandise retailer. He said,

> As mass merchants, we emphasize basic merchandise rather than discretionary purchases and stress value over fashion. . . . Our most important competitive strategy is to use discount pricing. Our store buildings and fixtures are designed and built, our merchandise assortments are selected, and our distribution systems are developed in order to offer a broad range of general merchandise at the lowest possible prices.

---

* This case was written from public sources by Constance M. Kinnear with the assistance of Thomas C. Kinnear. Copyright © 1987 by the authors.

K marts offered everything from clothing to housewares, from delicatessen foods to hardware, from sporting goods to stationery and toys. The product line also included such products as tires, batteries, building materials, and garden supplies not commonly carried by conventional department stores. In the first K marts, national brands composed approximately 50 percent of the merchandise mix, with the remainder being private K mart brands, sold at prices approximately 20 percent lower than national brands. K mart priced its goods with a margin of 25 to 26 percent over cost as opposed to regular retailers that priced at 38 to 40 percent over cost. K mart was not alone in the discount merchandising business. Its competitors included several small regional discount operations such as Mammoth Mart, Unishops, Giant stores, and Arlans. The competition also included new discount chains started by previously regular-only retailing firms. These included Federated's Gold Circle stores, Dayton-Hudson's Target stores, May Company's Venture stores, and Woolworth's Woolco stores. These stores offered little customer service, had a low-overhead, warehouse look, and made their profits through high-volume sales, with inventory turnover rates between six and eight times per year. When these stores were opened, their primary customers were blue-collar families with average to below-average incomes. The discounter's primary goal during this period of quick expansion was to convince its customers that it was safe and smart to save money. To this end, K mart offered only first-quality merchandise and a satisfaction-guaranteed return policy. Using low prices, K mart sought to accustom shoppers to a self-service, low-overhead store. Stores' location decisions were carefully made to make shopping K mart convenient for its customers. By 1984, not only were K marts present in over 80 percent of the standard metropolitan shopping areas of the country, but K mart surveys showed that 52 percent of the people in the country shopped at K mart at least once a month.

The K mart story was not one of totally untroubled success, however. Though sales increased annually, net income growth slowed in 1979 and actually decreased in 1980, 1981, and 1982. In 1982, sales growth itself was flat. Average sales per square foot of sales area were also falling. In 1981, K mart sold an average of $146 per square foot. In 1982, that figure dropped to $132 per square foot. In 1983, K mart average sales per square foot were up to $155, but this figure compared poorly to Target stores' figure of $172 per square foot that year. K mart also faced a falling inventory turnover figure. In 1981, inventory turned over only three and one half times, a sizable drop from the company's six times per year goal. Many factors within the retailing industry were affecting K mart's performance, factors which led K mart management to rethink its chain's position within that industry.

Changes in the Retailing Industry

The area of change in the retailing industry that had the most impact on K mart's performance had to do with an increasing demand on the part of consumers for quality in the products they bought. Mr. Fauber described the change in a speech to the New York Society of Security Analysts in 1983 by saying,

Today's consumer is much more experienced and wiser than in the 60s. Rising levels of education and consumerism and the impact of the media, particularly television, have resulted in a customer who knows how to determine good value for the money to a much greater extent than in the past. The more informed shopper has become a better shopper—not just for price, but also for value. Our research indicates that many more customers today would rather buy a better-quality product with the knowledge that it will provide a more useful economic life. But they still want these products at a good price.

Several different layers of customer wants, desires, and purchase preferences began to appear in the American retail scene. It was impossible for any one store to accommodate all these needs within one building. Many new retailers began to appear on the scene, zeroing in on changing lifestyles and tastes. These new store types were either upscale discounters or off-price specialty retailers, presenting customers with a new ambience and offering brand and designer merchandise priced some 20 to 70 percent below regular retail levels. Consumer loyalty to particular stores and convenient locations began to disappear as buyers shopped around for the best deals. This, in turn, increased competition among retailers to new heights. Retailers cut prices to boost store traffic and build store loyalties, but, in effect, they even further conditioned consumers to shop for value and price. The effects on K mart were expressed in an article in *Fortune,* which said,

> Regional discounters with more attractive stores and more fashionable products began to chip away at K mart's share of the market. New kinds of discounters picked off pieces of the company's domain: specialty stores began selling sports equipment, drugs and beauty products, books, apparel, and shoes. Catalog showroom houses moved in on small appliances and jewelry. . . . In this tough new market, K mart's style and quality did not keep pace with the public's taste.

The success of off-price retailers in the early 1980s rivaled that of K mart itself in the 1960s and 1970s. The total sales of off-price retailers were just $3 billion in 1979, but by 1982 sales totaled $7 billion, or nearly 6 percent of total industry sales in that year. Industry observers believed that this type of retail outlet would continue to grow by 30 to 35 percent annually through the end of the decade. This figure compared with a 10 percent expansion expected for the retail industry as a whole. As a result, it was estimated that off-price retailers could capture as much as 20 to 25 percent of total industry sales by 1987. Within the off-price group, growth rates were expected to be the highest for those retailers who were able to best capitalize on such demographic and economic trends as the new baby "boomlet," increasing numbers of households (especially one-person households), increasing numbers of elderly Americans, and a decline in the teenage population. In 1979, there were only a few hundred off-price retailers in the country. By 1984, it was estimated that there were between 4,000 and 5,000 such outlets operating in the United States. One industry analyst suggested why growth in this area would continue when he said, "I believe that every kind, every conceivable type of 'niche' retailing is going to be tested. More and more people are looking for the successful niche."

In general, off-price retailers served value-oriented middle- and upper-class consumers seeking upscale merchandise at discounted prices. Industry reports profiled the typical off-price shopper as "the suburban female in her 30s with a family income of $35,000."

Most discount retailers made changes that they hoped would appeal to the shoppers moving away from them to off-price stores. "Upscaling" by everyone became the name of the game. For many discounters, upscaling meant changing the selling environment of their stores with improved ambience, comfort, and convenience for shoppers. For most, it meant providing customers with a more appealing product mix with increased value in the products offered. To directly compete with the off-price and specialty discount operations, many discount chains began treating departments that were being chipped away by specialty stores or that fit defined demographic interests as "stores-within-a-store." Special attention was given to the layouts of these departments, giving them a newer, brighter, more separate appearance within the store. Also, the product mix within these departments was made deeper and broader than in departments that faced less competition from new types of retailers.

The goal of upscaling was to enhance competitive positions and attract a broader customer base. Upscaling was not meant to alienate customers who were already shopping discount stores, but instead was intended to make the stores also appeal to customers from higher economic levels. For example, apparel departments in discount stores began carrying an upgraded fashion mix, which included designer and brand name merchandise as well as improved private brands. In hard goods areas, inventories were being weighted more heavily toward branded goods, which provided increased product quality and customer satisfaction. This trend was summarized in the Standard & Poor's Retailing Industry Survey of July 4, 1985, as follows:

> In contrast to their off-price and department store counterparts, discounters have traditionally geared their mix to less affluent, less fashion-conscious shoppers, and stressed price over quality. More recently, however, leading chains have been "upscaling," both to accommodate the higher income level and shopping savvy of today's prototypical discount store shopper and to attract middle-income customers. Upscaling strategies generally entail adjusting the merchandise mix to include more name brands, lacing existing lines with higher-quality, pricier items, and reformatting and sprucing up the stores themselves.

The result of these upscaling activities was that everyone was copying everybody else, and all the stores began to resemble each other. They were all fighting for the same customers. As one president of a discount chain put it, "We are all selling things that can be purchased elsewhere."

All of these changes in retailing were taking place in conjunction with a long-term drop in per capita spending on general merchandise by U.S. consumers. Per capita spending on general merchandise had dropped 24 percent since the mid-1970s. Industry analysts, looking at this trend, pointed to the failure of several marginal retailing organizations and the subpar profitability of many others as proof that the retailing industry as a whole was "overstored."

The growing similarity of merchandise mix within discount stores, the desire to reach the same consumer groups, and the excess retailing space in the country led to a sharp increase in promotional competition within the retailing industry. Discount retailers began lowering prices on already-discounted products to gain customer traffic and maintain market share in dollar sales. This only encouraged consumers to search further for the best value for their dollar, forcing discounters to continue price promotions in order to maintain position within the industry.

K mart's Image

With the arrival of off-price and discount specialty stores, discount stores in general lost ground in the fight for consumer dollars. The situation was summarized by Fred Wintzer of Lehman Brothers' Kuhn Loeb in 1983 when he said,

> Consumers believed the merchandise carried by discounters was of less than high quality and that the stores were too often out of stock. When items were in stock, shoppers found them difficult to locate. Finally, discount stores were perceived as cluttered, as lacking the neatness of other general merchandise outlets. And K mart was the ''king'' of the discounters.

Though all discounters were in a fight to maintain sales and market share, K mart, as the largest discounter, had the most to lose and perhaps had to make the most changes if it was to maintain its leadership position. Mr. Norman G. Milley, K mart's executive vice president of merchandising and subsidiaries, assessed the company's position in the early 1980s when he said,

> We recognized a need to reanalyze the K mart position in the consumer's eyes. We took a great number of surveys and were able to determine that we had the price image but did not have the quality image. We had excellent locations, good traffic and customer acceptance, but we were not selling enough merchandise to many of our customers.
>
> We had narrowly defined the K mart customer and were not accepting the fact that these customers were going elsewhere to buy merchandise that we were not offering. We determined that we could sell those coming to K mart more kinds of products than we were carrying. Why could we not sell much higher-ticket merchandise if we presented it properly?

Low prices had always been K mart's strength. Now the image the company had tried to develop for itself when the chain first began was becoming a liability. Now shoppers were looking for value; yes, they were still looking for good prices, but for quality products at a good price. K mart had a very weak quality reputation among consumers. K mart had to take action in several areas to overcome this low-quality image.

K mart's Changes

K mart's consumer research showed that, although sales were leveling off and net income was falling in the early 1980s, the chain's customer count was not decreasing. Over half the people in the country still shopped a K mart at least once a month. People were still coming to K mart for basic needs, but they were not shopping in the store's more "ego-centered" departments like apparel or household furnishings. For these products, K mart shoppers were going else- where. The task for K mart was to convince customers to buy more products while in a K mart. The company decided to fight its long-standing image of a low-income, blue-collar store. The goal was to increase sales to the customer group composed of family members aged 25 to 44 with children by offering products that this group wanted. As Mr. Fauber explained it, K mart wanted to increase its interest to its more affluent customers, those who regularly popped into a K mart for the regular price advantage they found for such items as toothpaste or tennis balls. By updating K mart, it was hoped that these custom- ers would stay in the store longer and spend more money on a wider mix of goods.

As a first attempt to reach these goals, K mart's executives felt that all that was needed was an updating of the appearance of the stores and improved stocking methods. It was obvious to them that the stores were dull, and they believed that dull interiors reflected on the quality of the products in the store. Improving the appearance of the stores would improve the impression the stores gave the merchandise. This action was taken first since K mart executives believed that the major advantage regional discounters had over K mart were their clean, bright, modern interiors.

To improve appearance, continuous bands of poppy red, gold, and white were placed in the floor tiles to delineate department areas but yet to encourage shoppers to browse from area to area. Each department was located using the wall signs that continued the color theme used in the floor tile. Individual merchandise signs were standardized and displayed sparingly. Taller, graduated counters were installed. These made better use of vertical space and eliminated visual clutter. They promoted a sweeping view of K mart's merchandise variety. The goal was to present a "complete store" message. With a new simplified, low-key atmosphere, the aim was to let the merchandise speak for itself.

K mart management soon found that the decor changes were very unsuc- cessful. They soon came to the conclusion that the problem did not lie with the way in which the merchandise was displayed, but rather in the merchandise offered in the stores. Mr. Ed Willer, vice president of E. F. Hutton, described K mart's slowness at realizing the true problem when he said, "For a long time the mousetrap worked so well that it didn't even cross the minds of K mart management to change it. K mart didn't feel it was necessary to fundamentally change what they offered the American consumer." Mr. Fauber himself admit- ted that the company may have become so engrossed with adding square footage that it neglected a more vital ingredient of success, the stores' contents.

K mart's next changes were based on extensive studies of their customers. The management wanted to learn what K mart's customers wanted and what they were likely to want in the future. The first idea to come from these consumer studies was a belief that young homeowners were concerned with maintaining or improving the condition of their homes, as well as getting the best value possible in that work. The result of this was the development of the Homecare Center, a department that was given the status of a ''specialty'' shop and encompassed 15,000 square feet of space within a K mart store. The Homecare Center consolidated many former departments, including building materials, hardware, power tools, electrical equipment, and lighting, into one area with everything the home do-it-yourselfer would need for fix-up or repair projects. This department was given a distinctive blue-and-white sign to signify its store-within-a-store importance.

The Homecare Center was a great success. Its acceptance encouraged K mart to try other new product mixes. K mart buyers were told to experiment with product purchases and to buy what they thought could be sold. Several different product mix formulations were tried out in prototype stores in different parts of the country. Twenty-five such stores were called ''lead stores.'' In these, new product mixes featured a total selection of name brand products and designer apparel, with the elimination of all private label merchandise. Lead stores were located in higher-income neighborhoods. Other prototype stores, called ''future'' stores, offered ''better-priced'' merchandise made by some of the finest manufacturers in the country, but sold under labels other than those normally sold in department stores. The positive responses these trial stores received convinced K mart's management that K mart had not previously carried the products customers wanted on its shelves. The decision was made to stock the K mart chain with a combination of the two trial mixes. K marts would carry more name brand, more designer, and more high-quality private label goods. Although K mart management knew that there was great diversity among the economic status of the neighborhoods their stores served, they were committed to the idea that K mart was a national chain and that the vast majority of the goods carried by one K mart should be in all K marts. Consumers, they believed, should be presented with a national image of the K mart chain, knowing that products they expected in K mart would be found in all stores in the chain. Eighty percent of K mart's merchandise was standardized on a national basis. Store managers were left free to fine-tune 10 to 20 percent of the product mix in their stores in an effort to appeal directly to local markets, be they rural or urban, black or Hispanic, high or low income.

As higher-quality, higher-priced products were added to the K mart line, the traditional products and their low price points were retained. This policy was explained by Mr. Larry Parkin, chairman and CEO of K mart apparel. He said,

> The tactic is to add on at the top of the line, not to abandon the low end. People who bought in the middle of the range, the thinking goes, will step up. K mart will always have the lower price points because if we didn't have the $9 sweater, lots of people would have no sweater at all.

Items that traditional K mart customers expected to find in the store were still there. The new products were added to appeal to customers who wanted higher quality and who had gone elsewhere to find these products in the past.

More national brands began to appear in K marts. It became common to find such products as Armstrong Solarian no-wax tiles, Corelle dinnerware, Rogers stainless flatware, Libbey glassware, Sharp microwaves, and General Electric food processors in K mart stores. Seiko watches were now carried in the jewelry department along with the familiar K mart line of Timex watches. Casio and Sharp calculators could now be found in the electronics departments. Minolta 35-mm cameras were added to the familiar Kodak lines in the camera departments. Now 14k gold jewelry could be found at the jewelry counter near K mart's less expensive merchandise. More fashionable, brand name clothing was added to each apparel department. Brand names with higher price points became the rule and not the exception at K marts.

In order to make room for this line extension program, K mart began to make use of higher display fixtures, which allowed for additional cubic space usage. For example, in apparel departments, ''pipe run'' displays, which allowed only the shoulders of garments to be readily visible to customers, were replaced with open, circular racks. Using these racks, the entire front of a garment was plainly visible to the shopper. Other new types of fixtures, called ''waterfall'' displays, were trilevel and allowed the showing of coordinating slacks, blouses, and jackets on one display.

Other specialty departments began to appear and receive a store-within-a-store status. Housewares became The Kitchen Korner. This department now carried more than just low-cost kitchen utensils. Now the shopper could find cookware by such names as Farberware, Revere Ware, and Club Aluminum. Small kitchen appliances carried such brand names as General Electric, Sunbeam, Oster, and Norelco. Mixing bowls and utensils were now Pyrex. The belief was that the more knowledgeable consumer would know these brands and recognize the value that also came with the K mart price.

The linen department was now called the Bed and Bath Shop. This department was greatly expanded, using new display fixtures to better show off the improved variety and quality of the store's selection of sheets, blankets, towels, bathroom rugs, pillows, and bedspreads. Brand names made available included Pepperill and Springmaid.

Totally new product lines were also introduced. The new Home Electronics department carried name brand computer equipment priced below $500. Also carried were nationally advertised computer software, as well as national brand and private label TVs, VCRs, and a wide range of other video and audio equipment. Where it was believed that demand would be great enough, K mart introduced, expanded, or upgraded other departments, such as nutrition and health food centers, wicker shops, unpainted furniture, hard- and softcover book assortments, and stationery and greeting card departments. These were designed to take advantage of demographic trends. An expansion of the number of K mart pharmacies and automotive service departments was also begun.

Changes for K mart Corporation were not limited to adjustments within the company's discount store chain. The corporation began diversifying into other businesses designed to improve the company's profit performance. K mart Corporation purchased two cafeteria-style restaurant chains, Furr's Cafeteria and Bishop's Buffet, and began expanding the number of these outlets. This move was taken because K mart management believed that eating away from the home would continue to be a growing aspect of American life. Furthermore, these restaurant chains offered low-priced, homestyle cooking, something K mart management thought fit well with K mart's image. Following the lead of Sears, K mart introduced K mart Insurance Services to several stores in the South. The corporation was also moving into new forms of retailing to compete directly with the new off-price outlets. In 1982, K mart began opening off-price women's apparel stores, called Designer Depots, which offered only national brand clothing at discount prices. The company was also developing new discount gift shops, called Accents. These stores offered top-of-the-line home fashions and accessories, such as Limoge china and Oneida silver, at discount prices. K mart also entered into a joint venture with Hechinger Company of Washington, D.C., to develop large, free-standing warehouse-style discount home centers, to be called Builders Square.

Changes were also made in the message delivered by K mart's $580 million advertising budget. K mart advertising had long focused on telling customers of special low prices on specific items within the store. The goods advertised were often special loss-leader items designed to bring buyers into the stores, hoping that they would purchase other items while there as well as those products specially priced. In its change in advertising message, K mart began to advertise whole categories of goods or entire departments within the store. Especially featured in the ads were higher-ticketed, upscale merchandise. K mart wanted its customers to know that the chain now carried better-quality merchandise in departments that offered shoppers a wider range of goods to choose from than ever before.

K mart's Concerns

While trying to better attract those customers with higher incomes and an interest in purchasing products of higher price and value, K mart had to be careful not to alienate its traditional customers who came to its stores for low prices. K mart executives were concerned that the firm might have the same problems that W. T. Grant and Sears had when they upgraded the products in their stores. W. T. Grant's image with consumers became confused. Shoppers were not certain whether the chain was still in the discount business or was becoming a regular department store. W. T. Grant went out of business. When Sears increased the quality and price points on its merchandise, lower-income customers left Sears for discount stores. To win these shoppers back, Sears promoted bargains aggressively, but found its traditional shoppers returned to buy the bargains but little else. K mart did not want to confuse or alienate its traditional customer base. K mart's management was strong in its assertion that the chain was not "upscaling" as these competitors had done. It was not trying to bring in new shoppers, but just to provide the merchandise its present customers wanted. As explained by Mr. Fauber in late 1985,

> Many people studying K mart failed to understand the difference between "trading up," offering a higher-priced product at a higher margin, and K mart's approach of "updating," which was selling a higher-priced product, yes, but at our normal markup, and in the process giving the consumer a better value even than before.

K mart management was also concerned that a low-price, low-fashion, low-quality image could not be easily erased, especially during a period of high competitiveness within the industry. It was a difficult problem to balance the need to let consumers know that the stores had new merchandise of higher quality to offer while not stressing this message to the point where it alienated the company's traditional customer base. K mart needed to convince both the customers who had always relied on K mart for price and those that it was trying to attract more spending from that K mart had become a "smarter place to shop." This message would take time to get across to consumers.

The process of establishing a new image for K mart was made even more difficult by the time it took to make the physical changes in store layout, merchandise display, and merchandise purchasing for a chain of over 2,000 stores. One hundred and twenty-six crews were employed to transform the stores. In 1983, 715 Home Electronic Centers were in place, with another 750 planned for that year. In 1984, 650 Kitchen Korners, 125 Homecare Centers, and several hundred Bed and Bath departments were scheduled for completion. The entire changeover of the chain would take more than five years. The cost of refurbishing a store ran between $80,000 and $500,000. Three hundred million dollars was planned for this program in 1983 alone. The total cost of store renovations would be in excess of $1.25 billion for the period 1981 to 1986. Even spending at this pace, the length of time it took to complete the in-store changes delayed K mart's ability to present a new, chainwide image to the public. It would only confuse consumers to see brand name products in K mart ads if these products were not yet in their local store.

The question also remained as to how far K mart could go toward upgrading the quality and price of the products it sold. By 1984, the specialty departments within K marts were achieving and often surpassing management's goal of sales of $200 per square foot of sales space. Could the merchandise mix be even further raised, resulting in even better sales results? By continued merchandise mix trials, K mart management soon realized that there were limits to what consumers were willing to buy in a K mart store. For example, they found customers unwilling to purchase such items as down pillows or $50 blankets in K mart Bed and Bath departments. Shoppers who purchased items like these bought them in regular department stores or in linen specialty shops.

K mart shoppers looked for synthetic-filled pillows and blankets with a top price range of $25. K mart management believed that the stores had to carry predominantly common merchandise mixes across the country. This meant that products that were carried in K marts were carried in all 2,000 stores, and therefore were purchased in massive volumes. There was little room to take gambles on the merchandise to be purchased for the chain. Before an order for a certain product was placed, K mart management wanted to be sure the item would sell.

Opinions of K mart's Success

Opinions expressed in national retailing and business magazines and reports by executives in the retailing industry and industry analysts about what success K mart could expect from all the changes the company had made were as varied as the number of types of retail organizations that existed to serve the American consumer. Excerpts from some of these publications and reports are given below to show some of the controversy that existed regarding K mart's future.

> The hopeful view is that Fauber's moves will yield a resumption of K mart's swift growth and ample profitability. . . . The counterview is that K mart in 1983 is simply grasping for straws. Fauber seems to recognize that the old strategy of forced-draft expansion no longer works. But so far he's replaced it with assorted remedies, not with a well-defined growth strategy. Not with the kind of game plan that made K mart the retailing phenomenon of the 1960s and early 1970s.
>
> Stephen Taub
> *Financial World*
> March 31, 1983

> Other retailers have a stronger position, better profitability, know what they are doing, and have a game plan that's working.
>
> Jeffrey Edelman
> Smith Barney

> Will there be enough off-price merchandise available to meet K mart's huge needs? Will makers of quality-name clothes want to have their merchandise associated with the K mart image? Will the new, more label-conscious customers K mart hopes to attract respond to its bait?
>
> David Taylor
> Prudential-Bache

> The success of private labels hinges on the store's reputation for quality.
>
> Standard & Poor's Industry Surveys
> *Retailing Industry*
> July 4, 1985

> The demographic trends are not going K mart's way. To retailing analysts, the most attractive customer group in the near future will be the fast-growing popula-tion of 25- to 44-year-old college graduates living in suburbia and making

$20,000 to $35,000 a year from professional and managerial jobs. The typical K mart customer is a blue-collar high school graduate in the $15,000 to $25,000 income bracket. K mart is at the wrong place at the wrong time.

> Fred Wintzer, Jr.
> Lehman Brothers' Kuhn Loeb

On competition, I've seen a definite move toward upgrading. We're not doing that. We're trying to maintain our niche, while several competitors are going after more of the middle- and maybe slightly higher-than-middle-income customer. Hopefully, they will leave more customers on the lower end for us. What we are doing is emphasizing customer treatment, obviously making our store a nicer place to shop in. That's an important factor.

> President of Wal-Mart Stores
> *Discount Merchandiser*
> September 1985

Asked where the blue-collar people will go for their apparel, K mart replies: "We are still going to maintain those price points that K mart is famous for. They may be on the back of the rack, but they are going to be there. We are not going to avoid them."

> *Discount Merchandiser*
> July 1984

K mart sales per square foot improved 9 percent in 1983 to $155, following a 3 percent decline in 1982. A more upward movement is indicated by the 5.5 percent increase in comparable store sales for the first quarter of 1984. In the case of some remodeled stores, sales have been running 40 percent better than a year ago. How much of the improvement is due to remodeling and how much is due to a change in merchandise is a fine point, and not entirely relevant so long as productivity climbs.

> *Chain Store Age Executive*
> August 1984

People usually think of the K mart customer as a blue-collar worker whose wife works and has a household income of about $22,000 a year. But the K mart customer is the customer who works and lives near the store.

> Mr. Samuel G. Leftwich
> President of K mart Corporation

Our stores are changing faster than ever before. We're not doing Saks or Lord & Taylor or an upscale department store. We're upgrading, but keeping within our customers' price point.

> Larry Parkin
> Chairman and CEO of K mart Apparel

K mart feels that it has gained new and better-heeled customers. Citing Simmons' research, the company says that 23.3 percent of K mart customers in 1980 had family incomes from $25,000 to $40,000, but by the end of 1984, the new program and advertising had pushed that customer income figure up to 28.1 percent. Also, in 1980 only 8.3 percent of K mart's customers had annual incomes of $40,000 or more. Now, that share has risen to 18.9 percent, according to the company.

Chain Store Age Executive
August 1984

The notion of quality is, by no means, an easy one to nail down. As Fauber says, it is a concept influenced in a number of ways through "convenience, store ambience, advertising, availability of product, service, and employee attitude."

Discount Merchandiser
September 1985

The difficulty of K mart's task in presenting a new image to America can be shown by the round of applause and laughter the following jokes received when they were included in Johnny Carson's monologue in February 1986:

You know, K mart has made a lot of changes. They now offer valet parking at the front door for your pickup. Inside, I see that they have gotten rid of the used underwear bin. They've made a lot of new room by getting rid of the checkout where you could exchange livestock for household appliances. You notice the change right away—as soon as you walk in, you hear over the loudspeaker, "Pardonez moi, K mart shoppers. . . ."

Case 14

Otis NAO: Modernization*

In 1986, after months of bidding and negotiation, the Waldorf-Astoria Hotel in New York City awarded the Otis Elevator Company with a $5 million contract to modernize the hotel's 27 existing units. The contract (Otis's largest modernization job to date) called for the replacement of the old electro-mechanical controllers with Otis Elevonic® microprocessor controllers and the installation of new cabs made from exotic woods with custom-designed brass car controls. The modernization job was to take place in four phases, the first scheduled to begin in November 1986 and the last to be completed by September 1988. During the entire operation, the elevators in the Waldorf-Astoria had to be available for continual use, so Otis would need to schedule work around the hotel's busiest periods and ensure that some cars in each elevator bank were operational at all times.

Securing the Waldorf-Astoria modernization contract was a time-consuming and complex task. Otis escorted Waldorf-Astoria representatives to the prestigious Wrigley Building in Chicago, in order to demonstrate the superior performance of another Elevonic® system in operation. They also took trips to Eastern Car, Inc. in Cincinnati, Ohio (the vendor completing the cab renovations), to tour the assembly operations, and to Farmington, Connecticut, to meet with Otis senior management. Throughout the negotiations, several trips were made to Otis's main production facility in Bloomington, Indiana, to ensure that all phases of the job could be completed on time. According to Jack Taylor, who managed the modernization project for Otis in New York, "We got the job because we were the company that could best combine the hotel's tradition of

* This case was prepared by James M. Lattin, Associate Professor of Marketing and Management Science, Graduate School of Business, Stanford University, and George Von Klan, Branch Manager Far West Region, Otis Elevator Company. Financial figures do not represent the actual financial results or performance of the companies detailed herein. The actual names of competing firms, vendor companies, and individuals have been disguised. Copyright © 1989 by the Board of Trustees of the Leland Stanford University. All rights reserved. Used with permission.

elegance with state-of-the-art technology, and complete the project on time and within the established budget.'' In addition to the modernization job, the Waldorf-Astoria also signed a five-year, full-service maintenance contract with Otis.

Despite the success of the Waldorf-Astoria project, modernization had historically been a minor business segment for Otis (especially in North America). Otis was organized to manufacture and install equipment in new construction and to provide service and maintenance for existing equipment, and the company was a market leader in both areas. However, a recent study commissioned by Otis suggested that there might be considerable potential in the modernization market, and these findings gave Otis management cause to rethink the company's approach to modernization.

Otis Elevator: Company Background

Otis Elevator Company took its name from the inventor of the safety elevator, Elisha Graves Otis, who founded the firm in 1853. In subsequent years, the company introduced a number of elevator innovations, including the first electric elevator in 1889, the first gearless traction elevator in 1903, and the first use of signal control in 1924. Over the years, Otis developed its reputation as the industry leader, devoting itself to the design, manufacture, installation, and service of elevators, escalators, and moving sidewalks.

In 1985, Otis was the world's largest elevator company. In the global market, (estimated at $9.5 billion, 60 percent of which is service and the remainder new equipment), Otis recorded sales of $1.9 billion. Otis's share of the worldwide revenues from the sales of new elevator equipment was 22 percent. Otis also maintained approximately 17 percent of the 3.3 million elevators and escalators installed worldwide. Eight of the ten tallest buildings in the world used Otis elevators. The company carefully nurtured its reputation for high quality, and priced its products and services at a premium relative to its competition in most markets.

Otis was divided into four separate operating divisions: North American Operations, Latin American Operations, Pacific Area Operations, and Europe Transcontinental Operations. Unless specifically mentioned otherwise, the remainder of this case deals with the elevator market and Otis's activities in North America.

North American Operations (NAO)

NAO was comprised of the United States and Canada, with sales of new equipment and service totaling over $743 million in 1985 (approximately 40 percent of worldwide sales). NAO sold its products and services directly to the customer through a network of 180 district and branch offices (hereafter called *field offices*). Field offices performed activities at virtually every stage of the elevator life cycle: recommending the type and configuration of equipment initially sold to the customer, installing the equipment, maintaining the equipment over the life of the building, and in some cases refurbishing or upgrading the equipment (also called *modernization*). Field offices varied in size from two or three people in a small town to a few hundred people in a major metropolitan area. Field offices were operated as profit centers.

In addition to the field offices, NAO was divided into five regions whose function was to both direct and support the field offices. The organization is diagrammed in Exhibit 1. Regions were also operated as profit centers, and were headed up by a vice president who reported directly to the president—NAO. Regional offices supported the field offices by:

- Assisting with planning and control items like budgeting and payroll.
- Providing technical sales support in the form of engineering expertise.
- Performing ''value added'' processing activities such as drafting, contracting, estimation, and ordering.
- Overseeing sales activity for the various field offices.

EXHIBIT 1 Otis NAO: organization

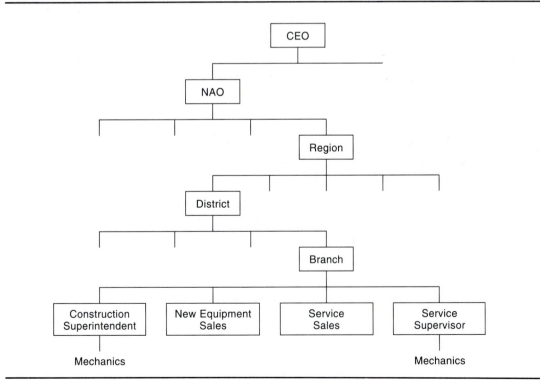

The marketing function at NAO was headed up by the vice president of marketing, whose staff consisted of about 30 individuals. The Communications Group made up the largest portion of the marketing department and was responsible for promotional materials, public relations activities, and employee newsletters. There were other smaller marketing departments, each made up of a handful of individuals, dealing with New Equipment Product Management, Service Operations, and Market Planning.

NAO Organization: New Equipment

New Equipment, as its name implies, consisted of selling and installing new elevators and escalators in newly constructed buildings. New equipment was not the most labor-intensive part of Otis's business. Materials generally accounted for about 60 percent of the costs associated with new equipment, with labor accounting for the remaining 40 percent. Different elevator technologies were appropriate for different end uses, including the following.

Hydraulic elevators. Designed for use in low-rise buildings (up to six stories), these elevators rarely exceeded speeds of 150 feet per minute. The hydraulic market was largely dependent upon construction of low-rise office buildings and apartments. In recent years Otis had increased hydraulic market share by introducing a standardized product of lower cost.

Geared elevators. These units, typically installed in mid-rise buildings (up to 20 stories), travelled at speeds up to 400 feet per minute. The geared market was dependent on both office and apartment construction. Recently, Otis had become concerned with the cost-competitiveness of its geared product offerings. NAO was planning to introduce a new geared product by late 1987 or early 1988.

Gearless elevators. These elevators were designed for buildings over 10 stories and travelled at speeds up to 1800 feet per minute. The gearless market was extremely dependent upon office space construction. In recent years competition in this category had been characterized by severe price pressure. Otis was the technological and market leader for gearless elevators, where its products offered superior performance, principally in speed and dispatching capabilities.

Escalators. Otis also manufactured and installed escalators. Escalator sales were dependent upon retail construction, which typically lagged residential construction.

The following table shows the product by applications mix for new elevators prevailing in 1985:

	Fewer than 5 floors	5–20 floors	More than 20 floors
Hydraulic	72%	28%	0%
Geared	22	76	2
Gearless	0	48	52

In 1985, the total size of the new equipment market (unit volume of elevators and escalators) was 19,679 (of which there were 1615 gearless elevators, 4,599 geared elevators, and 12,405 hydraulic elevators). In dollar terms, the new equipment market in 1985 was $1.364 billion (with $325 million in gearless, $468 million in geared, and $473 in hydraulic). Because of the competition in the industry, gross margins on new equipment were often less than 10 percent.

In 1985, Otis's approximate market share of the industry unit volume was 20 percent in the hydraulic and geared markets and 40 percent in the gearless market (down from its usually higher market share due to foreign competition entering the North American market).

Sales. New equipment was sold by a sales force of new equipment sales representatives who worked out of Otis's field offices, serving all building segments (apartments, offices, shopping centers, hospitals, hotels, airports, etc).

For smaller projects, such as a few hydraulic elevators, the elevator manufacturer was selected by either the general contractor, architect or building owner. As project size increased, such as for the construction of a high-rise office building, all three parties were often involved in making the decision about what company to buy elevators from. Also, as project size increased, factors such as technology, quality, and reputation became more important, and the complexity of the selling task increased. For these larger projects, new equipment representatives relied on OtisPlan®, a computer program used to simulate elevator performance. OtisPlan® helped determine the optimal elevator configuration for a building based on layout, population estimates, and traffic conditions, while still maximizing net rental space.

The sales process consisted of coming up with a bid proposal that would be accepted over the competition, based on price, equipment performance, and installation schedule. If a proposal was accepted, the new equipment representative was responsible for staying in contact with the customer until construction was completed and the elevator installation was turned over to the customer. Most new equipment included New Installation Service (NIS), an initial maintenance contract (typically for one year) included in the new equipment price. Once the equipment installation was finished and covered by NIS, the customer became the responsibility of a service sales representative.

Successful new equipment representatives developed a network of relationships with builders in their area to stay on top of new construction activity. They also relied on *Dodge Reports* for listings of new construction projects.

Market. The market demand for new elevators and escalators was highly dependent upon office and apartment construction. Together these construction segments comprised almost 80 percent of the total dollar value of elevator and escalator sales in typical years.

Sustainable demand for office space through 1991 was projected to average 250 million square feet annually. Actual new capacity additions had exceeded this amount over the past five years (since 1981). The accumulated surplus office space was reflected in high vacancy rates in most cities, with national rates at 16.5 percent in downtown areas and 22.0 percent in suburban areas. It was expected that it would take three or four years before the excess capacity could be absorbed. The high level of market saturation and the uncertainty arising from tax reforms (which might reduce the benefits of accelerated depreciation) were also expected to reduce the amount of new construction activity. According to DRI, office construction and apartment construction were forecast to decline through 1988 (see Exhibit 2). There was also some concern over the possibility of a recession around 1990.

EXHIBIT 2 DRI construction forecast
(million square feet)

Date	Office building	Apartment building
Actual		
1983	285	690
1984	320	760
1985	330	725
Forecast		
1986	260	640
1987	200	550
1988	170	510
1989	180	560

New equipment sales for Otis NAO had more or less followed construction activity from 1983 to 1985. With the forecasted decline in construction, new equipment sales were expected to drop to $289 million in 1986 and as low or lower in 1987 and 1988. Increasing pressure from competition was expected to keep margins on new equipment sales at low levels.

NAO Organization: Service

Service consisted of those activities that were performed after the elevator was installed and turned over to the customer. In contrast to new equipment, service was much more labor intensive. Roughly two-thirds of the costs associated with a full-service maintenance contract was labor; the remaining third was materials.

Two important types of service were contractual maintenance and repair. Contractual maintenance referred to contracts that were sold to building owners or property management firms to maintain the elevators in their buildings. In

NAO, contractual maintenance made up approximately 75 percent of service revenues and was the single-largest source of profits. Given that elevators usually lasted the life of the building, which could be 40 years or more, it was not surprising that maintenance was such an important business segment.

When evaluating different elevator companies, maintenance customers were typically concerned with minimizing service interruptions, reducing exposure to liability, and extending the life of their equipment. Otis maintenance was perceived by many to be the best in the industry, and was priced at a premium. Gross margins on service could run as high as 40 percent. The Otis "full service" contracts guaranteed that the elevators covered would be maintained to like-new performance specifications.

Otis tracked its net gains in maintenance contracts from year to year by adding up the number of contracts gained from *conversion* (those customers converted to Otis maintenance following the expiration of the initial NIS period) and *recapture* (those customers convinced to switch to Otis maintenance) and subtract the number of contracts lost to *cancellation*. Since 1983, the annual number of contracts gained from conversion approximately equaled the number of contracts gained from recapture. During the same period, the number of cancellations held steady at about 4,000 per year.

The major portion of Otis's maintenance portfolio consisted of equipment manufactured by Otis (see Exhibit 3). The standard term for a maintenance contract was five years, although contracts could be written for longer or shorter periods.

Repairs not covered by the Otis maintenance contract (which were performed at the customer's expense) were typically billed to the customer based on time and materials, with a markup for profit added on. If no major components of an elevator system were to be replaced and the total was less than

EXHIBIT 3 Installed elevators and escalators in North America
(by maintenance contract)

	1983	1984	1985
Maintained by Otis			
Otis	76,105	76,934	75,075
Other	8,954	9,734	12,537
Maintained by other major			
Otis	21,320	22,365	23,500
Other	142,680	145,533	150,650
Maintained by regional/independent			
Otis	42,101	42,588	45,200
Other	122,899	126,412	127,228
No maintenance contract			
Otis	28,189	27,763	32,404
Other	73,811	77,737	74,996
Total installed base			
Otis	167,715	169,650	176,179
Other	348,344	359,416	365,411
Total	516,059	529,066	541,590

Source: Company records.

$10,000, then work would usually be billed "open order." Open order repairs were rarely bid by competitors, and often consisted of routine items. Gross margins on open order repairs were similar to the margins on contractual maintenance. Open order work was usually completed fairly quickly.

Sales. Otis relied on its force of service sales representatives in its field offices to sell maintenance contracts. Service sales was usually an entry-level job in the Otis sales organization and once a service sales representative gained sufficient experience, he or she would often be promoted to new equipment sales. Service sales representatives covered a much larger customer base than new equipment representatives and the dollar value of the individual contracts they sold was smaller.

Market. Compared to new equipment, the contractual maintenance market was quite stable year to year, growing at an annual rate of less than 3 percent (see Exhibit 3). In 1985, the installed base of elevators and escalators in North America exceeded 540,000; in dollar terms, total industry service sales in 1985 totaled $1783 million.

For Otis NAO, service sales had been growing steadily over the past three years and were expected to continue to grow to $423 million in 1986.

NAO Organization: Field Operations

Otis had a substantial labor force of trained mechanics who performed construction and service work. Among NAO's 8,800 employees in 1985, 2,200 were new construction mechanics and 3,300 were service mechanics. Elevator mechanics were regarded as skilled tradespeople, and were paid accordingly, with wages over $30.00 per hour in some parts of the country. Otis was acknowledged to have the best-trained mechanics in the industry. All Otis mechanics were members of the International Union of Elevator Constructors (IUEC).

Mechanics working in new construction were the most affected by swings in the level of local construction activity, whereas mechanics working in service were usually employed throughout the year. Mechanics reported to a supervisor who was usually a former mechanic who had moved into management, and was responsible for providing technical and administrative support.

Maintenance mechanics were assigned a "route," which consisted of various buildings whose elevators the mechanic maintained, and the units within each route were assigned to one mechanic only. A typical route might have 50 or so units. The maintenance mechanic played an important role within Otis aside from performing maintenance, since he was continually in contact with the Otis maintenance customers on the route. Although profitability could be calculated by route, it was difficult to calculate the actual profitability of individual maintenance contracts. Informally, however, the maintenance mechanics and their supervisors were aware of which maintenance contracts were the most or least troublesome.

Once a year the maintenance supervisor visited each contractee to perform a maintenance survey, consisting of an inspection of the elevator and a review of the work completed by the mechanic. The survey also resulted in a letter to the customer identifying any work needed on the elevators but not included in the maintenance contract. Another, more limited review of maintenance was performed directly by NAO headquarters personnel, who inspected randomly selected contracts every two years in each field office. This served to ensure maintenance quality consistent with company and customer expectations.

One of the main issues facing the Otis service organization was the level of "callbacks" within Otis NAO. Callbacks were calls by maintenance customers to Otis due to a problem or interruption in service (such as an elevator shutdown) and were the greatest cause of customer dissatisfaction with Otis maintenance. In order to dispatch mechanics more effectively when callbacks occurred, OtisLine® was introduced in 1983. OtisLine® was a centralized 24-hour toll-free trouble-shooting and dispatching service operated out of NAO headquarters in Farmington. OtisLine® was also used to collect data on different types of callbacks by field office, cause of callback, and type of unit. It was estimated that there were five callbacks per unit per year within NAO, and that on average each callback consumed two to three hours of a mechanic's time.

Competition

Otis faced competition from several major elevator companies, as well as many smaller regional and independent companies.

Mason Elevator was Otis's strongest competitor in North America, with elevator-related profits in 1985 of $51.9 million. Mason was the market share leader in the hydraulic and geared new equipment, and number two in the gearless market. Mason's strengths were its proven products and its ability to price competitively to gain market share. Mason had been particularly successful at developing products that were easy to install, and in offering pre-engineered elevators that incorporated expensive options as standard. Mason's activity was limited primarily to North America, with only 6 percent of the global new equipment market.

Consolidated's Elevator Division was traditionally NAO's strongest competitor, although over the past decade its position had been deteriorating. Recently, Consolidated had acquired Trotter, one of the largest regional modernization contractors in the United States. Consolidated had the second largest installed base of elevators in North America.

Osaka, a Japanese elevator manufacturer, entered the U.S. market in 1982. They had been a vigorous competitor in the gearless markets in selected metropolitan areas, where they often bid jobs at substantially less than Otis's cost. Osaka seemed to be determined to establish a position in the North American market, despite the presence of well-established competitors and enormous start-up costs. Osaka focused on ride comfort and quietness as its main selling points, and was viewed favorably by building managers and developers regarding quality and technological capability. In 1985, Osaka had 15.7 percent share of the North American gearless market.

Winkler, headquartered in Europe, was the second-largest elevator manufacturer in the world, and was the number one player in many markets in Europe. Winkler had 11 percent of the global new equipment market; in recent years, they had become a more vigorous competitor in North America by acquiring smaller regional companies and pricing very competitively.

Nippon Elevator was the largest Japanese elevator manufacturer. Although Nippon's market share in North America was very small, its entry into the U.S. market was seen as a potential threat by Otis NAO. Nippon was offering technologically sophisticated products such as their latest variable frequency drive geared elevator and their new spiral-type escalator. Nippon had been concentrating its efforts on a limited number of new equipment projects in California. Nippon had 6 percent of the global new equipment market.

Regional contractors were smaller firms that limited their activity to a certain geographical area. Within the given area, they were often quite established. Regional firms were successful in hydraulic and geared new equipment, where they were able to offer a relatively simple product at a lower price than the major manufacturers. Regional firms also competed with the major national firms by offering maintenance contracts for name brand equipment. They typically offered less comprehensive maintenance than the major manufacturers at two-thirds the price.

Because major manufacturers such as Otis focused their efforts primarily on larger projects involving their own brand of equipment, regional contractors were often quite successful in addressing specialized market segments neglected by the major manufacturers. These firms often had capable engineering staffs which included modernization specialists. Some regional firms had developed preengineered modernization packages, which helped reduce the amount of time elevators had to be taken out of service when performing modernization work.

Regional firms had their own field force of mechanics (usually IUEC). Overall, regional contractors were able to offer competitive performance for projects that did not require state of the art technology or large financial resources.

In addition to the regional contractors, there were smaller, independent contractors, consisting typically of the owner, a designer and a few mechanics (maybe IUEC—non-union mechanics were paid substantially less than union mechanics and were less skilled). Independents usually had no engineering staff, and were not involved in the new equipment market. Their prices for maintenance contracts were 25 percent to 35 percent lower than the regional contractors.

Declines in Otis NAO service margins in recent years were attributed in part to increased costs (such as product liability, workers' compensation insurance, FICA, SUI, FUI, etc) and greater competition. Exhibit 4 provides additional information concerning new equipment and contractual maintenance market shares for Otis NAO and its competitors.

EXHIBIT 4 New equipment sales and contractual maintenance (by company): North America

New equipment sales (units)

	1983	1984	1985	1986*
Otis	4,442	4,868	4,714	3,833
Mason	6,264	6,326	6,786	5,878
Consolidated	2,374	1,985	1,948	1,523
American	1,659	1,428	1,623	1,431
Standard	731	327	338	284
Winkler	733	969	503	465
Osaka	43	261	460	496
Nippon Elevator	0	0	19	55
Other	3,661	3,023	3,288	2,753
Total	19,907	19,187	19,679	16,718

Contractual maintenance (units)

	1983	1984	1985	1986*
Otis	85,050	86,668	87,612	89,134
Mason	34,900	37,000	39,300	41,500
Consolidated	37,500	38,500	39,900	40,800
American	29,000	29,200	29,750	30,500
Standard	8,200	8,150	8,200	8,300
Winkler	23,400	24,750	25,400	26,000
Osaka	0	0	450	850
Nippon Elevator	0	0	0	0
Other Major	31,000	30,298	31,150	31,050
Regional/Independent	165,000	169,000	172,428	175,333

* Forecast.
Source: Company records.

Elevator consultants. In the past decade or so, elevator consulting firms had become a significant factor in the elevator industry. These were relatively small firms whose principals often had over 20 years experience in the elevator industry, usually with major manufacturers. They specialized in assisting building owners with elevator decisions (e.g., by recommending the carrying capacity, speed, location, and brand of elevators for a new building). There was sometimes an adversarial relationship between consultants and industry sales representatives.

Modernization

Modernization, simply defined, was the renovation of elevator systems to improve appearance or performance. The appearance of an elevator system could be enhanced by replacing or refurbishing cab interiors, lighting, hallway entrances, and fixtures (e.g., hall buttons and position indicators). The performance of an elevator system could be improved through the use of technological advances to decrease waiting times, reduce elevator crowding, and improve the comfort of the ride.

One of the most common performance modernization items involved upgrading the elevator controller (a device that controlled the acceleration, deceleration, and direction of the elevator; where there was more than one elevator, a "group" controller was needed to coordinate the dispatching of the elevators to calls at different floors). Replacing or overlaying an electromechanical controller with a microprocessor controller could result in a 25 percent to 50 percent improvement in elevator service. Performance modernization projects often also included upgrading or replacing door mechanisms, power supplies, hoist ropes, car frames, and rails.

Modernization projects varied in size from minor appearance improvements (costing a few thousand dollars per car) to very large performance projects involving replacement of one or more components in all the elevators of a large building (costing $100,000 to $200,000 per car). A large performance modernization project required at least eight months for design, bidding, and negotiation and another eight months to complete construction. Major projects also required considerable technical and marketing expertise. The variety and degree of customization of larger modernization projects made them more difficult to understand and manage than either new equipment sales or service sales.

Modernization appealed to building owners and managers because it allowed them to improve tenant satisfaction, retain and attract tenants, and increase lease revenues. Modernization sometimes also appealed to building owners and managers simply because they could no longer obtain parts for their old elevators.

In choosing a company to perform modernization work, owners and managers typically looked at a number of different characteristics:

- The contractor's reputation and skill in similar modernization jobs.
- Price.
- Bid responsiveness, with respect to scope, reaction time and follow up.
- Availability and price of subsequent maintenance contract (customers often purchased a maintenance contract from the firm that modernized their equipment).
- Familiarity with equipment through current service contract.
- Personal relationship with contractor.
- Referrals from other owners.
- Conformity with owner's schedule (there was usually a rush to complete modernization projects once they were started in order to minimize the disruption of elevator service to building tenants).

The Modernization Market

In the mid 1980s, the market for modernization began to attract the attention of Otis NAO. In 1984, management commissioned Industrial Marketing Consultants, Inc. (IMC) to do a study on the potential of the modernization market and the possible opportunities for Otis. IMC examined the characteristics and size of the modernization market in cities (including New York and Boston) where the installed base of elevators was older on average. In 1984, New York City had the largest installed base of elevators (nearly 52,500 units) of any city in North America. There were 22,500 elevators in place in 15,000 apartment/condo buildings, 11,000 elevators in 1,500 commercial office buildings, and 1,500 elevators in 500 hotels. In 1984, Boston's installed base was less than 7,000 units.

Market characteristics. In their survey, IMC found that customer attitudes toward modernization varied substantially, as shown in Exhibit 5. IMC

EXHIBIT 5   Customer Attitudes toward Modernization

Description	Agent	Service	Modernization attitudes
Residential			
Condos	Owners	O&G	Fix as breaks
Apartment building	Owners/Management	POG	Cosmetic; keep leased
Commercial			
Office/single	Direct maintenance	Full	Best; minimize time in elevator
Office/multi	Owner/Developer	Full	Cosmetic first; service to keep tenant
Hotel	Direct maintenance	Full	Stay competitive; highly cosmetic

Notes:

O&G stands for "oil and grease," the least expensive service offering.

POG stands for "parts, oil, and grease," about half the cost of full service maintenance.

Source: Industrial Marketing Consultants, 1984.

also found a wide range of modernization activity. In NYC, jobs ranged from as little as $5,000 or less (refurbishing cab interior) to as much as $200,000–$350,000 (complete cab, controller, door operator, and machine rehab). A list of modernization projects, and their approximate price ranges, is shown in Exhibit 6. IMC estimated that the likelihood of securing a maintenance contract following a modernization job varied with the size of the job. Following a small job (6 stop), the likelihood that Otis would come away with a maintenance contract was estimated to be 50 percent. However, the success rate increased to 85 percent for the larger performance modernization jobs.

EXHIBIT 6   Typical modernization projects in New York City in 1984

Project (number of stops)	Value (thousands)
Cab interior (6)	under $5
Controller and door operator (6)	$ 5–$15
Controller, door operator, and machine rehab (6)	$ 15–$40
Overlay and door operator (25)	$ 40–$60
Group controller and door operator (25)	$ 60–$100
Controller, door operator, and machine rehab (25)	$100–$150
Controller, door operator, and machine rehab (50)	$200–$350

Source: Industrial Marketing Consultants, 1984.

While studying the market in New York City, IMC found that the majority of modernization projects were relatively small in size (less than $40,000) and mostly in residential buildings. Projects over $40,000 were mainly commercial in nature. Exhibit 7 shows the price distribution of all 2,665 modernization projects undertaken in New York City in 1984. Over 80 percent of modernization revenues came from commercial buildings (average project size $100,000) and 20 percent from residential buildings (average project size $11,000). IMC estimated that New York City alone accounted for 20 percent to 25 percent of the modernization market in North America.

EXHIBIT 7 Distribution of modernization projects in New York City in 1984

Project Value (thousands)	Number of Projects	Approx Total Value (millions)
Under $5	600	$ 2
$ 5–$15	900	$ 7
$ 15–$40	300	$ 7
$ 40–$60	400	$ 20
$ 60–$100	150	$ 14
$100–$150	225	$ 32
$150–$200	50	$ 9
$200–$350	40	$ 9
	2,665	$100

Source: Industrial Marketing Consultants, 1984.

Competition. IMC found that regional contractors had traditionally been most successful in their pursuit of modernization. In NYC, for example, four regional contractors accounted for 46 percent of the modernization market in 1984 (each doing more modernization business than any major elevator company). In Boston, three regional contractors accounted for half of the 1984 modernization market.

Competitive margins on modernization varied dramatically, depending upon the size of the project. Very large performance modernization projects (those in excess of $150,000) were competitively priced like new equipment, with gross margins below 10 percent. Small appearance modernization jobs (less than $15,000) were priced more like full maintenance contracts, such that gross margins ranged from 25 percent to 40 percent. Projects in between were priced with gross margins ranging between 10 percent and 25 percent.

IMC found that elevator consultants played a very important role in the modernization decision. Elevator consultants were virtually always retained by owners for large modernization projects, since the consultants' expertise was often useful in understanding how to combine the older technology in a client's existing elevator system with various new technologies in order to increase the performance of the elevator system in a reliable, timely, and cost effective manner. In NYC, over 80 percent of the total contract value of modernization in 1984 involved elevator consultants.

Decisions on Modernization

In 1986, the important question for Otis NAO management was not *whether or not* to pursue modernization, but *how*. Several key questions needed to be answered.

- *What are the advantages for Otis of a full-scale modernization effort?* The first step for NAO management involved defining the company's strategic objectives with respect to modernization. Such a strategic direction was necessary before Otis could go about designing a modernization program and putting it into place.
- *How should Otis organize to pursue modernization?* Traditionally, Otis had organized to support its new equipment and service businesses. Should modernization be treated as a separate area or somehow be included into the existing organization? A closely related question involved the responsibility for selling modernization. Service sales representatives had the opportunity to identify new prospects for modernization through direct customer contact or by speaking with the route maintenance mechanic. However, because of the wide range of modernization possibilities, Otis service sales representatives were sometimes unfamiliar with modernization options available to the customer. They also tended to be less experienced than new equipment representatives in handling larger projects.
- *What market segments should be targeted and what modernization products should Otis develop?* For most of its modernization work, NAO either adapted its own new equipment components to modernization applications or purchased components from suppliers. National and local elevator equipment suppliers provided components such as cabs, door mechanisms, fixtures, relay logic controllers, and solid state controllers. Otis had been moderately successful replacing the relay logic controllers on older Otis equipment with its Elevonic® microprocessor controller. NAO was planning to introduce other, less costly products in 1986 designed to offer upgrades in elevator appearance and safety, such as the OtisVoice® (a programmable, electronically synthesized voice message) and the Lambda® door detector (an infrared sensor designed to reverse the elevator door without physical contact with the passenger). Both OtisVoice® and Lambda® had been developed as new equipment products. However, management was concerned that the adaptation of new equipment products might miss some of the opportunities that a dedicated modernization product development effort might catch. Furthermore, the mix of products under development would depend upon what segments of the modernization market were targeted.

Case 15

Leykam Mürztaler*

In February 1989, Dr. Gertrude Eder, marketing manager for Leykam Mürztaler AG, was reviewing a problem that had occupied her thoughts a great deal during the past few months. Although Leykam Mürztaler, like the paper industry in general, had been doing well in recent years, it was her opinion that it was time to think about ways to strengthen the company's ability to prosper as industry growth inevitably began slowing down. In particular, she was considering what recommendations to offer the executive board regarding the firm's branding strategy.

Leykam Mürztaler AG

The past few years had been good for the Leykam Mürztaler Group. Paralleling the industry's increased sales, the firm's total sales had risen from ASch4,842 million[1] in 1983 to ASch7,100 million in 1988, an increase of 47 percent. For Leykam Mürztaler AG, the principal operating component of the group, 1988 revenues had reached ASch 6,300 million, an increase over 1986 of 41 percent, enhanced by the successful startup of a new production line and by above-average growth in demand for high-grade coated woodfree printing papers, the firm's main sales segment.

Leykam Mürztaler AG, together with its predecessor companies, had been a producer of paper for over 400 years. Headquartered in Gratkorn, Austria, the firm produced coated woodfree printing paper and newsprint, with integrated pulp production. Principal mills and offices were located at Gratkorn and Bruck, Austria. Export sales offices for coated woodfree paper were headquartered in Vienna.

---

* This case was written by Professor H. Michael Hayes as a basis for class discussion rather than to illustrate either effective or ineffective handling of an administrative situation. Copyright © 1989 by IMEDE, Lausanne, Switzerland. Used with permission.

[1] ASch12.48 = U.S. $1.00 in December 1988.

In 1988, woodfree papers represented approximately 80 percent of sales, newsprint 13 percent and pulp 7 percent. Twenty-two percent of revenues came from Austria, 56 percent from Western Europe, and 22 percent from exports to the rest of the world (including Eastern Europe). The highest share of exports was for coated woodfree papers at approximately 90 percent.

(Production volumes in 1987 and 1988 are shown in Exhibit 1.) The large increase in production of printing and writing paper in 1988 (to 340,900 tonnes) reflected successful selling of the output of the new coated woodfree paper machine at Gratkorn, with a capacity of 138,000 tonnes per year. The decline in pulp production reflected a change in product mix. External sales of pulp were declining as the company's pulp production was further integrated into the company's own paper production.

EXHIBIT 1 Highlights of the development of the Leykam Mürztaler Group

	1987	1988	Percentage
Production (in tonnes):			
Printing and writing papers	272,900	340,900	+24.9%
Newsprint (Bruck)	98,200	99,200	+1.0
Paper total	371,100	440,100	+18.6
Chemical pulp	209,500	204,500	−2.4
Mechanical pulp	30,900	32,100	+3.9
Deink pulp	58,900	62,700	+6.4
Total sales (gross, in ASch mn):			
Leykam Mürztaler AG	5,234	6,300	+20.4
Export share	4,056	5,100	+25.7
Exports in percent	78%	81%	—
Leykam Mürztaler Group	5,906	7,100	+20.2
Capital expenditure and Prepayments for fixed assets (in ASch mn)	1,418	1,500	+5.8
Cash flow (in ASch mn)	1,020	1,500	+47.1
Employees (excluding apprentices) as of 31 December	2,825	2,865	+1.4

Source: Annual Report.

With the addition of the new production line, the company had become the European market leader in coated woodfree papers, with a market share of 8–10 percent. In December 1987 the supervisory board approved a project to establish a new production line at Bruck to produce mechanical coated printing papers (LWC) for magazines, catalogues, and printed advertising materials. Planned capacity was 135,000 tonnes, to be put into operation at the end of 1989.

Despite the increased level of investment, financial results were very good. In 1987, the last year for which complete financial details were available, profit was down slightly from the previous year (see Exhibit 2), reflecting the greatly increased depreciation charges associated with the new paper machine and the decision to use the reducing-balance method of depreciation for it and some other equipment. Cash flow, however, was close to an all-time record, results were "clearly better than originally forecast," and operating profits were

EXHIBIT 2 Financial results

	1983	1984*	1985†	1986	1987
Total sales (gross, in AS m)	4,842	5,367	5,420	5,187	5,906
Export sales (AS m)	2,973	3,413	3,537	3,331	4,062
Export share of Leykam Mürztaler AG (percent)	69%	72%	74%	74%	78%
Capital investment (AS m)	313	253	444	2,461	1,518
Total depreciation (AS m)	374	344	337	476	1,064
thereof: reducing-balance depreciation (AS m)	—	—	—	125	674
Cash flow (AS m)	373	1,025	959	871	1,020
Profit for the year (AS m)	1	422	81	101	67
Personnel expenditure (AS m)	1,096	993	1,046	1,076	1,231
Number of employees (excluding apprentices) as of 31 December	2,918	2,424	2,364	2,578	2,825
Dividend and bonus (AS m)	—	54	81	101	67
(Percentage)	—	4 + 4%	4 + 8%	4 + 8%	8

* Excluding Niklasdorf Mill.
† Excluding Frohnierten Mill from 1 April 1985.
Source: Annual Report.

near the top of the European woodfree paper producers, on a percentage of sales basis. Preliminary indications were that financial results for 1988 would be still better.

The company marketed its coated products under its MAGNO series brand (e.g., MAGNOMATT, MAGNOPRINT, MAGNOMATT K) principally through wholly owned merchants in Austria and other merchants throughout Western Europe. In addition, it sold to other kinds of merchants in Austria as well as to some printers and publishers directly. Paper merchants were contacted by sales representatives in Vienna and Gratkorn; sales subsidiaries in Germany, Italy, and France; and sales agents in other European countries. Some of its products were sold on a private brand basis to certain large merchants.

Although Leykam Mürztaler served paper markets on a worldwide basis, and planned to enter the LWC market, this case focuses on coated woodfree papers for printing applications in Western Europe.

The Pulp and Paper Industry in Western Europe[2]

Despite its maturity, the pulp and paper industry was undergoing major change. Characterized by high break-even volumes, small fluctuations in demand could significantly impact profits, and there was some evidence that capacity was

---

[2] Western Europe included the countries in the European Community plus Finland, Norway, Sweden, Austria, and Switzerland.

outgrowing demand. Despite the sophistication of paper-making technology, product differentiation was increasingly difficult to achieve. Some paper makers were integrating backwards to control the cost or ensure the supply of pulp. Others were integrating forward, buying paper merchants in order to have better control of marketing. Still others were integrating horizontally to have a more complete product line.

Other changes were affecting the industry as well. Customers were being merged, acquired, or reorganized, thus changing established purchasing patterns. Changes in advertising were impacting traditional usage patterns. Paper merchants were merging to gain economies of scale. Some were emphasizing private brands to reduce their dependence on paper makers. Markets were fragmenting as new, small businesses were forming at a record rate. Consumption patterns were changing. In Europe, consumption ranged from 233 kg per capita in Sweden to 60 in Portugal, but growth rates ranged from a high of 29.4 percent in Greece to a low of 2.4 percent in Denmark. There was some uncertainty about the implications of Europe's move toward a true common market in 1992, although trade barriers were not a significant factor in the industry.

Printing and Writing Paper

In the pulp and paper industry, the major and high-growth segment was printing and writing papers. Both coated and uncoated papers were produced from mechanically or chemically processed pulp to form four broad categories: coated woodfree, mechanical coated,[3] uncoated woodfree, and mechanical uncoated. To be defined as coated, a paper had to have a surface coating of at least 5 grams per square meter (gsm).

Coated woodfree papers represented the highest-quality category, in terms of printability, gloss, feel, ability to reproduce color, and many other characteristics. Grades of coated woodfree papers were not precisely specified, but the industry had established further categories such as cast coated, art paper, standard, and low coated. (See Exhibit 3 for categories and prices.) The standard grade represented the bulk of sales. Within this category, however, there were many gradations—the amount of whiteness, brightness, stiffness, and other characteristics. Leykam Mürztaler competed principally at the high end of the standard grade, but was planning to enter the art paper segment also.

Coated woodfree was the smallest printing and writing paper segment (17.8 percent of total consumption), but it was also the most dynamic, with an average growth rate of 8.4 percent from 1980 to 1987. Expectations were that 1988 consumption would exceed 3 million tonnes.

---

[3] Designated LWC or MWC, depending on the weight, although the dividing line was not precise.

EXHIBIT 3   Prices per tonne (U.S. dollars) of woodfree printing and writing papers in Western Europe (2nd quarter 1987, delivered)

Grade	West Germany	United Kingdom	France	Netherlands
Cast coated, sheets	$2,734	$2,324	$2,588	$2,480
Art paper, sheets	1,897	1,660	1,837	1,736
Standard, sheets	1,283	1,212	1,235	1,166
Standard, reels	1,199	1,145	1,169	1,091
Low coated, sheets	1,172	1,130	1,136	1,066

Note: Cast coated paper was estimated to represent 5 percent of the coated woodfree market, art paper 7–8 percent, standard coated 70 percent and low coated less than 20 percent. Within the standard coated category, actual transaction prices could vary as much as 25 percent as a function of quality and as much as 10 percent due to competitive or other factors.

Source: EKONO Strategic Study, September 1988.

Markets for Printing and Writing Paper

Principal markets for printing and writing paper were magazines (33 percent), direct mail (17 percent), brochures and general print advertising (15 percent), copy paper (11 percent), other office paper (9 percent), and books (5 percent). For coated woodfree papers, it was estimated that advertising, direct and indirect, accounted for 85–90 percent of consumption.[4]

On a country-by-country basis, there was significant variation in the mix of advertising expenditures, however. In the UK, for instance, the bulk of advertising expenditures went to newspapers and TV, whereas in Germany advertising expenditures were split somewhat evenly among newspapers, magazines, catalogues, and direct mail.[5] Major uses for coated woodfree papers were direct mail, brochures, annual reports, etc. The dynamic growth of coated woodfree papers in recent years was largely fueled by the rapid increases in "nonclassical" advertising. Changes in this mix could significantly affect country consumption patterns for coated woodfree papers.

Despite cost pressures and shifts in individual markets and end uses, coated woodfree papers were benefiting from demand for more and better four-color printing as advertisers sought ways to improve the impact of their messages.

The Printing Industry

The vast majority of orders for coated woodfree paper were placed by printers, either on the merchant or directly on the mill. In some instances, however, for very large orders, the order would be placed by either the printer or the publisher, depending on which seemed to have the strongest negotiating position with the supplier.

---

[4] ECC International, Limited, 1987.

[5] Papis Limited.

Selection of paper grade and manufacturer was a complex process that varied significantly according to end use, size of order, and sophistication of both the printer and the specifier or user. Almost without exception, the printer had the final say in the selection of paper make and could significantly influence the grade of paper as well. The specifier (ad agency) or user (advertiser, publisher, mail-order house, etc.) influenced paper selection, particularly with respect to grade, and could also influence selection of make, subject to final agreement by the printer.

For the printer, key paper characteristics were printability and runability. Surface characteristics, whiteness, and brightness were also important. Price was always important, especially when deciding between two suppliers with similar offerings or where paper costs represented a significant portion of the total cost of the printed product. Complaint handling, emergency assistance, speed, and reliability of delivery were key service components. Sales representative knowledge was also important. Within limits, relative importance of decision criteria varied from one country to another. In Italy and the UK, for instance, price and quality tended to be equally important, whereas quality and service factors tended to predominate importance rankings in Switzerland. There was some favoritism given producers for patriotic reasons, but seldom at the expense of quality or price.

The user or specifier considered many of the same characteristics as the printer. Printability and delivery were usually at the top of the list, but the major concern was the paper's suitability for the particular advertising message, within the constraints of the overall advertising budget.

Despite the apparent similarity of products offered by different mills, there was substantial variation in runability, which could only be determined by actual trial. According to one printer:

> The final test is how well the paper prints on our presses. This is a matter of ''fit'' between paper, ink, and press characteristics. We find there are variations between papers that meet the same specifications, which can only be determined by actual trial. This is not cheap as a trial involves printing 3,000 sheets. Because the paper characteristics cannot be completely specified, we like the idea of a mill brand. One time we tested two merchant brands that we thought were different. Then we found out that the paper came from the same mill, so we really wasted our time on the second test.
>
> The merchant's sales representative is important, but we don't need him [or her] to call all that frequently. We like to talk to him [or her] about trends or problems we're having, but when we need something quickly, we call the merchant.
>
> Once we have selected a paper, it is critically important that its quality be consistent. Most suppliers are pretty good. Except for obvious flaws, however, we find they tend to want to blame problems on the ink or the press.

Over the past several years, the number of printers remained relatively constant, at about 15,000–20,000, with decreases from mergers and acquisitions offset by a growth in instant print outlets. In the last 10 years, the number of commercial print customers doubled to over 500,000, half of whom used instant print outlets.

As the number of small businesses and the use of desktop publishing continued to grow, it was suggested that within 10 years traditional printers would perhaps only handle longer-run full-color work. Monochrome and spot color work would be produced in customers' offices, with the paper buying decision being made by people with little knowledge about paper or printing.[6] In-plant printing, however, was not expected to have a significant impact on the coated woodfree market.

Paper Merchants

Printers and publishers were reached in two principal ways: direct sales from the mill and sales from the mill through merchants, either independent or mill-owned. Direct sales were more common for high-volume products sold in reels, such as newsprint and LWC magazine paper. The pattern of distribution was influenced by characteristics of the transaction (see Exhibit 4) and the pattern varied significantly from one country to another (see Exhibit 5). For coated woodfree papers it was estimated that 70–80 percent of sales went through merchants.

EXHIBIT 4 Transaction characteristics—a comparison of the roles of manufacturers and merchants

Characteristics	Manufacturer	Merchant
Order size (kg)	less than 1,500	200–500
Items carried	Small	2,500–5,000
Fixed costs	High	Low
Stock level (kg)	less than 2,000/item	500–1,750
Delivery	Often slow	24 hours
Service	None	Possible
Cash flow	Low	Low

Source: The European Printing and Writing Paper Industry—1987.

EXHIBIT 5 Market shares per distribution channel (percentage)

	Country			
Form of distribution	UK	France	Germany	Italy
Paper mills	48%	50%	59%	80%
Mill-owned merchants	{ 52	50	—	{ 20
Independent merchants		—	41	

Source: The European Printing and Writing Paper Industry—1987.

---

[6] BIS Marketing Research Limited.

As with all wholesalers, stocking to provide quick delivery in small quantities was a principal merchant function. Fragmentation of the fastest-growing market segments (business and small printers) had decreased the average order size and increased demand for a wide choice of paper grades, making it more difficult for mills to directly access these customers.

In warehousing, larger merchants had introduced expensive computer-controlled logistical systems, which reduced delivery times and the cost of preparing orders for delivery. Predictions were made that electronic interchange of information between merchants and their suppliers and larger customers would be the norm within the next few years. Merchants in the UK were spearheading an initiative to achieve industry standards for bar codes throughout Europe.

Changes in end-user profiles and new customer needs had forced merchants to expand the scope of their activities and customer support functions. As a result, the merchants' role broadened to include a number of additional services, including technical advice on paper choice and broader printing problems.

Private branding, supported by advertising, had long been used by some merchants to differentiate their products and service. Some large merchants had also invested in testing apparatus, similar to that found in mills, to check conformance to specifications and to support their desire to become principals, with full responsibility for product performance.

Merchant margins varied with location, type of sale, and nature of the transaction. For sales from stock, margins ranged from a low of 12 percent in Italy and 15 percent in Germany to 25 percent in France and Switzerland. Margins reduced to about 5 percent, or less, when a merchant acted as the intermediary solely for invoicing purposes.[7] (A typical income statement for a paper merchant is shown in Exhibit 6.)

EXHIBIT 6 Typical income statement: paper merchant

Sales	100%
cost of goods sold	75
Contribution	25
other costs	23
Net profit	2
Depreciation	.5
cash flow	2.5

Source: The European Printing and Writing Paper Industry—1987.

---

[7] The European Printing and Writing Paper Industry—1987, IMEDE Case No GM 375.

Patterns of merchant ownership also varied from one country to another (see Exhibit 7). In the UK, for example, Wiggins Teape, a paper producer established in 1780, became a merchant in 1960 when existing merchants resisted introducing carbonless copy paper in the market. The company opened a network of offices to stimulate demand and provide technical support for the product. Between 1969 and 1984, the company acquired control of several major merchants operating in the UK, France, Belgium, Italy, and Finland. In 1984, sales of $480 million made Wiggins Teape the largest merchant in Europe.

EXHIBIT 7 Paper merchants: ownership and concentration per country

Country	Merchants totaling 80 percent of country sales	Ownership
Sweden	2	mill-owned
Denmark	3	mostly mill-owned
Netherlands	5	mill-owned
Belgium	5	mill-owned
Switzerland	5	mostly mill-owned
Austria	2 (70%)	mill-owned
France	6	mill-owned
West Germany	7	all independent
United Kingdom	few big and many small ones	partly mill-owned mostly independent

Source: *Paper Merchanting, the Viewpoint of Independent Merchant.*

On the other hand, Paper Union, one of the two largest merchants in Germany (turnover of $142 million and market share of 12 percent in 1984), was an independent merchant. It was formed in the early 1960s, from three smaller merchants, in an attempt to reach the critical size of 100,000 tonnes per year. Due to low margins in Germany, Paper Union had emphasized reducing operating costs and consistently fast delivery. Plans were being made, however, to introduce further services and advertising in an attempt to add value and increase customer awareness.

The move toward company-owned merchants was not without controversy. According to one independent merchant:

We believe that independent merchants are very much in the best interest of paper mills. We're aware, of course, that many mills are integrating forward, buying merchants in order to maintain access to distribution. It is our view, however, that this will cause a number of problems. No one mill can supply all the products that a merchant must offer. Hence, even mill-owned merchants must maintain relations with a number of other mills, who will always want to supply their full range of products to the merchant, including those that compete with the parent mill. This will create serious tensions and frequently will put the merchant in the position of having to choose between corporate loyalty and offering the best package to the customer. The parent can, of course, impose restrictions on the merchant with respect to selling competing products, but the salesforce would have serious problems with this.

Our strong preference is for exclusive representation of a mill. This is particularly important where there are strong influencers, such as advertisers, to whom it is important for us to address considerable promotional effort. Also, when we are an exclusive merchant, we provide the mill with extensive information on our sales, which allows the mill to do market analysis that both we and the mill find very valuable. We certainly would not provide this kind of information if the mill had intensive distribution. In a country like Switzerland, we can give the mill complete geographic and account coverage, so it's not clear to us why the mill needs more than one merchant. In our view, intensive distribution creates a situation where there is much more emphasis on price. While this first affects the merchant, it inevitably affects the mill as well.

If we do sell for a mill that has intensive distribution, we prefer to sell it under our brand, although we identify the mill, in small print. This is somewhat an historical artifact, going back to the days when mills did not attempt to brand their products, but if we're going to compete for business with another merchant, selling for the same mill, we feel having our name on the product helps us differentiate ourselves from the competitor.

At the same time, we should point out that we don't sell competing brands. There are about five quality grades within standard coated woodfree, and we handle two or three brands.

One industry expert predicted significant changes in distribution patterns.[8]

Looking to the future, it is predicted that there will be an increase in the number of paper grade classifications, moving from 4 just a few years ago to 20 or more. There will be an increasing number of different types of middlemen and distributors, and merchants will move into grades traditionally regarded as mill-direct products (e.g., newsprint and mechanical grades) to bring these grades to the smaller customers.

Just as we have seen a technological revolution hit the traditional printing industry, we must now see a marketing revolution hit the traditional paper industry. Selection of the correct channel of distribution and the development of an active working relationship with that channel will be vital.

Competition in Coated Woodfree Papers

In varying degrees, Leykam Mürztaler encountered at least 10 major European firms in the markets it served in Europe. Some, like KNP and Zanders, competed principally in coated woodfree papers. Others, like Stora and Feldmühle, produced a wide range of products, from coated woodfree papers to tissue to newsprint.

There was considerable variation in competitive emphasis among producers. Zanders, for instance, generally regarded as the highest-quality producer, mostly produced cast coated and premium art paper, competed only at the top end of the standard coated range, and was relatively unusual in its extensive use of advertising. Hannover Papier was particularly strong in ser-

---

[8] From a paper presented by BIS Marketing Research Limited.

vice, offering fast delivery. PWA Hallein, which had tended to emphasize price over quality, had recently improved its quality but was keeping prices low in an apparent effort to gain market share. Arjomari, the biggest French producer, owned the largest merchant chain in France and had recently purchased merchants in the United Kingdom and Southern Europe. It had recently entered the premium art paper segment, generally regarded as difficult to produce for. Burgo, a large Italian conglomerate, concentrated principally on the Italian market. (See Exhibit 8 for a report on the image of selected suppliers.)

Rapid growth in the coated woodfree market had stimulated capacity additions by existing producers and was also stimulating conversion of facilities from uncoated to coated. Nordland of Germany, for instance, switched 100,000 tonnes of capacity from uncoated to coated by adding a coater in October 1988. Excellent in service, there was, however, some question about its ability to produce high quality.

Branding was a relatively new aspect of the industry. All the major producers had established brand names for major products or grades. To date, however, only Zanders had actively promoted its brand to the trade or to advertisers.

EXHIBIT 8 Major mill reputation

Company	Comments on reputation
Zanders (Germany)	• Mercedes Benz in coated woodfrees • Excellent service • Strong promotion • Marketing activities have also been directed to advertising agencies, who can influence choice of brand
Leykam Mürztaler	• Reliable supplier • Good service
Arjomari (France)	• Strong positions in France due to its own merchants
Condat (France)	• Good and stable quality
Feldmühle (Germany)	• Stable quality • Rapid deliveries and good stocking arrangements
KNP (Netherlands)	• Flexible supplier, also accepts small orders • Good service
PWA Hallein (Germany)	• Competes with price
Scheufelen (Germany)	• Good and stable quality • Reliable deliveries
Stora Kopparberg (Sweden)	• Reliable deliveries • Quality and service OK

Source: EKONO Strategic Study, September 1988.

Marketing at Leykam Mürztaler AG

Marketing activities at Leykam Mürztaler were divided between the sales director, Wolfgang Pfarl, and the marketing manager, Gertrude Eder. Pfarl, a member of the executive board, was responsible for pricing as well as all personal selling activities, both direct and through merchants. Eder was responsible for public relations, advertising and sales promotion, and marketing research. As a staff member, she reported to Dr. Siegfried Meysel, the managing director.

Coated Woodfree Products and Markets

In coated woodfree papers, Leykam Mürztaler offered a comprehensive product line of standard coated papers under the MAGNO brand, for both sheet and web offset printing. These were produced in a wide variety of basis weights, ranging from 80–300 grams per square meter depending on the particular application. The firm targeted the high-quality end of the standard coated category by offering higher coat weights, better gloss and print gloss, and better printability.

Using Austria as its home market, Leykam Mürztaler focused its principal efforts on countries in Europe. The majority of sales revenues came, in roughly similar amounts, from Austria, Italy, France, and the United Kingdom, with somewhat higher sales in Germany. Belgium, Holland, Switzerland, and Spain were important but smaller markets.

The firm also sold in a number of other countries, including the United States. Penetration of the U.S. market by the European paper industry had been assisted by the favorable exchange rates during the early 1980s. The firm's policy, however, was to maintain its position in different countries despite currency fluctuations. As Gertrude Eder explained:

> We believe our customers expect us to participate in their markets on a long-term basis and to be competitive with local conditions. This may cost us some profits in the short term, as when we maintained our position in the United Kingdom despite the weak pound, but now that the pound is strong again, this investment is paying off. If we had reduced our presence when the exchange rate was unfavorable, it would have been very difficult to regain our position.

Channels of Distribution

Over the years, Leykam Mürztaler had sold most of its output through merchants. To some degree the method of distribution was influenced by the country served as the firm tended to follow the predominant trade practice in each country. In Switzerland, Germany, and the United Kingdom, all its business was done through merchants. In France, Italy, and Austria, there was a mixed pattern of distribution, but with a strong merchant orientation.

Merchants were carefully selected, and the firm did business only with stocking merchants who competed on service rather than price. In some countries (e.g., Holland) it used exclusive distribution, but this was not the normal pattern. Gertrude Eder explained:

> As a large producer, we have a volume problem. In the larger countries, one merchant simply can't sell enough product for us, plus we believe it is risky to commit completely to one merchant.

Similarly, Wolfgang Pfarl commented:

> In Germany, for instance, we could go to one merchant only, but to get the volume of business we need would require going into direct business with some nonstocking merchants, and that is something that neither we nor our stocking merchants want to happen.

To date, the trend toward mill ownership of merchants had not adversely affected the firm's ability to get good merchant representation. There was some concern, however, that with changing patterns of mill ownership, some merchants might be closed off to firms like Leykam Mürztaler in the future.

Service was also seen as a key to merchant relations. In this connection, the firm felt its computerized order system and new finishing facilities at the Gratkorn mill, highly automated, permitting flexibility in sheeting and packaging, and able to handle the total output of the new paper machine, provided great service capability and gave it a competitive advantage. As the mill superintendent put it:

> From a production standpoint, the ideal scenario is one in which we can run one grade of paper all year and ship it to customers in large reels. Reality is that meeting customer needs is critical, and I believe we have ''state-of-the-art competence'' in our ability to meet a tremendous variety of customer requirements efficiently.

Pricing

Pricing practices in the paper industry had a strong commodity orientation and, for coated woodfree papers, industry prices tended to serve as the basis for arriving at transaction prices. (See Exhibit 3 for information on industry prices and paper grades.) For sales to merchants, Leykam Mürztaler negotiated price lists, using the industry prices as a starting point, with final prices taking paper quality and other relevant factors into account. Price lists then remained in effect until there was a change in industry price levels. Routine orders were priced from the established price list. Large requirements, however, usually involved special negotiation.

According to one Leykam Mürztaler sales manager:

> We have some interesting discussions with our merchants about price. The customer knows we make a high-quality product, so his [or her] principal interest is in getting it at the lowest possible price. In Europe there is no uniform classification of coated papers, as there is in the United States of America and Japan, so a standard approach is to try to get me to reclassify my product to a lower grade, and so a lower price. To some extent, though, my customer's preoccupation with price simply reflects price pressures he [or she] is experiencing from his [or her] customers. Still, it is frustrating because we believe we offer a lot more than just price and a good product. But I think we do a good job for the firm in getting the highest price possible.

Branding

In recent years, Leykam Mürztaler had followed the industry practice of branding its principal products. It did, however, supply products to certain merchants for private branding, a practice that was established when mill branding was not the norm. In 1988, some 30 percent of sales carried a merchant brand, largely reflecting the volume from Germany and the UK, where private branding was customary. Recently, however, the firm had started to identify most of its products by using a typical Leykam Mürztaler packaging, even for private labels.

Brands had been promoted primarily by the salesforce, in direct contact with customers, using brochures and samples and by packaging. More recently, a series of superb visual messages was commissioned, using the theme, ''Dimensions in Paper,'' to suggest ways that high-quality paper combined with printing could produce more effective communication. The script accompanying the visual messages was designed to appeal to both the advertisers, with emphasis on communication, and printers with emphasis on paper finish, touch, color, absorption, contrast, and other key paper characteristics. On a limited basis, these messages had appeared in selected magazines and in brochures for customers. (See Exhibit 9.)

There was general agreement within the firm that more emphasis needed to be placed on branding as a way to achieve product differentiation and convey the desired high-quality image. There was less agreement on how much to spend promoting the brands or how to deal with merchants who were now buying Leykam Mürztaler products for sale under the merchants' labels. According to Gertrude Eder:

> Over the past few years we designed the corporate logo and corporate graphics and established blue, black, and white as the colors for all corporate communication. We have worked hard to establish a consistent presentation of our corporate identity. Feedback from customers and the sales department indicates that this has helped improve our visibility and image. Nevertheless, we are currently spending considerably less than 1 percent of sales on advertising. Zanders, on the other hand, a firm of about our size, has been spending a lot of money on advertising for years and as a result has better visibility than we do, particularly with advertising agencies, as well as an enviable reputation for quality and service.
>
> I don't know what the right number is for us, but we will need to spend substantially more if we are to establish the kind of brand awareness and image we desire. I think that to have any significant impact would take a minimum of ASch3–4 million for classical advertising (i.e., advertising in trade publications, in various languages) and ASch8–10 million for promotions, including brochures, leaflets, and trade fairs. In Western Europe we have to advertise in at least four to five languages, and sometimes more. In addition, the nature of the ads varies. In private brand countries, our ads emphasize the company name and focus on the Dimensions in Paper theme as well as the company's experience and modern production facilities. In other countries we emphasize the MAGNO brand.
>
> We are convinced that printers want to know what mill brand they are buying. Also, we believe that there is some subjectivity in selecting paper, particularly by the advertiser, and we want to convince the advertiser that his [or her] message will come across better on Leykam Mürztaler paper.

The decision on supplying Leykam Mürztaler products for private branding was even more complex. As Wolfgang Pfarl commented:

> I understand the position of the merchants who want to offer a private brand. The fact remains, however, that it is the mill that determines product characteristics and is responsible for meeting specifications. It is really a question of who is

EXHIBIT 9 MAGNOPRINT promotional piece (text)

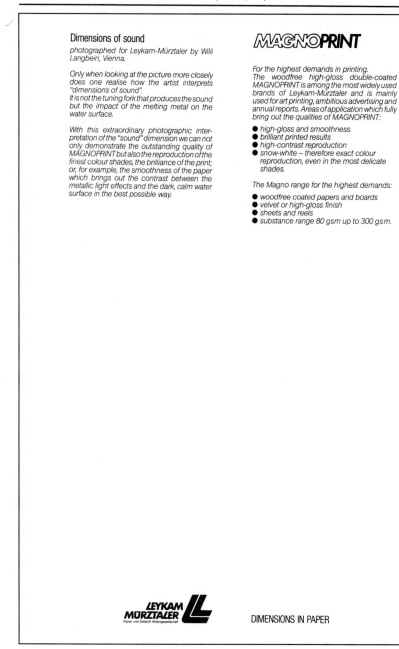

Dimensions of sound

photographed for Leykam-Mürztaler by Willi Langbein, Vienna.

Only when looking at the picture more closely does one realise how the artist interprets "dimensions of sound".
It is not the tuning fork that produces the sound but the impact of the melting metal on the water surface.

With this extraordinary photographic interpretation of the "sound" dimension we can not only demonstrate the outstanding quality of MAGNOPRINT but also the reproduction of the finest colour shades, the brilliance of the print; or, for example, the smoothness of the paper which brings out the contrast between the metallic light effects and the dark, calm water surface in the best possible way.

MAGNOPRINT

For the highest demands in printing.
The woodfree high-gloss double-coated MAGNOPRINT is among the most widely used brands of Leykam-Mürztaler and is mainly used for art printing, ambitious advertising and annual reports. Areas of application which fully bring out the qualities of MAGNOPRINT:

● *high-gloss and smoothness*
● *brilliant printed results*
● *high-contrast reproduction*
● *snow-white – therefore exact colour reproduction, even in the most delicate shades.*

The Magno range for the highest demands:

● *woodfree coated papers and boards*
● *velvet or high-gloss finish*
● *sheets and reels*
● *substance range 80 gsm up to 300 gsm.*

LEYKAM MÜRZTALER
Papier und Zellstoff Aktiengesellschaft

DIMENSIONS IN PAPER

adding the value. In my view the merchant ought to emphasize those things which he [or she] controls, such as local stocks, good sales representation, and service. Putting a merchant label on paper produced by Leykam Mürztaler misrepresents the value added-picture. Don't get me wrong. Our firm strongly believes in merchants. In fact, we avoid direct business wherever there are strong stocking merchants. It's just that we think mills and merchants have distinct roles to play, and they should not be confused.

Currently, we will still produce for a merchant's label, but we have started to insist that it also is identified as Leykam Mürztaler. The merchants aren't very happy about this, but we think it's the right thing to do.

Nevertheless, the situation with respect to existing merchants was difficult. As one of the senior sales managers said:

We have been supplying some of our merchants with paper to be sold under a private label for a long time, and they have invested substantial sums of money in establishing their own brands. I completely support the company's position on this, but I don't know how we can get the practice to change. If we insist on supplying products only under our own brand, there are a lot of competitors who would, I think, be happy to step in and take over our position with some merchants. If we can't convince a merchant to switch over to our brand, we could lose a lot of business, in one or two instances as much as 6,000 tonnes. On the other hand, if we aren't uniform on this, we will not be able to really exploit the potential of developing our own brands.

In addition to questions about branding policy, it was not clear how to capitalize on increased brand preference, if indeed it were achieved. As Wolfgang Pfarl said:

We might want to think in terms of higher prices or increased share, or some combination. Exactly what we would do could vary from market to market.

Personal Selling

Contact with merchants and with large, directly served accounts in Europe was mainly made by the company's own salesforce headquartered in Vienna, by sales representatives in subsidiary companies in Germany, Italy, and France, and by sales agents in other markets (e.g., the United Kingdom). Direct sales representatives numbered 20. Including clerical staff, Leykam had some 60 individuals in its sales department, most of whom had direct contact with customers.

The major activity of the salesforce was making direct calls on large customers and on merchants. In addition, sales representatives made occasional calls on a merchant's customers, generally accompanied by the merchant's sales representative. Objectives usually included negotiating long-term contracts, "selling" the existing product line, new product introduction, and a review of customer requirements for products and service.

It was the firm's belief that its salesforce was a major asset and that sales representatives could significantly influence relations with merchants. A major objective for all Leykam Mürztaler representatives was to do everything possible to develop close relations with assigned merchants. According to Wolfgang Pfarl:

> The average age of our salesforce is between 35 and 40, and most of the individuals have spent their entire career in sales with Leykam Mürztaler. They are really committed to serve the customer, with on-time deliveries or any other aspect of our relationship, and the customer really respects their high level of service. In addition, they are good negotiators and represent Leykam effectively during contract negotiations. They do not need to be technical experts, but they make sure that our technical people provide technical information as required. Also, they monitor shipping performance, make presentations to merchants, and may make joint customer calls with merchant sales representatives.

Mathias Radon, one of the Vienna-based sales managers, made the following comments:

> In total we call on about 100 merchants in Europe. I work with our sales offices in Italy, France and Belgium and handle five merchants personally in the United Kingdom, in cooperation with our representative there. I call on the merchants two to three times a year and have extensive phone contact with our sales offices and representatives from Vienna.
>
> In general, the customer wants to talk about quantity, price, and service. We have conversations about private labeling. The new merchants would like us to give them private labels, but I think they know they can't get it. On the other hand, the ones to whom we are currently providing private labels don't want to give it up. The problem varies from country to country. In France, for instance, it's not such a big problem
>
> One of my objectives is to encourage more stock business versus indent (merchant orders for direct mill shipment to the customer). This means we have to give them better service and provide back-up stocks.
>
> Some merchants handle mill brands that compete directly with Leykam Mürztaler, but most tend to do this under a private label.
>
> From time to time we work to develop a new merchant, but generally we work on building long-lasting relationships with existing merchants. We encourage trips by merchant personnel to the mill. I will make short presentations to merchant sales representatives when I call on the merchant, but generally they are pretty knowledgeable about paper. We've tried contests and other incentives with merchants and are still thinking about it, but I'm not sure if that's what we should do.
>
> From a quality standpoint, I try to stress whiteness, opacity, printability/ runability, and consistency. Lots of customers ask for lab figures, but I don't think you can rely just on lab reports. We have trial print runs every week by an independent printer to check our consistency. I think most printers feel the same way.
>
> We tend to have lots of small problems rather than any one large problem. Branding, for instance, pricing, friction when we appoint a new merchant, and country variations with regard to ways of doing business. I think branding will be important in all countries, but how we capitalize on it may have to vary.

After-Sales Service

Problems in printing could arise due to a number of circumstances. There might be variations or flaws in the paper or in the ink. Presses could develop mechanical problems. Even changes in temperature and humidity could negatively affect printing quality. Because of the complexity of the printing process, the cause of a problem was not always clear, and reaching an equitable settlement could be difficult.

When problems did arise, the printer turned to the merchant or mill for technical advice and frequently wanted financial compensation for lost production. According to Wolfgang Pfarl:

> When the printer encounters a production problem, it is important for us to be able to give him [or her] technical advice and work with him [or her] to solve the problem. Sometimes the sales representatives can do this. More often, we have to involve one of our technical people from the mill. All too often, however, the printer is just looking for someone to compensate him [or her] financially, and we have to be very tough or we're likely to find ourselves paying for a lot of other people's mistakes.

Future Issues

Looking to the future, the firm was focusing its attention on managing ''through the business cycle.'' As Wolfgang Pfarl put it:

> Our real challenge is to strengthen our market position in Western Europe. Most of our coated woodfree paper goes into advertising. We have seen extraordinary growth in this market in the last few years, but we have to expect there will be a significant downturn in one or two years and that advertisers will then look intensely at their costs. In many cases this means the printer will suggest a lower cost grade as a substitute for coated woodfree. Our task is to differentiate MAGNO from the generic category and position it as ''a paper for all seasons,'' so to speak. In other words, we want our customers to think of MAGNO as the ''right'' paper for high-quality advertising, separate from coated woodfree.
>
> In general, this means strengthening our corporate identity, being partners of the strongest merchants, and encouraging our merchants to support the MAGNO brand.

In a similar vein, Gertrude Eder commented:

> This is a business where the impact of the business cycle is made worse by the tendency of merchants to overstock in good times and destock in bad times. Our objective, I think, should be to position Leykam as the last mill the merchant or printer would think of cancelling in a downturn.

Part 5

Distribution Decisions

Marketers must make decisions on how to present the products they produce to their ultimate purchasers. Most producers do not present their products to end consumers themselves. They tend to make use of wholesalers and retailers.

The marketing decision maker has a number of decisions to make with respect to the distribution of a product. These include:

1. The types of wholesale and retail intermediaries to use.
2. The number of wholesale and retail intermediaries to use of each type.
3. The number of levels in the channel (degree of directness).
4. The ways to motivate existing channel members to perform effectively.

The first cases in this section deal with these issues. Beyond these decisions are a series of decisions concerning the physical distribution of the product. These include: customer service level, inventory size, order quantities, reorder points, warehouse locations, and transportation.

The next section of this note is a short reminder of some of the concepts related to each of these decision points.

Types of Intermediaries

There are many different types of wholesale and retail intermediaries. They vary on the types of products they carry and the services that they are able to perform. The decision on which types of intermediaries to utilize is related to the services that a firm desires to have performed. This is in turn related to the resources and skills of the firm and the needs and behavior of the ultimate consumer.

The Number of Intermediaries

The firm must decide whether to have intensive, selective, or exclusive distribution at the wholesale and retail levels. This decision is related to the quality of support these intermediaries will give in each situation, the ability of the firm to service the intermediaries, and the behavior of the ultimate consumer. For example, a wholesaler whom you want may only be willing to carry your products on an exclusive basis, or you may not be able to afford to contact all the retailers of a particular type. Alternatively, consumers may demand that your product be available at all outlets. This may force you into an intensive distribution situation.

Number of Channel Levels

The decision on how direct a channel from producer to ultimate consumer should be is related to the cost of alternative channels, the service and control provided, the characteristics of the end consumer in terms of their numbers and geographic location, the perishability and bulkiness of the product, plus the characteristics of the firm, and competitive activity.

Motivation

Once a channel is selected, motivating its members to perform effectively is an important activity. Motivating vehicles include monetary things such as margins, allowances, and cooperative programs; service activities such as training and technical advice, inventory taking, and display management; and provision of physical items such as racks. Also important here are the interpersonal relationships among the people in the intermediaries and in your firm.

Physical Distribution Management

Physical distribution management is a complex area where management science techniques have become important. In simple terms, the decision maker sets a customer service level (for example, deliver 95 percent of all orders within seven days) and then makes inventory, warehousing, and transportation decisions to reach this service level at minimum cost. The customer service level is set by considering costs, consumer behavior, and competitive activity.

Case 16

Chaebol Electronics Company, U.S.*

In mid-1984, Mr. Park Sung-Il, grandson of the founder of Chaebol Industries, Inc., and president of Chaebol Electronics Company, U.S., was deciding how his company should enter the U.S. videocassette recorder (VCR) market. As of March 1985, the agreement signed by his company—which gave it access to the proprietary technology of the Japanese company Japan Victor Corporation (JVC) for the manufacture of VCRs but limited sales to only the domestic Korean market—would expire. After that date, Chaebol was free to market VCRs worldwide. The decision had already been made to begin selling Chaebol VCRs in the United States as soon as possible. The decision Mr. Park faced was that of marketing his company's VCRs as it was already selling its televisions or positioning this new product line differently, selling it through different channels of distribution.

History of Chaebol Industries, Inc.

Chaebol Industries, Inc., had its beginnings with a small construction firm started by Mr. Park Kyung-Yung in 1945. After gaining several large port construction projects following the Korean War, Mr. Park expanded the firm into shipbuilding and through this into the exporting business. While Chaebol was growing in these areas, other large Korean conglomerates, such as Lucky-Goldstar, Samsung, and Hyundai, diversified their corporations into such fields as chemicals, oil refining, textiles, appliance manufacture, and electronics manufacturing. Each of these firms developed its own foreign distribution capabilities and became very successful in worldwide markets. As a result, these other Korean firms began to become strong competitors for Chaebol's exporting business.

* This case was prepared by Constance M. Kinnear, Research Associate, with the assistance of Thomas C. Kinnear, Professor of Marketing, both at the Graduate School of Business Administration, The University of Michigan. Copyright © 1986 by the authors.

In 1965, Mr. Park Kyung-Yung retired and his son, Mr. Park Taik-Cha, became president of Chaebol. Looking at the successes of his competitors and their impact on Chaebol's business, Mr. Park decided in 1966 that the time had come for Chaebol to expand its areas of operation into the electronics field. In 1967, Chaebol Electronics Company was established, and began producing black-and-white televisions. Room air conditioners, washing machines, refrigerators, and electric typewriters were added to Chaebol's list of products by 1970. As each new product was added to the Chaebol line, it was marketed only in Korea. However, the Korean market consisted of only 41 million people, with a per capita income of just under $2,000 per year. Faced with intense competition from the other large Korean conglomerates for its domestic market, Mr. Park soon became aware that his company would have to begin exporting its products to gain economies of scale in their manufacture.

Mr. Park hoped that Chaebol's long experience in exporting would give it a competitive advantage in foreign markets. To build on this experience, Chaebol first marketed its black-and-white TVs in the United States in 1975 through Johnson Importers of Atlanta, Georgia, the importer that had handled the export goods the company had transported for years. Since this importer was used to handling only low-cost items carried mainly by discounters, Chaebol offered only its lower-cost, lower-priced 12-inch and 19-inch black-and-white models for export. Johnson Importers found a market for 25,000 Chaebol sets in 1975, sold under the PKY brand name, in discount stores in Georgia, Alabama, and Florida. These stores on average priced the 12-inch sets at $105 and the 19-inch sets at $120 each. These stores included a 20 percent margin in these prices. Johnson Importers made a 15 percent margin on its sales of TVs to these outlets. Chaebol priced its 12-inch sets at $71.50 and its 19-inch sets at $81.50 each. Encouraged by this acceptance, Chaebol increased its production capacity in late 1975 from 300,000 to 400,000 sets per year.

In 1976, Johnson Importers was able to increase the sale of PKY sets to a total of 60,000 sets throughout the South. Mr. Park believed that similar success in the sale of Chaebol's TVs could be found in discount chains in other parts of the country. To achieve this, Mr. Park sent two Chaebol sales representatives to establish a sales office and arrange for warehousing facilities in Atlanta. These sales representatives received $25,000 in salary each, and it was budgeted that their sales expenses would come to another $15,000 each per year. These direct Chaebol employees contacted several large discount chains in the Northeast and Midwest. In 1977, sales to these chains, all employing private labels, were 50,000 units, increasing total company sales that year to 115,000 units. In 1978, Chaebol's salespeople were able to land the sale of 100,000 sets to K mart Corporation under K mart's KC brand name. As part of the arrangement for these sales, Chaebol agreed to open a service center to which sets could be sent by the retailer for repair. This center was located in Atlanta. As a result, total sales in 1978 jumped to 240,000 sets. Korean production capacity was increased to 600,000 units per year to handle these sales. In 1979, sales reached 275,000 units. In 1980, with additional private label sales to discounters in the

West and constantly increasing sales to previous customers, Chaebol sold 375,000 units.

In 1981, Chaebol increased its number of U.S. sales representatives to five and opened a second sales office, warehouse facility, and service center in Chicago. These sales representatives were now being paid a salary of $37,000 per year and had $20,000 a year in expenses each. Chaebol's salespeople began approaching large department store chains, such as Sears and Montgomery Ward, to increase sales. Again, the TVs sold to these accounts carried the retailers' own labels. 1981 total sales were 450,000 units. Of this total, only 100,000 sets carried the PKY brand name, and these were sold primarily to independent discounters who operated only a few stores each in regional areas.

In 1979, Mr. Park had directed Chaebol to begin manufacturing color TVs. As with Chaebol's previous products, these were first marketed only in Korea. By 1981, Mr. Park was ready to bring three color models, 9-inch, 13-inch, and 19-inch sets, to the United States. The decision to introduce color sets was brought on by a shift in sales patterns in the U.S. marketplace. By 1980, annual total sales of black-and-white TVs was dropping, by an average of 6 percent per year. Along with this drop in total sales, black-and-white set prices were dropping steadily, causing profit margins on the products to fall. Nineteen-inch black-and-white models were no longer desired in the market; buyers preferred to spend their money on a smaller color set than on a large black-and-white set. Furthermore, the color TV market was growing steadily, with growth rates of nearly 15 percent per year. Half of Chaebol's capacity was shifted to color TV production, and within black-and-white sets, 19-inch sets were dropped while small, portable 9-inch sets were added to the line. Cost information on Chaebol's export TV product line in 1981 is shown in Exhibit 1.

EXHIBIT 1   Cost information on 1981 export television sets

	Black-and-White		Color		
	9-inch	*12-inch*	*9-inch*	*13-inch*	*19-inch*
Direct material	$ 57.85	$32.70	$102.30	$121.35	$147.05
Labor	1.40	1.00	2.40	2.95	3.45
Overhead	2.50	1.40	4.00	5.00	5.80
Transportation	5.10	6.25	5.20	6.30	6.85
Duty	3.15	1.90	5.35	6.40	7.70
Total costs	$ 70.00	$43.25	$119.25	$142.00	$170.85
Chaebol's selling price to channel	$100.00	$60.00	$195.50	$232.00	$280.00
Average retail selling price of Chaebol sets	$125.00	$75.00	$230.00	$290.00	$350.00
Retail price of leading domestic brand	$156.00	$95.00	$271.50	$345.00	$415.00

Chaebol marketed its color TVs through the same discount channels it was using for its black-and-white models. However, with color, Chaebol's U.S.

EXHIBIT 2 Black-and-white TV market—retail brand shares and market size, 1981–1984

	1981	1982	1983	1984
Domestic manufacturers				
RCA	16.3	16.3	15.5	12.5
Zenith	15.5	15.4	13.6	10.2
General Electric	8.9	8.2	8.4	7.5
North American Phillips	5.8	6.9	8.2	10.3
Other domestic	2.6	2.0	2.7	2.7
Total domestic	49.1	48.8	48.4	43.2
Japanese				
Panasonic	6.0	5.9	7.0	8.1
Sony	4.4	3.9	3.5	5.3
Sanyo	3.6	3.2	3.3	3.2
Hitachi	1.3	0.9	0.7	0.5
Sharp	1.0	1.6	1.0	1.4
Toshiba	0.5	0.6	0.2	0.4
Other Japanese	1.0	1.4	0.8	0.4
Total Japanese	17.8	17.5	16.5	19.3
Far East				
Samsung (Korea)	2.1	2.4	2.9	3.5
Goldstar (Korea)	1.8	1.9	2.3	2.5
Chaebol (Korea)	1.7	1.9	2.5	3.3
Other Far East	0.5	0.6	0.9	1.2
Total Far East	6.1	6.8	8.6	10.5
Private label				
(Sears, J. C. Penney,				
Montgomery Ward,				
K mart, etc.)	20.2	20.0	18.5	17.5
All other	6.8	6.9	8.0	9.5
Market size				
in units (000)	5,806	5,597	5,488	4,717

salespeople were able to have its sets sold using the PKY label at K mart and two other large discounters. Color TV sales began with 100,000 units in 1981 and grew to 300,000 units in 1982. Forty percent of these color sets carried the PKY label. (See Exhibits 2 and 3 for competitive market shares).

In late 1982, Chaebol drastically changed its approach to the U.S. TV market. Great pressure in the press was being brought upon Korean TV producers, with many accusations of TV dumping by these companies within the U.S. market. In accusing them of dumping, it was being alleged that Korean manufacturers were selling TVs in the United States for prices below those charged for the same product in the domestic market. Mr. Park decided not to wait for the decision from the U.S. International Trade Commission on the dumping charges. He began construction in November 1982 of TV assembly and production facilities in Marietta, Georgia. Initial capacity of 100,000 units per year came online in June 1983. An additional 200,000 units of capacity was scheduled for 1985. Cost figures for 1983 production of 13-inch color TV sets in the United States as compared to in Korea was as follows:

EXHIBIT 3 Color TV market—retail brand shares and market size, 1981–1984

	1981	1982	1983	1984
Domestic manufacturers				
RCA	20.0%	20.1%	18.9%	18.1%
Zenith	18.7	18.9	16.8	16.2
General Electric	8.0	7.8	7.6	6.4
North American Phillips	12.4	11.8	10.5	10.2
Other domestic	4.7	3.8	3.9	3.5
Total domestic	64.0	62.4	57.7	54.4
Japanese				
Sony	7.7	6.9	7.5	6.7
Panasonic	2.6	3.7	4.0	3.9
Sharp	1.4	2.0	2.4	3.1
Hitachi	2.5	2.8	2.8	3.0
Sanyo	1.2	1.2	1.7	1.5
Other Japanese	3.1	3.0	3.0	4.2
Total Japanese	18.5	19.6	21.4	22.4
Far East				
Samsung (Korea)	0.2	0.5	1.6	1.6
Gold Star (Korea)	0.5	0.7	0.8	0.9
Chaebol (Korea)	0.7	1.1	1.3	1.7
Other Far East	0.5	0.8	0.7	0.8
Total Far East	1.9	3.1	4.4	5.0
Private label (Sears, J. C. Penney, Montgomery Ward, K mart, etc.)	13.4	12.7	13.2	12.9
All other	2.2	2.2	3.3	5.3
Market size in units (000)	10,641	11,567	13,608	15,646

	Korean production	U.S. production
Direct material	$101.20	$113.40
Labor	2.40	5.25
Overhead	4.25	5.85
Transportation	5.85	
Duty	5.35	
Total cost	$119.05	$124.50

Even though Chaebol's costs were higher when TVs were produced in the United States, management believed these U.S. costs were approximately 10 percent below those of domestic TV producers.

In conjunction with the establishment of U.S. production facilities, Mr. Park established Chaebol Electronics Company, U.S., and sent his son, Mr. Park Sung-Il, to the United States to head the company. The younger Mr. Park hired six new American sales representatives to work in three new sales offices in Denver, Los Angeles, and New York. Warehouse facilities and service centers were also established in these cities. Chaebol's five warehouses cost an average of $250,000 per year each. Service costs were one-quarter percent of sales in 1984. Mr. Park's goal was to expand TV sales into new markets. In late 1983, Chaebol U.S. succeeded in gaining contracts to sell its TVs in 9-inch black-and-white and 13-inch color to two major catalog showroom companies. These sets were all to carry the PKY label.

Chaebol's sales revenue in 1981 from sales of black-and-white TVs was $36.2 million. In 1983, sales revenue from black-and-white sets was $39.2 million, while sales of color sets brought in $83.75 million. Profit on these 1983 sales was $4.91 million.

The Electronics Market in 1984

Exhibit 4 shows the types of retail stores that sold electronic products in 1975 and 1984. It also shows the number of each type of store and the percentage of total electronic products sold in the United States in that year by that type of store. As the exhibit shows, there has been a significant increase not only in the total number of outlets selling electronic products but also in the variety of store types that carry this kind of product.

EXHIBIT 4 Types of electronics products sales outlets; number and percent of electronics market sales by type

Type of outlet	1975		1984	
	No. of stores	Percent sales	No. of stores	Percent sales
Radio/TV/appliance	50,152	31.4%	30,004	54.1%
Discount chains	17,887	25.0	5,764	12.4
Department stores	11,240	19.7	4,217	9.3
Furniture stores	38,732	15.9	29,609	3.7
Catalog/mail order	7,671	4.8	16,347	11.8
Auto/home supply	—	—	40,729	3.6
Drug/variety	—	—	60,516	3.3
Home centers	—	—	24,837	1.2
Hardware stores	—	—	19,870	0.6
Other	9,874	3.2	—	—
Total	135,556	100%	231,893	100%

Although Exhibit 4 shows that the total number of radio/TV/appliance stores has greatly decreased since 1975, the importance of this type of outlet within the electronics market grew to the point where radio/TV/appliance stores sold more of these products than all the other outlet types combined. The key characteristics of this type of store were wide selection, low price, and high volume. The major appliance stores stocked virtually every model of every major mass market line. It was common to find up to 150 different TV models and 100 VCRs. The stores advertised low prices and often guaranteed that they would meet any price offered by a competitor in their market area. The salespeople were usually quite knowledgeable and were paid on commission. Thus, they were aggressive in selling their higher-margin models. Price cutting was a necessity, and dealers often bought in large quantity lots, watching for deals, damaged-model sales, and other ways to cut costs. The average margin for this type of outlet was about 22 percent. These stores commonly had extensive service departments.

Discount chains, such as K mart stores, had been handling electronic products for 15 years. They bought in large quantity at lowest possible cost. The manufacturers were usually willing to cut prices in order to obtain large volume orders. Some of the larger chains also engaged in private branding, from which they were able to gain very favorable terms from manufacturers. For example, a U.S. manufacturer who engaged in private branding for one of the large chains obtained an average margin of 19 percent versus 34 percent for national brand sales. Chains usually required the customer to contact the company or independent service facility for warranty service. Some stores supported ''service centers,'' which would simply accept the set and send it on to the manufacturer for repairs. With low overhead and low margins (18 percent), the salespeople were usually few in number and rarely informed about electronics or the differences in major lines. These stores also carried very small lines of a few manufacturers, concentrating for the most part on the low end of the model line.

Department stores carried a limited variety of brands and models of electronic products. They usually did not carry either the lowest- nor the highest-priced models, but concentrated on the largest sales models of well-known brand names. The salespeople were quite knowledgeable, and engaged in a fair amount of trying to get the customer to ''trade up.'' Prices were sometimes discounted, particularly in larger chains. The department stores usually got about a 30 percent margin. In addition, they were eager to seek ''deals'' on quantity buys, closeouts, and so on. Only the national department store chains, such as Sears, J. C. Penney, and Montgomery Ward, had their own service facilities or carried their own private brands.

Furniture stores were involved only in the sales of console model TVs. Their salespeople were well informed about cabinetry and styling, but usually not too knowledgeable about electronics. These outlets usually sold at suggested retail price, and thus gained about a 37 percent margin on their sales. Furniture stores offered no in-store service facilities. With the introduction of the wide variety of electronic products since 1975, the importance of this type of outlet to the total sales of these products had decreased greatly.

Catalog/mail-order sales outlets usually sold a limited range of models from well-known brands. Unlike department stores, the range of models offered by catalog/mail-order stores went from the lower- to mid-priced models. It was also common for catalogs to offer lesser-known brands that could be priced at a significantly lower price than national brands as long as they offered high quality for that price. Catalog/mail-order outlets usually had a 15 percent margin on sales. Little selling at point of purchase was available. No repair services were offered. This type of sales outlet was of increasing importance for electronic product categories that had reached the point of mass acceptance in the marketplace.

Auto/home supply stores tended to carry only specialty products to fit the needs of small segments of the electronics market. Therefore, models and brands offered were limited, and prices and margins were relatively high. Salespeople were very knowledgeable, and these stores often offered repair services.

Drug/variety, home centers, and hardware stores had many characteristics in common. They all carried lower-priced, basic models of electronic products that were commonly purchased only through "special deals" so that low prices were possible. The variety of products and models sold by any given outlet in this group varied greatly from time to time, but usually they carried only radios, small black-and-white TVs, and accessory items like stereo speakers. The salespeople at these outlets had little knowledge of electronics. Margins for this group averaged 25 percent. No service facilities were offered on these products.

The VCR Market in 1984

The VCR market in the United States had grown very quickly from the time of the product's introduction in 1979. In 1981, 1.7 million units were sold. This number grew to 2.0 million units in 1982, 3.75 million units in 1983, and nearly 7.5 million units in 1984. The market shares of the major firms selling VCRs in 1984 are shown in the first part of Exhibit 5. The second part of the exhibit shows the number of brands and models of VCRs sold at each type of electronics outlet and the range of prices charged at each kind of store in 1984. Of the units sold in 1984, 48 percent sold for under $500, 20 percent for between $501 and $600, 17 percent for between $601 and $800, 13 percent for between $801 and $1,000, and only 2 percent for more than $1,000. The average price of VCRs sold in the United States had dropped by over $550 since their introduction in 1979. Typical features offered on low-, medium-, and high-priced VCRs in 1984 are shown below:

Low-priced models (under $400)	Medium-priced models ($400–$750)	High-priced models (over $750)
2 video heads	2 video heads	4 video heads
1 audio head	1 audio head	2 audio heads—stereo, hi-fi
Varactor tuner (preset 12–14 channels)	Varactor tuner (preset 80–99 channels)	Direct access quartz tuner
1-event/7-day programmability	4-event/14-day programmability	8-event/1-year programmability
8-hour/3-speed recording	8-hour/3-speed recording	8-hour/3-speed recording
8-function remote (many wired)	10-function wireless remote	13–17 function wireless remote
Not cable ready	107-channel cable capability	133-channel cable capability

EXHIBIT 5 U.S. videocassette recorder market—retail brand shares, 1984

	1984 share
Domestic manufacturers	
RCA (VHS)	15.1%
General Electric (VHS)	6.2
Quasar (VHS)	5.1
Magnavox (VHS)	4.1
Zenith (VHS/Beta)	3.2
Sylvania (VHS)	1.4
Curtis-Mathes (VHS)	1.3
Total domestic	36.4%
Japanese	
Panasonic (VHS)	12.8
Sony (Beta)	6.8
Sanyo (Beta)	6.3
Sharp (VHS)	4.6
Hitachi (VHS)	3.7
MGA (VHS)	2.7
JVC (VHS)	4.1
Toshiba (Beta)	1.6
Total Japanese	42.6%
Private label	9.5%
Other	11.1%

VCR market—Number of brands and models and price ranges by type of outlet

Type of outlet	No. of brands offered	No. of models offered	Price range
Radio/TV/appliance	12	60	$259–$1,100
Discount chains	5	7	$257–$459
Department stores			
National chains	3	11	$269–$599
Regionals and independents	6	12	$399–$799
Catalog/mail-order stores	6	9	$278–$650

The total U.S. market for VCRs in 1985 was expected to be between 11 and 12 million units. With this level of sales, VCRs will have succeeded in penetrating 25 percent of the product's total market potential (households with televisions) by the end of 1985. Because of the quickness with which VCR sales reached this sales level, industry analysts did not foresee much future growth for the product line, although they did predict sales levels maintaining a 10 million to 11 million unit-per-year pace for the next five years.

The quick growth of VCR sales has had long-reaching effects on the development of the market for these products. After only five years on the market, the demographics of VCR buyers were already broadening. Originally, VCRs were most commonly purchased by upper-income (over $32,000), well-educated, married heads of household between the ages of 35 and 49. In 1984, 27 percent of VCR units were purchased by 18-to-24-year-old singles with average income between $27,000 and $32,000. The amazing sales growth of VCRs attracted many new entrants to the market each year, so that by 1984 there were over 70 VCR brands available. Many brands offered extensive VCR lines. For example, RCA, the market share leader, offered 25 VCR models ranging in suggested retail price from $330 to $1,300. The more entrants there were to the market, the stronger price competition became. This led to progressively lower and lower margins and profitability for both manufacturers and retailers. This margin loss was greatest on the lower-price-range products. To counteract this, many manufacturers were adding VCRs with greater features and capabilities to their lines—VCRs that were higher priced but also more profitable.

In late 1984, market analysts expressed the belief that Korean VCR manufacturers would enter the U.S. market using the same strategy that had gained them market share in TV sales: that of offering low-priced products that would allow them to take advantage of their lower labor costs. Thus, their expectations were that Korean VCRs would be priced $50 to $75 below the 1984 $400 mid-priced Japanese units with the same features. Furthermore, analysts believed that this kind of price differential would require retailers to pick up the Korean models. However, many analysts felt retailers would only carry these models as advertising draws and would often try to get customers to buy up from these low-priced VCRs to more profitable models.

Chaebol's Decision

Mr. Park Sung-Il had narrowed down Chaebol's VCR entry strategy to between one of two alternatives.

Strategy I

The first entry strategy alternative involved using distribution channels and retail outlets for VCRs similar to those Chaebol had employed for TV sales. For VCRs, Mr. Park wanted to limit distribution to only high-volume buyers. Thus, if this strategy was employed, Chaebol would only seek sales to large discount chains and catalog/mail-order retailers. Mr. Park planned to produce three models for these outlets. All would be two video head, one audio head models, with varactor tuning allowing 12 stations to be preset. The lowest-cost model, Model CHA, would also feature one-event/one-week programmability, wired remote, auto rewind, and would not be cable ready. Model CHA would cost Chaebol $143.50 to produce. The next step up in Chaebol's offerings would be Model CHB, which would have 1-event/14-day programmability, an eight-function wireless remote, auto rewind, and be cable ready. Model CHB would cost $201 to manufacture. Model CHC, the highest-priced model offered under this strategy, would feature 1-event/14-day programmability, 12-function remote control, auto rewind, frame advance, a sharpness control, and would be cable ready. Model CHC would cost Chaebol $247.90. Mr. Park believed

Chaebol's costs on these products would allow its customers to price these models 15 percent below similar VCRs on the market.

Since Chaebol salespeople were already calling on these customers, Mr. Park believed this alternative would have few additional costs over Chaebol's present expenses. Additional warehouse space and service personnel would have to be acquired, but no new sales offices would be needed. Mr. Park believed that most of these sales would be low-priced, private brand VCRs, although he hoped that those customers who were purchasing PKY brand TVs would purchase PKY brand name VCRs. Mr. Park estimated he could sell 225,000 VCRs in 1985 with this strategy, 70,000 carrying the PKY name. He believed private label sales would carry a 27 percent gross margin for Chaebol, while the PKY brand sales would bring a 34 percent gross margin.

Strategy II

Mr. Park's alternative to the above strategy was to use Chaebol's cost advantage, arising from lower labor costs than either U.S. or Japanese competitors, to gain admission to the TV/radio/appliance outlets that had the largest share of VCR sales and sold only brand name products. Mr. Park believed Chaebol's cost advantage would allow it to produce VCRs that carried more features than competitors' products at each price point in the market. Selling VCRs in this channel would enable Chaebol's products to be distinguished from the 50 or more brands of low-cost, low-priced VCRs, and firmly establish the PKY brand name. In the future, he hoped to move Chaebol TVs into this channel where there were higher margins for producers and retailers. His dream was to have the PKY brand obtain the same quality reputation that Sony and Panasonic had achieved.

The models Chaebol would offer under this strategy were as follows:

Model	Chaebol cost	Features
CHC	$247.90	Two video heads, 1 audio head, 1-event/14-day programmability, varactor tuning for 12 preset stations, 12-function wireless remote, auto rewind, frame advance, sharpness control.
CH1A	$286.15	Two video heads, 2 audio heads, stereo, 5-event/14-day programmability, varactor tuning for 50 preset stations, 14-function wireless remote, auto rewind, tape memory, memory backup, time-remaining indicator, 107-channel cable ready.
CH1B	$367.90	Four video heads, 2 audio heads, stereo/hi-fi/Dolby, 8-event/1-year programmability, quartz tuning, 133-channel cable ready, 17-function wireless remote, auto rewind, tape memory, time-remaining indicator, one-touch recording, slow motion, frame advance, video dub, audio dub, sharpness control.
CH1P	$388.30	All of the features of the CH1B Model plus portable.

Mr. Park estimated that these models would sell at retail for considerably less than competitive products with similar features. On Model CH1B, he believed the retail price difference could be as much as $350. With this kind of differential, Mr. Park believed he would find many TV/radio/appliance store-owners eager to take on his products since they would allow the retailer to gain larger margins than other brands. Chaebol expected to make nearly a 44 percent gross margin on models sold to this type of outlet.

Mr. Park was considering two approaches to getting his company's VCRs in TV/radio/appliance outlets. The first was to sell directly to the owners of these stores. This approach would require a significant expansion of Chaebol's marketing organization. Since the number of TV/radio/appliance stores to be reached was large and geographically dispersed, new sales offices would have to be established in Boston, Indianapolis, Dallas, St. Louis, and Seattle. Each sales office would have three salespeople. In addition, three regional sales managers would have to be hired to help organize the now diverse and large sales function of the company. Furthermore, the establishment of a high recognition for Chaebol's PKY brand name would have to come from extensive advertising. Mr. Park estimated that the expenditure of $6 million on advertising in 1985 would be minimal to achieve the results he desired.

As an alternative, Mr. Park knew this market could also be approached through the employment of distributors who were already selling the VCRs of other manufacturers to TV/radio/appliance stores. Under this plan, no new sales offices would need to be opened, but one new salesperson would be added to the staff of each existing office. These five salespeople would be charged with maintaining relationships with the 10 geographically dispersed consumer electronics distributors that Chaebol's head office would choose to carry its VCRs. These distributors would work first on getting PKY brand VCRs into the largest regional and national TV/radio/appliance chains. Chaebol's salespeople would also call on PKY retailers in their areas, working on incentive programs with outlet salespeople, solving any problems that might arise, and checking that the services expected from the distributors were being adequately performed. Using distributors would cost Chaebol 11 percent of its margin; that is, the distributors would get an 11 percent margin on sales while Chaebol's margin would drop to approximately 33 percent on these sales. Under this approach, no additional warehouses over those proposed under Strategy I would be required. However, since this approach required the establishment of the PKY brand name, the advertising cost of $6 million would still be necessary.

Mr. Park believed Chaebol could achieve sales of 120,000 VCRs in 1985 using the direct approach and 150,000 VCRs using distributors. Though these figures were lower than the initial sales that could be achieved under the first strategy, Mr. Park believed the long-term strength of the company was better served by the firm establishment of a brand name and a strong position in TV/radio/appliance outlets.

A comparison of the costs involved in the plans considered by Mr. Park is shown in the table below:

Financial Analysis

Expense area	Cost of each new unit	Strategy I	Strategy II	
			Direct	Distributors
Sales offices	$ 25,000/yr.	—	5	—
Salespeople	$ 42,000/yr. salary $ 23,000/yr. expenses	—	18	5
Warehouses	$300,000/yr.	3	5	3
Service facilities		.25% sales	.33 sales	.33 sales
Average margins		27%, 34%	44%	33%
Advertising		$1.5 million	$6 million	$6 million

As Mr. Park worked on estimating the relative costs of these alternatives, he wondered if there was another approach to the market that might lead to success both now and in the future for Chaebol Electronics Company, U.S.

Case 17

Ito-Yokado Company*

In mid-March 1991, Masanori Takahashi, a senior strategy analyst for Ito-Yokado Company, was preparing to depart for Dallas, Texas. Once there, he would be leading a team of Japanese and American managers responsible for establishing transitional and long-term strategies for the Southland Corporation. After nearly an entire year of intense bargaining and negotiation with Southland and its creditors, Ito-Yokado acquired Southland on March 5, 1991.

Takahashi began working with Ito-Yokado in 1972 as an assistant manager of one of the company's superstores. He had advanced to the position of regional manager by 1979. In early 1981, Ito-Yokado's Operation Reform Project was conceived and Takahashi was asked to be a member of the team leading the project.

During the first few months on the team, Takahashi quickly understood certain crucial aspects of the new project, most notably the use of point-of-sale (POS) systems. Since implementation of the project advanced most rapidly in Ito-Yokado's 7-Eleven Japan subsidiary, he also had become familiar with the operating environment of convenience stores in Japan.

As Takahashi left his Tokyo office, he could not help but feel both excitement and apprehension regarding his new position. He had gained confidence while involved with the successful Operation Reform Project at Ito-Yokado's superstores and 7-Eleven Japan convenience stores. But this experience might or might not prove to be useful in respect to Southland.

Company Background

Ito-Yokado's founder, Masatoshi Ito, was born in 1924 and graduated from a commercial high school in Yokohama. He worked briefly at Mitsubishi Heavy Industries before joining Japan's war effort in 1944. After World War II, he worked with his mother and elder brother at the family's 66-square-foot

---

* This case was written from public sources by M. Edgar Barrett and Christopher D. Buehler as a basis for class discussion rather than to illustrate either effective or ineffective handling of an administrative situation. Copyright © 1991 by M. Edgar Barrett. Used with permission from M. Edgar Barrett.

clothing store in Tokyo.[1] The store was incorporated as Kabushiki Kaisha Yokado in 1958. By 1960, Ito was in sole control of the family business. During that same year he made his first visit to the United States.

In 1960, Ito visited National Cash Register (NCR) in Dayton, Ohio.[2] While in the United States, Ito was introduced to terms such as *supermarkets* and *chain stores* by NCR, which was interested in selling cash registers to Japanese retailers. In Japan, retailing was dominated by mom-and-pop stores and a handful of venerable department stores, with few types of retail outlets in between. At this time, Ito began to see the possible role of mass merchandisers in a society becoming ''mass-oriented.''

Ito soon opened a small chain of superstores in the Tokyo area. These stores carried a large selection of household goods, food, and clothing of generally lesser quality and lower price than either the mom-and-pop or department stores.[3] By 1965, Ito had opened eight superstores. In the same year, the name of the chain was changed to Ito-Yokado.

The Growth of Ito-Yokado as a Superstore

Ito's concept for the superstores was centered on having the rough equivalent of several types of retail stores contained within one multistory superstore. The initial stores were located near population centers and railroad stations in the Tokyo areas.[4] Often, several stores were located in close proximity in order to achieve ''regional dominance.''[5] The results were high name recognition, reduced distribution costs, and the effective squeezing out of competition.

Ito soon realized that social changes in Japan could create new opportunities for his retailing ideas. Younger and more mobile Japanese appeared to be less willing to spend a great deal of time shopping at numerous mom-and-pop stores. Also, the Japanese society was experiencing increased suburbanization. Ito decided to located stores in suburban prefectures. There are 47 prefectures (provinces) in Japan.

One reason for locating stores in suburban areas was the lower cost of real estate. This allowed Ito-Yokado to open larger stores with more parking spaces than competitors located in congested urban areas. Ito continued to use a strategy of ''regional dominance'' with these new openings, most of which were concentrated in the greater Kanto district, which consists of the Tokyo metropolitan area and surrounding cities. By the early 1970s, Ito-Yokado stores

---

[1] Andrew Tanzer, ''A Form of Flattery,'' *Forbes* (June 2, 1986).

[2] Jim Mitchell, ''Southland Suitor Ito Learned from the Best,'' *Dallas Morning News* (April 1, 1990).

[3] Ito was not the first to open this type of retail outlet. Isao Nakauchi opened the first Daiei superstore in the Osaka area a few years before the first Ito-Yokado store was opened. In 1990, Daiei was Japan's largest retailer in terms of gross sales.

[4] Mitchell, ''Southland Suitor.''

[5] Hiroshi Uchida, *First Boston/CSFB Report on Ito-Yokado, Ltd.* (April 20, 1988), p. 7.

were opening at the rate of four or five per year. By the late 1970s, 9 or 10 new stores were opened annually.[6] In early 1987, 101 of 127 Ito-Yokado superstores were located in the greater Kanto district.

Ito also adopted a strategy of leasing some properties for new stores. As of the mid-1980s, over 87 percent of Ito-Yokado's aggregate sales floor space, 10 of the company's 11 distribution centers, and the company headquarters in Tokyo were all leased.[7] Often, property prices were astronomical, or the owners of well-located sites would not part with their property for any price.

Constraints on Growth

The initial success of Ito-Yokado and the other superstores soon resulted in retaliatory action by a powerful competitor: the mom-and-pop store owners. These small retailers were said to "pull the strings of Liberal Democratic Party politicians at the local level."[8] The action initiated by the small retailers resulted in the 1974 Large Store Restriction Act, which was subsequently strengthened in 1979. The original act restricted the opening of stores with sales areas of over 1,500 square meters (16,500 square feet). In addition, the act restricted the hours of operation of new and existing large stores. A series of changes in 1979 added restrictions on stores with sales areas greater than 500 square meters (5,500 square feet). A Commerce Coordination Committee was established in each area in order to set policy regarding large-store openings and hours of operation. The committees were effectively controlled by the small retailers. By the early 1980s, Ito-Yokado was opening only four or five new stores annually.[9]

Factors other than the Large Store Restriction Act adversely affected Ito-Yokado. Japanese consumers' real disposable income decreased by a little over 1 percent during 1980–1981.[10] Japan experienced a general economic downturn in the early 1980s, as did the rest of the world, again serving to limit consumer purchasing power. Net income for Ito-Yokado—which had grown almost 30 percent per year between 1976 and 1981—grew by 9.7 percent in 1982 and by 0.9 percent in 1983.[11] The legal restrictions imposed on large stores, when combined with the economic downturn, led to both lower current earnings and a projection of reduced rates of growth in future earnings.

---

[6] Ibid., p. 6.

[7] Ibid., p. 7.

[8] Tanzer, "A Form of Flattery."

[9] Uchida, *First Boston*, pp. 7–8.

[10] Ibid.

[11] Ibid., p. 8.

Ito-Yokado as a Parent Company

During the early 1970s, Ito began pursuing new retailing interests. In 1972, he approached Dallas-based Southland Corporation in an attempt to secure a license to operate 7-Eleven stores in Japan. He was rebuffed.[12] He made a similar attempt in 1973 with the aid of a Japanese trading company, C. Itoh and Company, and was successful in obtaining the license. Concurrently, Ito was pursuing another U.S. firm, Denny's Restaurants, in an attempt to obtain rights for opening Denny's Restaurants in Japan. Both subsidiaries, Denny's Japan and 7-Eleven Japan (originally called York Seven but renamed 7-Eleven Japan in 1978), were established in 1973. The first 7-Eleven and the initial Denny's in Japan were both opened in 1974. Stock for each of the two majority-owned subsidiaries was traded independently on the Tokyo Stock Exchange. Both subsidiaries became profitable around 1977.[13]

Ito-Yokado in the 1980s

The Ito-Yokado group consisted of three business segments: Superstores and other Retail Operations, Restaurant Operations, and Convenience Store Operations. The Convenience Store Operations segment was made up of 7-Eleven Japan. The Restaurant Operations segment consisted of Denny's and Famil Restaurants. Ito-Yokado superstores, Daikuma discount stores, two supermarket chains (York Mart and York-Benimaru), Robinson's Department Stores, and Oshman's Sporting Goods Store made up the Superstores and other Retail Operations segment. Ito-Yokado's financial statements are shown in Exhibits 1 through 3.

Superstores and Other Retail Operations

York Mart and York-Benimaru

York Mart was a 100 percent owned subsidiary established in 1975. In 1990, it operated 40 supermarkets located primarily in the Tokyo area.[14] These stores sold mainly fresh foods and packaged goods, and competition was high in this geographic and retail area. Ito-Yokado's Operation Reform Program was implemented by York Mart in 1986 as a means to boost efficiency and profits. By 1990 sales were increasing at 6 percent per year.[15]

---

[12] Mitchell, ''Southland Suitor.''
[13] Uchida, *First Boston*, p. 8.
[14] Ibid., p. 8; and *Moody's Industrial Manual*, 1990, vol. 1, p. 1275.
[15] Ibid.

EXHIBIT 1 Ito-Yokado Company, Ltd., consolidated balance sheet (in millions of yen)

	As of February 28				
	1986	1987	1988	1989	1990
Assets					
Cash	¥ 26,188	¥ 25,596	¥ 32,527	¥ 31,566	¥ 32,529
Time deposits	32,708	64,894	55,631	125,809	163,524
Marketable securities	33,882	33,635	75,924	63,938	60,905
Notes and accounts receivable	16,570	16,582	19,042	26,949	24,195
Inventories	48,813	48,163	49,372	56,519	56,168
Other current assets	13,014	13,951	13,655	15,156	17,892
Total current assets	171,175	202,821	246,151	319,937	355,213
Investments and advertisement	18,097	21,642	24,352	25,589	33,779
Gross property and equipment	465,049	505,450	544,752	600,815	663,263
Less accumulated depreciation	160,409	183,185	207,561	237,079	262,958
Net property and equipment	304,640	322,265	337,191	363,736	400,305
Leasehold deposits	81,500	88,386	93,358	98,639	114,678
Total Assets	¥575,394	¥635,114	¥701,052	¥807,901	¥903,975
Liabilities and owners' equity					
Short term	¥ 23,577	¥ 22,425	¥ 17,815	¥ 20,090	¥ 20,140
Debt due	13,450	8,396	5,689	3,964	6,815
Accounts and notes payable	105,790	103,519	119,982	135,516	153,551
Accrued liability	40,892	45,217	53,654	61,077	65,941
Other current liability	12,777	13,523	17,297	20,458	25,404
Total current liabilities	196,486	193,080	214,437	241,305	271,851
Long-term debt	86,802	109,563	99,961	93,720	85,265
Accrued sev. indemnity	1,201	1,248	1,319	1,227	1,297
Deferred income taxes	1,912	2,036	969	0	2,150
Minority interests	45,011	51,974	60,619	83,102	95,920
Owners' Equity					
Common stock	17,364	18,184	22,462	28,913	33,328
Capital surplus	78,202	82,070	88,139	95,817	100,230
Other capital	9,292	9,292	9,292	16,210	16,210
Legal reserve	4,029	4,837	5,715	6,741	7,858
Retained earnings	135,307	163,042	198,351	241,078	290,078
Owner's equity	244,194	277,425	304,725	388,759	447,704
Less treasury stock	(212)	(212)	(1,423)	(212)	(212)
Net owners' equity	575,394	277,213	303,302	388,547	447,492
Total liabilities and owners' equity	¥243,982	¥635,114	¥701,052	¥807,901	¥903,975

Source: *Moody's Industrial Manual, 1990, vol. 1.*

EXHIBIT 2   Ito-Yokado Company, Ltd., consolidated income statement (in millions of yen)

	As of February 28				
	1986	*1987*	*1988*	*1989*	*1990*
Net sales	¥1,201,347	¥1,281,203	¥1,371,960	¥1,524,947	¥1,664,390
Cost of goods sold	829,077	875,343	923,771	1,025,839	1,113,659
Gross margin	372,270	405,860	448,189	499,108	550,731
Depreciation and amortization	27,328	31,106	32,064	33,777	37,695
Selling, general, and administrative expense	252,355	271,204	294,208	324,295	354,321
Operating income	92,587	103,550	121,917	141,036	158,715
Interest income	6,585	5,827	7,173	8,662	12,838
Interest expense	6,982	5,962	4,755	3,400	3,751
Foreign currency gains	2,089	488	74	—	—
Income before taxes	92,279	103,903	124,409	146,298	167,802
Income taxes					
Current	5,449	61,005	72,191	84,930	91,561
Deferred	1,153	106	(1,400)	(2,498)	3,183
Total income taxes	55,605	61,111	70,791	82,432	94,744
Minority interests	7,471	8,862	11,058	13,338	15,777
Equity in affiliated earnings	618	829	951	1,058	984
Net income	¥ 31,824	¥ 34,759	¥ 43,511	¥ 51,586	¥ 58,465
Opening retained earnings	¥ 109,717	¥ 135,307	¥ 163,042	¥ 198,351	¥ 241,078
Cash dividends	5,570	6,216	7,324	7,833	8,348
Transfer to legal reserves	664	808	878	1,026	1,117
Closing retained earnings	¥ 135,307	¥ 163,042	¥ 198,351	¥ 241,078	¥ 290,078
Per common share					
Net income	¥ 81.44	¥ 88.05	¥ 108.40	¥ 127.35	¥ 143.71
Cash dividends	¥ 15.70	¥ 18.18	¥ 19.55	¥ 20.00	¥ 23.00
Average number of shares	396,798	400,449	406,554	408,037	408,770

Source: *Moody's Industrial Manual*, 1990 vol. 1.

York-Benimaru was a 29 percent owned affiliate of Ito-Yokado, and was an independently managed regional supermarket chain. York-Benimaru operated 51 stores as of 1988. The stores were located in the Fukushima prefecture of Koriyama-city in northern Japan.[16] Like York Mart, York-Benimaru operated with a higher profit margin than the supermarket industry as a whole. York-Benimaru's earnings growth rate of 13 percent per year was expected to last into the 1990s, and Ito-Yokado's share of this profit was the major contribution to the "equity in earnings of affiliates" portion of Ito-Yokado's income statement (see Exhibit 2).[17]

Daikuma

Daikuma discount stores were consolidated into the Ito-Yokado group in 1986, when Ito-Yokado's ownership of Daikuma increased from 47.6 percent to 79.5

[16] Ibid.
[17] Ibid.

EXHIBIT 3 Ito-Yokado Company, Ltd., statement of cash flows (in millions of yen)

	As of February 28			
	1987	1988	1989	1990
Cash flow from operations				
Net income	¥ 34,759	¥ 43,511	¥ 51,586	¥ 58,465
Adjustments				
Depreciation and amortization	31,106	32,064	33,777	37,695
Minority interest	8,862	11,058	13,338	15,577
Undistributed earnings of affiliates	(603)	(719)	(811)	(732)
Deferred income tax and other	985	1,328	1,641	5,677
Increase in accounts and notes				
Receivable, less allowance	(12)	(2,140)	(10,675)	58
Decrease (increase) in inventory	650	(1,196)	(6,049)	740
Decrease (increase) in prepaid				
expenses	(2,194)	734	(1,109)	(8,875)
Increase in accounts and notes				
Payable and accrued liability	2,054	24,740	22,296	22,388
Increase in other liability	718	3,744	2,945	4,815
Net cash provided by operations	¥ 76,325	¥112,854	¥106,939	¥135,808
Cash flow from investing				
Increase in property and equipment	¥ (50,832)	¥ (50,075)	¥ (55,802)	¥ (72,927)
Increase in investments and				
advertising	(3,492)	(3,260)	(1,706)	(6,339)
Proceeds from disposal of property				
and equipment	1,460	731	1,991	1,442
Other	(6,206)	(5,629)	(5,878)	(13,888)
Net cash used by investing	¥ (58,620)	¥ (58,233)	¥ (61,395)	¥ (91,742)
Cash flow from financing				
Issue of long-term debt	¥ 37,859	¥ 7,692	¥ 9,755	¥ 10,135
Repayment of long-term debt	(15,331)	(9,321)	(6,472)	(7,112)
Proceeds from issuance of common				
stock by subs	0	0	18,554	0
Dividends paid	(6,216)	(7,324)	(7,833)	(8,834)
Other	(2,670)	(5,711)	(2,317)	(3,096)
Net cash provided by financing	¥ 13,642	¥ (14,664)	¥ 11,687	¥ (8,421)
Net change in cash equivalent	¥ 31,347	¥ 39,957	¥ 57,231	¥ 35,645
Cash equivalent at start of year	92,778	124,125	164,082	221,313
Cash equivalent at end of year	¥124,125	¥164,082	¥221,313	¥256,958

Source: *Moody's Industrial Manual, 1990 and 1989*, vol. 1.

percent.[18] In 1990, Daikuma was one of the largest discount store chains in Japan with 14 stores. While Daikuma was popular among young Japanese consumers, the discount stores attracted the critical attention of competing small retailers. Because the discount stores were regulated by the Large Store Regulation Act, intensive effort was required to open new stores. Despite these circumstances, and increasing competition, Daikuma opened two discount stores in 1989.[19]

[18] Ibid.
[19] *Moody's Industrial Manual*, p. 1275.

Robinson's Department Stores

In 1984, the Robinson's Japan Company was established to open Robinson's Department Stores in Japan. The Robinson's name was used under the terms of a license granted by the U.S. store of the same name. The Japanese company was 100 percent owned by Ito-Yokado, and the first Robinson's Department Store in Japan was opened in November 1985 in Kasukabe City of Saitama Prefecture.[20] This was a residential community north of Tokyo and was a rapidly growing area. Although an Ito-Yokado superstore was located nearby, Ito-Yokado's management believed that a niche existed for a slightly more upscale retail store. Ito-Yokado had "shattered traditional wisdom by opening up a department store in the suburbs, not in the center of Tokyo."[21] The location was expected to serve a population area of over 600,000 residents and to offer a broad selection of consumer goods at prices higher than superstores yet lower than the downtown Tokyo department stores.

Many of the strategies employed by Ito-Yokado in opening its Robinson's Department Store followed similar strategies employed in its superstores. The land was leased (in a suburb). Instead of purchasing goods on a consignment basis as most other department stores did, Robinson's managers were made responsible for the outright purchase of goods from suppliers. This allowed Robinson's to purchase goods at a significantly reduced price. Robinson's reported its first profit in fiscal 1989, approximately four years after opening.[22] In contrast, most Japanese department stores operate approximately 10 years before reporting a profit.[23] The single Robinson's location grossed about ¥28 billion (US$220 million) in fiscal 1989.[24] The second Robinson's Department Store opened in late 1990 in Utsunomiya, about 100 kilometers (60 miles) north of Tokyo.

Oshman's Sporting Goods

Ito-Yokado licensed the Oshman's Sporting Goods name from the Houston, Texas, parent company in 1985. That year, two stores were opened. One of the stores was located inside the original Robinson's Department Store.

Restaurant Operations

Famil

The Famil Restaurant chain was started in 1979 as an in-store restaurant to serve customers at Ito-Yokado superstores. It had, however, expanded to 251 loca-

---

[20] Uchida, *First Boston*, p. 10.
[21] Ibid.
[22] *Moody's Industrial Manual*, p. 1275.
[23] Uchida, *First Boston*, p. 10.
[24] *Moody's Industrial Manual*, p. 1275.

tions by 1988.[25] The Famil chain did not record its first positive earnings until 1986. In Famil's attempts to expand operations, the company had emphasized its catering business.[26] By 1990, the in-store operations (those located in Ito-Yokado superstores) accounted for 45 percent of Famil's sales, the catering business accounted for 32 percent of sales, and free-standing stores accounted for 23 percent of sales.[27]

Denny's Japan

Ito-Yokado opened the initial Denny's (Japan) Restaurant in 1974 with a license from Denny's of La Mirada, California. Ito-Yokado tailored the U.S. family restaurant to the Japanese market, and Denny's Japan became profitable around 1977. By 1981, 100 Denny's Japan restaurants had been established, [28] and in 1990 there were 320 such restaurants operated by Ito-Yokado.[29] In 1990, Ito-Yokado controlled 51 percent of Denny's Japan stock. In the early 1980s, Ito-Yokado decided that Denny's Japan should purchase all rights to the Denny's name in Japan. The purchase was made in 1984, and royalty payments to the U.S. parent were thereby discontinued.[30]

The fiscal year 1990 (March 1989, to February 1990), Denny's Japan reported a net annual sales increase of 10.9 percent, as compared to the 4.9 percent Japanese restaurant industry sales increase for the same period.[31] Exhibits 4 and 5 contain financial statements for Denny's Japan. In 1988, Denny's Japan began using an electronic order-entry system, which allowed managers of individual restaurants to quickly order food supplies based on trends in their own restaurant. It also allowed for the periodic updating of menus to reflect new food items.

Convenience Store Operations

7-Eleven Japan

Since the opening of the first 7-Eleven store in 1974, the chain had grown to over 4,300 stores located in virtually all parts of Japan by February 1990.[32] At

---

[25] Uchida, *First Boston*, p. 12.

[26] Ibid.

[27] *Moody's Industrial Manual*, p. 1275.

[28] Ibid.

[29] Yumiko Ono, "Japanese Chain Stores Prosper by Milking American Concepts," *Asian Wall Street Journal* (April 2, 1990).

[30] Ibid.

[31] *Moody's Industrial Manual*, pp. 1275–1276.

[32] James Sterngold, "New Japanese Lesson: Running a 7-11," *New York Times* (May 9, 1991), p. C1.

EXHIBIT 4 Denny's Japan Company, Ltd., consolidated balance sheet (in millions of yen)

	As of February 28		
	1988	1989	1990
Assets			
Cash	¥ 1,436	¥ 1,686	¥ 1,516
Time deposits	4,430	4,930	13,340
Marketable securities	104	0	14
Notes and accounts receivable	76	87	111
Inventories	562	569	617
Prepaid expenses	529	610	758
Short-term loans	4,527	6,241	5
Short-term leasehold deposits	267	286	300
Other current assets	414	233	341
Total current assets	12,345	14,643	17,092
Investments and advances	2,452	2,133	2,273
Gross property and equipment	18,894	21,291	23,739
Less: accumulated depreciation	9,108	10,397	11,937
Net property and equipment	9,786	10,894	11,802
Fixed leasehold deposits	5,177	5,334	5,496
Deferred charges other assets	4,449	3,940	3,380
Total assets	¥34,209	¥36,944	¥40,043
Liabilities and owners' equity			
Accounts payable	¥ 3,728	¥ 3,865	¥ 3,932
Accrued expenses	1,560	1,743	1,837
Income tax	2,009	2,210	2,140
Consumption tax withhold	328	0	653
Other current liabilities	0	383	299
Total current liabilities	7,625	8,201	8,861
Common stock	7,125	7,125	7,125
Additional paid-in capital	9,533	9,785	9,785
Legal reserves	233	286	345
Closing retained earnings	9,724	11,547	13,927
Owners' equity	26,584	28,743	31,182
Total liabilities and owners' equity	¥34,209	¥36,944	¥40,043

Source: *Moody's International Manual,* 1989, 1990, vol. 1.

that time, about 300 new stores were being opened annually.[33] Ito-Yokado owned approximately 50.3 percent of 7-Eleven Japan in 1990.

Originally, young urban workers represented the primary customer base. As 7-Eleven penetrated the Japanese market, however, almost everyone became a potential customer. In Tokyo, for example, utility bills could be paid at the chain's stores.[34]

The 7-Eleven stores were small enough, with an average of only 1,000 square feet, to effectively avoid regulation under the Large Store Regulation Act. This allowed 7-Eleven to compete with the mom-and-pop retailers on the

[33] Ono, "Japanese Chain Stores Prosper."
[34] Ibid.

EXHIBIT 5 Denny's Japan Company, Ltd., consolidated income statement
(in millions of yen)

	As of February 28		
	1988	*1989*	*1990*
Net sales	¥58,241	¥64,604	¥70,454
Interest income	317	434	650
Other revenue, net	223	236	290
Total revenue	58,781	65,274	71,394
Cost of sales	20,196	22,233	23,952
Gross margin	38,585	43,041	47,442
Sellings, administrative, and general expenses	32,444	35,990	40,177
Interest expense	19	9	17
Loss on sale of property	73	153	119
Income before taxes	6,049	6,889	7,129
Income taxes	3,521	3,894	4,074
Net income	¥ 2,528	¥ 2,995	¥ 3,055
Opening retained earnings	¥ 7,755	¥ 9,152	¥11,547
Cash dividends	508	535	588
Transfers to legal reserves	51	53	59
Closing retained earnings	¥ 9,724	¥11,559	¥13,955
Earnings per share (based on 26,741,000 weighted average shares)	¥ 94.50	¥112.40	¥114.20

Source: *Moody's International Manual*, 1989, 1990, vol. 1. The data are presented here as shown in Moody's. Some minor math errors exist.

basis of longer hours of operation and lower prices. Faced with this competition, many of the small retailers joined the ranks of 7-Eleven. By converting small retailers to 7-Eleven stores, Ito-Yokado was able to expand rapidly and blanket the country.[35]

7-Eleven Japan pursued a strategy of franchising stores instead of owning them. The franchise commission for 7-Eleven stores was approximately 45 percent of the gross profit of the store (the commission was 43 percent for 24-hour stores). Ito-Yokado provided most of the ancillary functions for each store (e.g., administration, accounting, advertising, and 80 percent of utility costs). In 1987, 92 percent of all 7-Eleven stores in Japan were franchised,[36] and by 1990, only 2 percent of the 7-Elevens were corporate owned.[37]

Within the Ito-Yokado group, 7-Eleven contributed 6.8 percent of revenues in 1990. With this relatively small portion of overall corporate revenues, however, 7-Eleven Japan contributed over 35 percent of the group's profit. Under its licensing agreement, 7-Eleven Japan paid royalties of 0.6 percent of

---

[35] Tanzer, "A Form of Flattery."

[36] Uchida, *First Boston*, p. 13.

[37] *Moody's Industrial Manual*, p. 1276.

EXHIBIT 6 7-Eleven Japan consolidated balance sheet (in millions of yen)

	As of February 28		
	1988	1989	1990
Assets			
Cash	¥ 11,868	¥ 15,739	¥ 14,373
Time deposits	23,440	31,090	65,510
Short-term loans	26,169	52,228	29,136
Notes and accounts receivable	2,343	2,517	2,582
Inventory	247	285	222
Prepaid expenses	223	285	124
Less: allowance for other debts	1,990	320	180
Other current assets	351	651	369
Total current assets	66,631	102,315	112,136
Investments and advances	3,534	3,382	9,355
Gross property and equipment	94,703	108,319	123,871
Less: accumulated depreciation	25,665	30,316	35,010
Net property and equipment	69,038	78,003	88,861
Fixed leasehold deposits	4,351	6,501	7,725
Other assets	1,460	2,213	8,248
Total assets	¥145,014	¥192,417	¥226,325
Liabilities and owners' equity			
Accounts payable	¥ 40,498	¥ 46,678	¥ 52,912
Accrued expenses	1,427	1,487	1,738
Advances	685	778	718
Income taxes	14,818	17,341	20,068
Other current liabilities	867	552	3,289
Total current liabilities	58,295	66,836	78,725
Long-term debt	1,612	1,781	1,933
Common stock	5,902	17,145	17,145
Additional paid-in capital	13,073	24,619	24,589
Legal reserves	1,142	1,491	1,919
Retained earnings	65,233	80,545	101,984
Owners' equity	85,107	123,800	145,667
Total liabilities and owners' equity	¥145,014	¥192,417	¥226,325

Source: *Moody's International Manual*, 1989, 1990, vol. 1.

gross sales to the Southland Corporation. In 1989 and 1990, 7-Eleven Japan paid royalties of about $4.1 million and $4.7 million, respectively. The financial statements for 7-Eleven Japan for the years 1986 to 1990 are shown in Exhibits 6 and 7.

Operation Reform Project

Ito-Yokado implemented the Operation Reform Project in late 1981 in a retail industry environment punctuated by reduced consumer spending and decreasing margins. The goals of the project were to increase efficiency and boost profitability by increasing the inventory turn while avoiding empty stores shelves. The plan was originally implemented in the Ito-Yokado superstores and the 7-Eleven Japan convenience stores.

EXHIBIT 7 7-Eleven Japan consolidated income statement (in millions of yen)

	As of February 28		
	1988	*1989*	*1990*
Revenue	¥96,236	¥102,314	¥118,490
Cost of goods sold	13,484	8,702	9,249
Gross margin	82,752	93,612	109,241
Selling, administrative, and general expenses	39,672	42,491	49,185
Loss on sale of property	232	(66)	(230)
Income before taxes	42,848	51,187	59,826
Tax expenses	23,911	28,882	33,599
Net income	¥18,937	¥ 22,305	¥ 26,227
Opening retained earnings	¥49,646	¥ 62,139	¥ 80,545
Dividends	3,054	3,495	4,280
Transfers to legal reserves	306	350	428
Officers' bonus	0	54	80
Closing retained earnings	¥65,223	¥ 80,545	¥101,984
Earnings per share (based on 179,569,000 weighted average shares)	¥ 129.1	¥ 126.7	¥ 146.1

Note: "Cost of goods sold" represents primarily the cost of merchandise sold in the 152 company-owned stores.
Source: *Moody's International Manual*, 1989, 1990, vol. 1.

The implementation of the project involved a coordinated effort of catering to rapidly changing consumer preferences while, simultaneously, monitoring merchandise flow more closely. This coordination was accomplished by making individual store managers more responsible for such decisions as what merchandise was to be stocked on store shelves, thus allowing managers to tailor merchandise selection in their individual stores to local preferences. Top Ito-Yokado regional managers held weekly meetings with store managers to monitor the implementation of the project. As late as 1988, these meetings were still held on a weekly basis.[38]

In order to avoid depletion of store stocks, Ito-Yokado established an online ordering system with vendors. In 1982, the ordering system reached only 400 vendors. By 1988, however, the system linked Ito-Yokado with 1,860 vendors.[39]

---

[38] Hiroaki Komatsu, *Nomura Securities Report on Ito-Yokado Co., Ltd.* (June 7, 1988), p. 4.
[39] Ibid.

Point-of-Sale System[40]

As implementation of the Operation Reform Project began, Ito-Yokado paid increased attention to the importance of obtaining information regarding the flow of merchandise through individual stores. The tool chosen to accomplish this task was the point-of-sale (POS) system. POS system usage was increasing in the United States in the early 1980s, but the systems were used primarily to increase productivity at the cash register.[41] In contrast, Ito-Yokado used similar systems as a part of the project by monitoring specific merchandise flow. As of the late 1980s, many retailers in the United States had begun utilizing POS in similar capacities, and some had begun to use POS to track the purchases of individual consumers.[42]

The first use of POS systems in Japan came in 1982, when 7-Eleven Japan began installing them in its stores. By 1986, every 7-Eleven store in Japan was equipped with such a system.[43] The systems available were sophisticated enough to monitor the entire stock of merchandise in a typical convenience store having about 3,000 items.[44] The systems could monitor the flow of every item of merchandise through the purchase, inventory, sale, and restocking stages.

In late 1984, Ito-Yokado decided to install POS systems in the superstores. The sophistication of those systems installed in convenience stores, however, was not adequate to handle the merchandise flow of a superstore, which could stock up to 500,000 items.[45] New POS systems were developed in

---

[40] POS systems are computer-based merchandise control systems. They can provide a variety of functions such as inventory monitoring, price identification and registering, and—in some circumstances—merchandise ordering.

The implementation of POS systems became a reality in the early 1970s, when IBM announced the creation of a merchandise system that later became the Universal Product Code (UPC). In 1974, Marsh Supermarkets became the first retail store to utilize UPC-based POS systems. Also in 1974, the European Article Number (EAN) system, which is virtually a superset of the UPC, was introduced in Europe. The EAN system was adopted by 12 European nations in 1977. In 1978, Japan joined the EAN association (EANA). By 1989, 40 countries were members of the EANA.

The Japanese domestic market utilizes the same bar-code system used in the United States and Europe for product marking under the EAN guidelines for product marking. The Japanese coding system for consumer goods is called Japanese Article Numbering (JAN). A similar system for product marking used by wholesalers and distributors in Japan is the value-added network (VAN). The first product utilizing the JAN code was introduced in Japan in 1978.

Source: Ryosuke Assano "Networks Raise Efficiency," *Business Japan* (October 1989), pp. 45–52; Radack et al., "Automation in the Marketplace" (March 1978); "Pointing Out Differences in Point-of-Sale," *Chain Store Age Executive* (October 1990), pp. 16B–17B.

[41] Tanzer, "A Form of Flattery."

[42] For an example of one such application, see Blake Ives et al., *The Tom Thumb Promise Club*, Edwin L. Cox School of Business, Southern Methodist University, 1989.

[43] Hiroaki Komatsu, *Nomura Securities Report on 7-Eleven Japan* (March 15, 1988), p. 4.

[44] Uchida, *First Boston*, p. 13.

[45] Ibid.

a coordinated effort by Ito-Yokado, Nippon Electric, and Nomura Computer Services.

The installation of POS systems in the existing superstores was completed in November 1985, with over 8,000 POS registers installed in 121 stores.[46] With 138 stores in 1990, Ito-Yokado had an estimated 9,000 POS registers in the superstores alone. In 1986, after the systems had been installed in all superstores and 7-Elevens, Ito-Yokado accounted for about 70 percent of the POS systems in use in Japan.[47] As of 1988, 7-Eleven Japan was the only major convenience store chain in Japan to have installed POS systems.[48] By August 31, 1989, Japan had 119,137 POS scanner-equipped registers in 42,880 stores, making it the country with the most POS systems in use.[49]

The POS systems used by 7-Eleven Japan and Ito-Yokado superstores were upgraded in 1986 to add a new dimension to Ito-Yokado's Operation Reform Project.[50] The upgraded systems allowed for bidirectional communication with the company headquarters. This feature essentially allowed information to flow not only from individual stores to a central location, but also from the central location back to individual stores. By linking the central system to other computer systems, more information than just sales of retail items could be transmitted. This capability allowed Ito-Yokado to increase the efficiency of deliveries by centralizing some orders. By increasing the total size of orders, Ito-Yokado increased its bargaining position with distributors. One result of this bargaining strength was more frequent deliveries of smaller volume. From 1987 to 1988, deliveries increased from one to three per week for stores in many regions of Japan, notably the Tokyo, Hokkaido, and Kyushu areas.

Using the POS systems, 7-Eleven began to offer customers door-to-door parcel delivery in conjunction with Nippon Express. In addition, some POS terminals were being used to issue prepaid telephone credit cards.[51] Since October 1987, Tokyo-area customers had been able to pay their electric bills at 7-Eleven; since March 1988, they had also been able to pay their gas bills.[52] Since women traditionally manage household finances in Japan, these services were designed to attract more women customers to the convenience stores.

Results

For the Ito-Yokado superstores alone, average days of inventory decreased from 25.8 in 1982 to 17.3 in 1987. By 1990, it was estimated to be 13 days.[53] The

---

[46] *Moody's Industrial Manual*, p. 1275.

[47] Tanzer, ''A Form of Flattery.''

[48] Komatsu, *Nomura Securities Report*, p. 4.

[49] *Business Japan* (October 1989), p. 51.

[50] Komatsu, *Nomura Securities Report*, p. 5.

[51] Ibid.

[52] Ibid.

[53] Uchida, *First Boston*, pp. 12, 22; and *Moody's Industrial Manual*, p. 1276.

EXHIBIT 8 Daiei, Inc. consolidated balance sheet (in millions of yen)

	As of February 28		
	1988	*1989*	*1990*
Assets			
Cash	¥ 60,409	¥ 61,096	¥ 55,529
Time deposits	89,090	61,866	85,713
Marketable securities	18,919	18,762	20,022
Net receivables	100,214	98,449	103,455
Inventories	95,924	90,203	108,241
Prepaid expenses and deferred income tax	7,784	11,149	15,338
Total current assets	372,340	341,525	388,298
Gross property and equipment	284,007	358,443	410,870
Less accumulated depreciation	108,540	120,955	141,172
Net property and equipment	175,467	237,488	269,698
Lease depreciation and loans to lessors	231,996	245,139	266,474
Investment and long-term receivables	118,009	170,676	164,853
Other assets	13,689	16,540	21,306
Total assets	¥911,501	¥1,011,368	¥1,110,629
Liabilities and owners' equity			
Short-term borrowings	¥256,539	¥ 338,188	¥ 350,274
Debt due	51,488	47,816	34,667
Notes and accounts payable	176,450	186,390	221,815
Accruals	18,370	18,274	21,256
Income taxes	7,872	7,284	8,445
Total current liabilities	510,719	597,952	636,457
Long-term debt	199,616	187,625	216,763
Lease deposits	52,656	56,750	60,489
Estimated retirement and term allowance	10,002	9,437	9,789
Reserve for investment losses	35,903	35,293	37,151
Deferred income	7,423	7,343	7,425
Other liabilities	1,636	4,604	7,314
Translation adjustment	2,179	1,979	1,754
Minority interests	663	692	2,794
Common stock (¥50)	18,144	25,649	33,783
Additional paid-in capital	82,748	92,426	100,664
Legal reserves	3,875	4,481	5,108
Deficit	(14,063)	(12,863)	(8,862)
Owners' equity	90,704	109,693	130,693
Total liabilities and owners' equity	¥911,501	¥1,011,368	¥1,110,629

Source: *Moody's International Manual*, 1990 and 1989, vol. 1.

effect on operating margins and net income for the entire Ito-Yokado corporation was equally dramatic. In 1982, the company's operating margin stood at 5.1 percent. It had increased to 8.1 percent by 1987. By 1990, the operating margin had climbed to 10.5 percent. Net income for the corporation increased from ¥14,662 million in 1982 to ¥34,649 million in 1987, and ¥58,465 million in 1990.[54]

---

[54] Ibid.

7-Eleven Japan recorded similar increases in operating margins and net income during the same period. In 1982, 7-Eleven Japan's operating margin was 20.7 percent. It had increased to 34.6 percent by 1987. Net income from the 7-Eleven operations increased from ¥7,837 million in 1982 to ¥33,000 million in 1987.[55]

As of 1990, the Ito-Yokado corporation was the second largest retailer in Japan, with ¥1,664,390 million of annual gross sales. The leading retailer was Daiei, with ¥2,114,909 million of revenues. Ito-Yokado was, however, the most profitable retailer in Japan, with net income of ¥58,465 million. In comparison, Daiei recorded net income of only ¥9,457 million for 1990. Financial statements for Daiei are shown as Exhibits 8 (p. 303), and 9.

EXHIBIT 9 Daiei, Inc. consolidated income statement (in millions of yen except earnings per share)

	As of February 28		
	1988	*1989*	*1990*
Net sales	¥1,718,886	¥1,880,825	¥2,114,909
Real estate revenue	0	21,235	22,790
Other revenue	45,588	37,623	55,171
Total operating revenue	1,764,474	1,939,683	2,192,870
Cost of goods sold	1,327,618	1,460,007	1,626,850
Gross margin	436,856	479,676	566,020
Selling, general, and administrative expenses	392,914	432,269	510,469
Operating income	43,942	47,407	55,551
Net interest expenditures	16,942	19,115	21,312
Other expenses	1,760	1,283	3,401
Income before taxes	25,240	27,009	30,838
Income tax	13,405	14,868	17,101
Minority interests	50	32	730
Equity losses	7,204	4,229	3,504
Translation adjustment	211	134	(46)
Net income	¥ 4,792	¥ 8,104	¥ 9,457
Opening retained earnings	¥ (13,929)	¥ (14,063)	¥ (12,863)
Decrease due to merger of chain store operations	0	0	1,497
Cash dividends	5,083	6,059	6,269
Transfer to legal reserves	73	606	627
Bonuses	114	141	143
Translation adjustment	(344)	8	(86)
Closing retained earnings	¥ (14,063)	¥ (12,863)	¥ (8,862)
Earnings per share	¥ 14.27	¥ 21.67	¥ 24.72
Shares outstanding	n/a	369,871,000	382,499,000

Source: *Moody's International Manual,* 1990 and 1989, vol. 1.

---

[55] Ibid.

The Southland Corporation[56]

The Southland Corporation began in Dallas, Texas, in 1927 when Claude S. Dawley consolidated several small Texas ice companies into the Southland Ice Company. This new company was under the direction of 26-year-old Joe C. Thompson, Sr. Under Thompson's guidance, Southland began to use its retail outlets (curb service docks) to sell products in addition to ice, such as watermelon, milk, bread, eggs, and cigarettes. With the addition of these products, the concept of the convenience store was born.

During the Great Depression and the 1940s, Southland's convenience store business added several more products, including gasoline, frozen foods, beauty products, fresh fruit and vegetables, and picnic supplies. Because the store opened at 7 A.M. and remained open till 11 P.M., the store name 7-Eleven was adopted during this time.

The 1950s were a period of substantial growth in terms of the number of stores and of 7-Eleven's geographical coverage. The first stores located outside of Texas were opened in Florida in 1954. During the same year, 7-Eleven's operating profit surpassed the $1 million mark for the first time. By 1959, the entire 7-Eleven empire constituted 425 stores in Texas, Louisiana, Florida, and several other East Coast states.

John Thompson became president of Southland when his father, Jodie Thompson, died in 1961. During the 1960s, a population migration toward the suburbs and changing lifestyles presented Southland with new growth opportunities. John Thompson led Southland on the path of expansion, and over 3,000 stores were opened in the decade. The product line of 7-Eleven also grew during this time, to include prepared foods, rental items, and some self-service gasoline pumps.

The 1970s were also a period of achievement for Southland. In 1971, the $1 billion sales mark was surpassed. Southland stock began trading on the New York Stock Exchange in 1972, and the 5,000th store was opened in 1974. It was at this time that Masatoshi Ito approached Southland with the prospect of franchising 7-Eleven stores in Japan.

During the 1970s and early 1980s, Southland's activities became more diversified. In 1986, the company had four operating groups: the Stores Group, the Dairies Group, the Special Operations Group, and the Gasoline Supply Division.

The Stores Group represented the largest of the operating groups in terms of sales through the 1980s. The Stores Group was responsible for the operating and franchising of convenience stores. At the end of 1985, there were 7,519 7-Eleven stores in most of the United States and five provinces of Canada. This group was also responsible for 84 Gristede's and Charles & Company food

---

[56] A more detailed history of Southland can be found in cases written by M. Edgar Barrett, of the American Graduate School of International Business: *The Southland Corporation (A)*, 1983, and *The Southland Corporation (B)*, 1990.

stores, 38 Super-7 outlets, and 7-Eleven stores operated under area licensees in the United States, Canada, and several Pacific Rim countries, including Japan.

The Dairies Group was one of the nation's largest dairy processors in 1986, and served primarily the Stores Group, although aggressive marketing in the 1980s targeted service to institutional dairy needs. This group operated in all of the United States and parts of Canada. The Special Operations Group consisted of Chief Auto Parts (acquired in 1979); Pate Foods (a snack food company); Reddy Ice (the world's largest ice company); and Tidel Systems (a manufacturer of cash dispensing units and other retailer equipment). The Gasoline Supply Division was formed in 1981 to serve the gasoline requirements of the over 2,800 7-Eleven stores handling gasoline. This division's history was punctuated by the 1983 acquisition of Cities Service Refining, Marketing, and Transportation businesses (CITGO) from Occidental Petroleum.

Southland's Recent Activities[57]

Southland's dramatic growth and diversification during the 1970s and early 1980s resulted in 7-Eleven having a dominant position in the convenience store industry. Despite this position, circumstances since the mid-1980s had greatly eroded 7-Eleven and Southland's strengths.

The oil price collapse of early 1986 was the sharpest drop of crude oil prices in history. The instability of crude oil and wholesale refined products, coupled with CITGO's inventory methods and various write-downs, resulted in only modest income for a previously very profitable company. The volatility of CITGO's financial position greatly affected Southland's earnings. Southland's equity interest in CITGO contributed to a $52 million loss for the entire corporation in 1986. In order to reduce the impact of an unstable crude oil market and the accompanying volatility of CITGO's earnings, Southland entered into a joint venture with Petroleos de Venezuela (PDVSA) in late 1986.

The joint venture with PDVSA had several components. Southland sold a half-interest in CITGO to a subsidiary of PDVSA for $290 million. In addition, PDVSA agreed to both supply CITGO with a minimum of 130,000 barrels of crude oil per day and provide its share of CITGO's working capital requirements.

A takeover attempt of Southland occurred in April 1987. Canadian financier Samuel Belzberg approached the Southland board of directors with an offer of $65 per share of common stock. Unwilling to relinquish control of Southland, the Thompson family tendered $77 per share for two-thirds of outstanding shares in July 1987. The other third of the shares would be purchased at $61 per share (plus $16 per share of new preferred shares) by the would-be private Southland Corporation.

Financing for this acquisition came from $2 billion in loans from a group of banks and a $600 million bridge loan from Goldman, Sachs and Salomon

---

[57] Barrett, *The Southland Corporation (B)*, offers more detailed information.

Brothers. An additional $1.5 billion was generated by the issue of subordinated debentures (junk bonds) in November 1987. This occurred after the stock and junk bond markets crashed in October 1987. Southland's investment bankers had to sell the bonds at a blended rate of almost 17 percent, instead of the anticipated rate of 14.67 percent. The Thompson family emerged from the buyout owning 71 percent of Southland at a total cost of $4.9 billion.

Paying the High Costs of a Leveraged Buyout

After Southland had been taken private through the leveraged buyout (LBO), significant changes occurred in both Southland and 7-Eleven operations. Southland was restructured, with the elimination of two levels of middle managers. During this time, Southland began selling more 7-Eleven stores than it opened in the United States and Canada. Due to the increased number of licensees opening stores overseas, however, the total number of stores worldwide continued to increase. 7-Eleven Japan was primarily responsible for this increase, with the opening of 340 stores in 1988 and 349 stores in 1989. Southland also divested itself of many large assets in the 1988 to 1990 period (see Exhibit 10). Significant in this group of divestments were the entire Dairy Group, over 100 7-Eleven stores in the continental United States, Southland's remaining interest in CITGO (sold to PDVSA), and 7-Eleven Hawaii, (purchased by 7-Eleven Japan).

In November 1989, 7-Eleven Japan purchased 58 stores and additional properties from Southland. These properties and stores, which were located in Hawaii, were exchanged for $75 million in cash. The 58 convenience stores were organized as 7-Eleven Hawaii, which was established as a subsidiary of 7-Eleven Japan.

As of December 31, 1990, Southland operated 6,455 7-Eleven convenience stores in the United States and Canada, 187 High's Dairy Stores, and 63 Quick Mart and Super-7 Stores. Southland owned 1,802 properties on which 7-Eleven stores were located. Another 4,643 7-Eleven stores in the United States and Canada were leased. In addition the company possessed 234 store properties held for sale, of which 109 were unimproved, 77 were closed stores, and 48 were excess properties adjoining store locations.[58]

Three of Southland's four food processing facilities were owned (the other was leased). The company owned six properties in the United States on which distribution centers were located. Five of the six distribution centers were company owned. The company also owned its corporate headquarters (called Cityplace) located near downtown Dallas.[59] Financial statements for Southland Corporation are shown in Exhibit 11 (p. 309), and Exhibit 12 (p. 310).

---

[58] Southland Corporation 1990 Form 10-K, pp. 21–23.
[59] Ibid.

EXHIBIT 10   Asset Divestitures of Southland, 1988–1990

Date Announced	Asset	Buyer	Amount
January 1988	Tidel Systems	D.H. Monnick Corp.	Undisclosed
February 1988	Chief Auto Parts	Management & Shearson Lehman	$130 million
March 1988	Movie Quik	Cevax U.S. Corp.	$51 million
March 1988	Reddy Ice	Reddy Ice	$23 million
April 1988	402 properties including 270 Houston-area 7-Elevens	National Convenience Stores	$67 million plus $13 million for related inventories
April 1988	473 7-Eleven stores in 10 states	Circle-K	$147 million
April 1988	Southland Dairy Group	Morningstar Foods	$242.5 million
July 1988	Snack Food Division	Undisclosed	$15 million
November 1988	79 San Antonio-area 7-Elevens	National Convenience Stores	Undisclosed
July 1989	184 7-Elevens in three states	Ashland Oil et al.	Undisclosed
October 1989	50% of CITGO	Petroleos de Venezuela S.A. (PDVSA)	$661.5 million
November 1989	58 7-Elevens in Hawaii, plus other properties	7-Eleven Japan	$75 million
April 1990	56 Memphis-area 7-Elevens	Undisclosed	$12.9 million
August 1990	28 7-Elevens in Florida, plus other properties	Undisclosed	$7.5 million
December 1990	Cityplace in Dallas	Oak Creek Partners	$24 million

Source: *Dallas Morning News* (November 15, 1989), p. D-1; *Dallas Morning News* (October 10, 1988), p. D-1; *Automotive News* (February 8, 1988), p. 108; *The Wall Street Journal* (February 19, 1988); *The Wall Street Journal* (January 28, 1988); *The Wall Street Journal* (March 4, 1988); *New York Times* (March 4, 1988); Southland Corporation, 1990 Form 10-K.

The Proposed Purchase of Southland by Ito-Yokado

The divestments of 1988, 1989, and 1990 constituted attempts by Southland to generate sufficient cash to service the massive debt incurred from the LBO of 1987. By early 1990, however, it was apparent that the cash generated from these divestments and Southland's operations was not sufficient to cover its interest expense. Some experts estimated that Southland's cash shortfalls would reach $89 million in 1990 and over $270 million in 1991.[60] Southland's long-

---

[60] Linda Sandler, "Southland's Junk Bonds Face Trouble," *The Wall Street Journal* (September 7, 1989).

EXHIBIT 11 Southland Corporation consolidated balance sheet (in thousands of dollars)

	As of December 31			
	1988	*1989*	*1990*	*1990**
Assets				
Cash and short-term inventory	$ 21,783	$ 8,045	$ 108,294	$ 351,678
Accounts and notes receivable	208,686	188,251	161,778	161,778
Inventories	428,098	276,112	301,756	301,756
Deposits and prepaid expenditures	25,929	25,483	64,075	44,889
Investment in CITGO	—	469,687	—	—
Total current assets	684,496	958,578	635,903	860,101
Property, plant, and equipment	2,632,060	2,620,137	2,504,090	2,504,090
Less depreciation	416,822	624,807	788,589	788,589
Net property, plant and equipment	2,215,238	1,995,330	1,715,501	1,715,501
Investment in CITGO	440,777	—	—	—
Excess acquisition costs	986,356	—	—	—
Other assets	534,644	484,847	447,638	397,349
Total assets	$4,861,511	$3,438,755	$2,799,042	$2,972,951
Liabilities and owners' equity				
Debt due	$ 527,174	$ 692,508	$3,522,647	$ 647,512
Accounts payable	692,596	723,694	647,512	9,145
Income taxes payable	377	139	9,145	171,729
Total current liabilities	1,220,147	1,416,341	4,298,119	828,386
Deferred credits	96,359	115,334	142,315	142,315
Long-term debt	3,787,578	3,457,015	182,536	3,118,797
Redeemable preferred stock	118,850	139,740	148,496	—
Redeemable common stock Purchase warrants	26,136	26,136	26,136	26,136
Common stock	2,050	2,050	2,050	41
Additional paid-in capital	18,318	18,318	20,364	594,146
Deficit	(407,927)	(1,736,179)	(2,018,926)	(1,736,870)
Total owners' equity	(387,559)	(1,715,811)	(1,998,560)	(1,142,683)
Total liabilities and owners' equity	$4,861,511	$3,438,755	$2,799,042	$2,972,951

* This depicts the balance sheet for Southland on December 31, 1990, as if the later buyout by Ito-Yokado had been completed.
Source: Southland Corporation 1990 and 1989 Forms 10-K.

term debt still totaled about $3.7 billion, and interest expense alone in the first three quarters of 1989 was almost $430 million.[61] In March of 1990, Southland announced that it was seeking "rescue" by Ito-Yokado.[62]

---

[61] Richard Alm, "Southland Seeks Rescue by Japanese Firm," *Dallas Morning News* (March 23, 1990).
[62] Ibid.

EXHIBIT 12 Southland Corporation consolidated income statement (in thousands of dollars)

	As of December 31		
	1988	1989	1990
Net sales	$7,950,284	$ 8,274,921	$ 8,347,681
Other income	40,213	76,962	62,375
Total revenues	7,990,497	8,351,883	8,410,056
Cost of sales	6,268,854	6,544,237	6,661,273
Gross margin	1,721,643	1,807,646	1,748,783
Selling, administrative expenses	1,543,090	1,607,312	1,664,586
Loss on assets sold	—	—	41,000
Write-off acquired assets	—	946,974	—
Interest expense	560,268	572,248	459,500
Employee benefits, etc.	15,416	13,372	13,653
Net before taxes	(397,132)	(1,332,260)	(429,956)
Income taxes	(111,900)	(11,984)	(128,459)
Loss from continuing operations	(285,232)	(1,320,276)	(429,956)
Discontinued operations			
Equity, CITGO	69,001	70,480	—
Loss, equity disposition	—	1,070	—
Loss before extraordinary charges	(216,231)	(1,250,866)	(301,497)
Extraordinary Charges	—	(56,047)	52,040
Effect of account change of medical benefits	(27,163)	—	(27,163)
Net income	$ (216,231)	$(1,306,913)	$ (276,620)
Opening retained earnings	$ (166,998)	$ (407,927)	$(1,736,179)
Dividends paid, redeemable preferred stock	(20,856)	(12,634)	(1,011)
Accretion	(6,706)	(8,257)	(7,744)
Currency translation adjustment	2,864	(488)	(2,628)
Deficit	$ (407,927)	$(1,736,179)	$(2,018,926)
Earnings per share data			
Loss, before extraordinary charges	$ (15.63)	$ (62.02)	$ (15.14)
Effect of extraordinary charges	—	(2.74)	2.54
Net loss	$ (12.19)	$ (64.76)	$ (13.93)
Year-end common shares (000)	205,042	205,042	205,042

Source: Southland Corporation 1990 and 1989 Form 10-K.

Proposed Acquisition of Southland by Ito-Yokado

Southland had "looked at possibilities of receiving assistance from other U.S. companies, but decided that . . . Ito-Yokado was the best potential partner."[63] The original proposal would have resulted in Ito-Yokado receiving 75 percent ownership of Southland for $400 million. This proportion of Southland would be split between Ito-Yokado and 7-Eleven Japan, with 7-Eleven Japan obtaining two-thirds of the 75 percent share.

---

[63] Karen Blumenthal et al., "Japanese Group Agrees to Buy Southland Corporation," *The Wall Street Journal* (March 23, 1990).

The deal was contingent on Southland's ability to swap its outstanding publicly traded debt for stock and zero-coupon (non-interest-bearing) bonds. The publicly traded debt amounted to approximately $1.8 billion. There were five classes of public debt, ranging in type and interest paid. The interest rate of the bonds varied from 13.5 percent to 18 percent. Ito-Yokado's offer was also contingent on 95 percent of all bondholders of each public debt issue accepting the swap. Under this original proposal, the Thompson family would retain a 15 percent stake in Southland, and the remaining 10 percent of the company would be held by bondholders.

The original proposal had a deadline of June 14, 1990, at which time either Ito-Yokado or Southland could cancel the agreement. Neither party indicated that such action would be taken, even though Southland's bondholders balked at the swap proposal. A bigger problem was facing the two companies: a rapidly approaching interest payment due on June 15, 1990. Southland's failure to pay the $69 million payment would result in Southland having a 30-day grace period in which to compensate bondholders. At the end of the 30-day period, unpaid bondholders could try to force Southland into bankruptcy court.[64]

Revisions to the Proposed Buyout

Southland did not make its scheduled interest payment that was due on June 15, 1990. Bondholders, meanwhile, had shown little regard for the original deal struck between Ito-Yokado and Southland.

Three more revisions of the proposed debt restructuring and terms for the buyout were submitted between mid-June and mid-July 1990. In each revision, either Ito-Yokado's or the Thompson family's stake in Southland was reduced and the share of Southland stock offered to bondholders increased. With each revision came increased bondholder support, yet this support was far short of either the two-thirds majority (as required in Chapter 11 restructuring cases) or the 95 percent acceptance rate dictated by Ito-Yokado. As revisions were submitted, the expiration dates of the debt restructuring and stock purchase by Ito-Yokado were extended.

On July 16, a bondholder filed suit against Southland for failure to pay interest on June 15, because on July 15 Southland's grace period had expired.[65] By September 12, a majority of bondholders had tendered their notes.[66] This majority was still far short, however, of the 95 percent swap requirement dictated by Ito-Yokado. The deadlines were extended to September 25 for both the debt swap offer by Southland and the stock purchase offer by Ito-Yokado.[67]

---

[64] Karen Blumenthal, "Southland Approaches 2 Crucial Dates in Plan to Rearrange $1.8 Billion in Debt," *The Wall Street Journal* (April 12, 1990).

[65] Ibid.

[66] Kevin Helliker, "Southland May Be Considering Seeking Chapter 11 Status, Thus Risking Bailout," *The Wall Street Journal* (September 14, 1990).

[67] Ibid.

As Southland was apparently headed for involuntary bankruptcy filing under Chapter 11, the proposal again seemed in jeopardy.

Acceptance of the Proposed Buyout

The deadline for Southland's debt swap offer was again extended. Bondholder approval was finally obtained in late October. Ito-Yokado's offer to buy out Southland was extended to March 15, 1991, pending court approval of the prepackaged bankruptcy deal.[68] The bankruptcy-court petition for approval of the prepackaged debt restructuring was filed on October 24, 1990.[69]

Although Southland did not have sufficient bondholder approval as dictated by Ito-Yokado, the bankruptcy court proceedings were swift. The last few bondholders who held out were placated in January when the Thompsons relinquished warrants for half of their 5 percent stake of Southland's stock.[70] On February 21, 1991, the U.S. bankruptcy court in Dallas approved the reorganization of Southland.[71] At that time, at least 93 percent of the holders of each class of debt issued by Southland had approved the reorganization.[72] On March 5, 1991, Ito-Yokado purchased 71 percent of Southland's stock for $430 million.[73] Two-thirds of this stock was purchased by 7-Eleven Japan, and the other third purchased directly by Ito-Yokado. The terms of the accepted debt-restructuring agreement between Southland and its bondholders are shown in Exhibit 13.

The Convenience Store Industry in the United States

The convenience store industry in the United States changed dramatically during the decade of the 1980s. The number of convenience stores in the United States, the gross sales of these stores, and the gross margins all increased during this time period. The net income of convenience stores, however, decreased significantly. This outcome was largely the result of the rapid expansion of several chains of convenience stores and the increased number of convenience stores opened by oil companies.

---

[68] Kevin Helliker, "Southland Says Reorganization Clears Hurdle," *The Wall Street Journal* (October 24, 1990).

[69] "Southland Chapter 11 Plan Needs Approval from SEC," *The Wall Street Journal* (December 6, 1990).

[70] David LaGeese, "Judge Approves Southland's Reorganization," *Dallas Morning News* (February 22, 1991), p. 1D.

[71] Ibid.

[72] Ibid.

[73] "Southland Sells 70 Percent Stake, Completing Reorganization, *The Wall Street Journal* (March 6, 1991), p. A2.

EXHIBIT 13   Southland Corporation debt restructuring terms for $1,000 principal debt of various classes as accepted by bondholders on February 21, 1991

	13.5% Senior notes	15.75% Senior notes	16.5% Senior notes	16.75% notes	18% Junior notes
Principal retained	$450	$300	$255	$200	$95
Interest rate of new debt received	12%	5%	5%	4.5%	4%
Number of shares of common stock received	86.5	40.5	35	28	11
Number of stock warrants received	1	7.5	6.5	6	6

Notes:

- "Principal retained" was in the form of newly issued bonds bearing interest as shown.
- Holders of 13.5% senior notes also received $57 cash per $1,000 principal of old debt.
- Holders of 16.5% notes may have received $250 of 12% notes with no stock warrants instead of $200 of 4.5% and 6 stock warrants (per $1,000 principal of old debt). In either case the holder would have been entitled to 28 shares of common stock.
- Stock warrants gave the holder the option to purchase one share of common stock per warrant for $1.75 per share from June 5, 1991, to February 23, 1996.

Source: Southland Corporation 1990 Form 10-K.

Aggregate Measures of the Industry

The number of convenience stores grew from about 39,000 in 1982 to over 70,000 in 1989. From 1985 to 1989, industry sales increased from $51.4 billion to $67.7 billion, an increase of 6.3 percent per year. Gross margins increased from 22.8 percent in 1985 to 26.2 percent by 1988. Despite such growth, convenience store operations experienced a decrease in net profit in the late 1980s. The total industry pretax profit peaked in 1986 at $1.4 billion, fell to $1.16 billion in 1988, and plummeted to $271 million in 1989. Some trends are shown in Exhibit 14.[74]

The expansion of convenience stores in the 1980s was led by large convenience store chains and oil companies. In addition to the growth experienced by the Southland Corporation's 7-Eleven, Circle-K, a Phoenix-based convenience store chain, expanded from 1,200 stores in 1980 to 4,700 stores in 1990.

The Role of the Oil Companies

The impact of oil companies on the convenience store industry has been significant. Virtually all of the major U.S. oil companies began combining convenience store operations with gasoline stations in order to boost profits. In 1984, Exxon opened its first combination convenience store and gas station. By

---

[74] This information is drawn largely from National Association of Convenience Stores (NACS), *1990 State of the Convenience Store Industry* (1990).

EXHIBIT 14 Industrywide convenience store performance, 1985–1989

	1985	1986	1987	1988	1989
Number of stores	61,000	64,000	67,500	69,200	70,200
Gross revenue (in billions)	$51.4	$53.9	$59.6	$61.2	$67.7
Net income (in billions)	$1.39	$1.40	$1.31	$1.16	$0.27
Average per-store profit before tax (in thousands)	$22.8	$21.9	$19.2	$16.8	$3.9

Source: National Association of Convenience Stores, *1990 State of the Convenience Store Industry*.

1989, it had 500. Texaco operated 950 Food Marts in the same year. From 1984 to 1989, the number of convenience stores operated by oil companies increased from 16,000 to 30,000.[75]

Since gasoline sold at a lower margin (about 6 percent in 1984) than nongasoline convenience store products (32 percent in the same year), the sale of convenience store items presented an opportunity for those gas stations with good locations (i.e., street corners) to increase profits. In order to capitalize on the potential for higher profits in retailing, the major oil companies boosted their marketing expenditures. In 1979, the petroleum industry spent about $2.2 billion for their marketing efforts. By 1988, these expenditures were almost $5 billion.[76]

The convenience stores operated by oil companies were growing in both number and size. In 1986, only about 20 percent of the oil company convenience stores were 1,800 or more square feet in size (the size of about 90 percent of traditional convenience stores). By 1990, however, over 50 percent of the oil company convenience stores were between 1,800 and 3,000 square feet in size.[77]

Merchandise Trends for Convenience Stores

Because of the intensified retailing efforts of oil companies and large convenience store chains, some trends (other than those mentioned above) evolved. In 1985, gasoline accounted for 35.4 percent of convenience store sales. By 1989, gasoline accounted for 40 percent of sales.[78] The gross profit margin for gasoline sales had increased from 7.3 percent to 11.7 percent over the same period.[79] Of the 61,000 convenience stores in the United States in 1985, 55 percent sold gasoline, and in 1989, 65 percent of 70,200 convenience stores

---

[75] Claudia H. Deutsch, "Rethinking the Convenience Store," *New York Times* (October 8, 1989).

[76] National Association of Convenience Stores, *Challenges for the Convenience Store Industry in the 1990s: A Future Study*, p. 194.

[77] Ibid., p. 198.

[78] NACS, *1990 State of the Convenience Store Industry*, p. 14.

[79] Ibid., p. 16.

sold gasoline. In 1989, 75 percent of the new convenience stores built were equipped to sell gasoline.[80]

Although gasoline sales and margins became an increasingly significant contributor to convenience store revenues, contributions of revenue from other merchandise stagnated. In 1985, merchandise (other than gasoline) sales for the convenience store industry amounted to $33.2 billion. In 1989, sales reached $40.6 billion.[81] This increase in merchandise sales, however, was offset by the large number of store openings. In 1985, the average yearly merchandise sales per store was $544,000. This number increased to only $578,000 in 1989.[82]

The Setting

While flying from Japan to the United States, Takahashi reflected on the success that both Ito-Yokado and 7-Eleven Japan had enjoyed over the course of many years. These achievements were the result of long-term strategies that were carefully tailored to the Japanese market. Could these same, or similar, strategies be the foundation for making Southland financially successful again? He realized that the convenience store industry in the United States was vastly different from that of Japan. Nevertheless, he was confident that, through careful and thorough planning, the goal of making Southland profitable could be achieved.

---

[80] Ibid., pp. 25–26.
[81] Ibid., p. 14.
[82] Ibid., p. 16.

Case 18

Laramie Oil Company: Retail Gasoline Division*

In April 1991 George Thomas, vice president in charge of domestic automotive gasoline distribution for the Laramie Oil Company, was considering what action he should take with regard to the company's 12,400 franchised and lessee-operated service stations. A number of developments that indicated discontent among franchisees and lessees had recently occurred. Although he was unsure as to what extent these developments indicated real widespread discontent, Mr. Thomas was wondering what might be causing it, and what action he should take at the present time, and in the long run.

Company Background

The Laramie Oil Company was a fully integrated petroleum company with operations in 21 countries. In 1990 domestic sales were $8.79 billion, and net income was $823.4 million. The Laramie product line included automotive gasoline, aviation fuels, distillates, lubricants, and assorted agricultural and industrial chemicals. Sales of automotive gasoline and related products accounted for 52 percent of revenues earned and 64 percent of net profit.

Both the international and domestic American head offices were situated in New York City. As distribution vice president, George Thomas had responsibility for the overall maintenance of a strong network of retail outlets. This responsibility involved the setting of policies concerning lease terms, the selection of dealers, the training of dealers, the motivation of dealers, the dismissal of dealers, and any other factors involving the maintenance of dealer morale and overall effectiveness. Mr. Thomas had responsibility only for the company's Laramie brand stations. Laramie Oil also operated about 50 discount outlets and expected to open more in the near future. These outlets operated under a different brand name.

---

* This case was written by Thomas C. Kinnear and C. Merle Crawford, Professor of Marketing, University of Michigan. Copyright © 1991 by Thomas C. Kinnear.

George Thomas described his objective as distribution vice president as follows:

> We've done a great deal of research to determine why gasoline purchasers use one brand of gasoline or another. In almost every instance, the consumer's perception of the gasoline retail outlet was a very significant determinant in brand selection. It appears that we're halfway to first base if we can keep our outlets modern and clean, plus provide the service that the consumer desires. By service, I mean more than just good, fast, competent pump island work. Service includes having outlets open when consumers need them, and making sure that outlets handle our national promotions. There is nothing more irritating to a customer who expects to receive a glass or coupon than to find that the station that he happens to be in isn't participating in the national promotion. That is one of the best ways to lose customers for good.
>
> Our whole retail distribution policy is directed toward providing a consistent type of physical outlet and service from one end of the country to the other. That's how gasoline is sold.

Implementation of Distribution Policies

George Thomas's control over the implementation of his department's policies was quite indirect. A general manager in each of five geographical divisions had responsibility for all marketing activities in his division, including retail distribution. Each division had a distribution manager whose responsibilities included the day-to-day implementation of corporate policies in regard to service station operations. The division distribution manager reported directly to the division general manager. The corporate and divisional distribution managers did, however, maintain informal contact with each other. Each divisional distribution manager had a number of district sales managers reporting directly to him. Direct contact with service station operators was maintained by company sales representatives, each of whom reported to a district sales manager. The sales representative was the final link in the chain of implementation between George Thomas's office and the service station operator. (See Exhibit 1 for a partial organization chart.)

Type of Service Stations

Laramie Oil Company distributed its automotive products through three types of service stations:

1. *Company operated.* These stations were owned or leased by Laramie Oil who hired the service station personnel to operate them on a straight salary basis. Laramie controlled the retail price and all other aspects of all products sold through these stations. About 100 of Laramie's 12,400 stations were operated in this manner.
2. *Franchised dealers.* The station site and all physical facilities of franchised dealer operations were owned by the dealers themselves. Laramie

EXHIBIT 1 Partial organization chart

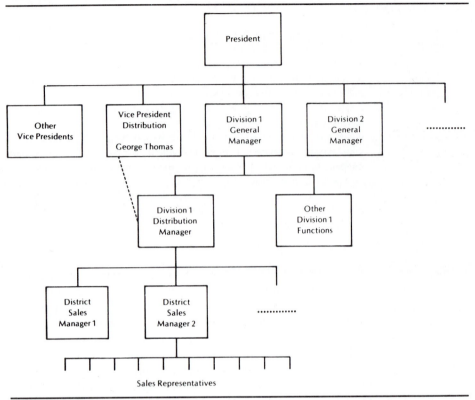

----- Indicates an informal communications link.

did, however, provide financing, so that an individual dealer could commence operation by putting up as little as $2,000. The company, or local financial institutions, held mortgages on the land and physical facilities. About 500 outlets were in this category.

3. *Lessee operated.* Lessee operators were dealers who leased their service station from Laramie Oil. The stations, in these cases, continued to be owned by Laramie Oil. The lessee purchased petroleum products from Laramie but was free to set his own operating policies as related to such things as hours, prices, and brands of accessories carried. The lessee's cost price of gasoline was based on a "tank wagon price" which included all taxes and delivery charges to the lessee's station. Typical lessee operators were charged per gallon, as shown in the accompanying table.

Transport price (except tax)	$0.660
Plus: State and federal taxes	0.450
Transport price (including tax)	1.110
Plus: Jobber margin	0.085
Tank wagon price	1.195
Plus: Rent paid to Laramie	0.055
Lessee's margin	0.070
Retail price	$1.320

The cost price of gasoline to franchised dealers closely approximated the lessee cost arrangement, except that rent charges were not included. For most franchisees, interest charges on their mortgages tended to make up this cost difference.

A Closer Look at Two Laramie Lessee Dealers

1. Jerry Williamson's Laramie service station, Dearborn, Michigan. Jerry Williamson's service station was located at one of the main intersections in the Detroit suburb of Dearborn. His customers were drawn mainly from local residents and commuters who drove through Dearborn on their way to and from their work in Detroit. Williamson was a class A automobile mechanic who had worked for a Ford dealership for eight years before becoming a Laramie dealer in 1974. He had put up $19,500 of his own money to obtain the right to be the Laramie lessee for his Dearborn location. Most of the $19,500 had been used to finance product inventories and tools, while some had been used to physically upgrade the station.

Williamson did a large automobile repair business. Over the years he had built up an excellent reputation among the residents of Dearborn for providing competent and reliable repair service. As a result of this business and his good location for attracting gasoline customers, he did an annual sales volume of slightly over $940,000. His profit statement for 1990 is presented in Exhibit 2.

Williamson took great pride in the fact that he had been able to build a very successful business operation. He thought of himself as being a part of the community as he took part in community work through his memberships in the Lion's Club and the Chamber of Commerce. In the latter organization he had risen to the position of vice president, and was looking forward to being president at some time.

When he was asked if there were any negative aspects to being a Laramie dealer, Williamson replied as follows:

> Well . . . not really; it's tough to complain a lot when you're making $63,000 a year. The only thing I really have to complain about is that Laramie

EXHIBIT 2   Percentage profit statements for Jerry Williamson's and Fred Shaw's service stations for 1990

	Jerry Williamson	Fred Shaw
Sales	100.00%	100.00%
Cost of goods sold	75.36	75.24
Gross profit	24.64	24.76
Expenses:		
Labor for outside work	0.46	0.29
Supplies	0.75	0.79
Wages (excluding owner)	8.38	8.69
Repairs and maintenance	0.34	0.24
Advertising	0.79	0.93
Delivery	0.41	0.42
Bad debts	0.02	0.02
Administrative	0.38	0.35
Miscellaneous	0.96	0.72
Rent	2.60	2.00
Insurance	0.47	0.46
Utilities	0.96	1.00
Taxes	0.74	0.66
Interest	0.10	0.11
Depreciation	0.60	0.65
Total expenses	17.96	17.33
Net profit	6.68%	7.43%
Inventory turnover × 1 year	17.26	12.88

pressures me to buy most of my repair parts and accessories from their own supply company or from company-approved jobbers. I think I could get slightly better margins from other jobbers, as the company takes a percentage rake-off from the approved jobbers. However, it's really a small complaint when you consider all the pluses that Laramie gives. Overall, I'm extremely pleased.

2. Fred Shaw's Laramie service station, Detroit, Michigan. Fred Shaw's service station was located in an industrial section of Detroit, with most of his customers being people who worked in the plants in the surrounding area. Prior to becoming the lessee of his current station, Shaw had worked as an employee in a suburban Laramie station. He had always wanted to be in business for himself, and whenever he heard that a station was available, he would approach the sales representative involved to see if he could obtain the station. Most of the stations had required too much capital, but finally he was able to obtain his current station by putting up $8,500 for the required inventories.

Although managing his station required long hours for Shaw, he preferred it to a very great extent over working for another dealer. It was in a very real sense to him the fulfillment of his dream of being his own boss.

Due to the nature of the surrounding environment, Shaw's station was quiet most of the day except when the shifts changed and then it was extremely busy. This constant changing from feast to famine made proper staffing extremely difficult, and required long hours to cover all shift changes.

Shaw's station was not as productive in either gasoline sales or repair service as was Jerry Williamson's. As a result, his 1990 sales volume was just under $390,000. Exhibit 2 presents his 1990 profit statement.

Hank Homes was the Laramie sales representative in Shaw's district, and on one of his weekly visits recently he asked Fred to take part in a special Bicentennial china giveaway promotion. Part of the conversation between the two men went as follows:

Hank: This looks to me to be one of the best promotions the company has ever put together. They're going to put about $2.5 million in advertising behind it. You should draw a pile of customers.

Fred: Come on, Hank. The type of customer who buys from my outlet isn't interested in bone china. It may be fine for other outlets, but I don't want in on this one. Besides, since the gasoline shortage of '79 and '80, I can't believe anyone wants to start these rotten giveaways again. Also, my customers are really mad about the big jump we've had in gasoline prices since the Kuwait invasion by Iraq.

Hank: I disagree, Fred. I'm sure you'd do well with it. Why don't you let me sign you up. I think you'd be pleased with the results. We pretested this in Denver and it went well. Think about it for a few minutes while we discuss a few other things. It looks to me as if your station could use a new coat of paint this spring. If we let it go any longer, it will chase customers away.

Fred: I don't think I can afford to put out for the paint right now, Hank. You know what a problem I'm having making ends meet here.

Hank: Well, maybe I can help you out on that score. If I work on them at the regional office, they might let me absorb part or even all of the expense for you. . . . Think about the china promotion, Fred, and I'll drop back tomorrow.

Franchisee and Lessee Discontent

The following dealer comments were taken from meetings of several Laramie retail dealer associations in various parts of the United States. Laramie retail dealer associations were groups of Laramie dealers who had gotten together on their own for such purposes as: the discussion of mutual problems, the collective purchasing of products from independent suppliers, and the undertaking of various social activities. Not all Laramie dealers belonged to associations and the strength and activity level of the associations varied greatly.

Lessee 1: The company claims that we can set our own prices, but that damn sales rep comes into my place and tells me I can't sell at more than a four-cent markup. I can hardly scrape from one week to the next at that rate. . . . I know for sure he'll drop my lease if I don't set these prices. Our dealer association has had economists do studies that showed that on the average it takes a gross profit margin of nine cents a gallon to operate profitably. Margins today run from about three cents to eight cents with the average at about five and a half cents. That's just not enough.

Lessee 2: What really bugs me is those stupid premium offers I have to put up with. They advertise them like mad on TV, so I have to carry them or the customers start screaming. . . . I don't get any more business with them—all my competitors are running some premium too—all they do is add to my costs. It's really frustrating. I thought the oil crisis had finished these things. I guess I was wrong.

Lessee 3: I couldn't be more satisfied. I make a really good living. If some of you guys stopped complaining and started working, you could do the same.

Lessee 4: You know I'd really like to close my place down at night . . . the only reason I'm open nights is 'cause the sales rep said he wouldn't renew my lease if I didn't keep his hours—imagine that, I've worked for Laramie for 15 years as a dealer and they'd drop me just like that. I can't afford to lose my station but I'm losing money by staying open.

Lessee 5: What's really got me worried is that they are going to turn my station into a company-owned and -operated outlet. Where would I be then?

Lessee 6: The company is more interested in their gallonage than our profits, and those one-sided leases let them dictate what we'll charge and what products we'll sell. They also use the lease to ride herd on our prices.

Lessee 7: I had hoped that the Supreme Court rulings prohibiting forcing their TBA (tires, batteries, and accessories) brands on us would have helped; however, all it's done is to make their methods more subtle.

Franchisee 1: I thought when I put up my bucks I was going to be in business for myself—fat chance—that sales rep is in my place all the time suggesting what hours to work, how to work, what price to set. . . . If I object, he starts talking about revoking my franchise. I know the Laramie name draws customers but some of his suggestions are unreasonable.

Franchisee 2: This business of them running their own discount stations in competition with me has really got me bugged, too.

Comments of Sales Representatives (SR)

The following comments were taken from individual interviews with selected sales representatives:

SR 1: Sure, I set hours and prices and procedures; if I didn't, some of those dolts would be out of business tomorrow.

SR 2: To get the volume out of my territory that the district manager demands, I have to pressure the dealers. Talking about the lease is always effective. However, I've never actually threatened any of my dealers with the loss of the lease.

SR 3: If you're honest and friendly with your dealers and show them what they will gain from following what you suggest, then you don't have to threaten them to get cooperation.

SR 4: You can bet your life I'm out pushing our TBA line to dealers. That right hasn't been taken away from us. However, that doesn't mean we're going to club them over the head if they don't.

Comments by George Thomas

(Made before a congressional committee.)

It isn't our policy to require dealers to maintain company-directed hours or prices. The whole idea is that the dealer has the right to establish his own hours and prices.

I'd fire any sales representative found pressuring dealers on matters like prices or hours or contests.

It seems to me that what we have here is a situation completely analogous to the normal arrangement between the landlord and tenant. We have up to $200,000 invested in large stations, and if the dealers are mismanaging them we have a right and a duty to protect our investment.

Developments in 1990

A number of developments that concerned George Thomas took place in 1990.

1. A group of dealers in Chicago filed a suit against Laramie, alleging that Laramie violated the Sherman Act by using short-term leases to intimidate the dealers into following suggested retail prices. No decision had been handed down yet by the court.

2. A Laramie Marketing Research Staff report indicated that the turnover rate among Laramie dealers had increased significantly in the last few years. This problem of dealer turnover was common throughout the oil industry. Estimates indicated that approximately one third of all service stations in the United States change management every year. The Laramie turnover rate was below the national average, but was still very high. This high turnover was considered to be a very serious problem by George Thomas. Also disturbing was the fact that a significant number of long-service Laramie dealers had left to join cut-rate chains who guaranteed station managers at least $2,500 income per month.

3. The Automotive Retail Trade Association had requested the Federal Trade Commission (FTC) to charge the seven major oil companies (including Laramie) with misrepresentation, breach of contract, and promotion of price wars. The writ alleged misrepresentation of "exclusive" franchise agreements and breach of contract because the oil companies have opened "off-brand" stations near franchise service stations. The association charged that the off-brand stations sell at prices lower than the wholesale prices charged to the franchise dealers. The association wants an injunction to stop oil companies from creating subsidiary stations in direct competition with franchised dealers.

    The writ also criticized the oil companies for nondisclosure of fees or profits received by oil companies from firms which supply automobile products to the service stations. The association wanted to know this information since service station lessees are requested to buy the accessories only from designated dealers.

Finally the writ criticized promotional gimmicks and giveaways as a financial burden to operators and alleged that oil companies ''demanded'' cooperation and participation under threat of nonrenewal of leases.

4. The Central States Automotive Retailers Association presented a brief to the governors of six states asking for legislation to prohibit gimmicks and giveaways connected with gasoline selling. The association alleged that an end to giveaways could reduce the selling price of gasoline by one or two cents a gallon. The brief also asked that oil companies be required to sell gasoline at one price to all customers. At present, wholesale price varies from customer to customer, with the highest charged to leased gas stations.

5. Laramie had recently closed many marginal stations. A group of dealers dispossessed in this process had brought suit against Laramie charging violations of their franchise agreement and conspiracy to restrain trade.

Mr. Thomas reflected on these developments and wondered what alternative courses of action were available to him, and what action he should take both in the short run and in the long run. He also wondered what factors had caused the current problems.

Case 19

American Airlines: SABRE Reservation System in Europe*

Toward the end of 1985, American Airlines decided to enter the European market with its computer reservation system (CRS). Three years before that, it had introduced its first flight to the Old World since September 1950, when American's president C. R. Smith had sold the subsidiary "American Overseas Airlines" to its only direct competitor, Pan American World Airways. Within three years, American offered flights to London, Paris, and Frankfurt. As European airline officials were beginning to talk about the liberalization of their skies, Robert Crandall, the newly elected CEO of the company, looked to gain a foothold in Europe by acquiring landing rights in as many cities as possible. By connecting European travel agents to SABRE, he also hoped to increase the airline's awareness overseas. This case shows the complexity of the CRS business in the rapidly changing airline industry.

The Early Years of American Airlines[1]

The birth of the commercial airline industry in the United States can be attributed in great part to the Kelly Act, which was passed by Congress in 1925. The act turned the airline business over from the Post Office Department to the private sector by requiring contractors to bid for each route. Until then, the U.S. Post Office Department was by far the biggest civil user of airplanes. It had hired 40 pilots in 1919 to fly its mail around the country. (Thirty-one of them had died in crashes by 1925.) There was also a handful of passenger airlines. One private shuttle flew Ford employees between Detroit and Chicago, while a sightseeing airline was run by the brother of Charlie Chaplin. But the number of airlines boomed after the Kelly Act was passed. Within weeks, the federal government received several hundred applications.

---

* This case was written with the cooperation of American Airlines by Martin Schreiber under the supervision of Thomas C. Kinnear. Copyright © 1990 by Thomas C. Kinnear.
[1] Historical data were found in Robert I. Sterling, *Eagle—The Story of American Airlines* (New York: St. Martin's Press, 1985).

One of the successful applications belonged to Robertson Aircraft Corporation. The company was awarded the route between St. Louis and Chicago (by way of Springfield and Peoria) and began its service April 15, 1926. In an old DH-4 biplane, The Lone Eagle—better known as Charles A. Lindbergh—made what became the first regularly scheduled flight of American Airlines.

American Airlines owes its existence to Sherman Fairchild, head of the Fairchild Airplane Manufacturing Company. In 1929, fearing the loss of a good customer to the competition, he tried to convince his board of directors to help the airline finance the acquisition of additional airplanes to service a recently awarded air mail route. The board of directors went much further: On March 1, 1929, a financing company, The Aviation Corporation (AVCO) was incorporated in Delaware; they sold 2 million shares at $17.50 each, raising $35 million.

Within one year, AVCO acquired majority interests in more than 80 companies: 5 airlines consisting of 13 carriers (one of them being the Robertson Aircraft Corporation of Charles Lindbergh), flying schools, aircraft and engine manufacturers, two airports, one motor bus line, even one broadcasting station. In 1930, AVCO's president, Frederic G. Coburn, consolidated all the domestic air transportation lines into a new corporation: American Airways. Realizing the dependency of the airline on the mail service (75% of its revenues), Coburn also helped develop a passenger plane. The airline, nevertheless, was losing about $1 million every year. The situation deteriorated even more when President Franklin D. Roosevelt cancelled all domestic air mail contracts in February 1934, when a federal investigation discovered that larger airlines had secretly been favored for air mail routes. But six months after the army had been assigned to fly the mail—and 66 of its planes had crashed causing 12 casualities—Congress quickly passed legislation returning the air mail business to the private sector. The Airmail Act, however, reduced the fares to be paid by the Post Office Department from 42.6 cents to 25.3 cents per flown mile. It also included two provisions: first, that airlines had to sell off their aircraft manufacturing subsidiaries; and second, no company involved in prior bidding was allowed to apply for the new air mail contracts. While sounding rather radical, the second provision was easily bypassed by the airlines: American Airways came back to the bidding table as American Airlines, United Aircraft & Transport as United Airlines, Eastern Air Transport as Eastern Airlines, and TWA with Incorporated added to its name.

If nothing else, the carriers had discovered the danger in their heavy dependency on government contracts. American Airlines was losing almost $2.5 million in 1934 and was looking for a strong leader to turn the business around. On October 26, 1934, a Texan was appointed as the new president of the company: Cyrus Rowlett Smith. Except for a period during World War II, he would remain president until 1963, when he became chairman and CEO, a position he held for five years.

C. R. Smith was committed to changing the airline into a passenger transportation business. His strategy consisted of:

- Targeting the business travelers.
- Improving service.
- Replacing old equipment with better and safer equipment.
- Excelling in marketing.

He began by training his employees in what he called esprit de corps. Realizing the importance of the flight attendants, he started a training program designed for stewardesses. In 1936, he convinced Donald Douglas, Sr., to design the DC–3, which became the first profitable all-passenger airplane. In the same year, he offered the first sleeper flights between New York and Los Angeles (via Memphis, Dallas, and Tucson) and introduced the industry to air traffic control systems. He even entered the catering business by opening several restaurants in airports. The strategy paid off: the airline showed its first profit after only two years and within three years, the revenue from mail service decreased from 71 percent to 31 percent of total revenue (Table 1). In 1938, Smith moved American's headquarters from the Chicago Midway Airport to the newly built LaGuardia Airport in New York City. There, he founded the first Admirals Club and opened a reservation school. By then, American's largest reservation office in New York was booking an average of 250 passengers a day.

TABLE 1 American Airways turns into a passenger airline

	Mail revenue	Passenger revenue
1933	$4,728,000	$1,885,000
1937	2,980,000	6,598,000

After serving in the Air Transport Command during World War II, Smith returned to American. He soon dazzled his competitors when he successfully offered the first family fares in the industry. On a 50-acre piece of land in Dallas that he won in a gin rummy game, he built a new learning center, where stewardesses went through a 20-day training program. On January 25, 1959, he introduced the first jetliner, a Boeing 707; seven years later, he retired American's last piston plane.

The Development of SABRE

Until 1946, reservation offices used large display boards, which listed entries and space availability. During the 50s, American introduced the Magnetronic Reservisor to keep track of seat inventories on all flights and to electronically format and send teletype messages to other airlines. This process required that reservations be routed to a keypunch operator, run through a sorting machine, and then processed by another machine which cut the paper tape in order to send the teletype message (prior to being filed).

During a flight in 1953, C. R. Smith met an IBM senior sales representative, R. Blair Smith. As C. R. Smith described the capacity and speed constraints American was encountering with their reservation system, Blair Smith quickly saw a wonderful business opportunity. In November of 1959, American Airlines and IBM announced a joint development project called Semi-Automated Business Research Environment, or in short form, SABRE. Introduced first in 1962 and expanded systemwide two years later, SABRE became the largest electronic data processing system designed for business use. Its computer center was located in Briarcliff Manor, New York. In one day the system could process:

85,000	phone calls.
30,000	requests for fare quotations.
40,000	confirmed passenger reservations.
30,000	queries to and from other airlines regarding seat space.
20,000	ticket sales.

The initial research, development, and installation was estimated at $40 million, the price of four Boeing 707 aircraft.

In the late 1960s, two other airlines came up with their own reservation systems. United introduced APOLLO, while TWA Inc. operated PARS.

Bob Crandall Improves SABRE

By 1974, C. R. Smith had been replaced as president and chairman of American Airlines by Albert V. Casey, a business school graduate with limited prior airline experience. "There are only four jobs in any company, regardless of what kind of business you're in," he once said. "You have one guy in charge of making the product, someone in charge of selling it, the third one's a bean counter who keeps score, and then there's the boss." In June of 1974, he placed Robert Crandall in charge of selling the product by appointing him senior vice president of marketing.

Bob Crandall was determined to utilize American's reservation system as a marketing tool for the airline. He ordered a new and improved SABRE to help analyze collected flight and booking data. American Airlines' yield management system emerged, which could predict booking trends on specific flights and monitor the effectiveness of various marketing strategies. SABRE also introduced new functions such as baggage tracing, crew management, inventory management, and financial analysis.

Together with American's chief of data processing, Max Hopper, Crandall introduced the concept of a joint industry computerized reservation system (JICRS). Travel agents would be able to subscribe to the system and thus quickly access information about any carrier. There had already been several separate efforts to set up an industry system (Table 2). The major purpose was

TABLE 2 Failed attempts to standardize the CRS industry

1967	Donnelly Official Airline Reservation System (BOARS)
1970	Automatic Travel Agency Reservation (ATARS)
1974	Joint Industry Computer Reservation System (JICRS)
1976	United, then American, pulls out of JICRS to market their own reservation systems
1976	Multi-Access Agent Reservation System (MAARS)
1980	American Express makes last major effort to establish an industry system

to eliminate continued duplication of investments and to reduce the reservations and sales cost by shifting the sales efforts from high-cost internal reservation offices to commission-paid travel agencies. Furthermore, before deregulation, all companies charged the same fare for the same service, and it took years to change prices and service. None of the attempts succeeded, however, for lack of capital, lack of agreement, or fear of government suspicions that a joint system would be anticompetitive within the industry. The JICRS concept would die as well, as United started to sell its own system to travel agents. American immediately followed suit and in May of 1976 installed its first SABRE terminal in a travel agency. Other airlines were allowed to offer their services through SABRE and were charged about 35 cents for ticketing through a competitor's system.

Strategically, the distribution of CRSs to travel agents proved to be a very successful move. Not only were airlines gaining increased sales exposure, they also enjoyed high entry barriers against competitors due to travel agency investments in hardware and training, as well as to certain restrictive contract terms.

Although successful, it was not until 1978, when legislation ordered the deregulation of the airline industry, that the reservation systems achieved the importance they enjoy today.

Deregulation

The Airline Deregulation Act of 1978 provided for a phased abolition of regulation on route entry and tariffs. Until then, both of these were issued under the authority of the Civil Aeronautics Board (CAB). However, during its 40-year reign, the CAB had allowed no new major passenger carrier (called a trunk carrier) to enter the industry. Only domestic local service air carriers, commonly called feeder airlines, had been allowed to enter minor markets, as they became uneconomical for trunk carriers to service with their larger planes. Before deregulation, most routes had been served by only one carrier. Prices were set for airlines to obtain a defined industry margin.

As the CAB gradually relinquished authority, the Department of Transportation (DOT) temporarily took over the remaining functions. (The public interest in airline operations was to pass to the Justice Department only in

1989.) New carriers were now allowed to enter the market, not on the basis of "convenience and public necessity," but if they were "fit, willing and able to perform air transportation." In addition, airlines could set their own prices according to supply and demand.

The cooperative attitude prevailing until 1981 quickly disappeared. Many former interline partners went into direct competition with each other. During the four years following deregulation, 119 new carriers entered the industry. As they began offering lower fares, a fierce price competition was launched, which ultimately lowered the average ticket price (Figure 1). In 1982, 80 percent of all tickets were sold at discount fares and the looming question became, who would survive the price war?

FIGURE 1   The effect of deregulation on airline ticket prices

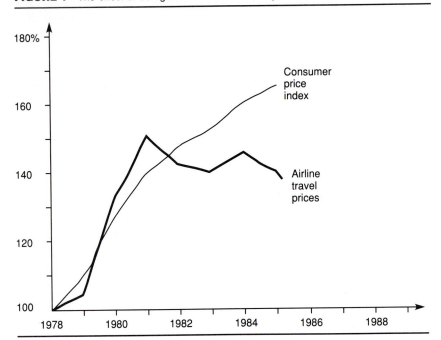

The impact of deregulation on airline operation was as far reaching as it was diverse.

Increase in Productivity

Increased competition forced established carriers to improve their productivity. Using larger, more fuel-efficient jets, they increased their average domestic route length. The incentive to replace their old aircraft with more fuel-efficient planes became even more pressing when fuel prices began to rise at the turn of the decade. Some of the used planes were put on the market and sold to smaller airlines seeking to increase the reach of their networks. Others were simply grounded. Sure enough, when oil prices dropped again, these older aircraft were put back into service.

As smaller, fuel-efficient planes were developed, productivity became less dependent on aircraft size than on maximum aircraft utilization, higher load factors, lower labor cost, and less restrictive work rules.

Lowering of Labor Cost

In order to survive, the large trunk carriers had to cut costs, and fast. With wages being the largest cost component (Figure 2), managers looked for ways to trim the high pre-deregulation salaries down to market rates and to allow for more flexible work rules.

FIGURE 2   American Airline's cost structure during 1985

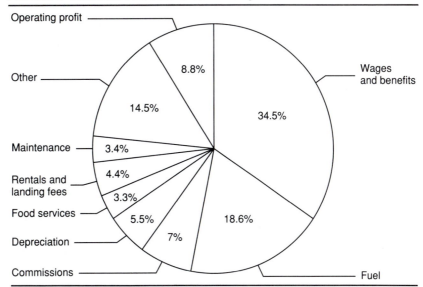

The most common practice was to engage in negotiations with unions. In March of 1983, Robert Crandall of American Airlines first reached an agreement with his employees in a deal that became the basis for negotiations at other carriers. (This is described in a later section.) Other airlines seeking concessions through negotiation were United, TWA, Delta, and Northwest. Pan American and Eastern, which were in more serious financial difficulties, were obliged to offer equity shares (10 percent and 25 percent) to their employees in exchange for wage and work rule concessions.

Two smaller airlines, Texas International and Frontier, tried to bypass the unions by starting their own low-cost nonunion subsidiary. Although initially successful, they were both later acquired by Texas Air Corp. shortly before being forced into Chapter 11 bankruptcy.

Finally, two other airlines, Braniff and Continental, chose the most extreme path to revise their labor costs. Braniff filed for bankruptcy in 1982 and Continental in 1983. In addition to restructuring their debt, both airlines defaulted on their labor contracts and started their operations again as nonunion companies.

Bankruptcies/Mergers

Originally, deregulation was intended to increase competition, but six years after the deregulation act, 75 carriers remained in the market, down from 105. The number contracted due to bankruptcies, mergers, and liquidations. The avalanche of mergers was facilitated by the fact that all regulatory authority had been given to the Department of Transportation, which in several cases overruled objections raised by the Department of Justice.

Pan Am and National were the first airlines to merge. The deal allowed Pan Am, which had been restricted to international air service prior to deregulation, to compete domestically.

Republic resulted from the second major post-deregulation merger. The airline consisted of North Central, Southern, and Hughes Airwest. Republic later merged with Northwest Airlines. Other mergers followed, and in 1985, the trend did not seem to have an end.

Hub and Spoke

As airplanes became more fuel efficient, the load factor became the most crucial variable for an airline's success. To increase the number of passengers per flight, airlines started to expand their hub airport utilization. Hub airports, operating as a central connecting point between city pairs (spokes) offered a competitive alternative to direct flights (Figure 3). By combining passenger traffic from different origins and with different destinations, the airline could increase the number of city pairs served, as well as the average number of passengers and corresponding revenue per flight. For flights to be attractive to customers, the connecting time at the hub had to be as short as possible. Airplanes would land in clusters and wait for all or most of the connecting passengers before taking off. As hubs grew in size and traffic (Table 3), passengers soon faced increasing delays.

FIGURE 3 The use of hub

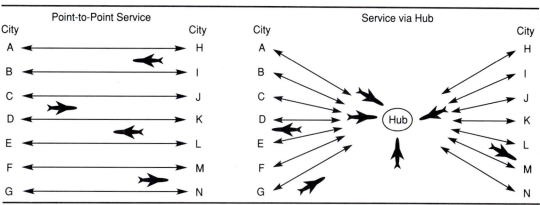

TABLE 3 Increased use of hub airports

Airline	Leading hub city in 1983	Percent of airline's domestic departures at hub	
		1978	*1983*
American	Dallas-Ft. Worth	11.2%	28.6%
Continental	Houston	12.8	22.9
Delta	Atlanta	18.3	21.4
Eastern	Atlanta	18.3	21.0
Northwest	Minneapolis-St. Paul	16.1	20.7
Pan American	New York	12.3	22.4
TWA	St. Louis	11.9	33.0
United	Chicago	16.0	18.9

International Growth—American Airlines Response to Deregulation

Robert Crandall was named American's president in 1980, three years after he had successfully introduced the Super Saver fares. Even so, as deregulation approached, many analysts predicted the end of American Airlines' existence. In his biography about American Airlines, Robert Serling wrote: "It was like assuming command of the Titanic the day she sailed." Albert V. Casey had tried to limit the damages by moving American's headquarters from New York to the Dallas/Ft. Worth area, but in 1980 the airline reeled under a $111.1 million loss (Table 4).

Crandall's strategy was to "grow a new, low-cost airline inside the old one." He started to lower American's labor cost. Through hard negotiations with unions, Crandall obtained concessions for a two-tiered wage scale, by

TABLE 4 American Airlines' income summary

	1978	1979	1980	1981	1982	1983	1984	1985
Operating results (in millions)								
Revenues								
Passengers	$2,329.5	$2,753.0	$3,154.4	$3,377.0	$3,414.2	$3,885.3	$4,335.8	$4,985.5
Other	406.0	499.5	551.7	546.6	563.0	647.1	751.6	873.8
Total operating revenues	$2,735.5	$3,252.5	$3,706.1	$3,923.6	$3,977.2	$4,532.4	$5,087.4	$5,859.3
Expenses								
Wages, salaries, and benefits	$1,083.4	$1,248.5	$1,372.7	$1,417.4	$1,472.9	$1,601.2	$1,748.7	$1,951.9
Aircraft fuel	514.7	801.5	1,114.8	1,115.7	1,115.7	1,038.6	1,091.8	1,141.8
Other	1,018.5	1,197.6	1,329.7	1,346.5	1,346.5	1,643.1	1,907.8	2,259.1
Total operating expenses	$2,616.6	$3,247.6	$3,817.2	$3,879.6	$3,935.1	$4,282.9	$4,748.3	$5,352.8
Operating income (loss)	$118.9	$4.9	($111.1)	$44.0	$42.1	$249.5	$339.1	$506.5
Operating statistics								
Revenue yield per passenger mile	7.96¢	8.17¢	11.12¢	12.13¢	11.04¢	11.39¢	11.81¢	11.30¢
Revenue passenger miles (in millions)	28,987	33,364	28,178	27,798	30,900	34,099	36,702	44,138
Passenger load factor	63.7%	67.4%	60.4%	61.4%	63.3%	65.0%	62.6%	64.6%
Number of operating aircraft at year-end	251	263	242	232	231	244	260	291

which American would pay newly hired employees only 50 percent of what present employees received. In return, Crandall guaranteed that there would be no layoffs and no pay cuts. His hard negotiating style earned him a reputation of "eating nails for breakfast." With the money saved, Crandall decided to expand the airline dramatically. "The faster we grow, the lower our average cost will be," he argued. Within four years, he bought almost 100 new planes, increasing American's old fleet by 41 percent. American started to build hubs in Dallas/Ft. Worth and Chicago. Both airports accounted for 80 percent of the airline's departures in 1983. The small, semiautonomous commuter airline, American Eagle, operated as a feeder airline funneling passengers from smaller outlying areas into American's route systems.

In 1983, while incorporated under AMR Corp., American began service to Europe with a flight from DFW to London (Braniff left the route open after filing for bankruptcy). By 1985, it had added flights to Paris and Frankfurt. Crandall also consolidated by selling off subsidiaries worth $60.3 million, which included its 45-year-old Sky-Chefs catering company and its AMR Energy Corp. In 1982, American lost $18.2 million, but one year later it registered an operating profit of $249.5 million. By 1985, American was credited with the largest market share (Table 5).

TABLE 5   1985 Market shares in passenger miles

Airline	Market share in revenue passenger miles
American	13.1%
United	12.4
Eastern	9.9
TWA	9.5
Delta	9.0
Pan American	8.1
Northwest	6.7
Continental	4.9
People Express	3.3
Republic	3.2
Western	3.1
USAir	2.9
Piedmont	2.4
Southwest	1.6
Others	9.9

Frequent Flier Programs

Deregulation cannot be discussed without mentioning the frequent flier programs. Designed to entice loyalty to one carrier, they would reward passengers with bonuses (usually a free trip) based on mileage flown and/or fares paid. Obviously, such programs were especially attractive with larger airlines serving many cities. American initiated the frequent flier wars when it introduced its

AAdvantage program. The entire service was run through SABRE. Two years after its introduction, American's competition developed similar programs of their own.

Increased Importance of the CRS Market

With deregulation, the number and complexity of airline fares increased, making reservation systems with their large databases more of a competitive tool. In 1977, before deregulation, travel agencies had booked only 38 percent of all tickets; in 1985, the percentage had jumped to 90 percent. As travel agents booked an increasing share of ticket sales, airlines doubled their efforts to place their CRS terminals with as many agents, particularly business travel specialists, as possible. The commission from ticket sales, which represented the agent's largest revenue source, jumped to 10 percent, even 13 percent in 1985, up from the CAB specified 7 percent. During the same time, the percentage of agencies automated with CRS terminals shot up from 5 percent to 90 percent (Table 6).

TABLE 6 Automatization of travel agencies

Year	Agents	Percent automated with CRS
1976	12,262	*
1977	13,454	5%
1978	14,804	*
1979	16,112	24
1980	17,339	*
1981	19,203	59
1982	20,962	75
1983	23,058	85
1984	25,748	*
1985	27,193	90

* Not available.

These five CRSs competed for market share (Figure 4):

SABRE of American Airlines. SABRE accounted for one third of American Airlines' $506 million in net earnings in 1985. However, as Robert Crandall testified before the Senate Aviation Subcommittee in March of the same year, SABRE had been profitable only since 1983 (Table 7). The accumulated investment in the CRS was estimated at $350 million.

APOLLO of United Airlines. With a 25 percent market share, APOLLO was the second largest system in the country. Along with SABRE, it was the most sophisticated CRS in the market. At the end of 1983, United's total investment in APOLLO was estimated at $250 million.

FIGURE 4 1985 market share of the major CRS vendors' installations

Market Share of the Five Major CRSs

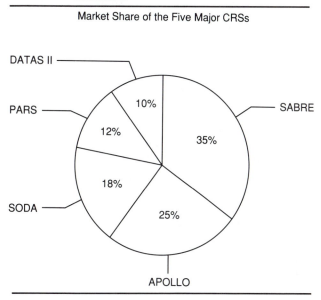

TABLE 7 Estimated operating results of SABRE (millions)

Year	Revenue	Expenses	Operating income (loss)
1976	$ 0.3	$ 4.4	$ (4.1)
1977	2.4	12.7	(10.3)
1978	6.0	24.5	(18.5)
1979	15.6	41.7	(26.1)
1980	32.0	56.6	(24.6)
1981	53.6	68.3	(14.7)
1982	82.9	92.4	(9.5)
1983	124.3	118.8	5.5
1984	179.0	136.2	42.8
1985	483.0	367.0	116.0

PARS of TWA. TWA had unveiled its reservation system to travel agents shortly after American and United had started selling their CRS service in 1976. A decade later, 12 percent of all 32,000 U.S. travel agency terminals were connected to PARS.

SODA of Eastern Airlines. Eastern Airlines had introduced SODA (System One Direct Access) shortly after Congress had passed the deregulation act. Thanks to Eastern's position as the third largest domestic carrier, SODA's market share rose to an impressive 18 percent by 1985.

DATAS II of Delta Air Lines. In 1979, Delta and United entered into an arrangement that allowed Delta to market the APOLLO system using its own name. Delta called its system DATAS. As the advantages of owning a CRS became apparent, Delta developed its own system and called it DATAS II. Its market share in 1985 was 10 percent.

Some other carriers, such as Alaska Air Lines, Pan Am, or USAir also maintained small CRS networks.

Prices charged to travel agents included three components: a one-time installation charge, a monthly hardware fee, and a monthly maintenance charge. To entice travel agents to join their networks, airlines offered financing and booking incentives (free hardware, software, or communication lines when processing a certain level of bookings through the system). Airlines were basing their efforts on the fact that an agent who had opted for their system would find it hard to switch to another system.

With travel agents selling most of the tickets, it became increasingly important for airlines to be listed on other airlines' CRS terminals. CRS vendors quickly raised their fees to about $1.75, up from the pre-deregulation fee of 35 cents. Charges were even higher around hubs of a CRS vendor due to the carrier's—and thus the reservation system's—monopoly position. (Travel agents would subscribe to the CRS that offered the most flights.) Other, mostly new carriers were facing difficulties in obtaining co-host status. Frontier Airlines, for instance, had to wait two years before having its flight information displayed on APOLLO. As travel agents demanded access to all other airlines' flight schedules through their system, CRS vendors were forced to comply.

They soon faced yet another charge: display bias. With many flights available, a standard terminal could not display all of them on one screen. The order by which flights were listed was defined by an algorithm written by the CRS vendor. Usually, nonstop and direct flights were listed first, followed by in-line and then off-line connecting flights.[2] Within each category, systems commonly would give priority to the flights of the CRS vendor. SABRE, for instance, listed the flights alphabetically, putting American with its acronym "AA" at the top of the list. Makes good business sense? Not for subscribing airlines. According to a survey, 90 percent of all travel agents' bookings were made from the first screen. In fact, 50 percent were made from the first line.

To get a more favorable screen display, certain non-CRS carriers offered to pay higher fees to the system operators, contributing to the discriminatory pricing in placement. Other carriers decided they could no longer wait for government regulations or the outcome of lawsuits and started to invest heavily in their own CRS systems. But as they tried to sell their systems to agencies, they faced restrictive contracts prohibiting travel agents from installing more than one system. The only way to gain market share was to convince agencies to change systems. As new systems encroached on their territory, established CRS

---

[2] In-line connections refer to two flights of the same airline. Off-line connections refer to two flights of different airlines.

vendors began to include liquidated damage clauses in the contracts, and sue for damages in case of breach.

In November 1984, six weeks before closing its doors, the CAB issued a final ruling over computer reservation systems.

- The regulation banned both explicit and indirect bias in search routines. CRS vendors were ordered to disclose their algorithms.
- CRS vendors were forbidden to tie travel agents for more than five years. They also were not allowed to force travel agents to book most of their tickets on the CRS's airline.
- Charges to participating airlines could not be ''unfair or discriminatory.''

In spite of these rules, co-host airlines still faced another bias called the halo effect: Travel agents, who were heavily dependent on the CRS vendor for training and maintenance, seemed to favor flights of the CRS vendor over nonvendor flights by a margin of about 10 percent.

The most common algorithms now listed the flights according to flight duration. To be on the top of the list, some airlines published unrealistic flight times, while others focused on shortening connecting times in hubs, causing an inadvertent flood of delays.

Trying to expand their system, CRS vendors enticed hotels and car-rental companies to offer their services through the reservation system. They also added ''backoffice'' software packages that would automate agents' billing and accounting procedures. The airline's task was to create a virtual circle. The more products it could put on its system for people to reserve, the more people would want to hook their terminals to the network. Conversely, the more people on the system, the more economically feasible it would be to offer a diversity of services (e.g., hotel and car reservation). Every new service also increased the dependency of travel agents on their CRS system.

With the increased demand for PCs, dumb terminals were replaced with intelligent workstations. To make the CRS compatible with PCs, connectivity and compatibility problems had to be resolved.

Marketing finally became an integral part of the CRS business. Government agencies and larger agency chains, for instance, were discovered to be very profitable market niches. Both, because of their size, were highly attractive to CRS vendors. On the other hand, they also enjoyed a strong negotiating position.

International Consequences of Deregulation

The international passenger service accounts for a large share of aggregate airline revenue. While the numbers vary among airlines, all U.S. carriers combined have transported roughly 50 percent of all passengers traveling to and from the United States during the last 10 years. An estimated 46.6 million passengers have traveled between the United States and foreign countries (excluding Canada); 40.7 percent of these were crossing the North Atlantic (Table 8).

TABLE 8 International traffic

Region	Passengers (millions)	Share percent
All countries	46.6	100.0%
Central America and Mexico	6.8	14.6
Caribbean	8.8	18.9
South America	2.4	5.2
Europe	19.0	40.7
Africa/Middle East	1.1	2.4
Far East	7.0	15.0
Oceania	1.5	3.2

Bilateral Agreements

In the early days of the airline industry, carriers had to negotiate directly with foreign governments in order to obtain landing rights and to offer services between the United States and a foreign country. It was not until 1943 that the U.S. government took over the responsibility of negotiating bilateral treaties with foreign countries for common air routes. A year later, government representatives from 52 countries tried to define a standard framework for international air service. Because they failed to agree on a multilateral transport agreement, bilateral negotiations between the governments of two countries remained the only way for airlines to obtain the rights to provide service to a foreign country. A typical bilateral agreement would define:

- The right of each government to designate the airline to serve the foreign country.
- The destinations available to the designated airlines.
- The type of traffic the designated airlines are allowed to carry (Table 9).

TABLE 9 The freedoms of the air

1. The right to use the airspace of another country without landing.
2. The right to land in another country for servicing and other noncommercial purposes.
3. The right to discharge in a foreign country passengers and cargo coming from the home country.
4. The right to pick up in another country passengers and cargo bound for the home country.
5. The right to pick up passengers and cargo in a foreign country and convey them to yet another country.
6. The right to transport passengers and cargo from one to another foreign country by routing through the home country.

- The capacity allowed for the designated airlines.
- The pricing of international services.
- Provisions concerning profit repatriation, access to local distribution (CRS) channels, ground handling, airport charges, aviation safety, and other ancillary issues.

Early agreements between the United States and European countries were rather favorable to the United States. One reason lay in the technical superiority of U.S. carriers, which had the capacity to fly more passengers than their European counterparts. Another reason could be found in the large geographical size of the United States. While American airliners could fly to every smaller country with which their government had an agreement, each European carrier was restricted to only a limited number of American gateways.

In an effort to extend deregulation to international air service, the U.S. government in 1978 urged far more liberal agreements. It offered access to new American cities in exchange for fifth-freedom rights. With these rights, American carriers could enter in direct competition with European carriers on inter-European routes. As transatlantic flights were offering high margins, the short flights between foreign gateways would count only as marginal revenue, putting the airline in a position to offer relatively low fares. To no one's surprise, many European airlines opposed the exchange of these rights and instead demanded cabotage rights in the United States (i.e., rights to fly passengers and cargo within the United States). These rights were strongly protected in most countries. Some voices in the EC argued that the European Community was to be regarded as one country, which would change fifth-freedom rights to cabotage rights. But in 1985, a united European transportation system was far from being established.

European Air Transportation

Geographically speaking, Europe consists of 34 countries, each having its own language, currency, and laws. Only 22 of these are listed as members of the European Civil Aviation Conference (ECAC) (Table 10). West Germany, France, and Great Britain represent the largest economies; accordingly, they are also registering the largest demand for scheduled flights. From these countries, most of the tourists travel to the hot spots of Italy, France, and Spain.

Route Length

While the average route length in the United States is over 800 miles, the European average is a mere 465 miles. The longest European route (between London and Athens) is only two thirds the distance between New York and Los Angeles. European carriers thus have a higher percentage of smaller planes than

TABLE 10 ECAC and AEA membership

ECAC members	AEA members
Austria	Austrian
Belgium	Sabena
Cyprus	
Denmark	SAS
Finland	Finnair
France	Air France
	UTA
Greece	Olympic
Iceland	Icelandair
Ireland	Air Lingus
Italy	Alitalia
Luxemburg	Luxair
Malta	
Netherlands	KLM
Norway	
Portugal	TAP
Spain	Iberia
Sweden	
Switzerland	Swissair
Turkey	
United Kingdom	British Airways
	British Caledonian
West Germany	Lufthansa
Yugoslavia	Jugoslav

their American counterparts. They also pay a higher percentage for landing fees and are subject to airspace usage charges throughout the Continent. With these constraints, European airliners are estimated to have operating costs 20 percent higher than U.S. carriers. This is not enough, however, to account for the ticket price difference. During the 1980s, the average ticket price in Europe was 35–40 percent more expensive than in the United States for a comparable stretch.

Government Ownership

In 1985, most European airlines were completely or partially owned by their respective governments and received financial subsidies. In return they were bound to provide a public transportation service. This service included connecting a country's cities, even when demand would not justify it. Government ownership goes back to when operating an airline was thought to add international prestige to the country. Airlines were long considered the commercial ambassadors of their country. This attitude was still predominant during the first half of the 1980s, although some governments, such as Great Britain, were starting to talk about selling a share of their ownership.

Partly because of their relationship with the government, European airlines were heavily unionized. In addition, many countries had strict rules regarding layoffs. In France, for instance, the newly elected socialist government recently passed a law making any firing in the country dependent on governmental approval.

Charter Flights

Passengers in Europe had three options to avoid paying regular fares:

1. Buy a discount ticket offered by regular carriers (Table 11).

TABLE 11   The importance of discount fares in Europe and the United States

	Discount fares issued as a percent off total traffic	Average discount below full fare
Europe	57%	40%
United States	85	56

2. Buy a ticket in the gray market, consisting of second-hand and stand-by tickets.
3. Fly with a deregulated, nonscheduled carrier (charters).

Charters offered complete tours, which included flight and accommodations. Since they were excluded from bilateral agreements, they escaped many price regulations. Unlike in the United States, nonscheduled travel (charter) plays a very important role in Europe. In the United States, the market share of charter service dropped from 27 percent in 1977 to 8 percent in 1985. In Europe, by contrast, 43 percent of all passengers flying within the Continent during 1985 took charters for 55 percent of the total passenger miles. Spain and Greece registered particularly heavy charter traffic. During 1984, 19.9 million passengers used nonscheduled services to visit Spain, while only 4.4 million passengers used scheduled services.

Once scheduled carriers realized the vast opportunity that charter operations could offer, they began buying shares of existing charter carriers. The result was a complicated network of ownership.

Rail Transportation

Europe's air transportation is also exposed to fierce competition from the rail system, particularly over shorter distances. While the U.S. rail system accounts for only 0.5 percent of domestic traffic, European trains carry about 13 percent of all passenger traffic. Like the airlines, the rail systems are regarded as a public utility and, thus, are heavily subsidized by their respective governments. Traveling by train is usually cheaper but takes more time than air travel. With the development of faster trains, rail systems have increasingly been able to compete on longer routes. Probably the most prominent high speed train is the French TGV ("train à grande vitesse") that, at a speed of over 170 mph, connects Paris and Lyon within three and a half hours.

Bilateral Agreements

European bilaterals on scheduled services were relatively rigid:

- Only one airline from each country was usually permitted to service a route.
- The two selected airlines were allowed to offer no more than a designated percentage of the total capacity. Usually, carriers had to share the capacity 50–50; a more liberal bilateral between France and Great Britain allowed for capacity shares between 45 percent and 55 percent.
- The two selected airlines were to share the revenue in proportion to the capacity allocated to them.
- Fares had to be accepted by the regulatory body of both countries.

Liberalization—The role of the EEC

The European Economic Community (EEC) has its origin in the Treaty of Rome, signed in 1957. During the fall of that year, government representatives of 12 countries agreed to work toward economic integration. The community was to establish conditions which would ensure fair competition among businesses of different countries by eliminating state boundaries for businesses. Without directly naming the airline industry, the treaty nevertheless included provisions that applied to any kind of business, like an article guaranteeing the freedom to supply services in any of the given countries. The community also was to establish a common transportation policy. Finally, Articles 85–90 prohibited cartels and anticompetitive practices.

Until 1985, however, the treaty had been mostly overlooked by airline authorities. Most carriers held that the treaty did not address the airline industry. Articles 85–90 applied specifically to acts of enterprises. Carriers, on the other hand, were owned by autonomous governments. Even if the carriers wished to deregulate Europe's skies, they had no authority to do so. The Treaty of Rome had assigned the power of decision over air transportation to a Council of Ministers and not to the AEA. Lastly, deregulation did not make much sense as long as governments were subsidizing their airlines.

Nevertheless, as of 1985, most European carriers agreed to the idea of liberalization, while remaining undecided about the pace by which this liberalization should come about.

The CRS Market in Europe

During the 70s, European airlines had discovered the use of computerized reservation systems. Each carrier had developed its own system offering diverse functions. A 1983 survey on the world's largest reservation systems (Table 12) clearly showed that European CRSs were not as sophisticated as American ones. Backoffice systems, for instance, were not offered by any of the European airlines.

TABLE 12 Survey of major CRSs

	Air France	British Airways	Finnair	Icelandair	KLM	Lufthansa	Sabena	SAS	Swissair	TAP-Air Portugal	American Airlines
Reservations	I	I	I	I	I	I	C	I	I	C	I
Check-in	I	I	C	—	I	I	C	I	I	C	I
Ticketing	I	I	I	I	I	I	C	I	I	—	I
Fare quote	I	I	—	—	I	I	C	—	I	—	I
Hotel reservations	I	I	I	—	I	I	C	—	I	—	I
Car rental	I	C	—	—	I	—	C	—	—	—	I
Baggage trace	I	C	C	—	C	C	C	I	C	—	I
Scheduling	I	I	—	—	I	I	—	I	I	—	I
Crew management	I	I	I	I	I	I	I	I	I	I	I
Flight planning	I	I	I	—	I	I	I	I	C	—	I
Weight and balance	I	I	C	—	I	I	I	I	I	C	I
Inventory management	I	I	I	I	I	I	I	I	I	I	I
Maintenance schedule	I	I	I	I	I	I	I	I	I	I	I
Performance analysis	I	I	—	I	I	I	I	I	I	I	I
Financial	I	I	I	I	I	I	I	I	I	I	I
Cargo control	I	I	I	I	I	I	I	I	I	I	I
Management information	I	I	I	I	I	I	I	I	I	I	I

I = In-house.
C = Contracted.
— = Not available.

Although travel agents accounted for the majority of ticket sales, not all of the airlines offered their systems to travel agents. The airlines that did, did so only to agencies within their respective countries, since the systems generally displayed only flights for the domestic airline. Travel agents wishing to book a reservation on a foreign carrier had to call the other airline's reservation office, ask for seat availability, and if available, ask to have the ticket sent.

SABRE's 1986 European Marketing Plan

Having a 35 percent share of the nearly saturated U.S. travel agency market in 1985, American decided to expand further and to "focus its attention on sales and service of its SABRE system internationally."[3] The 1986 marketing plan for sales and service outlined the strategic steps to successfully enter foreign markets. Besides offering additional revenue generated by new subscribers, the expansion into foreign markets would lead to increased visibility for American Airlines and would generate useful data for yield management concerning international flights.

At American, the foreign network was divided into three areas:

Area I: Central America, South America, and Caribbean.
Area II: Europe, Africa, and the Middle East.
Area III: Australia, New Zealand, Pacific, and South East Asia.

Although trying to expand worldwide, the early phases of the plan concentrated on Europe. Accordingly, we will focus only on the marketing plan as it relates to Europe.

The introduction to the plan also stated the following:

A most effective premise upon which this entire plan is built relates to positive interaction with the International Passenger Sales Division of American Airlines . . . so that, hand in hand, both organizations may identify new opportunities leading to worldwide SABRE distribution.

Competitive Environment

SABRE faced competition from both local systems and CRSs of U.S. carriers. Furthermore, the European market was practically unaware of SABRE. "They may have heard the name, but in their own minds, they do not differentiate its functionality from APOLLO or any other U.S. system."

The marketing plan went on describing several competitive advantages of local systems over SABRE:

- Unlike SABRE, all local systems could issue tickets. Most of them did so through a Bank Settlement Plan (BSP).[4] American was in the process of receiving BSP specifications from each country that offered such a procedure. In non-BSP countries such as France, ticketing capability was administrated through the national carrier.

---

[3] This and the following quotes are taken from the SABRE 1986 Marketing Plan.

[4] The Bank Settlement Plan (BSP) is a unified procedure by which travel agents give the coupons of the tickets they sold to an organization, which manages for a fee the money transfer to the different airlines. In certain cases, a travel agent can strike a deal with an airline and pay the ticket revenue (minus commission) directly to that airline, therefore avoiding the BSP fee.

- Local systems were able to quote fares more accurately than SABRE. To quote fares through SABRE, reliable sources for fare information had to be determined and the information continually updated.
- Most local systems had booking and ticketing capabilities for national rail services. American had just started to negotiate with its first rail participants—the French SNCF and Swiss Rail.
- Local systems maintained nationalistic arguments to promote the use of their systems. They were also backed by the national flag carriers, which objected to the use of foreign CRSs.

Special attention was lavished upon reservation systems in the United Kingdom, Germany, and France, because of the large size of their market (Table 13). In Scandinavia, the reservation system of SAS (Scandinavian Airlines System) represented the major competitor of SABRE. Unknown to American at that time were the operating procedures in Switzerland, Austria, Spain, Belgium, the Netherlands, and Italy.

TABLE 13 Major European CRS competitors

Country	United Kingdom	Germany	France	Scandinavia
CRS	TRAVICOM	START	ESTEREL	
BSP	Yes	Yes	No	No
Special features	Comprehensive fares and quoting capabilities, telex capabilities	Ticketing capabilities for rail system, backoffice system	Ticketing capabilities for rail system	

Other U.S. CRS vendors had already entered the European market (Table 14). United Airlines was by far the most aggressive vendor. Promoting APOLLO, United had placed sales representatives throughout Europe and built a large demonstration facility in Paris. It also offered free installation, several months of free equipment rental, and special override commissions for flight segments booked on United.

TABLE 14 Position of major U.S. CRSs in Europe

CRS	APOLLO	DATAS II	PARS
Airline	United/Covia	Delta Airlines	TWA
Main location	Paris	Germany	London
Comments	Agressive marketing and pricing	Services U.S. military bases	

Objectives and Goals

While never expressively stated, the objectives were obvious: first, to acquire significant international market share to become the worldwide leader in the distribution of travel information; second, to collect through SABRE market information about competitors' operations and pricing, enabling American Airlines to increase its presence on international routes.

> The key is to get SABRE's "foot in the door." As we establish our distribution and enhance functionality, bookings will increase. Optimum revenue potential to American will be long term in nature. Significant booking fee revenue potential exists once the system eases into the role of a primary system and additional CRTs are installed.[5]

The goal was to install SABRE in 310 European locations by the end of 1986 and to achieve a penetration of 4 percent in the worldwide IATA travel agency market (Table 15).[6]

> The focus of the initial sales effort will concentrate primarily on IATA locations. Depending on the particular sensitivities which are present from one country to another, a decision may be reached to automate non-IATA locations as well.

TABLE 15   SABRE's objectives in Europe

	SABRE locations	IATA agencies	Percent
United Kindgom	65	3,155	2.1%
Norway	25	233	10.7
Sweden	25	262	9.5
Denmark	20	150	13.3
Finland	24	300	8.0
Germany	40	1,342	2.9
France	30	1,200	2.5
Switzerland	17	355	5.0
Belgium	14	180	3.0
Holland	20	250	8.0
Other Europe	30	300	10.0
	310	7,777	4.0

Global Strategies

Until SABRE could offer ticketing capabilities and cater to local travel habits, it could be promoted and sold only as a secondary system. Subscribers could only book flight segments in the United States and order tickets to be sent by mail.[7]

---

[5] Cathode-ray tube; commonly used to design computer workstations.

[6] The International Air Transport Association (IATA) is the airlines' own trade association. Until 1984, among other duties, it assumed the jobs of determining equitable fares and controlling the distribution part of the business. It still is assigned to the latter duty. Under its Standard Agency Agreement of 1952, travel agents accredited under the agreement (i.e., those meeting the necessary criteria of competence, financial soundness, and suitable premises) get the right to issue IATA's interlinable air tickets plus the opportunity (if available in their country) to participate in its Bank Settlement Plan (BSP).

[7] Subscribers, such as travel agents, are customers who are using SABRE to process reservations.

While the system would be gradually upgraded to meet the requirements for a primary system, sales were to focus on the technological superiority of the product and price the system at a level competitive with existing U.S. systems. American was considering two ways to enter the local markets: first by getting local travel agents to connect to SABRE, and second, by licensing the sophisticated SABRE software to national carriers. Thus, while advertising the system as a competitive alternative to local CRS systems, the sales and service departments also had to consider every opportunity to make SABRE the CRS standard in each country.

> It should be noted that direct sales activity will be supplemented by on-going Prime Host discussions with key selected carriers. In the event that a Prime Host opportunity is successful, direct sales of SABRE to locations with the national carrier system will cease.

During this early stage, product development was to focus its efforts on:

- Expanding ticketing capabilities.
- Permitting booking and ticketing capabilities for rail and small regional air services.
- Adapting travel agency backoffice accounting software to national standards.
- Offering billing in foreign currencies.

SABRE specialists were scheduled to visit travel agents in order to help them increase their bookings. Agents were also to be offered repeated training and invited to various workshops. Agency sales were also to induce European hotel chains, car rental companies, and other local travel firms to become associates and list their services through SABRE for a fee.[8]

Once all necessary enhancements would be customized for a single-country market, SABRE would finally be promotable as a primary system to compete directly with local CRSs.

Configuration Strategy

Two major competitive disadvantages for SABRE were its high communication costs and its long response time. With the mainframe in Tulsa, Oklahoma, long distances had to be traversed when processing a booking in Europe. The low efficiency was especially evident when an incorrect command was sent by a European travel agent to the mainframe only to be answered, after a long delay, with an error message. It also was very inefficient to have a service used mainly by Europeans (e.g., Swissair shuttle between Zürich and München) being listed and managed in Tulsa. To avoid wasteful communication costs, a European

---

[8] Associates, such as hotel chains, are customers who are offering their services through the reservation system to the subscriber.

mini-mainframe could be designed to filter the messages and send to Tulsa only those which it could not process by itself. Such a system, however, was not feasible in the near future and a study of different alternatives continued.

Initial Research

In March of 1986, three senior analysts were to be hired to conduct a three-month marketing study to determine the potential subscriber base in each region and country. The research would also provide specific country by country information about:

- Current operating methods and procedures for travel agencies.
- Import/export regulations and other documentation requirements.
- Cultural and business practices.
- Communication requirements, and installation and maintenance procedures.
- Language requirements to develop a comprehensive sales, marketing, and installation program.
- Legal ramifications for operations.

The research was also expected to indicate recommendations for:

- Staffing and sales representation.
- Time frames for implementing the sales and installation efforts.
- Training requirements.
- SABRE functional enhancements.
- Promotion strategies.

Sales Staffing

New personnel would be added to headquarters as well as to the overseas staff. Each of the three foreign regions would be controlled by a regional manager. The regional manager of Europe would be based in London and report to the vice president of automation at headquarters. Four country managers would report to the regional manager (Figure 5). They would be responsible for the United Kingdom, France, Germany, and Scandinavia, and oversee one sales and one product specialist as well as one marketing service representative. Further recruiting would be necessary for the product development and training areas (eight analysts) and for the finance department (eight analysts).

Training and HELP Desk

Comprehensive training for travel agents would be crucial for the success of SABRE in Europe. The training had to not only be comprehensive in nature but also be offered in the native languages of travel agents. While located first in

FIGURE 5 Organization chart of European SABRE operations

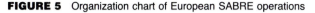

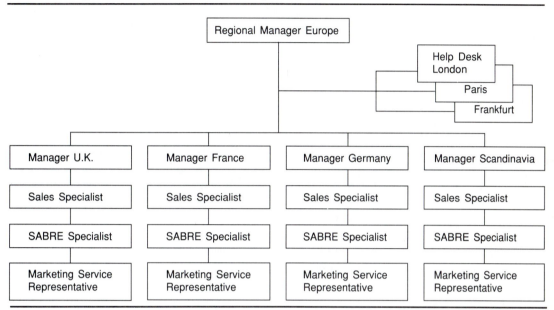

Dallas, the training was later to take place in London. Immediate assistance would be available through Help desks, consisting of two SABRE specialists located in London, Paris, and Frankfurt. The desks could be contacted by phone or electronic mail. "During the third quarter, an in-depth evaluation will be undertaken to determine the feasibility of adding additional Help desks in the cities of Paris, Frankfurt, and Stockholm."

For internal training, regional meetings between the regional manager and all SABRE field personnel would be held on a quarterly basis. "The meetings will be a forum for discussion of current corporate objectives, analysis of results, planning of strategies, and solicitation of feedback and input relating to the international marketplace."

A training session for international passenger sales would also be conducted quarterly to increase awareness and confidence among the sales force.

Advertising and Promotion

New brochures and a video presentation were being developed to highlight the international functionality and the broad features of SABRE for potential subscribers. SABRE was also represented at various air, travel, and computer trade shows throughout Europe. Additionally, the SABRE subscriber conference, which was held in the United States annually, would target international subscribers more actively and highlight its new international enhancements.

During the third quarter, an analyst from advertising and promotion would be charged with the development of international advertising and sales promotion. ''This analyst will address the individual customs, cultures, and language requirements of each respective country and coordinate these efforts with the local advertising agency.''

Legal Issues

The contract administration department of American Airlines faced working around many different contract laws and government regulations in Europe. In conjunction with the legal, financial controls, and international SABRE sales and service departments, it had to ensure the administration of highly comprehensive and enforceable agreements in each country. As SABRE's presence grew in the European market, contract administration would be required to move into each foreign location in order to address the local legal issues more effectively.

The legal and financial control departments were facing yet another issue: foreign currency billing.

Pricing

As noted earlier, SABRE would be priced at a competitive level. The rates of competing U.S. systems had to be matched immediately.

Conclusion

As American prepared itself to relive SABRE's success story in Europe, many questions remained unanswered. Many of them addressed the local marketplace, others were more concerned with global issues. In particular,

- How long would it take SABRE to reach the status of a primary system in each country?
- On which strategy should American focus its efforts, direct sales to travel agents or software licensing to national carriers?
- How would the competition react to SABRE's entry?
- How would the liberalization movements in EEC countries impact SABRE's attempt to become a major CRS in Europe?

''Alea iacta sunt.'' Like Caesar when he crossed the Rubicon, Crandall had thrown the dice in the air; now only the future would tell whether his plans would end successfully.

Part 6

Promotion Decisions

A. Advertising Decisions

Advertising is the most visible and controversial activity carried on in marketing. The first seven cases in this section focus their attention on this function.

Advertising is defined as all paid, nonpersonal forms of communication that are identified with a specific sponsor. It, therefore, includes expenditures on radio, television, newspaper, magazines, and outdoor billboards, plus the Yellow Pages. The largest absolute dollar spenders on advertising tend to be big consumer products companies, like Procter & Gamble, General Foods, and General Motors. The industries that spend the highest percentage of their sales on advertising are the drug and cosmetic companies, followed closely by packaged food products and soaps.

The marketing decision maker has a number of decisions to make with respect to advertising for a product. These include:

1. Setting advertising objectives.
2. Determining the advertising budget.
3. Deciding on what creative presentation should be used.
4. Selecting what media vehicles to use.
5. Selecting what scheduling pattern should be used.
6. Deciding how the advertising should be evaluated.

In the cases that follow in this section, the reader will work to make decisions in most of these areas. The next section of this note is a short reminder of some of the concepts related to each of these decision points.

Advertising Objectives

Advertising objectives should be stated in qualified terms with a specific time period designed for a specific market target. The objective may be in terms of profits, sales, or communications measures such as awareness, interest, and preference. The objective: "increase brand awareness" is obviously not as good a statement as "increase brand awareness to 85 percent of all women 18–40, in the next six months."

Advertising Budgets

Advertising budgets are difficult to set. That is why companies have fallen into using rule of thumb methods such as (1) the "all we can afford" method; (2) the percentage of sales method; and (3) the matching competitors method. We would prefer decision makers to proceed by defining the task they hope to accomplish and then have them calculate the cost of doing this. This is called the task approach. To do this method the advertiser must understand the functional relationship between his or her task and advertising expenditures.

Creative Development

Creative activity is usually done by an advertising agency. The final product is usually the result of much copy testing on dimensions such as attention getting and persuasiveness.

Media Decision

Media decisions are of two types. The first is the selection of broad classes of media to be considered for future analysis. This is done by matching the media characteristics with the needs of the advertiser. For example, television allows for good visual demonstration. This may be a desired characteristic for the campaign at hand.

The second stage involves the selection of specific media vehicles, for example, the NFL football game versus "All in the Family" versus a page in *Fortune*. The procedures for doing this are complex. Simply stated, vehicles are compared on the basis of their cost per thousand (CPM) target audience persons reached. The vehicle with the lowest CPM is selected. Audience sizes are then adjusted to allow for duplication between vehicles and new CPMs are calculated. Then the lowest CPM vehicle at that point is selected. This process continues until the budget is used up. A number of computer algorithms have been developed to handle the many calculations made in this process.

Scheduling Patterns

The advertisers must decide whether to (1) spend their budget continuously throughout the period; (2) concentrate it at a short interval; or (3) spend it intermittently throughout the period. There are no good rules of thumb to answer this question. The advertisers must experiment to find out which pattern makes the most sense for their products.

Evaluating Advertising

If the advertiser has specified quantitative objectives, one is then in a position to measure to see if the objectives were met. The procedure used should be specifically designed to fit the type of objective stated.

B. Sales Management Decisions

The last three cases in this section of the book deal with the management of the personal selling function. Personal selling is defined as all paid, personal forms of communication that are identified with a specific organization.

Organizations in the United States spend over one and one half times as much money on personal selling as they do on advertising. Effective management of personal selling activity is thus very important.

The marketing decision maker has a number of decisions to make with respect to personal selling for a product. These include:

1. Defining the selling job to be performed.
2. Establishing the desired characteristics of the salespersons who will do this job.
3. Determining the size of the sales force.
4. Recruiting and selecting salespersons.
5. Training salespersons.
6. Organizing the sales force.
7. Designing sales territories.
8. Assigning salespersons to territories.
9. Motivating salespersons.
10. Compensating salespersons.
11. Evaluating salespersons.

In the three sales management cases that are in this section, the reader will work to make decisions in most of these areas. Again, the next section of this note is a short reminder of some of the concepts related to each of these decisions.

Definition of the Selling Job

The beginning point of all sales management decisions is the definition of the selling job to be performed. For example, is the job basically just order taking or are there complex engineering presentations involved? In defining a particular selling job, one must keep in mind the role of personal selling in the overall marketing strategy and understand well the needs of the buyer or buyers involved. The competitive and physical environments of the job are also important considerations.

Desired Characteristics for Salespersons

Out of the definition of the selling job, the manager is able to establish a set of criteria for determining the type of person who should perform the selling job. One should list the personal background and individual skills and qualifications that are necessary to effectively perform the defined job. For example, in selling complex electrical equipment, the criteria might include the holding of a degree in electrical engineering, with strong oral communications skills to make presentations to customers.

Sales Force Size

Determining the necessary size of a sales force involves determining the effort level capabilities of an average salesperson and dividing that into a measure of the total selling job to be done. In doing so, judgments must be made on how many total accounts to serve, how often to call on them, and how many accounts an average salesperson can effectively handle.

Recruiting and Selecting Salespersons

The selection of the right salespersons basically involves generating a pool of prospects and evaluating those prospects using the criteria established for the selling job. Information is collected on prospects using application forms, personal interviews, and psychological tests.

Training

The basic objective of training is to bring a salesperson up to the required level of competence in those areas of the defined selling job that were deficient upon hiring. These might include product knowledge, oral presentation skills, field procedures, and so on. Decisions must be made as to who should do the training and where it should be done. Do we let current salespersons do the training in the field or have special people to do it at the office, or some combination?

Organizing the Sales Force

The sales force may be organized on a geographical, product, market, or some combination of these factors basis. If a salesperson can effectively handle all the company's products in a given geographic area, then the geographical structure probably makes the most sense. Otherwise, the product or market basis seem appropriate. The selection between these two approaches depends on whether product or market knowledge is the most important.

Case 20

South-West Pharmaceutical Company*

In August, Frank Van Huesen, vice president of the New Orleans-based advertising agency, Advertising Associates, was sitting in his skyscraper office contemplating a meeting scheduled for the next week. At that time, he was to meet with Mr. Lewis Spring, president of South-West Pharmaceutical Company (S.W.P. Company), to discuss agency recommendations for Gentle Care advertising for the next year. Although advertising expenditures for Gentle Care, a skin conditioner for pregnant women, were relatively small, the client was an important account for Advertising Associates, with about $700,000 in billings. Even though the number of pregnant women had been declining, Gentle Care had been experiencing a sudden, unexpected surge in sales. Therefore, planning its future strategy posed a definite challenge to Van Huesen's marketing and advertising expertise. Before the meeting, he had to come up with sound answers to such questions as: "How much to spend for advertising?"; "What media mix to employ?"; and "What to say in messages for Gentle Care?"

Company Background

The S.W.P. Company of New Orleans, Louisiana, is the oldest manufacturer of proprietary medicine products in the United States. It all began in Iberville, Louisiana, in 1826 when Captain N. L. Denard obtained the "formula" for a tonic from the Choctaw Indians. Formulation took place on south Louisiana plantations for many years until 1860 when Charles Thomas Spring, a pharmacist, bought the formula for $25 and started making and selling bottles of the tonic for $5. The company was moved to New Orleans in 1874 because of the city's better transportation facilities, and growth continued in a sporadic way. In 1955, the Stanfield Company was absorbed and with it another unique product, Gentle Care, joined the S.W.P. product line.

* This case was prepared by Kenneth L. Bernhardt and John S. Wright, Professor of Marketing, Georgia State University. Copyright © 1987 by Kenneth L. Bernhardt.

EXHIBIT 1 Product and price list for S.W.P. Company

Wholesale discounts: 18 percent on net billing	Quantity: 150-pound minimum prepaid shipment. Any assortment of S.W.P. Company products in original case lots can be combined to meet these shipping requirements.		Resale to retailers. At list less applicable wholesaler's cash discount when earned. Terms: 2 percent if paid within 30 days from date of invoice. Net and due after discount period.		

Product	Unit size	List dozen	List	Packed case	Case weight
Gentle Care liquid	3 oz.	$29.60	$3.70	3 doz.	9½ lbs.
Gentle Care cream	2 oz.	29.60	3.70	1 doz.	3 lbs.

The company now manufactures and sells three principal products: Spring's Tonic, Ease Eye Drops, and Gentle Care. Exhibit 1 shows a partial product list, which includes package sizes, prices charged to retailers per dozen items, suggested "list" prices to be charged customers by retailers, as well as case sizes and weights. Wholesalers selling the products receive an 18 percent discount for performing their functions. Sales volume for the company was at an annual rate of less than $5 million, and had been growing about 10 percent per year.

The firm's products have traditionally been sold in retail drugstores, which received the merchandise through drug and specialty wholesalers. The company employs one salesman who calls upon present and prospective customers, primarily in the Southwest. Mr. Spring is active in several trade associations and spends much time traveling to cement trade relations. Management is keenly aware that customer buying patterns are changing and, therefore, efforts are being made to have company products stocked in discount stores, supermarkets, and chain drugstores. Consequently, many "direct" sales are made to large retailers and to rack jobbers. Of its 3,000 active accounts, 500 are large retail chains, and the remaining 2,500 are to a variety of middlemen including wholesale grocers, rack jobbers, and specialty jobbers.

The Product and Its Market

Gentle Care is also very old as products go, having been first sold in 1869. The product, which is a skin conditioner especially formulated for use during pregnancy to relieve tight, dry skin, was originally provided in liquid form. When massaged on the skin, it has a very soothing and relaxing effect on the muscles. Gentle Care's basic ingredients include winter-pressed cottonseed oil, soft-liquid soap, camphor, and menthol.

In 1967, a line extension of the product was devised in the form of Gentle Care cream, whose ingredients include cottonseed oil, laury, myrestyl, cetyl, stearyl in absorption base, glycerin, sorbitol, perfume, and color. Currently the cream form comprises a small but growing percentage of Gentle Care sales.

Mr. Van Huesen describes the industry as "body lotions and creams for use during pregnancy." Exhibit 2 shows the few other companies in the industry, along with the pricing they employ. It should be noted that the other brands are very small in comparison to Gentle Care, are sold primarily through maternity shops, and have only regional or local distribution. None advertises, nor do the brands pose a competitive threat to Gentle Care, which is believed to have better distribution for its sales volume than any other drug product in the United States. By its very nature, the product is a "slow-mover" at the store level, and smaller outlets order the product in half-dozen lots. No deals have been made available to the middlemen in the past; however, an experiment was planned for the fall when retailers would be offered a "one free in five" package deal.

EXHIBIT 2 Industry and pricing structure—body lotions and creams for use during pregnancy

Company	Product	Size	Retail price	Wholesale price per dozen
S.W.P. Company, New Orleans, La.	Gentle Care (liquid)	3 oz.	$3.70	$25.60
	Gentle Care (cream)	2 oz.	3.70	25.60
Leading Lady Foundations, Inc., Cleveland, Ohio	Anne Alt Body Lotion	8 oz.	3.00	n.a.
Mothers Beautiful, Miami Beach, Fla.	Mothers Beautiful Body Lotion	8 oz.	2.50	n.a.
Shannon Manufacturing Co., North Hollywood, Calif.	Mary Jane Maternity Lotion	8 oz.	3.00	n.a.
Maternity Modes, Niles, Ill.	Maternity Modes Protein Body Creme	4 oz.	3.00	n.a.

n.a. = not available.

Isolating the target market for Gentle Care may appear to be an obvious exercise—it consists of all pregnant women. Within that category of womankind, however, Mr. Van Huesen thought the prime target for such lotions and creams should be the first-time mother-to-be. If she decides to use such a product at that time, it is quite likely she will again use it during succeeding pregnancies. What role is played by "influencers" (the expectant mother's mother, older mothers in the neighborhood, aunts, nurses, maternity shop personnel, and so forth) in the purchase and use decision is not known.

Birthrates in the United States have been declining precipitously, and the United States is approaching a state of zero population growth, a point where

EXHIBIT 3 Birthrate by age of mother and color, United States, 1961–1971

Ago (years)	Nonwhite			White		
	Ten years ago	Now	Percent change	Ten years ago	Now	Percent change
15–19	15.3%*	12.9%	−16%	7.9%	5.4%	−32%
20–24	29.3	18.5	−37	24.8	14.5	−42
25–29	22.2	13.6	−39	19.4	13.5	−30
30–34	13.6	8.0	−41	11.0	6.6	−45
35–39	7.5	4.0	−47	5.3	2.7	−49
40–44	2.2	1.2	−45	1.5	0.6	−60

* Table is read as follows: Ten years ago, of all nonwhite women between 15 and 19 years of age, 15.3 percent gave birth.

deaths and births are in balance. Reference to Exhibit 3 shows, nevertheless, that one woman in seven in the 20–24 age range does have a baby in a given year.

Little is known about the consumer decision to use these lotions and creams during pregnancy. How do women learn about such products? Are influencers important to the decision, or does advertising inform the expectant mother of the product's availability? In the absence of specific research into this area of consumer behavior, it was assumed by both Mr. Spring and Mr. Van Huesen that advertising plays a significant, if not *the* critical, role. The product recently had been experiencing large increases in sales, with this year's sales expected to be about 50 percent greater than the level of two years earlier, in spite of a decline in the market potential for the product category. Exhibit 4 gives the sales of Gentle Care for the previous seven years, as well as the advertising-to-sales ratio for that period. The large sales increases were being achieved by both the liquid and cream forms of Gentle Care.

EXHIBIT 4 Gentle Care—advertising-to-sales ratios

	Sales	Advertising	A/S ratio
Seven years ago	$189,578	$140,512	0.74
Six years ago	195,664	82,092	0.42
Five years ago	205,102	69,390	0.34
Four years ago	250,314	69,050	0.28
Three years ago	253,818	40,902	0.16
Two years ago	264,286	68,176	0.26
Last year	315,918	65,706	0.21
Current year	400,000 (projected)	75,000	0.19

Marketing Strategy

The marketing strategies employed by S.W.P. Company are reflections of the marketing philosophy of its president, Lewis Spring. Before joining the firm in

1969, Spring worked in promotional jobs in the petroleum and entertainment industries and he views promotion as an important part of his job. Technical people are hired to handle the manufacturing and physical distribution sides of the business, while Spring concentrates on the marketing-sales-advertising operations.

This circumstance simplifies Van Huesen's job. There are no layers of bureaucratic approval of S.W.P. Company. Once Van Huesen and Spring agreed on a strategy to be followed, it was implemented. The process involved a combination of Spring's ideas on how proprietary drugs should be promoted and Van Huesen's understanding of how advertising can be used to achieve the company's goals.

For a long time, Spring has maintained great faith in the importance of package design to the sales success of the kind of products manufactured by his company. The company once changed advertising agencies over this issue; Spring thought the Gentle Care package needed changing, while agency personnel felt that such a change would destroy the product's "image with the consumer."

Another of Spring's marketing guidelines is that the smaller company "must find the one single most important use for the product" and build the promotional program around that point. Closely related is another philosophical belief, namely that the firm "should do what the competition is not doing," whether it is in the area of media selection, creative strategy, or other promotional concerns.

The Advertising Budget

The company management does not have any "cut-and-dried" formula for arriving at the advertising budget. Advertising's importance to the sales of company products is recognized by Lewis Spring; nevertheless, as Exhibit 4 reveals, the advertising-to-sales ratio has been declining over the past decade without a consequent decline in sales. The relatively large budget seven years ago was due to the simultaneous introduction of the cream and a change in package design, which was accompanied by an increased budget to help secure greater distribution. The drastic cutback in advertising expenditures three years ago was due to an unsuccessful diversification into the cosmetic business that necessitated a recoupment of financial resources. The relative cutbacks this year and last year were in response to tight money conditions at the time and to a management decision to "make this year a year of profit." Spring believes, however, that such cutbacks can be only a temporary phenomenon; in respect to advertising he holds that "you must be everlastingly at it."

Media Strategy

As has been characteristic of the proprietary drug industry for generations, Gentle Care was traditionally advertised by means of small space ads placed in newspapers. Twenty years ago it was realized that for a product whose market is as highly segmented as that for Gentle Care, this media strategy resulted in a great deal of "wasted circulation" of the advertising message; thereafter, advertising for the product was concentrated solely in magazines.

As shown in Exhibit 5, there exists an appreciable number of magazines which can be characterized as "baby oriented." Of course, within the category, those read during the prenatal stage are desired by the producers of pregnancy body skin conditioners. Once the child is born, the product is no longer needed, although it is possible that the woman will continue to use the product for other skin care purposes.

EXHIBIT 5 Baby-oriented magazines

Magazine	Frequency of publication	Circulation	CPM (B/W)	Page rate (B/W) one insertion
American Baby	Monthly	1,108,700	8.92	$ 9,890
Baby Care	Quarterly	575,785	7.49	4,310
Baby Talk	Monthly	1,021,693	8.28	8,460
Congratulations	Annually	2,624,120*	n.a.†	20,670
Expecting	Quarterly	855,013	9.11	7,790
Good Housekeeping	Monthly	5,703,732	3.94	22,765
Modern Romances	Monthly	752,339	3.48	2,645
Mothers' Manual	Bimonthly	913,085	8.77	8,010
Parents' Magazine and				
Better Family Living	Monthly	2,017,029	6.52	13,565
Redbook's Young Mother	Annually	1,519,888	4.77	19,345

* Distributed to specific places; CPM not determinable.

† n.a. = not available.

Source: SRDS *Consumer Magazines and Farm Publications.*

For many years, Gentle Care was featured in smaller-sized ads (one-sixth page to one-half page) in 8 or 10 magazines, one or two insertions per year. In other words, the emphasis was placed on the *reach* strategy—trying to get the message before as many different prospects as possible for a given expenditure of advertising dollars. This strategy was replaced with one aiming at greater *frequency;* fewer publications were used with more insertions in each magazine over the year. The rationale behind this change was based on the fact that there is no seasonality in the product's use; women become pregnant throughout the 12 months.

The current advertising schedule for Gentle Care is shown in Exhibit 6. One key change made last year was switching out of *Redbook,* where the product had been advertised every other month adjacent to the magazine's "expectant mother's" column. To ensure that position, larger space had to be purchased, so for the same amount of money, the entire McFadden Group of eight magazines was available, although for small-sized ads. The agency's media department felt that the McFadden Group would be a better match with the target market for Gentle Care than would *Redbook. Parents' Magazine* was

EXHIBIT 6 Gentle Care—current advertising plan

Magazine	Size ad	Cost per ad	Number ads	Total cost
Expecting	½ page (2¼ × 6¹⁵/₁₆ inches)	$6,620	2	$13,240
American Baby	1 col. (2⅜ × 5 inches)	3,640	3	10,920
Mothers' Manual	⅓ page (4⁹/₁₆ × 5 inches)	3,600	2	7,200
Parents' Magazine	1 col. (2¼ × 5 inches)	5,330	2	10,660
McFadden's Group True Story Photoplay TV-Radio Mirror True Confessions Motion Picture True Romance True Experience True Love Redbook	⅓ page (2¼ × 5¹/₁₆ inches)	6,082	4	24,328
Reserve for special regional availabilities				4,000
				$70,348
Estimated production				4,652
				$75,000

included in the media schedule primarily to allow the company to use the seal of approval in Gentle Care advertising, even though its impact on sales was undetermined.

Creative Strategy

Before Advertising Associates took over the account five years earlier, Gentle Care was advertised through ads which featured the product jar. A typical ad, as created by the former agency, is shown in Exhibit 7. This ad shows an attractive woman's head with her hand apparently rubbing her shoulder. The headline is very general in content; it is not until the reader sees the subheading does she learn that Gentle Care is for use during pregnancy. Seals of approval from two well-known certification agencies were also featured, which meant that advertisements had to be placed in *Good Housekeeping* and *Parents' Magazine*. Exhibit 8 shows the first advertisement in company history which prominently displays that the product is for use during pregnancy.

The new campaign inaugurated by Advertising Associates, an example of which is shown in Exhibit 9, was more direct; the reader could readily determine who used the product and for what purpose. One seal of approval, that of *Good Housekeeping* magazine, was dropped in the belief that the magazine's

EXHIBIT 7 Pre-Advertising Associates
ad for Gentle Care

Any
Body
Enjoys
Soothing

Gentle
Care
**BODY SKIN
CONDITIONER CREAM**

**ESPECIALLY RECOMMENDED
FOR USE DURING PREGNANCY**
Enjoy a beauty massage! Keep tight,
dry skin soft and supple with GENTLE
CARE Body Skin Conditioner Cream.
This new cream has an active mois-
turizer and emollient which helps
counteract dry skin problems. Easily
absorbed by the skin, this luxurious
non-greasy cream soothes dry tissues,
relaxes that stretched feeling. Also in
Original Formula Liquid on Cosmetic
Counters at Drug Stores Everywhere.

EXHIBIT 8 First Gentle Care ad prominently
featuring use during pregnancy

PREGNANT?

Make Yourself Comfortable.

Treat your skin to a soothing beauty massage with Gentle Care. The rich lubricating liquid helps tight, dry skin stay
soft and supple. It brings you ease and
comfort while you wait. Look for
Gentle Care at your Drug Counter. It's
the Body Skin Conditioner that's especially recommended during pregnancy.

Gentle Care

EXHIBIT 9 First ad in the Advertising
Associates campaign

Make Yourself Comfortable.

Treat your skin to a soothing beauty
massage with GENTLE CARE. It's the
body skin conditioner that's especially
recommended during pregnancy. The rich,
lubricating liquid helps tight, dry
skin stay soft and supple. It
brings you ease and comfort
while you wait. Look for
GENTLE CARE
at your drug
counter.

Gentle
Care

audience was much older than the target market for Gentle Care. The decision was discussed at length because the role of older women in the purchase and use of the product was not known.

Changing standards and values in our society are reflected in the current campaign as shown in Exhibit 10. Here a nude model is seen actually applying the product as it would be done by the purchaser. Furthermore, the headline is direct and to the point. The *Parents' Magazine* seal is again featured, and the product package is illustrated in a subordinate position.

EXHIBIT 10 Example of current advertising for Gentle Care

Don't let your tummy get out of shape while you're pregnant.

Give your tight, dry skin a soothing massage with Gentle Care. Its special formula will help relieve the taut feeling and minimize itching. And it will help your skin stay soft and supple. So make yourself comfortable. Look for Gentle Care in cream or liquid form at your drug counter.

The New Advertising Plan

In mulling over the advertising history of his client, Van Huesen jotted down several questions which he felt needed answering before he could design the new advertising plan for Gentle Care:

1. What level of advertising should be recommended for next year?
2. What changes, if any, should be made in media strategy? Are specialized magazines the best media choice for Gentle Care? If so, are ''baby-oriented'' publications the best choice?
3. Is the frequency rather than the reach strategy to be continued for Gentle Care advertising next year?
4. Should the *Parents' Magazine* seal be retained?
5. What changes, if any, should Mr. Van Huesen recommend in the creative strategy for the product?

Once these questions were answered, Mr. Van Huesen felt he was ready to meet with Mr. Spring to present his recommendations for the Gentle Care advertising. Van Huesen knew from past experience that he could anticipate some probing questions from Mr. Spring concerning how the effectiveness of the advertising for Gentle Care could be measured.

Case 21

Zantac (A)*

It was July 1989. Dr. Martin Preuveneers, international marketing director for Zantac[1] Glaxo's £1.3 billion[2] antiulcer drug, the world's best-selling pharmaceutical product, was preparing recommendations in order to ensure that Zantac would reach the £2 billion sales goal that Glaxo's directors had set for June 1993. Zantac had achieved its leadership after an intense, five-year global battle against Tagamet, another antiulcer drug made by SmithKline Beecham and the industry's previous best seller. The challenge now was to sustain Zantac's leadership. Losec, a new antiulcer product from the Swedish company Astra, first introduced in Sweden during 1988, looked like the most serious competitor. Dr. Preuveneers wanted to make sure that Losec would not be able to do to Zantac what Zantac had done to Tagamet.

Company Background

Zantac is a product of Glaxo Holdings plc, a UK-based company with headquarters in London. In 1989 Glaxo was the world's third-largest pharmaceutical company (Exhibit 1), and one of the most profitable (Exhibit 2). Zantac accounted for 50 percent of its sales.

---

* This case was written by Reinhard Angelmar and Christian Pinson, Professors at INSEAD, with the assistance of Hugh Dixson, MD, MBA, and the cooperation of Glaxo Holdings plc. It is intended to be used as a basis for class discussion rather than to illustrate either effective or ineffective handling of an administrative situation. Although the case is based on a real situation, some names and figures have been disguised. The information in this case has been obtained from Glaxo, public sources, and industry interviews. Zantac is a registered trademark of Glaxo; Tagamet is a registered trademark of SmithKline Beecham; Losec is a registered trademark of Astra. Copyright © 1992 INSEAD, Fontainebleau, France. Used with permission. Financial support from the INSEAD Alumni Fund European Case Programme is gratefully acknowledged.

[1] Zantac's generic name was ranitidine hydrochloride (*ranitidine*). Although Glaxo's policy was to use the same brand name worldwide, due to conflicts with locally registered brand names and comarketing arrangements, ranitidine was also marketed under the following brand names: Antak (Brazil); Azantac and Raniplex (France); Zantic and Sostril (Germany); Ranidil, Trigger, and Ulcex (Italy); Zinetac (India); Azantac (Mexico); and Coralen, Quantor, Ranidin, and Ranix (Spain).

[2] During 1989, the average US $ / £ sterling exchange rate was $1.64 to £1.

EXHIBIT 1 1989 world rankings

Ethical pharmaceutical products

1989 Rank	Product	Company	Indication	Share of all ethical pharmaceuticals (percent)	Sales growth*		
					1986–1987 (percent)	1987–1988 (percent)	1988–1989 (percent)
1	Zantac	Glaxo	Ulcer	1.8%	35%	27%	21%
2	Tagamet	SmithKline Beecham	Ulcer	0.9	5	2	–1
3	Renitec/Vasotec	Merck	Hypertension	0.9	210	78	31
4	Adalat	Bayer	Hypertension	0.8	31	20	11
5	Capoten	Bristol-Myers/Squibb	Hypertension	0.8	48	34	15
6	Voltaren	Ciba-Geigy	Inflammation	0.7	17	11	44
7	Tenormin	ICI	Hypertension	0.7	16	15	9
8	Naprosyn	Syntex	Inflammation	0.6	15	25	8
9	Cardizem	Marion Merrell Dow	Angina	0.5	66	53	30
10	Feldene	Pfizer	Inflammation	0.5	–2	13	3
			Industry growth:		11%	14%	11%

* Based on constant exchange rates.

Ethical pharmaceutical companies

1989 Rank	Company	Home country	Share of all ethical pharmaceuticals (percent)	Sales growth*		
				1986–1987 (percent)	1987–1988 (percent)	1988–1989 (percent)
1	Merck & Co	US	3.8%	20%	22%	16%
2	Bristol-Myers/Squibb	US	3.5	18	21	14
3	Glaxo	UK	3.3	29	28	22
4	SmithKline Beecham	US/UK	3	11	8	4
5	Ciba-Geigy	Switzerland	2.9	11	9	13
6	Hoechst	Germany	2.7	3	11	8
7	American Home	US	2.6	7	7	6
8	Bayer	Germany	2.3	13	18	23
9	Eli Lilly	US	2.2	12	5	18
10	Sandoz	Switzerland	2.1	19	14	14
			Industry growth:	11%	14%	11%

* Based on constant exchange rates.

Source: *Glaxo.*

EXHIBIT 2 Glaxo Holdings plc key financial figures (in £ millions) (the financial year ends on June 30)

	1989	1988	1987	1986	1985	1984	1983	1982	1981
Total group sales	2,570	2,059	1,741	1,429	1,186	915	779	663	537
Pharmaceuticals sales	2,557	2,027	1,698	1,361	1,060	779	615	504	414
*Ranitidine sales**	*1,291*	*989*	*829*	*606*	*432*	*248*	*97*	*37*	*—*
Ranitidine's sales growth	31%	19%	37%	40%	74%	156%	162%	—	—
Ranitidine's share of group sales	50%	48%	48%	42%	36%	27%	12%	6%	—
After-tax profit	688	571	496	400	277	169	109	80	61
R&D expenditure	323	230	149	113	93	77	60	50	40
Net assets	2,318	1,809	1,471	1,108	846	697	565	481	442
Shareholders' equity	2,291	1,784	1,450	1,090	827	675	542	428	382
Return on net assets (†)	44%	47%	52%	56%	49%	39%	35%	31%	22%
Return on shareholders' equity (‡)	30%	32%	34%	37%	33%	25%	20%	19%	16%
Number of group employees	28,710	26,423	24,954	24,728	25,634	25,053	27,768	28,106	28,218

* This includes the sales of ranitidine to licensees and associates.

† Based on profit before taxes and interest (EBIT).

‡ Based on after-tax profit.

Dr. Preuveneers was responsible for the analysis of all Zantac-relevant market and product information worldwide, and for the formulation of Glaxo marketing strategies for Zantac. Although he had no responsibility for results and no formal authority over any other department or country, his position as the interface between Glaxo's senior management, Glaxo's R&D company, and the operating companies allowed him to influence all decisions regarding Zantac.

Glaxo's operating companies decided how to position Zantac, when to introduce which line extensions, how much marketing resource to devote to Zantac versus other products, and the promotional mix. Marketing costs amounted on average to 25 percent of operating company sales. Of these, about 60 percent were spent on the salesforce (medical representatives), 5 percent on salesforce promotional material (e.g., visual aids), 5 percent on advertising (medical journals, direct mail, etc.), 5 percent on scientific congresses and educational events, 5 percent on clinical studies with local opinion leaders, 10 percent on product sampling, and the remaining 10 percent on the cost of the operating company marketing department.

Industry Background

All new pharmaceutical products have to obtain approval from each country's health or regulatory authorities before market introduction. Manufacturers have to provide data from tests on animal and human subjects (clinical trials) that demonstrate the efficacy and safety of the product. The approval decision can take two to three years for products based on new chemical entities. The terms of approval are highly specific, and define: (1) the indication(s) for which the drug is approved; (2) the presentation (e.g., a 300 mg tablet); (3) the dosage (e.g., once a day); and (4) the length of treatment (e.g., four weeks). Any change in these specifications requires new data, and a new application and approval. Approval of changes generally takes less than one year.

Zantac was approved for distribution only in pharmacies and hospitals, and patients needed a doctor's prescription to obtain it. This differentiates so-called "ethical" products like Zantac from "over-the-counter" (OTC) or "self-medication" products like aspirin and antacids.

General practitioners (GPs) account for about 85 percent of all antiulcerant prescriptions. Specialists, especially those practicing in research hospitals, play an important role by carrying out clinical trials, and as opinion leaders. Manufacturers' medical representatives are the main source of information about drugs for many GPs:

> The representative helps me memorize the indications, the treatment regimen, and the interactions; that's what I need for prescribing. I am not competent enough to match the subtle differences between patients with the subtle differences between different products; I want the rep to explain this.

> (from a market research study)

Contact time per visit varies between 5 and 15 minutes, during which up to four products are promoted. Visits are carefully scripted, and presentations supported by visual aids, PC presentations, and the like. The danger is to appear somewhat mechanical and depersonalized:

> You always know what's in the visual aids: "Our curve is higher than—'s"; it's written in large letters—you feel like they are teaching us to read. They are like trained monkeys: they recite their lesson, without comprehending it; when you ask a question about another indication for their product, they are lost.

> (from a market research study)

What the representatives say to doctors, as well as other aspects of drug promotion, are highly regulated. For example, representatives are obliged to provide doctors with a health-authority-approved data sheet comprising the following information: (1) indication(s); (2) dosage and treatment length; (3) drug interactions, when present; (4) side effects, when present; and (5) warnings, when appropriate. If a company detects a violation by a competitor it can obtain a discontinuation of the promotion in question. Brand advertising of ethical drugs to the general public, for example via network TV, is generally forbidden.

In countries that operate a reimbursement system for prescription payments, Zantac is rated for at least 60 percent reimbursement. The U.S. market constitutes an exception, with more than 50 percent of the prescriptions being paid for directly by the patients. Few doctors have an accurate perception of drug costs, and high prices tend to be seen as indicating high quality. Due to spiraling health care costs, price sensitivity is increasing, especially in the hospital market.

Ulcer Disease

Ulcers are erosions in the mucous membrane that lines the muscular walls of the gastrointestinal tract. Ulcers that appear in the upper and lower part of the stomach are called *peptic ulcers*. Reflux, another form of ulcer, occurs at the lower end of the esophagus as a result of backward flow, or reflux, of acid gastric juice from the stomach. Ulcers cause stomach pain attacks that last for a few hours and tend to occur daily for some days or weeks. They then disappear only to recur a few weeks or months later. Ulcer complications, like bleeding and stomach perforation, can be lethal. In the UK, as many people die from peptic ulcer every year as are killed on the roads.

Approximately 1–2 percent of the adult population in Western society has an ulcer in any one year, and about 10–15 percent of the population has an ulcer at some time during their lives. Factors thought to be important for developing an ulcer include smoking, and frequent use of aspirin and nonsteroidal anti-inflammatory drugs (NSAIDs), which are prescribed to relieve the symptoms of arthritic conditions. While ulcer occurs in men and women of all ages, its incidence is significantly higher in people over 60 years old.

Patients usually come to GPs when self-treatment of stomach pain fails. Because symptoms are not always clear-cut, it is often difficult to distinguish ulcer from nonulcer stomach problems like dyspepsia and gastritis.[3] Accurate diagnosis requires referring the patient to a gastroenterologist for a test. Initial prescriptions of antiulcerants are usually made without testing. Fast pain relief is the most important treatment objective for doctors and patients, followed by rapid healing and product safety. The disappearance of pain does not guarantee that the ulcer is actually healed. This poses ''compliance'' problems, since some patients stop treatment as soon as the pain disappears. Most doctors are now requesting tests after treatment.

The H2-Blocker (H2-Antagonist) Revolution in Ulcer Treatment

Each day, the body produces one to two litres of gastric juice, with acid peaks occurring around meal times and in the early morning hours. Gastric juice plays a part in the digestive process, kills microorganisms, and helps solubilize certain minerals, especially iron and calcium. But excessive gastric acidity has traditionally been seen as the major direct cause of ulcer.

---

[3] *Dyspepsia* refers to a diverse group of symptoms (e.g., abdominal pain, heartburn, flatulence) that patients may have whether or not an ulcer is present; *gastritis* refers to an acute or chronic inflammation of the stomach.

Prior to the introduction of Tagamet, antacids such as Tums and Maalox were the main nonsurgical ulcer treatment. Antacids neutralize acid already in the stomach and provide short-term pain relief but do not accelerate healing, unless very large and frequent doses are used. The only really effective treatment for serious ulcer disease prior to Tagamet was surgery. While offering a significant reduction in ulcer recurrence (only 10–20 percent over a five-year period), surgery was unpleasant, costly, and always involved some risk.

Tagamet (whose generic name is cimetidine) was the first of a new class of antiulcerants called H2-blockers or H2-antagonists. Instead of merely neutralizing already existing acids, H2-blockers reduce the level of acid production (see Exhibit 3). They do this by blocking the histamine (H2) receptor, which is an important controller of gastric acid production. Tagamet was the brainchild of Dr. James Black, working in the British laboratories of the U.S.-based pharmaceutical company Smith, Kline & French (SmithKline). Dr. Black was subsequently awarded the Nobel Prize in medicine for his discovery of Tagamet and another breakthrough drug.

EXHIBIT 3   How antiulcerant products work

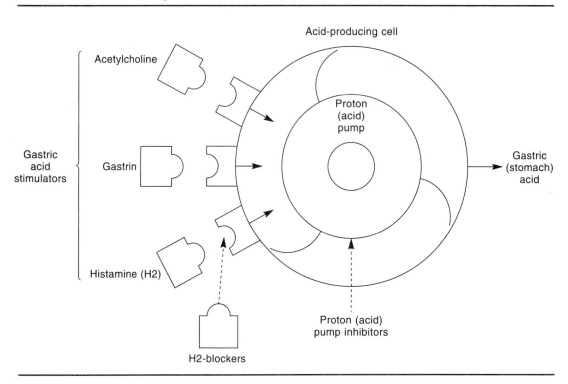

In November 1976, Tagamet was launched first in the United Kingdom, followed rapidly by launches in other countries, including the United States, where the regulatory authority rated it a "major therapeutic gain," an accolade given to a mere 3 percent of new drugs. Tagamet was priced far above any other frequently prescribed drug. Its 1982 introduction in Japan completed Tagamet's worldwide launch.

Tagamet and SmithKline in 1981

Tagamet's success exceeded SmithKline's wildest dreams. By 1981, Tagamet had not only become the favoured medical ulcer treatment, but had also put the stomach surgeons out of business. The total market for antiulcerants exploded from £100 million in 1976 to £600 million in 1981, thereby making Tagamet the world's best-selling ethical pharmaceutical product, sold exclusively by SmithKline's own, fast-growing country organizations. Thanks to Tagamet, SmithKline had become a darling of Wall Street, which had coined a new word: *Tagamania*.

To ensure the company's future beyond Tagamet, SmithKline targeted other indication areas for similar breakthroughs, and acquired companies outside pharmaceuticals. But Tagamet still accounted for about 65 percent of SmithKline's 1981 $1.2 billion ethical pharmaceutical sales, 39 percent of the corporation's $2 billion sales, and an estimated 60 percent of its $370 million corporate net profits.[4]

Tagamet came mainly in the form of pale green tablets, which patients were to take four times per day: three times a day with meals, and again at bedtime. Although SmithKline had obtained UK approval for a simpler twice-daily regimen, it did not actively promote it.

Tagamet produced pain relief after several days of treatment. Its healing rate was 80 percent (i.e., 80 percent of the patients entering treatment were healed) after six weeks of treatment. Ulcers recurred in two-thirds of the healed patients within a year. SmithKline had obtained approval for long-term maintenance treatment, but did not strongly promote this concept.

The data sheets mentioned the possibility of side effects like gynaecomastia (tenderness and swelling of the breasts in males), reversible liver damage, and mental confusion in the elderly and very ill, as well as possible interactions with other drugs such as the tranquilizer Valium. Researchers had discovered these side effects and drug interactions, the incidence of which was estimated at 1 percent of the treated persons, only after several years of widespread use of Tagamet—by 1981, over 11 million patients around the world had been treated with Tagamet. But most practitioners had never encountered these side effects, and those who had often attributed them to other

---

[4] During 1981, the average US $ / £ sterling exchange rate was $2 to £1.

factors. Tagamet's safety was generally seen as very high, as evidenced by the lack of serious consequences in cases of extreme overdose, and by several ongoing long-term studies in Europe and the United States. Whether Tagamet produced male sexual dysfunctions like impotence and reduced sperm production was the subject of as yet inconclusive debate among researchers.

Physicians prescribed Tagamet for a myriad of digestive disorders, turning it into "the ultimate cure for belly-ache." Nonapproved uses added up to an estimated 30 percent of Tagamet's sales. Patients were so convinced of its superiority that doctors felt they had little choice but to prescribe Tagamet.

Development of Zantac

When Glaxo's researchers learned of Dr. Black's breakthrough in 1972, they quickly redirected their own antiulcer project. The new objective was to improve on Tagamet. They discovered that a part of the molecule, previously regarded as vital to Tagamet's effectiveness, could be replaced with different chemical structures. Exploration of an alternative structure, thought to be more selective in its action, hence producing fewer side effects, resulted in the chemical synthesis of ranitidine in August 1976. In October 1981, Zantac was ready for launch.

To achieve this unusual speed, Glaxo had to abandon its traditional sequential development approach in favour of a parallel, simultaneous process:

- A multimillion pound investment in production facilities was made before the animal trials were finished, that is, before Zantac's safety was established.
- Clinical trials were started in November 1978 in over 20 countries. Previously, trials had commenced in the United Kingdom first, and then started gradually in other countries.
- Time-saving considerations entered all decisions, including the choice of tablet colour: "We wanted to avoid any registration problems as a result of the colour we chose. After all, different colours have different significance in different markets. We went for white to play it safe," explained one member of the development team.
- In March 1981, the approval package was put together, with 26 countries serviced within two months.

The UK and Italian health authorities happened to be the first ones to approve Zantac for acute and maintenance treatment of peptic ulcers and reflux. No clinically significant side effects and drug interactions were noted (see Exhibit 4).

SmithKline was not alarmed by Zantac ("How can you improve on Tagamet?" was their official position), nor were they impressed by Glaxo. Industry analysts shared this attitude, citing the following arguments:

EXHIBIT 4 Main characteristics of Tagamet and Zantac, 1981

	Tagamet (cimetidine)	Zantac (ranitidine hydrochloride)
Product and indications		
Presentations	Pale green tablets: 200 mg, 300 mg, 400 mg	White tablet: 150 mg
	Ampoule for injection	Ampoule for injection
Relative potency, active substance	1	5
Approved main indications	Acute and maintenance treatment of peptic ulcers; acute treatment of reflux	Acute and maintenance treatment of peptic ulcers; acute treatment of reflux
Acute treatment (peptic ulcer)		
Total daily dosage	1,000 mg 1,200 mg (North America)	300 mg
Number of administrations per day	4 (3 × 200 mg with meals plus 400 mg at night) (in North America: 4 × 300 mg) 2 (2 × 400 mg)	2 (2 × 150 mg)
Approved treatment length	4 to 6 weeks	4 weeks
Maintenance treatment (peptic ulcer)		
Number of tablets per day	1 or 2 × 400 mg	1 × 150 mg at night
Other aspects		
Efficacy	80% of patients healed after 6 weeks	80% of patients healed after 4 weeks
Side effects	Breast swelling in males (gynaecomastia) Reversible liver damage Mental confusion in the elderly and very ill	No serious side effects have been reported
Drug interactions (products whose effects are influenced by the antiulcerant)	Anticoagulants and valium	No clinically significant interactions have been reported
Cautions	Reduced dosage in patients with impaired kidney function	Examine patients with severe kidney impairment

Source: Medical literature and industry sources.

The first major drugs in new therapeutic classes normally do far better than newer products unless the therapeutic benefits of the follower are very noteworthy.

Tagamet's known side effects are not major deterrents to prescribing so that, even if Zantac's side effect profile proves to be lower, doctors may well prefer to prescribe a product perceived as having a longer track record of large-scale usage.

Tagamet's economies of scale will be so enormous by the time Zantac is launched that Zantac may not be able to be marketed at a more competitive price.

About 40 percent of Tagamet's current sales arise in the United States, where Glaxo representation is considerably lower than that of SmithKline.

On the most optimistic realistic assumption . . . we would be most surprised if Zantac's eventual sales ever exceeded £100m worldwide.

(from an industry analysis; 1980)

Key Decisions for Zantac

Glaxo UK, the UK operating company, recommended that Zantac be priced 10 percent below Tagamet's daily treatment cost, to allow Zantac to capture 10 percent of the UK antiulcerant market. The recommendation was based on a considerable amount of market research showing that doctors saw Zantac basically as a "me-too" product with no significant medical benefits compared to Tagamet.

Although in theory Glaxo UK was just one of many subsidiaries, the tradition of UK-led product development and launch had always given the UK operating company a strong influence on global marketing policy. With a 27 percent share of Glaxo's total sales, the UK was also by far the most important market for Glaxo. Glaxo's international coverage reflected Britain's colonial heritage. For example, Glaxo's sales were larger in Nigeria than in the United States.

For Glaxo's senior management, the Zantac situation evoked memories of Ventolin, an asthma drug launched by Glaxo some years earlier. Although Ventolin became a rather successful product, one senior executive expressed Glaxo's hindsight regret:

> With proper commercial exploitation Ventolin could have become one of the world's largest pharmaceutical products. First, Ventolin was underpriced. We simply never appreciated how different it was from existing products. We just priced it at their levels. Second, we didn't have sufficient geographical presence.

Glaxo's track record of outstanding research but poor marketing had earned it a reputation as "the only university quoted on the Stock Exchange." But Sir Paul Girolami, Glaxo's chief executive, was determined that Glaxo would never again fail on product exploitation. Born in Venice, Italy, educated in Britain, and qualified as a chartered accountant, Sir Paul had entered Glaxo in 1965 as a financial controller, before becoming its financial director in 1976 and chief executive in 1980.

In a fiery meeting of senior executives, Sir Paul ignored the carefully compiled market research of Zantac and, despite the perception that Tagamet was already priced as high as the market would bear, ordered that Zantac be launched at a significant premium over Tagamet. Sir Paul reasoned that if Glaxo's own marketing organization did not recognize the superiority of its new drug by charging a substantial premium, then no one else would. To ensure that Zantac would not suffer from Glaxo's weak position in the major countries, Sir Paul decided to enter marketing alliances with other pharmaceutical companies wherever necessary.

While these decisions delighted Glaxo's researchers, they provoked little enthusiasm among the operating companies. Many were sceptical and waited to see the results from the first countries where Zantac was about to be launched, namely the United Kingdom and Italy.

The UK Launch of Zantac

Tagamet's position in the United Kingdom, where it commanded a 90 percent market share, was extremely strong. The discovery and development of this breakthrough drug in Britain were the pride of the British medical community, and its extensive patient base had generated a flood of publications testifying to the drug's effectiveness and safety. These were also the dominant themes in SmithKline's advertising (Exhibit 5).

Several months prior to Zantac's launch, SmithKline's 75-member salesforce, about the same size as Glaxo UK's, began to warn doctors about the arrival of this new drug, which they claimed had no advantages over Tagamet and a much shorter safety record. This created significant awareness (31 percent unaided awareness among GPs) and interest in Zantac prior to its launch. SmithKline also started to promote its twice-daily regimen in order to preempt Zantac. The difference between the newly promoted twice-daily dosage (800 mg) and the habitual four-times-a-day dosage (1000 mg), plus the yet different U.S. dosage (1200 mg), created uncertainty and doubts in doctors' minds.

Glaxo UK enjoyed an above average reputation for research, effective products, and the quality of its medical information. They were able to obtain health authority agreement for a price of £ 0.91 for a day's treatment, compared to £0.52 for Tagamet. This resulted in a 17 percent price premium for the approved four week treatment cycle over Tagamet's habitual six-week treatment cycle. In fact, most doctors ended up prescribing Zantac for the habitual six weeks.

For Zantac's launch in October 1981, Glaxo hosted a conference of gastroenterologists from around the world. Senior Glaxo R&D managers were very active, giving interviews to the business press and other media. A sample of press echoes follows: "Super-pill from Glaxo" (*Newcastle Evening Chronicle*, October 15); "Drug cuts out sex problems" (*Darlington Evening Despatch*, October 15); "A new anti-ulcer drug which does not affect people's sex lives, was launched in Britain today by Glaxo" (*Oxford Mail*, October 14).

The launch campaign positioned Zantac as a new, advanced H2-blocker that was "fast, simple and specific" (Exhibit 6), which doctors interpreted to mean "faster, simpler, and safer" than Tagamet. SmithKline responded by emphasizing its "tried and trusted" reputation and extensive safety record (Exhibit 7).

Zantac's Launch in Italy

Tagamet, which was promoted by SmithKline's 95 medical representatives, had a 39 percent share of the Italian antiulcerant market. Because of the lack of effective patent protection in Italy, 10 copies of Tagamet had another 16 percent of the market.

EXHIBIT 5   Tagamet: Selected United Kingdom campaigns prior to Zantac's launch, 1977–1981

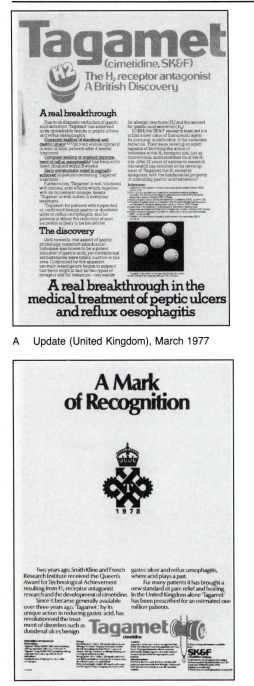

A   Update (United Kingdom), March 1977

B   World Medicine (United Kingdom), May 5, 1979

C   Doctor (United Kingdom), February 21, 1980

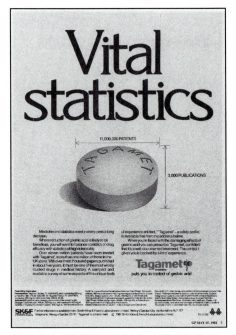

D   General Practitioner (United Kingdom), May 15, 1981

EXHIBIT 6   Zantac: United Kingdom launch campaign, 1982

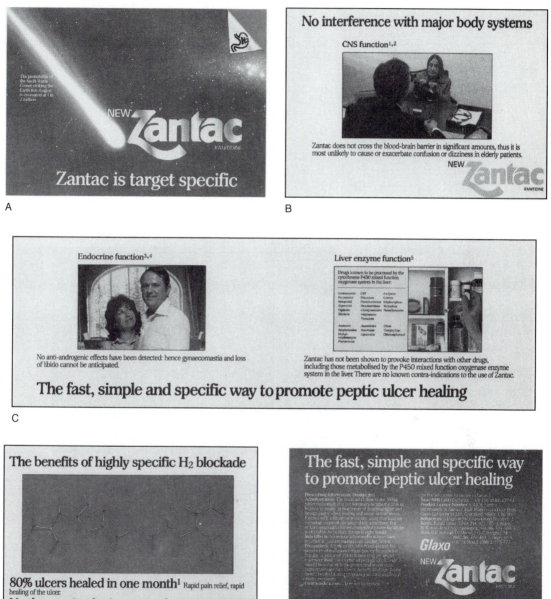

EXHIBIT 7 Tagamet: selected campaigns following Zantac's launch, United Kingdom, 1981–1983

A

General Practioner, (United Kingdom), October 30, 1981

B

General Practioner, (United Kingdom), December 11, 1981

C

General practitioner, United Kingdom, November 4, 1983

D

To preempt copiers and increase promotional presence, it was decided to enter a comarketing agreement with the Italian company Menarini. Glaxo sold ranitidine to Menarini, whose 220 representatives promoted it under the brand name Ranidil. In parallel, Glaxo Italy's 250 representatives promoted ranitidine under the brand name Zantac. Both brands were priced identically, at more than twice Tagamet's daily treatment cost.

Zantac was launched in October 1981, at about the same time as in the United Kingdom. Each doctor was exposed every two to three weeks to Glaxo's ranitidine, compared to every three months for SmithKline's Tagamet. Glaxo Italy managed to involve Italian opinion leaders, and carried out extensive sampling and advertising (see Exhibit 8).

Zantac and Ranidil took off at an incredible speed, capturing 80 percent of the Italian H2-blocker market one year after the launch, with Zantac's share slightly exceeding that of Ranidil. Meanwhile, Glaxo UK obtained a 23 percent share for Zantac (see Exhibit 9). The speed with which Tagamet was blown out of the market in Italy silenced the sceptics inside Glaxo.

Zantac's Worldwide Launch

In Germany, ranitidine was launched in October 1982 by Glaxo GmbH in parallel with a company set up jointly with the German company E. Merck, by a total salesforce of 160, as against 100 for SmithKline. The two ranitidine brands, Zantac and Sostril, were priced at a 60 percent price premium (daily treatment cost) over Tagamet, and made good inroads against Tagamet (Exhibit 9).

News from Europe slowly made its way to the SmithKline organization in the United States, where Tagamet held a 90 percent share. The news tended to emphasize Tagamet's continued sales progression in Europe, and its good showing in the UK. While SmithKline increased its U.S. salesforce from 725 to 850, Glaxo concluded a copromotion agreement with Roche Inc., under which the latter's 700 representatives and Glaxo Inc.'s 450 representatives were to launch the same brand, namely Zantac.[5] A growing number of articles talked about this forthcoming new antiulcerant product.[6]

When the U.S. regulatory authority finally approved Zantac, it gave it a "C" rating, indicating that it made "little or no" contribution to existing drug therapies. Zantac was launched in the United States in June 1983, at a 20

---

[5] According to industry sources, the arrangement was as follows: (1) each year all sales up to an agreed level went to Glaxo, irrespective of which company made the sales; (2) sales above this level were split between Glaxo and Roche, with Roche having the larger share; and (3) the agreed level for Glaxo's "front sales cut" increased each year.

[6] Broad coverage was given to a study in which impotence and breast swelling in 9 out of 19 men treated with Tagamet disappeared when these patients were subsequently given Zantac. Experts were quick to point out that all of the patients in the study were suffering from a rare gastric disease and given nearly four times the recommended dose of Tagamet. Nevertheless, a warning that high Tagamet doses could cause reversible impotence in men was added to Tagamet's data sheet.

EXHIBIT 8 Zantac: selected launch campaigns outside the United Kingdom, 1981–1983

A   Italy, 1981–1982

B   Italy, 1981–1982

C   Germany, 1982

D   Germany, 1982

EXHIBIT 8 *(continued)* Zantac: selected launch campaigns outside the United Kingdom, 1981–1983

Visual Aid, United States, 1983

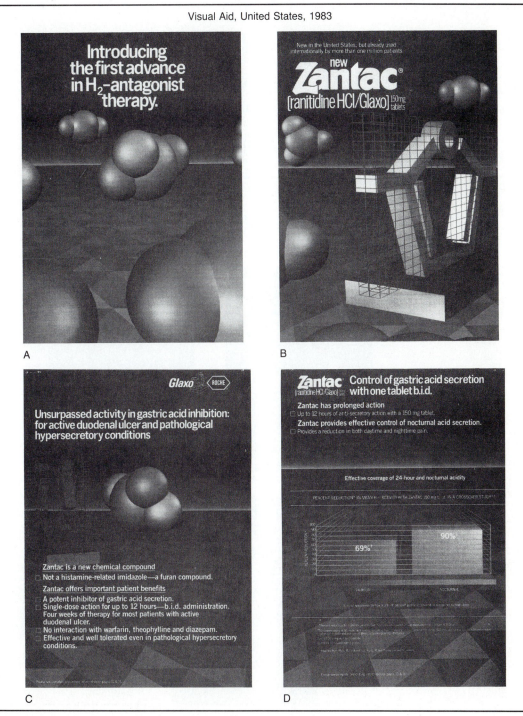

A

B

C

D

Note: Two pages with medical prescribing information are not shown here.

EXHIBIT 8 *(concluded)* Zantac: selected launch campaigns outside the United Kingdom, 1981–1983

Visual Aid *(concluded)*

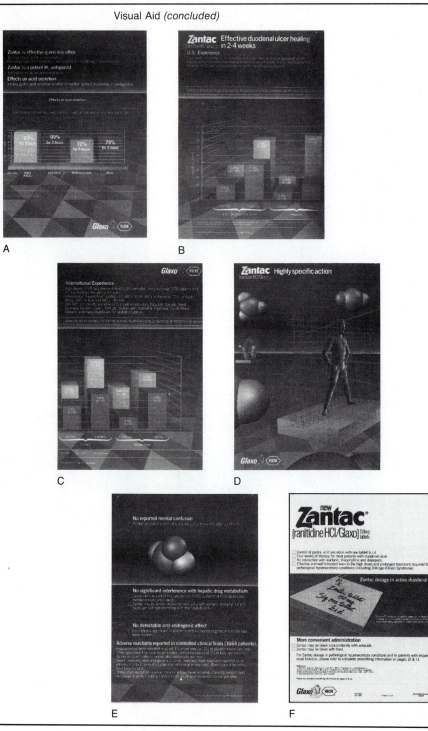

EXHIBIT 9 Zantac penetration of H2-blocker market in five major countries

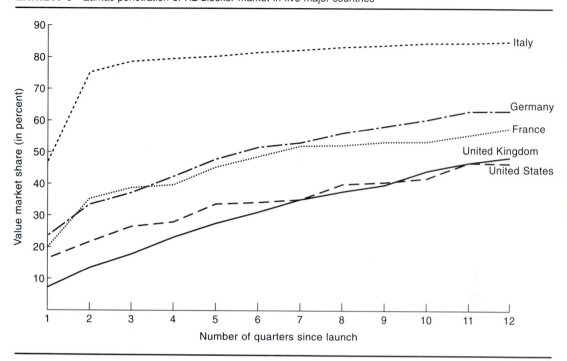

Source: Glaxo.

percent price premium (daily treatment cost) over Tagamet. It was positioned as a more potent, more convenient, and safer product (see Exhibit 8). SmithKline responded by emphasizing Tagamet's safety: "Tagamet's side effects are generally low in incidence, well defined, mild in nature, and reversible. Zantac is a new drug in the United States and it hasn't been on the market that long. Its clinical profile is still evolving," argued Tagamet's product director at the time of Zantac's U.S. launch. Medical experts generally agreed with SmithKline. To counter Zantac's twice-a-day convenience argument, SmithKline presented a study showing no difference in compliance among patients taking tablets twice or four times a day. Even so, SmithKline applied to the FDA for approval of a twice-a-day dosage for Tagamet. In mid-1984, one year after its introduction, Zantac obtained 28 percent of the U.S. H2-blocker market.

In order to increase barriers for Zantac's anticipated launch in France, SmithKline signed a comarketing agreement with the French company Pharmuka, which resulted in the launch of a second cimetidine brand (Edalène), shortly before Zantac's entry in November 1984. Glaxo concluded a comarketing agreement with the French company Fournier. They launched Zantac and Raniplex at a 50 percent price premium (daily treatment cost) over cimetidine. Their combined salesforce outnumbered the cimetidine sales force by 70 percent, partly because Glaxo France doubled its own sales force by hiring a "mercenary" freelance salesforce. French doctors were generally aware that the four H2-blocker brands in reality represented only two different products. They accepted the two ranitidine brands, choosing between them on the basis of chance ("Representative X was the first to visit me"), nationality ("I prefer to prescribe the French ranitidine"), merit ("Glaxo invented it; I favour the firm that has done the research"), or like/dislike for a specific representative. But the new cimetidine brand Edalène was seen as a mere commercial manipulation and never took off:

> I would be deceiving patients if I told them that Edalène is a new product. It isn't. I've been prescribing Tagamet for years. One needs a reason for switching, and I don't see any.
>
> (from a market research study)

With Zantac's launch in Japan in November 1984, in cooperation with the Japanese company Sankyo, Glaxo virtually completed Zantac's worldwide launch in a record three years.

Zantac's Postlaunch Moves

Postlaunch clinical comparisons showed that the ulcer healing rate of Zantac (twice daily) was 6 percent higher than that of Tagamet (four times daily). Comparison of the twice-daily regimens resulted in a still greater 12 percent superiority for Zantac. Two studies published in leading U.S. and UK medical journals in 1984 and 1985 showed that the annual relapse rate during maintenance treatment (i.e., the percentage of healed patients who experienced an ulcer recurrence during the following year despite continuous treatment) was about twice as high for Tagamet (30 percent) as with Zantac (12–15 percent). Glaxo used these two studies throughout the world as proof of Zantac's superior effectiveness, particularly in maintenance,[7] and set out to persuade doctors that ulcers needed long-term maintenance treatment (see Exhibit 10). They wanted to change the way doctors thought about and treated ulcers: from an acute, curable disease to a chronic, lifelong illness requiring treatment forever.

Glaxo also pioneered a further simplification of the dosage regimen, from twice daily to once a day at bedtime. This was based on the discovery that nighttime reduction of acidity mattered most. The once-a-day regimen, which initially required patients to take two 150 mg tablets at the same time, became even simpler when Glaxo launched a once-a-day 300 mg tablet.

---

[7] It was later realized that the differences in effectiveness resulted probably from the differences in potency between the recommended dosage regimens. Because Zantac was five times more potent than Tagamet, the equivalent Tagamet dosage for acute treatment should have been 1500 mg versus 800 mg (for the actually recommended twice-daily regimen), and for maintenance treatment it should have been 750 mg (versus the approved 400 mg).

EXHIBIT 10   Zantac: example of maintenance campaign (visual aid), United Kingdom, 1984

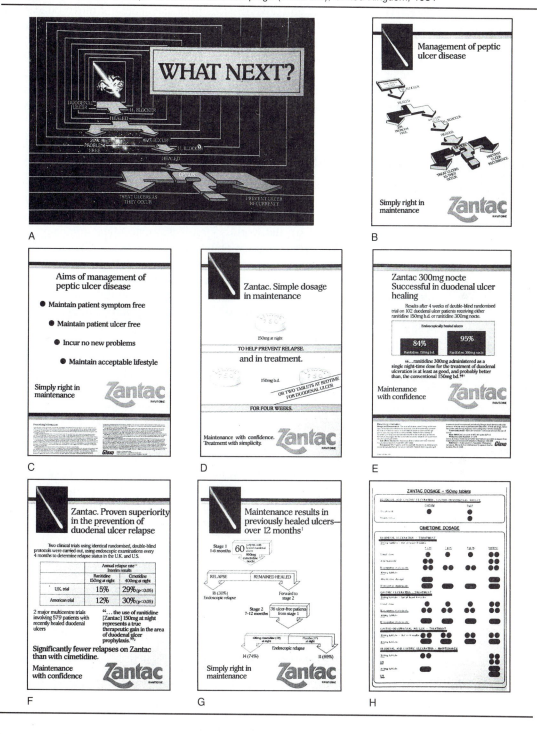

SmithKline followed with its own once-a-day 800 mg tablet. They reduced Tagamet's price and advertised its price advantage, a move unheard of for a branded ethical pharmaceutical manufacturer. SmithKline also obtained official approval to promote Tagamet for nonulcer dyspepsia (see Exhibit 11).

Zantac, however, was first to obtain U.S. approval for reflux during 1986, a memorable year for Glaxo. Zantac overtook Tagamet in terms of global sales, thus becoming the biggest pharmaceutical product worldwide and the first to ever hit the $1 billion sales landmark. This earned Zantac an entry to the *Guinness Book of World Records*. But competition was heating up.

Challenges from Other H2-Blockers

July 1986 saw the launch of a third H2-blocker, whose generic name was *famotidine*. Famotidine was developed and first launched in Japan by the Japanese company Yamanouchi. In most other countries it was marketed by the U.S.-based Merck & Co., the world's largest pharmaceutical company, under the brand name *Pepcid*[8] at a price about 10 percent below Zantac. Merck's promotional support appeared to be limited, due to internal competition with other higher margin and more exciting products. Famotidine was 7 to 8 times more potent than Zantac but appeared to have no other significant differentiating feature vis-à-vis Zantac. Its worldwide launch was virtually completed in early 1989, and its global market share was 12 percent.

The U.S. based company Eli Lilly launched another H2-blocker under the brand name *Axid*,[9] first in the United Kingdom in mid-1987, and subsequently in other major markets. Axid was similar to Zantac and priced about 10 percent below. Like Zantac and famotidine, it was rated as making "little or no" contribution to existing drug therapies by the U.S. regulatory authority. Axid's 1989 global market share was 2 percent.

SmithKline maintained its price aggressiveness, and the expiration of Tagamet's patents during 1992 was expected to focus attention even more on price.[10] They further extended Tagamet's indications and stepped up line extensions, offering the greatest variety of presentations among all H2-blockers. Most of these achieved only minute market shares, while some succeeded but might have hurt Tagamet's image:

The launch of Tagamet's 200 mg effervescent tablet put Tagamet in the same category as antacids. In some countries, Tagamet has become the Alka-Seltzer of the rich.

(a Glaxo manager)

---

[8] Other major brand names for famotidine were: Pepdine (France), Ganor and Pepdul (Germany), and Gaster (Japan).

[9] Other major brand names for this product were: Nizax (Italy, Denmark), Cronizat and Zanizal (Italy), Nizaxid (France), Calmaxid (Switzerland), and Naxidine (Netherlands).

[10] Zantac's patents would be challenged in 1995, but Glaxo was confident of being able to maintain patent protection for Zantac until 2002.

EXHIBIT 11   Tagamet: selected promotional material, United Kingdom, 1985

General practitioner, United Kingdom, May 24, 1985

EXHIBIT 12 Worldwide antiulcerant market size and shares, 1981–1989

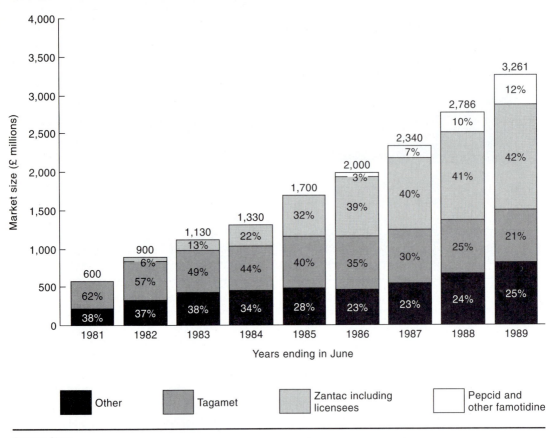

Source: Glaxo.

A 1988 U.S. copromotion agreement with DuPont led to a 10 percent increase in Tagamet's U.S. salesforce effort. SmithKline's mid-1989 merger with the UK-based pharmaceuticals company Beecham, resulting in a new company called SmithKline Beecham, was also expected to strengthen Tagamet.

The four main H2-blockers (Zantac, Tagamet, Pepcid, and Axid) accounted for 75 percent of global 1989 antiulcerant sales (Exhibit 12). The remaining 25 percent were shared by various products such as sucralfate (strong in the United States under the name of *Carafate* and in France as *Ulcar*), seaweed extracts (Japan), and by niche products like the recently launched Cytotec from the U.S. company Searle, which was targeted mainly at NSAID-induced ulcers.

Zantac in 1989

Zantac's global share was 42 percent, with country shares varying significantly (Exhibit 13). Glaxo maintained a strong salesforce presence (Exhibit 14). One-third of all Glaxo visits were exclusively devoted to Zantac. During multi-product visits, Zantac was usually promoted in first position. Glaxo rarely promoted more than two products during a visit and preferred to multiply its salesforce. In some countries, each GP was visited by three different Glaxo representatives, each belonging to one of three separate Glaxo GP sales forces with their own management. Each salesforce emphasized a different aspect of Zantac: one focused on Zantac's use in acute peptic ulcer, the second on maintenance treatment, while the third talked about reflux. Hospitals were visited by dedicated hospital salesforces.

Different visual aids were developed for each salesforce. As other companies emulated Glaxo's salesforce and brand multiplication strategies, some doctors developed strong negative reactions. Signs saying "Comarketers keep out" appeared on some doctors' doors!

To monitor salesforce call frequency, behaviour during the visit, and salesforce communication effectiveness, a representative sample of doctors was surveyed every one to two weeks and asked to recall visits, brand names, key messages, and other aspects of the visits (e.g., samples and promotional material left behind). To monitor the impact on sales, Glaxo tracked the relation between salesforce and market share (Exhibit 15).

Glaxo also carefully evaluated the effectiveness of its advertising (see Exhibits 16 to 18 for examples of advertising research in Germany, the United Kingdom, and the United States, respectively).

Astra's Losec: A New Type of Antiulcerant

In March 1988, the Swedish company Astra launched Losec,[11] the generic name of which was *omeprazole*, in Sweden. Losec presented itself in pink/brown gelatine capsules containing coated 20 mg granules to be taken once a day before breakfast. Astra was the largest Northern European pharmaceutical company with 1988 sales of 6.3 billion krona (US $1 billion), and net profits of 682 million krona. Northern Europe accounted for 27 percent of Astra's sales, the United States and Japan each for 10 percent, and Italy for 1 percent. Prior to Losec, Astra's small gastrointestinal business (1.4 percent of 1987 sales) consisted mainly of antacids.

Losec represented a new class of drugs called *proton (acid) pump inhibitors*. Proton pump inhibitors follow the same general treatment strategy as H2-blockers, namely to heal ulcers by reducing gastric acidity. The major differ-

---

[11] Other major brand names of this product were: Antra (Germany), Mopral (France), and Prilosec (United States).

EXHIBIT 13 Antiulcerant market shares (in value) in six major countries, 1986–1989

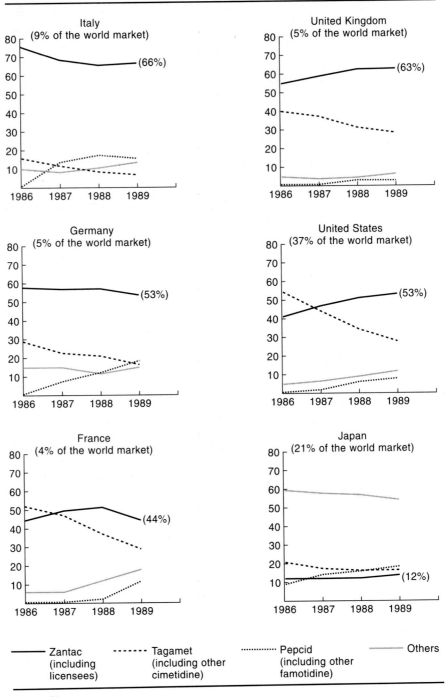

Source: Glaxo.

EXHIBIT 14 Size of antiulcerant salesforces in five major countries, 1989

	Germany		France		Italy		UK		US	
	Number of reps	Share of reps	Number of reps	Share of reps	Number of reps	Share of reps	Number of reps	Share of reps	Number of reps	Share of reps
Zantac	240	16%	285	21%	432	14%	191	24%	2,600	31%
Other ranitidine	220	14	200	15	741	23	—	—	—	—
Total ranitidine	460	30%	485	36%	1,173	37%	191	24%	2,600	31%
Tagamet†	100	7	200	15	173	5	120	15	1,330	16
Pepcid	350	23	240	18	681	21	218	28	1,500*	18
Losec	160	10	130‡	10	478	15	65	8		
Other	462	30	300	22	691	22	199	25	2,850	35
Total	1,532	100%	1,355	100%	3,196	100%	793	100%	8,280	100%

* Losec was to be marketed in the United States by Merck, whose salesforce was currently promoting Pepcid.

† The figures for Tagamet do not include Beecham's salesforce.

‡ This figure does not include potential comarketers or copromoters.

Source: Glaxo and industry interviews.

EXHIBIT 15 Zantac: sales force visit share (SFS) and unit market share (UMS) in a major country, 1988

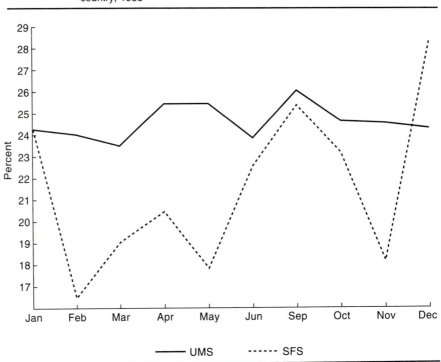

Source: Glaxo.

ence is that they act directly on the final site of gastric acid production, the so-called proton or acid pump (Exhibit 3). Their impact on gastric acid reduction is more powerful and of longer duration than that of H2-blockers. Several other companies were known to be developing proton pump inhibitors, whose launch was expected from 1993 on. Lansoprazole, by the Japanese company Takeda, seemed the most interesting and advanced proton pump inhibitor under development.

Clinical comparisons between Zantac and Losec showed the following picture (Exhibit 19):

- Several studies claimed faster pain relief for Losec.
- In peptic ulcer, Losec produced significantly higher healing rates after two and four weeks of treatment, but after eight weeks of treatment there was no significant difference.
- In reflux, Losec had superior healing rates at all points in time.
- Losec was able to heal ulcers that could not be healed by H2-blockers, so-called *refractory ulcers*.
- Patients relapsed at the same rate as after treatment with Zantac.

EXHIBIT 16   Zantac: attention and eye movement ad tests, Germany, 1985–1987

A

B

Source: Glaxo.

Translation and test results

Date: 16/10/85

What has a hamburger got to do with Zantac?

Be at the office on time in the morning. No time for breakfast. A quick cup of coffee standing up, then off.

By lunchtime, the stomach is making itself heard. Thank goodness for the hamburger. It fills you up and doesn't take much time. The next appointment is pressing.

Day in, day out, rushing around, no time to eat. The toughest stomach could not hold out.

Explain to your patients the connection between nutrition, stress and stomach pain. Tell them to take time for their meals. And prescribe against acid and pain in an H2-blocker that works quickly and safely.

Studies: (30 doctors, 20 advertisements studied)

	Recall	Recognition
Zantac	10/30	28/30
Best ad	10/30	28/30
Worst ad	0/30	3/30

Date: 3/6/87

What has the workplace got to do with Zantac?

In Germany each year more than 750,000 people suffer from duodenal and stomach ulcers.

For these patients in the past this has meant a long sick-leave, possibly an even longer hospital stay and even the risk and expense of a surgical operation.

Now with Zantac 300 they are soon free of pain and quickly cured. The number of hospital stays and operations can be drastically reduced. From the patient's point of view the cost of ulcer treatment can be greatly diminshed.

Studies: (30 doctors, 16 advertisements studied)

	Recall	Recognition
Zantac	13/30	16/30
Best ad	13/30	19/30
Worst ad	4/30	6/30

Source: Glaxo Gmbll and Institut für Kommunikationś-forschung von Keitz GmbH.

Figures in red show percent of doctors who looked at this element at all, figures in blue show average time they spent looking at each element (in seconds).

Figures show percent of doctors who looked at this element first.

Note: Subjects were asked to go through an issue of the *Arzte Zeitung* (a medical periodical). Their eye movements were recorded by a special camera.

EXHIBIT 17   Zantac: tests of the "Volcano" and "Ball of String" ads, United Kingdom, spring and autumn 1989

	Spring 1989	Fall 1989	Spring 1989	Fall 1989	Spring 1989	Fall 1989	Average Values					
							All ads on the database†		All ads on database running		All ads on database in same therapy class	
							Spring 1989	Fall 1989	1-3 months	10-12 months	Spring 1989	Fall 1989
• Recall from visual (brand blanked out)*	54%	67%	60%	75%	59%	68%	50%	51%	51%	67%	61%	62%
• Recall from complete ad	60%	68%	60%	75%	55%	56%	50%	50%	51%	63%	59%	61%
• Product associated with "blanked out visual"‡												
Zantac	28%	38%	36%	52%	30%	41%	25%ᵈ		25%§		N.A.	
other	7%	10%	4%	7%	4%	5%						
don't know/N.A.	17%	7%	19%	11%	21%	20%						
not seen ad	46%	40%	40%	25%	41%	32%						
• Main messages conveyed by complete ad (unprompted)												
ulcers can reoccur	21%	26%	32%	33%	18%	10%						
ulcer treatment	34%	30%	24%	25%	9%	14%						
long term treatment		9%	7%	14%	20%	20%						
healing		9%	14%	13%								
for burning pain	24%	16%	9%	12%	17%	19%						
lifelong treatment					14%	12%						
ulcers last forever												
ulcer craters	14%		17%									
painful	10%		14%									
effective			10%									
no message	2%	2%	4%	3%	15%	9%						
• Interest‖	0.91	0.7	0.8	0.71	-0.44	-0.14	-0.07	-0.06	-0.1	0.16	-0.01	0.06
• Impact	1.2	1.03	1.03	1.12	-0.62	-0.24	-0.05	-0.04	-0.07	0.23	0.02	0.12
• Attractiveness	0.77	0.56	0.75	0.68	-0.7	-0.59	0	0.01	-0.05	0.29	-0.12	-0.06
• Informativeness	0.6	0.6	0.58	0.67	-0.28	-0.14	0.06	0.07	0.08	0.22	0.27	0.28
• Credibility	0.83	0.83	0.83	1.07	0.44	0.51	0.27	0.28	0.28	0.47	0.45	0.51
• Relevance	1.09	1.19	1.15	1.11	0.67	0.63	0.52	0.53	0.52	0.7	0.63	0.7
• Ulcer disease is a chronic condition#	1.08	1.34	1.39	1.59	N.A.	0.66						
• Zantac should be used long term to reduce risk of relapse	0.48	0.74	0.69	1.00	N.A.	0.71						

* With all means of brand/manufacturer recognition removed from the advertisement, subjects were asked whether ad has been seen prior to interview.

† MARS (volcano) and MRO (ball of string) databases.

‡ When presented with the blanked-out ad, the GPs were asked to state which product they associated with the visual.

§ Average product identification values for all ads in the MARS/MRO databases.

‖ Interest and six other dimensions below were rated on a scale of 2 to -2.

Agreement with statement was rated on a scale of 3 to -3.

Source: Glaxo Pharmaceuticals Ltd, 1989.

EXHIBIT 18 Zantac: ad tests among doctors, USA, 1989

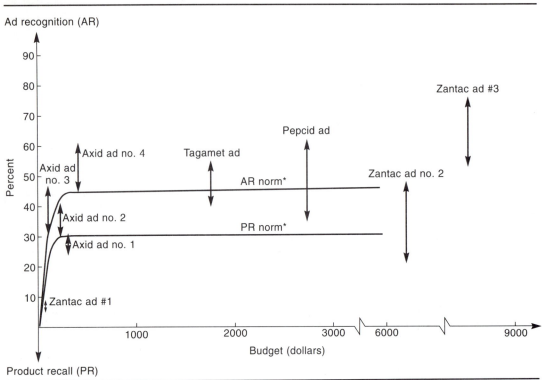

* Ad recognition and product recall norms correspond to average recall values of 67 ad observations (same therapeutic class).

Source: Glaxo.

- As with Zantac, no clinically significant side effects had been reported.
- Losec had similar potential drug interactions as Tagamet, but so far, actual clinical evidence was limited.

In mid-1989, Losec was already approved for sale in 15 countries and launched in 10, accounting for approximately 5 percent of global antiulcerant sales. Of the major countries, only France and the United Kingdom had approved Losec until now. Approvals generally were for acute treatment of peptic ulcer and reflux. The United Kingdom provided the exception, allowing Losec only for acute treatment of refractory peptic ulcer (''second-line treatment''). Maintenance treatment was not approved anywhere.

Astra's short-term intention was to obtain approval for acute ulcer and reflux treatment in all countries; longer term, it intended to obtain approval for maintenance treatment as well. Because of the need for extensive, long-term studies, maintenance approvals were unlikely before 1992 at the earliest.

The important and highly visible United States was one of the many countries in which the approval decision was still pending. On March 15, 1989,

EXHIBIT 19 Main characteristics of Zantac and Losec, 1989

	Zantac (ranitidine hydrochloride)	Losec (omeprazole)
Pain relief		Claimed to be faster
Acute ulcer healing rates:		
Peptic ulcer (average)		
After 2 weeks	52%	67%
After 4 weeks	80%	92%
After 8 weeks	92%	92%
Typical approved treatment length	Four weeks	Two to four weeks
Reflux oesophagitis (range)		
After 4 weeks	27–67%	67–85%
After 8 weeks	38–65%	85–96%
Typical approved treatment length	Six weeks	Four to eight weeks
Relapse rates	Both products have similar relapse rates	
Side effects	No significant side effects have been reported for either product	
Drug interactions	None of clinical significance	Potentially the same as for Tagamet

Source: Medical literature and industry sources.

the Advisory Committee to the U.S. registration authority recommended that Losec be approved only for refractory reflux. This highly restrictive recommendation was motivated by concerns about a potential cancer risk.

Data sheets for some countries indeed mentioned the possibility of carcinoid risk and explicitly cautioned against maintenance usage. Trials of Losec had been suspended in 1984 for about a year when carcinoids (i.e., benign tumours) were observed in the acid-producing cells in the stomach of rats after prolonged administration of Losec. It appeared that these carcinoids were the ransom for Losec's superior potency: when acid completely disappeared from the stomach, other substances increased that eventually produced the stomach carcinoids in rats but, so far, not in other animals or humans.

Astra's entry strategy was similar across countries. Losec was priced between 50 percent and 100 percent above Zantac for daily treatment cost. Positioning emphasized the following themes: (1) Losec is a breakthrough product; (2) Losec has a "precise mechanism of action"; and (3) Losec provides fast pain relief and healing (see Exhibit 20). Involvement of opinion leaders in clinical trials and conferences created awareness and image for Losec prior to the actual launch. Its image was that of an innovative product with side effects (among GPs), or which relieves pain and heals (among gastroenterologists). Lansoprazole was perceived to be very similar to Losec (see Exhibit 21). During launch, Astra typically targeted hospitals first, followed by GPs.

Data from the European launch countries showed that Losec achieved a 12 percent value share of the antiulcerant market six months after launch, of which about 6 share points came from Zantac. Three-fourths of the Losec prescriptions were for reflux.

EXHIBIT 20 Losec: selected launch campaigns, 1988-1989

A
Sweden, 1988

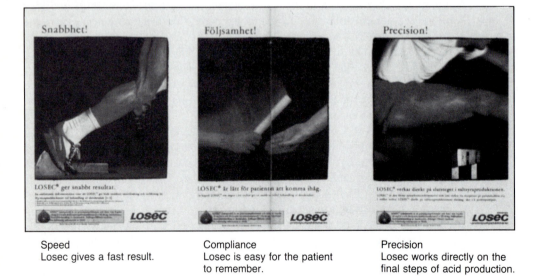

Speed	Compliance	Precision
Losec gives a fast result.	Losec is easy for the patient to remember.	Losec works directly on the final steps of acid production.

B
Sweden (1989).

EXHIBIT 20 *(concluded)*   Losec: selected promotional material, 1989

A   "How reserved are you about the discovery of a new therapeutic class?" The Netherlands, 1989

Above is the title of the Dutch launch ad for Losec. The ad continues: "The discovery or creation of a completely new therapeutic class: every pharmaceutical scientist dreams about it."

The ad goes on to say that Astra have succeeded with the discovery of omeprazole and describes it as a breakthrough in the treatment of acid-related diseases.

"Losec works faster. And more rapidly. In more patients." And concludes: "Therefore we have let our last reservations go." The illustration was commissioned by Astra from a Dutch artist.

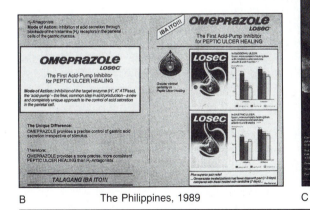

B   The Philippines, 1989

C   United Kingdom, 1989

EXHIBIT 21 Perceptual maps of leading antiulcerant brands in France, 1989

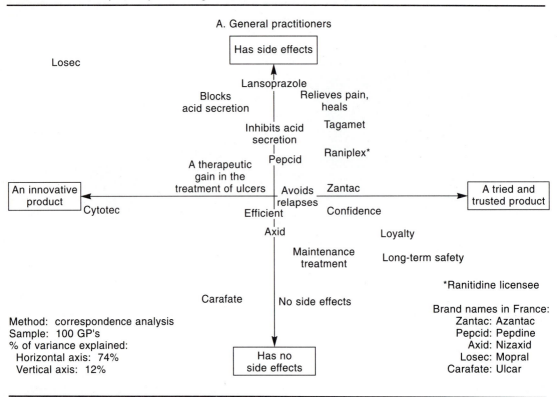

A. General practitioners

Losec

Has side effects

Lansoprazole

Blocks
acid secretion

Relieves pain,
heals

Tagamet

Inhibits acid
secretion

Raniplex*

A therapeutic
gain in the
treatment of ulcers

Pepcid

An innovative
product

Cytotec

Avoids
relapses

Zantac

A tried and
trusted product

Efficient

Confidence

Axid

Loyalty

Maintenance
treatment

Long-term safety

*Ranitidine licensee

Carafate

No side effects

Brand names in France:
Zantac: Azantac
Pepcid: Pepdine
Axid: Nizaxid
Losec: Mopral
Carafate: Ulcar

Method: correspondence analysis
Sample: 100 GP's
% of variance explained:
Horizontal axis: 74%
Vertical axis: 12%

Has no
side effects

Source: Glaxo France.

Astra already had, or was expected to conclude, marketing partnerships in the United States, Japan, Italy, France, and some other countries. In the United States, Losec registration and marketing was handled by Merck & Co., which already marketed Pepcid. Exhibit 14 includes estimates of the size of the salesforces expected to promote Losec in five major countries.

Issues for Zantac

Reviewing events since 1981, Dr. Preuveneers sought the real reason behind Zantac's rise to become the world's number one pharmaceutical product. Was Zantac simply a clearly superior product? Had SmithKline made so many blunders that victory had been easy? Was it merely luck on Glaxo's part? Or was there another explanation?

Over the last eight years, Glaxo had been transformed from a UK-centered company to one with a truly international outlook. This was reflected in Glaxo's

EXHIBIT 21 **(concluded)** Perceptual maps of leading antiulcerant brands in France, 1989

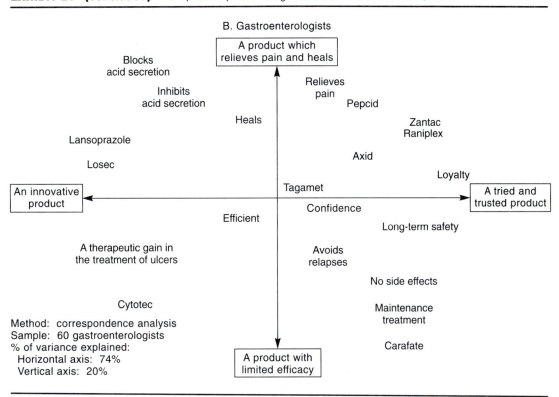

B. Gastroenterologists

Method: correspondence analysis
Sample: 60 gastroenterologists
% of variance explained:
  Horizontal axis: 74%
  Vertical axis: 20%

Source: Glaxo France.

international board of directors, and in the operating companies throughout the world, where local managers had replaced the British expatriates. The influence of the United States, which accounted for 41 percent of Glaxo's total 1989 sales, was on the rise, as indicated by the recent appointment of Dr. Ernest Mario, an American and previously head of Glaxo, Inc., to the position of Glaxo chief executive.

Looking to the future, Dr. Preuveneers was concerned about possible declining commitment to Zantac within Glaxo. Some argued that Glaxo's resources should be concentrated on the promising new products nearing market introduction (see Exhibit 22). Dr. Preuveneers wondered how he could demonstrate the importance of Zantac for Glaxo's future growth.

A second issue was what segments he should emphasize. While total antiulcerant sales were predicted to grow at an average 15 percent during the coming four years, growth prospects of different geographic and indication areas varied (Exhibit 23). In the peptic ulcer area, 65 percent of sales were for

EXHIBIT 22 Glaxo's new product pipeline, 1989

Brand name/indication areas	Estimated number of worldwide patients (millions of patients)	Estimated launch date	Estimated annual sales three years after worldwide launch (£ million)
Zofran: for severe nausea and vomiting associated with cancer therapy such as chemotherapy and radiation	1	End of 1989	£ 75
Flixonase: nasal spray for hayfever	35	End of 1989	£ 175
Cutivate: cream ointment for skin rashes	35		(both products)
Imigran: for migraine and cluster headache	35	First half of 1991	£ 450
Severent: a long-acting treatment for asthma	25	First half of 1992	£ 250

Source: Industry analyses.

EXHIBIT 23 Antiulcerant indication and geographic segments: 1989 segment size, and average future growth rates

	Peptic ulcer (in percent)	Reflux (in percent)	Non-ulcer (in percent)	Total (in percent)	Total (£ millions)	Average future growth (per annum)
United States	13%	7%	17%	37%	£1,207	16%
Europe	18	7	8	33	£1,076	17
Japan	14	0	5	19	£620	11
Rest of world	9	2	0	11	£358	15
Total	54%	16%	30%	100%		
Total (£ millions)	£1,761	£522	£978		£3,261	
Average future growth (per annum)	13%	23%	15%			15%

Source: Glaxo.

acute, and 30 percent for maintenance treatment. The remainder went for preventative treatment of NSAID-induced peptic ulcers via coprescriptions of antiulcerants, a recent indication area that might grow anywhere between 13 percent and 40 percent per annum. Zantac's share was similar across all indication segments.

The challenge for Zantac as industry leader was to continue to develop the market and, at the same time, to defend its share against new entrants. Not everybody within Glaxo was taking Astra seriously. How likely was it really that Astra would be able to repeat the success with Losec that Glaxo had achieved with Zantac, and what could Glaxo do to prevent this from happening?

Dr. Preuveneers's task was now to formulate recommendations enabling Zantac to maintain its leadership and achieve the objectives set by Glaxo's directors.

Case 22

Suburban CableVision*

Kim Harrison had joined Communications Industries, Inc., six months ago, following her graduation from a well-known midwestern business school. Now, in late 1986, she had been promoted to marketing manager for Suburban CableVision, a New England subsidiary of Communications Industries (CI), with the responsibility for marketing cable services in four suburban communities. Suburban CableVision had just been acquired, and a new management team had been put in place.

Ms. Harrison had been assigned the task of developing a marketing plan for 1987. Given that the new year was only a few weeks away, she realized that she did not have much time. The problem was complicated by the regulatory changes that were due to take place on January 1. The new regulations allowed considerably greater flexibility in packaging and pricing cable TV services. As she began to review the marketing files left by her predecessor, she realized that this holiday season was going to be very busy for her and very different than the previous few years when she was on Christmas break from her university studies.

Background on the Cable TV Industry

The cable television industry was born in 1948. At that time, Ed Parsons of Astoria, Oregon, lived at the foot of a mountain. The mountain was between his home, which contained a TV set with nothing but snow on the screen, and the transmitters for the television stations he wanted to watch. Parsons climbed the mountain with antenna in hand, secured it at the top, and strung a wire all the way back down to his TV set. As the only person in town with good picture quality, he soon had friends and neighbors at his house all of the time. When neighbors asked him if he would hook up their sets to his wire, he quickly

* This case was prepared by Kenneth L. Bernhardt and James Novo. Copyright © 1987 by Kenneth L. Bernhardt.

agreed, allowing him and his wife to have time alone together for the first time since he had climbed the mountain.

After this birth of cable television, the industry grew very slowly. In areas where TV reception was poor, people put up towers and ran cable to those households willing to pay for better reception. By 1975, only about 10 percent of U.S. television households were cable subscribers. RCA launched the first communications satellite, SATCOM I, in 1975. Programs from the East Coast could now be received by the West Coast instantaneously. Home Box Office became the first company to provide programming specifically aimed at cable subscribers. Others followed, and today there are over 150 programming sources. The rapid increase in programming led to a rapid growth in the number of cable subscribers.

Consumers were expected to spend more than $10 billion on cable television in 1986, more than they spend on going to the movies or renting home video programs. More than 77,000 people were employed by cable systems. The number of subscribers had doubled during the previous five years, and now totaled 42 million. More than three fourths of all TV households now had cable available to them, but only about 60 percent of those households able to receive cable actually chose to buy it.

The number of subscribers had grown at a compound annual growth rate of 14.2 percent between 1980 and 1985. This rate was expected to slow to under 5 percent between 1986 and 1990. An Arthur D. Little study indicated that spending on new cable systems would decline from a peak of $1.4 billion in 1982 to $160 million by 1990. Ms. Harrison recognized that the future of the industry lay in increasing the number of subscribers and revenue from existing systems rather than from laying new cable in areas that previously did not have cable TV available.

Planning for 1987 was complicated by the Cable Communications Policy Act of 1984 (CCPA). The act took away the power of state and local authorities to regulate the rates that cable companies charge subscribers for basic cable service. At the same time, the Federal Communications Commission was phasing out such regulations as the requirement that local cable systems carry all available local channels. Thus, starting January 1, 1987, local systems were free to raise rates and to put whatever programming they wanted on the channels.

The amount of money the average U.S. subscriber paid for cable TV services nearly doubled between 1980 and 1986, to $21 per month. One leading cable TV analyst recently estimated that the average monthly fee would grow to $28 in 1990 and $39 by 1995. Others in the industry were afraid that higher prices could drive away potential new subscribers and cause some existing subscribers to drop cable. A number of premium channels—such as Home Box Office (HBO), Showtime, and The Movie Channel—were already experiencing a slowing in their growth patterns as consumers appeared to be rejecting expensive cable bills that included multiple premium services.

Background on Communications Industries and Suburban CableVision

Communications Industries (CI) owned and operated four cable television systems servicing 43 cities in the states of Delaware, Connecticut, Rhode Island, and Massachusetts. The four systems had cable passing 315,000 homes, 196,000 of which subscribed to basic cable programming services. More than 113,000 (62 percent) also subscribed to premium programming services, such as movie channels or pay sports channels. CI was the 35th largest cable company but was very small compared to the larger firms in the industry (see Exhibit 1). Total revenues for CI were in excess of $100 million from four television stations, six radio stations, and outdoor advertising services in addition to the cable TV revenues.

EXHIBIT 1 1985 Statistics on Communications Industries, Suburban CableVision, and 10 largest cable companies

Rank	Company	Basic subscriptions (million)	Pay units (million)	Homes passed (million)	Percent basic /Homes passed*	Percent premium† /Basic
1	Tel-Communications	3.7	2.7	6.4	57	73
2	ATC (Time Inc.)	2.6	2.3	4.6	56	91
3	Group W	2.0	1.6	3.9	53	76
4	Cox Communications	1.5	1.5	2.7	57	97
5	Storer	1.5	1.5	2.7	56	95
6	Warner-Amex	1.2	.9	2.7	45	75
7	Times-Mirror	1.0	.8	2.0	49	87
8	Continental	1.0	1.1	1.8	54	114
9	Newhouse	.9	1.0	1.5	62	107
10	Viacom	.8	.6	1.5	54	78
35	Communications Industries	.2	.2	.3	62	83
NA	Suburban CableVision	.01	.02	.02	64	119

* Basic penetration = $\dfrac{\text{Basic subscribers}}{\text{Homes passed (those with access to cable)}}$

† Premium-to-basic ratio = $\dfrac{\text{Premium services subscribed to}}{\text{Basic subscribers}}$

Suburban CableVision marketed cable services in four communities. As described in Exhibit 2, the communities had very different profiles. Downing was a blue-collar, industrial town. Suburban had penetrated 75 percent of the homes in Downing with access to cable, which was the highest penetration of any of the cities in the area. However, the number of premium service subscriptions was lower than in the other areas. Some of the Suburban managers attributed this to the lower incomes of Downing's households—many could not afford basic plus several pay channels. They felt that the basic penetration was

EXHIBIT 2   Profile of four towns

	Downing	Anderson	North Lexington–Middletown	
Basic penetration*	75%	58%	61%	
Premium-to-basic ratio†	1.00	1.26	1.26	
Proportion of total households	one third	one third	one third	
Demographics	Blue-collar, industrial	Very white-collar, managerial, elderly	Rural, farm areas rapidly being developed into far-out suburban subdivisions; young families; mixed demographics.	
Number of years system in operation	5	4	3	2

$$* \text{ Basic penetration} = \frac{\text{Basic subscribers}}{\text{Homes passed (those with access to cable)}}$$

$$† \text{ Premium-to-basic ratio} = \frac{\text{Premium services subscribed to}}{\text{Basic subscribers}}$$

high because TV was a major form of entertainment for these people, and they were willing to pay for basic cable service.

The town of Anderson had a high percentage of the population employed in white-collar and managerial jobs. There was also a large elderly population. Suburban managers felt that these people would drive some distance to attend plays and the opera, so TV was less important to them. Those who did subscribe to basic cable, however, were likely to buy more pay services because of their relatively high incomes.

The towns of North Lexington and Middletown were rural, farm areas just beginning to be developed. Although these suburbs were relatively far from the downtown metropolitan area, a number of subdivisions were being created and many young families were moving into the area. The basic penetration and purchase of premium services were similar to the rates experienced in Anderson.

Although the population in Suburban's market area was growing relatively slowly, the company had experienced rapid growth. During 1985–86 the number of households with access to cable increased by only 1.4 percent. The system as a whole comprised 22,675 households, and 14,600 (64 percent) of these were basic cable subscribers. Although the number of basic subscribers had grown by 7.8 percent in the previous year, the number of pay channel subscriptions, 17,200, was up only 2 percent over the previous year.

Channels 2 through 42 contained a wide variety of basic cable programming. Included were several news channels, network and independent broadcast stations, and specialized channels devoted to local programming, movies, children's programs, and music and culture (see Exhibit 3). On channels 44

EXHIBIT 3   Guide to the satellite and premium channels

Channel	Title	Description
2	Local origination	Programming produced locally for all subscribers.
3	Eternal Word	"Inspirational programming"; Catholic Cable Network.
4	Lifetime	Women-oriented programming; many subscriber call-in shows; exercise, lifestyles, star interviews.
5 and 6 (seen on 55 and 56)	Reuters News & Sports	(5 and 6 are a "channel lock," which keeps other channels in tune.) News and financial reports.
7	The Weather Channel	Local and world weather reports.
8	CNN (Cable News Network)	Live coverage of national and world news.
9	CNN Headline	"Around the world in 30 minutes"; for the busy news viewer.
10	C-SPAN (Cable Satellite Public Affairs Network)	Senate and House committee meetings from start to finish; viewer call-in programs.
11	Public access	"Your community channel"; Suburban CableVision supplies the equipment and training free of charge to anyone in the community who wishes to produce and cablecast a television show or event for the community.
12	Educational access	Channel reserved for use by the school system of the community.
13	Middletown College	Channel reserved for use by local college.
14–29		These channels are the network and independent broadcast stations in the area.
30	WOR 9, New York	Movie classics and television programming from the late 60s and 70s; New York news and sports with Nicks, Rangers, Islanders, Devils, Jets, and Mets.
31	CKSH 9, Canada	Canadian television station; broadcasting in French; programming similar to U.S. network stations.
32	WTBS (Turner Broadcast System)	Movie classics and TV programming from the late 60s and 70s.
34	CBN (Cable Broadcast Network)	Family programming; specializes in movies and early television shows from the 50s and 60s.
35	Nickelodeon	Cable channel for kids of all ages; quality nonviolent entertainment.
37	SPN	From movies to music to international entertainment.
38	Nashville Network	Sports, comedy, dance, and news about country-western favorites.
39	MTV–Music Television	Video music, music news, interviews with the stars.
40	Arts & Entertainment	Cultural programming.
41	USA Network	TV series from the 70s no longer seen on broadcast television.
42	ESPN	The total sports network.
44	Sports Channel	The best of Eastern sports; all home Celtics games live.
45	Bravo	International award-winning films; exciting theater productions featuring the world's best performers; opera, symphony, and ballet.

EXHIBIT 3 *(concluded)*

Channel	Title	Description
46	Showtime	Latest box office hits.
47	HBO	Hollywood blockbusters; original HBO premier films.
48	Cinemax	More movies than HBO and Showtime; late-night, adult-only films.
49	TMC (The Movie Channel)	More movies than HBO and Showtime.
50	HTN (Home Theatre Network	Family programming; the movie channel that doesn't have sex and violence.
51	Disney	Disney movies and classic cartoons.
52	NESN	New England's Sports Network; exclusive live coverage of Bruins and Red Sox.

through 52, a number of premium channels were available for an extra charge above the basic cable service.

Pricing

Suburban's pricing structure was very complex (see Exhibit 4). Basic service was broken down into five tiers. The lowest level of service generally available, basic service, consisted of tiers 1 and 2 (channels 2 through 29). Subscribers signing up for this basic service were charged $7.25 per month. The three other tiers available had options to add super stations (tier 3, $2.05 per month), family stations (tier 4, $3.10), and sports stations (tier 5, $2.35). In addition, eight premium channels were available at prices ranging from $7.95 per month to $11 per month.

EXHIBIT 4 Pricing structure

Basic tiers/premium channels	Channels	Service	Cost/month
Tiers 1 and 2	2–29	Basic service	$ 7.25
Tier 3	30–32	Super stations	2.05
Tier 4	34–40	Family stations	3.10
Tier 5	41, 42	Sports stations	2.35
Sports Channel	44	Celtics and eastern sports	6.95
Bravo/HBO/Showtime/ Movie Channel/Cinemax	45–49	Movie channels	11.00 each
HTN	50	Family movies	7.95
Disney	51	Disney movies and cartoons	11.00
NESN	52	Bruins and Red Sox	7.95

Note: If subscribers order basic tiers 1–4, they get a $1 discount off of all $11 services (movie channels plus Disney) and HTN. If subscribers order any three premium channels, they get Bravo free.

Exhibit 5 shows a breakdown by level of service. Only 1,000 subscribers, 6.9 percent, subscribed to tiers 1 and 2 only. Ms. Harrison believed that the

EXHIBIT 5   Breakdown by level of basic service

	Number of subscribers	Percent of subscribers
Tiers 1 and 2 only	1,000	6.9%
Tiers 1, 2, and 3 only	4,550	31.1
Tiers 1, 2, and 4 only	100	.7
Tiers 1, 2, 3, and 4 only	2,950	20.2
Tiers 1, 2, 4, and 5 only	300	2.1
Tiers 1, 2, 3, and 5 only	150	1.0
Tiers 1, 2, 3, 4, 5	5,550	38.0
	14,600	100.0%

current system was much too complicated and caused problems in the development of advertising copy. In addition, it was difficult for Suburban's telephone sales representatives to explain the system to potential new subscribers. Thus, she felt that it was important to create a new system now that the company had the ability to change rates without having to get approval from each city council. She wondered whether she should include tier 3 as part of a basic subscriber package and felt that there was a marketing opportunity to simplify the system into basic and super basic (consisting of all five tiers). Other systems typically charged between $5 and $15 for basic service and anywhere from $7 to $12 for premium channels.

Ms. Harrison believed that Suburban made more money on basic service than on premium channels. The cost to Suburban for most of the premium movie channels was about $4 per subscriber per month, some being slightly more and some slightly less. The premium sports channels cost about $3. Many of the basic channels did not cost Suburban anything, and most of the others only cost about 25 cents per subscriber per month. Counting all costs for billing, maintaining subscriber records, and programming costs, the average variable cost per month for basic subscribers (tiers 1 through 5) was about $5.

Some cable executives believed that "basic subscriptions pay for the fixed costs of the system, and you make your profit from premium channel sales." Others felt that subscribers perceived more value in the basic channels and that premium channels were already priced about as high as they could be. In fact, many felt that if basic channel rates were raised, then premium channel rates should be decreased to prevent pricing people out of the cable market. These managers believed that instead of downgrading their service (for example, having one of the premium channels disconnected), many people would simply have the total cable service disconnected. Ms. Harrison had heard that some systems had substantially increased sales of the Disney channel by lowering the price to $7.95. Ms. Harrison knew that she would have to give considerable thought to the issue of how she packaged the channels together and how she priced them.

Advertising

Exhibit 6 contains a copy of the newspaper advertising that Suburban had been running. The campaign had been only moderately successful, and Ms. Harrison wondered whether newspaper advertising was just not effective or whether it was the copy itself that caused the poor results.

Suburban had been experimenting recently with the use of direct mail in cooperation with premium channel programming suppliers. For example, it had recently completed a test of a promotion with the Disney channel. The promotion, run in September, was centered around a free preview weekend. Direct mail and print ads informed consumers that they could preview the Disney

EXHIBIT 6 Sample newspaper ad

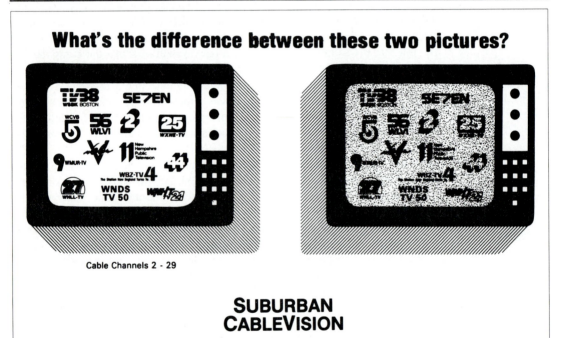

Helen
Kordalis

channel for free, and if they decided to sign up, a 50 percent discount ($5) was given toward the $10 installation charge. While she had not had time to fully evaluate the promotion, she felt that it had been a success. The advertising and mailing costs had been $2,160, but the Disney co-op rebate had covered $783 of this. The Suburban customer service representatives were given 50 cents per new Disney subscriber as their commission. The gross margin (revenue less cost of programming) was $6 per subscriber per month. In addition, Suburban received the $5 installation fee per new subscriber to the Disney channel and incurred only about 25 cents in actual costs for the installation. Over the course of the promotion, 188 subscribers took advantage of the offer and added the Disney channel to their service. This represented a 14 percent increase in the number of people subscribing to the Disney channel.

A similar offer from HBO and Cinemax was far less successful. This promotion was communicated to subscribers via print advertising only. Only 12 subscribers added HBO as a result of the offer, and nobody added Cinemax.

During the fall, Suburban also tested a heavy newspaper advertising campaign for adding The Movie Channel. New subscribers were given an AM/FM radio premium. Only 18 sales were attributable to the campaign, and Ms. Harrison thus had questions about the effectiveness of newspaper advertising and premiums.

A second direct mail campaign was tested, promoting the Sports Channel and the New England Sports Network. Sales of these two premium channels increased 25 percent and 17 percent, respectively, at a cost per new subscriber of $2.58. No discounts or premiums were used.

As a result of the successes with the premium channel direct mail promotions, Ms. Harrison decided to test targeted direct mail for basic subscriber acquisition. Eleven hundred mailers were sent to apartment addresses that had never had cable service. The mailers cost 25 cents each, and 3 percent of those receiving them signed up. In addition, the mailer was sent to 321 homes where cable had been disconnected because the residents were moving. These homes represented 30 percent of the moves; the other 70 percent had been reconnected when the new residents moved in. One sixth of those receiving the mailing signed up for cable. Ms. Harrison thought that there might be potential with direct mail targeted to subsegments of the nonsubscriber base, including the elderly, educators, managers, and those who disliked network TV.

In the early days of cable, there were a number of ''truck chasers''— consumers who would actually chase after the cable television truck when it was in their neighborhood laying cable. They would beg to get hooked up immediately, and direct salespeople were used extensively to make door-to-door sales calls in neighborhoods where cable was being laid. With changing demographics, two-income families, and increased customer sophistication, Ms. Harrison doubted whether door-to-door salespeople would be effective today, but she wondered whether it would be worth testing. A good salesperson would probably cost $25,000, including benefits.

She also wondered whether it might make sense to use public relations to help sell cable subscriptions. She was aware of Toys For Tots campaigns in various cities. In return for bringing in a toy for an orphan, the installation fee for new subscribers would be waived.

Ms. Harrison's predecessor had recommended a public relations program shortly before he left, but a decision had not been made on the program. He had recommended that Suburban sponsor a telethon in North Lexington in support of raising money for the renovation of the local library. There were 1,200 households in North Lexington that had never subscribed to cable, and anyone from these households who donated $25 or more to the telethon would be given free cable installation. Ms. Harrison made a note to review this plan to see whether by changing or keeping its present form it would be a good promotional vehicle for the coming year.

Other Potential Segments

Ms. Harrison was unsure about exactly which segments should be targeted. Much emphasis in the industry had been devoted to increasing the amount of revenue per cable household. Adopting this as a goal would mean that efforts should be directed at increasing the number of services to each current subscriber household, thus increasing the total revenue.

One industry leader believed instead that it's easier to acquire a nonsubscriber than to get someone who is already paying $20 a month to pay $30. This person recommended that cable systems target the "Young and Busies," conveying the message that cable provides a sense of control over one's viewing habits. He also recommended going after TV lovers already predisposed to the product category and promoting cable's variety and choices.

Still another target market recommended by others in the industry was videocassette recorder (VCR) owners. A recent study had shown a relationship between VCR ownership and cable subscriptions. Only 18.5 percent of nonsubscribers owned a VCR versus 27 percent for basic-only subscribers. The percent owning a VCR increased to 33 percent for those who subscribed to one premium service, and to 34 percent for those who subscribed to two services.

Another recent study indicated that VCR ownership was related to cable subscriber behavior, depending on the degree to which the VCR owner rented tapes. As shown in Exhibit 7, light renters of VCR tapes were more likely than average to upgrade (add premium services), and much less likely than average to downgrade (cancel premium channels) or disconnect the cable service. Ms. Harrison had read in a trade journal about one leading cable company that had been testing a strategy of positioning itself as an expert consultant on video electronics. This cable company promoted a $15 VCR hook up kit, and even offered to come out and hook up a subscriber's VCR for a fee. The company offered technical assistance over the telephone to its subscribers, and had begun selling GE VCRs in several markets. The trade journal article reported that the

EXHIBIT 7 Impact of VCR ownership on subscriber behavior (indexed against all cable subscribers)

	All cable subscribers	Non-VCR owners	VCR owners	Heavy renters	Light renters
Downgrade rate	100	100	100	115	50
Disconnect rate	100	105	89	114	55
Upgrade rate	100	112	88	54	132

Source: *Cable Television Administrative and Marketing Society Newsletter* 1, no. 3 (1985).

company had sold 389 VCRs in one and one half months in a four-market test. Special discounts were offered, tied to a pay channel upgrade campaign. Given that industry projections indicated that 50 percent of the population would soon have VCRs, she wondered whether Suburban should target VCR owners in its advertising and promotional efforts.

Another potential market that she thought should be given some consideration was former subscribers. She thought a direct mail campaign targeted toward these households might have a high payoff. Many in the industry were concerned about "churn." Churn was a result of households downgrading their service or having it totally disconnected, and was computed by dividing the number downgrading or disconnecting each month by the total number of subscribers at the beginning of the month. Depending on the season (it was higher in the summer and lower in the winter), the churn percentage for Suburban had been running between 2 and 3 percent for basic service, and between 4 and 6 percent for premium channels. If she chose to concentrate on increasing retention of subscribers (thus reducing churn), there were a number of promotional techniques that could be used. Some cable systems had experienced success in mailing letters to new subscribers that explained all aspects of cable. Thus these better educated people were able to get more out of their subscriptions. She felt that it would be important to beef up customer service, since some people disconnected in frustration after having trouble getting billing and reception problems taken care of promptly and competently. Finally, she had heard that some cable systems had had some success in reducing churn by using advertising to inform people about programs on cable channels. Apparently, bringing these programs to the attention of subscribers through advertising made them appreciate the service more, and thus they were less likely to downgrade or disconnect. Suburban's churn rate was about average for the industry, and she wondered whether it made any sense to use her promotional budget to reduce churn.

Other Considerations

Suburban's system used the latest technology and was an "addressable" system. This meant that the subscriber's service could be changed by merely pushing a button at the central office. It also allowed the use of pay-per-view

(PPV) television. Basically, PPV is just what the name implies—cable TV customers call their cable company and order a particular movie (or other program, such as a sports event) at one of the times it is offered. The cable company transmits the movie and bills the customer accordingly. This means that cable companies can offer subscribers the ability to watch a movie at home without having to pay a full month's price for such services as Home Box Office or Showtime. It is also more convenient than renting a videotape: You don't have to have a VCR, and you don't have to leave your house.

One leading industry consultant estimated that by the end of 1986, 2.6 million households will have PPV available, and industry revenues are projected to reach $70 million. The same consultant predicts that by the end of the decade, PPV will reach nearly 10 million cable subscribers and generate revenues of more than $350 million. The typical price of a PPV movie is $4.50 (ranging from $3.95 to $4.95, depending on the particular movie).

Currently, movies are shown first in the movie theaters and then are released on videotape to the tape rental stores. Finally, they become available on premium movie channels, such as HBO. With PPV it is sometimes shown on cable TV before it is released on videotape for rental. Suburban's technology would allow the introduction of PPV movies, and Ms. Harrison wondered whether that was the direction in which to go.

Thinking about all of the available alternatives, Ms. Harrison recognized the challenging opportunity in front of her. She realized that putting together the marketing plan for the new management team would be quite a job, and thought that she had better get started.

Case 23

Rich's Department Store*

The Executive Committee meeting had been a lengthy session, lasting through most of the morning, but Mr. Dick Mills, vice president and sales promotion director of Rich's Department Store, had returned to his office knowing that a major advertising decision was still not ready to be made. And Mr. Mills realized that it would be his responsibility to submit a final recommendation on media strategy at the next meeting.

Mr. Mills stared at the two neatly bound research reports that he had placed side by side on his desk. The pair of documents represented summaries of the two presentations that had been made to the Rich's Executive Committee that morning. These studies had been based on exactly the same data, drawn from the same in-store survey of Rich's customers. Each report had been prepared by an experienced and professional marketing researcher. Mr. Mills had expected the strong self-interests of the researchers to be reflected in their presentations and interpretations of the survey results, but he was confident that neither person would misrepresent the actual facts.

Mr. Mills had to admit to himself that he had been very surprised at the apparent major contradictions between the two presentations that he had heard earlier that morning. Mr. Mills and the research director of Rich's, who had also attended the morning presentations by the two outside researchers, had discussed the situation briefly after the meeting. The two had decided to separately review the written reports and, then, to meet later in the afternoon to decide what additional steps to take.

Before rereading the reports, Mr. Mills thought back over the events of the past three months that had eventually led to this situation.

Rich's Department Store was both the largest merchant and the largest single advertiser in Atlanta, Georgia. The store had been founded in 1867 and had grown to an annual sales volume of approximately $200 million through its downtown store and six branch stores located in major suburban shopping

* This case was prepared by Kenneth L. Bernhardt. Copyright © 1990 Kenneth L. Bernhardt.

centers. The Rich's market share was 40 percent of department store sales in Atlanta and 25 percent of all general merchandise sales.

The Rich's advertising strategy in the past had been to emphasize newspaper advertising for specific sales items and to utilize broadcast media primarily for image purposes. Newspaper was also used for some image-oriented advertising, with occasional direct mailings used to promote specific sales items of merchandise. Rich's is the largest local advertiser in both print and broadcast media.

The two principal daily newspapers in Atlanta are *The Atlanta Journal* (evenings) and the *Atlanta Constitution* (mornings). These are two of the largest circulation newspapers in the South, and both have distinguished journalism traditions, including Pulitzer Prizes. Although both newspapers are owned by the same company, Atlanta Newspapers, Inc., there is little overlap of readership except for the combined Sunday morning edition.

There are 6 TV stations and 40 radio stations in the Atlanta market. However, broadcast media are dominated by WSB-TV and WSB Radio, both of which are owned by Cox Broadcasting Corporation.

Mr. Mills recalled that several months earlier, executives of Cox Broadcasting and of their two local stations had met with key executives of Rich's. One topic discussed at that meeting had been possible use of broadcast media to promote individual sales items. WSB had offered to participate with Rich's in a market test to determine the abilities of different media to sell specific items of merchandise.

As a result of these discussions, Mr. Mills had held a series of meetings with Mr. Jim Landon, research director of WSB-TV and Radio, and Mr. Ferguson Rood, research director of the Atlanta Newspapers, Inc., to design the market test. It was eventually decided to conduct the test during Rich's annual Harvest Sale, which has been the merchandising highlight of the year since 1925. This sale runs for two weeks each fall. The test was to center on 10 specific items of merchandise which would be advertised in both print and broadcast media during the first three days of the sale. During this same period, in-store interviews would be conducted by professional interviewers, with all purchasers of these 10 items in three representative stores (see appendixes for detailed survey design, sample questionnaire, and media plan).

At the conclusion of the survey period, the Research Departments of both Atlanta Newspapers, Inc., and WSB were furnished duplicate computer card decks by Rich's containing survey data. It was this data that served as the basis for the presentations that Jim Landon and Ferguson Rood had made to the Rich's Executive Committee. Excerpts from *The Atlanta Journal* and *Constitution* report are in Appendix A, and excerpts from the WSB report are presented in Appendix B.

These were the two presentations that Mr. Mills would have to reconcile to arrive at a decision about future media strategy for Rich's. Mr. Mills knew that a decision would have to be made quickly, in view of TV production lead times, if any change in media mix were to be considered for the upcoming Christmas sales season.

Appendix A **An Analysis of a Rich's In-Store Study of Advertising
Effectiveness on Specific Purchase Decisions***

Foreword

This report is the result of an innovative research study conducted by Rich's
Department Store in partnership with Atlanta Newspapers, Inc. and Cox Broadcasting Corporation.

The study was designed to measure:

1. The relative performance of newspapers, television, and radio as a source
   of influence on shoppers' decisions to purchase specific items.
2. Shoppers' exposure to specific item advertising messages.

The advertising period covered in this study consisted of three days
(beginning Sunday, September 20) prior to Rich's annual Harvest Sale.

A total of 2,176 interviews were made on Monday and Tuesday, September 21 and 22. The interviews were made in three of Rich's seven stores—
Downtown, Lenox Square, and Greenbriar, and focused on the 10 departments
in each store where the advertised items were sold.

An Atlanta interviewing firm was employed by Rich's to interview shoppers in each department immediately after they made their purchase. To qualify
for the survey, shoppers had to purchase the specific advertised item or a
directly related item.

Summary and Interpretation

More than 9 out of 10 shoppers covered in this survey had the specific
purchase in mind before going to Rich's, or knew it was *on special*.

Three fourths of all shoppers recalled being recently exposed to advertising messages for specific items.

More than half of all shoppers' decisions to purchase specific items were
attributed to advertising.

Attributions to newspapers were more than twice those of television and
radio combined in influencing specific item purchase decisions (71
percent versus 33 percent).

Dollar for dollar . . . newspapers delivered more than three times the
influence on specific item purchase decisions than television and radio
combined.

The advertising schedule placed in newspapers . . . was conspicuously
more effective and more efficient . . . in influencing specific purchase decisions . . . than the saturation schedule placed on television
and radio.

---

* Presented by *The Atlanta Journal* and *Constitution* Research & Marketing Department.

See Exhibits A–1 through A–16.

EXHIBIT A-1 Newspaper advertising schedule*

	Sunday Journal and Constitution (inches)	A.M. Constitution (inches)	P.M. Journal (inches)
Sunday	1,064		
Monday		172	247
Tuesday	___	0	505
Total	1,064	172	752

* 1,989 column inches, the equivalent of 11.6 pages, made up the newspaper schedule covered in this survey.

EXHIBIT A-2 Broadcast schedule*

	Television			Radio		
	Sunday	Monday	Tuesday	Sunday	Monday	Tuesday
6 A.M.		X			X	X
7		X			X	X
8		X	X		X	X
9		X	X	X	X	X
10		X		X	X	X
11		X			X	X
12		X	X	X	X	X
1 P.M.	X	X	X	X	X	X
2	X	X	X	X	X	X
3	X	X	X	X	X	X
4	X	X	X	X	X	X
5	X	X	X	X	X	X
6	X	X		X	X	
7	X	X		X	X	
8	X	X				
9	X	X				
10	X	X				
11	X	X				
Total spots	42	86	49	53	121	87
Average number per schedule hour	3.8	4.8	6.1	5.3	8.6	7.2

* 438 30-second spots were scheduled to run on five television and five radio stations, for an average of 8 spots per hour, between 6 A.M. and 11 P.M., over the three-day period.

EXHIBIT A-3 Comparison of advertising schedule and budget

	Broadcast spots			Newspaper space
	TV	Radio	Total	(inches)
Hard goods:				
Mattress	12	19	31	35
Carpeting	12	23	35	150
Draperies	16	26	42	407
Vacuum sweeper	15	22	37	172
Color television*	0	0	0	150
Soft goods:				
Handbags	15	27	42	189
Girdles†	15	27	42	0
Shoes	15	27	42	398
Shirts*	56	64	120	86
Pant suits	21	26	47	400
Total 10 departments:				
Sunday	42	53	95	1,064
Monday	86	121	207	420
Tuesday	49	87	136	505
Total	177	261	438	1,989
Budget			$27,158	$16,910

* The original broadcast schedule included 20 TV and 24 radio spots for the color television sets to run Tuesday. Since all the sets were sold on Monday, this commercial time was switches to shirts.

† While no Playtex girdle ads were scheduled to run in newspapers, other foundation advertising during the test period supported the influence.

EXHIBIT A-4 Interviews

	Number	Percent
Total	2,175	100%
Women	1,764	81
Men	380	18
Couples	31	1
Under 35	963	44
35–49	817	44
50 and older	394	18
White	1,966	90
Nonwhite	209	10
Hard goods	527	24
Mattress	71	3
Carpeting	45	2
Draperies	123	6
Vacuum sweeper	134	6
Color television	154	7
Soft goods	1,649	75
Handbags	284	13
Girdles	249	11
Shoes	393	18
Shirts	483	22
Pant suits	240	11
Distribution of interviews by store		
Downtown	683	31
Lenox Square	848	39
Greenbriar	645	30

EXHIBIT A-5

"Before coming to Rich's today, did you have in mind buying this specific brand/item, or did you decide after you came into the store?"

63 percent of all shoppers had the specific purchase in mind before going to Rich's.

These shoppers described the following as sources of influence on their buying decision when asked: "What was it that gave you the idea to buy this brand/item?"

Advertising	52%
Needed or wanted it	23
Past experience with it	16
Outside source suggestion	6
Other	7

EXHIBIT A-6

"Was the store having a special on this specific brand/item today, or were they selling at the regular price?"

84 percent of all shoppers said the brand/item was on special.

These shoppers gave the following sources when asked: "Where did you learn about that?"

Advertising	63%
Store display/crowds	27
Outside source	6
Other	4

EXHIBIT A-7   Advertising influence

55 percent of all shoppers attributed their specific purchase decision to advertising. Of these, 71 percent attributed their purchase to newspapers, 33 percent to broadcasts (28 percent to television and 9 percent to radio), and 9 percent to mail circulars.

Newspapers and broadcast accounted for 94 percent of all advertising influence. 61 percent of these influences were attributed to newspapers exclusive of broadcast. 23 percent were attributed to broadcast exclusive of newspapers, and 10 percent were attributed to both.

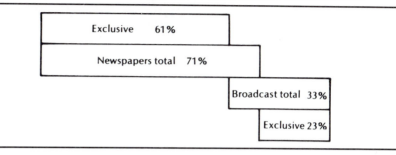

EXHIBIT A-8   Advertising influence

Newspapers and television accounted for 90 percent of all advertising influence. 62 percent of these influences were attributed to newspapers exclusive of television. 19 percent were attributed to television exclusive of newspapers, and 9 percent were attributed to both.

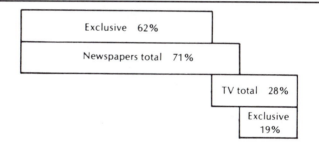

Newspapers and radio accounted for 77 percent of all advertising influence. 68 percent of these influences were attributed to newspapers exclusive of radio. 6 percent were attributed to radio exclusive of newspapers, and 3 percent were attributed to both.

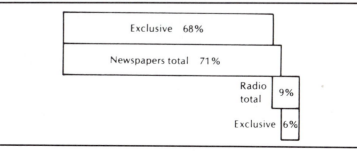

EXHIBIT A-9 Advertising influence—by shopper demographics (among the 55 percent of all shoppers who were influenced by advertising)

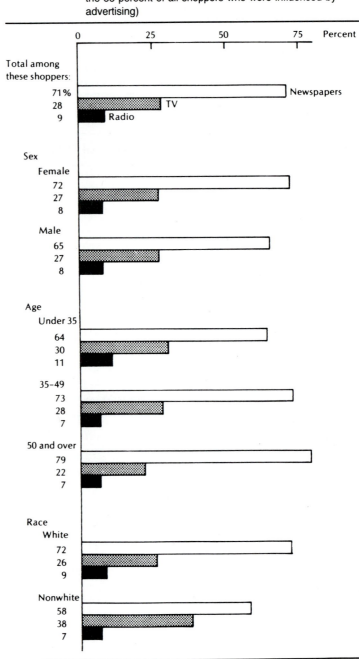

EXHIBIT A-10 Advertising influence—by shopping patterns (among the 55 percent of all shoppers who were influenced by advertising)

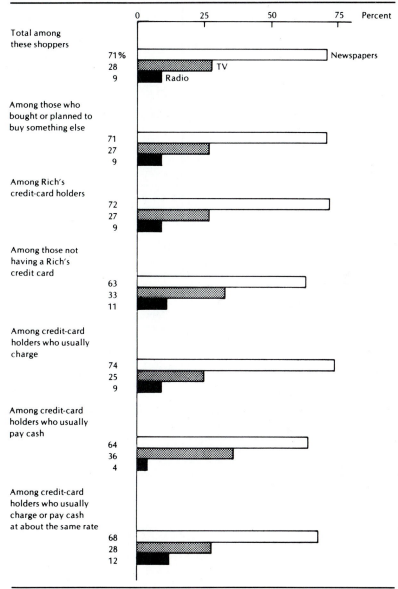

EXHIBIT A-11 Share of budget versus share of influence

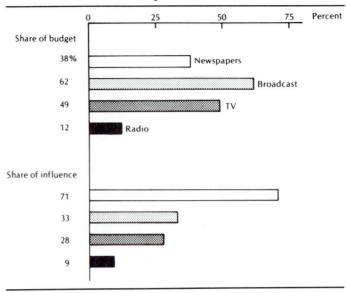

EXHIBIT A-12 Newspapers/broadcast—share of influence
versus share of budget by departments

	Newspapers		Broadcast	
	Share of influence	Share of budget	Share of influence	Share of budget
Total	71%	38%	33%	62%
Hard goods	77	45	30	55
Mattress	43	11	69	89
Carpeting	83	39	23	61
Draperies	83	56	22	44
Vacuum sweeper	70	25	45	75
Color TV	99	100	1	—
Soft goods	68	34	34	66
Handbags	68	41	27	59
Girdles	28	—	74	100
Shoes	87	54	25	46
Shirts	63	12	36	88
Pant suits	82	53	16	47

EXHIBIT A-13 Comparison of advertising schedule/budget/
shopper influence*

| | Total 10 departments | | | | |
| | Broadcast spots | | Newspaper space | | |
	TV	Radio	Journal—Constitution	Constitution	Journal
Schedule					
Sunday	42	53	1,064		
Monday	86	121		172	248
Tuesday	49	87		0	505
	177	261	1,064	172	753

* 438 broadcast spots versus 1,989 inches; budget—$27,158 for broadcast spots versus $16,910 for newspaper space; and shopper influence—33 percent for broadcast spots versus 71 percent for newspaper space.

EXHIBIT A-14 Advertising exposure

74 percent of all shoppers recalled being exposed to specific advertising messages within the past day or two. Of these, 79 percent recalled newspapers, 53 percent recalled broadcasts (46 percent television, 18 percent radio), and 24 percent recalled mail circulars.

Newspapers and broadcast accounted for 96 percent of all advertising messages. 43 percent recalled newspapers exclusive of broadcast. 17 percent recalled broadcast exclusive of newspapers, and 36 percent recalled both.

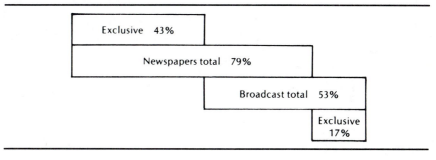

EXHIBIT A-15   Advertising exposure

Newspapers and television accounted for 93 percent of all advertising messages. 47 percent recalled newspapers exclusive of television. 14 percent recalled television exclusive of newspapers, and 32 percent recalled both.

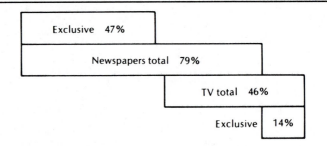

Newspapers and radio accounted for 85 percent of all advertising messages. 67 percent recalled newspapers exclusive of radio. 6 percent recalled radio exclusive of newspapers, and 12 percent recalled both.

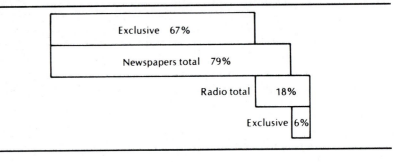

Questionnaire   HARVEST SALE IN-STORE CUSTOMER SURVEY

Interviewer Name: _____ (1-2)   STORE: ...... Downtown ..... Lenox .... Greenbriar   (3)
                                                      1   2   3

DATE: M   T   W   TIME OF INTERVIEW: _____   DEPARTMENT: _____   (6)
       1   2   3   (4)   (5)

Hello. We're conducting a short survey among RICH'S customers:

1.   What did you happen to buy in this department today? _____
                                          (PROBE, BRAND, STYLE)
                                                                 (7-8)

2.   Before coming to RICH'S today, did you have in mind buying this specific brand/item, or did you decide after you came into the store?

       HAD IN MIND.... (☐) 1   DECIDED IN STORE..... (☐) 2   SKIP TO Q. #3   (9)

       What was it that gave you the
       idea to buy this brand/item? _____

       (IF APPROPRIATE, ASK: Where did you learn about that?) _____

                                                                       (10-11)

3.   Was the store having a special on this specific brand/item today, or were they selling at the regular price?

       SPECIAL....... (☐) 1   REGULAR PRICE....... (☐) 2   SKIP TO Q. #4   (12)

       Where did you learn about that? _____

                                                                       (13-14)

4.   Do you recall seeing or hearing any advertising within the past day or two on radio or television or in the newspapers or in a mail circular that may have reminded you or helped you decide to buy this _____ today?

       YES......... (☐) 1   NO............... (☐) 2   SKIP TO Q. #5   (15)

       a. Where did you see or hear it? _____   (16)

	4a. UNAIDED RECALL	5. AIDED RECALL		
		YES	NO, DK	
RADIO...............	1	1	2	(17)
NEWSPAPERS..........	2	1	2	(18)
TELEVISION..........	3	1·	2	(19)
MAIL CIRCULAR........	4	1	2	(20)
OTHER, DON'T KNOW....	5			

ASK FOR EACH MEDIUM NOT CHECKED IN Q. #4a.

5.   Did you happen to see or hear any of the following within the past day or two:
A radio commercial for this specific _____? A newspaper ad for this specific _____? A television commercial for this specific _____? A mail circular for this specific _____?

6.   Have you bought anything else at RICH'S today, or do you plan to buy anything else at RICH'S today?

       YES....... (☐) 1   NO............... (☐) 2

7.   Do you (or your wife/husband) have a RICH'S credit card?   (21)

       YES....... (☐) 1   NO............... (☐) 2   (22)

       a. Do you usually charge or pay cash for most of your purchases at RICH'S?

       CHARGE .... (☐) 1   CASH............... (☐) 2   SAME..... (☐) 3   (23)

8.   What is the name of the county where you live? _____ OUT-OF-STATE .. (☐)   (24-25-26)

ESTIMATE AGE: UNDER 35 YEARS.. (☐) 1   SEX: FEMALE... (☐) 1   RACE: WHITE..... (☐) 1   (27)
                   35 - 49......... (☐) 2   MALE..... (☐) 2   NON WHITE. (☐) 2   (28)
                   50+.......... (☐) 3   (29)

Appendix B **Analysis of Rich's In-Store Survey***

Introduction

First, we would like to state that WSB television and radio were pleased to have the opportunity to participate in this research effort with Rich's. We have one basic characteristic in common with Rich's—both WSB-TV and WSB Radio, like Rich's, are dominant in the Atlanta market. Like Rich's, we are an Atlanta institution and have enjoyed dominance since our origination.

In this presentation, we will not attempt to interpret the results of your research from a marketing standpoint. You have your own market research department, and we are sure that they have done a capable job of analyzing and interpreting the results of the study from that aspect. Instead, we will concentrate on interpreting the results from a media standpoint, which is our particular area of experience.

The following pages contain our detailed analysis of this research for Rich's management.

Pre-Harvest Sale Advertising Weight

Rich's Pre-Harvest Sale was heavily promoted with a ''mix'' of three media: radio, TV, and newspaper.

On the broadcast side, Rich's ran 261 radio spots on five stations and 177 TV spots on five stations promoting 10 different items during a three-day period. It can be estimated that the total radio campaign reached about 90 percent of the Atlanta adult metro population, with the average listener exposed to seven commercial announcements (all products combined). The total television campaign also reached an estimated 90 percent of the Atlanta adult population, with the average viewer exposed to 10 commercial announcements.

The newspaper campaign consisted of 13 ads for the specific items and 11 ads for related[1] items, or a total of 24 ads representing 1,987 inches of space in the *Journal* and *Constitution*. Rich's also ran 6,140 inches of other newspaper advertising during the three-day period. We have no way of estimating the reach and frequency of the newspaper ads.

Pre-Harvest Sale a Success

Rich's total advertising effort helped make the store's pre-Harvest Sale a tremendous success.

Monday, September 21, and Tuesday, September 22, were two of Rich's biggest days of the year according to traffic and sales volume. As far as we

---

* Presented by WSB-TV, WSB Radio, and Cox Broadcasting Research.
[1] Same item but different price than in the radio and TV commercial.

know, the departments participating in the test were all up considerably in sales volume compared to a year ago.

Unfortunately, sales results for the *specific items* tested were not available. However, it is our understanding that the departmentwide sales results reflected the success of the individual items in those departments that were tested.

The advertising effort for the pre-Harvest Sale represented one of the few times that Rich's has used a media-mix for *item selling*. Radio and TV have been used extensively by Rich's for institutional advertising and to announce sale events, but item selling has been limited in the past primarily to newspaper and direct mail. *The media-mix for item selling worked from a sales results standpoint.*

Summary of Media Recall Findings

After analyzing the results of the survey, we found the following to be the most significant findings:

1. Because of the confusion and particularly the conditioning factor regarding newspaper, the three media cannot be completely compared in recall.
2. Recall for both radio and TV was significantly higher on Tuesday versus Monday, indicating that the broadcast media were building in impact on customers. Sales results were also generally better on Tuesday versus Monday.
3. Both radio and TV did *best* in recall (compared to newspaper) for items having the *least* amount of newspaper advertising. Radio and TV did *poorest* for items having the *greatest* amount of newspaper advertising.
4. In general, items where radio and TV did *best* in recall (compared to newspaper) had better sales results than items where radio and TV did poorest.
5. All three media performed better among high-priced items and for items where customers decided to buy before coming into the store.
6. Radio and TV balanced newspaper quite well by reaching younger adults than the print medium.

See Exhibits B–1 through B–3.

EXHIBIT B–1   Summary of newspaper recall

Item	Budget	Day/ads	Got idea	Learned of special	Direct recall
Draperies	$4,412	Sun.–2, Tues.–2	48%	68%	81%
Pant suits	3,359	Sun.–2, Mon.–1, Tues.–3	50	56	63
Shoes	2,834	Sun.–1, Mon.–2, Tues.–1	48	55	72
Handbags	1,670	Sun.–1, Tues.–1	30	30	60
Carpeting	1,503	Sun.–1	61	63	80
Color TV	1,503	Sun.–1	62	68	66

EXHIBIT B-1 *(concluded)*

Item	Budget	Day/ads	Got idea	Learned of special	Direct recall
Dress shirts	859	Sun.–1	40%	40%	54%
Vacuum cleaner	780	Mon.–4	36	62	64
Mattresses	260	Tues.–1	30	37	54
Career shirts	—	—	19	27	45
Girdles	—	—	12	15	16
Averages, all items*			42	51	64

* Excludes girdles (no ads), but includes career shirts because of ads for dress shirts, a related item.

EXHIBIT B-2 Summary of television recall

Item	Budget	Adult audience (000)	Got idea	Learned of special	Direct recall
Career shirts	$2,998	1,373.4	15%	16%	27%
Draperies	2,714	776.5	11	15	37
Pant suits	2,494	885.4	8	9	39
Playtex girdles	2,364	752.1	25	34	32
Dress shirts	2,028	824.8	16	16	29
Handbags	1,922	649.2	10	10	34
Shoes	1,909	724.7	11	14	41
Vacuum cleaner	1,867	627.4	19	36	42
Carpeting	1,790	624.5	8	12	29
Mattresses	1,627	691.9	40	48	49
Color TV	—	—	0	0	5
Averages, all items*			16	21	36

* Excludes color TV (no commercials).

EXHIBIT B-3 Summary of radio recall

Item	Budget	Adult audience (000)	Got idea	Learned of special	Direct recall
Career shirts	$903	489.1	2%	6%	17%
Draperies	560	654.3	1	2	8
Shoes	544	566.8	5	6	14
Pant suits	539	633.9	1	2	12
Carpeting	513	590.9	8	7	24
Dress shirts	498	496.4	4	5	12
Girdles	482	553.0	6	9	11
Mattresses	477	527.6	11	23	29
Handbags	476	475.1	2	3	20
Vacuum cleaner	453	482.1	7	8	10
Color TV	—	374.2	—	1	2
Averages, all items*			5	7	16

* Excludes color TV (no commercials).

Three Types of Media Recall in the Study

The questionnaire used in Rich's in-store survey obtained information about customers' recall of advertising media in three areas:

1. Idea to Buy

For customers purchasing the item being tested, those that indicated having in mind buying that specific merchandise before coming to the store were asked *what gave them the idea to buy the item.* In this question, answers involving media came from top-of-mind recall (not aided). Nonmedia answers to this question, such as "needed" item, "wanted" item, or "had past experience" with item were accepted.

2. Learned of Special

Those customers who were aware of the store having a special on the specific item purchased were asked *where they learned about it.* In this question, answers involving media also came from top-of-mind recall and nonmedia responses such as "saw on display" or "friend told me" were accepted.

3. Direct Recall

Customers were also asked if they recalled seeing or hearing any advertising that may have reminded them or helped them decide to buy the specific item. If they answered in the affirmative, they were then asked *where they saw or heard it.* If radio, newspaper, TV, or mail circular were not mentioned by the respondent, they were also asked if they happened to hear a radio commercial, see a newspaper ad, and so on (aided recall). For purposes of analyzing the results, the unaided and aided answers to direct recall have been combined in this question.

Effect of Confusion and "Conditioning"

First, we would like to emphasize three points that should be taken into consideration when evaluating each advertising medium's performance based on the recall results of the study:

1. Because of the heavy amount of Rich's advertising activity in all media during the three-day period of interviewing, there was a certain amount of confusion that occurred among the customer-respondents regarding where they saw or heard advertising. This fact will be documented in the pages to follow.
2. Because Rich's traditionally has done the vast majority of its *item* advertising in newspaper, customers are "conditioned" to this particular medium;

i.e., more inclined to think of Rich's merchandise being advertised in a newspaper.

3. During the three-day period of the study, *other department stores* were also running *newspaper* ads for items similar to Rich's items being tested. Some newspaper ad recall in this study could have been due to confusion with other stores' ads.

These points can all be substantiated by the following results.

Only Slight Confusion for Radio Commercials

There were *no* radio commercials for color TV sets, since the spots were canceled before they were scheduled to run on Tuesday afternoon.

0%	Claimed they got the idea to buy a color TV set from radio commercials.
1%	Thought they learned of color TV sets being on sale from radio commercials.
2%	Said they recalled hearing radio commercials for color TV sets.

Only Slight Confusion for TV Commercials

There were *no* TV commercials for color TV sets, since the spots were canceled before they were scheduled to run on Tuesday afternoon.

0%	Claimed that they got the idea to buy a color TV set from TV commercials.
0%	Thought they learned of color TV sets on sale from TV commercials.
5%	Said they recalled seeing TV commercials for color TV sets.

Some Confusion and "Conditioning" for Mail Circular

In the mail circular that Rich's distributed to its customers the week prior to the survey, there were *no* ads for any specific items, yet among the total sample of customer-respondents purchasing any of the 11 items tested:

3%	Claimed they got the idea to buy the specific item from a mail circular.
5%	Thought they learned of the specific item being on sale from a mail circular.
18%	Said they recalled seeing a mail circular for the specific item.

Greater Confusion and "Conditioning" for Newspaper Ads

There were *no* Rich's newspaper ads for Playtex girdles, yet:

12%	Claimed they got the idea to buy girdles from newspaper ads.
15%	Thought they learned of girdles being on sale from newspaper ads.
16%	Said they recalled seeing newspaper ads for girdles.

There were *no* Rich's newspaper ads for mattresses on either Sunday or Monday of the survey, yet among customers interviewed on Monday:

27%	Claimed they got the idea to buy a mattress from newspaper ads.
30%	Thought they learned of the mattress being on sale from newspaper ads.
49%	Said they recalled seeing newspaper ads for mattresses.

Caution in Comparing Media by Recall!

As you can see, the extent of erroneous recall of newspaper advertising ranged from a low of 12 percent to a high of 49 percent. For this important reason, it is impossible to derive any accurate yardstick for measuring the separate value of each medium, dollar for dollar. In addition, these results cannot be converted to any type of advertising-to-sales ratio.

Radio May Have Been Higher with More WSB Spots

Due to the problem created by trying to find enough availabilities on WSB only in morning and evening drive time (because of the agency's buying criteria) to handle commercials for 11 different items in three days, Atlanta's dominant radio station was not able to contribute as much weight as it should have to most of the media schedules. As a result, a higher proportion of spots ran on WQXI (primarily teens), WAOK (primarily ethnic), WRNG (primarily 50 + listeners), and WPLO (lower socioeconomic level). A brief analysis of the number of radio commercials that ran for each item, showing the light proportion of WSB spots, is shown in the accompanying table.

	Total spots	WSB spots	WSB morning drive spots*
Career shirts	48	10	0
Carpeting	23	6	3
Color TV	—	—	—
Draperies	26	7	2
Dress shirts	15	6	2
Girdles	27	5	1
Handbags	27	5	1
Mattresses	19	6	2
Pant suits	26	8	2
Shoes	27	6	2
Vacuum cleaner	22	5	2
Total	260	64	17

* Monday or Tuesday.

Television versus Newspaper

While TV budgets were fairly even, newspaper budgets ranged from $260 for mattresses up to $4,412 for draperies. TV versus newspaper performance in all types of recall showed a good relationship to the amount of money spent in newspaper. The smaller the newspaper budget versus TV, the better TV performed versus newspaper in recall, and vice versa:

1. TV did *best* in all types of recall *compared to newspaper* for mattresses, career shirts, and vacuum cleaners. These items had the *smallest amount* of advertising space in the newspaper compared to the others.
2. TV did *poorest* in all types of recall *compared to newspaper* for draperies, pant suits, shoes, and carpeting. These items had the *greater amount* of advertising space in the newspaper.

Radio versus Newspaper

Again, radio budgets were fairly even compared to the wide range in newspaper budgets. Radio versus newspaper performance in all types of recall also showed a fairly strong relationship to the amount of money spent in newspaper. The smaller the newspaper budget versus radio, the better radio performed versus newspaper in recall, and vice versa:

1. Radio did *best* in all types of recall *compared to newspaper* for mattresses, vacuum cleaners, and career shirts. These items generally had the least newspaper space.
2. Radio did *poorest* in all types of recall *compared to newspaper* for draperies, pant suits, and handbags. These items generally had the greatest newspaper space.

Less Newspaper Space—No Harm to Sales Volume

We have just indicated that, as newspaper space was reduced, both radio and TV did better in recall.

How about Rich's Sales Volume?

There appeared to be little, if any, correlation between the amount of newspaper space and sales volume as measured by department sales increases. If anything, the reverse occurred:

	Monday	Tuesday
TV and radio did best (least newspaper space):		
Girdles	+7%	+92%
Career shirts	+151	+349
Mattresses	+43	+76
Vacuum cleaners	+98	+222
TV and radio did poorest (most newspaper space):		
Draperies	−0	+9
Pant suits	+17	+46
Shoes	−19	+14
Carpeting	−9	+526

Idea to Buy versus Direct Recall

One probable indication of the "conditioning" of Rich's customers to newspaper advertising comes from comparing initial "idea to buy" recall, where media responses came purely from top of mind, to the direct recall that came later in the interview, concentrating on each medium. All three media gained in regard to the proportion of customers recalling (from idea to buy to direct recall), but newspaper, having been recalled more from top of mind, gained the least, while TV and especially radio, in the background during top of mind "idea to buy," came to the surface more in the direct recall.

	Average recall, all items*		
	Idea to buy	Direct recall	Percent increase
Newspaper	42%	64%	+52%
TV	16	36	+125
Radio	5	16	+220

* Girdles were eliminated for newspaper and color TV sets were eliminated for radio and TV because of no advertising.

First Day versus Second Day Recall

Analysis of the direct recall results by day of interview produced an interesting fact. The impact of newspaper was initial, while both radio and TV performed significantly better on the second day. This is probably due to the nature of the broadcast media, which gain impact and effectiveness with *increased frequency* (as listeners and viewers are exposed to more commercials). In addition, sales results for all items were generally better on Tuesday than on Monday, compared to a year ago. This also indicates that, if spots had been spread more evenly over Sunday, Monday, and Tuesday (rather than concentrated on Sunday and Monday in most cases), and if interviewing had been extended through Wednesday, both radio and TV would have performed better in recall, at no increase in budget for either medium.

	*Average recall, all items**		
	Monday	*Tuesday*	*Tuesday percent difference*
Newspaper	66%	62%	−6%
TV	33	38	+15
Radio	13	18	+38

* Mattresses were eliminated for newspaper as an invalid comparison, since there were no ads on Sunday or Monday. However, even though there were no radio or TV commercials for career shirts on Sunday or Monday, and no newspaper ads at all, this item was included in this comparison because there was advertising for dress shirts, a related item. Also girdles were eliminated for newspaper and color TV for radio and TV because of no advertising.

High-Priced versus Low-Priced Items

In order to analyze media performance by item *price range,* the items were divided into either a high-price (carpeting, color TV, draperies, mattresses, and vacuum cleaners) or a low-price (career shirts, dress shirts, girdles, handbags, pant suits, and shoes) group. All three media performed better among high-priced items compared to low-priced merchandise, especially radio and TV. However, the differences were greater regarding "idea to buy" recall and "learned of special" recall than with the direct recall. Customers who had made up their minds to buy a large ticket item were apparently more persuaded by advertising than those coming to Rich's for lower priced merchandise. However, whether in the market for high- or low-priced items, both type customers were exposed to advertising, as indicated in the direct recall.

	High-priced items	Low-priced items	High-priced percent difference
Idea to buy:			
Newspaper	47%	37%	+27%
TV	20	14	+43
Radio	7	3	+133
Learned of special:			
Newspaper	60	42	+43
TV	28	16	+75
Radio	10	5	+100
Direct recall:			
Newspaper	69	59	+17
TV	39	34	+15
Radio	18	14	+29

"Had in Mind" versus "Decided in Store"

In order to analyze media performance by the extent to which customers had in mind to buy the item before coming to the store, the items were divided into two groups: "had in mind" and "decided in store," based on results to the question covering this aspect of purchasing. The four items where roughly half of the customers indicated deciding in the store (pant suits, dress shirts, career shirts, and handbags) were placed in the "decided in store" group. The other seven items, where significantly less customers indicated deciding in store, were placed in the "had in mind" group. All three media performed significantly better among items in the "had in mind" group, that is, for items where a greater proportion of customers made their decision in advance. The differences were greater regarding "idea to buy" and "learned of special" recall than with the direct recall.

	"Had in mind" items	"Decided in store" items	"Had in mind" percent difference
Idea to buy:			
Newspaper	48%	35%	+37%
TV	19	12	+58
Radio	6	2	+200
Learned of special:			
Newspaper	59	38	+55
TV	26	13	+100
Radio	9	4	+125
Direct recall:			
Newspaper	70	56	+25
TV	38	32	+19
Radio	16	15	+7

Broadcast Media Recall Reflected Younger Adults

By analyzing media recall by age of customer, it was determined that radio and TV balanced newspaper quite well by reaching younger adults. In all three types of recall, the under-35 age group was proportionately higher for broadcast, especially radio, than for newspaper. These figures are based on all items combined.

Age	Radio	TV	Newspaper
Got idea:			
Under 35	56%	44%	36%
35–49	31	38	44
50 and over	13	18	20
Learned of special:			
Under 35	50	43	36
35–49	34	41	41
50 and over	16	16	23
Direct recall:			
Under 35	49	44	41
35–49	33	38	41
50 and over	18	18	18

Note: Read table. Of those customers indicating that they "got the idea" to buy an item from radio commercials, 56 percent were in the under 35 age group.

Rich's Dominant Position in Atlanta

In concluding this presentation, we would like to announce the results of separate research that we have just completed that indicates the extent to which Rich's dominates the department store market in Atlanta, a domination that we feel is due to:

Outstanding management.

Quality of merchandise.

Attention to customer service and satisfaction.

Efficient use of advertising and promotion, *especially the use of a media-mix.*

Presentation Summary

1. With use of media-mix for item selling, the pre-Harvest Sale was a success. All departments participating in the test were up in sales volume.
2. Because of confusion and conditioning factors, recall results are not completely comparable between media.
3. In general, as the amount of newspaper space was reduced, the proportion of recall for both TV and radio was increased, and sales results were generally more favorable.

4. Sales volume was up significantly on Tuesday versus Monday in all departments, indicating a relationship with broadcast media recall, also up significantly on Tuesday as frequency increased.
5. All media had higher recall for higher-priced items and items where customers generally decided in advance.
6. Separate research confirms Rich's dominance of the Atlanta market, especially versus Davison's. Rich's uses radio and TV effectively, Davison's uses very little broadcast media.

Case 24

Exercise in Print Advertising Assessment*

One of the most important and most difficult marketing decisions is the choice of creative executions in advertising. The purpose of this exercise is to help you develop skills in determining what is a good and a bad creative execution.

In preparation for your class session using this exercise, we would like you to spend time looking at *print* advertising (newspaper and magazine advertising). We would like you to select what you think is the "best ad" you have seen and the "worst ad" you have seen. To aid you in this task you might ask yourself the following questions:

1. What is the sponsor's apparent target segment(s)?
2. What are the objectives of the ad?
3. Are the basic appeal, theme, and copy approach appropriate for these purposes?

To the bottom of each ad you selected attach a small piece of paper containing the following information:

1. Sponsor of the ad.
2. Publication in which the ad appeared.
3. Publication date.
4. Your reason(s) for selecting that ad as the best or worst.
5. Your name.

Staple or tape this information to the bottom of the ad but don't obscure any of the ad. Turn in your ads to your professor as required. In the class session you will get a chance to compare your choice of ads with those of your classmates.

Case 25

Allied Food Distributors*

In April 1990, Ms. Elizabeth Ramsey, the district sales manager for the upper Midwest district of Allied Food Distributors, was preparing to hire a new salesperson for the southwest Indiana sales territory. The current salesperson in this territory was leaving the company at the end of June. Ms. Ramsey had narrowed the list of potential candidates to three. She wondered which of these applicants she should select.

Company Background

Allied Food Distributors was one of the largest food wholesalers in the United States. The company carried hundreds of different packaged food items (fruits, vegetables, cake mixes, cookies, powdered soft drinks, and so on) for sales to supermarkets and grocery stores. Allied carried items in two different circumstances. First, some small food companies had Allied carry their entire line in all areas of the United States. Allied was in essence their sales force. Second, some large food companies had Allied carry their lines in less populated parts of the country. These areas were not large enough to sustain a salesperson for each food company.

Allied operated in all 50 states. The country was divided into 20 sales districts. Ms. Ramsey's sales district included Michigan, Indiana, and Illinois. Each district was divided into a number of sales territories. A salesperson was assigned to each territory.

The Southwest Indiana Territory

The sales territory for which Ms. Ramsey was seeking a salesperson was located in the southwest corner of Indiana. Exhibit 1 presents a map of the territory. It was bordered on the south by the Ohio River and the state of Kentucky, on the west by the Wabash River and the state of Illinois, and on the

---

* This case was written by Thomas C. Kinnear. Copyright © 1990 Thomas C. Kinnear.

EXHIBIT 1 A map of the southwest Indiana territory

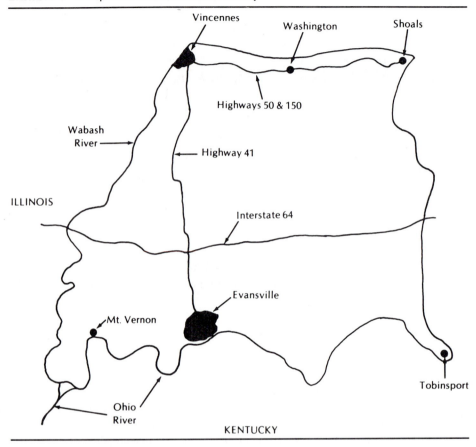

east by the Hoosier National Forest. The northern boundary ran a few miles north of Highways 50 and 150 that ran from Vincennes in the west through Washington to Shoals in the east. Evansville was the largest city in the area with a population of about 140,000. The salesperson for the territory was expected to live in Evansville, but would spend about three nights a week on the road. The only other reasonably large population concentration was in Vincennes with a population of about 20,000. Vincennes was located about 55 miles straight north of Evansville on Highway 41. Interstate Highway 64 ran the 80 miles east-west through the territory about 15 miles north of Evansville. Evansville was 165 miles southwest of Indianapolis, 170 miles east of St. Louis, Missouri, and 115 miles southwest of Louisville, Kentucky. The territory was very rural in character with agriculture being the dominant industry. The terrain was quite hilly, with poor soil. As a result, the farms in the area tended to be economically weak. There were many small towns and villages located throughout this basically rural environment.

The Selling Task

Allied maintained 75 active retail accounts in the southwest Indiana territory. About 10 of these accounts were medium- to large-sized independent supermarkets located in Evansville and Vincennes. The rest of the accounts were small, independent general food stores located throughout the territory.

The salesperson was expected to call on these accounts about every three weeks. The salesperson's duties included: checking displays and inventory levels for items already carried, obtaining orders on these items, informing retailers about new items, attempting to gain sales orders on these items, setting up special displays, and generally servicing the retailers' needs. Often, the salesperson would check the level of inventory on an item, make out an order, and present it to the retailer to be signed. The salesperson generally knew the store owner on a first name basis. The ordered goods were sent directly to the retailer from a warehouse located in Indianapolis.

The Selection Process

The responsibility for recruiting salespersons for the territories within a district was given to the district sales manager. The process consisted of the following steps:

1. An advertisement for the job was placed in newspapers in the state in question.
2. Those responding to the ad were sent job application forms.
3. The returned application forms were examined and certain applicants were asked to come to the district sales office for a full day of interviews.
4. The selection was then made by the district sales manager, or all applicants were rejected and the process started again.

Training

Allied did all its salesperson training on the job. The salesperson on the territory to which a new person would be assigned was given the task of training. Basically, this involved having the new person travel the territory to meet the retailers and to be shown how to obtain and send in orders. The district sales manager usually assisted in this process by traveling with the new salesperson for a few days.

Compensation

The current salesperson on the southwest Indiana sales territory was earning a straight salary of about $43,000 per year plus fringe benefits. Ms. Ramsey indicated that she was willing to pay between $25,000 and $50,000 for a new person depending on the qualifications presented.

The Choices

On the basis of application forms and personal interviews, Ms. Ramsey had narrowed the field of applicants down to three. A summary of the information on their application forms along with the comments she had written to herself are contained in Exhibits 2, 3, and 4. She wondered which person she should select for the position.

EXHIBIT 2   Information on Mr. Michael Gehringer

Personal information

Born July 15, 1948; married; three children ages 14, 16, and 19; height 5 feet, 10 inches; weight 205; excellent health; born and raised in Indianapolis.

Education

High school graduate; played football; no extracurricular activities of note.

Employment record

1. Currently employed by Allied Food Distributors in the warehouse in Indianapolis; two years with Allied; job responsibilities include processing orders from the field and expediting rush orders; current salary $2,600 per month.
2. In 1987–88 employed by Hoosier Van Lines in Indianapolis as a sales agent; terminating salary was $550 per month; left due to limits placed on salary and lack of challenge in the job.
3. In 1985–87 employed by Main Street Clothiers of Indianapolis as a retail salesperson in the men's department; terminating salary $1,500 per month; left due to boring nature of this type of selling.
4. Between 1968 and 1985 held six other clerical and sales type jobs, all in Indianapolis.

Applicant's statement

I feel that my true employment interest lies in selling in a situation where I can be my own boss. This job seems just right.

Ms. Ramsey's comments

Seems very interested in job as a career.

Well recommended by his current boss.

Reasonably intelligent.

Good appearance.

Moderately aggressive.

EXHIBIT 3 Information on Mr. Carley Tobias

Personal information

Born February 12, 1961; married; two children ages 1 and 4; height 6 feet, 2 inches; weight 170; excellent health; born in San Francisco; raised in Cleveland, Ohio.

Education

High school and Community College graduate in business administration; student council president at Community College; plus belonged to a number of other clubs.

Employment record

1. Currently employed by The Drug Trading Company in Cincinnati as a salesperson; job responsibility involves selling to retail drugstores; seven years with Drug Trading; current salary $3,300 per month.
2. In 1981–84 U.S. Army private; did one tour of duty in Germany.

Applicant's statement

I am seeking a new position because of the limited earning potential at Drug Trading, plus my family's desire to live in a less populated city.

Other information

He is very active in civic and church organizations in Cincinnati; he is currently president of the Sales and Marketing Executives of Cincinnati.

Ms. Ramsey's comments

Very personable.

Reasonably intelligent.

Good appearance.

He seems to like Cincinnati a lot.

Good experience.

EXHIBIT 4   Information on Mr. Arthur Woodhead

Personal information

Born May 26, 1968; single; height 6 feet; weight 180; excellent health; born and raised in Chicago.

Education

Will graduate in May 1990 from the University of Illinois, Chicago, with a B.B.A. Active in intramural athletics and student government.

Employment record

Summer jobs only; did house painting and gardening work for his own company. Earned $1,600 per month in summer of 1989.

Applicant's statement

I really like to run my own affairs, and selling seems like a good position to reach this objective.

Ms. Ramsey's comments

Well dressed and groomed.

Very intelligent.

Management potential, not career salesperson.

Not very aggressive.

Case 26

Outdoor Sporting Products, Inc.*

The annual sales volume of Outdoor Sporting Products, Inc., for the past six years had ranged between $6.2 million and $6.8 million. Although profits continued to be satisfactory, Mr. Hudson McDonald, president and chief operating officer, was concerned because sales had not increased appreciably from year to year. Consequently, he asked a consultant in New York City and the officers of the company to submit proposals for improving the salespeople's compensation plan, which he believed was the basic weakness in the firm's marketing operations.

Outdoor's factory and warehouse were located in Albany, New York, where the company manufactured and distributed sporting equipment, clothing, and accessories. Mr. Hudson McDonald, who managed the company, organized it in 1956 when he envisioned a growing market for sporting goods resulting from the predicted increase in leisure time and the rising levels of income in the United States.

Products of the company, numbering approximately 700 items, were grouped into three lines: (1) fishing supplies, (2) hunting supplies, and (3) accessories. The fishing supplies line, which accounted for approximately 40 percent of the company's annual sales, included nearly every item a fisherman would need such as fishing jackets, vests, caps, rods and reels of all types, lines, flies, lures, landing nets, and creels. Thirty percent of annual sales were in the hunting supplies line, which consisted of hunting clothing of all types including insulated and thermal underwear, safety garments, shell holders, whistles, calls, and gun cases. The accessories line, which made up the balance of the company's annual sales volume, included items such as compasses, cooking kits, lanterns, hunting and fishing knives, hand warmers, and novelty gifts.

While the sales of the hunting and fishing lines were very seasonal, they tended to complement one another. The January–April period accounted for the bulk of the company's annual volume in fishing items, and most sales of hunt-

---

* Adapted from a case written by Zarrel V. Lambert, Auburn University, and Fred W. Kniffin, University of Connecticut, Stamford. Used with permission.

ing supplies were made during the months of May through August. Typically, the company's sales of all products reached their lows for the year during the month of December.

Outdoor's sales volume was $6.57 million in the current year with self-manufactured products accounting for 35 percent of this total. Fifty percent of the company's volume consisted of imported products, which came principally from Japan. Items manufactured by other domestic producers and distributed by Outdoor accounted for the remaining 15 percent of total sales.

Mr. McDonald reported that wholesale prices to retailers were established by adding a markup of 50 to 100 percent to Outdoor's cost for the item. This rule was followed on self-manufactured products as well as for items purchased from other manufacturers. The resulting average markup across all products was 70 percent on cost.

Outdoor's market area consisted of the New England states, New York, Pennsylvania, Ohio, Michigan, Wisconsin, Indiana, Illinois, Kentucky, Tennessee, West Virginia, Virginia, Maryland, Delaware, and New Jersey. The area over which Outdoor could effectively compete was limited to some extent by shipping costs, since all orders were shipped from the factory and warehouse in Albany.

Outdoor's salespeople sold to approximately 6,000 retail stores in small- and medium-sized cities in its market area. Analysis of sales records showed that the firm's customer coverage was very poor in the large metropolitan areas. Typically, each account was a one- or two-store operation. Mr. McDonald stated that he knew for a fact that Outdoor's share of the market was very low, perhaps 2 to 3 percent; and for all practical purposes, he felt the company's sales potential was unlimited.

Mr. McDonald believed that with few exceptions, Outdoor's customers had little or no brand preference and in the vast majority of cases they bought hunting and fishing supplies from several suppliers.

It was McDonald's opinion that the pattern of retail distribution for hunting and fishing products had been changing during the past 10 years as a result of the growth of discount stores. He thought that the proportion of retail sales for hunting and fishing supplies made by small- and medium-sized sporting goods outlets had been declining compared to the percent sold by discounters and chain stores. An analysis of company records revealed Outdoor had not developed business among the discounters with the exception of a few small discount stores. Some of Outdoor's executives felt that the lack of business with discounters might have been due in part to the company's pricing policy and in part to the pressures which current customers had exerted on company salespeople to keep them from calling on the discounters.

Outdoor's Sales Force

The company's sales force played the major role in its marketing efforts since Outdoor did not use magazine, newspaper, or radio advertising to reach either the retail trade or consumers. One advertising piece that supplemented the work of the salespeople was Outdoor's merchandise catalog. It contained a complete listing of all the company's products and was mailed to all retailers who were either current accounts or prospective accounts. Typically, store buyers used the catalog for purposes of reordering.

Most accounts were contacted by a salesperson two or three times a year. The salespeople planned their activities so that each store would be called upon at the beginning of the fishing season and again prior to the hunting season. Certain key accounts of some salespeople were contacted more often than two or three times a year.

Management believed that product knowledge was the major ingredient of a successful sales call. Consequently, Mr. McDonald had developed a "selling formula," which each salesperson was required to learn before taking over a territory. The "formula" contained five parts: (1) the name and catalog number of each item sold by the company; (2) the sizes and colors in which each item was available; (3) the wholesale price of each item; (4) the suggested retail price of each item; and (5) the primary selling features of each item. After a new salesperson had mastered the product knowledge specified by this "formula" he or she began working in the assigned territory and was usually accompanied by Mr. McDonald for several weeks.

Managing the sales force consumed approximately one third of Mr. McDonald's efforts. The remaining two thirds of his time was spent purchasing products for resale and in general administrative duties as the company's chief operating officer.

Mr. McDonald held semiannual sales meetings, had weekly telephone conversations with each salesperson, and had mimeographed bulletins containing information on products, prices, and special promotional deals mailed to all salespeople each week. Daily call reports and attendance at the semiannual sales meetings were required of all salespeople. One meeting was held the first week in January to introduce the spring line of fishing supplies. The hunting line was presented at the second meeting, which was scheduled in May. Each of these sales meetings spanned four to five days so the salespeople were able to study the new products being introduced and any changes in sales and company policies. The production manager and comptroller attended these sales meetings to answer questions and to discuss problems which the salespeople might have concerning deliveries and credit.

On a predetermined schedule each salesperson telephoned Mr. McDonald every Monday morning to learn of changes in prices, special promotional offers, and delivery schedules of unshipped orders. At this time the salesperson's activities for the week were discussed, and sometimes the salesperson was asked by Mr. McDonald to collect past due accounts in the territory. In addition, the salespeople submitted daily call reports, which listed the name of each account contacted and the results of the call. Generally, the salespeople planned their own itineraries in terms of the accounts and prospects that were to be contacted and the amount of time to be spent on each call.

Outdoor's sales force during the current year totaled 11 full-time employees. Their ages ranged from 23 to 67 years, and their tenure with the company

EXHIBIT 1 Salespeople: Age, years of service, territory, and sales

Salespeople	Age	Years of service	Territory	Sales Previous year	Sales Current year
Allen	45	2	Illinois and Indiana	$ 330,264	$ 329,216
Campbell	62	10	Pennsylvania	1,192,192	1,380,240
Duvall	23	1	New England	—	414,656
Edwards	39	1	Michigan	—	419,416
Gatewood	63	5	West Virginia	358,528	358,552
Hammond	54	2	Virginia	414,936	414,728
Logan	37	1	Kentucky and Tennessee	—	447,720
Mason	57	2	Delaware and Maryland	645,032	825,088
O'Bryan	59	4	Ohio	343,928	372,392
Samuels	42	3	New York and New Jersey	737,024	824,472
Wates	67	5	Wisconsin	370,712	342,200
Salespeople terminated in previous year				1,828,816	—
House account				257,384	244,480
Total				$6,478,816	$6,374,816

ranged from 1 to 10 years. Salespeople, territories, and sales volumes for the previous year and the current year are shown in Exhibit 1.

Compensation of Salespeople

The salespeople were paid straight commissions on their dollar sales volume for the calendar year. The commission rate was 5 percent on the first $300,000, 6 percent on the next $200,000 in volume, and 7 percent on all sales over $500,000 for the year. Each week a salesperson could draw all or a portion of his or her accumulated commissions. McDonald encouraged the salespeople to draw commissions as they accumulated since he felt that they were motivated to work harder when they had a very small or zero balance in their commission accounts. These accounts were closed at the end of the year so each salesperson began the new year with nothing in the account.

The salespeople provided their own automobiles and paid their traveling expenses, of which all or a portion were reimbursed by per diem. Under the per diem plan, each salesperson received $70 per day for Monday through Thursday and $42 for Friday, or a total of $322 for the normal workweek. No per diem was paid for Saturday, but a salesperson received an additional $70 if he or she spent Saturday and Sunday nights in the territory.

In addition to the commission and per diem, a salesperson could earn cash awards under two sales incentive plans that were installed two years ago. Under the Annual Sales Increase Awards Plan, a total of $10,400 was paid to the five salespeople having the largest percentage increase in dollar sales volume over the previous year. To be eligible for these awards, a salesperson had to show a sales increase over the previous year. These awards were made at the January sales meeting, and the winners were determined by dividing the dollar amount

EXHIBIT 2   Salespeople's earnings and incentive awards in the current year

Salespeople	Sales		Annual sales increase awards		Weekly sales increase awards (total accrued)	Earnings*
	Previous year	Current year	Increase in sales (percent)	Award		
Allen	$ 330,264	$ 329,216	(0.3%)	—	$1,012	$30,000†
Campbell	1,192,192	1,380,240	15.8	$3,000 (2d)	2,244	88,617
Duvall	—	414,656	—	—	—	30,000†
Edwards	—	419,416	—	—	—	30,000†
Gatewood	358,528	358,552	(0.1)	400 (5th)	1,104	18,513
Hammond	414,936	414,728	—	—	420	30,000†
Logan	—	447,720	—	—	—	30,000†
Mason	645,032	825,088	27.9	4,000 (1st)	3,444	49,756
O'Bryan	343,928	372,392	8.3	1,000 (4th)	1,512	19,344
Samuels	737,024	824,472	11.9	2,000 (3d)	1,300	49,713
Wates	370,712	342,200	(7.7)	—	612	17,532

* Exclusive of incentive awards and per diem.
† Guarantee of $600 per week or $30,000 per year.

of each salesperson's increase by his or her volume for the previous year with the percentage increases ranked in descending order. The salespeople's earnings under this plan for the current year are shown in Exhibit 2.

Under the second incentive plan, each salesperson could win a Weekly Sales Increase Award for each week in which his or her dollar volume in the current year exceeded sales for the corresponding week in the previous year. Beginning with an award of $4 for the first week, the amount of the award increased by $4 for each week in which the salesperson surpassed his or her sales for the comparable week in the previous year. If a salesperson produced higher sales during each of the 50 weeks in the current year, he or she received $4 for the 1st week, $8 for the 2d week, and $200 for the 50th week, or a total of $4,100 for the year. The salesperson had to be employed by the company during the previous year to be eligible for these awards. A check for the total amount of the awards accrued during the year was presented to the salesperson at the sales meeting held in January. Earnings of the salespeople under this plan for the current year are shown in Exhibit 2.

The company frequently used "spiffs" to promote the sales of special items. The salesperson was paid a spiff, which usually was $4, for each order obtained for the designated items in the promotion.

For the past three years in recruiting salespeople, Mr. McDonald had guaranteed the more qualified applicants a weekly income while they learned the business and developed their respective territories. During the current year five salespeople, Allen, Duvall, Edwards, Hammond, and Logan, had a guarantee of $600 a week, which they drew against their commissions. If the year's cumulative commissions for any of these salespeople were less than their cumulative weekly drawing accounts, they received no commissions. The commission and drawing accounts were closed on December 31 so each salesperson began the new year with a zero balance in each account.

The company did not have a stated or written policy specifying the maximum length of time a salesperson could receive a guarantee if commissions continued to be less than his or her draw. Mr. McDonald held the opinion that the five salespeople who currently had guarantees would quit if these guarantees were withdrawn before their commissions reached $30,000 per year.

Mr. McDonald stated that he was convinced the annual earnings of Outdoor's salespeople had fallen behind earnings for comparable selling positions, particularly in the past six years. As a result, he felt that the company's ability to attract and hold high-caliber professional salespeople was being adversely affected. He strongly expressed the opinion that each salesperson should be earning $50,000 annually.

Compensation Plan Proposals

In December of the current year, Mr. McDonald met with his comptroller and production manager, who were the only other executives of the company, and solicited their ideas concerning changes in the company's compensation plan for salespeople.

The comptroller pointed out that the salespeople having guarantees were not producing the sales that had been expected from their territories. He was concerned that the annual commissions earned by four of the five salespeople on guarantees were approximately half or less than their drawing accounts.

Furthermore, according to the comptroller, several of the salespeople who did not have guarantees were producing a relatively low volume of sales year after year. For example, annual sales remained at relatively low levels for Gatewood, O'Bryan, and Wates, who had been working four to five years in their respective territories.

The comptroller proposed that guarantees be reduced to $250 per week plus commissions at the regular rate on all sales. The $250 would not be drawn against commissions as was the case under the existing plan but would be in addition to any commissions earned. In the comptroller's opinion, this plan

EXHIBIT 3   Comparison of earnings in current year under existing guarantee plan with earnings under the comptroller's plan*

Salespeople	Sales	Existing plan			Comptroller's plan		
		Com-missions	Guar-antee	Earnings	Com-missions	Guar-antee	Earnings
Allen	$329,216	$16,753	$30,000	$30,000	$16,753	$12,500	$29,253
Duvall	414,656	21,879	30,000	30,000	21,879	12,500	34,379
Edwards	419,416	22,165	30,000	30,000	22,165	12,500	34,665
Hammond	358,552	18,513	30,000	30,000	18,513	12,500	31,013
Logan	447,720	23,863	30,000	30,000	23,863	12,500	36,363

* Exclusive of incentive awards and per diem.

would motivate the salespeople to increase sales rapidly since their incomes would rise directly with their sales. The comptroller presented Exhibit 3, which showed the incomes of the five salespeople having guarantees in the current year as compared with the incomes they would have received under his plan.

From a sample check of recent shipments, the production manager had concluded that the salespeople tended to overwork accounts located within a 50-mile radius of their homes. Sales coverage was extremely light in a 60- to 100-mile radius of the salespeople's homes with somewhat better coverage beyond 100 miles. He argued that this pattern of sales coverage seemed to result from a desire by the salespeople to spend most evenings during the week at home with their families.

He proposed that the per diem be increased from $70 to $90 per day for Monday through Thursday, $42 for Friday, and $90 for Sunday if the salesperson spent Sunday evening away from home. He reasoned that the per diem of $90 for Sunday would act as a strong incentive for the salespeople to drive to the perimeters of their territories on Sunday evenings rather than use Monday morning for traveling. Further, he believed that the increase in per diem would encourage the salespeople to spend more evenings away from their homes, which would result in a more uniform coverage of the sales territories and an overall increase in sales volume.

The consultant from New York City recommended that the guarantees and per diem be retained on the present basis and proposed that Outdoor adopt what he called a "Ten Percent Self-Improvement Plan." Under the consultant's plan each salesperson would be paid, in addition to the regular commission, a monthly bonus commission of 10 percent on all dollar volume over his or her sales in the comparable month of the previous year. For example, if a salesperson sold $40,000 worth of merchandise in January of the current year and $36,000 in January of the previous year, he or she would receive a $400 bonus check in February. For salespeople on guarantees, bonuses would be in addition to earnings. The consultant reasoned that the bonus commission would motivate the salespeople, both those with and without guarantees, to increase their sales.

He further recommended the discontinuation of the two sales incentive plans currently in effect. He felt the savings from these plans would nearly cover the costs of his proposal.

Following a discussion of these proposals with the management group, Mr. McDonald was undecided on which proposal to adopt, if any. Further, he wondered if any change in the compensation of salespeople would alleviate all of the present problems.

Case 27

Puritan Drug Company*

On May 1, 1984, David Thomas transferred to the Syracuse Division of the Puritan Drug Company as divisional sales manager. Prior to his transfer, Thomas served as assistant to the vice president of sales in the company's New York headquarters location.

At the conclusion of Thomas' first month-end sales meeting held on June 6, 1984, Harvey Brooks, a salesperson in one of the division's rural territories, informed Thomas of his wish to retire, effective the following month. Thomas was surprised by Brooks' announcement because Robert Jackson, the division manager, informed him that Brooks had recently requested and received a deferment of his retirement until he reached his 66th birthday in July 1985. Brooks' sole explanation was that he had "changed his mind."

Brooks' retirement posed a significant territorial reassignment problem for Thomas.

Background of the Syracuse Division

David Thomas became the divisional sales manager at the age of 29. He had joined Puritan Drug as a sales trainee after his graduation from Stanford University in 1978. From 1978 to 1980 he worked as a salesman. In the fall of 1980, the sales manager of the company made Thomas one of his assistants. Thomas assisted the sales manager in arranging special sales promotions of the lines of different manufacturers.

Thomas' predecessor in Syracuse, Harry L. Schultz, had served as divisional sales manager for 15 years before his death in April 1984. "H. L.," as Schultz was called, had also worked as a salesman for the drug wholesale house

* Copyright © 1985 by the President and Fellows of Harvard College

This case was prepared by Rowland T. Moriarty, Jr., as the basis for class discussion rather than to illustrate either effective or ineffective handling of an administrative situation. Reprinted by permission of the Harvard Business School.

that merged with Puritan Drug in 1964 and became its Syracuse Division. Although Thomas had made Schultz's acquaintance in the course of business, he did not know Schultz well. Over the past month many members of the divisional sales force often expressed their admiration and affection for Schultz. Several sales reps made a point of telling Thomas that "Old H. L." knew every druggist in 12 counties by their first name. Schultz, in fact, had died of a heart attack while trout fishing with the president of the Syracuse Pharmacists' Association. Robert Jackson remarked that most of the druggists in town attended Schultz's funeral.

The Syracuse Division of Puritan Drug was one of 74 wholesale drug divisions in the United States owned by the firm. Each division acted as a functionally autonomous unit maintaining its own warehouse, sales, buying, and accounting departments. While the divisional manager was responsible for the performance of the division, there were a number of line functions performed by the regional and national offices of Puritan Drug. As divisional sales manager, for example, David Thomas maintained a relationship with the regional office in Albany, which was responsible for assisting him in implementing marketing policies established by the central office in New York.

As a wholesaler, the Syracuse Division sold to retail druggists a broad product line of approximately 18,000 items. The product line consisted of just about anything and everything sold through drugstores except fresh food, tobacco products, newspapers, and magazines. In the Syracuse trading area, Puritan Drug competed with two other wholesalers; one carried substantially the same line of products as Puritan Drug, and the other carried a more limited line of drug products.

The Syracuse Division operated as a profitable family-owned wholesale drug house before its merger with Puritan Drug in 1964. While the division operated profitably since 1964, it had not shown a profit on sales equal to the average for the other wholesale drug divisions of Puritan Drug. From 1973 to 1984 the net sales of the division rose each year. However, because competitors did not make available their sales figures, it was impossible to ascertain whether this increase in sales represented a change in the competitive situation or merely a general trend of increasing business volume in the Syracuse trading area. While Schultz was of the opinion that the increase had been at the expense of competitors, the Albany office maintained that since the trend of increase was less than that of other divisions in the northern New York region, the Syracuse Division may have actually lost ground competitively. A new technique for calculating the potential wholesale purchasing power of retail drugstores, adopted shortly before Thomas' transfer, indicated that the share of the wholesale drug market controlled by the Syracuse Division was below both the median and the mean for other Puritan Drug divisions.

Only a handful of the division's current work force was employed by the family-owned firm prior to its merger with Puritan Drug in 1964. H. L. Schultz was the one remaining executive whose employment in the Syracuse Division antedated the merger; only two sales reps, Harvey Brooks and Clifford Nelson, had sold for the predecessor company.

Many of the company executives and sales reps, although not employed by the predecessor company, nevertheless had employment histories with Puritan Drug going back to the 1960s and 1970s. Of those employees hired prior to 1974, only Robert Jackson, the division manager, had an undergraduate degree, earned at a local YMCA evening college. The more recently hired employees were, without exception, university or pharmacy college graduates. None of the younger employees were promoted when recent vacancies occurred for the jobs of divisional warehouse operations manager and divisional merchandise manager in Syracuse. Two of the younger employees, however, had recently been transferred to similar positions in other divisions.

The Syracuse Division Sales Force

From the time Thomas assumed Schultz's duties in early May, he had devoted four days a week to the task of traveling through each sales territory with the sales rep who covered it. He had made no changes in the practices or procedures of the sales force. Brooks' retirement request provided the first occasion where Thomas could make a nonroutine decision.

When Thomas took charge of the Syracuse Division sales force, it consisted of nine sales reps and four trainees. Four of the sales reps (Frederick Taylor, Edward Harrington, Grace Howard, and Linda Donnelly) had joined the company under the sales training program for college graduates initiated early in the 1970s. The other five sales reps had been with the company many years. Harvey Brooks and Clifford Nelson were the most senior in service. William Murray joined the company as a warehouse employee in 1960 at the age of 19. He became a sales rep in 1965. Walter Miller joined Puritan Drug as a sales rep in 1965 when the wholesale drug firm that he had previously worked for went out of business. Miller, who was 48 years old, had been a wholesale drug sales rep since the age of 20. Albert Simpson came to Puritan Drug after working as a missionary salesman for a manufacturer. Simpson, who joined the company in 1968 at age 26, had earlier served as an officer in the Army Medical Corps.

The four sales trainees graduated from college in June 1983. When Thomas arrived in Syracuse, they were in the last phase of their 12-month training program and were spending much of their time traveling with the experienced sales reps. Thomas believed that Schultz hired the trainees to cover anticipated turnover of sales reps and trainees and to implement the New York office's policy of getting more intensive coverage of each market area. The trainees expected to receive territory assignments, either in the Syracuse Division or elsewhere, on the completion of their training period at the end of June 1984.

Thomas had not seen very much of the sales reps as a group. His acquaintance with them had been formed by the one month-end sales meeting he attended and through his travels with them through their territories.

Walter Miller. Thomas was of the opinion that Walter Miller was a very easy-going, even-tempered person. He seemed to be very popular with the other sales reps and with his customers. Thomas thought that Miller liked him because he had commented to Thomas several times that his suggestions had been very helpful.

Harvey Brooks. Harvey Brooks had not been particularly friendly. Thomas observed that Brooks was well liked because of his good humor and friendly manner with everyone. Thomas did notice, however, that Brooks intimated that the sales manager should defer to Brooks' age, experience, and judgment. Brooks and his wife lived in the town of Oswego.

On June 4, 1984, Thomas traveled with Brooks, and they visited five of Brooks' accounts. Thomas filed a routine report with the Albany office on the sales rep's field work:

Points requiring attention: Not using merchandising equipment; not following weekly sales plan. Pharmaceutical business going to competitors because of lack of interest. Too much time spent on idle chatter. Only shows druggists what "he thinks they will buy." Tends to sell easy items instead of profitable ones.

Steps taken for correction: Explained shortcomings and demonstrated how larger, more profitable orders could be obtained by following sales plan—did just that by getting the biggest order ever written for Carthage account.

Remarks: Old-time "personality." Should do terrific volume if trained on new merchandising techniques.

On a similar form completed by H. L. Schultz on the basis of his travels with Brooks on March 3, 1984, the following comments were made:

Points requiring attention: Not getting pharmaceutical business. Not following promotion plans.

Steps taken for correction: Told him about these things.

Remarks: Brooks made this territory—can sell anything he sets his mind to—a real drummer—very popular with his customers.

Grace Howard. Grace Howard (age 29) was the oldest of the sales reps who had passed through the formal sales training program. Thomas considered her earnest and conscientious. Howard had increased her sales each year. Although Thomas did not consider Howard to be the "sales rep type," he noted that Howard was quite successful in using the merchandising techniques that Thomas wanted to implement.

William Murray. William Murray handled many of the big accounts in downtown Syracuse. Thomas believed that Murray was an excellent sales rep who considered himself "very smooth." Thomas had been surprised at the affront Murray had taken when he had offered a few suggestions to improve Murray's selling technique. William Murray and his wife were good friends of the Jacksons, as well as the merchandise and operations managers and their wives. Thomas suspected that Murray had expected to be Schultz's successor.

Clifford Nelson. Clifford Nelson appeared to Thomas to be an earnest and conscientious sales rep. He had been amiable, but not cordial to Thomas. Thomas' report on Nelson's calls on 10 accounts on June 5, 1984, contained the following statements:

Points requiring attention: Rushing calls. Gets want book and tries to sell case lots on wanted items. Carries all merchandising equipment, but doesn't use it.

Steps taken for correction: Suggested change in routing; longer, better-planned calls; conducted presentation demonstration.

Remarks: Hard-working, conscientious, good salesman, but needs to be brought up-to-date on merchandising methods.

Schultz's comments on his observations of Nelson on March 4, 1984, were:

Points requiring attention: Uses the want book on the basis of most sales. Not pushing promotions.

Steps taken for correction: Discussed shortcomings.

Remarks: Nelson really knows how to sell—visits every customer each week. Hard worker— very loyal—even pushes goods with very low commission.

On the day Thomas traveled with Nelson, the sales rep suggested that Thomas have dinner at the Nelsons' home. Thomas accepted the invitation, but at the end of the day Nelson took him to a restaurant in Watertown instead, explaining that he did not want to inconvenience his wife because his two daughters were home from college on vacation.

Albert Simpson. Albert Simpson caused Thomas considerable concern. Simpson continually complained about sales management procedures, commission rates, the "lousy service of the warehouse people," and similar matters at the sales meeting. Thomas believed that while most of his complaints were valid, the matters were usually trivial, and that the other sales reps did not complain about any of these matters. Thomas mentioned his difficulties with Simpson to Robert Jackson, the district manager. Jackson replied that Simpson had been very friendly with Schultz. Simpson seemed quite popular with his customers.

Frederick Taylor. Frederick Taylor was, in Thomas' opinion, the most ambitious, aggressive, and argumentative sales rep in the division. He had been employed by the company since his graduation from the University of Rochester in 1980, first as a trainee, and then as a sales rep. Taylor had substantially increased the sales volume of his territory. He persuaded Schultz to assign him six inactive hospital accounts in July 1982. Within six months, he was able to generate sales to these accounts in excess of $50,000. While the other sales reps considered Taylor "cocky" and a "big spender," Thomas regarded Taylor's attitude as one of independence. If Taylor agreed with a sales plan, he worked hard to achieve its objectives; if he did not agree, he would not cooperate. Thomas thought that he had been successful in working with Taylor.

Linda Donnelly. Linda Donnelly impressed Thomas as being unsure of herself, confused, and overworked. Thomas attributed these difficulties to Donnelly's attempts to serve too many accounts in too large a territory. Donnelly was very receptive to Thomas' suggestions on how to improve her work. Thomas believed that, at age 24, Donnelly would improve with proper guidance. Donnelly had raised her sales to a point enabling her to move from salary to commissions in March 1984.

Edward Harrington. Edward Harrington (age 25) was the only sales rep who continued to work on a salary basis. His sales volume was insufficient to sustain the income of $1,500 a month, the company minimum for sales reps with more than one year's experience. Harrington was very apologetic about being on a salary. Thomas believed that Harrington's determination to "make good" would be realized through his conscientiousness. When he was assigned the territory in 1982, it consisted largely of uncontacted accounts. The volume of sales in the territory tripled over the past two years. Thomas felt that Harrington appreciated all the help given and that, in time, Harrington would be an excellent salesman.

Commission and Turnover Rates at Puritan Drug

Sales commission rates were paid to the sales force as follows:

Brooks and Nelson	2.375%
Miller and Donnelly	2.25
Murray and Simpson	2.125
Howard and Taylor	2

Expense accounts amounted to about .75 percent of sales. Thomas explained the differences in commission rates in terms of the differential product commissions set by the company. Higher commission rates were given on items the company wished to "push," such as pharmaceuticals and calendar promotion items.

While all four trainees seemed to be good prospects, they were somewhat of an unknown quantity to Thomas. He had held training conferences with them, and thought they performed rather poorly. He was concerned that Schultz had neglected their training, yet the reps were eager for assigned territories. They indicated this desire to Thomas at every possible opportunity.

The turnover of the Syracuse Division sales force had been quite low among the senior sales reps. Only six of the graduates of the sales training program had left the division since 1979. Two were promoted to department heads in other Puritan Drug divisions. The remaining four left to work for drug manufacturers. Drug manufacturers valued sales reps with wholesaling experience, and wholesalers who competed with Puritan Drug did not offer any training programs. Consequently, there were many opportunities for a sales rep who left Puritan Drug.

Sales Management at Puritan Drug

Throughout the month of May, Thomas devoted considerable thought to improving the sales performance of the Syracuse Division. He had accepted the transfer to this job at the urging of Richard Topping, vice president in charge of sales and his prior boss. Thomas was one of a dozen young employees whom Topping had brought into the New York office as assistants to the top sales executives. None of these young assistants remained in the New York office for more than three years. Topping had made a policy of offering them field assignments so that they could "show their stuff."

Thomas had observed the performance records of other divisional sales managers while he worked in New York. He knew that some sales managers had achieved substantial improvements on the past performances of their divisions. Thomas believed that the sales performance of his own division could be enhanced by improving the sales management plan. He also knew that the share of the Syracuse market for wholesale purchases of retail drugstores[1] held by Puritan Drug was 20.05 percent, compared to a 48 percent share for some of the other divisions.

Thomas remembered that Topping had regularly focused his staff's attention on the qualitative aspects of sales policy. Thomas had assisted Topping in implementing merchandising plans to utilize the sales reps' efforts to minimize the handling cost of their sales, and to maximize the gross margin.

The company promoted a three-step sales plan for increased profitability:

1. Sales of larger average value per line of the order were encouraged because the cost of processing and filling each line of an order was practically constant.
2. Sales of larger total value were encouraged because the delivery cost for orders having a total weight between 20 and 100 pounds was practically constant.
3. Because some manufacturers offered margins considerably larger than others, sales of higher margin items were encouraged. Sales commissions

---

[1] The New York market analysis section calculated the potential wholesale sales for retail drugstores. This market estimate, called the PWPP (potential wholesale purchasing power), was calculated for each county by adjusting retail drugstore sales to an estimate of the purchases of goods from wholesalers.

varied with the margins available to Puritan Drug on the products the sales reps sold.

The headquarters office also sought to increase the effectiveness of Puritan Drug promotions by setting up a sales calendar. The sales calendar coordinated the activities of all Puritan Drug divisions so that during a given calendar period, every company account could be solicited for those specific items which yielded attractive margins. The sales calendar required that the sales reps in each division follow a fairly prescribed pattern in selling to each individual account. The divisional sales managers were responsible for the coordination of the activities of their sales reps. Thomas believed that his predecessor had never really accepted the sales patterns prescribed by the New York office.

The national office also required each division to keep uniform sales and market analysis records. In the New York office, Thomas had developed a familiarity with the uses of these records. He inherited from Schultz a carefully maintained system of sales department records.

The division trading area formed the basis of the sales and market analysis record system. The economics of selling costs, transportation costs of delivery, and sales reps' traveling expenses determined the limits of the trading area. Thomas knew from his own experience, however, that delineation of trading areas was heavily influenced by tradition, geography, number of sales reps, number of possible sales contacts, estimated market potential, competition, and agreements with adjacent Puritan Drug divisions. The Rochester and Albany trading areas bordered the Syracuse Division on the east, south, and west; Canada bordered the division in the north. (A map of this division is included as Exhibit 1.)

Since his arrival, Thomas had formed the opinion that the present territories had been established without careful regard for the number of stores in the area, the sales potential, or the travel involved. Although he had not yet studied any one territory carefully, Thomas suspected that all his sales reps skimmed the cream from many of their accounts. He believed that they simply did not have adequate time to do a thorough selling job in each store. Exhibit 2 provides information on sales and sales potential by county. Exhibits 3 and 4 provide selected data on individual territory assignments and performance.

Sales Territories of Harvey Brooks and Clifford Nelson

Harvey Brooks' sales territory included accounts scattered through small towns in four rural counties northeast of Syracuse (see Exhibit 5). Brooks originally developed the accounts for the predecessor company. At the time he undertook this task in 1954, a competing service wholesaler had established a mail-order business with the area's rural druggists. Brooks "took to the road" to build sales with personal service. He had been hired specifically for this job because he was a native of the area and an experienced "drummer."

EXHIBIT 1 Syracuse Division trading area in upstate New York. Salespeople's assignments

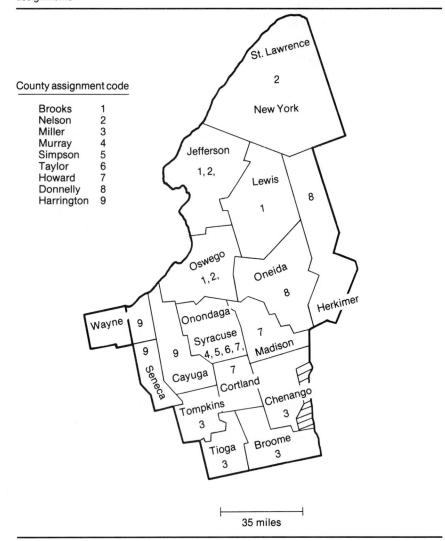

County assignment code

Brooks	1
Nelson	2
Miller	3
Murray	4
Simpson	5
Taylor	6
Howard	7
Donnelly	8
Harrington	9

35 miles

EXHIBIT 2 Selected data on sales and sales potentials, by counties

				Retailers								Hospitals			
County	Salesperson[a] code	Population (000s)	Percent of division	Sold	Inactive accounts	Accounts not sold	Total	Potential wholesale purchasing power (000s)	Percent of division PWPP	Sales[b] (000s)	Sales percent of PWPP	Sold	Not sold	Sales (000s)	Miscellaneous sales (000s)
St. Lawrence	2	117.2	6.3%	23	1	2	26	$ 2,725	4.4%	$ 1,020	26.9%	2	4	$ 20	$ 15
Jefferson	1,2	90.2	4.9	34	—	—	34	3,265	5.3	918	28.2	2	2	10	10
Lewis	1	24.8	1.3	8	—	—	8	653	1.0	215	32.2	—	1	—	8
Herkimer	8	69.3	3.7	10	6	1	17	1,560	2.5	245	15.7	1	2	—	—
Oswego	1,2	97.8	5.3	25	1	—	26	3,350	5.5	933	27.1	—	2	—	25
Oneida	8	285.4	15.5	46	14	12	72	8,700	14.2	838	10.5	—	13	—	18
Wayne	9	76.6	4.1	4	—	1	5	618	1.0	138	22.3	—	—	—	—
Cayuga	9	75.6	4.1	12	4	—	16	1,403	2.3	253	18.0	2	—	10	68
Onondaga	4,5,6,7	474.8	25.8	98	9	13	120	19,118	31.2	5,415	28.7	6	9	270	480
Madison	7	59.7	3.2	12	2	3	17	3,125	5.1	653	20.9	—	2	—	—
Seneca	9	34.4	1.9	6	1	3	10	1,395	2.3	210	15.0	2	1	15	60
Cortland	7	45.4	2.5	6	2	1	9	1,275	2.1	403	31.5	—	2	—	—
Chenango	3	48.2	2.6	4	2	6	12	1,420	2.3	158	11.1	—	3	—	—
Tompkins	3	75.7	4.1	9	1	4	14	2,038	3.3	330	16.2	—	5	—	—
Tioga	3	46.2	2.5	4	—	7	11	805	1.3	200	24.8	—	—	—	—
Broome	3	225.3	12.2	22	2	13	37	9,925	16.2	633	6.4	—	8	—	45
Totals		1,846.6	100.0%	323	45	66	434	$61,375	100.0%	$12,562	20.5%	15	54	$325	$719

[a] County assignment code: Brooks – 1 Murray – 4 Howard – 7
Nelson – 2 Simpson – 5 Donnelly – 8
Miller – 3 Taylor – 6 Harrington – 9

[b] Excludes miscellaneous sales, sales to hospitals, and house sales.

EXHIBIT 3 Selected data on sales reps' territory assignments by county

Sales rep	County	Sales 1984[a]	Active[b] accounts	PWPP[c]	Assigned[b] accounts
Miller	Chenango	$ 154,755	4	$ 1,417	15
	Tompkins	332,250	9	2,038	19
	Tioga	199,195	4	805	11
	Broome	675,750	22	9,928	45
Total		1,361,950	39	14,188	90
Brooks	Jefferson	365,085	16	2,265	18
	Lewis	215,985	8	653	9
	Oswego	924,650	25	2,675	28
Total		1,150,720	49	5,593	55
Howard	Onondaga	572,543	14	2,275	14
	Madison	652,125	12	3,125	19
	Cortland	402,500	6	1,275	11
Total		1,627,168	32	6,675	44
Murray	Onondaga	1,890,383	33	5,563	44
Total		1,890,383	33	5,563	44
Nelson	St. Lawrence	1,020,440	25	2,725	32
	Jefferson	556,298	20	1,000	20
	Oswego	6,950	1	675	1
Total		1,583,688	46	4,400	53
Simpson	Onondaga	1,834,815	29	7,520	48
Total		1,834,815	29	7,520	48
Taylor	Onondaga	1,595,183	29	3,760	29
Total		1,595,183	29	3,760	29
Donnelly	Herkimer	242,650	10	1,560	19
	Oneida	937,500	46	8,700	85
Total		1,180,150	56	10,260	104
Harrington	Wayne	136,000	4	618	5
	Cayuga	317,500	14	1,403	18
	Seneca	271,950	8	1,395	13
Total		725,450	26	3,416	36
Hospitals	Taylor (Syracuse)	270,000			
	Nelson/ Harrington	55,000			
House accounts		$ 1,322,530			
Total division sales		$14,951,910			

[a] The figure by sales rep includes sales to chain and independent drugstores and to miscellaneous accounts, but does not include sales to hospitals or house accounts indicated at the foot of the table.

[b] Includes hospitals and other recognized drug outlets in the territory.

[c] No potential is calculated for hospitals or miscellaneous sales. However, where a county is divided among several sales reps, the potential sales figure for each rep is obtained by allocating the county potential in proportion to the total *number* of potential drugstore and miscellaneous accounts in that county assigned to that rep.

EXHIBIT 4 Summary data on sales reps' performance

	1984 sales (000s)	Percent of total sales	1984 PWPP[a] (000s)	Percent of total PWPP	Sales percent of PWPP	1984 active accounts[b] No.	Percent	1984 assigned accounts[b] No.	Percent	Active accounts percent of assigned	1984 sales per active account	PWPP per assigned account[c]	1984 commissions
I													
Miller	$ 1,363	10.2%	$14,188	23.2%	9.6%	39	11.5%	90	17.9%	43.4%	$35,000	$157,750	$30,675
Brooks	1,505	11.3	5,593	9.1	27.0	49	14.5	55	10.9	89.0	30,750	101,500	35,725
Murray	1,890	14.2	5,563	9.1	34.0	33	9.8	44	8.8	75.0	57,250	126,250	40,200
Nelson	1,585[d]	11.9	4,400	7.2	36.0	46	13.6	53	10.5	85.0	34,500	83,000	38,500
Simpson	1,835	13.8	7,520	12.2	24.5	29	8.6	48	9.5	60.5	63,375	156,750	39,000
Subtotal	$ 8,178	61.4%	$37,264	60.8%	22.0%	196	58.0%	290	57.6%	67.2%	$58,450	$128,500	
II													
Howard	$ 1,628	12.2	$ 6,675	10.9%	24.4%	32	9.5%	44	8.7%	72.7%	$50,900	$151,500	$ 3,300
Taylor	1,595[d]	12.0	3,760	6.1	42.4	28	8.3	29	5.8	96.5	66,750	129,500	31,900
Donnelly	1,180	8.9	10,260	16.7	11.5	56	16.5	104	20.7	53.8	21,050	98,750	26,550
Harrington	725[d]	5.5	3,415	5.5	21.3	26	7.7	36	7.2	72.3	27,875	95,000	18,000
Subtotal	$ 5,128	38.6%	$24,110	39.2%	21.3%	142	42.0%	213	42.4%	66.7%	$36,188	$113,250	
Total	$13,306[d]	100.0%	$61,374	100.0%	21.7	338	100.0%	503	100.0%	67.0%	$39,325	$122,000	
Hospital sales by:													
Taylor	$ 270												
Nelson	30												
Harrington	25												
House sales:	1,322												
Grand total	$14,953												

a No potential is calculated for hospital or miscellaneous sales. However, where a county is divided among several sales reps the potential sales figure for each rep is obtained by allocating the county potential in proportion to the total *number* of potential drugstore and miscellaneous accounts in that county assigned to that rep.

b Includes hospitals and other recognized drug outlets in the territory.

c Understated since hospitals and miscellaneous accounts are included in the assigned accounts listed but not in the potential.

d Excluding hospital sales.

EXHIBIT 5 Counties sold by Brooks and Nelson

In 1959, Clifford Nelson, a friend of Brooks, became a division sales rep. At the suggestion of Brooks, he covered other accounts in the same four-county area. Nelson previously had been a sales rep for a proprietary medicine firm. He was seven years younger than Brooks. Since 1955, Brooks and Nelson each had had a number of accounts in the four-county area. (The list of their accounts appears as Exhibits 6 and 7.) Thomas noticed that the commission incomes Brooks and Nelson received had been stable over the years.

EXHIBIT 6 Accounts sold by Harvey Brooks, by counties, with 1984 purchases

Jefferson County			Oswego County			Lewis County		
Adams Center	D	$ 8,925	Calosse	D	$ 4,273	Beaver Falls	D	$ 9,525
(Alexandria Bay)	D	45,750	Central Square	D	4,643	Croghan	D	61,493
(Alexandria Bay)	D	39,475	Constantia	M	180	Harrisville	D	46,290
Bellville	D	5,250	Cleveland	M	975	Lowville	D	59,220
(Carthage)	D	152,500	(Fulton)	D	37,800	Lowville	D	10,785
Chaumont	D	1,510	(Fulton)	D	61,275	Lyons Falls	D	15,060
(Clayton)	D	26,575	(Fulton)	D	69,500	Port Leydon	D	5,813
(Clayton)	D	41,000	(Fulton)	D	96,000	Turin	M	7,800
Deferiet	D	923	Hannibal	D	9,725	County total:		$215,986
Dexter	D	29,175	Hastings	M	9,600	Territory total: $1,505,724		
Ellisburg	D	590	Lacona	M	1,155			
LaFargeville	D	1,305	Mexico	D	39,750			
Plessis	D	2,200	Oswego	D	30,188			
Redwood	M	270	(Oswego)	D	51,900			
Rodman	D	8,025	(Oswego)	D	60,250			
Sackets Harbor	D	1,613	(Oswego)	D	102,500			
County total:		$365,086	(Oswego)	D	109,750			
			(Oswego)	D	56,075			
			Oswego	H	38			
			Parish	M	12,900			
			Phoenix	D	24,325			
			(Pulaski)	D	21,875			
			(Pulaski)	D	72,700			
			Sandy Creek	D	35,325			
			West Monroe	D	11,950			
			County total:		$924,652			

Code: D = Independent drugstore; M = miscellaneous account; H = Hospital.

Note: Accounts in parentheses are those indicated by Nelson as the ones he wanted from Brooks. These accounts total $1,044,963 (87.7 percent of Brooks' sales in Jefferson County, 80 percent in Oswego County, or 69.4 percent of the territory total). Added to Nelson's 1983 sales, this would increase his volume 65 percent to $2,658,018. Brooks' old territory would be left with $460,758 in sales.

A Visit from Clifford Nelson

On the morning of June 9, three days after the June sales meeting, Thomas saw Clifford Nelson come in the front door of the Syracuse Division offices. Although Nelson passed within 30 feet of Thomas' desk, he did not appear to notice Thomas. Nelson walked through the office area directly to the partitioned space where Robert Jackson's private office was located. Twenty minutes later, Nelson emerged from the division manager's office and made his way to Thomas' desk.

"Hi there, young fellah!" he shouted as he approached.

"Howdy, Cliff. Sit down and chat awhile," Thomas replied. "What got you out of bed so early?" he asked, knowing that Nelson must have risen at 6 o'clock to make the drive to Syracuse from his home in Watertown.

Nelson squeezed his bulky frame into the armchair next to the desk. "It's a shame Harvey is retiring," he said. "I never thought he could stand to give it

EXHIBIT 7   Accounts sold by Clifford Nelson, by counties, with 1984 purchases

St. Lawrence County			Jefferson County			Oswego County		
Canton	D	$ 98,100	Adams	C	$ 4,713	Pulaski	C	$6,825
Edwards	D	5,040	Carthage	C	5,325			
Edwards	M	14,138	Evans Mills	D	5,525			
Gouverneur	D	1,695	Philadelphia	D	9,450			
Gouverneur	D	70,373	Watertown	D	75,500			
Gouverneur	D	123,898	Watertown	D	11,850			
Heuvelton	D	810	Watertown	D	22,000			
Massena	D	84,443	Watertown	D	76,700			
Massena	D	25,478	Watertown	D	46,100			
Massena	C	18,360	Watertown	D	65,750			
Massena	C	16,688	Watertown	D	95,500			
Massena	H	285	Watertown	D	57,500			
Madrid	D	10,740	Watertown	D	24,250			
Morristown	D	20,483	Watertown	D	2,135			
Norfolk	D	22,463	Watertown	D	28,300			
Norwood	D	23,543	Watertown	C	9,075			
Ogdensburg	D	60,675	Watertown	C	14,925			
Ogdensburg	D	169,163	Watertown	M	1,700			
Ogdensburg	D	54,023	Watertown	H	315			
Ogdensburg	D	25,350	Watertown	H	9,000			
Ogdensburg	M	1,118	County total:		$565,613			
Ogdensburg	H	19,898						
Potsdam	D	115,830						
Potsdam	C	55,283						
Potsdam Falls	D	2,753						
County total:		$1,040,630						

Territorial total: $1,613,068

Code: D = Independent drugstore; C = Chain drugstores; M = Miscellaneous account; H = Hospital.

up. I never knew anyone who enjoyed selling as much as Harvey—except maybe me." Nelson continued praising Brooks and telling anecdotes which illustrated his point until Thomas began to wonder whether Nelson thought that he was biased in some way against the retiring sales rep. Thomas recalled that he had made some critical remarks about Brooks to Jackson, but he could not recall any discussion of Brooks' shortcomings with the man himself, or any of the other sales reps. Nelson ended his remarks by saying, "Old H. L. always said that Harvey was the best damn wholesale drug salesman he'd ever known."

There was a brief silence, as Thomas did not realize that Nelson was finished. Finally Thomas said, "You know, Cliff, I think we ought to have a testimonial dinner for Harvey at the July sales meeting."

Nelson made no comment on Thomas' suggestion; instead, he went on to say, "None of these green trainees will ever be able to take Harvey's place. Those druggists up there are old-timers. They would resent being high pressured by some kid blown up to twice his size with college degrees. No sir! You've got to sell 'em right in those country stores."

Thomas questioned whether Nelson's opinion of the adaptability of the younger, college-educated sales reps was justified by the available evidence. He recalled that several of them with rural territories performed better against their May sales quotas than either Brooks or Nelson. Thomas was proud of his self-restraint when he commented, "Selling in a rural territory is certainly different."

"That's right, Dave. I wanted to make sure you understood these things before I told you." Nelson was nervously massaging his double chin between his thumb and forefinger.

Thomas looked at him with a quizzical expression. "Told me what?"

"I have just been talking to Robert Jackson. Well, I was talking to him about an understanding between Harvey and me. We always agreed that if anything should happen to the other, or he should retire, or something—well, we agreed that the one who remained should get to take over his choice of the other's accounts. We told H. L. about this and he said, 'Boys, what's OK by you is OK by me. You two developed that territory and you deserve to be rewarded for it.' Well, yes sir, that's the way it was."

Without pausing, Nelson went on, "I just told Jackson about it. He said that he remembered talking about the whole thing with H. L. 'Yes,' he said, 'Tell Thomas about it,' he said, 'Tell Thomas about it.' Harvey and I went over his accounts on Sunday. I went over his list of accounts with him and checked the ones that I want. Here is the list with the accounts all checked off.[2] I already know nearly all the proprietors. You'll see that—"

"Wait a minute, Cliff! Wait a minute!" Thomas interrupted. "You've lost me completely. In the first place, if there is any assignment of accounts to be made I'll do it. It will be done on a basis that is fair to the sales reps concerned, and profitable to the company. You know that."

"Dave, I'm only asking for what is fair." Nelson's face was flushed. Thomas noticed that the man he had always believed to be deliberately confident and self-possessed was now so agitated that it was difficult for him to speak. "I don't want my territory chopped up and handed to some green kid!"

Thomas noticed that everybody in the office was now watching Nelson. "Calm down, Cliff," he whispered to the sales rep, indicating with a nod of his head that others were watching.

"Don't talk to me that way!" replied Nelson. "I don't care. A man with 25 years' service deserves some consideration!"

"You're absolutely right, Cliff. You're absolutely right." As Thomas repeated his words, Nelson settled back in his chair. The typewriters started clattering again.

"Now, first of all, Cliff," as Thomas tried to return the conversation to a

---

[2] Nelson's selected accounts are the accounts in parentheses in Exhibit 6.

friendly basis. "Where did you get the idea that your territory was going to be 'chopped up'?"

"You said so yourself. You said it at the sales meeting the other day when you made that speech about how you were going to boost sales in Syracuse." Nelson emphasized his words by pounding the side of the desk with his masonic ring.

Thomas reflected for a moment. He recalled his speech at the sales meeting called, "How We Can Do a Better Job for Puritan Drug." The speech was a restatement of the merchandising policy of the New York office. He had mentioned that getting more profitable business would require that a larger percentage of the purchases of each account would have to come to Puritan Drug; that receiving a larger share of the business from each store would require more selling time in each store; and that greater concentration on each account would require reorganization of the sales territories. He realized that his future plans entailed reorganization of the territories. He had not anticipated, however, Nelson's reaction.

Finally, Thomas said, "I do plan to make some territorial changes—not right away—at least not until I have looked things over pretty darn carefully. Of course, you understand that our first duty is to make greater profits for the company. Some of our territories would be a great deal more profitable if they were organized and handled in a different manner."

"What are you going to do about Harvey's territory?" asked Nelson.

Since Thomas had not yet looked over the information about the territory, he was anxious not to commit himself to any course of action relating to it. "Well, I just haven't had a chance to study the situation yet," he replied. "If I could make the territory more profitable by reorganizing it, I guess that is what they would expect me to do."

"What about the promises the company made to me about letting me choose the accounts I want?" Nelson asked.

"You don't mean the company's promise; you mean Schultz's promise," Thomas corrected him.

"Well, if Schultz wasn't 'the company,' I don't see how you figure that you are!" Nelson's face resumed its flush.

"OK, Cliff. How about giving me a chance to look over the situation. You know that I want to do the right thing. Let me go over the list of the accounts you want. In a few days I can talk intelligently about the matter." Thomas felt that there was no point in carrying the discussion further.

"All right, Dave," said Nelson, rising. The two men walked toward the front entrance of the office. As they reached the top of the steps leading to the front door, Nelson turned to Thomas and offered his hand. "Look, Dave, I'm sorry I got so mad. You just can't imagine what this means to me. I know you'll see it my way when you know the whole story." Nelson's voice sounded strained.

Thomas watched the older man leave. He felt embarrassed, realizing that Nelson's parting words had been overheard by several manufacturers' representatives standing nearby.

A Conversation with the Division Manager

Thomas decided he would immediately discuss his conversation with Nelson with Jackson. He walked over to Jackson's office, and hesitated upon reaching the doorway. Jackson looked up, and indicated with a gesture that Thomas should take a seat.

Thomas sat down and waited for Jackson to speak. Jackson was occupied for the moment unwrapping a cigar. After a few moments of silence, Thomas opened the conversation. "Clifford Nelson just stopped by to speak to me."

"Yeah?" said Jackson, removing bitten flakes of tobacco from the end of his tongue.

"He said something about getting some of Harvey Brooks' accounts when Harvey retired," Thomas said in a deliberately questioning manner.

"Yeah."

Thomas continued, "Well, this idea of his was based on a promise that he said H. L. had made."

"Yeah. He told me that, too."

"Did Schultz make such a promise?" Thomas inquired.

"Hell, I don't know. It sounds like him." Jackson tilted back in his swivel chair.

"What shall I do about it?"

"Don't ask me; you're the sales manager." Jackson paused, holding his cigar away from his lips as if he were about to speak. Just as Thomas was about to say something, Jackson lurched forward to flick the ashes from his cigar into his ash tray. "Look here, Dave. I don't want any morale problems around here. You're the first of the 'wonder boys' to be put in charge of a department in this division. I don't want you to do anything to mess up the morale. We never had any morale problems when Schultz was around. We don't want anything like that in this division."

Thomas was momentarily bewildered. He knew from the way that Jackson used the phrase "wonder boys" that he was referring to the managers brought into the organization by Richard Topping.

Jackson went on, "Why the devil did you tell the reps that you were going to reassign the sales territories without even telling me?"

"But you were there when I said it."

"Said what?"

"Well, at the sales meeting, that one of the ways we were going to get more business was to reorganize the sales territory," Thomas replied.

"I certainly don't remember anything like that. Dave, you gave a good inspirational talk, but I sure can't remember anything about reassigning territories."

"Actually, I just mentioned the reorganization of territories in passing," Thomas smiled.

"I'll be damned. That sort of thing is always happening. Here everybody is frothing at the mouth about something that they think we are going to do and we haven't the slightest idea why they think we're going to do it. You know, probably the real reason Harvey Brooks is retiring, instead of staying on as he planned, was this fear of sales territory reorganization. Both he and Nelson know that their retirement pension is based on earnings from their last five years of active employment. Now that I think of it, three or four of the other sales reps have stopped during the last couple of days to tell me what a fine job they were doing. They probably had this territory reassignment stuff on their minds, too."

Jackson's cigar was no longer burning. He began groping under the papers on his desk for a match. Thomas took advantage of this pause in the conversation. "Mr. Jackson, I think there are some real advantages to be won by adjusting the sales territories. I think—"

"You still think that after today?" the division manager asked in a sarcastic tone.

"Why, yes! The profit made on sales to an individual account is related closely to delivery expense. The larger the total proportion of the account's business we get, the more profit we make because the delivery expense remains more or less constant."

"Look, Dave, you college computer types always have everything figured out, but sometimes that doesn't count. Morale is the important thing. The sales reps won't tolerate having their territories changed. I know that you have four trainees that you'd like to put out on territories. If you put them out on parts of the territories belonging to some of the more experienced reps—bam! God knows how many of our good sales reps would be left. I've never had any trouble with sales force morale since I've been manager of this division. Old Schultz, bless his soul, never let me down. He wasn't any damn Ph.D., but he could handle sales reps. Don't get off on the wrong foot with them, Dave. With the labor situation in the warehouse being what it is, I've just got too much on my mind. I don't want you creating more problems than I can handle. How 'bout it, boy!"

Jackson ground out his half-smoked cigar, looking steadily at Thomas.

Thomas was extremely upset with the division manager's implication that he lacked concern for sales rep morale. He had always thought of himself as very considerate. He realized that at the moment his foremost desire was to get away from Jackson.

Thomas rose from his chair, saying, "Mr. Jackson, you can count on me. I know you are right about this morale business."

"Atta boy," said the division manager. "It does us a lot of good to talk like this once in a while. Now, see if you can make peace with the sales reps. I want you to handle everything yourself."

"Well, thanks a lot," said Thomas, as he backed out of the office door.

As he walked through the office, he saw two manufacturers' representatives with whom he had appointments. His schedule of appointments that day prohibited him from doing more than gathering the material pertaining to the Nelson and Brooks territories.

Thomas Goes Home

Thomas left the office shortly after 5 o'clock to drive to a suburb of Syracuse. It was a particularly hot and humid day. Pre-Fourth of July traffic lengthened the drive home by nearly 20 minutes. When he finally turned into his own driveway, he felt as though his skin were caked with grime and perspiration. He got out of the car and walked around to the terrace at the rear of the house. Beth, his wife, was sitting in a deck chair, working on some papers.

"Hello, Dave. You're late," she said, looking up with a smile.

"I know it. Even the traffic was bad today." He dropped his suit coat on a glass-topped table and sprawled out full length on a chaise lounge. "I'm exhausted. And, boy, I am disgusted with myself."

"Bad day?"

"Awful. You just can't imagine how discouraging it is trying to get this job organized. You would think it would be obvious to everyone that what ails the Syracuse Division is the organization of the sales force," said Thomas, arranging a pillow under his head.

"I didn't realize that you thought anything was wrong with the Syracuse Division."

"Well, what I mean is that we now get only 20 percent of the potential wholesale business. If I could organize the sales force my way—well, God knows, maybe we could get 40 percent of the business. That is what the New York office watches for. The sales manager who increases his division's share of the market gets the promotions when they come along. I know Topping transferred me to this division because he knew these possibilities existed."

"I don't understand. Is Mr. Topping still your boss, or is Mr. Jackson?"

"Beth, it's terribly discouraging. While Jackson is my boss, I'll never get anywhere in Puritan Drug unless Topping and the other people in New York promote me."

"Don't you like Mr. Jackson?"

"I had a run-in with him today."

"You didn't!" she said as she laid her papers aside.

Thomas didn't anticipate his wife's reaction. He gazed up at the awning as if he did not notice her intent expression. "We didn't argue particularly. He just—well, he doesn't know too much about sales management. He put his foot down on my plans to reorganize the territories.''

''I can't understand why you would go and get yourself into a fight with your boss when you haven't even been here two months.''

''Honest, Beth, I didn't have any fight. Everything is OK. He just—well, do you want me to be a divisional sales manager all my life?''

''You're tired,'' she said sympathetically. ''Why don't you go up and shower.''

''That sounds wonderful,'' he said, raising himself from the chaise lounge.

An Unexpected Caller

Thomas had just stepped out of the shower when he heard his wife calling to him. ''Dave, Fred Taylor is here to see you.''

''Tell him I'll be down in just a minute. Offer him a drink, Beth.''

As he dressed, Thomas wondered why Fred Taylor had chosen the dinner hour to call. During the month since he had moved into his new home, no other sales rep had ever dropped by uninvited.

When Thomas came downstairs, he found Taylor sitting on the living room couch, a gin and tonic in his hand.

''Hello, Fred,'' said Thomas, crossing the room with his right hand extended. ''You look as if you had a hot day. Why don't you take off your coat? If we go out to the terrace, you may get a chance to cool off.''

''Thanks, Dave,'' the visitor said as they moved out to the terrace. ''I'm sorry to barge in this way, but I thought it was important.''

''Well, what's on your mind?'' asked Thomas as they sat down.

''I heard about what happened at the office today. I thought I'd come over and tell you that we stand behind you 100 percent.''

Thomas was perplexed by Taylor's words. He realized that Taylor probably was referring to his meeting with Nelson. Thomas said, ''I'm not sure what you mean, Fred.''

''I heard that you and Nelson had it out this morning about changing the sales territories,'' Taylor replied.

Thomas smiled. Two thoughts entered his mind. He was amused at the proportions that the brief morning conversation had assumed. At the same time, he was curious to know how Taylor, who had presumably been in the field selling, had heard about the incident so quickly. Without hesitation he asked, ''Where did you hear about this, Fred?''

''Bill Murray told me! He was down at the warehouse with Walter Miller when I stopped off to pick up a special narcotics order for a customer. They are all excited about this territory business. Murray said Nelson came out to his house at lunch time and told him about it. Everybody figured that you were going to change the territories when you started traveling around with each of the reps, especially after what you said at the sales meeting.''

"Well, the reason I went on the road with each of the reps, Fred," said Thomas, "was so that I could learn more about their selling problems while, at the same time, meet the customers.''

Taylor smiled, "Sure, but when you started filling out a rating sheet on each account, I couldn't help thinking you had some reason for it.''

Thomas realized that Taylor had spoken with irony in his voice, but he thought it was better to let the matter pass. Since he was planning to use the information he had gathered for the reorganization of the sales territories, he decided that he would be frank with Taylor. To find out what the young sales rep's reaction might be to territorial changes, he said, "Fred, I've thought a lot about making some changes in the territories—"

Taylor interrupted him. "That's terrific. I'm sure glad to hear that. I don't like to speak ill of the dead, but old Schultz really gave the trainees the short end of the stick when he put us on territories. He either gave us a territory of uncontacted accounts where it was like beating our heads against a stone wall. Some of us actually quit, like the two guys who trained with me. Or, Schultz gave us replacement territories where some of the best accounts had been handed over to the older reps. Well, I know for a fact that when I took over my territory from Mike Green, Bill Murray and Albert Simpson got 12 of Green's best accounts. And, damn it, I got more sales out of what was left than Green ever did; Murray and Simpson's total sales didn't go up. It took me a while, but I had the laugh at every sales meeting when our monthly sales figures were announced.''

"Is that right?" said Thomas.

"Damn right! And I wasn't the only one. That's why those old duffers are so down on the four of us that have come with the division since the mid-1970s. We've beaten them at their own game.''

"Do you think that Harrington and Howard and Donnelly feel the same way?" asked Thomas.

"Think, hell! I know it! That's all we ever talk about. If you reorganize those territories and give us back the accounts that Schultz took away, you'll see some real sales records. Take, for example, the Medical Arts Pharmacy out by Mercy Hospital. Bill Murray got that one away from my territory and he calls there only once a week. If I could get that one back, I'd get in there three times a week, and get five times as much business.''

Thomas had to raise his hands in a gesture of protest. "Don't you have enough accounts already, Fred, to keep you busy?"

"Dave, I spend 50 hours a week on the road and I love it; but I know damn well that if I put some of the time I spend in the 'two-by-four' stores into some of those big juicy accounts like Medical Arts Pharmacy, I'd do even more business.''

Thomas commented, "I'm not particularly anxious to argue now, but if you start putting time into Medical Arts Pharmacy, what's going to happen to your sales to the two-by-four stores?"

Taylor quickly replied, "Those druggists all know me. They'd go right on buying."

Thomas did not agree with Taylor. He thought that Taylor realized this.

After a moment of silence, Taylor rose from his chair, saying, "I'd better scoot home. My family will be furious with me for being late when we have plans for the weekend."

The two men walked to Taylor's car. As Taylor climbed into his car, he said, "Dave, don't forget what I said. Harrington, Howard, Donnelly, and I stand behind you 100 percent. You won't ever hear us talk about going over to a competitor!"

"Who's talking about that?" asked Thomas.

"Well," said Taylor as he started the motor and shifted into gear, "I don't want to tell tales out of school."

"Sure," Thomas said quickly. "I'm sorry I asked. So long, Fred. I'll see you soon."

Part 7

Pricing Decisions

The cases in the pricing section of this book involve several different kinds of decisions. A firm's pricing strategy is extremely important because of the quickness with which a change can be implemented, because of the importance of price to consumers in their purchase decisions, and because of the direct impact of prices on profits.

The first important consideration in establishing a price for a product is the firm's pricing objectives. A firm striving for growth may utilize a totally different strategy from one who is seeking to discourage others from cutting prices or to desensitize consumers to price. Firms with objectives oriented around maximizing long-run profits may utilize different strategies than firms who are seeking to maximize short-run profits. Thus, the first step in establishing a price should be to clearly identify what the objectives are.

Two alternative strategies often utilized are skimming and penetration. A skimming strategy is one in which a high initial price is set, and the product is sold to all those consumers willing to pay this price. The price is then lowered somewhat, and the product is sold to those consumers willing to pay that price. This process continues for some time, "skimming the cream" off the top of the market with each price change. For example, when electronic calculators were first introduced, they were priced at more than $300. A number of scientific and engineering related organizations were willing to purchase the product at this price. The price was then lowered to the neighborhood of $150 to $200, and a number of other organizations were willing to purchase the product. Later, the price was reduced to the $50 to $100 range, and very many more buyers entered the market. Eventually, the price was lowered still further, and many more consumers entered the market.

A skimming strategy is appropriate when there are no close substitutes for the product and the demand is inelastic with respect to price. It is a very conservative policy allowing the marketer to recover as much of the costs as possible quickly in the event that demand is not that great. It also allows the marketer to accumulate money for aggressive penetration later when competition enters the market. A skimming strategy is an effective way to segment the market, as in the calculator example and in the case of the book market where a skimming strategy is used for hardcover books, and the paperback edition is later introduced using a penetration strategy.

A penetration strategy utilizes a low initial price in the hopes of penetrating a large proportion of the market in a short period of time. This strategy would be used when one or more of the following conditions existed:

a. High short-run price elasticity (for example, the low price of the Model-T Ford allowed many people to purchase a car for the first time).
b. Large economies of scale in production.
c. The probability of quick public acceptance.
d. The probability of quick competitive imitation.

The specific pricing decisions that have to be made include the price level to set, price variation including discount structure and geographic price differences, margins to be given to various intermediaries in the channels of distribution, and the determination of when to change the price structure.

A number of different pricing methods are utilized by organizations. Some use the cost-plus method, whereby a certain percentage is added to the firm's costs to establish their pricing. This method is often used by industrial marketers and by wholesalers and retailers. Other organizations use break-even analysis, marginal cost analysis, and/or marginal revenue analysis to determine their pricing structure. Still other organizations are price followers and use a strategy of meeting the prices of competitors.

The ideal way to determine the price that should be charged involves analyzing a number of variables before actually setting the price. Included would be:

1. *Consumer buying patterns.* What price would consumers expect to pay for this type of product? What are the important price points or price lines that different segments of the market desire?
2. *Product differentiation.* In what ways is the company's product different from the others on the market? What advantages does the product offer the consumer?
3. *What is the competitive structure* of the industry, and what stage of the product life cycle is the product in?
4. *How price sensitive* is total industry demand, and how price sensitive is demand for the individual firm's product? What is the size of the total market and what is the likelihood of economies of scale?
5. *What is the economic climate forecast,* and how sensitive is the demand of the product to changes in the economic climate?

6. *Legal and social considerations.* New interpretations of the Robinson-Patman Act (prohibiting price discrimination) and various state laws governing pricing must be taken into consideration.
7. *Cost structure of the firm.* The relationship between fixed costs and variable costs is extremely important in pricing decisions, as is the cost structure of the firm compared to competitors' pricing structure. Pricing strategy for a hotel, with a very low variable cost ratio, will of necessity be quite different than pricing strategy for a clothing manufacturer, which has a very high variable cost ratio.
8. *The overall marketing strategy for the product.* It is important to recognize that the pricing strategy must be consistent with all the other elements of the firm's marketing strategy.

Case 28

Royale Suites*

"It's a great day for sitting outside eating crabs." Bill Abbott and his New Property Planning Team were enjoying a lunch break on a sunny July day in 1991. After lunch they would return to developing a marketing plan for the new Royale Suites Baltimore Hotel. The 12-story, 325-room hotel, opening in 18 months, was located within three blocks of the financial district and Inner Harbor tourist sites. Although only a few rooms would have an Inner Harbor view, they expected to capitalize on the already successful Royale Suites concept. "We've only got two days to bring our plan together before we present it to Corporate Marketing. Where do we stand now?"

The Royale Suites Concept

Royale Suites was one of the early entries into the all-suite hotel segment. Recognizing the increasing demand by businesspeople to conduct small meetings in their hotel rooms and families' desires for larger and more private hotel rooms, Royale Suites opened their first property in the early 1980s. Additional units had been opened in most of the largest cities in the United States. Baltimore was one of the few prime locations remaining to Royale Suites. Royale Suites Real Estate staff had been fortunate to locate and acquire an outstanding site.

The typical Royale Suite property is from 8 to 12 stories high, including from 225 to 350 two-room suites. A typical floor plan is shown in Exhibit 1. Kitchen facilities are not included since they are believed to be of little interest to business people and created significant additional equipment and cleaning costs.

---

* Prepared by Professor Ronald Stiff, University of Baltimore, 1420 N. Charles, Baltimore, Maryland, 21201, USA as the basis for class discussion rather than to illustrate either effective or ineffective handling of an administrative situation. This case contains disguised data and names. Used with permission.

EXHIBIT 1   Typical room layout

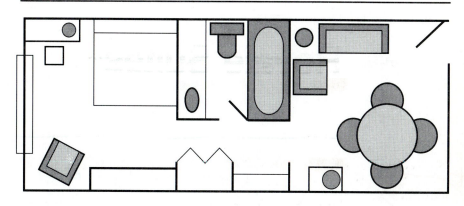

Interior decorations are adapted to specific markets and local, classical themes were encouraged. The Baltimore Royale Suite would have two meeting rooms seating 60 persons in each. They could be combined into a larger room seating 100 and used for meals.

The New Properties Planning Team

Royale Suites uses a New Properties Planning Team to plan the opening of all new properties. This team consisted of planning managers for each of the major departments in the hotel (Exhibit 2). Often those on the planning team continue on as the operating managers for the site.

EXHIBIT 2   New properties planning team

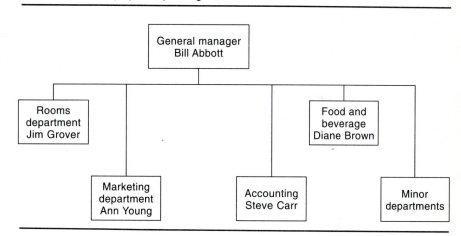

The team was headquartered in a building overlooking Baltimore's Inner Harbor. They were charged with developing the marketing plan for the hotel opening and the first year of service.

Competition

About 15 percent of downtown hotel rooms were suites. These were either in local hotels or included as part of the room inventory of national chains (Exhibit 3). As a result, suites received little promotion both locally and nationally. This was a relatively untapped product in the downtown market area.

Serving as mainly upscale rooms within nonsuite hotels, suites were generally priced higher than standard rooms in these hotels.

(inc these prices by 5% twice)

EXHIBIT 3 Competitor rates last year (price increases of 5 percent per year are expected)

Name	Number of employees	Number of rooms	Low rate	High rate	Number of suites	Low rate	High rate
Omni Inner Harbor	500	688	$125	$145	16	*216.09* $196	$196 *216.09*
Stouffer Harborplace		562	99	185	60	*192.94* 175	175 *192.94*
Marriott Inner Harbor	500	527	135	175	12	*148.84* 135	175 *192.94*
Hyatt Regency Baltimore	515	487	145	185	25	*159.86* 145	185 *203.96*
Lord Baltimore Radisson	362	417	110	175	26	*248.06* 225	225 *248.06*
Holiday Inn Inner Harbor	200	374	80	114	3	*88.20* 80	114 *125.69*
Sheraton Inner Harbor	270	339	135	180	20	*148.84* 135	180 *198.45*
Days Inn Inner Harbor	76	251	90	90	8	*104.74* 95	95 *104.74*
Harbor Court	270	203	140	175			
Comfort Inn		194	60	80			
Belvedere		179	85	180			
Peabody Court		104	115	135			
Harrison's Pier 5		71	120	165			
Brookshire					90	*109.15* 99	144 *158.76*
Tremont					60	*115.76* 105	125 *137.81*
Tremont Plaza	225				220	*104.74* 95	115 *126.79*
Total	2,918	4,396			540		
Average		338	$111	$153		$135 *148.84*	$157 *173.09*

Consumer Behavior

Ann Young noted that reservations were made in several ways:

Pure transient: Tourist or business travelers who either dropped in or made reservations direct to the Baltimore site. This group paid the rack rate (published rate charge).

Computer reservations: Customers who made reservations through Royale Suites's national toll-free number.

Government: Government employees on relatively low per diem.

Bus tours: Contracts with travel agents for tour groups at negotiated rates.

Corporate groups: Corporation and association meetings. These consisted of very small groups that could meet in the suites and larger groups that attended meetings in the Convention Center or in other hotels.

✳ *Airlines*: Contracts with airlines as a part of a vacation plan and also with flight crews.

✳ *Weekend packages*: Two-night weekend plans, including some special services to make them attractive.

A customer survey was available to the planning team that suggested parity between major all-suite hotels (Exhibit 4). However, these data did not break down quality perceptions for specific market segments. It was not clear what attributes were most important to these segments and how the chains compared in the minds of these segments.

Comparison with competitors

EXHIBIT 4   Relative quality evaluations

Overall satisfaction	Residence Inn	Embassy Suites	Royale Suites
Very satisfied	42%	40%	38%
Satisfied	53	56	57
Dissatisfied	5	4	5
Specific attributes (5 = Comparatively satisfied; 1 = Comparatively dissatisfied)			
Staff	4.1	3.2	3.7
Food	N/A	2.9	3.3
Room quality			
Cleanliness	4.2	3.8	4.1
Size	4.8	4.7	4.6
Bed comfort	2.9	3.1	2.9
Climate	3.1	2.8	3.2
Noise	3.3	3.4	3.1
Amenities	2.8	3.1	2.8
Sample size	209	243	256

A second survey provided some overall insights into service attributes that were important to all hotel consumers and consumer's beliefs in hotel's performance on these attributes (Exhibit 5). Ann felt that this might provide some guidance in positioning Royale Suites.

The Marketing Mix

Product

The physical product was fixed by corporate architectural and planning standards as adapted to the specific Baltimore site. There were a number of possible services that could be offered.

Although most Royale Suites offered free breakfasts and happy hours, this was no longer a standard corporate policy or included in corporate advertising. Diane Brown estimated the cost of breakfast to average $4.00 per occupied room and a happy hour at $1.00 per occupied room.

Diane favored these services. "Although happy hours and breakfasts have become pretty standard through the all-suite industry, this is not yet the standard

EXHIBIT 5 Hotel service attributes—importance and perceived performance
(November 1988; includes managers and executives only)

Hotel service attribute	Importance to customer	Consumer belief of actual performance
Billing accuracy	91	83 •
Efficient check-in	80	55
Reliable message and wake-up service	79	76 •
Cares about the consumer	77	54
Competitive room rates	72	52
Reasonable charge for in-room phone	72	37
Express checkouts	68	63
Attractive and generously sized rooms	59	55
Fast breakfast service	54	48
Well-lighted and ample workspace	48	51
Availability of no-smoking rooms	47	49
Quality frequent-traveler program	41	34
Multiple dining and lounge facilities	36	54
Late-evening room service	24	38

Scores: Percentage who answer 8, 9, or 10 on a 1 to 10 scale.
Source: Opinion Research Corporation Executive Travel Tracking Service, 1990.

in Baltimore. If we introduce this as a standard feature we can be a pace setter here and avoid playing catch-up if others introduce these later.''

Ann Young replied, ''It's a great marketing feature. However, will it lead us to charging noncompetitive room rates? Our consumers are sensitive about prices and there are plenty of alternatives for breakfast and booze downtown. I'm also concerned about our restaurant—its services may be very important to our customers.''

Restaurant Policy

Royale Suites had a flexible policy on restaurants. Throughout the chain they are both owned and leased. Diane Brown stated, ''We have built a reputation for having restaurants with a little local flair. We don't just 'cookie-cut' our food services, they are adapted to each site either by opening our own facility or leasing our space to a local restaurant with a good reputation.'' Diane Brown felt that the contribution to profits would be about the same either owning or leasing the restaurant and the primary concern must be to design food services that enhanced the image of the Baltimore Royale Suite with its customers. Brown also believed that although hotel restaurants traditionally were mainly used by guests, careful design and positioning had increased their potential to attract customers from outside the hotel.

Prices

Steve Carr commented: We pay 1½ percent of room revenues into the corporate computer system. This would seem to be a lot just to book rooms. However, it provides us an opportunity. As you know, we can implement a yield management pricing system using the corporate computer (see Appendix A for a description of yield management). The information system permits us to do much more than we could last year. We can develop a set of pricing rules and update them in just a minute or two. If we make all our advance, group, and transient booking through corporate's computer we can fully implement a yield management pricing program.

Let me give you some background on this. When we opened our first units we stressed a single-price policy nationwide. This made a lot of sense to the consumer and it made a lot of sense to us. However, as competition got tougher we all learned that each city is a unique, local market with different costs and competition. Market pricing became a necessity. This made accountants into marketers and marketers into accountants—probably a good idea. Our computer has turned us into an airline in a pricing sense. If we were clever enough every room would be booked and profits would be maximized. Of course, every room might have a different price. We have to start somewhere, so let's develop a fairly simple set of pricing rules.

pricing →

To simplify this, let's develop rules that give us average prices and occupancy rates for Monday to Thursday, Friday, Saturday, and Sunday. These can be used in our pro forma. We can make use of competitor's prices (Exhibit 3) and some of our historic prices and occupancy rates (Exhibit 6). Let me propose a starting point. There are 52 Sundays with 16,900 rooms available. Perhaps 25 percent of these will be sold at rack rate. How do we price and sell the remaining rooms?

EXHIBIT 6 Occupancy rates—Royale Suites last year—selected sites
(room rate increases of from 5 percent per year are expected)

(rates of other R.S. in other cities and their occupancy rate)

Some similar weekday/weekend some have drops

		Royale Suites Average Occupancy Rate					
		August		September		Annual	
City	Average Room Rate	Monday–Thursday	Friday–Sunday	Monday–Thursday	Friday–Sunday	Monday–Thursday	Friday–Sunday
Chicago	$85.00	56.1%	51.1%	63.4%	61.7%	62.3%	56.8%
Dallas	90.00	55.5	57.4	63.2	58.7	60.2	58.1
Denver	90.00	61.5	57.4	67.8	59.2	63.5	58.8
Detroit	90.00	68.4	61.5	70.2	60.2	69.3	61.4
New Orleans	90.00	68.4	56.4	71.4	62.4	70.4	58.8
Phoenix	85.00	68.4	47.7	73.2	51.4	71.2	49.2
San Francisco	95.00	75.2	76.0	80.2	73.5	78.2	75.5
Average	89.29	64.8%	58.2%	69.9%	61.0%	67.9%	59.8%
Weekly average—7 sites			62.9%		67.4%		65.6%
Weekly average—all sites			61.5%		64.7%		63.7%

Profitability vs. loss

© high weekend and week (tourism)   *competition*

Advertising, Sales, and Public Relations

Corporate accesses each Royale Suite 2 percent of room revenues for national advertising. This is used to position Royale Suites, provide information about its features and locations, and promote the toll-free reservations number. Media includes national TV, consumer and business magazines, airline flight magazines, and travel trade publications.

Each Royale Suite location is responsible for any national or local advertising featuring its specific property. Media rates for magazines and newspapers

Media Selections

EXHIBIT 7 Media rates and circulation

Magazine	Rate	Circulation	CPM (cost per 1,000 circulation)
Time—national	$120,130	4,339.029	$ 27.69
Time—eastern	63,290	1,457,910	43.41
Time—national business	73,500	1,679,998	43.75
Newsweek—national	100,980	3,180,011	31.75
Newsweek—eastern	39,278	951,000	41.30
Newsweek—national business	42,460	753,043	56.38
New Yorker	32,275	622,123	51.88
Business Week—national	56,700	889,535	63.74
Business Week—northeast	21,210	199,316	106.41
Business Week—mid-Atlantic	14,380	131,813	109.09
Fortune—national	40,900	668,972	61.14
Fortune—northeast	19,360	160,135	120.90
Fortune—mid-Atlantic	11,500	85,175	135.02
Forbes	45,550	743,533	61.26
Baltimore Magazine	4,760	55,442	85.86
The Wall Street Journal—national	99,384	1,835,713	54.14 b&w
The Wall Street Journal—eastern	43,956	757,483	58.03 b&w
Baltimore Sun—morning	11,241	238,533	47.13 b&w

Rates: Color, full-page ads, one insertion.

under consideration are given in Exhibit 7. Ann addressed her concerns about advertising:

> We have to develop a plan that creates a favorable awareness in the minds of our target market segments. An opening kick-off is a must and then we must sustain interest and expand awareness through the rest of the year. Our budget is limited so we should be very creative with our public relations for the opening. It's important that we're noticed among all the other attractions here.
>
> I'm also concerned about our sales effort. Salary and expenses will average $50,000 per salesperson. This includes a car and quite a bit of travel. We should be able to trade some travel with the airlines. However, we must be much more specific about our target market segments before we allocate our budget between advertising and salespersons. Are we a business hotel or are we aggressively going after other segments? Help me to define the targets and I'll define the promotional plan.

Financial Analysis and Final Marketing Plan

Steve had produced a first cut at an income statement based on these initial ideas of the market situation and marketing mix (Exhibit 8). "This just isn't good enough. Most other units are averaging over 10 percent profits as a percent of revenues and several are at 15 percent."

Bill concurred, "I know we've done a lot of work on this project and now we have to concentrate and focus our efforts on a specific marketing plan that provides a realistic, reasonable return to Royale Suites. This is a good location and I know we can build a top performer. Let's see how we can improve this."

CPU = selling price − Variable costs

Breakeven = Total Fixed Costs / cpu
analysis

Prob James
1-(914) 631-0544

projected
Fake

EXHIBIT 8 <u>Pro forma income statement for new Royale Suite Hotel</u>

2,400,000 / 98,93 × 138.79 = $3,366,986.76

Summary

Average daily rate =	$113.59	$138.79
Pre-tax income =	$515,460	
Percent of revenues =	3.6%	
Occupancy rate =	62.6%	58.4%
Number of rooms	325	

	Monday–Thursday	Friday	Saturday	Sunday	Average
1 → Average daily rate	$120.00	$105.00	$105.00	$105.00	$113.59 138.79
2 → Occupancy rate (est.)	66.0% 61.25%	58.0% 57.45%	58.0% 57.45%	58.0% 57.45%	62.58% 58.4%
Days	209	52	52	52	365
Variable costs					
Housekeeping	$30.00 per room per day				
3 → Breakfast	$ 4.00 per room per day				
4 → Happy hour	$ 1.00 per room per day				
Advertising charge	2.0% of room revenues				
Computer charge	1.5% of room revenues				

} (roughly $40 p/r) + (3.5% of room revenue)

	Percentage of revenue	Annual total
Revenues		
Rooms	58.7%	$ 8,467,290
Food	25.0	3,606,171
Beverages	10.0	1,442,468
Other (telephone, gifts, newspapers, etc.)	6.3	908,755
Total	100.0%	$14,424,685

weighted avg. selling price

	Percentage of revenue	
Expenses		
Rooms		
Variable costs		
Housekeeping	15.4%	$ 2,227,095
Advertising charge	1.2	169,346
Computer charge	0.9	127,009
Food & beverages		
Fixed costs	16.6	2,400,000
Variable costs (varies directly as percentage of total revenue)	10.5	1,514,592
Breakfast/Happy Hour	2.6	371,183
Undistributed expenses		
Administration	10.4	$ 1,500,000
5 → Marketing	5.5	800,000
Operations/Maintenance	10.4	1,500,000
Other (telephone, property tax, etc.)	9.0	1,300,000
Depreciation	13.9	2,000,000
Total	96.4	$13,909,225
Income before taxes	3.6	$ 515,460

Salesforce and/or advertising expenses

not outrageous

Notes: Those rows numbered 1 through 5 on the left can be revised.

1 & 2 Average daily rates and occupancy rates are weighted average of all available rates.

3 & 4 Breakfast and Happy Hour costs must include all expected costs. These rows can also be used to include any other variable costs in your market plan. Specify these to the right of your cost.

5 Includes all advertising and salesforce costs. This row can also be used to include any other fixed costs in your market plan. Specify these to the right of the cost.

[handwritten: Don't charge the same rate for all rooms (discounting)]

Appendix A Yield Management Pricing*

[handwritten: high season. low season]

Airline deregulation, coupled with large computer reservations systems, encouraged the development of the first computerized yield management systems. The principle of yield management is recognition of the price sensitivities of specific market segments. Ideally as many full-fare seats as possible are sold and then unfilled seats are sold at decreasingly lower prices until occupancy approaches 100 percent and profits are maximized. Competition ensures that full fares will seldom be achieved for 100 percent of capacity. Therefore, a block of lower-fare seats can be made available for advance purchase. Seat inventory is monitored to expand or reduce this block of seats before the advance reservations deadline or to open them again closer to flight time. This requires computers to manage the seat as a perishable commodity. Some large airlines make over 30,000 fare changes daily.

The yield management system must have specific rules to match prices to the demands of different segments. These can include services provided, time of day for the flight, day of week, length of stay, how far in advance the ticket is purchased, and other factors. Penalties are often required to minimize high-price segments' use of low-price tickets. These are generally advance payment and loss of all or part of the fare when canceling.

Airlines, like many services, have low variable costs. Any seat priced above variable costs contributes to fixed costs or profits. Empty seats are lost contribution. Low variable costs permit significant added contribution, even from deeply discounted seats. Frequent flyer awards only cost an airline the variable cost of the seat provided the awards do not displace a paying fare. Thus, travel restrictions are placed on free seat awards.

Yield management pricing has been adopted by communications companies, banks, car rental companies, hotels, and other service firms.

Hotel Room Yield Management

Relihan (1989) describes yield management applied to hotel rooms. Hotel guests can be grouped into a wide variety of market segments. At the most general level, business and leisure segments must be served. The leisure segment tend to plan ahead, booking earlier than the business segment, and are more price sensitive. Business consumers often are unable to book ahead and are more concerned with availability of a room than price. The hotel must accurately forecast demand to maximize the contribution produced by these segments. The basis for this is accurate reservations history information.

Reservations history can provide the occupancy rate as a function of the average room rate for the total property and for specific market segments. An

---

* Walter J. Relihan, ''The Yield-Management Approach to Hotel-Room Pricing,'' *The Cornell Hotel and Restaurant Administration Quarterly* (May 1989), pp. 40–45.

EXHIBIT A-1   Revenues and occupancy as a function of average room rate

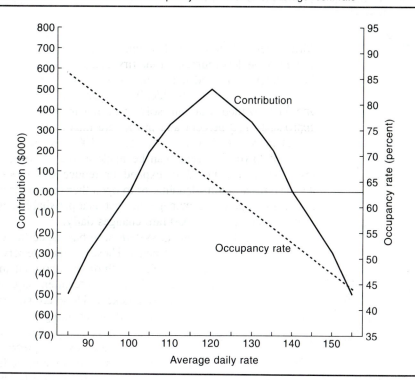

example of occupancy rate as a function of average room rate is given in Exhibit A-1. Occupancy rates and average room rates can be entered into an income statement to estimate the expected total contribution as shown in Exhibit A-1. In this example, contribution is maximized at an average room rate of $120 with an expected occupancy rate of 65 percent. Break-even occurs at any rate between $100 and $140. However, profits are very sensitive to room rates at this hotel and decline rapidly at rates other than $120. Lower rates produce low unit contribution margins and higher rates drive away too many consumers.

Case 29

Techtronics Limited*

In late 1993, the FCC is expected to decide on the broadcast standard for high-definition television (HDTV) in the United States. Subsequently, manufacturers of HDTV sets expect the first consumer sets to be available about two years later. Mr. Mark Leeds, the founder and president of Techtronics Limited (TL), has committed a significant amount of time and resources to TL's new HDTV product and is now faced with a major pricing decision with respect to it. "Based on the new technologies developed in our labs, I believe Techtronics Limited is in a strong position to compete in the market. However, I haven't been able to develop an effective pricing strategy," Mr. Leeds exclaimed.

Company History

Techtronics Limited was founded in White Plains, New York, in 1970 by Mr. Leeds. Mr. Leeds, an electrical engineer, founded TL to manufacture and market products that incorporated inventions he had developed while earning his PhD at Columbia University. In recent years, TL's revenues have been mostly derived from sales to the military of video screen televisions, having screen sizes from 8 to 10 feet diagonally. Sales revenues grew from $250,000 in 1970 to $35 million in 1992. Profits in 1992 were $4.7 million.

HDTV Project

The end of the Cold War has brought about a reduction in military spending. As a result, Mr. Leeds is looking for ways to diversify to ensure future viability, and he believes HDTV set production is one such way. Because Techtronics Limited has been producing video screen TVs for a number of years, it finds itself in a strong position to make the transition to HDTV set production. Additionally, TL has been experimenting with various digital data compression

---

* This case was written by Brian Murray and Thomas C. Kinnear. Copyright © 1993 by Thomas C. Kinnear.

techniques in order to enhance the speed and quality of its fax machines. Leeds expects the new technology to be very similar in its application. Since the company's inception, TL has prided itself on technological innovation for the high-end video market. Mr. Leeds expounded on the new patented innovation that he feels will give TL an initial competitive edge:

> Our lab, in conjunction with Columbia University, has developed a breakthrough in eliminating the edge effect. Presently, reception worsens the farther away from the broadcast tower the set is located. The edge effect refers to the digital signal limitation of getting a crystal-clear picture or no picture at all depending on the strength of the signal. Where the signal cuts out also depends partly on the weather. Thus, sets in outlying areas may suddenly go blank. This work will allow our sets to be marketed to consumers in rural areas or areas with volatile weather patterns.

High Definition Television

Under the present analog system, a wave is converted to 525 horizontal lines, which comprise the picture. Due to inefficiencies inherent with this process, broadcasters are forced to lower the resolution to about 350 lines in order to produce a continuous picture. These inefficiencies also produce the ghosts or double images that sometimes appear. Conversely, the new HDTV system is all digital. A series of 1s and 0s are transmitted to sets equipped to interpret this code. Additionally, over 1,000 horizontal lines per screen are going to be transmitted 30 or 60 times per second (the standard has not yet been set) for increased definition equivalent to 35 mm film. Moreover, the new HDTV format enables manufacturers to employ a greater screen aspect ratio (the ratio of the screen's width to its height). The new ratio of 16:9 as compared to the previous standard's 4:3 removes the box perception of the current television and allows standard 35 mm movies to be viewed uncropped. Thus, a viewer will see more of the picture at a clarity level of more than twice what is currently offered. By employing a digital signal, the sound quality will be akin to that of a compact disc. Overall, the viewer will ultimately feel more a part of the program. This is especially true for sporting events.

It should be noted that detractors of HDTV technology point out that in order to appreciate the enhanced definition, sets must be at least 32 inches across. Moreover, studies have concluded that the average viewer cannot notice the effects of HDTV from 9 feet away, a typical viewing distance.

This new technology will soon be replacing the existing system, and the FCC has mandated the eventual extinction of our present system. By 2008, broadcasters will be switched to a completely digital signal. Until then, broadcasters will broadcast in both digital and analog with a greater percentage of programs produced for HDTV as sets become widely available. Consumers unwilling or unable to purchase HDTV sets will be able to purchase a converter box, at a nominal price, which will allow their old sets to receive the digital signals.

Consequently, television manufacturers will eventually convert or be forced out. Presently, major television manufacturers like Sony, Mitsubishi, Thompson, and Zenith are among the best positioned to enter the U.S. HDTV market, due to the fact that they already make high definition televisions for the Japanese market. This market, however, uses a different standard for the HDTV signal. Thus, the manufacturers are still required to make major adjustments in production for the U.S. market. TL, being a small company with related technological and production experience, can quickly move into set production without incurring the large switching costs a larger manufacturer may face. Moreover, it is expected that other low-cost manufacturers, such as Korean manufacturers, will enter the market as HDTV becomes more affordable to the consumer.

Costs

Mr. Leeds expects that TL's direct manufacturing costs will vary depending on the volume produced. Specifically, he believes direct labor costs will fall at higher production levels because of increased automation of the process and improved worker skills. Likewise, less waste is expected, due to automation and will lower material costs. Exhibit 1 presents the estimates. The equipment costs necessary to automate the product process are $90,000 to produce between 0 and 5,000 units, an additional $120,000 to produce 5,001 to 10,000 units, and an additional $170,000 to produce between 10,001 and 20,000 units. The useful life of the equipment is set at five years. Moreover, R&D expenses are estimated at one to two million dollars per year. Because other competitors have begun compensating for edge effects in a less cost effective manner, Mr. Leeds is confident that TL's production costs are substantially below current competitors. Mr. Leeds is unwilling to produce over 20,000 units per year in the first few years due to the limited cash resources of the company to support inventories.

EXHIBIT 1   Estimated production costs of TL's HDTV sets

Volume	0–5000	5,000–10,000	10,001–20,000
Raw materials	$ 480	$460	$410
Direct labor	540	320	115
Total direct costs	$1,020	$780	$525

* R&D is estimated at $1–$2 million.

Market Studies

Despite the fact that Mr. Leeds believes that the initial market for HDTVs is going to be in the commercial sector, especially bars and hotels, he feels that establishing a long-term position in the consumer market will afford a much greater potential. With this in mind, Mr. Leeds has hired a small economic research consulting firm to perform a consumer study on the likely reactions to alternative retail prices for the set. After extensively interviewing potential HDTV purchasers and examining the sales and pricing histories of similar products, the consultants have concluded that TL's sets would be highly price elastic across the range of prices from $500 to $5,000, both in the primary and secondary senses. They also reported the estimated price elasticity of demand in the range to be between 4.0 and 6.5.

Pricing

Mr. Leeds relates the following situation facing him: "In the Japanese market, only a few thousand were sold in the first year. Manufacturers have been forced, due to this lack of sales, to cut prices from the $30,000–$40,000 range to the $5,000–$10,000 range. I believe that when HDTV sets are introduced into the U.S. market, the initial median price will be around $3,000." Experts feel that by the late 1990s the price will come down to around $1,000, at which price the general public will begin to purchase HDTV sets.

In terms of numbers, Zenith projects one million sets could be sold in the first two years of production. Other, more conservative, estimates predict HDTV set makers won't sell their millionth set until seven or eight years after introduction. This 1 percent of the market benchmark will then be reached in about the same amount of time it took color television. The long-term outlook projects that HDTV sets will have penetrated between 25–56 percent of the consumer market by 2008.

Furthermore, Mr. Leeds figures that about 50 percent of the suggested retail selling price will go to wholesaler and retail margins. Subsequently, he is considering a number of different pricing options to ensure profitability. "My marketing staff has given me valid arguments for pricing anywhere from above Sony to below the impending Korean products," he says.

Case 30 _____

Big Sky of
Montana, Inc.*

Introduction

Karen Tracy could feel the pressure on her as she sat at her desk late that April afternoon. Two weeks from today she would be called on to present her recommendations concerning next year's winter season pricing policies for the Big Sky of Montana, Inc.—room rates for the resort's accommodation facilities as well as decisions in the skiing and food service areas. The presentation would be made to a top management team from the parent company, Boyne U.S.A., which operated out of Michigan.

"As sales and public relations manager, Karen, your accuracy in decision making is extremely important," her boss had said in his usual tone. "Because we spend most of our time in Michigan, we'll need a well-based and involved opinion."

It'll be the shortest two weeks of my life, she thought.

Background: Big Sky and Boyne U.S.A.

Big Sky of Montana, Inc., was a medium-sized destination resort[1] located in southwestern Montana, 45 miles south of Bozeman, and 43 miles north of the west entrance to Yellowstone National Park. Big Sky was conceived in the early 1970s and had begun operation in November 1974.

The 11,000-acre, 2,000-bed resort was separated into 2 main areas: Meadow and Mountain Villages. The Meadow Village (elevation 6,300 feet) was located 2 miles east of the resort's main entrance on U.S. 191 and 7 miles

---

* This case was prepared by Anne Senausky and Professor James E. Nelson for educational purposes only. It is designed for classroom purposes and not for purposes of research nor to illustrate either effective or ineffective handling of administrative problems. Some data are disguised. Copyright © 1978 by the Endowment and Research Foundation at Montana State University. Used with permission.

[1] Destination resorts were characterized by on-the-hill lodging and eating facilities, a national market, and national advertising.

from the ski area. The Meadow Village had an 800-bed capacity in the form of 4 condominium complexes (ranging from studios to 3-bedroom units) and a 40-room hostel for economy lodging. Additional facilities included an 18-hole golf course, 6 tennis courts, a restaurant, post office, a convention center with meeting space for up to 200 people, and a small lodge serving as a pro shop for the golf course in the summer and cross-country skiing in the winter.

The Mountain Village (elevation 7,500 feet) was the center of winter activity, located at the base of the ski area. In this complex was the 204-room Huntley Lodge offering hotel accommodations, 3 condominium complexes (unit size ranged from studio to 3-bedroom), and an 88-room hostel for a total of 1,200 beds. The Mountain Mall was also located here, next to the Huntley Lodge and within a five-minute walk of 2 of the 3 condominium complexes in the Mountain Village. It housed ticket sales, an equipment rental shop, a skier's cafeteria, two large meeting rooms for a maximum of 700 persons (regularly used as sack lunch areas for skiers), two offices, a ski school desk, and ski patrol room, all of which were operated by Boyne. Also in this building were a delicatessen, drug store/gift shop, sporting goods store/rental shop, restaurant, outdoor clothing store, jewelry shop, a T-shirt shop, two bars, and a child day-care center. Each of these independent operations held leases, due to expire in two to three years.

The closest airport to Big Sky was located just outside Bozeman. It was served by Northwest Orient and Frontier Airlines with connections to other major airlines out of Denver and Salt Lake City. Greyhound and Amtrak also operated bus and train service into Bozeman. Yellowstone Park Lines provided Big Sky with three buses daily to and from the airport and Bozeman bus station (cost was $4.40 one way, $8.40 round trip), as well as an hourly shuttle around the two Big Sky villages. Avis, Hertz, National, and Budget offered rent-a-car service in Bozeman with a drop-off service available at Big Sky.

In July 1976 Boyne U.S.A., a privately owned, Michigan-based operation, purchased the Huntley Lodge, Mountain Mall, ski lifts and terrain, golf course, and tennis courts for approximately $8 million. The company subsequently invested an additional $3 million into Big Sky. Boyne also owned and operated four Michigan resort ski areas.

Big Sky's top management consisted of a lodge manager (in charge of operations within the Huntley Lodge), a sales and public relations manager (Karen), a food and beverage manager, and an area manager (overseeing operations external to the lodge, including the mall and all recreational facilities). These four positions were occupied by persons trained with the parent company; a fifth manager, the comptroller, had worked for pre-Boyne ownership.

Business figures were reported to the company's home office on a daily basis and major decisions concerning Big Sky operations were discussed and approved by "Michigan." Boyne's top management visited Big Sky an average of five times annually, and all major decisions such as pricing and advertising were approved by the parent for all operations.

The Skiing

Big Sky's winter season usually began in late November and continued until the middle of April, with a yearly snowfall of approximately 450 inches. The area had 18 slopes between elevations of 7,500 and 9,900 feet. Terrain breakdown was as follows: 25 percent novice, 55 percent intermediate, and 20 percent advanced. (Although opinions varied, industry guidelines recommended a terrain breakdown of 20 percent, 60 percent, and 20 percent for novice, intermediate, and advanced skiers, respectively.) The longest run was approximately three miles in length; temperatures (highs) ranged from 15 to 30 degrees Farenheit throughout the season.

Lift facilities at Big Sky included two double chairlifts, a triple chair, and a four-passenger gondola. Lift capacity was estimated at 4,000 skiers per day. This figure was considered adequate by the area manager, at least until the 1980–81 season.

Karen felt that the facilities, snow conditions, and grooming compared favorably with those of other destination resorts of the Rockies. "In fact, our only real drawback right now," she thought, "is our position in the national market. We need more skiers who are sold on Big Sky. And that is in the making."

The Consumers

Karen knew from previous dealings that Big Sky, like most destination areas, attracted three distinct skier segments: local day skiers (living within driving distance and not utilizing lodging in the area); individual destination skiers (living out of state and using accommodations in the Big Sky area); and groups of destination skiers (clubs, professional organizations, and the like).

The first category was comprised typically of Montana residents, with a relatively small number from Wyoming and Idaho. (Distances from selected population centers to Big Sky are presented in Exhibit 1.) A 1973 study of four Montana ski areas performed by the advertising unit of the Montana department of highways characterized Montana skiers as:

1. In their early 20s and males (60 percent).
2. Living within 75 miles of a ski area.
3. From a household with two skiers in it.
4. Averaging $13,000 in household income.
5. An intermediate to advanced ability skier.
6. Skiing five hours per ski day, 20 days per season locally.
7. Skiing four days away from local areas.
8. Taking no lessons in the past five years.

Karen was also aware that a significant number of day skiers, particularly on the weekends, were college students.

EXHIBIT 1

A. Population centers in proximity to Big Sky (distance and population)

City	Distance from Big Sky (miles)	Population (U.S. 1970 Census)
Bozeman, Montana	45	18,670
Butte, Montana	126	23,368
Helena, Montana	144	22,730
Billings, Montana	174	61,581
Great Falls, Montana	225	60,091
Missoula, Montana	243	29,497
Pocatello, Idaho	186	40,036
Idaho Falls, Idaho	148	35,776

B. Approximate distance of selected major U.S. population centers to Big Sky (in air miles)

City	Distance to Big Sky*
Chicago	1,275
Minneapolis	975
Fargo	750
Salt Lake City	375
Dallas	1,500
Houston	1,725
Los Angeles	975
San Francisco	925
New York	2,025
Atlanta	1,950
New Orleans	1,750
Denver	750

* Per passenger air fare could be approximated at 20 cents per mile (round trip, coach rates).

Destination, or nonresident skiers, were labeled in the same study as typically:

1. At least in their mid-20s and males (55 percent).
2. Living in a household of three or more skiers.
3. Averaging near $19,000 in household income.
4. More an intermediate skier.
5. Spending about six hours per day skiing.
6. Skiing 11–14 days per season with 3–8 days away from home.
7. Taking ski school lessons.

Through data taken from reservation records, Karen learned that individual destination skiers accounted for half of last year's usage based on skier days.[2] Geographic segments were approximately as follows:

---

[2] A skier day is defined as one skier using the facility for one day of operation.

Upper Midwest (Minnesota, Michigan, North Dakota)	30 percent
Florida	20 percent
California	17 percent
Washington, Oregon, Montana	15 percent
Texas, Oklahoma	8 percent
Other	10 percent

Reservation records indicated that the average length of stay for individual destination skiers was about six or seven days.

It was the individual destination skier who was most likely to buy a lodging/lift package; 30 percent made commitments for these advertised packages when making reservations for 1977–78. Even though there was no discount involved in this manner of buying lift tickets, Karen knew that they were fairly popular because it saved the purchaser a trip to the ticket window every morning. Approximately half of the individual business came through travel agents, who received a 10 percent commission.

The third skier segment, the destination group, accounted for a substantial 20 percent of Big Sky's skier day usage. The larger portion of the group business came through medical and other professional organizations holding meetings at the resort, as this was a way to "combine business with pleasure." These groups were typically comprised of couples and individuals between the ages of 30 and 50. Ski clubs made up the remainder with a number coming from the southern states of Florida, Texas, and Georgia. During the 1977–78 season, Big Sky drew 30 ski clubs with membership averaging 55 skiers. The average length of stay for all group destination skiers was about four or five days.

A portion of these group bookings were made through travel agents, but the majority dealt directly with Karen. The coordinator of the professional meetings or the president of the ski club typically contacted the Big Sky sales office to make initial reservation dates, negotiate prices, and work out the details of their stay.

The Competition

In Karen's mind Big Sky faced two types of competition, that for local day skiers and that for out-of-state (i.e., destination) skiers.

Bridger Bowl was virtually the only area competing for local day skiers. Bridger was a "nonfrills," nonprofit, and smaller ski area located some 16 miles northeast of Bozeman. It received the majority of local skiers including students at Montana State University, which was located in Bozeman. The area was labeled as having terrain more difficult than that of Big Sky and was thus more appealing to the local expert skiers. However, it also had much longer lift lines than Big Sky and had recently lost some of its weekend business to them.

Karen had found through experience that most Bridger skiers usually "tried" Big Sky once or twice a season. Season passes for the two areas were mutually honored at the half-day rate for an all-day ticket, and Big Sky occasionally ran newspaper ads offering discounts on lifts to obtain more Bozeman business.

For out-of-state skiers, Big Sky considered its competition to be mainly the destination resorts of Colorado, Utah, and Wyoming. (Selected data on competing resorts is presented in Exhibit 2.) Because Big Sky was smaller and newer than the majority of these areas, Karen reasoned, it was necessary to follow an aggressive strategy aimed at increasing its national market share.

EXHIBIT 2 Competitors' 1977–1978 package plan rates,* number of lifts, and lift rates

	Lodge double (2)†	Two-bedroom condo (4)	Three-bedroom condo (6)	Number of lifts	Daily lift rates
Aspen, Colo.	$242	$242	$220	19	$13
Steamboat, Colo.	230	230	198	15	12
Jackson, Wyo.	230	242	210	5	14
Vail, Colo.	230	242	220	15	14
Snowbird, Utah	208	none	none	6	11
Bridger Bowl, Mont.	(no lodging available at Bridger Bowl)			3	8

* Package plan rates are per person and include seven nights lodging, six lift tickets (high season rates).

† Number in parentheses denotes occupancy of unit on which price is based.

Present Policies

Lift Rates

It was common knowledge that there existed some local resentment concerning Big Sky's lift rate policy. Although comparable to rates at Vail or Aspen, an all-day lift ticket was $4 higher than the ticket offered at nearby Bridger Bowl. In an attempt to alleviate this situation, management at Big Sky instituted a $9 "chair pass" for the 1977–78 season, entitling the holder to unlimited use of the three chairs, plus two rides per day on the gondola, to be taken between specified time periods. Because the gondola served primarily intermediate terrain, it was reasoned that the chair pass would appeal to the local, more expert skier. A triple chair serving the bowl area was located at the top of the gondola, and two rides on the gondola would allow those skiers to take ample advantage of the advanced terrain up there. Otherwise, all advanced terrain was served by another chair.

However, if Big Sky was to establish itself as a successful, nationally prominent destination area, Karen felt the attitudes and opinions of all skiers must be carefully weighed. Throughout the season she had made a special effort to grasp the general feeling toward rates. A $12 ticket, she discovered, was thought to be very reasonable by destination skiers, primarily because Big Sky was predominantly an intermediate area and the average destination skier was of intermediate ability; also because Big Sky was noted for its relative lack of lift lines, giving the skier more actual skiing time for the money. "Perhaps we should keep the price the same," she thought, "we do need more business. Other destination areas are likely to raise their prices and we should look good in comparison."

Also discussed was the possible abolition of the $9 chair pass. The question in Karen's mind was if its elimination would severely hurt local business or would it sell an all-lift $12 ticket to the skier who had previously bought only a chair pass. The issue was compounded by an unknown number of destination skiers who opted for the cheaper chair pass too.

Season-pass pricing was also an issue. Prices for the 1977–78 all-lift season pass had remained the same as last year, but a season chair pass had been introduced which was the counterpart of the daily chair lift pass. Karen did not like the number of season chair passes purchased in relation to the number of all-lift passes and considered recommending its abolition as well as an increase in the price of the all-lift pass. "I'm going to have to think this one out carefully," she thought, "because skiing accounted for about 40 percent of our total revenue this past season. I'll have to be able to justify my decision not only to Michigan but also to the Forest Service."

Price changes were not solely at the discretion of Big Sky management. As is the case with most larger western ski areas, the U.S. government owned part of the land on which Big Sky operated. Control of this land was the responsibility of the U.S. Forest Service, which annually approved all lift pricing policies. For the 1976–77 ski season, Forest Service action kept most lift rate increases to the national inflation rate. For the 1977–78 season, larger price increases were allowed for ski areas which had competing areas near by; Big Sky was considered to be such an area. No one knew what the Forest Service position would be for the upcoming 1978–79 season.

To help her in her decision, an assistant had prepared a summary of lift rates and usage for the past two seasons (Exhibit 3).

Room Rates

This area of pricing was particularly important because lodging accounted for about one third of the past season's total revenue. It was also difficult because of the variety of accommodations (Exhibit 4) and the difficulty in accurately forecasting next season's demand. For example, the season of 1976–77 had been unique in that a good portion of the Rockies was without snow for the initial months of the winter including Christmas. Big Sky was fortunate in receiving as much snow as it had, and consequently many groups and individuals who were originally headed for Vail or Aspen booked in with Big Sky.

Pricing for the 1977–78 season had been made on the premise that there would be a good amount of repeat business. This came true in part but not as

EXHIBIT 3

A. 1977–78 lift rates and usage summary (136 days operation)

Ticket	Consumer cost	Skier days*	Number season passes sold	
Adult all-day all-lift	$ 12	53,400		640,800
Adult all-day chair	9	20,200		181,800
Adult half day	8	9,400		75,200
Child all-day all-lift	8	8,500		68,000
Child all-day chair	5	3,700		18,500
Child half day	6	1,200		7,200
Hotel passes†	12/day	23,400		280,800
Complimentary	0	1,100		
Adult all-lift season pass	220	4,300	140	30,800
Adult chair season pass	135	4,200	165	22,275
Child all-lift season pass	130	590	30	3,900
Child chair season pass	75	340	15	1125
Employee all-lift season pass	100	3,000	91	9100
Employee chair season pass	35	1,100	37	1295

B. 1976–77 lift rates and usage summary (122 days operation)

Ticket	Consumer cost	Skier days	Number season passes sold	
Adult all-day	$ 10	52,500		525,000
Adult half day	6.50	9,000		58,500
Child all-day	6	10,400		62,400
Child half day	4	1,400		5,600
Hotel passes†	10/day	30,500		305,000
Complimentary	0	480		0
Adult season pass	220	4,200	84	18,480
Child season pass	130	300	15	1,950
Employee season pass	100	2,300	70	7000

* A skier day is defined as one skier using the facility for one day of operation.
† Hotel passes refers to those included in the lodging/lift packages.

983930

EXHIBIT 4

A. Nightly room rates,* 1977–1978

	Low season range	High season range	Maximum occupancy
Huntley Lodge			
Standard	$ 42–62	$ 50–70	4
Loft	52–92	60–100	6
Stillwater Condo			
Studio	40–60	45–65	4
One-bedroom	55–75	60–80	4
Bedroom w/loft	80–100	90–100	6
Deer Lodge Condo			
One-bedroom	74–84	80–90	4
Two-bedroom	93–103	100–110	6
Three-bedroom	112–122	120–130	8
Hill Condo			
Studio	30–40	35–45	4
Studio w/loft	50–70	55–75	6

EXHIBIT 4 *(concluded)*

B. Nightly room rates, 1976–1977

	Low season range	High season range	Maximum occupancy
Huntley Lodge			
Standard	$ 32–47	$ 35–50	4
Loft	47–67	50–70	6
Stillwater Condo			
Studio	39–54	37–52	4
One-bedroom	52–62	50–60	4
Bedroom w/loft	60–80	65–85	6
Deer Lodge Condo			
One-bedroom	51–66	55–70	4
Two-bedroom	74–94	80–100	6
Three-bedroom	93–123	100–130	8
Hill Condo			
Studio	28–43	30–45	4
Studio w/loft	42–62	45–65	6

* Rates determined by number of persons in room or condominium unit and do not include lift tickets. Maximums for each rate range apply at maximum occupancy.

much as had been hoped. Occupancy experience had also been summarized for the past two seasons to help Karen make her final decision (Exhibit 5).

As was customary in the hospitality industry, January was a slow period and it was necessary to price accordingly. Low season pricing was extremely important because many groups took advantage of these rates. On top of that,

EXHIBIT 5

A. 1977–1978 Lodge-condominium occupancy (in room-nights*)

	December (26 days operation)	January	February	March	April (8 days operation)
Huntley Lodge	1,830	2,250	3,650	4,650	438
Condominiums†	775	930	1,350	100	90

B. 1976–1977 Lodge-condominium occupancy (in room-nights)

	December (16 days operation)	31 January	28 February	31 March	April (16 days operation)
Huntley Lodge	1,700	3,080	4,525	4,300	1,525
Condominiums‡	600	1,000	1,600	1,650	480

C. Lodge-condominium occupancy (in person-nights§)

December 1977 (1976)	January 1978 (1977)	February 1978 (1977)	March 1978 (1977)	April 1978 (1977)
7,850 (6,775)	9,200 (13,000)	13,150 (17,225)	17,900 (17,500)	1,450 (4,725)

* A room-night is defined as one room (or condominium) rented for one night. Lodging experience is based on 124 days of operation for 1977–78 while Exhibit 3 shows the skiing facilities operating 136 days. Both numbers are correct.
† Big Sky had 92 condominiums available during the 1977–78 season.
‡ Big Sky had 85 condominiums available during the 1976–77 season.
§ A person-night refers to one person using the facility for one night.

groups were often offered discounts in the neighborhood of 10 percent. Considering this, Karen could not price too high, with the risk of losing individual destination skiers, nor too low, such that an unacceptable profit would be made from group business in this period.

Food Service

Under some discussion was the feasibility of converting all destination skiers to the American Plan, under which policy each guest in the Huntley Lodge would be placed on a package to include three meals daily in a Big Sky-controlled facility. There was a feeling both for and against this idea. The parent company had been successfully utilizing this plan for years at its destination areas in northern Michigan. Extending the policy to Big Sky should find similar success.

Karen was not so sure. For one thing, the Michigan resorts were primarily self-contained and alternative eateries were few. For another, the whole idea of extending standardized policies from Michigan to Montana was suspect. As an example, Karen painfully recalled a day in January when Big Sky "tried on" another successful Michigan policy of accepting only cash or check payments for lift tickets. Reactions of credit card carrying skiers could be described as ranging from annoyed to irate.

If an American Plan were proposed for next year, it would likely include both the Huntley Lodge Dining Room and Lookout Cafeteria. Less clear, however, were prices to be charged. There certainly would have to be consideration for both adults and children and for the two independently operated eating places in the Mountain Mall (see Exhibit 6 for an identification of eating places in the Big Sky area). Beyond these considerations, there was little else other than an expectation of a profit to guide Karen in her analysis.

The Telephone Call

"Profits in the food area might be hard to come by," Karen thought. "Last year it appears we lost money on everything we sold." (See Exhibit 7.) Just then the telephone rang. It was Rick Thompson, her counterpart at Boyne Mountain Lodge in Michigan. "How are your pricing recommendations coming?" he asked. "I'm about done with mine and thought we should compare notes."

"Good idea, Rick—only I'm just getting started out here. Do you have any hot ideas?"

"Only one," he responded. "I just got off the phone with a guy in Denver. He told me all of the major Colorado areas are upping their lift prices one or two dollars next year."

"Is that right, Rick? Are you sure?"

"Well, you know nobody knows for sure what's going to happen but I think it's pretty good information. He heard it from his sister-in-law who works in Vail. I think he said she read it in the local paper or something."

EXHIBIT 6 Eating places in the Big Sky area

Establishment	Type of service	Meals served	Current prices	Seating	Location
Lodge Dining Room*	A la carte	Breakfast	$2–5	250	Huntley Lodge
		Lunch	2–5		
		Dinner	7–15		
Steak House*	Steak/lobster	Dinner only	6–12	150	Huntley Lodge
Fondue Stube*	Fondue	Dinner only	6–10	25	Huntley Lodge
Ore House†	A la carte	Lunch	.80–4.00	150	Mountain Mall
		Dinner	5–12		
Ernie's Deli†	Deli/restaurant	Breakfast	1–3	25	Mountain Mall
		Lunch	2–5		
Lookout Cafeteria*	Cafeteria	Breakfast	1.50–3.00	175	Mountain Mall
		Lunch	2–4		
		Dinner	3–6		
Yellow Mule†	A la carte	Breakfast	2–4	75	Meadow Village
		Lunch	2–5		
		Dinner	4–8		
Buck's T-4†	Road house restaurant/bar	Dinner only	2–9	60	Gallatin Canyon (2 miles south of Big Sky entrance)
Karst Ranch†	Road house restaurant/bar	Breakfast	2–4	50	Gallatin Canyon (7 miles north of Big Sky entrance)
		Lunch	2–5		
		Dinner	3–8		
Corral†	Road house restaurant/bar	Breakfast	2–4	30	Gallatin Canyon (5 miles south of Big Sky entrance)
		Lunch	2–4		
		Dinner	3–5		

* Owned and operated by Big Sky of Montana, Inc.
† Independently operated.

EXHIBIT 7 Ski season income data (percent)

	Skiing	Lodging	Food and beverage
Revenue	100.0	100.0	100.0
Cost of sales:			
Merchandise	0.0	0.0	30.0
Labor	15.0	15.9	19.7
Maintenance	3.1	5.2	2.4
Supplies	1.5	4.8	5.9
Miscellaneous	2.3	0.6	0.6
Operating expenses	66.2	66.4	66.7
Net profit (loss) before taxes	11.9	7.0	(25.2)

''That doesn't seem like very solid information,'' said Karen. ''Let me know if you hear anything more, will you?''

''Certainly. You know, we really should compare our recommendations before we stick our necks out too far on this pricing thing. Can you call me later in the week?'' he asked.

''Sure, I'll talk to you the day after tomorrow; I should be about done by then. Anything else?''

''Nope—gotta run. Talk to you then. Bye,'' and he was gone.

''At least I've got some information,'' Karen thought, ''and a new deadline!''

Case 31

Procter & Gamble Inc.: Downy Enviro-Pak*

In February 1989, Grad Schnurr, the brand manager for Downy fabric softener at Procter & Gamble (P&G) Inc., needed to work fast to develop plans to launch a refill pouch called an Enviro-Pak for the Downy product line. The introduction of such packaging would result in a reduction in the solid waste created by the Downy fabric softener. Several key decisions had to be made regarding pricing and promotion. Senior management had a keen interest in this project, especially after seeing the success of Loblaws's Green Product line. The environment was now a significant concern to consumers, and P&G Inc. wanted to be the first major consumer goods company in the market with their response.

Company History

Procter & Gamble was founded in Cincinnati, Ohio, in 1837 when William Procter, a candlemaker, and James Gamble, a soap maker, formed a partnership that grew to become a leading international company. By 1988, P&G was selling more than 160 brands in 140 countries and was a global leader in household cleaning, health care, personal care, and food product markets. Total sales exceeded $20 billion in 1988. P&G's leading brands include Tide laundry detergent, Pampers diapers, Ivory soap, Downy fabric softener, Crest toothpaste, Crisco oil, Duncan Hines baking mixes, and Vicks cold care products.

Procter & Gamble Inc. opened its first Canadian plant in 1915 in Hamilton, Ontario. It subsequently added three manufacturing sites in Belleville and Brockville, Ontario, and Pointe Claire, Quebec. P&G Inc. experienced substantial growth during the 1980s, with net sales doubling between 1978 and 1988; 1988 sales exceeded $1.2 billion, with net income of $78.9 million.

* This case was prepared by Janet Lahey, MBA student, and Chris Lane under the supervision of Professor Adrian B. Ryans for the sole purpose of providing material for class discussion at the Western Business School. Certain names and other identifying information may have been disguised to protect confidentiality. It is not intended to illustrate either effective or ineffective handling of a managerial situation. Any reproduction, in any form, of the material in this case is prohibited except with the written consent of the School. Copyright 1990 © The University of Western Ontario. Used With permission.

P&G Inc. was organized into four divisions: Laundry and Cleaning Products, Health and Beauty Care, Food, and Paper Products. In an effort to push down decision making and increase responsiveness to the market, the company was organized on a category basis within each division (e.g., fabric softeners within the Laundry and Cleaning Products division). Each category had managers from Marketing, Finance, Sales, Product Supply, and Marketing Research assigned to it.

Marketing was organized on a brand management basis, with a brand manager and one or two assistant managers concentrating on the business of one product/brand, such as Tide detergent or Downy fabric softener. Promotions and projects within a brand were executed by business teams, which involved the other functional managers responsible for the category. During significant new product launches or promotions, these teams would meet every three or four weeks to review the critical path and discuss their progress.

Downy

Downy was a popular liquid fabric softener used in the washing machine to soften clothes, remove static from clothes, and leave them with a fresh scent. In early 1989, regular Downy was being sold in 1-liter, 1.5-liter, and 3-liter plastic jugs, and concentrated Downy was being sold in 500-milliliter, 1-liter, and 2-liter sizes. Overall, Downy was the number two brand in Canada in the liquid fabric softener category with a 12 percent share of the market. Its major competition consisted of a similar product called Fleecy, manufactured by Colgate-Palmolive, as well as fabric softener dryer sheets, which Procter & Gamble produced. There was little growth in this market segment, and competition usually took place on a price or incremental improvement (scent, efficacy) basis.

Pricing

The 3-liter bottle of Downy generated a contribution margin of 23 percent and was sold directly to the retail trade at $5.99. The average retail shelf price of $7.30 reflected typical retail trade margin levels of 18 percent (calculated on retail price). When Downy was on deal, the retail shelf price would fall to about $5.99 (retailers would still receive an 18 percent margin on the deal price). Downy appeared to be priced at a premium versus its competition, but on a price-per-use basis was on par with the major competitor.

Promotion

The 1989 Downy marketing plan included several promotions and incentives at both the consumer and trade levels. Events were scheduled to take place approximately every two months and would generally last four weeks. Approximately 70 percent of Downy was sold to the trade on deal.

Environmental Concern

In 1989, the environment had become a significant issue to Canadian consumers. David Nichols of Loblaws gained celebrity status when he launched an innovative line of "Green Products," which claimed to be "environmentally friendly." In Ontario alone, Loblaws sold more than $5 million of Green Products. It was clear that these products had a wide appeal. Business magazines were running articles concerning environmental management on a regular basis. One environmental concern, which was the primary focus of several lobby groups and which could be most readily addressed by consumers, was solid waste.

Landfill sites in urban communities like Toronto were projected to be full by the mid-90s. This posed a serious problem for government officials in determining locations for new sites, since "NIMBY" (not in my back yard) protests by the residents close to proposed landfill locations were increasingly effective. People were becoming aware of how much solid waste was being buried in the ground. As a result, some communities had started up "Blue Box" curbside recycling programs, which were run by the government and partially funded by industry. Household residents stored particular types of waste, such as newspapers, soft drink bottles, and tin cans in a blue plastic box, which were collected and sorted by municipal operators. The overwhelming success of these programs, with participation rates over 80 percent, indicated that citizens were highly concerned about protecting their environment and were willing to make an effort to reduce the amount of solid waste being sent to landfill sites.

Government Action

The Ontario Government had legislated new regulations for the soft drink industry, under the Environmental Protection Act, requiring specific percentages of recyclable bottles. It had also stated a goal of a 25 percent reduction in the use of landfill sites by 1992. Other industries were speculating that the provincial government would soon require funding from them for recycling programs and were aware that legislation similar to the soft drink industry might also follow. Ontario was seen to be the leading province in dealing with environmental issues. Other provinces were expected to introduce similar programs after they had been proven in Ontario.

Procter & Gamble's Environmental Policy

P&G Inc. considered itself to be a community leader in terms of being a responsible business organization that contributed to the well-being of the environment. By 1989, it had already undertaken a number of environmental initiatives, including:

1. Using recycled materials for P&G product cartons and shipping containers. Laundry detergent cartons were made of 100 percent recycled paper.

2. Introducing a paper recycling program in the corporate head office.
3. Eliminating heavy metals from printing inks to facilitate safer incineration.

P&G Inc.'s efforts in the solid waste area were a major responsibility of a division general manager and the director of product development. The corporate policy followed the generally accepted ranking of waste management priorities: source reduction, reuse, and recycling.

European Enviro-Paks

In early 1989, Procter & Gamble Inc. was receiving consumer complaints regarding solid waste at an increasing rate. Disposable diapers were a particular area of concern. Calls about the environment had doubled in frequency over the past few months. P&G subsidiaries in Germany, Switzerland, and France had recently introduced ''stand-up'' pouches as refills for previously purchased bottles of Downy. These pouches (a type of Enviro-Pak) significantly reduced the solid waste generated by the Downy product. Grad Schnurr decided to review the results of the European launches to help him develop a strategy for a Canadian introduction (see Exhibit 1).

EXHIBIT 1 Procter & Gamble Inc.: Downy Enviro-Pak

	European Enviro-Pak results	
	Downy Enviro-Pak market share	Enviro-Pak share of Downy business
Germany	11.2%	26%
France	2.3	14
Switzerland	4.1	19
Austria	3.1	31
Spain	0.7	12
Italy	0.7	8

Source: Company records.

Product

A number of market research studies conducted in Europe indicated that the success of the pouch could be attributed primarily to its convenience and cost relative to the bottled Downy. Packages that reduced the amount of solid waste could generate further savings to German consumers, who were faced with financial penalties for excess garbage disposal.

Promotion

In Germany, the Downy pouch had been launched with substantial consumer and trade promotions, including in-store refill demonstrations and give-aways, trade samples followed by telephone calls for orders, shopping bag advertising, trade incentives for display, and direct delivery of display pallets.

EXHIBIT 2   Procter & Gamble Inc.: Downy Enviro-Pak

	Downy sales to the trade in Canada	
	Shipments (000 cases)*	*Market share (in percentage of dollar sales)*
1988		
July	79	
August	72	13.8%
September	91	
October	78	12.6
November	95	
December	69	12.5
1989		
January	139	
February	96	12.6
March†	89	
April†	70	14.2
May†	73	
June	100	11.8

* 3-litre Downy was packed 6 bottles to a case.

† Forecast.

Source: Company records.

Pricing

The most popular package size for Downy in Europe was a 4-litre bottle. The European pouch had been originally priced at a 5 percent discount to this bottled version with very disappointing repurchase results. The problem stemmed from the promotional price of the 4-liter bottle, which often made the consumer price of the pouch more expensive. The trade was not reducing the pouch prices because they wished to retain the good margins they provided. P&G conducted a test market in one city with the pouch priced at a 15 percent discount to the bottle on a per-usage basis. This resulted in a significant volume improvement, with the pouch reaching a market share of 17 percent versus its previous share of 10 percent.

Share Results and Cannibalization

The pouch had been introduced in Germany and had achieved an 11 percent market share (see Exhibit 1). Although this was accompanied by a drop in the partner 4-litre size, the overall market share for Downy grew, taking Downy's share from 20 percent to 25 percent after the pouch was launched. Grad Schnurr wondered whether the same effect would occur in Canada, and what implications this had for the pricing of the pouch.

EXHIBIT 3   Procter & Gamble Inc.: Downy Enviro-Pak, proposed package

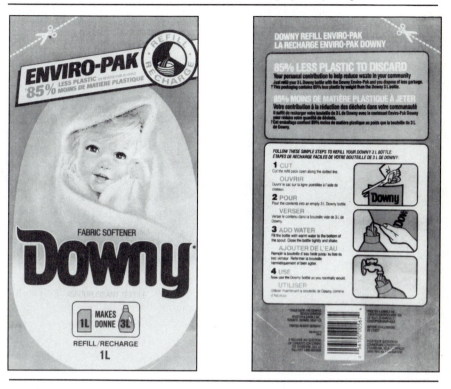

The Downy Enviro-Pak

The Downy pouch or Enviro-Pak provided a significant reduction in solid waste after use, containing 85 percent less plastic than the 3-litre bottle it would refill. The pouch was similar to a plastic milk bag, but had a gusseted bottom so it could stand upright on the shelf. A consumer would cut the corner of the pouch off and then pour the product through a funnel into an empty 3-litre bottle. He or she would then add two litres of water, shake the bottle, and have three litres of fabric softener ready for use.

Grad Schnurr thought the Downy Enviro-Pak offered benefits for both consumers and the trade. Consumers would be attracted to the product for two reasons. First, by using the Enviro-Pak, they would be reducing the amount of household solid waste they generated. Second, the price could be lower than that of the regular bottle. Grad Schnurr recognized that the pouch represented a small inconvenience to consumers, as they had to do some preparation before they could use the product. Some consumers would also be concerned about spillage when they were refilling the bottle. These factors would need to be addressed through the Enviro-Pak's price and promotion plan.

The trade would also benefit in two ways. The pouches would attract environmentally conscious shoppers to their stores, away from competitors who did not carry such products. Also, the unique design of the Enviro-Pak provided more efficient use of space versus the bottled Downy. This second feature would provide decreased retailer handling and inventory costs.

Competitive Activity

Downy's three major competitors had also launched refill versions in Europe. No such activity had taken place in North America, but Canada would be a logical target for the next expansion, given the growing concern about the environment. However, Mr. Schnurr was unsure as to how applicable the German market results would be in predicting the response to the new package in Canada.

The logistics of the product launch also remained to be worked out. Given the likelihood of competitive activity in developing a more environmentally friendly package for Downy fabric softener, Grad Schnurr wasn't sure whether he should conduct a test market first or launch the Enviro-Pak in parts of Canada immediately. This decision was further complicated with trade rumours that Colgate-Palmolive was about to launch an environmental package. It would be much tougher trying to get retailers to list the Enviro-Paks if they already carried competitive versions. The brand that was able to introduce its environmental package first would gain an enviable reputation as a leading force in fighting the war on solid waste.

Manufacturing Issues

The manufacturing business team members estimated that their production schedule could support an August launch in Ontario and Quebec. These provinces were chosen for a number of reasons, including rising environmental awareness, potential volume, distribution time from plant, and competitive activity. The Hamilton plant estimated that it would take them an additional four months to get enough volume to fill the distribution pipeline and support ongoing shipments for the rest of the country. The cost of a packing line capable of producing 300,000 cases[1] annually of Enviro-Paks was estimated at $600,000.

Given the unique nature of this product, there was a high degree of uncertainty about the shipment forecasts. The last thing Grad Schnurr wanted was to have an overwhelming response to the Enviro-Pak with orders that P&G could not fill due to lack of supply.

Pricing

Grad Schnurr knew it would be vital to maintain the pouch price point below the comparable price of the 1.5-litre and 3-litre bottles. The pouch design provided

---

[1] Each case would contain 12 Enviro-Paks.

a significant savings in the cost of goods sold. Its total delivered cost was 10 Percent less than the 3-litre bottle. Grad Schnurr had to consider the total contribution of the brand and how much of this saving should be passed on to the trade and consumer. He was considering two options:

1. *An everyday low retail price ($6.29).* This option would give the Enviro-Pak a discount versus the regular price of the 3-litre size ($7.30) using a cost-per-use comparison. The price to retailers would be either $5.16 or $4.74, depending on whether they were offered an 18 percent or 25 percent margin. The higher margin would help ensure fast acceptance, as retailers traditionally received 18 percent margins on the Downy bottle. To gain additional retailer support during the introductory period, retailers would be given a purchase allowance of $1.00 off each case. This amounted to an eleven-cent saving per bottle.

   In this scenario, there would be no special promotion or discount periods when the regular Downy product was on deal. One concern Grad Schnurr had with this option was that the Enviro-Pak would be priced above the 3-litre bottles when the bottles were featured on promotion at $5.99.

2. *A moderately lower retail price ($7.00), with featuring.* Under this scenario, the trade would be offered discount pricing for the Enviro-Pak coinciding with the regular Downy promotion schedule. The regular trade price would be $5.74, while the promotional offers would provide for a 20 percent discount, or a price of $4.59 for the trade and $5.60 for consumers.

Promotion

Grad Schnurr had put together a preliminary promotion plan, including trade discounts and television, radio, and print advertising. He was also considering using displayable shipping containers. These containers enabled retailers to build a display out of the Downy shipping containers by cutting off the top portion of each container and stacking them at aisle ends. The incremental cost of this style of container would be $0.95 per case.

Given the unique environmental properties of the Downy Enviro-Pak, the launch would need some extra consideration to ensure the product was accepted by environmental groups, as well as the trade and consumers. This was evident in the problems Loblaws had faced when some of its Green Products were disputed by environmental groups such as Pollution Probe and Friends of the Earth. Grad Schnurr wanted to make sure that consumers accepted the Enviro-Pak as a valid environmental package without giving the impression that P&G was exploiting this concern for the sake of profits. He wondered how to go about this tactical issue. Should some of the environmental lobby groups be consulted before the launch? What if they did not support the idea? Would early consultation risk the security of the launch plans? Grad Schnurr need to consult with Barry Smith, P&G Inc.'s public relations manager, to start planning their approach.

Part 8

Public Policy and Ethical Aspects of Marketing

The current environment of the marketing manager is undergoing rapid change and transition. Probably the most noteworthy of these developments, whether for better or for worse, is the increasing pervasiveness of public influences on marketing institutions and decision making. In this context, public influences are generally defined to include different levels of government (acting through legislation, regulation, or moral suasion), organized public groups (the consumerism movement, for example), individual advocates of change, and the force of changing public attitudes and opinion.

The cases in this section seek to develop an improved understanding of some of these trends and developments, and to provide practice for students in rendering decisions in the contemporary environment. The specific objectives of the cases are as follows:

1. To improve capacity for marketing decision making in situations where public influences and ethical considerations are involved.
2. To explore the nature and extent of public and ethical influences on marketing institutions and decision making.
3. To develop conceptual foundations leading to an improved understanding of contemporary developments in marketing.

Approaches to decision making in the area of marketing and public policy are not well established. One possible approach makes the following three assumptions:

1. Marketing and public policy decisions are made in a bargaining arena containing many interest groups.
2. Either explicit or implicit bargaining takes place among the interest groups in this arena whenever a marketing decision involves public influences.

3. Better decisions will be made if the objectives, motivations, and behaviors of each interest group are understood.

With these assumptions in mind, we present an approach to decision making in this area:

1. List and/or diagram the interest groups involved in a particular decision context. Note the interrelationships among them.
2. Identify the behavior of each group.
3. Attempt to explain this behavior by examining the objectives, motivations, and values of the people comprising the groups.
4. Identify what each group stands to lose or gain in the bargaining.
5. Identify what each group might be most willing to give up. What would they most want in return?
6. Based upon this analysis, predict the likely strategies of each group.
7. Make a decision based upon the anticipated reaction of each group to the alternatives you are considering. Be sure to have a contingency in case their reactions are not as you anticipated.

The ethical aspects of marketing are varied and complex. They fall in the so-called gray area of marketing decision making and behavior. The decision or behavior is itself legal, but may not be the right thing to do. The development of an approach to marketing ethics falls beyond the scope of this book. However, in this section we do present cases that explicitly raise ethics questions for marketers. Ethical issues are also present in some of the cases in other parts of the book.

Case 32

Nestlé and the Infant Food Controversy (A)*

In October 1978, Dr. Fürer, managing director of Nestlé S.A., headquartered in Vevey, Switzerland, was pondering the continuing problems his company faced. Public interest groups, media, health organizations, and other groups had been pressuring Nestlé to change its marketing practices for infant formula products, particularly in developing countries. Those groups had used a variety of pressure tactics, including consumer boycott in the United States over the past eight years. Critics of Nestlé charged that the company's promotional practices not only were abusive but also harmful, resulting in malnutrition and death in some circumstances. They demanded Nestlé put a stop to all promotion of its infant formula products both to consumers and health personnel.

Nestlé management had always prided itself on its high quality standards, its efforts to serve the best interests of Nestlé customers, and its contribution to the health and prosperity of people in developing countries. Nestlé management was convinced their infant formula products were useful and wanted; they had not taken the first signs of adverse publicity in the early 1970s very seriously. By 1978, massive adverse publicity appeared to be endangering the reputation of the company, particularly in Europe and North America. Despite support from some health officials and organizations throughout the world, Nestlé management in Vevey and White Plains, New York (U.S.A. headquarters) were seriously concerned. Dr. Fürer had been consulting with Mr. Guerrant, President of Nestlé U.S.A., in an effort to formulate a strategy. Of immediate concern to Nestlé management was the scheduled meeting of the National

* This case was written by Aylin Kunt, research assistant under the supervision of Professors Christopher Gale and George Taucher in 1979. The earlier work of Professor James Kuhn of Columbia University is gratefully acknowledged. This version is a substantial revision of the earlier case and was prepared by Professor Michael R. Pearce. Copyright © 1981 by l'Institut pour l'Etude des Methodes de Direction de l'Enterprise (IMEDE), Lausanne, Switzerland and The School of Business Administration, University of Western Ontario, London, Ontario, Canada. It is intended for classroom discussion and is not intended as an illustration of good or bad management practices.

Council of Churches (USA) in November 1978. On the agenda was a resolution to support the critics of Nestlé who were leading the consumer boycott against Nestlé products in the United States. The National Council of Churches was an important, prestigious organization which caused Nestlé management to fear that NCC support of the boycott might further endanger Nestlé.

Also of concern was the meeting of the World Health Organization (WHO) scheduled in the fall of 1979 to bring together the infant food manufacturers, public interest groups, and the world health community in an attempt to formulate a code of marketing conduct for the industry. Nestlé management, instrumental in establishing this conference, hoped that a clear set of standards would emerge, thus moderating or eliminating the attacks of the public pressure groups.

Dr. Fürer was anxious to clear up what he thought were misunderstandings about the industry. As he reviewed the history of the formula problem, he wondered in general what a company could do when subjected to pressure tactics by activist groups, and in particular, what Nestlé management should do next.

Nestlé Alimentana S.A.

The Swiss-based Nestlé Alimentana S.A. was one of the largest food products companies in the world. Nestlé had 80,000 shareholders in Switzerland. Nestlé's importance to Switzerland was comparable to the combined importance of General Motors and Exxon to the United States. In 1977, Nestlé's worldwide sales approximated 20 billion Swiss francs. Of this total, 7.3 percent were infant and dietetic products; more specifically, 2.5 percent of sales were accounted for by infant formula sales in developing countries.

Traditionally a transnational seller of food products, Nestlé's basic goal had always been to be a fully integrated food processor in every country in which it operated. It aimed at maintaining an important market presence in almost every nation of the world. In each country, Nestlé typically established local plants, supported private farms and dairy herds and sold a wide range of products to cover all age groups. By the end of 1977, Nestlé had 87 factories in the developing countries and provided 35,610 direct jobs. Nestlé management was proud of this business approach and published a 228-page book in 1975 entitled *Nestlé in Developing Countries*. The cover of this book carried the following statement:

> While Nestlé is not a philanthropic society, facts and figures clearly prove that the nature of its activities in developing countries is self-evident as a factor that contributes to economic development. The company's constant need for local raw materials, processing, and staff, and the particular contribution it brings to local industry, support the fact that Nestlé's presence in the Third World is based on common interests in which the progress of one is always to the benefit of the other.

Although it neither produced nor marketed infant formula in the United States, the Nestlé Company, Inc. (White Plains) sold a variety of products such as Nescafé, Nestea, Crunch, Quik, Taster's Choice, and Libby and McNeil & Libby products throughout the United States.

With over 95 percent of Nestlé's sales outside of Switzerland, the company had developed an operating policy characterized by strong central financial control along with substantial freedom in marketing strategy by local managers. Each country manager was held responsible for profitability. Through periodic planning meetings, Nestlé management in Vevey ("the Centre") reviewed the broad strategy proposals of local companies. One area of responsibility clearly reserved by Vevey was the maintenance of the overall company image, although no formal public relations department existed. Marketing plans were reviewed in part by Vevey to see if they preserved the company's reputation for quality and service throughout the world.

Nestlé and the Infant Formula Industry

The international infant formula industry was composed of two types of firms, pharmaceutically oriented ones and food processing ones. The major companies competing in the developing countries were as follows:

Company	Brands
A. Pharmaceutical	
(U.S.) Wyeth Lab (American Home Products)	SMA, S26, Nursoy
(U.S.) Ross Lab (Abbott Laboratories)	Similac, Isomil
(U.S.) Mead Johnson (Bristol-Myers)	Enfamil, Olac, Prosobee
B. Food processing	
(U.S.) Borden	New Biolac
(Swit.) Nestlé	Nestogen, Eledon, Pelargon Nan, Lactogen
(U.K.) Unigate	

In addition to these six firms, there were about another dozen formula producers chartered in 1978 throughout the world.

The basic distinction between pharmaceutically oriented formula producers and food processing oriented producers lay in their entry point into the formula business. In the early 1900s, medical research laboratories of major pharmaceutical firms developed "humanized formulas," leading their parents into marketing such products. Essentially, a humanized formula was a modification of normal cow's milk to approximate more closely human milk. Generally speaking, the food processing companies had begun offering infant food as an extension of their full milk powdered products and canned milk.

As early as the 1800s, Nestlé had been engaged in research in the field of child nutrition. In 1867, Henri Nestlé, the founder of the company and the great-grandfather of infant formula, introduced the first specifically designed, commercially marketed infant weaning formula. An infant weaning formula is basically a cereal and milk mixture designed to introduce solids to a child of five–six months of age.

As of the 1860s, both Nestlé and Borden had been producing sweetened and evaporated milk. Nestlé very quickly recognized the need for better artificial infant food and steadily developed a full line of formula products in the early 1900s (for example, Lactogen in 1921, Eledon in 1927, Nestogen in 1930). Although it was a food processing company, Nestlé's product development and marketing were supervised by physicians.

In the United States in the early 1900s, the infant formula products developed by the medical laboratories were being used primarily in hospitals. Over time, the industry developed the distinction of formula products for "well babies" versus for "sick babies." In the latter category would be included special nutritional and dietary problems, such as allergies to milk requiring babies to have totally artificial formulas made from soybeans. Approximately 2 percent of industry volume was formula designed for "sick babies."

In the late 19th century and early years of the 20th century, Nestlé had developed a commanding position in the sweetened and evaporated milk market in the developing countries (also referred to as "the Third World"). Demand for these products was initially established among European colonials and gradually spread throughout the world and into the rising middle classes in many nations. Nestlé's early marketing efforts focused on switching infant feeding from the previously common use of sweetened and condensed milk to a more appropriate product, humanized infant formula.

By promoting a full product line through doctors (medical detailing), Nestlé achieved an overwhelmingly dominant market position in the European colonies, countries which later became independent "Third World" countries. Meanwhile, most of the competition developed quickly in the industrialized countries, so much so that Nestlé stayed out of the U.S. formula market entirely. Only late in the 1950s did significant intense competition, mainly from American multinationals, develop in Nestlé's markets in developing countries. These markets with their high birth rates and rising affluence became increasingly attractive to all formula producers. After the entry of American competitors, Nestlé's share of markets began to erode.

As of 1978, Nestlé accounted for about one third to one half of infant formula sales in the developing countries while American companies held about one fifth. The size of the total world market for infant formula was not exactly known because data on shipments of infant formula were not separated from other milk products, especially powders. Some sources guesstimated world sales to be close to $1.5 billion (U.S.), half of that to developing countries.

Traditional Methods of Promotion

Several methods had been used over the years to promote infant products in developing countries. Five major methods predominated:

1. Media advertising—all media types were employed including posters in clinics and hospitals, outdoor billboards, newspapers, magazines, radio, television, and loudspeakers on vans. Native languages and English were used.
2. Samples—free sample distribution either direct to new mothers or via doctors was relatively limited until competition increased in the 1960s. Mothers were given either formula or feeding bottles or both, often in a "new mother's kit." Doctors in clinics and hospitals received large packages of product for use while mother and baby were present. The formula producers believed this practice helped educate new mothers on the use of formula products, and hopefully, initiated brand preference. In some instances, doctors actually resold samples to provide an extra source of income for themselves or their institutions.
3. Booklets—most formula marketers provided new mothers with booklets on baby care which were given free to them when they left the hospitals and clinics with their newborn infants. These booklets, such as Nestlé's *A Life Begins,* offered a variety of advice and advertised the formula products and other infant foods, both Nestlé and home made.
4. Milk nurses—milk nurses (also known as mothercraft nurses) were formula producer employees who talked with new mothers in the hospitals and clinics or at home. Originally, they were all fully trained nurses, instructed in product knowledge, then sent out to educate new mothers on the correct use of the new formula products. This instruction included the importance of proper personal hygiene, boiling the water, and mixing formula and water in correct quantities. These became a major part of many firms' efforts; for example, at one time Nestlé had about 200 mothercraft employees worldwide. The majority of milk nurses were paid a straight salary plus a travel allowance, but over time, some were hired on a sales-related bonus basis. Some companies, other than Nestlé, began to relax standards in the 1960s and hired nonnursing personnel who dressed in nurses' uniforms and acted more in a selling capacity and less in an educational capacity.
5. Milk banks—milk bank was the term used to describe a special distribution outlet affiliated with and administered by those hospitals and clinics which served very low income people. Formula products were provided to low income families at much reduced prices for mothers who could not afford the commercial product. The producers sold products to those outlets at lower prices to enable this service to occur.

PAG 23

Nestlé management believed the controversy surrounding the sale of infant formula in developing countries began in the early 1970s. Many international organizations were concerned about the problem of malnourishment of infants in the developing countries of South Asia, Africa, and Latin America. In Bogota (1970) and Paris (1972), representatives of the Food and Agricultural Organization (FAO), the World Health Organization (WHO), UNICEF, the International Pediatric Association, and the infant formula industry including Nestlé all met to discuss nutrition problems and guidelines. The result was a request that the United Nations Protein-Calorie Advisory Group (PAG), an organization formed in 1955, set guidelines for nutrition for infants. On July 18, 1972, the PAG issued Statement 23 on the "Promotion of special foods for vulnerable groups." This statement emphasized the importance of breast-feeding, the danger of over-promotion, the need to take local conditions into account, the problem of misuse of formula products, and the desirability of reducing promotion but increasing education.

Statement 23 included the following statements:

Breast milk is an optimal food for infants and, if available in sufficient quantities, it is adequate as the sole source of food during the first four to six months of age.

Poor health and adverse social circumstances may decrease the output of milk by the mother . . . in such circumstances supplementation of breast milk with nutritionally adequate foods must start earlier than four to six months if growth failure is to be avoided.

It is clearly important to avoid any action which would accelerate the trend away from breast-feeding.

It is essential to make available to the mother, the foods, formulas, and instructions which will meet the need for good nutrition of those infants who are breast-fed.

Nestlé management regarded PAG 23 as an "advisory statement," so management's stance was to see what happened. None of the developing countries took any action on the statement. Nestlé officials consulted with ministers of health in many developing countries to ask what role their governments wished Nestlé to play in bringing nutrition education to local mothers. No major changes were requested.

At the same time, Nestlé Vevey ordered an audit of marketing practices employed by its companies in the developing nations. Based on reports from the field, Nestlé management in Vevey concluded that only a few changes in marketing were required which they ordered be done. In Nigeria, the Nigerian Society of Health and Nutrition asked Nestlé to change its ads for formula to stress breast-feeding. Nestlé complied with this request, and its ads in all developing countries prominently carried the phrase "when breast milk fails, use . . ."

The British Contribution

In its August 1973 issue, the *New Internationalist,* an English journal devoted to problems in developing countries, published an article entitled "The Baby Food

Tragedy.'' This was an interview with two doctors: Dr. R. G. Hendrikse, Director of the Tropical Child Health Course, Liverpool University, and medical researcher in Rhodesia, Nigeria, and South Africa, and Dr. David Morley, Reader in Tropical Child Health, University of London. Both doctors expressed concern with the widespread use of formula among impoverished, less literate families. They claimed that in such cases, low family incomes prevented mothers from buying the necessary amount of formula for their children. Instead, they used smaller quantities of formula powder, diluting it with more water than recommended. Further, the water used was frequently contaminated. The infant thus received less than adequate nutrition, indeed often was exposed to contaminated formula. The malnourished child became increasingly susceptible to infections, leading to diarrheal diseases. Diarrhea meant the child could assimilate even less of the nutrients given to him because neither his stomach nor intestines were working properly. This vicious cycle could lead to death. The two doctors believed that local conditions made the use of commercial infant formula not only unnecessary, but likely difficult and dangerous. Breast-feeding was safer, healthier, and certainly less expensive.

The article, in the opinion of many, was relatively restrained and balanced. However, it was accompanied by dramatic photographs of malnourished black babies and of a baby's grave with a tin of milk powder placed on it. The article had a strong emotional impact on readers and reached many people who were not regular readers of the journal. It was widely reprinted and quoted by other groups. The journal sent copies of the article to more than 3,000 hospitals in the developing nations.

The two doctors interviewed for the article had mentioned Nestlé and its promotional practices. Accordingly, the editors of the *New Internationalist* contacted Nestlé S.A. for its position. The company response was published in the October issue of the *New Internationalist* along with an editorial entitled ''Milk and Murder.''

Nestlé S.A. responded in part as follows:

> We have carefully studied both the editorial and the interviews with Dr. Hendrickse and Dr. Morley published in the August edition of the *New Internationalist*. Although fleeting references are made to factors other than manufacturers' activities which are said to be responsible for the misuse of infant foods in developing countries, their readers would certainly not be in a position to judge from the report the immense socioeconomic complexities of the situation. . . .
>
> It would be impossible to demonstrate in the space of a letter the enormous efforts made by the Nestlé organization to ensure the correct usage of their infant food products, and the way in which the PAG guidelines have been applied by the Nestlé subsidiaries. However, if the editor of the *New Internationalist* (or the author of the article in question) wishes to establish the complete facts as far as we are concerned, then we should be happy to receive him in Vevey on a mutually agreeable date in the near future. We should certainly welcome the opportunity to reply to some of the sweeping allegations made against Nestlé either by implication or by specific references.

The editor of the *New Internationalist* refused the invitation to visit Nestlé's Vevey headquarters. Further they maintained that PAG 23 guidelines were not being observed and did not have any provisions for enforcement.

In March 1974, War on Want published a pamphlet entitled *The Baby Killer*. War on Want was a private British group established to give aid to Third World nations. In particular, they were devoted "to make world poverty an urgent social and political issue." War on Want issued a set of recommendations to industry, governments, the medical profession, and others to deal with the baby formula problem as they saw it. See Exhibit 1.

EXHIBIT 1 War on Want's recommendations

Industry

1. The serious problems caused by early weaning onto breast milk substitutes demand a serious response. Companies should follow the Swedish example and refrain from all consumer promotion of breast milk substitutes in high risk communities.
2. The companies should cooperate constructively with the international organisations working on the problems of infant and child nutrition in the developing countries.
3. Companies should abandon promotions to the medical profession which may perform the miseducational function of suggesting that particular brands of milk can overcome the problems of misuse.

Governments of developing countries

1. Governments should take note of the recommendations of the Protein Advisory Group for national nutrition strategies.
2. Where social and economic conditions are such that proprietary infant foods can make little useful contribution, serious consideration should be given to the curtailment of their importation, distribution, and/or promotion.
3. Governments should ensure that supplies are made available first to those in need—babies whose mothers cannot breast feed, twins, orphans, etc.—rather than to an economic elite, a danger noted by the PAG.

British Government

1. The British Government should exercise a constructive influence in the current debate.
2. The Government should insist that British companies such as Unigate and Glaxo set a high standard of behaviour and it should be prepared to enforce a similar standard on multinationals like Wyeth who export to developing country markets from Britain.
3. The British representative on the Codex Alimentarius Commission should urge the commission to consider all aspects of the promotion of infant foods. If necessary, structural alterations should be proposed to set up a subcommittee to consider broader aspects of promotion to enable the commission to fulfill its stated aims of protecting the consumer interests.

EXHIBIT 1 *(concluded)*

Medical profession

There is a need in the medical profession for a greater awareness of the problems caused by artificial feeding of infants and of the role of the medical profession in encouraging the trend away from breast-feeding.

Other channels

Practicing health workers in the Third World have achieved startling, if limited, response by writing to local medical journals and the press about any promotional malpractices they see and sending copies of their complaints to the companies involved. This could be done by volunteers and others not in the medical profession but in contact with the problem in the field.

In Britain, student unions at a number of universities and polytechnics decided to ban the use of all Nestlés products where they had control of catering following the initial exposé by the *New Internationalist* magazine. Without any clear objective, or coordination, this kind of action is unlikely to have much effect.

However, if the companies involved continue to be intransigent in the face of the dangerous situation developing in the Third World, a more broadly based campaign involving many national organisations may be the result. At the very least, trade unions, women's organisations, consumer groups, and other interested parties need to be made aware of the present dangers.

There is also a clear need to examine on a community scale, how infant feeding practices are determined in Britain today. There is a long history of commercial persuasion, and artificial feeding is now well entrenched.

As has been shown, there are still risks inherent in bottle feeding even in Britain. The available evidence suggests that both mother and child may do better physically and emotionally by breast-feeding. An examination of our own irrational social practices can help the Third World to throw a light on theirs.

The Baby Killer was written by Mike Muller as an attempt to publicize the infant formula issue. Mr. Muller expanded on the *New Internationalist* articles, and in the view of many observers, gave reasonable treatment to the complexity of the circumstances surrounding the use of formula products in the developing countries. On the whole, it was an attack against bottle-feeding rather than an attack against any particular company.

Part of *The Baby Killer* was based on interviews the author had with three Nestlé employees: Dr. H. R. Müller, G. A. Fookes, and J. Momoud, all of Nestlé S.A. Infant and Dietetics Division. These Nestlé officials argued that Nestlé was acting as responsibly as it could. Further, they said that abuses, if they existed, could not be controlled by single companies. Only a drastic change in the competitive system could check abuses effectively. Mr. Muller apparently was not impressed by this argument, nor did he mention Nestlé management's stated willingness to establish enforceable international guidelines for marketing conduct. In *The Baby Killer,* Mr. Muller revealed he was convinced that Nestlé was exploiting the high birth rates in developing countries by encouraging mothers to replace, not supplement, breast-feeding by formula products. Mr. Muller offered as support for his stance a quotation from Nestlé's 1973 Annual Report:

> . . . the continual decline in birth rates, particularly in countries with a high standard of living, retarded growth of the market. . . . In the developing countries our own products continue to sell well thanks to the growth of population and improved living standards.

Dr. Fürer's reaction to *The Baby Killer* was that Mr. Muller had given too much weight to the negative aspects of the situation. Mr. Muller failed to mention, for example, that infant mortality rates had shown very dramatic declines in the developing countries. Some part of these declines were the result of improved nutrition, Dr. Fürer believed, and improved nutrition was partly the result of the use of formula products. Despite his strong belief that Nestlé's product was highly beneficial rather than harmful, Dr. Fürer ordered a second audit of Nestlé's advertising and promotional methods in developing countries. Again, changes were made. These changes included revision of advertising copy to emphasize further the superiority of breast-feeding, elimination of radio advertising in the developing world, and cessation of the use of white uniforms on the mothercraft nurses.

At the same time, on May 23, 1974, WHO adopted a resolution that misleading promotion had contributed to the decline in breast-feeding in the developing countries and urged individual countries to take legal action to curb such abuses.

The Third World Action Group

In June 1974, the infant formula issue moved into Switzerland. A small, poorly financed group called the Third World Action Group located in Bern, the capital of Switzerland, published in German a booklet entitled *Nestlé Kills Babies (Nestlé Totet Kinder)*. This was a partial translation of the War on Want publication *The Baby Killer*. Some of the qualifying facts found in Mr. Muller's booklet were omitted in *Nestlé Kills Babies*, while the focus was changed from a general attack on bottle-feeding to a direct attack on Nestlé and its promotional practices.

Nestlé top management was extremely upset by this publication. Dr. Fürer immediately ordered a follow-up audit of Nestlé's marketing practices to ensure stated corporate ethical standards were being observed. Nestlé management also believed that the infant formula issue was being used as a vehicle by leftist, Marxist groups intent on attacking the free-market system, multinational companies in general, and Nestlé in particular. Internal Nestlé memoranda of the time reveal the material available to management that supported their belief that the issue went beyond infant formula promotion. For example:

Having a closer look at the allies of the AG3W in their actions, we realize that they happen to have the same aim. There are common actions with the leninist progressive organizations (POCH), who are also considered to be pro-Soviet, with the Swiss communist party (PdA) and the communist youth organization (KJV), as well as with the revolutionary marxist alliance (RML). Since the AG3W has tried to coordinate the support of (only pro-communist) liberation movements with representatives of the communist block, it is not surprising that they also participate at the youth festival in Eastern Berlin.[1]

Believing the issue to be clearly legal, Nestlé management brought suit in July 1974 against 13 members of the Third World Action Group and against two newspapers who carried articles about *Nestlé Kills Babies*. Nestlé charged criminal libel, claiming that the company had been defamed because "the whole report charges Nestlé S.A. with using incorrect sales promotion in the third world and with pulling mothers away from breast-feeding their babies and turning them to its products." More specifically, Nestlé management claimed the following were defamatory:

The title "Nestlé Kills Babies."

The charge that the practices of Nestlé and other companies are unethical and immoral (written in the introduction and in the report itself).

The accusation of being responsible for the death or the permanent physical and mental damage of babies by its sales promotion policy (in the introduction).

The accusation that in less developed countries, the sales representatives for baby foods are dressed like nurses to give the sales promotion a scientific appearance.

The trial in Bern provided the Third World Action Group with a great deal of publicity, giving them a forum to present their views. Swiss television in particular devoted much time to coverage of the trial and the issues involved. The trial ended in the fall, 1976. Nestlé management won a judgment on the first of the libel charges (because of lack of specific evidence for the Third World Action Group), and the activists were fined 300 Swiss Francs each. Nestlé management dropped the remaining charges. In his judgment, the presiding judge added an opinion that became well-publicized:

The need ensues for the Nestlé company to fundamentally rethink its advertising practices in developing countries as concerns bottle-feeding, for its advertising practice up to now can transform a life-saving product into one that is dangerous and life-destroying. If Nestlé S.A. in the future wants to be spared the accusations of immoral and unethical conduct, it will have to change its advertising practices.

---

[1] Third World Action Group (AG3W) *Der Zürichbieter*, August 15, 1973.

The Controversy Spreads

While the trial was in process, various interest groups from all over the world became interested and involved in the infant formula controversy. In London, England, Mr. Mike Muller founded the Baby Foods Action Group. Late in 1974, the World Food Conference adopted a resolution recommending that developing-nation governments actively support breast-feeding. The PAG had been organizing a number of international regional seminars to discuss all aspects of the controversy. For example, in November 1974, during the PAG regional seminar in Singapore, the PAG recommended that the infant formula industry increase its efforts to implement Statement 23 and cooperate to regulate their promotion and advertising practices through a code of ethics.

The world health organizations kept up the pressure. In March 1975, the PAG again met:

> to discuss together the problem of deteriorating infant feeding practices in developing countries and to make recommendations for remedying the situation. The early discontinuance of breast-feeding by mothers in low-income groups in urban areas, leading to malnutrition, illness, and death among infants has been a serious concern to all.

In May 1975, WHO at its 14th plenary meeting again called for a critical review of promotion of infant formula products.

In response, representatives of the major formula producers met in Zürich, Switzerland, in May 1975 to discuss the possibility and desirability of establishing an international code of ethics for the industry. Nine of the manufacturers, with the notable exceptions of Borden, Bristol-Myers, and Abbott, created an organization called the International Council of Infant Food Industries (ICIFI) and a code of marketing conduct. This code went into effect November 1, 1975. Some firms also adopted individual codes, including Nestlé, with standards higher than the ICIFI code.

The ICIFI code required that ICIFI members assume responsibility to encourage breast-feeding, that milk nurses be paid on a strict salary basis and wear company uniforms, and that product labels indicate breast milk as the best infant food. At this time, Nestlé began to phase out use of mass media for infant formula in developing countries, but continued to distribute educational materials and product information in the hospitals and clinics. Nestlé management believed such advertising and promotion was of educational value: to ensure proper use of formula and to decrease usage of sweetened and condensed milk for infant feeding.

ICIFI submitted its code of ethics to the PAG who submitted it to a number of third parties. On the basis of their opinions, the PAG refused to endorse the code saying it did not go far enough, that substantial amendments were required. ICIFI rejected these suggestions because of difficult antitrust considerations, so the PAG withheld its approval of the code.

An important exception to ICIFI membership was Abbott Laboratories. While Abbott representatives had attended the meeting that led to the establishment of ICIFI, they decided not to join. Abbott, having recently had difficulties with the U.S. Food and Drug Administration regarding the marketing of cyclamates and artificial sweeteners, felt ICIFI was not an adequate response to the public pressure:

> The most important area is to reduce the impact of advertising on the low-income, poorly educated populations where the risk is the greatest. The ICIFI code does not address this very important issue.
>
> Our company decided not to join ICIFI because the organization is not prepared to go far enough in answering this legitimate criticism of our industry. We feel that for Abbott/Ross to identify with this organization and its code would limit our ability to speak on the important issues.

Abbott acted largely independently of the other producers. Later in 1977, Abbott management announced its intention to commit about $100,000 to a breast-feeding campaign in developing nations and about $175,000 to a task force on breast-feeding, infant formula, and Third World countries.

Developments in the United States

Although Nestlé U.S. neither manufactured nor marketed formula, management found itself increasingly embroiled in the controversy during the mid-1970s. The first major group to bring this matter to the public was the Interfaith Center on Corporate Responsibility (ICCR). The ICCR, a union of 14 Protestant denominations and approximately 150 Catholic orders and dioceses, was a group concerned about the social responsibility behaviour of corporations. The ICCR advised its members on this topic to guide decisions for the members' combined investment portfolio of several billion dollars. Formerly known as the Center of Corporate Responsibility, the ICCR was established under the tax-exempt umbrella of the American National Council of Churches when the U.S. Internal Revenue Service revoked the CCR tax exemption.

The ICCR urged its members to investigate the marketing practices of the leading American formula producers, American Home Products, Abbott Laboratories, and Bristol-Myers. Stockholder groups demanded from these companies, as they were entitled to do by American law, detailed information regarding market shares, promotion and advertising practices, and general company policies concerning the infant formula business.

Nestlé management believed that the ICCR was interested in ideology more than in baby formula. As support, they pointed to a statement made in a January edition of ICCR's *The Corporate Examiner:*

> The motivations, ethos, and operations of transnational corporations are inimical to the establishment of a new economic order. Both justice and stability are undermined in the fulfillment of their global vision.

Perhaps the major vehicle used by ICCR to get attention was a half-hour film entitled *Bottle Babies*. Well-known German filmmaker Peter Krieg began this film shortly after the Bern trial began. Nestlé Vevey management believed that the film was partially sponsored by the World Council of Churches to provide a public defense for the Third World Action Group position. Most of the filming was done in Kenya, Africa, in 1975 in a "documentary" style, although Nestlé management pointed out that the film was scripted and in their opinion, highly emotional and misleading. A letter (Exhibit 2) that Nestlé management later received written by Professor Bwibo of the University of Nairobi supported management's views about the *Bottle Babies* film.

ICCR distributed copies of the *Bottle Babies* film to church groups throughout the United States. Typically, the film was shown to a gathering of church members followed by an impassioned plea to write letters of protest and a request for funds to further the campaign. Since the film singled out Nestlé for attack in its last 10 minutes, Nestlé became symbolic of all that was wrong in the infant formula controversy in the minds of these religious groups. Nestlé management, however, was seldom asked for, or given an opportunity to present, its position on the issues.

While Nestlé felt the growing pressure of *Bottle Babies,* the major American formula producers faced a variety of ICCR-shareholder initiatives. ICCR requested detailed information from American Home Products, Abbott Laboratories, and Bristol-Myers. Each company responded differently.

American Home Products.   After refusing to release all the information ICCR requested, AHP faced a resolution to be included in its proxy statement. ICCR dropped the resolution the day before printing, when AHP management agreed:

To provide the requested information.

To send a report to its shareholders saying that many authorities believe misuse of infant formula in developing countries could be dangerous, that the company promotes breast-feeding while making available formula for mothers who cannot or do not choose to breast-feed, that the company would promote to medical professionals only and that AHP was a member of ICIFI which was developing a voluntary code of promotional practices.

Abbott Laboratories.   After a year and a half of meetings with ICCR, Abbott released most of the information ICCR wanted. Still, to obtain the rest of the data, ICCR shareholders filed a shareholder resolution. This proposal received less than the three percent of the vote required by the Securities and Exchange Commission (SEC) in order to resubmit the proposal at a later time. Thus, it was not resubmitted.

Bristol-Myers.   Bristol-Myers would not cooperate with ICCR so one church shareholder with 500 shares, Sisters of the Precious Blood, filed a

EXHIBIT 2

14th April, 1978

Miss June Noranka
644 Summit Avenue
St. Paul
Minnesota 55105

Dear Miss Noranka:

Following your visit to Kenya and my office I write to inform you, your group, your colleagues, and any other person interested that the film Peter Krieg filmed in this department and the associated teaching areas, did not represent the right aspects of what we participated in during the filming.

The film which was intended to be a scientific and educational film turned out to be an emotional, biased, and exaggerated film—and failed to be a teaching film. It arouses emotions in people who have little chance to check these facts. No wonder it has heated the emotions of the Activists groups in America and I understand now spreading to Europe. I wish I was in an opportunity to be with your groups and we view the film together and I comment.

As a pediatrician, I would like to put on record that I have not seen the Commercial baby food companies pressure anybody to use their brands of milk. As for Nestlé, we have discussed with their Managing Directors, starting much earlier than the time of the film in 1971, as to the best way of approaching baby feeding and discussed extensively advertisement especially the material to be included. The directors have followed our advice and we are happy with their working conditions.

We are interested in the well-being of our children and we are Medical Scientists. So anything of scientific value we will promote but we will avoid imagined exaggerated and distorted views.

I am taking the liberty to copy this letter to Mr. Jones, managing director of Food Specialty in Nairobi who produce and make Nestlé's products here, for his information.

Yours sincerely,

NIMROD O. BWIBO
Professor & Chairman

shareholder resolution in 1975 asking that the information be released. After receiving 5.4 percent of the vote and having aroused the concern of the Ford Foundation and the Rockefeller Foundation, it appeared the resolution would be launched again the next year. In August 1975, Bristol-Myers management published a report "The Infant Formula Marketing Practices of Bristol-Myers Co. in Countries outside the United States." The 1976 proxy included the Sisters' resolution and a statement entitled "Management's Position." The Sisters maintained the statement was false and misleading and filed suit against management; statements appearing in a proxy statement are required by law to be accurate.

In May 1977, a U.S. district court judge dismissed the case, saying the Sisters had failed to show irreparable harm to themselves as the law requires. The judge would not comment on the accuracy of the company's proxy report. The nuns appealed with the support of the SEC. In early 1978, the management of Bristol-Myers agreed to send a report outlining the dispute to all shareholders and to restrictions on company marketing practices including a ban on all consumer-directed promotion in clinics, hospitals, and other public places and a stop to using milk nurses in Jamaica.

In 1977, Abbott management agreed to revise their code of marketing conduct and to eliminate the use of nurses' uniforms by company salespeople despite the fact some were registered nurses.

ICCR and its supporters also persuaded Representative Michael Harrington, Democrat–Massachusetts to cosponsor a federal resolution requiring an investigation of U.S. infant formula producers.

The campaign against the formula producers took on a new dimension in mid-1977. A group called the Third World Institute, led by Doug Johnson at the University of Minnesota, formed the Infant Formula Action Coalition "INFACT" in June 1977. INFACT members were encouraged by ICCR and the Sisters, but felt that significant progress would not be made until Nestlé was pressured to change. INFACT realized that legal and shareholder action against a foreign-based company would be futile, so on July 4, 1977, INFACT announced a consumer boycott against those infant formula companies whose marketing practices INFACT found abusive. Despite the boycott's original target of several companies, Nestlé was the main focal point especially after the other major companies made concessions to ICCR. INFACT began the boycott in front of Nestlé's Minneapolis offices with a demonstration of about 100 people. INFACT urged consumers to boycott over 40 Nestlé products.

Nestlé management in White Plains was not sure what response to take. Nestlé U.S. was not at all involved with infant formula, but was genuinely concerned about the publicity INFACT was getting. Nestlé S.A. management on the other hand originally did not think the boycott campaign would amount to anything, that it was a project of some college kids in the United States based on misinformation about events in other parts of the world.

In September and October 1977, Nestlé senior managers from Vevey and White Plains met with members of INFACT, ICCR, the Ford Foundation, and other interested groups. Nestlé management had hoped to resolve what they thought was a problem of poor communication by explaining the facts. Nestlé management argued the company could not meet competition if it stopped all promotion, which would mean less sales and less jobs in the developing nations. Further, management claimed: ''We have an instructional and educational responsibility as marketers of these products and, if we failed in that responsibility, we could be justly criticized.'' INFACT members stated they found the talks useful in clarifying positions, but concluded Nestlé was unwilling to abandon all promotion of its formula products.

In November 1977, INFACT decided not only to continue the boycott, but also to increase it to a national scale. INFACT held a conference in Minneapolis on November 2–4, for more than 45 organizers from 24 cities. These organizers represented women's groups, college hunger-action coalitions, health professionals, church agencies, and social justice groups. A clearinghouse was established to coordinate boycott efforts and information collection. The group also agreed to assist ICCR in its shareholder pressure campaign and to press for congressional action. Later, INFACT petitioned all U.S. government officials, state and federal, for support of the boycott. On November 21, the Interfaiths Hunger Coalition, a group affiliated with INFACT, demonstrated in front of Nestlé's Los Angeles sales office with about 150 people chanting ''Nestlé kills babies.'' This demonstration received prominent media coverage as did other boycott activities. The combination of INFACT's boycott, ICCR's shareholder efforts, the exhibition of *Bottle Babies,* and the strong support of other U.S. activists (including Ralph Nader, Cesar Chavez, Gloria Steinem, and Dr. Benjamin Spock), resulted in an increasingly high profile for the infant formula controversy, even though Nestlé management believed there had been as yet no adverse effect on sales.

In early 1978, an unofficial WHO working group published the following statement:

> The advertising of food for nursing infants or older babies and young children is of particular importance and should be prohibited on radio and television. Advertising for mother's milk substitutes should never be aimed directly at the public or families, and advertising for ready-made infant food preparations should show clearly that they are not meant for less than three-month-old infants. Publicity for public consumption, which should in any case never be distributed without previous recommendation by the competent medical authority, should indicate that breast milk should always constitute the sole or chief constituent of food for those under three months. Finally, the distribution of free samples and other sales promotion practices for baby foods should be generally prohibited.

Nestlé management met again with INFACT representatives in February 1978. No progress was made in reconciling the two sides. Nestlé management could not accept statements from INFACT such as:

> The corporations provide the product and motivate the people to buy it, and set into motion a process that may cause the death of the baby. The corporations are responsible for that death. When the outcome is death, the charge against the corporation is murder.

Nonetheless, management learned what INFACT wanted:

> Stop all direct consumer promotion and publicity for infant formula.
>
> Stop employing "milk nurses" as sales staff.
>
> Stop distributing free samples to clinics, hospitals, and maternity hospitals.
>
> Stop promoting infant formula among the medical profession and public health profession.

To further publicize their campaign, INFACT representatives and their allies persuaded Senator Edward Kennedy, Democrat–Massachusetts, to hold Senate hearings on the infant formula issue in May 1978. CBS decided to make a TV report of the entire affair. To prepare for the hearings, INFACT organized a number of demonstrations across the United States. At one meeting on April 15, 1978, Doug Johnson said:

> The goal of the Nestlé's Boycott Campaign and of the entire infant formula coalition is to get the multinationals to stop promotion of infant formula. We're not asking them to stop marketing; we're not asking them to pull out of—out of the countries; we're simply asking them to stop the promotion, and in that I think we're—we're in agreement with a number of prestigious organizations. The World Health Organization recently asked the corporations to stop consumer advertising and to stop the use of free samples, and the International Pediatric Association did that several years ago. So, I think we're asking a very reasonable thing: to stop promoting something which is inappropriate and dangerous.

CBS filmed these demonstrations, but did not air them until after the Kennedy hearings.

The Kennedy Hearings and CBS Report

Senator Kennedy was chairman of the Subcommittee on Health and Scientific Research on Infant Nutrition. Both critics and members of the infant formula industry appeared before the Kennedy Committee in May 1978. Nestlé S.A. management decided not to send headquarters management or management from Nestlé U.S. Instead, they asked R. Oswaldo Ballarin, president and chairman of Nestlé, Brazil, to represent Nestlé at the hearings. Dr. Ballarin began with a statement prepared by Nestlé U.S., but Senator Kennedy soon interrupted him as the following excerpt from the testimony indicates:

Dr. Ballarin: United States Nestlé's Company has advised me that their research indicates this is actually an indirect attack on the free world's economic system: a worldwide church organization with its stated purpose of undermining the free enterprise system is at the forefront of this activity.

Senator Kennedy: Now you can't seriously expect . . . [Noise in background: gavel banging] We'll be in order . . . we'll be in order now please. We'll be in order. Uh, you don't seriously expect us to accept that on face value, after we've heard as . . . as you must've, Doctor . . . if I could just finish my question . . . the . . . the testimony of probably 9 different witnesses. It seemed to me that they were expressing a very deep compassion and concern about the well-being of infants, the most vulnerable in this . . . face of the world. Would you agree with me that your product should not be used where there is impure water? Yes or no?

Dr. Ballarin: Uh, we give all the instructions . . .

Senator Kennedy: Just . . . just answers. What would you . . . what is your position?

Dr. Ballarin: Of course not. But we cannot cope with that.

Senator Kennedy: Well, as I understand what you say, is where there's impure water, it should not be used.

Dr. Ballarin: Yes.

Senator Kennedy: Where the people are so poor that they're not gonna realistically be able to continue to purchase it, and which is gonna . . . that they're going to dilute it to a point, which is going to endanger the health, that it should not be used.

Dr. Ballarin: Yes, I believe . . .

Senator Kennedy: Alright, now . . . then my final question is . . . is what do you . . . or what do you feel is your corporate responsibility to find out the extent of the use of your product in those circumstances in the developing part of the world? Do you feel that you have any responsibility?

Dr. Ballarin: We can't have that responsibility, sir. May I make a reference to . . .

Senator Kennedy: You can't have that responsibility?

Dr. Ballarin: No.

Dr. Ballarin's testimony continued (for example of excerpts, see Exhibit 3), but Nestlé management believed little attention was paid to it. Mr. Guerrant, president of Nestlé U.S., was very angry and wrote a letter to Senator Kennedy on May 26, 1978, protesting against the way he had treated Dr. Ballarin (Exhibit 4).

CBS aired its program on July 5, 1978. Again, Nestlé management was upset. In their view CBS had selected portions of the testimonies to make Nestlé management look inept and confused. Mr. Guerrant wrote a letter of protest to CBS president Richard Salant (Exhibit 5).

Following the Kennedy hearings, representatives of Nestlé S.A., Abbott, Bristol-Myers, and American Home Products met privately with Senator Kennedy to explore a suggestion for a further hearing. Meanwhile, the president of ICIFI wrote Kennedy, pointing out that this was an international and not a U.S. domestic issue—and should therefore be discussed at a forum sponsored by WHO. Kennedy accepted ICIFI's suggestion and requested the Director Gen-

EXHIBIT 3   Further excerpts from Dr. Ballarin's testimony

Nestlé recognized that even the best products will not give the desired results if used incorrectly. We, therefore, placed great weight on educational efforts aimed at explaining the correct use of our product. Our work in this field has received the public recognition and approval of the official Pediatric Associations in many countries. Such educational efforts never attempt to infer that our product is superior to breast milk. Indeed, we have devoted much attention to the promotion of breast-feeding, and educational material has always insisted that breast-feeding is best for the baby.

Nevertheless, many factors militate against exclusive breast-feeding in the rapidly growing cities of Brazil as well as other developing countries, and our products are seen today as filling a valid need, just as they did when they were first introduced over 50 years ago. In recognition of this, all such products are subject to strict price control, while in many countries which do not have a local dairy industry, they are classified as essential goods and imported free of duty. In many cases, official agencies establish what they consider to be a fair margin for the manufacturers.

It must be stressed that many problems remain to be solved. Our production is far from reaching the total needs of the population. Hence, many mothers in the poorer population groups continue to supplement breast-feeding with foods of doubtful quality. Owing to the lack of adequate medical services, especially in the rural areas, misuse of any supplement can occur and we are very conscious of the need to improve our efforts. These efforts depend on continued cooperation between the infant food industry and health professionals. We have to be more and more conscious of our responsibility to encourage breast-feeding while researching new foods and safer methods for feeding babies who cannot be exclusively breast-fed. The dilemma facing industry and the health service alike, is how to teach these methods without discouraging breast-feeding.

EXHIBIT 4   Excerpts from Mr. Guerrant's letter to Senator Kennedy

I am angry but more important deeply concerned about the example of our governmental processes exhibited this week by the Human Resources Subcommittee on Health and Scientific Research.

It was the general consensus of several people in the audience that your position toward the manufacturers was "you are guilty until you prove your innocence." Objectivity would have been more becoming, Senator.

Secondly, it seemed equally probable that prior to the hearing the prepared statements were reviewed and you were quite prepared to rebuff Dr. Ballarin on his statement "undermining the free enterprise system." Unaccustomed to television and this type of inquisition, Dr. Ballarin, who appeared voluntarily, was flustered and embarrassed.

Probably, for this gathering, the statement was too strong (though nothing to compare with their theme "Nestlé kills babies") and should have been more subtle. But the point is well made, and your apparent denial of this possibility concerns me.

As you may know, this whole issue gained its greatest momentum a few years ago in Europe fostered by clearly identified radical leftist groups. Their stated purpose is opposition to capitalism and the free enterprise system. I submit that they are not really concerned with infants in the Third World but are intelligent enough to know that babies, especially sick and dying, create maximum emotional re-

EXHIBIT 4 *(concluded)*

sponse. Further, they are clever enough to know that the people most easy to "use" for their campaign, to front for them, are in churches and universities. These are good people, ready to rise against oppression and wrong-doing without, regrettably, truthful facts for objective research. I know, as my father is a retired Presbyterian minister, and I have a very warm feeling toward members of the church, Protestant and Catholic.

People with far left philosophies are not confined to Europe and are certainly represented in many accepted organizations here and abroad. (Please take the time to read the enclosed report of the 1977 Geneva Consultation of the World Council of Churches.) Associated with the World Council is the National Council of Churches, and one of their units is the Interfaith Centre for Corporate Responsibility. One of their major spokespersons appears to be Leah Margulies, who was present in your hearing.

Now, just briefly to the very complex infant food issue. As the U.S. Nestlé Company does not manufacture or sell any infant food products, we are unhappy with the attempted boycott of our products—at least 95 percent of these manufactured in the United States. The jobs and security of about 12,000 good U.S. employees are being threatened.

From our associates in Switzerland, and Nestlé companies in the Third World, we have gathered hundreds of factual documents. Neither Nestlé nor the U.S. companies in this business claim perfection. Companies are comprised of human beings. However, virtually every charge against Nestlé has proved to be erroneous. Distorted "facts" and just pure propaganda have been answered by people with undeniable integrity and technical credentials. Quite some time ago, because of the accusations, Nestlé world headquarters in Switzerland studied every facet of their total infant food business, made immediate changes where warranted and established new and very clear policies and procedures regarding the conduct of this business.

I might add that Nestlé infant foods have undoubtedly saved hundreds of thousands of lives. There is not even one instance where proof exists that Nestlé infant food was responsible for a single death. The products are as essential in the Third World as in the industrialized world. Though the accusers use some statements by apparently qualified people, there is an overwhelming amount of data and number of statements from qualified medical, technical, and government representatives in the Third World confirming Nestlé's position.

At your hearing this week were the same identical charges made against Nestlé and the others years ago. These people will not recognize the changes made in marketing practices nor the irrefutable facts of the real infant health problems in the Third World. They continue to push the U.S. Nestlé boycott and continue to distribute the fraudulent film "Bottle Babies." (Please read Dr. Bwibo's letter enclosed.) Sincere, well-meaning church people continue to be used, as they have not had all the real facts available for analysis.

The above situation made me believe that the organizers must have some motivation for this campaign other than what appears on the surface. If it could possibly be what I think, then our representatives in government should proceed with caution, thorough study, and great objectivity, as your ultimate position can be of critical consequence. I am not a crusader, but I do feel the free enterprise system is best.

EXHIBIT 5 Excerpts from Mr. Guerrant's letter to CBS President Salant

In the first minute of the program the infant formula industry has been tried and convicted of causing infant malnutrition. The remainder of the program is devoted to reinforcing Mr. Myer's conclusion. Tools of persuasion include the emotionality of a needle sticking in a child's head and the uneasy answers of cross-examined industry witnesses who are asked not for the facts but to admit and apologize for their "guilt."

But CBS Reports chose to concentrate on the "rhetoric of concern" and the claims which permeate the rhetoric. Industry's response to the rhetoric is not glamorous but hits into the root causes of infant malnutrition—the poverty, disease, and ignorance existing in the areas of developing and developed countries. Those conditions are not easy for anthropologists, economists, scientists, or medical people to trace or explain. And certainly the reasons for them are not as identifiable as a major corporation. But in 30 minutes Mr. Myers and Ms. Roche identified four companies as a major reason for infant malnutrition.

One way Nestlé has attempted to meet the responsibility is by making capital investments in and transferring technology to the developing countries. Nestlé began this effort in 1921 in Brazil and now has almost 40,000 local employees working in 81 manufacturing facilities in 25 developing countries. Not only does Nestlé have a beneficial impact on those directly employed, the company also encourages and assists the development of other local supporting industries, such as the dairy industry and packaging plants.

Another way Nestlé meets its responsibility is to work with local governments and health authorities in educating consumers. Clinics, pamphlets, posters, books, and product labels emphasize the superiority of breast-feeding, demonstrate proper sanitation and diet for breast-feeding, and show in words and pictures how to correctly use formula products.

Neither of these positive approaches was covered in CBS Reports nor was there mention of the fact that infant mortality has declined worldwide over the past 30 years, nor that lack of sufficient breast milk is a major cause of infant malnutrition, nor that tropical diseases cause millions of deaths per year in developing countries. Any one of these facts would have provided some balance to the Myers-Roche report.

---

eral of WHO to sponsor a conference at which the question of an international code could be discussed.

A consensus emerged that a uniform code for the industry was required and that Kennedy and ICIFI would suggest that WHO sponsor a conference with that aim in mind. The conference would be comprised of WHO officials, ICIFI members and other companies, health and government officials from the developing countries, and all appropriate concerned public groups. WHO accepted the idea and announced the conference date in the fall of 1979. Shortly after Nestlé management met with Kennedy, the National Council of Churches, comprised of about 30 major religious groups in the United States, announced that the question of supporting INFACT and ICCR would be discussed and decided at the NCC national conference in November 1978.

The Situation in October 1978

Dr. Fürer knew all senior Nestlé management felt personally attacked by critics of the industry. Not only was this the first major public pressure campaign ever encountered by Nestlé, but also Nestlé management felt its critics were using unfair tactics. For example, again and again they saw in boycott letters and articles a grotesque picture of a wizened child with a formula bottle nearby. Eventually this picture was traced to Dr. Derrick Jeliffe, an outspoken critic of the industry. He admitted to *Newsweek* he had taken the picture in a Caribbean hospital in 1964. Even though it seemed the media and many respected companies were against Nestlé, Dr. Fürer stated publicly:

> No one has the right to accuse us of killing babies. No one has the right to assert that we are guilty of pursuing unethical or immoral sales practices.

Nonetheless, under U.S. law a company is regarded as a public person which meant that the First Amendment applied; that is, Nestlé could not get legal relief against charges made by the critics unless the company could prove those charges were both wrong and malicious.

Further, Dr. Fürer was struck by the fact that all the demands for change were coming from developed countries. In fact, Nestlé had received many letters of support from people in the developing countries (Exhibit 6). Mr. Ernest Saunders, Nestlé vice president for infant nutrition products summarized his view as follows:

> Government and medical personnel tell us that if we stopped selling infant foods we would be killing a lot of babies.

EXHIBIT 6 Examples of support for Nestlé

1. I have been associated with the medical representatives of Nestlé in Kenya for the last five years. We have discussed on various occasions the problems of artificial feeding, in particular the use of proprietary milk preparations. We have all been agreed that breast-feeding should always come first. As far as I am aware, your representatives have not used any unethical methods when promoting Nestlé products in this country.

   M. L. Oduori, Senior Consultant
   Pediatrician
   Ministry of Health
   Kenyatta National Hospital, Nairobi
   Kenya, Dec. 23, 1974

2. You are not "killing babies," on the contrary your efforts joined with ours contribute to the improvement of the Health Status of our infant population.
   We consider your marketing policies as ethical and as not being opposite to our recommendations. We note with pleasure that you employ a fully qualified nurse and that during discussions with mothers she always encour-

EXHIBIT 6 *(continued)*

ages breast-feeding, recommending your products when only natural feeding is insufficient or fails.

> Dr. Jerry Lukowski
> Chief Gynecologist, Menelik Hospital
> Ethiopia, Dec. 3, 1974

3. Over several decades I have had direct and indirect dealings with your organisation in South Africa in relation to many aspects of nutrition among the nonwhite population who fall under our care, as well as the supply of nutriments to the hospital and peripheral clinics.

    I am fairly well aware of the extent of your Company's contributions to medical science and research and that this generosity goes hand in hand with the highest ethical standards of advertising, distribution of products, and the nutrition educational services which you provide.

    At no time in the past have my colleagues or I entertained any idea or suspicion that Nestlé have behaved in any way that could be regarded as unethical in their promotions, their products or their educational programmes. On all occasions when discussion of problems or amendments to arrangements have been asked for, full cooperation has been given to this department.

    Your field workers have given and are giving correct priorities in regard to breast feeding, and, where necessary, the bottle feeding of infants.

    The staff employed to do this work have shown a strong sense of responsibility and duty towards the public whom they serve, no doubt due to the educational instruction they have themselves received in order to fit them for their work.

> S. Wayburne, Chief Pediatrician
> Baragwanath Hospital
> Associate Professor of Pediatrics,
> Acting Head of Department of
> Pediatrics, University of
> Witwaterbrand/South Africa
> Dec. 18, 1974

4. I have read about the accusation that "Nestlé Kills Babies" and I strongly refute it, I think it is quite unjustifiable.

    On my experience I have never seen any mother being advised to use artificial milk when it was not necessary. Every mother is advised to give breast foods to her baby. It is only when there is failure of this, then artificial foods are advised.

    I, being a working mother have brought up my five children on Nestlé Products and I do not see anything wrong with them. I knew I would have found it difficult to carry on with my profession if I had nothing to rely on like your products.

    Your marketing policies are quite in order as I knew them and they are quite ethical. As they stress on breast milk foods first and if this is unobtainable then one can use Nestlé's Products.

> Mrs. M. Lema, Nursing Officer
> Ocean Hospital
> Dar-es-Salaam/TANZANIA
> Dec. 16, 1974

EXHIBIT 6 *(concluded)*

5. On behalf of the Sisters of Nazareth Hospital, I thank you heartily for your generous contribution in giving us the Nestlé products in a way that we can assist and feed many undernourished children freely cured and treated in our hospital.

   Trusting in your continuous assistance allow me to express again my sincerest thanks, and may God bless you.

   > Nazareth Hospital
   > Nairobi, Kenya
   > September 9, 1978

6. I am very grateful for this help for our babies in need in the maternity ward.

   Another mission has asked me about this milk gift parcels, if there would be any chance for them. It is Butula Mission and they have a health centre with beds and maternity and maternal child health clinics. There is a lot of malnutrition also in that area, so that mothers often do not produce enough milk for their babies. It would be wonderful if you could help them also.

   > Nangina Hospital
   > Medical Mission Sisters
   > Funyula, Kenya
   > June 15, 1976

7. As a doctor who has practiced for 18 years in a developing country, I was angered by the collection of half-truths, judiciously mixed with falsehoods put out by the Infant Formula Action Coalition as reported in the *Newsweek* article on breast-feeding. Whether we like it or not, many mothers cannot or will not resort to breast-feeding. I do not believe that advertising has played any significant part in their decision. It is an inescapable necessity that specific, nutritionally balanced formulas are available. Otherwise, we would witness wholesale feeding with products that are unsuitable.

   I carry no brief for companies like Nestlé, but have always found it to be a company with the highest regard to ethical standards. Infant formulas have saved many thousands of lives. What alternative are their critics proposing?

   > D. C. Williams, M.D.
   > Kuala Lumpur
   > Malaysia

8. Surely, Nestlé is not to blame. There have been similar problems here but through the efforts of the Save the Children Fund and government assistance, feeding bottles can only be purchased through chemists or hospitals by prescription. In this way, the decision of whether to breast-feed or not is decided by qualified personnel.

   I would think that Americans would have better things to do than walk around disrupting commerce with placards.

   > Gail L. Hubbard
   > Goroka, Papua New Guinea

Dr. Fürer also believed that the scientific facts underlying the breast versus bottle controversy were not being given adequate attention (for example, see Exhibit 7) nor were the changes Nestlé and the other companies had made. Nestlé's policies regarding infant formula products were apparently not well known. Exhibit 8 includes excerpts from the latest edition, dated September 1, 1977.

EXHIBIT 7 Examples of supplementary information on breast-feeding versus bottle-feeding

1. Findings of the Human Lactation Center (HLC).

The HLC is a scientific research institute, a nonprofit organization dedicated to worldwide education and research on lactation. The HLC entered the breast/bottle controversy between the infant formula industry and the anti-multinational groups in an attempt to clarify certain issues. Eleven anthropologists, all women, studied infant feeding practices in 11 different cultures, ranging from a relatively urbanized Sardinian village to a very impoverished Egyptian agricultural village. Their findings:

Poverty is correlated with infant morbidity (disease). Child health is associated with affluence.

Infant mortality had decreased in the three decades prior to 1973 when food prices began to escalate.

Breast milk is the best infant food but breast-feeding exclusively for most *undernourished* women in the less developed countries is inadequate beyond the baby's third month. Lack of sufficient food after this time is a major cause of morbidity and mortality whether or not the infant is breast-fed.

Mixed feeding is an almost universal pattern in traditional cultures; that is, breast-feeding and supplementary feeding from early on and often into the second year.

The preferred additional food for the very young child is milk. Most milk is fresh milk, unprocessed.

Most women still breast-feed though many do not. The popular assumption that breast-feeding is being reduced has not been verified.

Third World women with the least amount of resources, time or access to health care and weaning foods, have no choice but to breast-feed.

More than half the infants they bear do not survive due to lack of food for themselves and their children.

Women who are separated from close kin, especially the urban poor, lack mothering from a supportive figure. They find themselves unable to lactate adequately or lose their milk entirely. Without suitable substitutes, their infants die.

Middle class women in the less-developed countries, market women, the elite and professional women are moving towards bottle feeding with infant formula in much the same way women turned from breast to bottle feeding in the western countries.

EXHIBIT 7 *(continued)*

The current literature on breast-feeding in the developing countries is meager. Information on mortality, the incidence of breast-feeding, the content of infant food, and the amount of breast milk, tend to be impressionistic reports by well-meaning western or western trained persons often unaware of the complexities of feeding practices and insensitive to the real-life situation of the mothers. Judgments for action based on these inconclusive data could be dangerous.

Mothers have a sensitive and remarkable grasp of how best to keep their infants alive. Neither literacy nor what has been called "ignorance" determine which infants live and which die except as they are related directly to social class.

In seeking solutions to the problems of infant well-being in the developing world, we must listen to the mothers and involve them in the decisions which will affect their lives.

2. *The Feeding of the Very Young: An Approach to Determination of Policies,* report of the International Advisory Group on Infant and Child Feeding to the Nutrition Foundation, October 1978:

"Two basic requirements of successful feeding are: (1) adequate milk during the first four to six months of life, and (2) adequate complementary foods during the transition to adult diets. It is imperative that all societies recognize these requirements as a major component of nutrition policy. The extent to which mothers are able to meet both of these requirements will vary under different cultural and sociological circumstances. In all societies there will be some proportion of mothers who will not be able to meet them without assistance, and policy must be developed to protect those children who are at risk of malnutrition resulting from inadequacy in either one or both of these basic requirements."

Source: Nestlé memoranda.

EXHIBIT 7 *(concluded)*

Trends in infant mortality:
Developed countries

Trends in infant mortality:
Developing countries

Guide: Art

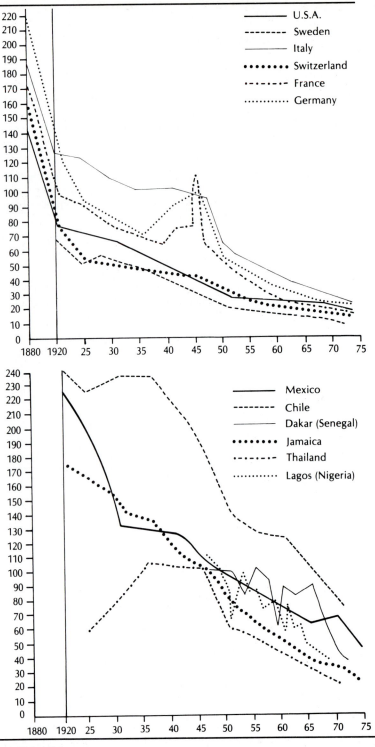

Source: Demographic Yearbook, United Nations.

EXHIBIT 8   Excerpts from Nestlé directives on infant and dietetic products policy

Infant milks

It is recognized that breast milk is the best food for a baby. Our baby milks are therefore not intended to compete with breast milk, but to supplement breast feeding when the mother's own milk can no longer cover the baby's needs or to replace it when mothers cannot, or elect not to breast feed.

Three to four months after birth, the quantities of breast milk produced by the average mother become insufficient to satisfy the growing needs of the baby. The baby needs a supplement of water and food. From this moment on, in the poor communities of developing countries this baby is in danger because water is sometimes polluted and local foods, like plantain or manioc, are nutritionally inadequate. They are starchy foods with little food value and a young baby cannot digest them. Thus the highest infant mortality occurs precisely in areas where babies receive only mother's milk plus a supplement of unboiled local water and/or starchy decoctions.

This is not a Nestlé theory. This is a fact known by every Third World doctor and recently scientifically demonstrated by British researchers working in Africa.

The alternative to traditional local supplement is a properly formulated breast milk substitute, preferably a humanized formula. It is true that there is a risk of misuse, but these risks exist with a local supplement too, although the baby has a better chance of survival when the starting point is of high quality.

It is precisely to reduce the risks of misuse and thereby increase the chances of survival that we had developed over the years a comprehensive programme of information and education: contact with doctors, educative advertising, booklets, nurses; all this had the purpose of making the alternative to local supplements known and ensuring a proper and safe use of our products when needed. Nestlé policies are designed to avoid the unnecessary replacement of breast milk.

The real issue is not breast milk versus formula, as so often pictured, but breast milk plus formula plus education versus traditional foods like manioc.

Products must be in line with internationally recognized nutritional criteria and offer definite consumer benefits.

Distribution policy

It is a rule that PID products are never sold to mothers directly by us; distribution aims at making products available to prescribers and users under optimum safety and price conditions.

Within the limits set by the law and by the distribution structure, we practice mixed distribution (pharmacies and general food stores) and use the normal market channels. On the other hand, dietetic specialties and products designed for delicate or sick babies, which are basically sold on medical prescription, are sold only through pharmacies, unless special local conditions warrant mixed distribution.

Communication policy—direct contact with mothers

Medical representatives must not enter into direct contact with mothers, unless they are authorized to do so in writing by a medical or health authority and provided that they are properly qualified. Films may be shown with the agreement of the medical or public health authorities concerned.

EXHIBIT 8 *(concluded)*

Visits to mothers in their homes are not allowed unless the responsible medical authority has made a written request for a visit to take place.

Personnel policy

The main task of the medical promotion personnel consists in contacting the medical and paramedical professions and hospitals. They are not concerned with direct sales to mothers and cannot sell dietetic products other than, exceptionally and exclusively, to the trade or institutions.

Specialized training must be given to such staff, to enable them to render a genuine service to the medical and paramedical professions and give them scientific and unbiased information on product characteristics and utilization.

No sales-related bonus will be paid to any staff engaged in medical promotion or having direct contact with mothers. If a bonus is to be paid, it must depend on elements other than sales, such as personal qualities and qualifications.

Many members of management believed the attack against Nestlé was ideologically based. They gathered information about and quotations from many of the activist groups to support their position (for example, see Exhibit 9). Whatever their foundation, the critics seemed to Dr. Fürer to be gaining publicity and momentum. INFACT claimed at least 500 separate action committees in the United States, support in about 75 communities in Canada, as well as support in about 10 other countries. "The movement is snowballing," reported Gwen Willens of INFACT. "We're getting over 300 letters of support every day."

As Dr. Fürer consulted with senior management in Nestlé, he wondered what further steps Nestlé might take to deal with the controversy surrounding the marketing of infant formula products in the developing countries.

EXHIBIT 9   Examples of comments concerning the ideology of the activist group

Sue Tafler and Betsy Walker, "Why Boycott Nestlé?" in *Science for the People,* January/February 1978.

Unfortunately, the power in many developing countries is not held by the people themselves, and local ruling elites often want to encourage corporate investment. . . . What the boycott will not do is overthrow capitalism. . . . The boycott can unite well-meaning groups that see themselves as apolitical with more openly political groups. . . . We can have the effect of politicizing others working in the coalition. If Nestlé does make some concessions to the demands of the boycott, the sense of victory can give encouragement to the organizers of the boycott to continue on to larger struggles.

T. Balasusiya, Centre for Society and Religion, Colombo, Sri Lanka, participant at the World Council of Churches meeting, January 1977.

EXHIBIT 9 *(concluded)*

The capitalist system is the main cause of the increasing gap and within that system multinationals are a main form. Ideology of wealth is the practical religion of capitalist society. Churches are legitimizers of the system, so their first job is self-purification. There can be no neutrality between money and God.

Our function is not to judge persons, but we have to judge systems. . . . What alternative solutions do countries propose that have rejected the capitalist system, e.g., USSR, China, Cuba, Tanzania? Capitalism is inherently contradictory to the Gospel.

M. Ritchie, at a conference, "Clergy and Laity Concerned," August 1978.

It's not just on babies, it's not just multinational corporations, it's class conflict and class struggle. Broadening the constituency both of people interested in the infant formula issue . . . how the infant formula campaign and the people there link up completely in terms of support and action with other types of campaigns. . .

I think ultimately what we're trying to do is take an issue-specific focus campaign and move it in conjunction with other issue-specific campaigns into a larger very class-wide very class-conscious campaign and reasserting our power in this country, our power in this world.

Douglas Johnson of INFACT, at an address in Washington, September 1978.

Our hope is that we can use this [boycott] campaign as the forerunner of legislation for control of multinational corporations.

Source: Nestlé internal memoranda.

Case 33

Country Lass Fashions*

As New England regional manager for Country Lass Fashions, Jonathan Frank recognized that he was low man on the totem pole. Having recently earned his masters in retailing from Columbia University, he knew that his opinion was not regarded very highly yet in the organization, but he also knew that his company was in trouble.

Country Lass had been in business for over 30 years. With a reputation for good-quality products, the company's sales had slowly grown to over $9 million. But while its founders understood production and sales, Country Lass exhibited very little understanding of the market. Through ignorance or neglect, it appeared to violate all the standard practices of the industry. Country Lass made no funds available for cooperative advertising, permitted no returns of unsold merchandise, and had a policy of no markdown allowances. Its promotion was limited to advertising in high-circulation national magazines and major metropolitan newspapers. In short, in an industry known for good relations between manufacturers and retailers, Country Lass was conceding nothing.

This negative internal attitude was complicated by external pressures. Foreign producers, with much lower material and labor costs, were flooding the market with high-quality, inexpensive goods. Tariffs designed to keep foreign competitors away from the United States market also drove up the cost of imported fabric and textile machinery. In any event, these tariffs were replete with loopholes and were being scaled down and repealed by the federal government ostensibly to achieve a free-market economy. Finally, popular-priced competitors were offering stylish products which were currently very successful.

In this environment Frank had to try to sell women's fashion goods. Inventory was piling up, especially blouses. Frank decided to take a chance with an idea he had been considering for some time. He had a good working relationship with Mary Blake, fashion editor for the *Boston Times*. If Blake

* This case was prepared by Mort Ettinger and Daniel Lindley of Suffolk University, Boston, Massachusetts. Used with permission.

could write a fashion page featuring Country Lass blouses, Frank was sure he could sell two pages of advertising to retailers who carried Country Lass blouses. Retailers who purchased space would be eager to order blouses in advance of the publicity and tie-in advertising. Fliers could be prepared by the *Times* based on the story and the ads and sent to the retailers for display and distribution in their stores.

After talking with Blake and *Times* advertising manager Art Lester, Frank was sure he was on to something. The *Times* had once been a major newspaper in the Boston area, but it had suffered at the hands of its two major competitors, the *Globe* and the *Herald*. In fact, its single biggest advertiser was Lambert and Vaccaro, a large Boston department store, and one of Country Lass' largest accounts. Frank, Blake, and Lester were convinced that this idea would benefit all parties.

The next task facing Frank was to sell the advertising. The cost of display advertising was $74.65 per column inch; each page contained five 14-inch columns. The cost of two full pages came to $10,451. Frank figured that the top of each page could carry two 2½ by 3½ display ads at $653 each. The rest of each page could be divided into 35 boxes (1 by 1½) and sold for $112 each.

Frank decided to sell the four display ads himself. Convinced that Lambert and Vaccaro would buy, Frank decided to save that store until last. The three remaining major department stores in Boston were easy to sell. Emmanuel's and Truman's did not want to be excluded. Flutey's was eager to be represented if Lambert and Vaccaro would be in the ad. But when Frank called on Muriel Lincoln, the head buyer for Lambert and Vaccaro, he ran into a problem he had not anticipated. Lincoln said she wanted nothing to do with the ad if Flutey's would appear in it.

By now nearly all the small ads had been sold. Many participating advertisers had already received tear sheets of the ad to display on the shopping floor and in dressing rooms of their stores and to send to preferred customers. Frank was in a tough spot. An idea came to him. He walked over to Flutey's and went straight to the buyer's office. "I'm in trouble," he said and explained the problem. Flutey's buyer reacted as he had hoped; she offered to buy the space that had been reserved for Lambert and Vaccaro in addition to the space already purchased.

Frank wasted no time in getting over to the *Boston Times* composing room. Within 30 minutes he had a final mock-up of the ad. Taking a short-cut to his office through Lambert and Vaccaro, Frank ran into Muriel Lincoln. He could not resist showing her the story and the accompanying ad. "Look how impressive this is. And to think, you could have been in it," he told her. She gave him an icy stare as they parted company.

When Jonathan Frank returned to his office there was an urgent phone message to call Art Lester. He could tell there was trouble when Lester's secretary forwarded the call. "I've got bad news," Lester started. "We have to pull the ad. Don't ask me why; I can't tell you. You have to trust me that there are important reasons. Don't take this personally."

Frank could not believe what he was hearing. After arguing, pleading, and, finally, reminding Lester of their close professional relationship over the years, Frank learned that Lincoln had threatened to discontinue advertising with the *Times* if the ad and story ran. By now, inventory had been shipped. Retailers were planning in-store promotions and tie-ins to correspond to the advertising. If no large consumer response materialized, loyal retailers risked getting stuck with a large volume of perishable fashion merchandise, and salespeople risked antagonizing good customers.

Frank made two more phone calls. His attorney advised, ''Never sue a newspaper.'' His insurance broker was only too happy to sell him a $1 million liability policy.

Case 34

California Valley Wine Company*

Introduction

On a March night in 1988, Maxwell Jones, new products/special project manager for California Valley Wine Company, leaned back in his chair in the office headquarters in Fresno, California. He glanced at the clock. It was already 10:30 P.M. on Wednesday. Max had been in the office since morning, but he was not sure that he was any closer to resolving the dilemma. Max had to make a recommendation which would shape the future of California Valley Wine Company (CVWC).

In recent years the company experienced diminishing sales and declining profitability (Exhibit 1). Several new product ideas were under consideration by CVWC management. Max received instructions to make a recommendation on what the new product was to be. For several months Max worked on the new product project and struggled with the decision. He gathered a large amount of information from trade sources, field salespeople, and executives at CVWC. By the end of the week, Max's recommendation was due to the New Product Evaluation Committee.

EXHIBIT 1 Sales and Profit for CVWC, 1980–1987 ($ millions)

Year	1980	1981	1982	1983	1984	1985	1986	1987
Sales	18.2	19.6	21.9	22.0	21.1	21.2	20.9	19.5
Earnings before taxes	2.1	1.8	1.9	1.6	.9	1.0	(.5)	.05

Background of California Valley Wine Company

CVWC was established in early 1934, shortly after the repeal of Prohibition. The founders, two cousins, George and Frank Lombardi, grew table grapes in

---

* This case was prepared by John E. Bargetto, MBA student, and Patrick E. Murphy, professor of marketing, University of Notre Dame. This case is written to facilitate classroom discussion rather than to illustrate either effective or ineffective corporate decision making. Copyright © 1990 by Patrick E. Murphy. Used with permission.

Fresno, California, and saw the sudden demand in wine as a good opportunity to enter the wine business. The Lombardis purchased an old winery that had been vacated during Prohibition and they began fermenting in the fall of 1934. In the early years they sold their wines mainly in barrels to restaurants, hotels, and liquor stores. In 1950 they constructed a major, modern winery on the outskirts of Fresno and planted additional vineyards.

In 1988 CVWC owned 1,600 acres of grapes, mostly Chenin Blanc, Thompson Seedless, and Ruby Cabernet. They marketed the wines in 1.5 and 3.0 liter bottles which retailed for $3.59 and $6.79, respectively. The three wines sold were Chenin Blanc (a white wine made from Chenin Blanc grapes), a Mountain Burgundy (a red wine made from Ruby Cabernet grapes), and a Mountain Rose (a rose wine made from a blend of red wine and Thompson Seedless).

Contemporary Wine Industry Conditions

In recent years the wine business in California (where 90 percent of U.S. wine is produced) experienced particular difficulties. The so-called wine boom of the 1970s, when consumption levels of wine rose steadily, was over; per capita wine consumption recently declined (see Exhibit 2). The highest-ever consumption level occurred in 1985 and 1986, at 2.43 gallons per capita. However, in 1987 for the first time in 25 years, per capita consumption of wine decreased. Max knew well the reasons for the decline: growing health consciousness in society, greater awareness of physical problems associated with alcohol consumption, stiffer DUI laws and a rising drinking age, and the popularity of soft drinks with the younger generation. After 15 years of solid growth, total wine consumption (including coolers) in 1987 slipped to 581 million gallons.

EXHIBIT 2   Apparent wine consumption in the United States 1934–1987

| Year | Population* | | Wine consumption† | | Per capita wine consumption | |
	1,000 Persons	Percent Change	1,000 Gallons	Percent Change	Gallons	Percent Change
1934	126,374	—	32,674	—	0.26	—
1935	127,250	0.7%	45,701	39.9%	0.36	38.5%
1936	128,053	0.6	60,303	32.0	0.47	30.6
1937	128,825	0.6	66,723	10.6	0.52	10.6
1938	129,825	0.8	67,050	0.5	0.52	0.0
1939	130,880	0.8	76,647	14.3	0.59	13.5
1940	131,954	0.8	89,664	17.0	0.68	15.3
1941	133,121	0.9	101,445	13.1	0.76	11.8
1942	133,920	0.6	133,038	11.4	0.84	10.5
1943	134,245	0.2	97,501	−13.7	0.73	−13.1
1944	132,885	−1.0	98,955	1.5	0.74	1.4
1945	132,481	−0.3	93,975	−5.0	0.71	−4.1
1946	140,054	5.7	140,316‡	49.3	1.00‡	40.8
1947	143,446	2.4	96,660‡	−31.1	0.67‡	−33.0
1948	146,093	1.8	122,290	26.5	0.84	25.4

EXHIBIT 2 *(concluded)*

Year	Population* 1,000 Persons	Percent Change	Wine consumption† 1,000 Gallons	Percent Change	Per capita wine consumption Gallons	Percent Change
1949	148,665	1.8	132,567	8.4	0.89	6.0
1950	151,235	1.7	140,380	5.9	0.93	4.5
1951	153,310	1.4	126,514	−9.9	0.83	−10.8
1952	155,687	1.6	137,620	8.8	0.88	6.0
1953	158,242	1.6	140,796	2.3	0.89	1.1
1954	161,164	1.8	142,156	1.0	0.88	−1.1
1955	164,308	2.0	145,186	2.1	0.88	0.0
1956	167,306	1.8	150,039	3.3	0.90	2.3
1957	170,371	1.8	151,881	1.2	0.89	−1.1
1958	173,320	1.7	154,633	1.8	0.89	0.0
1959	176,289	1.7	156,224	1.0	0.89	0.0
1960	179,979	2.1	163,352	4.6	0.91	2.2
1961	182,992	1.7	171,632	5.1	0.94	3.3
1962	185,771	1.5	168,082	−2.1	0.90	−4.3
1963	188,483	1.5	175,918	4.7	0.93	3.3
1964	191,141	1.4	185,625	5.5	0.97	4.3
1965	193,526	1.2	189,677	2.2	0.98	1.0
1966	195,576	1.1	191,176	0.8	0.98	0.0
1967	197,457	1.0	203,403	6.4	1.03	5.1
1968	199,399	1.0	213,658	5.0	1.07	3.9
1969	201,385	1.0	235,628	10.3	1.17	9.3
1970	203,984	1.3	267,351	13.5	1.31	12.0
1971	206,827	1.4	305,221	14.2	1.48	13.0
1972	209,284	1.2	336,985	10.4	1.61	8.8
1973	211,357	1.0	347,481	3.1	1.64	1.9
1974	213,342	0.9	349,465	0.6	1.64	0.0
1975	215,465	1.0	368,029	5.3	1.71	4.3
1976	217,563	1.0	376,389	2.3	1.73	1.2
1977	219,760	1.0	400,972	6.5	1.82	5.2
1978	222,095	1.1	434,696	8.4	1.96	7.7
1979	224,567	1.1	444,375	2.2	1.98	1.0
1980	227,255	1.2	479,628	7.9	2.11	6.6
1981	229,637	1.0	505,684	5.4	2.20	4.3
1982	231,996	1.0	514,045	1.7	2.22	0.9
1983	234,284	1.0	528,076	2.7	2.25	1.4
1984	236,477	0.9	554,510	5.0	2.34	4.0
1985	238,736	1.0	580,292	4.6	2.43	3.8
1986	241,096	1.0	587,064	1.2	2.43	0.0
1987§	243,400	1.0	580,933	−1.0	2.39	−1.6

* All ages resident population in the United States on July 1.

† All wine, including wine coolers, entering distribution channels in the United States.

‡ Figures reflect excessive inventory accumulation by consumers and the trade in 1946, and subsequent inventory depletion in 1947; therefore, data for these years do not accurately reflect consumption patterns.

§ Preliminary.

Sources: Prepared by Economic Research Department, Wine Institute, on behalf of the California Wine Commission. Based on data obtained from reports of Bureau of Alcohol, Tobacco, and Firearms, U.S. Treasury Department, and Bureau of the Census, U.S. Department of Commerce.

During the 1970s, with its steady growth and romantic appeal, the wine industry drew many interested investors. The number of California wineries grew from 240 in 1970 to over 600 by 1980. While most of these were smaller wineries with whom CVWC did not compete directly, some aggressive competitors did enter the market. For example, in 1977 Coca-Cola purchased Taylor California Cellers and employed the same sophisticated marketing techniques— segmentation and slick advertising campaigns—used to sell Coke. (Coke sold Taylor to Seagrams in 1983 but Coke left behind the impact of much greater advertising expenditures by the entire wine industry.) With all of these new entrants, inventories swelled in most wineries and the industry suffered from excess supply.

To make matters worse, during the first half of the 1980s the dollar was overpriced in international markets. The wine market became flooded with inexpensive foreign wines, mainly from Italy, France, and Germany. In 1984, imports held 25.7 percent of the total wine market in the United States. Italian wines (such as the well-known brands of Riunite and Soave Bolla) dominated in the United States with 51 percent of the imported wine market.

During the 1980s consumption of hard booze such as whiskey and vodka dropped significantly. At the same time, low-alcohol wines (7–9 percent) as well as nonalcoholic wines entered the market. These changes reflected a growing concern about the need for greater moderation regarding the consumption of alcoholic beverages. Increased desire for good health and concern about the high caloric content of alcoholic beverages also discouraged alcoholic beverage consumption in the United States during the 1980s. In fact, a Gallup Poll taken in 1987 showed that 63 percent of Americans "occasionally drink alcohol" while a 1989 poll indicated that the percentage fell to 56 percent.

Social activist groups had recently directed consumers' attention toward the need for more moderate alcohol consumption. The growing attention about the dangers of alcohol use while driving gave rise to organizations such as MADD (Mothers Against Drunk Driving) and SADD (Students Against Driving Drunk). One organization, Stop Marketing Alcohol on Radio and Television (SMART), embarked on a major lobbying effort to restrict advertising of beer and wine because of health problems associated with alcoholic beverages and the companies' appeal to younger and underage drinkers.

From his vantage point within the industry, Max was clearly aware that all these factors pointed to the changing attitude that Americans had toward the use of all alcoholic beverages. CVWC's sales had been affected by all of these developments. The sales of its red, white, and rose table wines bottled under the brand name California Valley continued to lose market share (Exhibit 3). It was time that CVWC did something and it was Max's responsibility to evaluate new product possibilities. He had been with CVWC since 1962 when he joined as a sales representative. Over the years he was promoted to sales manager and eventually became the western states regional director of sales.

EXHIBIT 3 CVWC market share of jug wines
(1980–1987)

	Market Share
1980	14.0%
1981	15.0
1982	15.1
1983	14.9
1984	14.1
1985	14.6
1986	13.2
1987	10.4

Two Possible Products

After considering several possible products, including sparkling wines, fruit wines, and blush wines, Max narrowed the field to two: a wine cooler or an inexpensive dessert wine. A wine cooler is a blend of carbonated water, fruit juice, and wine with an alcohol level of 4–6 percent. While wine coolers had been consumed for years, sometimes in the form of sangria, the surge in popularity had been a recent phenomenon (Exhibit 4). Coolers were first introduced as a commercial beverage in the early 1980s by California Cooler

EXHIBIT 4 Total cases of wine coolers sold, 1981–1987 (millions)

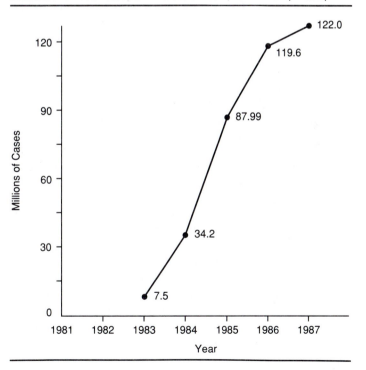

and there were numerous brands on the market. One concern expressed by the president at CVWC was the relatively high caloric content (225 per 12-ounce bottle) of the wine cooler. By 1987, the wine cooler segment of the wine industry had swelled to a $1.7 billion business representing 20 percent of the wine market.

The majority of the cooler market was divided between five market leaders. In 1987, Seagram's Wine Cooler and Gallo's Bartles and Jaymes together commanded nearly 48 percent of the market (Exhibit 5). Miller Brewing Company made a major product introduction of Matilda Bay malt-based cooler in 1987. Max was uncertain whether wine coolers were merely a fad or if they would become a permanent beverage option for consumers.

EXHIBIT 5   Wine cooler market share (1987)

Cooler	Share
Seagrams	24.0%
Bartles & Jaymes	23.4
California Cooler	13.1
Sun Country	9.2
White Mountain	7.1
All others	23.2
Total	100.0%

Although the rapid growth of the cooler market had ended, it represented a tremendous potential for sales. However, if CVWC were to enter this market, it would meet tough competition. A large advertising budget would be required to take market share from those brands already established, such as Bartles & Jaymes and Seagrams. For instance, Gallo allotted $80 million in 1985 to introduce its new cooler product.

CVWC could easily produce wine coolers from excess bulk wine. Other ingredients needed to make coolers are easily obtained. The same wine wholesalers through which CVWC sold its table wine can be utilized to distribute the cooler product. For example, the company used wholesalers and also sold directly to large retailers such as the Liquor Barn (a chain of California discount liquor stores) and out-of-state distributors in other places.

The Dessert Wine Option

Wines containing more than 14 percent alcohol are known as fortified or dessert wines because brandy has been added during the fermentation process to yield a beverage with higher alcohol content than table wines. Dessert wines can be contrasted with table wines that usually have an alcohol content of 10–14 percent. The most important advantage of the fortified wine option is profitability; the 22 percent net margins on these wines were larger than the 13 percent net margin on wine coolers. The varieties of grapes that CVWC grew were ideal for fortified wines, both for making the wine and the brandy required. Max had estimated that for $20,000 CVWC could set up an in-house brandy distillery which could supply all the brandy required to make fortified wines.

Although the same distributors could be used to get this product onto the market, Max was aware that some of the biggest liquor stores in California refused to carry low-end dessert wine products. In the words of a manager at one Liquor Barn, ''We don't carry those products because we do not want that clientele in our store.''

Dessert wines included a whole range of products from high-end Portugese ports ($15/bottle) to low-end muscatels ($1.99 bottle). During the 1940s and 1950s, these sweet ports and sherries represented a sizable portion of the wine consumed and they continued to grow until about 1970. The tastes of typical wine consumers for these sweet wines moved to a preference for drier table wines and the market for fortified wines began to erode. In recent years, the majority of the fortified wines consumed were inexpensive brown bag purchases by street drunks. Although the image of these wines has changed, dessert wines have a noble past.

History of fortified wines.   Fortifying wine with the addition of brandy is a practice that dates back to the Roman period. The fortification process solved a practical problem of wine spoilage in ancient times. Wine spoilage especially posed a problem for those traveling who did not have the luxury of a cool cellar to protect the wine from damaging heat. Winemakers of that early era discovered that if wine was fortified by adding a concentrated spirit (like brandy) it would age longer. This practice was copied by the British living in Madeira, Portugal, who found that this fortification process allowed the wine to hold up better for the long sea journey home.

During the decades following the repeal of Prohibition in 1933, fortified wines such as sherries and ports represented a major portion of the wine consumed in the United States. These wines were typically enjoyed as an aperitif or as a dessert. However, as tastes changed and the variety of wines available broadened, wine drinkers began to consume more table wines. In 1970 dessert wines represented 27.7 percent of the wine market, but by 1986 they accounted for only 7.5 percent of the total wine market. Inexpensive fortified wine products are classified as special natural wines. As measured in volume, consumption of this product has been quite steady during the years 1968–1986 (Exhibit 6). Table wines saw a big increase in consumption during the 1970s and represented the vast majority of the nearly 600 million gallons consumed in the United States.

The Dilemma

Max was well aware, however, of the problems involved with entering the fortified wine market. Fortified wines presently available in the market were typically associated with the type of wines consumed by the destitute alcoholics

EXHIBIT 6 Wine consumption in the United States, 1968–1986

Year	U.S.-produced other special natural wine over 14 percent alcohol consumed in the United States	All U.S.-produced wine consumed in the United States (1,000 gallons)	Percent of type
1968	12,591	191,447	6.6%
1969	12,221	210,936	5.8
1970	11,665	237,328	4.9
1971	11,631	269,065	4.3
1972	11,823	289,942	4.1
1973	10,944	292,041	3.7
1974	9,653	298,071	3.2
1975	10,918	318,071	3.4
1976	11,994	317,470	3.8
1977	12,396	331,766	3.7
1978	11,104	340,620	3.3
1979	10,084	352,206	2.9
1980	10,008	377,120	2.7
1981	10,288	390,971	2.6
1982	10,293	391,956	2.6
1983	11,055	397,070	2.8
1984	10,807	412,099	2.6
1985	11,724	441,034	2.7
1986	13,698	477,891	2.9

who roamed the streets. Max was struck by an article he read some time ago in *The Wall Street Journal*. He reached for a copy of the article he placed in a file folder and reread it closely. (The text of the article is shown in Exhibit 7).

He was particularly sensitive about alcoholism because his father had suffered from the disease. He knew that many street drunks depended on these inexpensive fortified wines because it was the cheapest source of alcohol available. However, Max was not really sure what percentage of fortified wines were purchased by public drunks.

Max had wondered for some time about the ramifications of offering a fortified product to the market and whether or not it would add to the serious problem of alcoholism in this country. After reading *The Wall Street Journal* article, Max contacted the Wine Institute in San Francisco. The Wine Institute is an industry-funded organization whose purpose is to represent the California wineries and promote their wines. The reply regarding this question of the so-called misery market came in a written letter.

We reject the notion, however, that availability of "over 14 percent wine" encourages and/or causes abuse of the product. We know from a wide range of literature that alcohol abuse is a complex medical and social problem evolving from a vast array of generic biochemical predispositions, cultural norms, behaviors, expectations, and beliefs. We believe the most effective way to address alcoholism is through intervention, education, treatment, and prevention programs.

EXHIBIT 7

Misery Market

Winos & Thunderbird Are a Subject Gallo Doesn't Like to Discuss

It, Other Vintners Disavow Wines' Appeal to Drunks, But the Money Is Good

Night Train to the Bowery

By ALIX M. FREEDMAN
Staff Reporter of THE WALL STREET JOURNAL

NEW YORK—In the dim light of a cold February morning, a grizzled wino shuffles into the Bowery Discount liquor store muttering, "Thunder-chicken, it's good lickin.'" Fumbling for some change, he says: "Gimme one bird." Raymond Caba, the store clerk, understands the argot and hands over a $1.40 pint of Thunderbird, the top seller in what he calls "the bum section."

The ritual is repeated a thousand times a day in dead-end neighborhoods across the country. Cheap wines with down-and-dirty names—and an extra measure of alcohol—are the beverage of choice among down-and-out drunks. But winos are a major embarrassment to the big companies that manufacture these wines. With rare exceptions, they aren't eager to acknowledge their own products.

Thunderbird and Night Train Express are produced by the nation's largest wine company, E.&J. Gallo Winery, though you'll not learn that from reading the label on the bottle. MD

20/20 is made by Mogen David Wine Corp., a subsidiary of Wine Group Ltd., which refuses to talk about its product. Richards Wild Irish Rose Wine, the very best seller in the category, is produced by Canandaigua Wine Co. Canandaigua is volubly proud of the wine but quick to point out that it enjoys wide popularity with people who aren't alcoholics.

The Biggest Bang

People concerned about the plight of street alcoholics are critical of the purveyors of dollar-a-pint street wines made with cheap ingredients and fortified with alcohol to deliver the biggest bang for the buck. At 18% to 21% alcohol, these wines have about twice the kick of ordinary table wine, without any of the pretension.

The consumption of alcohol in the U.S. *is* declining in virtually every category, but the best selling of the low-end brands keep growing, in large part be-

(continued)

EXHIBIT 7 (continued)

cause customers can't stop drinking. Says Paul Gillette, the publisher of the Wine Investor in Los Angeles: "Makers of skid-row wines are the dope pushers of the wine industry.

Vintners generally try hard to filter their wines through the imagery of luxury and moderation, stressing vintage, touting quality. So they are understandably reluctant to be associated in any way with what some call a $500 million misery market.

Suppliers deny that the most popular street wines sell as well as they do because they appeal to dirt-poor, hardcore drinkers. Companies contend that their clientele is not like that at all, and, besides, any alcoholic beverage can be abused. (The wine people say they face stiff competition from high-alcohol malt liquor and 200-milliliter bottles of cheap vodka.) The future for the high-proof business, vintners say, isn't particularly rosy in any case. The wine category they call "dessert" or "fortified"— sweet wines with at least 14% alcohol— has lost favor with drinkers.

Markedly Profitable

Wino wines are inexpensive to produce. They come in no-frills, screw-top packaging and require little or no advertising. Although they generally aren't the major part of vintners' product lineups, they are especially profitable. All told, net profit margins are 10% higher than those of ordinary table wines, Canandaigua estimates. Gallo says that isn't true for its products, but it won't say what is true.

The wines are also a rock-solid business. Of all the wine brands in America, the trade newsletter Impact says, Wild Irish Rose holds the No. 6 spot, Thunderbird is 10th and MD 20/20 is 16th. In contrast to the lackluster growth of most other wine brands, unit sales of the leading cheap labels, Wild Irish Rose and Thunderbird are expected to be up 9.9% and 8.6% respectively this year, Jobson's Wine Marketing Handbook estimates.

So unsavory is this market that companies go to great lengths to distance themselves from their customers. If suppliers are willing to talk about the segment—and few are—they still don't acknowledge the wino's loyal patronage. Gallo and Canandaigua leave their good corporate names off the labels, thus obscuring the link between product and producer.

The 'No-Name Market'

"This is the market with no name," says Clifford Adelson, a former executive director of sales at Manischewitz Wine Co., which once made low-end wines and was recently acquired by Canandaigua. "It's lots and lots of money, but it doesn't add prestige."

Cheap wines typically aren't even sold in many liquor stores. For instance, Frank Gaudio, who owns the big Buy-Rite Twin Towers Wine & Spirits store in New York's World Trade Center, doesn't stock any of these brands, though many homeless alcoholics spend their days just outside his door. "We don't want that clientele in our store," he says. "We could sell [fortified wines] and probably make money, but we don't." The wines, however, are staples of the bulletproof liquor stores of low-income neighborhoods. While you can't say the whole market for items like Thunderbird and Night Train consists of derelicts, down-and-outers do seem to be its lifeblood. Fifty current and reformed drinkers interviewed for this article claim to have lived on a gallon a day or more of the stuff.

EXHIBIT 7 (continued)

Misery Market: Catering to Winos Isn't a Subject Vintners Discuss

"The industry is manufacturing this for a select population: the poor, the homeless, the skid-row individual," says Neil Goldman, the chief of the alcoholism unit at St. Vincent's Hospital in Manhattan's Greenwich Village.

* * *

Dawn finds a small bottle gang near the Bowery, chasing away the morning shakes with a bottle of Thunderbird they pass from hand to hand. Mel Downing tugs up the pant leg of his filthy jeans to reveal an oozing infection on his knee. He is drinking, he says, to numb the pain of this "wine sore" and other ones on his back before he goes to the hospital later in the morning. "We're used to this stuff," the 39-year-old Mr. Downing quickly adds. "We like the effect. We like the price."

A cheap drunk is the main appeal of the wines that winos call "grape" or "jug," but most often just "cheap." Winos say that these wines, even when consumed in quantity, don't make them pass out as readily as hard liquor would.

Walter Single, a recovering alcoholic, recalls that on a daily diet of nine pints of Wild Irish Rose, he still was able "to function well enough to panhandle the money he needed to drink all day and still have enough left for a wake-up in the morning."

Some drinkers say the high sugar content of the wines reduces their appetite for food, so they don't have to eat much. Others say they still can drink wine even after their livers are too far gone to handle spirits. Still others appreciate the portability of pint bottles. "I feel more secure with a pint,"

explains Teddy Druzinski, a former carpenter. "It's next to me. It's in my pocket." Canandaigua estimates that low-end brands account for 43 million gallons of the dessert category's 55 million gallons and that 50% is purchased in pints.

Many people in the wine industry eschew producing skid-row wines. "I don't think Christian Brothers should be in a category where people are down on their luck—where some may be alcoholics," says Richard Maher, the president of Christian Brothers Winery in St. Helena, Calif. Mr. Maher, who once was with Gallo, says fortified wines lack "any socially redeeming values."

"The consumers are we alcoholics," agrees Patrick Gonzales, a 45-year-old wino who is undergoing a week of detoxification at a men's shelter on New York's Lower East Side: "You don't see no one sitting at home sipping Mad Dog [MD 20/20] in a wine glass over ice."

Market Profile

Major producers see their customers otherwise. Robert Huntington, the vice president of strategic planning at Canandaigua, says the Canandaigua, N.Y., company sells 60% to 75% of its "pure grape" Wild Irish Rose in primarily black, inner-city markets. He describes customers as "not supersophisticated," lower middle-class and low-income blue-collar workers, mostly men.

Daniel Solomon, a Gallo spokesman, *(continued)*

EXHIBIT 7 (continued)

maintains that Thunderbird "has lost its former popularity in the black and skid-row areas" and is quaffed mainly by "retired and older folks who don't like the taste of hard products."

According to accounts that Gallo disputes, the company revolutionized the skid-row market in the 1950s after discovering that liquor stores in Oakland, Calif., were catering to the tastes of certain customers by attaching packages of lemon Kool-Aid to bottles of white wine. Customers did their own mixing at home. The story goes that Gallo, borrowing the idea, created citrus-flavored Thunderbird. Other flavored high-proof wines then surged into the marketplace. Among them: Twister, Bali Hai, Hombre, Silver Satin and Gypsy Rose. Gallo says that the Kool-Aid story is "a nice myth" but that Thunderbird was "developed by our wine makers in our laboratories."

Vintners advertised heavily and sought to induce skid row's opinion leaders—nicknamed "bell cows"—to switch brands by plying them with free samples. According to Arthur Palombo, the chairman of Cannon Wines Ltd. and one of Gallo's marketing men in the 1950s and '60s, "These were clandestine promotions." He doesn't say which companies engaged in the practice.

Today, such practices and most brands have long since died out. Companies now resort to standard point-of-sale promotions and, in the case of Canandaigua, some radio and television advertising. There still is an occasional bit of hoopla. In New Jersey, Gallo recently named a Thunderbird Princess, and Canandaigua currently is holding a Miss Wild Irish Rose contest. But to hear distributors tell it, word of mouth remains the main marketing tool.

The market is hard to reach through conventional media. Winos will drink anything if need be, but when they have the money to buy what they want, they tend to hew to the familiar. (Sales resistance may help explain why the handful of low-end products that companies have tried to launch in the past 20 years mostly have bombed.) Besides, "it would be difficult to come up with an advertising campaign that says this will go down smoother, get you drunker and help you panhandle better," says Robert Williams, a reformed alcoholic and counselor at the Manhattan Bowery Corp.'s Project Renewal, a half-way house for Bowery alcoholics.

Companies see no reason to spend a lot of money promoting brands they don't want to be identified with. "Gallo and ourselves have been trying to convey the image of a company that makes fine products," says Hal Riney, the president of Hal Riney & Associates, which created the TV characters Frank Bartles and Ed Jaymes for Gallo's wine cooler. "It would be counterproductive to advertise products like this."

Richards Wild Irish Rose purports to be made by Richards Wine Co. The label on a bottle of Gallo's Night Train reads "vinted & bottled by Night Train Limited, Modesto, Ca." Gallo's spokesman, Mr. Solomon, says "The Gallo name is reserved for traditional [table] wines."

Industry people chime in that it isn't at all uncommon for companies to do business under a variety of monikers. But they also agree with Cannon's Mr. Palombo: "Major wine producers don't want to be associated with a segment of the industry that is determined to be low-end and alcoholic."

Winos have their own names for what they buy, Gallo's appellations notwithstanding. When they go to buy Night Train, they might say, "Gimme a ticket." They call Thunderbird "pluck," "T-Bird" or "chicken." In street lingo, Richards Wild Irish Rose is

(continued)

EXHIBIT 7 *(concluded)*

known as "Red Lady," while MD 20/20 is "Mad Dog."

If skid-row wines are cheap to market, they are even cheaper to make. They are generally concocted by adding flavors, sugar and high-proof grape-based neutral spirits to a base wine. The wine part is produced from the cheapest grapes available. Needless to say, the stuff never sees the inside of an oak barrel.

"They dip a grape in it so they can say it's made of wine," says Dickie Gronan, a 67-year-old who describes himself as a bum. "But it's laced with something to make you thirstier." Sugar probably. In any event, customers keep on swigging. Some are so hooked that they immediately turn to an underground distribution system on Sundays and at other times when liquor stores are closed. "Bootleggers," often other alcoholics, buy cheap brands at retail and resell them at twice the price. The street shorthand for such round-

the-clock consumption is "24-7."

At nightfall, Mr. Downing, the member of the bottle gang with the leg infection, is panhandling off the Bowery "to make me another jug," as he puts it. As his shredded parka attests, he got into a fight earlier in the day with his buddy, Mr. Druzinski, who then disappeared. Mr. Downing also got too drunk to make it, as planned, to the hospital for treatment of his "wine sores."

A short while later, Mr. Druzinski emerges from the shadows. He has a bloodied face because he "took another header," which is to say he fell on his head. Nevertheless, in the freezing darkness, he joins his partner at begging once again.

"I'm feeling sick to my stomach, dizzy and mokus," Mr. Downing says. "But I still want another pint." He scans the deserted street and adds: "Another bottle is the biggest worry on our minds."

In doing some more research about the social implications of fortified beverages, Max had found an article in the *British Journal of Addiction*.[1] The article was titled, "A Ban of Fortified Wine in Northwestern Ontario and Its Impact on the Consumption Level and Drinking Pattern." The article described an experiment in which fortified wines were removed from store shelves in 10 communities in Ontario. The brands removed were those in the lower-price category, and considered to be the more popular beverage of public inebriates, many of whom were Native Indians. The researchers sought to compare the drinking patterns of people living in these 10 delisted communities with those in 18 communities where these fortified wines continued to be available. The researchers found that the ban of these fortified wines only led to an increased consumption of table wines, vodka, and Liquor Board wines and in some cases created additional social problems. Max felt that the presence of fortified wines in the American market did not cause alcoholism, but felt bothered by the idea

---

[1] "A Ban of Fortified Wine in Northwestern Ontario and its Impact on the Consumption Level and Drinking Patterns," *British Journal of Addiction,* 76 (1981), pp. 281–88.

that a large proportion of the customers for a CVWC fortified product might be these public drunks.

Marketing Strategy

Whether Max recommended CVWC to enter the fortified wine market or the wine cooler market, he would be responsible for developing the appropriate marketing strategy. Max had a fairly clear vision in his mind of what the two potential products could be. In the case of the fortified wine, it would be made from the Thompson Seedless and French Colombard grapes and would contain about 15 percent sugar while having 18 percent alcohol. He thought perhaps the product could have an added orange or cherry flavor.

Given the potential image problems that a market for a fortified product could create for CVWC, Max felt that if they were to enter this market it would be best for CVWC to utilize an alternative brand name and a DBA (doing business as). The DBA is the name of the producer which, by law, has to be listed on the label. To protect the image of California Valley Wine Company, the bottom of the label could read ''Produced and Bottled by CVWC Cellars,'' thereby disguising the producer of the wine. In addition to the DBA, as the *TWSJ* article mentioned, many wineries in California used second labels in order to protect the image of their main brand. For example, Gallo bottles its wines under a whole myriad of brand names: Carlo Rossi, Andre, and Polo Brindisi. Exhibit 8 lists the brand names, producers, and market shares of the leading fortified wine products. Although Max had not given much consideration to possible brand names for the fortified wine, Warm Nights had been tossed around by some of the salespeople.

EXHIBIT 8 U.S. fortified wine industry (fortified wines are sweet wines with at least 14 percent alcohol.)

Wine	Producer	Market share (percent)
Wild Irish Rose	Canandaigua	22%
Thunderbird	Gallo	18
All other Gallo dessert wines		16
MD 20/20	Wine Group Ltd.	7
Cisco	Canandaigua	4
Night Train Express	Gallo	3
All others: imported dessert wines, other domestic brands		30

Source: Industry estimates.

Max felt that perhaps an upscale product with a distinctive label could be developed, one that commanded a higher price in the market and which in turn would yield a greater margin. It could be bottled in 750 milliliter bottles and positioned distinctively away from the low-end competition of MD 20/20 and Thunderbird. Examples of packaging options are shown in Exhibit 9. Certainly

EXHIBIT 9

part of the reasons these wines were favorites of the public drunks was the inexpensive price. A 375-milliliter bottle of Night Train retailed for $1.09. The 750-milliliter bottles of Thunderbird and Wild Irish Rose could be purchased for as little as $1.99 and $2.32, respectively.

He wondered if the flat-shaped, pint-size bottle of Night Train had been intentionally designed to fit into a coat pocket. He thought that CVWC—in order to avoid the misery market—could market a product packaged with a fancy label in a corked bottle, and sell it for a higher price, for example, $5.50. It could be positioned more as a sophisticated dessert wine. But then Max questioned whether or not customers would be willing to pay for this.

Max believed that the fortified wine was a liquor store item. Perhaps it would be feasible to selectively market this product, focusing on suburban stores. In this way the inner-city liquor stores, often frequented by public drunks, could be avoided. Max knew that once the product is out on the store shelves, the producer cannot influence who buys the product or how it is used. One idea that came to mind was that CVWC could print on the bottom of the labels "ENJOY IN MODERATION" like some other alcoholic beverage producers had done.[2] Perhaps this would help discourage abuse of the product. Max had bounced the idea off one of the salespeople, who replied, "Hey, Max, that's not our responsibility."

Promotion of fortified wines posed a particularly difficult problem. Max wondered how CVWC could promote the product and which product attributes could be highlighted. Max pulled out his *Code of Advertising Standards* that wine industry members were to voluntarily abide by. The following is a paragraph from the first section:

> Subscribers shall not depict or describe in their advertising: The consumption of wine or wine coolers for the effects their alcohol content may produce or make direct or indirect reference to alcohol content or extra strength, except as otherwise required by law or regulation.

There were certainly problems with promotion of this product, but one thing was certain. If CVWC was not able to promote the product it would be difficult to take market share away from the competition.

Of course, if Max were to recommend entering the wine cooler business, the problems associated with fortified wines would be avoided. If CVWC was to be successful in the wine cooler business, it would require some innovation. Max had thought that CVWC could develop a cooler with new flavors, for example, pomegranate or wild berry. They could be packaged in six packs potentially leading to greater sales over the typical four pack. He believed women could be targeted for this new product which could be sold as low calorie. Max considered whether CVWC might get some nationally known TV star to endorse the new product.

---

[2] "Alco Beverage Company and Moderation Advertising," HBS case 9–387–070.

EXHIBIT 10   Projected CVWC sales (1989–1991)

	Wine Cooler		
	1989	*1990*	*1991*
Sales (millions)*	5.00	6.00	7.00
Expenses			
Cost of goods sold	3.00	3.60	4.20
Selling and administrative	0.20	0.20	0.20
Salaries	0.15	0.17	0.19
Advertising	0.90	0.90	0.90
Interest	0.20	0.25	0.25
Total expenses	4.45	5.12	5.74
Earnings before taxes	0.55	0.88	1.26
	Fortified Wine		
Sales (millions)†	2.50	3.50	5.50
Expenses			
Cost of goods sold	1.00	1.40	2.20
Selling and administrative	0.20	0.20	0.20
Salaries	0.10	0.11	0.12
Advertising	0.20	0.20	0.20
Interest	0.15	0.15	0.15
Total expenses	1.65	2.06	2.87
Earning before taxes	0.85	1.44	2.63

* Based on $11.42/case selling price.

† Based on $14.75/case selling price.

He turned on the PC near his desk and stared at the projections for both the fortified wine and wine cooler options. Exhibit 10 contains the actual numbers generated by the spreadsheet program. Both alternatives seemed to be viable and would help the bottom line of CVWC. He thought the numbers might even be a bit conservative.

Max was even more confounded by all of these considerations. But then again it was his responsibility to give the recommendation to the committee. Not only was he expected to present his recommendation regarding the new product to the New Product Evaluation Committee but he was also asked to discuss his strategy with the Social Responsibility Committee. This committee had been established in 1976 to oversee the activities of the various departments at CVWC because of its involvement in the alcoholic beverage industry.

When looking for some misplaced statistics on his cluttered desk, Max found a memo he had received from the vice president of marketing earlier in the day. The memo was marked "urgent" in red ink. It instructed Max to have his recommendation available by noon tomorrow. The memo concluded with a "Are there any other new product options you haven't explored? Max, see me in the morning." Max took a long breath and reached for the articles on the wine industry that covered his desk. Thumbing through them he hoped that a clear strategy would come to mind, one that he could sleep with.

Part 9

Marketing Programs and Strategy

This section contains seven cases which are comprehensive in nature, requiring the student to make a number of decisions in several different marketing decision areas. Thus, a great deal of integration is necessary. A decision in one of the marketing areas may have a significant impact on the other decisions which must be made to complete the marketing program.

In developing a complete marketing program for a product, one must start with the firm's overall goals and objectives. Then all the environmental factors such as demand, competition, marketing laws, distribution alternatives, and cost structure must be analyzed. At this point, a number of opportunities as well as potential problems will have been identified, and specific marketing objectives can be established.

The marketer must make a clear definition of the target market(s) to be served. This can be determined only after a thorough evaluation of all the alternative segments of the market, their needs, wants, attitudes and behavior, the strengths and weaknesses of the firm's products and those of competitors, and the potential profitability of various alternatives.

The next step in developing the marketing program is to search for the optimal marketing mix; that is, what is the best combination of product strategy, pricing strategy, promotion strategy, and distribution strategy? Typically, there will be a number of possible alternatives for each of these, so the marketer must determine the interrelationships among them and choose the optimal combination based upon a complete situation analysis.

The last step in the development of a marketing program is to create a plan for implementing the program. Without adequate implementation, even the best-designed plans will fail.

Case 35

Aldus Corporation*

In August 1988, the sales and marketing executives of Aldus Corporation met at a Massachusetts resort to begin their strategic marketing planning for 1989. At the meeting, Richard Strong, marketing manager for Aldus Europe, proposed that Aldus split its product family into two distinct product lines: the Aldus Executive Series, which would include PageMaker, Persuasion, and additional new products that would be aimed at the business market; and the Aldus Professional Series, which would include a new professional version of Page-Maker, Aldus Freehand, Aldus Snapshot, and additional new products that would be aimed at the creative graphics professional market. Richard Strong argued that his proposal would allow Aldus to develop two separate, focused product and market strategies for these two major market segments.

The initial response to Richard's proposal was cautiously favorable. On the surface, it would solve a lot of problems. It would allow Aldus to clarify the positioning of each of its major products, while helping the company establish a strong and unique company identity in each of its two major market segments. However, the company had based its success to date on offering a single product line that bridged the gap between business and creative professionals. A 1988 advertisement for Aldus PageMaker had emphasized this positioning (see Exhibit 1). Furthermore, it was not at all clear how the multibranding decision would be implemented at the sales and distribution levels, either domestically or internationally.

The Aldus corporate marketing staff was given the challenge of evaluating Richard Strong's proposal and developing a detailed implementation plan if the multibranding decision was recommended for adoption.

* This case was prepared by Professor Adrian B. Ryans for the sole purpose of providing material for class discussion at the Western Business School. Certain names and other identifying information may have been disguised to protect confidentiality. It is not intended to illustrate either effective or ineffective handling of a managerial situation. Any reproduction, in any form, of the material in this case is prohibited except with the written consent of the School. Copyright 1990 © the University of Western Ontario. Used with permission.

EXHIBIT 1   Advertisement for Aldus PageMaker

Aldus Corporation

Aldus Corporation was founded in February 1984, to develop a cost-effective and easy-to-use software tool that would perform on a microcomputer many of the page layout and design functions of a workstation-, minicomputer-, or mainframe-based publishing system. The result was PageMaker, which allowed people to design, edit, and produce printed communications electronically, thereby reducing the time and expense associated with traditional publishing techniques. This new microcomputer-based publishing soon became known as "desktop publishing," a term coined by Aldus's founder and president, Paul Brainerd.

Before founding Aldus, Paul Brainerd had been a vice president with a company that manufactured dedicated publishing systems for newspapers and magazines. Prior to that, Brainerd was editor-in-chief of the *Minnesota Daily* and assistant to the operations director for the Minneapolis Star and Tribune Company.

Aldus Corporation shipped its first copies of PageMaker for the Apple Macintosh in July 1985, and by 1988, it had become the international standard for desktop publishing software. Both the Macintosh version of PageMaker and the PC version, which was first shipped in January 1987, had been translated into more that 10 languages. A Japanese Kanji version of PageMaker for the Macintosh was scheduled for introduction in September 1988. This would be the first Asian-language desktop publishing software product from a U.S. company.

In June 1987, Aldus completed a successful public offering of 2,240,000 shares of common stock, raising approximately $31 million to support future growth. Later in 1987, Aldus became a multiproduct company with the acquisition of the marketing and distribution rights to two new products: Aldus FreeHand, a drawing tool for the Apple Macintosh, and Aldus SnapShot, an electronic photography program for the PC. In July 1988, the company announced its fourth major product, Aldus Persuasion, a desktop presentation software program for the Macintosh, scheduled to be released late in 1988. While the new products gave Aldus a more diversified portfolio, PageMaker was still accounting for about 80 percent of Aldus's sales in mid-1988. The financial highlights of Aldus's first five years of operations are shown in Exhibit 2.

Aldus Corporation derived its name from Aldus Manutius, a fifteenth-century Venetian scholar who founded the Aldine Press, the first modern publishing house. He was also known for having invented italic type and for standardizing the rules of pronunciation.

Business Strategy

Paul Brainerd attributed a great deal of Aldus's early success to its effective use of strategic alliances, the development of a motivated and educated network of resellers, and a highly successful public relations campaign.

From the beginning, one of Aldus Corporation's basic business strategies had been to forge strategic alliances with other vendors for both technical and marketing purposes. The strategic alliance with Apple was particularly important. In 1985 Aldus, which was then working on its first version of PageMaker, employed a total of 15 people. The marketing function was comprised of one salesperson, a part-time marketing consultant, and Paul Brainerd. As Paul Brainerd later commented: "The name of the game was clearly leverage—how could we at Aldus leverage off our very limited resource base?" The initial version of PageMaker was designed to run on an Apple Macintosh computer. In 1984, Apple had about 2,000 dealers in the United States and Canada. It was clear to the management team at Aldus that, if PageMaker was successful, one sale of the software package could result in several thousands of dollars of hardware sales (in computers, printers, and other peripheral equipment). If Apple could be convinced of the potential value of PageMaker as a means of generating hardware sales, it had the financial and organizational resources to be of great assistance to Aldus.

At the same time that Aldus was looking at Apple, Apple was facing some significant problems of its own. Apple had been developing a laser printer, the

EXHIBIT 2 Aldus Corporation selected financial highlights

Consolidated condensed balance sheet

(Handwritten annotations: "Current ratio = C/A / C/L"; "Net profit = Net Income / Sales revenue")

Assets	July 1, 1988	Dec. 31, 1987	Dec. 31, 1986	Dec. 31, 1985
Current assets				
Cash and marketable securities	$33,429,006	$31,736,569	$3,159,937	$ 903,039
Other current assets	18,790,193	10,266,492	2,051,494	594,966
Total current assets	52,219,199	42,003,061	5,211,431	1,498,005
Equipment and leasehold improvements, net	4,833,736	4,004,413	791,443	174,186
Capitalized software development costs	2,986,854	2,387,685	377,960	—
Other assets, substantially all intangible assets	570,237	592,283	—	1,620
	$60,610,026	$48,987,442	$6,380,834	$1,673,811
Liabilities and shareholders' equity				
Current liabilities				
Accounts payable and accrued liabilities	$ 5,944,218	$ 3,929,736	$1,071,546	$ 185,335
Deferred technical support revenue	672,392	334,874	116,722	62,062
Income taxes payable	1,012,000	—	1,433,000	167,000
Total current liabilities	7,628,610	4,264,610	2,621,268	414,397
Lease obligations	127,325	218,783	144,000	6,000
Deferred income taxes	1,157,000	1,168,000	3,615,566	1,253,414
Shareholders' equity	51,697,091	43,336,049	$6,380,834	$1,673,811
	$60,610,026	$48,987,442		
Working capital	$44,590,589	$37,738,451	$2,590,163	$1,083,608

Consolidated condensed statement of income

	6 months ending July 1, 1988	Dec. 31, 1987	Year ending Dec. 31, 1986	Dec. 31, 1985	Dec. 31, 1984
Net sales	$35,075,105	$39,542,200	$11,135,688	$2,234,424	$ —
Operating expenses					
Cost of sales	7,494,841	8,600,441	1,066,417	161,890	121,590
Selling, general, and administrative	14,700,460	16,597,433	5,518,519	1,120,948	117,750
Research and development	3,798,793	2,502,337	590,401	297,637	
Income from operations	$ 9,081,011	$11,841,989	$3,960,351	$ 653,949	$(239,340)
Interest income, net	810,746	972,483	151,801	37,138	21,854
Other expenses	(474,549)	(253,377)	—	—	—
Income before provision for income taxes	$ 9,417,208	$12,561,095	$4,112,152	$ 691,087	$(217,486)
Extraordinary credit	—	—	—	80,000	—
Provision for income taxes	2,982,000	4,755,500	1,750,000	253,000	
Net income	$ 6,435,208	$ 7,805,595	$2,362,152	$ 518,087	$(217,486)
Net income per share of common stock	$.50	$.66	$.21	$.05	$(.02)

LaserWriter, to complement the Macintosh computer. This project was running into considerable opposition within Apple. The organization was still smarting from the demise of the expensive Lisa computer, and some Apple managers were questioning the wisdom of marketing a printer selling for $7,000. At this price, it would cost twice as much as the basic computer. In addition, there were no applications that fully utilized its capabilities. However, Steve Jobs continued to support the laser printer project and Apple was already working with Adobe Systems and its PostScript graphics language that would be a crucial element in taking full advantage of the LaserWriter's capabilities. In July 1984, Aldus demonstrated a prototype of PageMaker to the Apple project manager for the LaserWriter. An informal alliance was formed. Apple would provide the workstation and the laser printer, Adobe the PostScript language, and Aldus the business application.

Over the next year, Paul Brainerd visited Apple at least once every four to six weeks. Bruce Blumberg, the Apple project manager for the LaserWriter, informally introduced him to many Apple employees, and through corridor and office conversations Paul developed an understanding of their needs. Aldus played the lead role in developing marketing materials that would demonstrate to potential users the possible applications of desktop publishing. Apple often played the lead role in advertising and promoting these applications to potential users, featuring desktop publishing applications in its business media advertising for the Macintosh. A sample early PageMaker advertisement is shown in Exhibit 3. Together, Apple and Aldus wrote Apple's marketing plan for penetrating the publishing market.

The project took on a new urgency within Apple with the increased emphasis John Sculley, the new president of Apple Computer, was placing on the penetration of the business market. The only "solutions-oriented" application with a detailed marketing plan ready for implementation was desktop publishing. Some people within Apple were sceptical about the size of the segment, but both Sculley and Jobs felt instinctively that desktop publishing could be very successful with businesses. Potentially it could revolutionize the printing business within organizations by eliminating the need for having documents typeset, "pasted-up," and printed. It promised to bring centralized electronic publishing to the desktop. As the marketing of desktop publishing gained momentum, it became apparent that it was the perfect "Trojan horse" for Apple. Desktop publishing provided Apple with an entry into businesses. As it became established in an organization, individuals recognized the "user-friendliness" of the Macintosh's graphical interface and began using the Macintosh for new applications, and in some organizations the Macintosh began spreading from department to department.

The strategic alliance with Apple resulted in Aldus gaining access to Apple's 2,000-dealer reseller network in North America. In order to develop this dealer network into an effective marketing organization for desktop publishing, Aldus and Apple jointly determined the tasks that needed to be done, prioritized them, and then allocated each of the high-priority tasks to one of the

EXHIBIT 3   Early PageMaker dealer advertisement

two partners. One outcome of this process was a very successful series of seminars that provided dealer personnel with a ''hands-on'' experience with desktop publishing. Apple promoted the seminars within its dealer network and provided facilities and hardware. Aldus provided the software and two teams of people to mount the seminars across North America. Each of the teams visited

10 cities over a two-week period. Thus, by leveraging off the resources and facilities of Apple, Aldus was quickly able to gain visibility with key dealers and in the marketplace.

The third key element that Paul Brainerd felt had contributed to the early success of Aldus PageMaker was an extensive public relations effort. Given his experience in the publishing business as an editor, Paul knew the potential influence of people in the media. Paul identified the top 10 computer press people and contacted them about the potential of desktop publishing. He explained to them the product concept and demonstrated the product to them. Fortunately, most of them were familiar with the difficulties of the traditional printing process and many, seeing the potential of desktop publishing, became excited about the product and wrote extensively about it.

Looking back on the first couple of years of Aldus's history, Paul attributed a great deal of the company's success to having a very clear plan, having a set of priorities, and having focused the company's very limited resources on these priorities.

The Desktop Publishing Business

Businesses, which produced a wide variety of printed material for internal and external distribution, had generally utilized in-house publication departments or commercial printers to perform design, paste-up, proofing, and typesetting of high-quality printed communications. Historically, topographic-quality publications had been produced by large commercial printers utilizing typesetters and software pagination systems based on mainframes or minicomputers. Such systems required users to have considerable skill and training in page layout and makeup and were expensive, with prices ranging from $30,000 to over $200,000. Consequently, such systems had been sold primarily to large newspapers, magazines, corporate communication departments, and commercial typesetters.

Advances in microcomputers and graphics technology, combined with the availability of low-cost laser printers and the development of page composition software, had facilitated the advent of relatively low-cost, microcomputer-based publishing solutions. These systems allowed the integration of text and graphics and the production of typeset-quality printed communications. A typical desktop publishing system, consisting of a microcomputer, a laser printer, and the PageMaker software, cost approximately $8,000 to $12,000 in 1988. Desktop publishing solutions offered users increased control over the printing process and improved quality and timeliness of printed material. Because desktop publishing systems were affordable and easy to use, they had significantly expanded the market for publishing systems and were becoming increasingly popular with a broad range of small businesses, large corporations, government agencies, educational institutions, graphic designers, and business professionals. Typical applications included business communications, such as newsletters, reports to shareholders, and in-house magazines; advertising materials, including ads, brochures, and other promotional materials; sales and marketing materials, such as catalogues, price lists, and directories; manuals and other forms of documentation; and presentation graphics. Industry analysts expected the market (in $ terms) for desktop publishing systems based on microcomputers to more than double by 1992.

Market Segmentation and Customers

Aldus management viewed the desktop publishing market as being divided into four major segments based on the computer operating system used (Apple Macintosh or IBM PC AT or compatible) and whether or not the user was a business person or a creative graphics professional. A creative graphics professional was defined as anybody who bought typesetting services, or physically prepared documents for publication. The four segments are shown in Exhibit 4.

Aldus first introduced PageMaker into Segment 1 (see Exhibit 4) in 1985. PageMaker offered this segment of users a substitute technology for manual ways of working or for buying outside typesetting services. The second segment (Segment 2 in Exhibit 4) attracted to PageMaker was a group of Macintosh technology enthusiasts in the business market who were graphically oriented and wished to incorporate graphics into their documents, or who simply wanted their documents to look more attractive. This segment began to develop in 1986, and its growth accelerated with the increasing availability of laser printers in the office environment. The innovators and early adopters in both Segments 1 and 2 had a high degree of technical competence and were prepared to invest the time and effort to learn how to use the relatively complex desktop publishing software. The third segment PageMaker began to penetrate in 1987, after the release of the PC version of the product, was the PC business segment (Segment 3 in Exhibit 4). Part of this segment's growth was due to some businesspeople being impressed with the attractiveness of documents developed with a desktop publishing system on the Macintosh and wanting to be able to produce similar documents on their IBM AT or compatible. The fourth segment was the PC creative graphics professional. Some industry observers wondered why this

EXHIBIT 4 Segmentation of the desktop publishing market

Type of user	Type of operating system	
	PC (MS-DOS)	Macintosh
Business	Segment 3	Segment 2
Graphics professional	Segment 4	Segment 1

segment continued to exist, since the ease-of-use of the graphically oriented Macintosh suggested that they would be better served by a Macintosh-based desktop publishing system. However, there were a number of reasons for the segment's continued existence: some companies were totally committed to IBM or IBM-compatible computers, other companies were attracted to IBM-compatible desktop publishing systems because they could be cheaper than Macintosh ones, and still other companies because the choice of the computer had been made on the basis of the availability of other software packages. The OS/2 system, which had been announced by IBM and Microsoft, promised to make IBM or compatible systems more attractive systems for desktop publishing.

In Segment 1, PageMaker dominated the market with about a 70 percent market share. Quark's Xpress and Letraset's Ready-Set-Go owned much of the rest of the market and Quark's market share was increasing. Market research conducted by Aldus suggested that less than 20 percent of the potential graphics art market had ''come down'' to desktop publishing by the summer of 1988. One Aldus marketing executive suggested that the potential creative graphics professional market might be fully tapped in three to five years.

PageMaker totally dominated Segment 2. By 1988, Aldus's sales into this segment were increasingly tied to new Macintosh installations, since most of the Macintosh-installed base that had a use for PageMaker had already bought desktop publishing software. Future sales of PageMaker in this segment were highly dependent on Apple's continued ability to develop new customers and to increase its penetration of its existing customer base.

Segment 3 was believed to be a huge potential market given the large PC-installed base and the increasing availability of laser printers. Aldus believed that the real competition in this segment was advanced word processors, or low-end desktop publishing software. Ventura Publishing and PageMaker had roughly equal shares of the high-end desktop publishing market in this segment.

PageMaker had a strong market share position in Segment 4, but, for the reasons suggested above, this was not a large segment. The aggregate market shares for Aldus and other major players in the Macintosh and MS-DOS desktop page layout markets in 1987 are shown in Exhibit 5.

In small- and medium-sized organizations the decision to move to desktop publishing was often made by high-level managers. The decision about which software package to purchase was often left to the judgment of the individuals who would be directly using the software. In large organizations, a variety of different buying processes were evident with major differences between organizations being attributable to the degree of centralization in the information systems function. Perhaps the most common buying pattern observed, for a niche application like desktop publishing, was for the individual department or function using desktop publishing to select one of the available packages. However, the organization would only provide support for one, or perhaps two packages.

EXHIBIT 5 World desktop page layout market, 1987

MS-DOS units and value

Software vendor	Units	Unit share	Value (millions)	Dollar share
Aldus	69,062	30.5%	$30.87	42.4%
Ventura	60,090	26.6	32.87	45.2
Software Publishing Corp.	39,521	17.5	2.98	4.1
DRI	7,667	3.4	2.35	3.2
Unison World	27,278	12.1	1.29	1.8
Springboard	16,201	7.2	0.77	1.1
AT	2,951	1.3	0.53	0.7
Other	3,355	1.5	1.08	1.5
Total	226,145		72.74	

Macintosh units and value

Software vendor	Units	Unit share	Value (millions)	Dollar share
Aldus	38,148	53.9%	$12.37	54.0%
Letraset	14,504	20.5	4.37	19.1
Quark	9,612	13.6	3.46	15.1
Orange Micro	8,466	12.0	2.73	11.9
Total	70,729		22.93	

Source: International Data Corporation.

Marketing

Product Line

In addition to PageMaker, Aldus had a number of other software products in its product line or under development. However, PageMaker still accounted for over 80 percent of Aldus Corporation's sales.

In July 1987, Aldus had acquired the marketing rights to a PostScript-based Macintosh drawing program that was introduced into the market in November 1987 as Aldus FreeHand. Aldus FreeHand was launched as a direct competitor to Adobe System's Illustrator product and it enjoyed substantial early market success by offering the ''power of Illustrator with the ease of use of MacDraw.'' By the late summer of 1988, version 2.0 of FreeHand was engaged in a highly competitive battle with Adobe Illustrator 88 for market dominance in the PostScript drawing program category. At the same time, Aldus was attempting to expand the market for FreeHand beyond that category by also positioning its offering against MacDraw II, a higher-priced and more sophisticated version of the original MacDraw program.

In September 1987, the company acquired both the marketing and development rights to a personal computer-based ''electronic photography'' application that was introduced to the market in November 1987. Aldus SnapShot was a more troubled software product due to the restricted availability of the hardware required to run it on its MS-DOS platform. The concept of ''electronic photography'' had failed to capture the market's imagination in the way that ''desktop publishing'' had done and Aldus had been unable to forge the strategic alliances with hardware vendors that would be required to make the product an unqualified market success.

In February 1988, Aldus acquired both the marketing and development rights to a desktop presentation product that was introduced in August 1988 as Aldus Persuasion, and was scheduled to be shipped in the fourth quarter of 1988. This acquisition was particularly important to Aldus for several reasons. First, the product itself was believed to be superior to any other desktop presentation product on the market, capable of ''setting the standard'' for desktop presentation products in much the same way that PageMaker had done for desktop publishing products. Second, the desktop presentation market was believed to meet or exceed the market opportunity represented by desktop publishing—and was significantly larger than the potential market for FreeHand or SnapShot. Third, the desktop presentation market was clearly perceived as a ''business market.'' Thus, it was hoped that Aldus Persuasion would help to position Aldus Corporation as a player in the mainstream business software market rather than the smaller graphic arts niche.

In August 1988, Aldus was actively seeking additional acquisitions and was also engaged in the internal development of new software products for the business market.

Pricing

One of the crucial early marketing decisions made by Aldus was the pricing of PageMaker for the Macintosh. In 1984, the most expensive piece of Macintosh software was Excel, a spreadsheet program, which had a list price of $395. After some debate, Aldus management decided to price PageMaker at $495, feeling that any lower price would result in it not being viewed as a serious business tool. There was no visible resistance in the market to the price. Subsequently, when Aldus introduced Version 3.0 of PageMaker for the Macintosh in 1987, the price was raised to $595.

The PC version of PageMaker was expensive to develop and Aldus's management believed it would be more expensive to sell and service in the market. With some trepidation they priced this version of PageMaker at $695, a $200 premium over the then-current Macintosh version price. Xerox's Ventura Publisher for the PC was announced almost simultaneously and was priced at $895, although Xerox's higher channel discounts resulted in its retail price being $795, a $100 premium over PageMaker. Aldus moved the price of the PC version of the product to $795 when Version 3.0 was introduced.

Distribution and Sales

Aldus distributed its products primarily through retail dealers and original equipment manufacturers (OEMs). OEMs and large retailers paid about 50 percent of the suggested retail price. The company had been selective in both authorizing and retaining dealers who were committed to supporting its products. No single dealer, chain, or OEM accounted for more than 10 percent of sales.

Domestic Retail Distribution

When Aldus first began marketing PageMaker, the desktop publishing product category did not exist. Aldus knew that there were some graphic arts customers with a need for the product, but that it would have to play the major role in developing dealers to sell desktop publishing solutions. The Aldus salesforce began working directly with the dealers to educate them on the benefits of desktop publishing and to help them develop sales materials and sales programs for desktop publishing. In choosing dealers for PageMaker, Aldus used three major criteria: the dealer must have a storefront, must sell hardware and software in order to provide a total solution, and must be focused on a vertical market. The company marketed PageMaker through independent dealers and large-volume chains such as Businessland, ComputerLand, Entre, Sears Business Centers, Inacomp, Computer Factory, Nynex, and others. More recently, Aldus had begun marketing PageMaker through value-added resellers (VARs), who distributed Aldus's products with other hardware and software products in various configurations designed to best meet specific end-user needs.

By late 1986, the dealer network in North America had grown to 1,200 dealers for the Apple Macintosh version of PageMaker. With the introduction of the PC version Aldus authorized an additional, largely new, set of dealers for the product. With almost 3,000 dealers by early 1987, it became increasingly difficult for the small Aldus salesforce to maintain all these relationships. Therefore, in March 1987, Aldus signed an agreement with Microamerica to serve as its primary third-party distributor of PageMaker to authorized dealers in the domestic retail market. PageMaker was the first software product carried by Microamerica. Aldus selected Microamerica because it did carry hardware and because it had invested in developing training facilities around the United States. Although Aldus continued to sell directly to retail dealers, this arrangement permitted small independent authorized dealers to purchase directly from Aldus or from Microamerica. Microamerica offered delivery within 24 hours of an order, minimizing the inventory carrying costs for small dealers. By August 1988, the company had over 3,100 separate authorized dealer locations.

Domestic Sales Force

By the summer of 1988, Aldus had a seven-person corporate salesforce in the United States to do missionary selling, but these individuals did not make any direct sales. This corporate salesforce was devoting a lot of its energies on trying to persuade major corporations to standardize on PageMaker. In addition, a salesforce of about 40 dealer account managers and associate sales representatives was deployed throughout the country to stimulate dealer and VAR sales and to assist dealers and VARs with market education and development. The full cost of an Aldus salesperson in the United States, including salary, commissions, benefits and office costs, was about $100,000 in 1988. The sales organization in the United States was divided into three regions, with the regional sales managers reporting to the vice president of marketing and sales (see Exhibit 6).

EXHIBIT 6   Organization chart

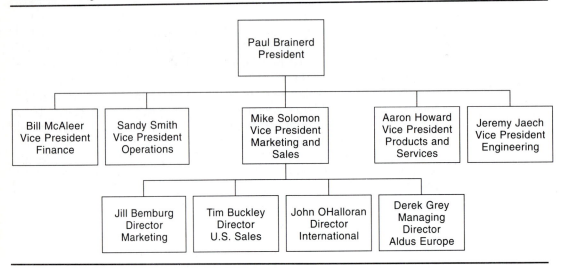

International Distribution

Aldus made an early commitment to marketing its products globally. Even before the first product was shipped in the United States, the first distributor was signed up in Europe. Distribution developed differently in the international market than it had in the United States. In Europe, the typical Aldus approach in a country was to appoint a lead distributor, who was typically one of the top five distributors in the country and who had a network of resellers. In early 1987, Aldus established a marketing, distribution, and support joint venture corporation in Scotland. Aldus U.K. was 50 percent owned by Aldus and 50 percent owned by the two individuals who held the exclusive license to distribute Aldus's products in the United Kingdom and Ireland. Later, in 1987, Aldus bought the other 50 percent of the joint venture and this became Aldus Europe. Aldus Europe provided a coordinating function for all Aldus's activities in Europe. In the next two years, subsidiaries were set up in the United Kingdom, Sweden, and West Germany. The subsidiaries were established to provide the marketing function for Aldus that the distributors were not providing and to allow Aldus to build real cooperative relationships with the IBM and Apple organizations in the major countries. By mid-1988, Aldus was supporting 10 localized versions of PageMaker and five translations of Aldus FreeHand in close to 40 countries. For calendar 1988, it was estimated that about 40 percent of Aldus's sales would come from its international operations.

OEM Distribution

The company had entered into OEM distribution agreements with Hewlett-Packard, DEC, Wang, Olivetti, and IBM. The OEM agreements typically granted the right to distribute the company's prepackaged products with the OEM's microcomputers and, in some cases, related peripheral hardware, such as printers. The products were distributed under Aldus's trademarks.

In October 1986, Aldus entered into a cooperative marketing agreement with Hewlett-Packard and Microsoft. The three companies agreed to jointly market and promote a desktop publishing solution based on the Hewlett-Packard Vectra microcomputer and its LaserJet printer family, Microsoft Windows graphical operating environment and Microsoft Word word processing software, and the PC version of PageMaker. The three companies planned to promote their products through a one-year advertising campaign, dealer training programs, trade show exhibits, seminars, and other activities.

Marketing Budgets

The total marketing and sales budget for Aldus amounted to about 20 percent of sales. In 1988, the company expected to spend about $1.5 million on media advertising. New product launches and launches of major new releases of a current product were becoming increasingly expensive. Aldus management believed that by 1988 a major launch or relaunch cost about $750,000 in the Macintosh market and $1.5–2.0 million in the PC market. These figures included advertising, dealer rollout expenses, public relations, collateral materials, demonstration materials (such as diskettes or videos), and third-party marketing programs (such as joint promotions with vendors of complementary hardware or supplies).

Technical Support and Service

Aldus provided technical support, service, and training to the market through several channels, including the use of an ''800'' telephone support center. It offered direct technical support to individuals and corporations through several different programs. In addition, it had developed a U.S. network of over 70 authorized trainers to offer training and consulting in major U.S. markets. Finally, an additional informal network of over 200 ''service bureaus'' had sprung up in the United States to offer typeset-quality desktop publishing output using Linotronic imagesetters.

Competition

The desktop publishing market was highly competitive and had been subject to rapid change, which was expected to continue in the future. The company believed that the principal competitive factors in the desktop publishing market included product features and functions, ease of understanding and operating the software, product reliability, price/performance characteristics, brand recognition, and availability and quality of support and training services. Aldus competed within the desktop publishing software industry with small independent software vendors and large corporations. Some of Aldus's actual and potential competitors had financial, marketing, and technological resources greater than those of Aldus.

To date, price competition had not been a major factor among producers of desktop publishing software. However, suppliers of word processing, database, and spreadsheet applications software programs had experienced significant price reductions through the use of "site licenses" (permitting copying of the program and documentation) and discount pricing for large-volume corporate customers.

The Macintosh version of PageMaker competed with software from a variety of independent vendors. Partly as a result of Aldus's close alliance with Apple, PageMaker soon gained ascendancy over its early competitors: Boston Software's MacPublisher and a product called Scoop, which was marketed by Tangent. By mid-1988, Ready-Set-Go from Letraset, a company well-known to the graphics market as a supplier of press type, had been relegated to the position of a well-financed also-ran. The major competitive threat in 1988 was Quark Xpress priced at $795, which had become a strong contender in the high end of the market. Quark had a similar distribution system to Aldus, relying heavily on retailers and VARs, but its network was not as extensive as Aldus's. Quark Xpress had a somewhat higher level of typographic sophistication than PageMaker. The software design was more modular than PageMaker's and it was possible for VARs to customize the software to meet the specific needs of particular end-use markets. For example, a VAR that was targeting weekly newspapers might use the standard Quark Xpress page composition software but add a software module that would allow the newspaper to quickly "dummy" in advertisements. At the corporate level Quark was not believed to provide the same level of customer support as Aldus. By August 1988, Quark enjoyed more than a 15 percent share of the total Macintosh market for desktop publishing, and a much higher share in the creative graphics professional segment. Some Aldus executives attributed part of its success to its exclusive focus on this segment, while both PageMaker and Aldus Corporation attempted to appeal to a much broader market.

The PC version of PageMaker competed primarily with the software offered by several vendors including the Xerox Corporation, which held exclusive marketing and distribution rights to Ventura Publisher. Ventura had beaten the PC version of PageMaker to the market by about three months. Ventura

Publisher targeted customers who prepared long, structured documents that incorporated both text and graphics. Training materials, such as manuals, reference materials, and certain types of proposals, were typical applications. This was in contrast to PageMaker, which was better suited to applications with a higher design content. While Ventura focused largely on the product development task, Xerox handled the marketing. Ventura benefitted from its association with the Xerox name and Xerox's existing retail presence due to its typewriter, copiers, and printer product lines. Xerox viewed Ventura Publisher as an opportunity to leverage hardware sales into the desktop publishing market. Prior to the introduction of Ventura Publisher there was no MS-DOS desktop publishing product. Xerox had set up a separate business unit, Xerox Desktop Software (XDS), to market Ventura Publisher and other similar products. From Aldus's perspective, the relationship between Xerox and Ventura had not lived up to its full potential. XDS seemed to have some difficulty getting top management support and attention and Xerox had not been as successful as it had hoped in developing personal computers and low-cost printers that would benefit from XDS's efforts. In fact, Xerox had withdrawn from the personal computer market. Nevertheless, the Ventura product was selling well against the MS-DOS version of PageMaker and was making unchallenged claims of ''market leadership on the PC platform,'' which ran the risk of becoming a self-fulfilling prophecy.

In addition to competition within the desktop publishing category, Aldus faced competition from three other sources: low-end competitors, led by Software Publishing's First Publisher; dedicated larger-scale electronic publishing systems; and a variety of word processing software programs, which were increasingly incorporating low-end desktop publishing features. The dedicated electronic publishing systems, provided by companies such as Interleaf Corporation and Atex, were designed for publication and engineering departments and other groups requiring additional composition and pagination features. In general, the cost of a stand-alone workstation, or a centralized minicomputer or mainframe-based publishing system, was substantially higher than for microcomputer-based desktop publishing systems. Of these indirect competitors for PageMaker, Aldus executives believed that the word processors represented the most significant threat because of their ability to address the needs of the business market, which had by now eclipsed the creative graphics professional segment as the dominant portion of the market. Word processing programs were generally less expensive than desktop publishing software and were easier to use. However, word processing programs generally lacked the flexibility and features of PageMaker, such as the ability to set up elaborate layouts including mixed columns and to integrate text and graphics from other software programs.

Aldus also competed with other companies in the microcomputer software market for dealers and distributors, and for alliances with other hardware and software vendors. The principal considerations for distributors and dealers in determining which products to offer include profit margins, product support and service, and credit terms.

The Proposal

By the summer of 1988, Richard Strong and others believed they were witnessing some troubling trends. As PageMaker became a more sophisticated product that met the evolving needs of the high-end user, this made the product less attractive to the less sophisticated business segment of the market. Unfortunately, the primary distribution channels, the retail dealers, lacked the sophistication to support the high-end user. Thus, Richard Strong believed that Aldus was in danger of serving neither segment of the market well. The situation was exacerbated in Europe by the weaker position of the Apple Macintosh, which made Aldus's sales in Europe much more heavily dependent on the MS-DOS version of PageMaker and the other products. Given the relatively small size of the MS-DOS graphic arts professional segment of the market, Aldus Europe was particularly dependent on the business segment of the market for growth.

As he looked to the future, he saw the needs of the business user and the creative graphics professional continuing to diverge. The creative graphics professionals would demand increasing sophistication (including more control over typography), more features and greater power, access to more sophisticated support and technical assistance, and greater compatibility with the other software and hardware (such as sophisticated scanners and image setters) they used in their businesses. As the business segment of the market for desktop publishing continued to expand, attracting less technically sophisticated users, the demand for greater ease of use, greater automation, and reduced training periods for new users to become proficient would be key needs. With user-friendly and well-documented software, the need for technical assistance for this segment of the market would probably diminish.

Richard Strong believed that trying to meet the divergent needs of these segments with PageMaker and one product line was placing huge demands on the software development people. The program code required for a program like PageMaker was huge (over 1 million lines of code). The complexity of the product would complicate the program upgrade task and probably delay upgrade schedules. Internally, there was conflict in the organization. Some of the software development people were oriented to the business market and some were oriented to the graphics market, but both groups could only respond to their markets' needs through one product.

Richard Strong proposed that Aldus be split into two divisions focused on the business and the professional segments of the market. Given the relative size of the two markets, the business division would probably be three times the size of the graphics division in terms of staff. In particular, he suggested that the professional product line be anchored around a version of PageMaker priced around $2,000. This sophisticated, powerful desktop publishing product would be complemented by a number of other software tools for the graphic arts professional. The effective sales, distribution, and other sales service and support for this product line would require a new high-end distribution channel.

The business product line would be anchored around a $500 version of PageMaker. The product line would contain a range of easy-to-use software tools for the office worker, and would be distributed through a broad distribution network.

These product line and organizational decisions were being made in the context of what many industry executives saw as increasing polarization of the software distribution industry. The ''mass market'' was increasingly being served by superstores, software-only retailers, mail-order firms, and telemarketers. The high end was served increasingly by VARs and other boutiques that could provide needs assessments, consulting, training, and after-sales service and support. Traditional independent hardware dealers, who also sold software, seemed to be becoming a much less viable channel for software.

While others at the meeting saw merit in Richard's proposal, they pointed out a number of areas of concern. From a technical perspective, a brand split would be difficult to do given the way the computer code had been written for PageMaker. The code was not split into distinct modules, which meant that a brand split would require a major software development effort. Already the software engineering resources were being strained with new product development efforts already underway and the work on the development of the next release of PageMaker (Release 4.0), which was due in less than eighteen months. While a divisional structure had merit, several executives felt such a dramatic move was premature given Aldus's financial and human resources. In addition, the marketing costs of launching and supporting two product lines would not be trivial. There was also the question of whether the creative graphics professional market was large enough to support a separate division.

At the conclusion of the sales and marketing meeting, the Aldus corporate marketing staff were asked to evaluate the proposal and to develop a specific set of recommendations. If the decision were made to split the product line, a plan would have to be developed to address some of the concerns raised by Richard Strong. In particular, how could the marketing communications mix (advertising, direct mail, collateral materials, and personal selling) be developed to address the two market segments most effectively. If the decision were made to split the product line, then the marketing strategies for the two markets would have to be specified. In addition, in the latter case, a communications strategy would be required to explain the split to Aldus's current resellers, the industry infrastructure, the trade press, and the financial community.

Case 36

Dutch Food Industries Company (A)*

In early September, Jan de Vries, product manager for Dutch Food Industries' new salad dressing product, was wondering what strategy to follow with respect to this new product. His assistant had prepared information concerning alternative promotional methods to use to introduce the new product, and he was concerned with exactly which of these he should recommend for the product's introduction. He also wondered what price the new product should retail for and when the company should introduce the new product. Mr. de Vries had to decide these issues in the next couple of days, as his report containing his recommendations on the introduction of the new salad dressing was due on the desk of the director of marketing the following Monday.

Company Background

The Netherlands Oil Factory of Delft, The Netherlands, was founded in 1884. This firm, which supplied edible oils to the growing margarine industry, merged in 1900 with a French milling company. The new firm then operated under the name Dutch Food Industries Company (DFI).

From this origin, the brand name DFI became increasingly strong and was eventually given to all of the company's branded products. More recently, the name was registered for use internationally.

In the course of the 1920s, DFI became an important factor in the margarine market. The company was a troublesome competitor for the Margarine Union, the company formed by the merger in 1927 of the two margarine giants, Van den Bergh and Jurgens. In 1928, an agreement was reached by which DFI joined the Margarine Union.

In 1930, the interests of the Margarine Union were merged with those of International Industries Corporation—a large, diversified, and international

* This case was written by Kenneth L. Bernhardt and James Scott assisted by Jos Viehoff, graduate student, Netherlands School of Economics. Copyright © 1990 by Kenneth L. Bernhardt.

organization. It was in this way that DFI became a part of the International Industries complex of companies.

International Industries Corporation (IIC) is a worldwide organization with major interests in the production of margarine, other edible fats and oils, soups, ice cream, frozen foods, meats, cheeses, soaps, and detergents.

The total sales of IIC were more than $1 billion.[1] Profits before taxes were $56 million.

Within IIC, DFI proceeded with its original activities after its margarine factory was closed, namely developing its exports of oils and fats, its trade in bakery products, as well as a number of branded food products. The following list indicates the range of consumer products which the company marketed: table oil, household fats, mayonnaise, salad dressing (several varieties), tomato ketchup, peanut butter, and peanuts.

DFI's total annual sales were between $14 million–$28 million. Profits before taxes were between $1.4 million–$2.8 million.

Background on the Dressing Market

A large and growing percentage of Holland's population eats lettuce, usually with salad dressing, with their meals. Estimates indicated that 82 percent of the people ate lettuce with salad dressing regularly. The salad dressing market has extreme seasonal demand as shown in Exhibit 1. This seasonal pattern coincides with the periods of greatest production of lettuce in Holland. Thus, 50 percent of the total year's volume for the salad dressing market occurs in the four months beginning in April. During this period, lettuce is plentiful and sells for approximately $0.46 per head.

The total salad dressing market was growing at approximately 7 percent per year. DFI's share of the market had declined from 20.7 percent to 16.6 percent over the last five years. The total market for salad dressings at manufacturer's level was currently estimated at between $7 million and $8.4 million. The company was looking for ways to halt the decline in market share and, in fact, increase DFI's share of the growing market.

Historically, the salad dressing market was composed of two segments. The first was a 25 percent oil-based salad dressing, which comprised 90 percent of the total market. The other 10 percent of the market consisted of 50 percent oil-based salad dressing, a slightly creamier product. Previously, DFI, in an effort to increase its market share, had introduced a new product which was 50 percent oil based. Up to that time, DFI sold only 25 percent oil-based salad dressing. The product, called Delfine, was not successful in obtaining the desired volume and profit. While DFI still marketed Delfine, almost all of DFI's volume came from its 25 percent oil-based product, Slasaus.

A research study was conducted to help the DFI marketing executives determine why Delfine was not successful. Several reasons emerged:

---

[1] All financial data in this case are presented in U.S. dollars.

EXHIBIT 1 Seasonal analysis of salad dressing market (percentage of annual total market sales—bimonthly periods)

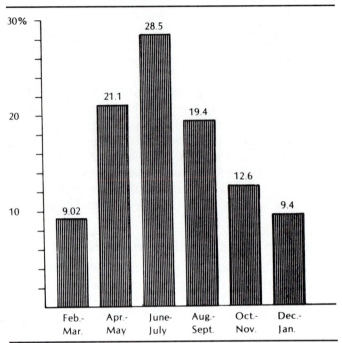

1. The potential of the 50 percent oil-based market was much smaller than originally anticipated, and only a small percentage of the total population was even interested in this product.
2. The consumers could detect only a small difference between the 25 percent oil-based and the 50 percent oil-based varieties when blind-tested. The difference was not noticeable enough for the consumers to prefer the 50 percent oil-based product.
3. The 50 percent oil-based salad dressing was more expensive, and the consumer was not willing to pay the difference for an apparently almost imperceptible difference.

Because the Delfine sales were well below expectations, DFI removed the heavy promotion support which it had been giving the product. The executives decided to wait for a significant breakthrough of a product with unique advantages. The Delfine experience indicated to them that it would take a totally new type of product for DFI to increase its market share significantly.

Background and Development of Slamix

Every two years, the company conducted a housewives' habits study in which a panel of 700 consumers was asked about their household and their food preparation habits. In August two years before, the company received the most recent study, called PMC-11. The housewives were asked how they prepared their lettuce and what ingredients they used. The results showed that an extremely large percentage of the housewives added not only salad dressing to lettuce, but also added other ingredients such as salt, pepper, eggs, onion, gherkins, and so on. Thus DFI executives got the idea that putting some of these ingredients in the salad dressing would result in a real convenience for the housewife, and DFI would have the significant new product for which they had been searching. The laboratory, in August of the same year, began developing a "dressed" salad dressing which included some of the ingredients which many housewives were accustomed to adding.

Early in the next year, a committee called the Slamix Committee,[2] was formed to make sure that every part of the company was involved in the development of this new product. The committee, which was headed up by the product manager, had representatives from various parts of the company, including development, production, and marketing. The committee studied production problems, laboratory findings, and in general, was charged with the responsibility of seeing that the development progressed as scheduled. The committee did not have decision-making powers but either invited decision makers to important meetings or wrote reports to the people who were in a position to make the required decisions.

After several product tests concerned with taste and keeping properties were conducted at the factory, the company, one year after laboratory work began, undertook its first consumer test of the new "dressed" salad dressing. A panel of housewives was shown a bottle of the new product which was a salad dressing containing pieces of gherkins, onions, and paprika. Several conclusions emerged from this study:

1. The "dressed" salad dressing was seen by the housewives as more than a salad dressing with ingredients. It was seen as a completely new product.
2. There were two sides to this newness:
    a. By looking at the product, they thought that it had a new taste.
    b. The convenience aspect was strongly stressed by the housewives.
3. The housewives thought that the new product would be good for decorating the lettuce. With its new color (light red with colorful ingredients), they thought that they could decorate the lettuce much better than with present salad dressings which were creme-colored and very similar to mayonnaise.
4. When asked about the ingredients, one half of the housewives were favorable toward paprika, and half were against it. This apparently was a troublesome ingredient. However, because of the convenience aspect, gherkins and onions were favored by the housewives.

Later, a second consumer study was conducted by the Institute of Household Research in Rotterdam. A sample of 140 housewives who actually used

---

[2] Literally translated, Slasaus means "lettuce sauce," and Slamix is literally "lettuce mix."

salad dressing on lettuce was given a bottle of the new product to take home. Then, they were visited in their homes. Much useful information emerged from this study. After looking at the product, but before trying it, the housewives said that it looked like a fun product, it made them happy, and they thought that it would taste good. When asked what they thought the product contained, they said tomatoes, red paprika, celery, gherkins, and green paprika.

However, the company was disappointed with the housewives' overall evaluation of the product. Only 20 percent of the housewives said that they thought the product was very good, 11 percent did not like the product, and 69 percent of the housewives said that there were some favorable and some unfavorable aspects of the product. The main reason for the 80 percent unfavorable reaction was the consistency of the new salad dressing. It was too thin. The housewives could pour it too easily and it rapidly went to the bottom of the bowl. Because it fell to the bottom, the housewives said that it was much harder to decorate their salad. It was also uneconomical because they felt that they would put too much on if the product was that thin. There were also problems with taste. Many of the housewives thought it was too sour or too sharp. The paprika was the main reason for the dissatisfaction.

In spite of the above problems, there were several aspects of the study which encouraged the company to proceed with the development of this new product. When asked how they would change the ingredients in the "dressed" salad dressing, only 47 percent of the housewives suggested changes. Most recommended that more onions be added. The housewives were asked for their preference between DFI's Slasaus and the new "dressed" salad dressing. As shown in Exhibit 2, the housewives preferred the new product, except for its consistency. Sixty percent of the housewives said that they would buy the product if it were possible to buy it in the store. Since this was a very high positive response, the company was very encouraged.

EXHIBIT 2 Preference test: Slasaus versus "dressed" salad dressing

Prefer	Taste	Appear-ance	Decoration aspects	Con-sistency	Con-venience
"Dressed" salad dressing	59%	73%	46%	18%	50%
Slasaus	38	20	44	65	20
No preference/no difference	3	7	10	17	30
	100%	100%	100%	100%	100%

The marketing, production, and development groups, coordinated by the Slamix Committee, began work on incorporating the required changes made evident by this consumer study. DFI's development group experimented with changes in the consistency, taste, and ingredients. The production group experimented with a new production process. DFI had intended to introduce the new "dressed" salad dressing in a few months. However, the top corporate executives decided that, before the new product could be introduced, an extensive test of its keeping properties (vulnerability to deterioration) would have to be conducted.

The keeping-properties test showed that after several months the light red-colored product changed to a pink color. The difference in color was only slight, but DFI executives thought that the consumer reaction to this change should be tested. They decided that at the same time they would conduct a consumer test to find a name for this new product. A sample of 180 housewives from the Institute of Household Research was used to get at these questions. Only 2 out of the 180 housewives saw that there was a difference in color between the two bottles of the new product. When they were told that there was a slight difference and were shown the two bottles together, most of the housewives could not see the color change, and those that could were not unhappy about it.

The housewives were then asked what the name for this product should be. The phrase ''mixed salad dressing'' kept coming up. The housewives were then asked what they thought of two names which the company had screened, ''Slamix'' (lettuce mix) and ''Spikkeltjessaus'' (sauce with little spots). Eighty-one percent thought that Slamix was a very good name. Only 26 percent thought that Spikkeltjessaus was a good name. The name Slamix was chosen for the new product. Interestingly, that was the name that the company had used internally for the new product when it was first being developed.

A short time later, DFI had solved the color-change problem. The company now thought that it had a product ready to be marketed, so a final consumer test was undertaken to test the effect of all of the changes that had been made during the previous year.

Two versions of Slamix, a white one and a pink one, were tested at the Institute for Household Research. One hundred eighty housewives were asked what they thought of the product and whether they would buy it or not. The negative reactions to the product were minimal. Almost no negative comments were voiced. The problems of consistency, color, taste, and ingredients had apparently been solved. When asked if they would buy the product, 76 percent of those shown the pink product, and 70 percent of those shown the white product responded in a positive manner. After tasting the two versions of Slamix, the housewives revealed a strong preference for the pink Slamix. The DCI executives felt that the product was now ready to be marketed.

DFI executives next reviewed the financial projections prepared by Mr. de Vries, the product manager. Almost no capital investment would be required as the Slamix would be produced by using present production facilities. Only a few machines, at a total cost of $11,000, would be required.

At an early stage in the development of the product, Slamix sales had been forecasted at 3.7 percent of the total market at the end of the first year. Encouraged by the results of the consumer tests, DFI executives revised their estimate of sales. The new forecast was for approximately 6.7 percent of the market. (See Exhibit 3.)

EXHIBIT 3 Forecast sales of Slamix

Year	Share of market (percent)
Original estimates	
Year 1	3.7%
Year 2	3.9
Year 3	4.4
Revised estimates	
Year 1	6.7
Year 2	11.7

The directors of the company thought that they finally had the product for which they had been waiting. The consumer tests were complete, and the product had found very high favor with the consumers. There was significant technological development involved in the product, and DFI executives thought that it would take considerable time for the competition to duplicate the product. The product manager's projected sales seemed reasonable. Mr. de Vries was asked to prepare a comprehensive report concerning the introductory marketing strategy to be used to introduce the new product.

Pricing Strategy

The first problem that the product manager had to resolve concerned the suggested retail price that the company should charge for Slamix. To help Mr. de Vries make his recommendation, the assistant product manager had made a list of the following considerations:

1. The company's total cost for a 0.30-liter-size bottle of Slamix was $0.20. This was 20 percent higher than DFI's regular salad dressing, Slasaus.
2. The gross margin for Slasaus was 22 percent. Because of the unique qualities of Slamix, large development costs, and possible substitution with Slasaus, a higher gross margin for Slamix might be considered.
3. DFI gave the wholesalers a 12.5 percent margin and retailers a 14.3 percent margin for Slasaus. Possibly these should be increased for Slamix to encourage greater acceptance and promotion by the trade channels of distribution.
4. The two leading salad dressings, Salata by Duyvis and Slasaus, both had a retail price of $0.28 for the 0.30-liter bottle. The retail price for the 0.60-liter bottle was $0.48. Private label salad dressings were $0.22 for a 0.30-liter bottle. The average price for all salad dressings was approximately $0.26.
5. DFI had conducted some research on the optimal price of Slamix. After using a sample of the product, 140 housewives were asked what price they would be willing to pay for Slamix. Their responses, by percent, were:

	Percent
$0.31 or less	45%
Between $0.31 and $0.40	41
$0.40 or more	14
Total	100%

The average price mentioned was $0.34.

The assistant product manager also prepared the table shown in Exhibit 4. The first column shows the retail price, and gives data that allows one to calculate trade margins and gross margin for Slasaus. The remaining six columns show alternative retail prices for Slamix, resulting from different trade margins and gross margins. Mr. de Vries wondered which of these prices he should recommend to the board of directors.

EXHIBIT 4   Alternative prices for Slamix*

		Slamix					
	Slasaus	1	2	3	4	5	6
Retail price	$0.28	$0.32	$0.34	$0.34	0.36	$0.37	$0.38
Price to retailer	0.24	0.28	0.28	0.29	0.295	0.31	0.316
Price to wholesaler	0.21	0.25	0.25	0.26	0.26	0.28	0.28
Cost	0.165	0.20	0.20	0.20	0.20	0.20	0.20

* Selected figures in this table have been disguised.

Promotion Alternatives

The board of directors told the product manager that he had $203,000 for his promotion budget. Of this, $7,000 was to be allocated as Slamix's share of the general corporate advertising which aided all DFI products. The $203,000 was determined by using a percentage of the "expected gross profit of the first year" for Slamix.[3] DFI's policy was to break even in the third year of the new product, attaining a total payback within five years. The company was generally willing to spend the gross profit for the first year as part of the total investment.

The company had already given considerable thought to the sales message and the brand image desired for Slamix. The information below was sent to the advertising agency to help in planning the promotional program of the company:

> *Sales message.* It is now possible, in a completely new way, to make delicious salad. Sla + Slamix = Sla Klaar. (Lettuce + Slamix = Lettuce Ready)

---

[3] It was possible that the percentage could be greater than 100 percent. This would mean that the company was willing to spend more than the first year's gross profit for initial promotion.

Supporting message. Slamix is a salad dressing with pieces of onion, gherkins, and paprika.

Desired brand image. With Slamix you can make, very easily and very quickly, a delicious salad that also looks nice. Slamix is a complete, good, handy product. DFI is a modern firm with up-to-date ideas.

Thus, the company wanted to get across three principal points. They are (1) that Slamix is a completely new product, (2) that it is convenient, and (3) that it is a salad dressing with ingredients making it a complete salad dressing.

The product manager was undecided as to how to divide the $196,000 among the following alternatives:

1. Television.
2. Radio.
3. Newspaper advertising.
4. Magazines.
5. Sampling.
6. Coupons.
7. Price-off promotion.
8. Key chain premiums.
9. Trade allowances.

Television

The product manager thought that television would be advantageous because of the ability to show the product in actual use—a housewife pouring Slamix onto the lettuce. The cost of using the television medium is shown in Exhibit 5. The company did not have a choice among the seven blocks of time, but had to take whatever was available. For planning, however, they figured an average cost of a 30-second ad would be $1,800. Mr. de Vries felt that at least 25 advertisements were necessary before the TV advertising would have maximum impact.

EXHIBIT 5 Data on Dutch television media

Station	Block number	Time	Cost of 30-second ad
Nederland 1	1	Before early news	$2,300
Nederland 1	2	After early news	2,300
Nederland 1	3	Before late news	2,950
Nederland 1	4	After late news	2,950
Nederland 2	5	After early news	500
Nederland 2	6	Before late news	840
Nederland 2	7	After late news	840
Average cost per 30-second TV ad			$1,800
Production cost for a TV ad			7,000

TV coverage per 1,000 households = 850 or 85 percent. Only about one half of the homes can receive Nederland 2.

Radio

The chief attraction of radio was its extremely low price. Each 30-second radio ad cost $126 on Radio Veronica, a popular station during the daytime. Production costs for a radio ad were approximately $840. Only 60 percent of the households could receive Radio Veronica, mainly in the western part of the country. Mr. de Vries felt that if radio were used, a minimum of 100 spots should be purchased.

Newspapers

Mr. de Vries thought the main advantages of newspapers would be the announcement effect and its influence with the local trade. Nationally, the cost of each half-page insertion would be $14,000.

Magazines

Magazines would be a desirable addition to the promotional program for several reasons. Due to the ability to use color, the company could show the product as it actually looked on the shelf. By using several women's magazines, the company could reach a select audience of people reading the magazine at its leisure. Data on selected Dutch magazines are shown in Exhibit 6. Mr. de Vries thought that if they were to use a magazine campaign, at least 10 insertions would be necessary before the advertising would be very effective. Of the possibilities in Exhibit 6, the agency thought that the combination of *Eva*,

EXHIBIT 6 Data on selected Dutch magazines

Magazines	Type	Circulation	Frequency	Price for full-page ad		Cost per 1,000 circulation*
				Black and white	Color	
Eva	Women's	375,000	Weekly	$ 770	$1,408	$3.75
Margriet	Women's	825,000	Weekly	2,100	3,440	4.15
Libelle	Women's	570,000	Weekly	1,416	2,340	4.10
Prinses	Women's	213,000	Weekly	660	1,175	5.55
Panorama	General	403,000	Weekly	1,300	2,150	5.40
Nieuwe Revu	General	261,000	Weekly	920	1,540	5.90
Spiegel	General	175,000	Weekly	710	1,325	7.55
Het Beste	Digest	325,000	Monthly	965	1,615	4.90
Studio	TV guide	575,000	Weekly	1,525	2,420	4.20
NCRV-gids	TV guide	482,000	Weekly	1,420	2,290	4.75
Vara-gids	TV guide	504,000	Weekly	1,500	2,370	4.70
AVRO-Televizier	TV guide	950,000	Weekly	2,600	3,870	4.05
Combination of Eva, Margriet, and AVRO-Televizier				4,900	7,785	3.65

* Cost of one-page color ad, divided by circulation in thousands. With *Eva* as an example, cost per 1,000 circulation = $1,408/375 = $3.75.

Margriet, and *AVRO-Televizier* would be most effective for DFI, since the combination would reach a large number of people at a relatively low cost.

Sampling

Although he realized that it was very expensive, Mr. de Vries considered the use of direct-mail sampling. A small 12 cm. by 18 cm. (approximately 5 × 7 inches) folder could be mailed to Holland's 3.7 million households for $20,000. The cost, however, would increase substantially if a small bottle of the product were to be included in the direct mailing. This cost would be 20 cents for handling, plus 75 cents for the actual sample. Thus, it would cost $980,000 to sample the whole country.

Coupon

Mr. de Vries was considering whether or not to include a coupon good for $0.04 off the purchase of Slamix with one of the other DFI products—mayonnaise, for example. He estimated that 900,000 coupons would be distributed. At a redemption rate of 5 percent, the cost would, thus, be approximately $1,700.

Price-Off Promotion

DFI made use of a reduced retail price for most of its new product introductions. Thus, the product manager thought it quite normal to consider the use of reducing the retail price by U.S. $0.07 per bottle and identifying this price reduction on the label of the product. It was felt that this reduced price would encourage the housewives to try Slamix. It was also quite normal to follow up this sales promotion with a similar price reduction approximately five months after the product was introduced. This would encourage those who had still not tried the product to purchase a bottle and would encourage those who had already bought one bottle to continue purchasing the new product. The cost of this price-off promotion is shown in Exhibit 7.

EXHIBIT 7

Introduction:	
720,000 bottles at 25 cents (U.S. $0.07) off each	$50,400
Handling and display materials	2,800
Total	$53,200
Follow-up five months later:	
600,000 bottles at 25 cents (U.S. $0.07) off each	$42,000
Handling and display materials	2,800
Total	$44,800

Key Chain Premium

It was very unusual to use a free premium to introduce a new product, but Mr. de Vries was considering this alternative for several reasons. Many products in Holland at this time were using key chains as a premium. As shown in Exhibit 8, an extremely large percentage of the people in Holland were collecting key chains. The details of the research showed that mothers and daughters were more likely to collect key chains, especially if the children were between 8 and 11 years of age. Mr. de Vries felt that if he used key chains as premiums for the introduction of Slamix he could have a follow-up promotion five months later using either key chains or price-off deals. Selected cost information on the key chain promotion is shown in Exhibit 9.

EXHIBIT 8 Percentage of households collecting key chains

	June	July	September
Households with children	45	n.a.	n.a.
Households without children	5	n.a.	n.a.
Total (weighted average)	34	37	41

n.a. = not available.

EXHIBIT 9

Introduction:	
720,000 bottles = about 220 metric tons	
750,000 key chains at $0.056	$42,000
Handling costs and display materials	16,800
Total	$58,800
Follow-up five months later:	
600,000 bottles = about 180 tons	
625,000 key chains at $0.056	$35,000
Handling costs and display materials	14,000
Total	$49,000

Trade Allowances

The product manager also considered the use of trade allowances to encourage the retailers to accept and promote the new product. The company traditionally offered $0.28 per case of 12 bottles. Thus, if it was decided that trade allowances were desirable, the cost would be $16,800 for the initial introduction and an additional $14,000 used during the follow-up promotion five months later. Trade allowances could be used together with either the price-off promotion or the key chain promotion. The product manager felt that trade allowances would not be very effective without one of the two consumer sales promotions.

Distribution

Outside of the question of what trade margins to use and whether or not to use trade allowances during the consumer sales promotions discussed above, Mr. de Vries did not see any problems with distribution. DFI had a sales force of approximately 50 persons who regularly called on 10,000 outlets in Holland. It was felt that the sales force could handle the introduction of the new product with no problem.

The last problem the product manager faced concerned the timing of the introduction of Slamix. The product would be ready for introduction in October. Mr. de Vries wondered whether the seasonal nature of the demand for the product would make it more desirable to hold off the introduction until March of the next year.

Case 37

I've Got a Swatch*

It was mid-1986 and Chris Keigel had only recently returned from military service to become European marketing manager for Swatch, the new watch concept that had revolutionized the watch industry and brought Swiss watchmaking out of a 40-year slump. He knew that Swatch management in Biel, Switzerland, was concerned about maintaining sales growth and agreeing on long-term international strategy. Existing watch brands were renewing their strategies and new competitors inspired by Swatch were mushrooming worldwide. Chris Keigel had been requested to gather background information for an upcoming top management meeting called to arrive at a consensus on the very concept of Swatch, its international positioning, and viable product line extensions.

Company Background

Swatch watches were manufactured by ETA S.A., a century-old Swiss watch movement firm and a subsidiary of SMH (Société Micromécanique et Horlogère), the world's second-largest watchmaking concern after the Japanese firm Seiko. SMH was the result of a merger in 1983 between ASUAG (Allgemeine Schweizer Uhrenindustrie) and SSIH (Société Suisse pour l'Industrie Horlogère), Switzerland's two major watch manufacturers rescued from bankruptcy by the major Swiss banks. In addition to Swatch, the SMH product line included the well-known brands Omega, Longines, Tissot, and Rado. Swatch A.G. was a subsidiary set up in 1984 to handle the international marketing of Swatch watches. Its Executive Committee was composed of President E. T. Marquardt, Vice President American Operations Max Imgrüth, Vice President Continental Operations Felice A. Schillaci, and Vice President Australian Operations H. N. Tune.

---

* This case was prepared by Helen Chase Kimball, Research Associate, under the supervision of Christian Pinson, Associate Professor, INSEAD, as a basis for class discussion rather than to illustrate either effective or ineffective handling of an administrative situation. It was in part inspired by a report prepared by R. J. Burnett, INSEAD MBA student. Certain proprietary data have been disguised. Copyright © INSEAD/CEDEP 1987. Used with permission.

Watch Technology

Until the late 1950s, all watches were *mechanical* (i.e., spring-powered, with movements comprising a hundred or more parts). In 1957, the first electric watch was marketed in the United States. A few years later, the American firm, Bulova, developed a *tuning-fork* watch, battery-powered and accurate to within one minute per month. The *quartz* (i.e., electronic) watch was invented in Switzerland in 1968 but first marketed in the United States by Hamilton. It improved accuracy to unheard-of levels. The quartz watch display was either of the traditional ''analog'' type with hands moving around a face, or ''digital'' with numbers appearing in a frame. Exhibit 1 gives a rough description of the components of four watch types.

EXHIBIT 1   Major components of four watch types

	Mechanical	Tuning fork	Quartz digital	Quartz analog
Energy source	Hairspring	Battery	Battery	Battery
Time base	Balance-spring	Tuning fork	Quartz crystal	Quartz crystal
Electronic circuit	—	Simple	Integrated circuit	Integrated circuit
Transmission	Gears	Gears	Gears	Stepping motor/gears
Display	Hands	Hands	Numbers	Hands

The first digital watches used either light-emitting diodes (LEDs) or a liquid crystal display (LCD), which consumed less energy. By 1986, most quartz digital watches had LCDs. The switch to quartz was spectacular: whereas 98 percent of all watches and movements produced in 1974 were mechanical and only 2 percent were quartz, in 1984 the breakdown was 24 percent mechanical and 76 percent quartz.

The Watch Industry

Watchmaking was first developed in Switzerland by Swiss goldsmiths and French Huguenots fleeing religious persecution during the Reformation. During the Industrial Revolution the Swiss industry branched into a two-tier system with component manufacturing separate from watch assembling. Swiss watchmakers were masters of precision workmanship and ''Swiss made'' had become synonymous with quality. By 1970, however, the Swiss contribution to world watch production had dropped considerably. This trend continued into the 1980s as less expensive and more accurate quartz watches and movements, mainly from Japan and Hong Kong, flooded the market. In 1984, 60 percent of quartz watches and movements produced were from Hong Kong, 30 percent from Japan, and only 7 percent from Switzerland.

Starting in the 1950s, the production operations of the major American firms (Timex, Bulova, Hamilton) gradually shifted overseas. By 1986, domestic production was considered virtually nil. (See Exhibit 2.) While Switzerland's estimated contribution to American import volume decreased from 99 percent in 1950 to 4 percent in 1984, the percentage of import volume from Asia increased from 10 percent in 1970, primarily from Japan, to 92 percent in 1984, mostly from Hong Kong.

EXHIBIT 2 Estimated breakdown of world watch production

	World production*	Switzerland	Japan	Hong Kong	USA	Rest of world
1948	31	80%	—	—	—	20%
1970	174	43	14%	—	11%	32
1975	218	34	14	2%	12	38
1980	300	29	22	20	4	25
1985	440	13	39	22	0.4	25

* Million watches and movements
Source: Federation of the Swiss Watch Industry.

The Japanese industry was highly concentrated with the two major firms, Hattori Seiko and Citizen, stressing the development of automated production lines and maximum vertical integration of operations. Compared with the multitude of Swiss watch brands, the combined product lines of these two plus Casio, the third major Japanese watchmaker, did not exceed a dozen brands. In contrast, the industry in Hong Kong was highly fragmented, with several manufacturers producing 10–20 million watches per year, and hundreds of small firms producing fewer than 1 million annually. These firms could not afford to invest in quartz analog technology but with virtually no barriers to entry for watch assembly, they produced complete analog watches from imported movements and modules, often Swiss or Japanese. Design costs were also minimized by copying Swiss or Japanese products. The competitive advantages of the Hong Kong firms were low-cost labor, tiny margins, and the flexibility to adapt to changes in the market.

The spectacular rise of Japan and Hong Kong, particularly in the middle- and low-price categories, was primarily due to their rapid adoption of quartz technology, a drive to achieve a competitive cost position through accumulation of experience and economies of scale. Whereas in 1972 the digital watch module cost around $200, the same module cost only $.50 in 1984. The Asian watchmaking industry had been ensuring a chronic state of world oversupply, mainly in the inexpensive quartz digital range. This had been the cause of a number of bankruptcies and had incited watch manufacturers to turn to the quartz analog market, where added value was higher. Since, in contrast to quartz digital technology, quartz analog technology was available only within the watch industry, the hundreds of watch assemblers scattered throughout the world were increasingly dependent on the three major movement manufacturers—Seiko, ETA, and Citizen.

The Watch Market

According to one industry analyst, the European OECD member countries represented around 30 percent of total world watch sales volume, the United States approximately 20–30 percent, and the Japanese market around 10 percent. Estimated annual market growth was approximately 4 percent.

Industry experts estimated 1984 wristwatch purchases in the United States to be 90–95 million units, a 400 percent increase over 10 years. By 1985, Americans were buying a new watch once every two years, compared with once every 6–10 years a decade earlier. However, the U.S. market was considered to be near saturation with an average of 3.5 watches per owner. Buying habits had changed in Europe also, with the 8–20 year age group representing nearly half of all watch sales in 1985. When commenting on buying habits, industry experts pointed out that the industry was increasingly committed to the quartz analog, stressing the different meanings the digital and the analog had for the consumer (Exhibit 3). However, some of the more expensive Swiss watch manufacturers seemed to believe in a future trend back to mechanical.

EXHIBIT 3 A semiotic comparison of digital and analog watches

Digital	Analog
1. Time is represented by a *sign*	1. Time is represented by a *symbol*
2. The focus is on	2. The focus is on
—The instant	—Length of time
—Numerical code	—A pictorial code
—Discontinuity	—Continuity
—Linearity and periodicity	—Circularity and cyclical character
3. Signification	3. Signification
—The time display is precise	—Time display is imprecise
—Time is imposed	—Time can be negotiated
—Monosemy: only one meaning	—Polysemy: several meanings

Source: Adapted from Michel-Adrien Voirol, "Un Problème d'Evolution du Produit Horloger," in "Les Apports de la Sémiotique au Marketing et à la Publicité," IREP Seminar, 1976.

The watch market was generally divided into five retail price segments (Exhibit 4). Swiss watches fell mostly in the mid- to expensive price ranges. To protect its mid-price niche, Seiko had adopted a multibrand strategy, offering cheap watches under the Lorus, Pulsar, and Phasar brands, with more expensive watches under the Credor, Seiko, and Lassale brand names.

EXHIBIT 4 Watch industry price segments (Swiss franc), 1984

Segment	Retail price	Percentage units	Percentage value	Examples
A	$ 8–$30	60%	10%	Hong Kong LCDs, some cheap mechanicals
B	$ 30–$100	15	15	Swatch, Timex, Casio, Guess, Lip, Lorus, Dugena, Junghans, Yéma, Jaz, Pulsar, Hamilton
C	$ 80–$250	20	45	Tissot, Seiko, Citizen, Casio, Lip, Yéma, Jaz, Pulsar, Dugena, Junghans, Bulova, Hamilton, Herbelin
D	$120–$450	4	15	Omega, Longines, Eterna, Seiko, Citizen, Certina, Rado, Movado, Bulova
E	$450+	1	15	Rolex, Piaget, Cartier, Audemars Piguet, Certina, Rado, Lassale, Ebel

Dollar/Swiss franc exchange rates: 1983 = 2.10, 1984 = 2.20, 1985 = 2.30, 1986 = 1.84.
Source: compiled from Federation of the Swiss Watch Industry records.

Development of Swatch

Dr. Ernst Thomke joined ETA S.A. as president in 1978 after proving his success in the marketing department of Beecham Pharmaceuticals. He had been an apprentice in the production division of ETA before taking a PhD in chemistry and a medical degree. In early 1980, after considering the sorry state of the Swiss watch industry, Thomke concluded that the future was in innovative finished products, aggressive marketing, volume sales, and vertical integration of the industry. Quartz analog technology was more complex than digital, but as ETA was known for the technology it possessed for the production of high-priced, ultra-thin "Delirium" movements, Thomke decided to develop a "low-price prestige" quartz analog wristwatch that could be mass produced in Switzerland at greatly reduced cost. Two ETA micromechanical engineers specializing in plastic injection molding technology, Jacques Müller and Elmar Mock, were given the challenge of designing a product based on Thomke's concept. This required inventing entirely new production technology using robots and computers for manufacture and assembly. By 1981, a semi-automated process had been designed to meet Thomke's goal of a 15 SF ex-factory price and seven patents were registered. The watch's movement, consisting of only 51 instead of the 90–150 parts in other watches, was injected directly into the one-piece plastic case. The casing was sealed by ultrasonic welding instead of screwed, precluding servicing. The watch would be simply replaced and not repaired if it stopped. The finished product, guaranteed for one year, was shock resistant, water resistant to 100 feet (30 meters), and contained a three-year replaceable battery.

In April 1981, Thomke took his idea to Franz Sprecher, a marketing consultant who had worked at Nestlé before setting up his own consulting firm. As background for ETA's project, Sprecher studied prestige products like perfumes, successful mass-market brands like Bic, and both designer and ready-to-wear fashion. He worked closely with advertising agencies in the United States on product positioning and advertising strategy. In addition to the name "Swatch," a snappy contraction of "Swiss" and "watch," this research generated the idea of downplaying the product's practical benefits and positioning it as a "fashion accessory that happens to tell time." Swatch would be a second or third watch used to adapt to different situations without replacing the traditional "status symbol" watch.

Launch

Dr. Thomke arranged to have Swatch distributed in the United States by the Swiss Watch Distribution Center (SWDC) in San Antonio, Texas, an American firm in which ETA held a minority interest and whose chairperson, Ben Hammond, had been instrumental in setting up and building Seiko distribution in the Southwestern states. Swatch was test marketed in December 1982 at 100 Sanger Harris department stores in Dallas, Salt Lake City, and San Diego, without any advertising, public relations, or publicity. The original test product line consisted of 12 rather conventional watches in red, brown, and tan. Opinions on test results were mixed, but the ETA team continued undaunted. Swatch was officially launched in Switzerland in March 1983, and then gradually worldwide. Exhibit 5 shows the Fall 1983 collection as pictured in sales brochures.

Max Imgrüth, a graduate of the State University of New York's Fashion Institute of Technology, took over as president of SWDC in April 1983, and arranged a second test market in December 1983 through both the Zale jewelry chain in Dallas and the New York department store Macy's, with television support created by Swatch's advertising agency, McCann-Erickson. Test market conclusions were that most of the watches in the 1983 Fall/Winter collection were not acceptable for the U.S. market. Imgrüth recalled:

> Nothing happened. I tried to figure out what was wrong. The product was not very distinctive. It was not just the ad, it was the watches. It was too close to the traditional watch. First of all . . . was its positioning, second the product, third pricing, fourth advertising. Basically, I ran down the marketing mix.

Imgrüth became increasingly involved in product design and local adaptation of Swatch communication. He was appointed president of the newly created American subsidiary Swatch Watch USA in early 1984. The American pricing strategy was modified and a direct salesforce organized to replace SWDC that year. Managers hired to run Swatch Watch USA included Vice President Operations Don Galliers, formerly in the watch strap business, and Marketing Manager/Creative Director Steve Rechtschaffner, 27, a former member of the U.S. freestyle skiing team with experience in sales promotion. Exhibit 6 gives the perceived advantages and disadvantages of Swatch, in December 1984, in four countries.

Price

There were initially three prices for the Swiss launch: 39.90 SF for a model with only two hands, 44.90 SF for three hands, and 49.90 SF for three hands and a calendar display. In the United States, however, Swatch was first marketed at seven price points, ranging from $19.95 to $37.50. Consumers did not seem to understand why certain watches cost more than others so American prices were reduced to three in 1984: $25, $30, and $35. In 1986, one Swatch retail price was set throughout the world, based on the price in the United States of $30.00. Exhibit 7 presents the results of a survey on perceptions of Swatch retail prices in four countries.

From the start Thomke and Sprecher had decided that product contribution would have to be sufficient to finance massive communication. Manufacturing costs had been reduced substantially and wholesaler and agent margins could be decreased some. Retail margins would have to be kept high enough to motivate retailers. Exhibit 8 gives a comparison of costs and margins for traditional moderate-price Swiss and Japanese watches, low-price Hong Kong watches, and Swatch in 1982–1983.

EXHIBIT 5 Swatch international launch collection

EXHIBIT 6   Perceived advantages and disadvantages of Swatch in 1984

	Total n = 800	United States n = 200	France n = 200	Great Britain n = 200	West Germany n = 200
Positive features					
Pretty shape	34.5*	34.0	33.5	20.0	50.5
Amusing, original	28.6	9.0	31.5	28.0	46.0
Waterproof	28.4	37.5	29.5	29.5	17.0
Fashionable, modern	24.5	7.5	30.5	24.0	36.0
Pretty, varied colors	22.6	31.0	13.5	18.5	27.5
Strong, resistant	22.1	24.5	27.5	24.5	12.0
Can be worn by anyone	16.0	30.5	9.0	12.5	12.0
Quality watches	14.8	28.0	8.0	4.0	19.0
Low price	14.5	3.5	32.0	5.0	17.5
Can be worn anywhere	12.6	13.5	13.5	11.0	12.5
Negative features					
Uncomfortable plastic strap	16.0†	13.5	13.0	17.5	20.0
Too fashionable, too modern	10.3	2.0	6.5	9.5	23.0
Looks like a gadget, a toy	9.9	3.5	10.0	8.5	17.5
Does not match all styles of dress	8.4	1.0	4.0	14.0	14.5
Fragile	8.1	0.5	12.0	3.0	17.0
Too-sophisticated face	7.4	6.0	3.0	8.5	12.0
Too much plastic	6.6	1.0	7.5	-	18.0
Too noisy	3.6	-	12.5	1.0	1.0

* Percentage of respondents indicating this feature in response to the question: "What, in your opinion, are the advantages of Swatch watches in comparison with other watches?"

† Percentage of respondents indicating this feature in response to the question: "And what would be their disadvantages?"

Source: Delta International Market Study, December 1984.

EXHIBIT 7 Actual and perceived 1986 retail prices of Swatch

United States—actual price = $30

Perceived price ($)	Total n = 290	Buyers n = 99	Potential buyers n = 140	Nonbuyers n = 51
<20	8*	3	9	16
21–30	57	62	56	49
31–40	26	25	26	25
41–50	6	7	6	2
51–60	2	3	2	2
>60	1	—	1	2

United Kingdom—actual price = £24

Perceived price (£)	Total n = 202	Buyers n = 68	Potential buyers n = 83	Nonbuyers n = 51
<10	4	—	4	12
11–15	10	3	14	14
16–20	39	44	36	35
21–25	22	38	16	12
26–30	8	4	10	12
31–35	1	1	1	2
36–40	2	—	4	2
>40	1	1	—	—

France—actual price = FF 250

Perceived price (FF)	Total n = 200	Buyers n = 66	Potential buyers n = 99	Nonbuyers n = 35
<100	10	2	11	20
100–150	9	2	12	14
151–200	17	8	23	17
201–250	41	74	32	3
251–300	7	9	5	9
301–400	4	3	4	3
>400	2	3	1	3

West Germany—actual price = 65 DM

Perceived price (DM)	Total n = 200	Buyers n = 67	Potential buyers n = 74	Nonbuyers n = 59
<20	3	3	—	7
21–40	11	6	12	14
41–60	38	27	42	44
61–80	39	58	34	22
81–100	7	4	8	8
101–200	3	2	3	3
>200	1	—	1	2

* Percentage of total responses to the question: "All the [Swatch] watches have the same price—could you estimate that price?"

Source: Qualitest A.G. Market study, Zurich, August 1986, and company records.

EXHIBIT 8 Breakdown of low- to moderate-price watch costs and margins

	Swiss	Japanese	Hong Kong	Swatch
Retail price = 100%	100%	100%	100%	100%
− (Retail margin)	(50)	(55)	(50)	(45)
Wholesale price	50	45	50	55
− (Wholesale/agent margin)	(25)	(16)	(18)	(11)
Ex-factory price	25	29	33	44
− (Contribution)	(4)	(12)	(3)	(24)
Manufacturing cost	21	18	29	20

Source: Company records.

Product Line

Two Swatch collections of 12 different models each were marketed per year, in spring and in fall. Styles were based on four major targets groups geared to social behavior and trends: "classic," "hi-tech," "sports," and "fashion." Collections were designed by Käthi Durrer and Jean Robert in Zurich, with fashion consultants in New York, Milan, and Paris. At first there was only one large-size model, enabling mass production. In 1984, a smaller size was added. Limitation of sizes to these two enabled substantial reductions in production costs. Variations in the collections were made possible through face and watch-band graphics and style. In the spring of 1984, Max Imgrüth decided to name individual watches (e.g., "Pinstripe," "Black Magic," "McSwatch," "Dotted Swiss"), and tie each collection in with specific themes, starting with the "Skipper" line of sailing-inspired sport watches. Subsequent themes ranged from "Street Smart" paisleys and plaids to "Kiva" American Indian designs. Exhibit 9 illustrates selected watches from the 1984–1986 collections.

By Fall 1984, Swatch management realized that a continuous system for pretesting the 80 to 100 models presented by the designers for each collection was essential for constant collection renewal. Franz Sprecher commented:

> The strategy should be to create bestsellers. This doesn't mean keeping the same collection for five years but improving the collection by identifying weak models and knowing whether to revamp them or create new models that will be leaders.

EXHIBIT 9   Selected watches from the 1984–1986 collections

A. Cresta Run
   spring–summer 1985

B. spring–summer 1984

C. Granita di Frutta
   spring–summer 1985

D. Street Smart
   fall–winter 1985–1986

E. Color Tech
   fall–winter 1985–1986

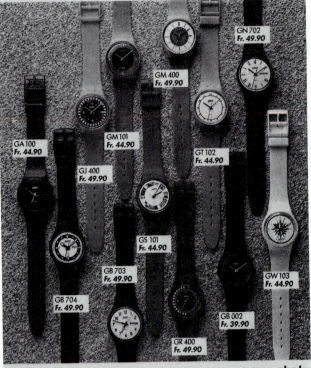

B

A

C

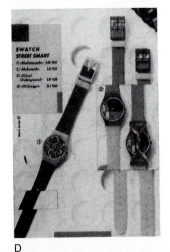

D

E

EXHIBIT 9 *(concluded)*   1986 Collections

A   Coats of Arms

B   Devil's Run

C   Kiva

D   Aqua Love

E   Jellyfish

F   Nefertiti

G   Morgans

H   Classics

I   Calypso Beach

EXHIBIT 10 Preferences, purchase intentions and sales data for 1985 spring/summer Swatch collection (France, West Germany, Great Britain, United States)

Swatch code	Most preferred models*			Least preferred models†	Purchase intentions‡				Ex-factory sales worldwide (000 units)
	Total $n = 800$	Men $n = 400$	Women $n = 400$	Total $n = 800$	For self			Gift	
					Total $n = 800$	Men $n = 400$	Women $n = 400$	Total $n = 800$	
GB 101	41.1	63.3	19.0	2.0	33.6	57.0	10.3	27.0	147
GA 102	36.1	58.8	13.5	3.9	28.4	48.5	8.3	26.0	149
LB 106	20.6	6.5	34.6	1.5	16.6	2.8	30.6	18.3	140
LM 104	20.4	3.3	37.6	2.3	18.1	1.0	35.3	21.0	70
GM 401	19.0	24.8	13.3	3.1	15.9	21.3	10.5	15.0	67
LW 104	18.3	3.8	32.8	3.5	15.1	1.3	29.1	16.6	246
LA 100	17.4	6.5	28.3	1.4	15.1	3.3	27.1	17.3	207
GN 401	17.3	31.8	2.8	4.3	15.1	28.3	2.0	11.8	63
GB 705	13.3	22.8	3.8	8.5	10.5	19.3	1.8	7.8	106
GW 104	12.9	11.8	14.0	7.9	8.0	5.8	10.3	9.9	221
GB 706	10.3	16.3	4.3	10.0	7.5	12.5	2.5	8.0	121
GK 100	9.9	11.5	8.3	48.9	6.3	7.3	5.3	8.0	286
GT 103	9.8	9.3	10.3	5.1	5.6	5.0	6.3	6.8	53
LT 101	9.5	1.8	17.3	3.1	7.1	0.3	14.0	10.3	53
LB 107	6.9	1.8	11.8	6.8	5.5	0.5	10.3	5.6	88
LW 107§	6.1	1.0	11.3	27.5	4.5	0.8	8.3	7.1	322
GJ 700	5.8	7.3	4.3	37.4	3.6	4.5	2.8	4.4	104
LN 103	4.1	0.8	7.3	2.6	3.3	—	6.5	5.6	64
LW 105§	3.9	0.8	7.0	17.3	3.0	0.3	5.8	4.6	213
GM 701	3.9	5.0	2.8	22.3	2.8	4.0	1.5	2.3	108
GB 403	3.5	4.5	2.5	13.9	2.5	3.5	1.5	2.9	78
LW 106§	2.4	0.8	4.0	27.1	1.5	—	3.0	3.1	152
LS 102	1.8	1.0	2.5	28.9	1.1	0.3	2.0	2.1	107
LB 105	1.5	0.8	2.3	5.0	1.3	0.8	1.8	1.6	118
LB 104	1.1	0.5	1.8	3.5	0.6	0.3	1.0	2.3	125

* Percentage of total responses to the question, "Here are a number of new Swatch watches. They come in two sizes, standard and small. Which are the three you like best?"

† Percentage of total responses to the question, "Which are the three watches you like least?" Responses were virtually the same regardless of sex.

‡ Percentage of total responses to the question, "Would you consider buying such a watch for yourself or as a gift?"

§"Granita di Frutta": 69.9% of those interested in these models as gifts claimed the recipient would be a girl under 15 years of age.

Source: Delta International Market Study, December 1984, and company records.

The collection illustrated in Exhibit 10, including the three scented "Granita di Frutta" models[1], was pretested in December 1984. Test results, presented with the actual ex-factory sales figures for the collection, revealed no significant differences between the four countries involved.

Distribution

Until the mid-1970s, most medium- and high-priced watches were sold through jewelry and specialist shops. The Swiss watchmakers, later followed by Seiko,

---

[1] A line of aromatic Swatches geared to the teenage consumer and consisting of pastel pink, blue, and yellow watches emitting strawberry, mint, and banana fragrances; it represented 80 percent of sales in the United States for the first two months of 1985.

EXHIBIT 10 *(concluded)*

1985 Spring–summer collection

A | GB 101 | GB 403 | GT 103 | GB 705 | GB 706 | GJ 700 | GN 401 | GM 701 | GA 102 | GM 401 | GW 104 | GK 100
Carlton | Coral Reef | Plaza | Plaza | Plaza | Coral Reef | Plaza | Coral Reef | Carlton | Plaza | Coral Reef | Jellyfish

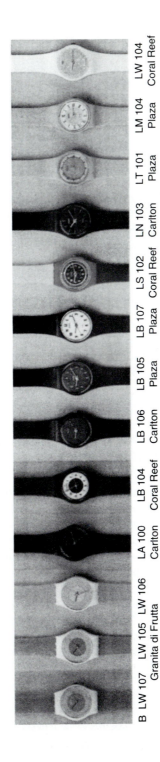

B | LW 107 | LW 105 | LW 106 | LA 100 | LB 104 | LB 106 | LB 105 | LB 107 | LS 102 | LN 103 | LT 101 | LM 104 | LW 104
Granita di Frutta | Carlton | Coral Reef | Carlton | Plaza | Plaza | Coral Reef | Carlton | Plaza | Plaza | Coral Reef

had always placed emphasis on after-sales service and set up dealerships allowing jewelers to take up to 250 percent markups. As prices slipped, however, a grey market[2] developed, fired by a drive for volume and lack of control over distribution channels.

In the United States (Exhibit 11), Swatch watches were sold primarily in "shop-in-shops" at up-market department stores, some specialized watch retailers, sports shops, and boutiques, while in Europe Swatch was sold by the few existing up-market department stores but mostly by traditional jewelers and some specialized sports, gift, and fashion boutiques, mail-order houses, and duty-free shops. In France, as part of his launch strategy, the Swatch distributor Raymond Zeitoun, previously with Seiko, persuaded the prestigious jeweler Jean Dinh Van on rue de la Paix in Paris to sell Swatch for a few days. When the jeweler accepted "for the fun of it" and sales boomed, others followed suit. Zeitoun spoke of Swatch in France:

> Granted, it's an item without much of a margin but the profession has to change and widen its horizons. The advantage of Swatch is that it brings a lively atmosphere and a younger clientele to the store.

Discounting by distributors was not allowed, and the trade was warned to keep an eye out for counterfeits (Exhibit 12). Swatch Watch USA spent close to $1 million in 1984 to buy back Swatches displayed at less than the set price. Don Galliers recalled:

> We purchased 80–85 percent of the grey market watches. Counterfeits appeared in 1985. We set up an international brand protection program with a very sophisticated information network. All new styles were copyrighted, counterfeiters caught at the source, and "confusingly similar" watch marketers taken to court. If we were spending $16 to $18 million a year on advertising, we could spend a couple of million to protect the brand.

Merchandising was considered fundamental and included sales promotional activities designed to catch the consumer's eye. Backed by two-meter "maxiSwatches," expensive and carefully designed display racks were "color-blocked," that is, arranged in rows of color. In-store videos played pop or rock music and sales brochures were available in ample supply. In all countries, parties for the trade were organized for each collection launch to create a feeling of a "Swatch Club," encouraging retailers to give Swatch prime window space and exposure in spite of lower margins. One of Swatch's selling points with distributors was its very low return rate[3] (i.e., 0.3 percent in 1984 compared with the industry average of 5 percent), which virtually eliminated after-sales service problems and customer dissatisfaction.

---

[2] Parallel importing and distribution through unauthorized channels.
[3] Percentage of watches returned on warranty.

EXHIBIT 11   Swatch distribution channels

Channel	Switzerland		United Kingdom		France		West Germany		United States	
	1985	1986	1985	1986	1985	1986	1985	1986	1985	1986
Department stores	10*	10	6	9	3	11	19	22	82	71
Jewelers	85	78	87	78	95	79	73	59	3	2
Sports shops	—	—	0.1	0.1	—	—	6	16	1	2
Fashion shops	5	12	6	12	—	—	2	4	6	12
Others†	—	0.2	0.4	0.5	2	10	—	—	8	14
Total number of stores (including branches)	590	511	1708	1273	2634	2266	1030	511	6437	4634

* Percentage of total number of outlets.

† Gift and card shops, drugstores, college bookstores, military exchanges, catalogues, etc.

Source: Company records.

In general, the attitude of the distributors toward Swatch watches was very positive with the few negative comments limited to low profit margin, production-related delivery problems, skepticism about long-term success, and lack of distributor exclusivity. Don Galliers commented on Swatch's distribution strategy in the United States:

> Swatch's success was built on limited distribution. We should not sell more than 5 million Swatches in the United States in any single year, to keep it rare, in demand. You can't always get what you want so when you see it you'd better buy it. For a trendy article like this, if you accelerate too much into the market you risk making it become a fad.

Product Line Extensions

While its major competitors, Seiko, Citizen, and others were diversifying into other applications of electronics and "superwatches," complete with televisions, computers, or health-monitoring systems, Swatch, mainly through the initiative of Swatch Watch USA, had moved into a range of accessories and ready-to-wear apparel (Exhibit 13) designed to express a "Swatch" lifestyle (Exhibit 14).

One of the reasons given for expanding into accessories and apparel was the need to fill out the available space in the shop-in-shops. "Funwear" and "Fungear," manufactured in Hong Kong and the United States, were designed by Renée Rechtschaffner, Steve's wife and the winner of a Swatch-organized contest at the Fashion Institute of Technology. By the last quarter of 1985, nonwatch items accounted for one-third of Swatch sales in the United States.

EXHIBIT 12 Example of Swatch counterfeit alert program

SAM SWATCH® SEZ...

SALES PERSONS

"CUSTOMS AGENTS..."
BE ON YOUR TOES!"

NOT ALL WRIST WATCHES BEARING THE SWATCH® ✛ NAME ARE THE **REAL McCOY!**

1 Note the difference between a SWATCH® and a clever phony: the *real* SWATCH® has three plastic divisions at the hinge. The *phony* has only two!

SWATCH®   PHONY

2 *Real* SWATCH® watches have battery hatches located *off-center*. Phony SWATCH® watches have *centered* hatches.

BE A SWATCH®-WATCHDOG!
DON'T ACCEPT A PHONY AS A WARRANTY RETURN!

EXHIBIT 13 Swatch clothing and accessories

Date	Product	Description	Retail Price
Fall 1984	Swatch Guard	Protective, decorative device for watches	$3
Fall 1984	Maxi-Swatch	2-meter Swatch wall-clock	$150
Spring 1985	Shields	Sunglasses	$35
Spring 1985	Chums	Eyeglass holders	$5
Spring 1985	Signature line	Umbrellas, T-shirts, sweats with watch graphics	$12–$38
Spring 1985	Gift set	Keyholder and Swiss penknife	$45
Spring 1985	Parafernalia	Italian pens, stationery items, key rings, safety razors	$7–$15
Fall 1985	Fungear line	Knapsacks, belts, bags	$10–$65
Fall 1985	Funwear line	Unisex casual wear (pants, tops, sweats, shirts, shorts, skirts) linked to watch themes	$12–$65

EXHIBIT 14 Swatch accessories and apparel (USA)

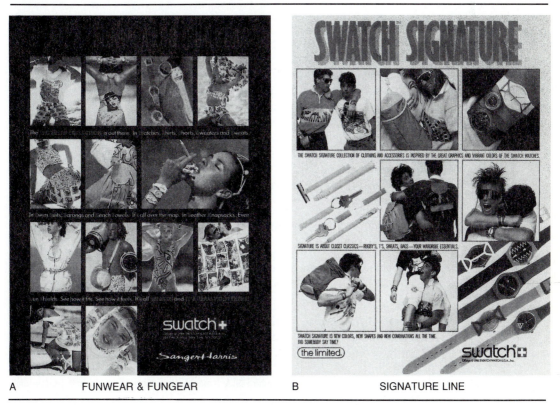

A   FUNWEAR & FUNGEAR   B   SIGNATURE LINE

Aided awareness scores for Swatch accessories, available only in the United States, are presented in Exhibit 15.

EXHIBIT 15 Aided awareness of Swatch accessories, USA—1985

	Total Sample (n = 895)	Age		
		12–18 (n = 219)	19–24 (n = 234)	25–34 (n = 442)
Shields	17*	43	13	8
Bags	16	37	12	8
T-shirts	15	36	13	6
Guards	11	27	10	4
Gift sets	9	20	10	3
Chums	8	20	6	3
Beach boxes	8	18	4	5
Maxi-Swatch	8	17	7	3
Pocket knives	6	15	5	2
Pens and pencils	6	13	3	3
Razors	3	5	3	1

* Percentage of respondents indicating this accessory in response to the question: "Please tell me which of the following Swatch accessories you are aware of."
Source: "Attitude and Awareness of Swatch in Various Markets" study, McCann-Erickson, July 1985.

Fashion retailing in the United States was stimulated by six "Market Weeks" per year to launch each new season (i.e., spring, spring-summer, summer, back-to-school, fall-winter, holiday) and introduce products to retailers nationwide. At Swatch Watch USA, preparation of each market week began almost a full year in advance with market and sales analyses, fashion forecasts, and theme development (watches and accessories) covering approximately two months for each season, followed by gradual decisions and presentations throughout the rest of the year on design, color, prints, prices, quantities, range, advertising, public relations, and promotion. Coordination of production and delivery with "fickle fashion" was tricky business that relied on very short lead times. Perpetual innovation was also difficult to maintain. Don Galliers commented:

> We don't have the flexibility of the traditional watch industry where if you miss it this year you can launch it next year. We also don't have the normal 18-month development time to field the watch after a one-year design time. Our whole cycle is built on the concept that every six weeks there is something new at the Swatch counter.

In the spring of 1986, under license from the Coca-Cola company, the American subsidiary also started marketing a line of Coca-Cola watches. They contained traditional ETA and not Swatch technology quartz movements and did not bear the name Swatch.[4]

---

[4] Another SMH subsidiary, Endura S.A., manufactured private label and promotional watches with conventional movements.

Communication

Thomke and Sprecher had adopted a global communication strategy for Swatch to establish a distinctive brand personality. The company issued strict directives on use of the Swatch logo, baselines, layout, and the Swiss cross. The Swatch communication budget was split more or less evenly between advertising/store promotion (50 percent) and public relations/special events (50 percent). Local agencies were in charge of public relations, promotion, publicity, and special events including contests, concert tours, and sports events. McCann-Erickson in Zurich was in charge of all advertising, designed for local adaptation in different countries through the use of voice-overs for commercials and strips of copy in the respective languages for print ads (Exhibits 16 and 17). Roger Guyard, regional manager for France, explained:

> We want to have a global image with the same image in England as in Australia. Where we are different from the others is in our launch events and promotions, adapted to each country and each population.

The Swatch communications target audience was described by McCann-Zurich as "all men and women between 15 and 39 years of age, particularly between 20 and 29, opinion leaders/trend-setters, extroverts who were nonetheless group-dependent, young fashion wearers and both active and passive sports fans." For Felice Schillaci, vice president continental operations, Swatch was "a brand for the young at heart, no age group, no 18 to 29, it's a state of mind, an attitude."

Public Relations

Heavy emphasis was placed on testimonials and endorsements by opinion leaders as well as special events including sponsoring of musicians and artists, exhibitions, and competitions at which gadgets, leaflets, and "Swatch Magazines" were distributed (Exhibit 18). Swatch promotion was often unsolicited such as when Princess Diana wore not only her husband Prince Charles's watch at a polo match but also two Swatches, just when Swatch was introducing the ideas of man-size watches for women and "multiple Swatch accessorizing." Swatch also benefited from massive publicity through the press. According to Elmar Mock:

> Management's stroke of genius was not to hide its engineers. We were on great terms with the newspapers who created an advertising effect, quite naturally, without the slightest solicitation.

Limited-edition watches were launched with elaborate parties. The first was designed by Kiki Picasso and distributed to 100 celebrities at a cocktail party in Paris. There was the diamond-studded "Limelight" ($100) available in both Europe and the United States. Then there was the Breakdance watch ($30)

EXHIBIT 16 Swatch international TV commercials

"Hero" —1983 launch campaign

A *Text:* "Watch! Swatch! La Nouvelle Swatch! Swatch, Swiss quartz, water-resistant, shock-resistant, imported from Switzerland. It's come a long way since the cuckoo clock. Swatch, the new wave in Swiss watches."

"New Cut II —1984

B *Text:* "Watch! Swatch! La Nouvelle Swatch! Portable Swiss quartz watches that are more than water-resistant, shock-resistant: Swiss watches that are more than precise. These days it's fashion that makes us tick. Swatch, the new wave in Swiss watches!"

"Streetlife" —1986

C *Text:* "Swatch! (Swatch. . . .) Always different, always new! (Swatch!) Fashionable (Swatch!), water-resistant, shock-resistant, Swiss-made (Swatch!). Swatch, the new wave in Swiss watches!"

EXHIBIT 17   International adaptation of Swatch print ads

A   France

B   West Germany

C   Canada

D   Norway

EXHIBIT 18   Major special events organized or sponsored by Swatch

Date	Country	Event
March 1984	Germany	13-ton giant Swatch on Commerzbank building, Frankfurt.
April 1984	France	"Urban Sax" saxophonist group at the "Eldorado" theater in Paris to celebrate launch; first *Swatch Magazine*.
August 1984	USA	Ivan Lendl U.S. Tennis Open.
September 1984	USA	World Breakdancing Championship: "The Roxy," New York.
September 1984	France	First street art painting show with the French artists "Les Frères Ripoulin," "Espace Cardin" theater, Paris.
November 1984	USA	The Fat Boys music sponsorship, "Private Eye's," New York, to introduce "Granita di Frutta" to the trade.
October 1984– January 1985	USA	New York City Fresh Festival: breakdancing, rapping, graffiti artists.
January 1985	USA	World Freestyle Invitational/Celebrity Classic, Brekenridge, Colorado.
March 1985	France	IRCAM "copy art" show, Paris; limited edition (119) Kiki Picasso design watches; second *Swatch Magazine*.
Spring 1985	USA	Hi-fly freestyle windsurfing team sponsorship.
May 1985	England	Second street art painting show, Covent Garden, London, with Les Frères Ripoulin and English street artists.
June 1985	Switzerland	Art fair in Basel; third street art painting show with 50 European artists.
Summer 1985	Sweden	Oestersjö Rallyt (Segel-Rallye).
September 1985	France	Cinema festival, Pompidou Center, Paris with Kurosawa's film *Ran;* Mini City Magazine.
September 1985	France	"Le Défile": Jean-Paul Gaultier & Régine Chopinot fashion/dance show, "Pavillon Baltard," Paris.
September 1985	England	Andrew Logan's Alternative Miss World, London.
October 1985	Belgium	"Mode et Anti-Mode" fashion show, Brussels.
Fall 1985	USA	Thompson Twins concert tour sponsorship.
November 1985	Spain	Swatch launch party, the "Cirque," Barcelona.
November 1985	USA	Limelight launch party, Los Angeles (for trade).
November 1985	International	Freestyle World Cup sponsorship.
November 1985	Japan	Giant Swatch in Tokyo for launch of Swatch.
January 1986	USA	Fashion show: "Private Eye's," New York (for trade).
January 1986	USA	Pierre Boulez orchestra concert tour.
January–November 1986	England	"Time & Motion Competition," Royal College of Art, London.
February 1986	England	Feargal Sharkey tour.
February 1986	France	First World Freestyle Ski Championships, Tignes.
February–March 1986	Germany	Swatch Freestyle World Cup, Oberjoch.
March 1986	Switzerland	"Arosa" freestyle skiing weekend with retailers.
March 1986	Austria	"Exposa" jewelry fair with Swatch balloons.
March 1986	France	"Waterproof Paris": Daniel Larrieux's subaquatic ballet performance.
April–October 1986	Canada	Giant Swatch, Swill Pavilion, Expo 86, Vancouver.
May–September 1986	Sweden	Swatch Funboard Cup sponsorship.
June 1986	France	Fourth street art painting show, fourth Swatch Magazine.
June 1986	Italy	"Sssswatchgala Mailand," launch event.
July 1986– February 1987	Switzerland	First International Swatch Freestyle Youth Camp, Zermatt.
July 1986	International	Second Himalaya Super Marathon sponsorship.
July 1986	Netherlands	Drachenflug Festival sponsored by Swatch.

EXHIBIT 18 *(concluded)*   Swatch special events

A   Japan

B   France

C   USA

D   France

E   West Germany

F   France

G   USA

H   USA

I   Switzerland

and four other watches designed by New York artist Keith Haring ($50) marketed in the United States only. Swatch's French public relations agency claimed that the strategy behind these serial watches was to manage the production-related scarcity by "creating a frenzy through rarity." Organization of advertising and events revolved around the development of a "Swatch cult" and using connections. In 1984, for instance, Max Imgrüth organized a celebrity advertising campaign through a photographer in California who persuaded a number of stars to be in Swatch ads in exchange for a Rolex or Piaget gold watch. These included Lauren Hutton, Donna Mills, Lee Majors, and Ivan Lendl.

Advertising

Swatch advertising and promotion budgets are given in Exhibit 19 with industry media expenditure in the United States. Don Galliers explained that Switzerland had a strict policy whereby roughly 30 percent of the product's retail price would go to advertising. Swatch advertising relied primarily on films for television and cinema (Exhibit 20). Print ads, accounting for approximately one-third of total advertising expenditure, were used worldwide to reinforce awareness of each collection and current trend themes. They ran from April to June and from September to December every year. Swatch print media plans included sport, fashion, and avant-garde magazines (e.g., *Vogue, Elle, Cosmopolitan, Sports Illustrated, L'Equipe, Rolling Stone, The Face, City*) as well as magazines geared to the young (e.g., *Just 17, Jacinte, Mädchen, Seventeen*) and occasionally general news publications (e.g., *Stern, Der Spiegel, Figaro Magazine, Tiempo*).

Swatch Watch USA had an in-house department that adapted the McCann ads and created its own ads (Exhibit 20). Max Imgrüth commented on global advertising:

> We adapted the spots in a way that made sense, different wording, cut them a little bit with McCann here, knowing full well that what the Swiss wanted to achieve, a brand created and sent in directly from Switzerland, was impossible. A watch is not consumed like Coca-Cola. It is not a daily need. This is emotional and you have to play local emotions.

Felice Schillaci explained that the loyal Swatch customer in the United States fell in the 10–16 age bracket. Reliable data on the Swatch buyer profile in Europe were not available but buyer age group brackets in the United Kingdom were estimated to be 20 percent under 18, 40 percent between 18 and 24, 30 percent between 25 and 34, and 10 percent over 34. Management in the United States felt that by catching consumers at an early age they would stick with Swatch as they grew up and the enthusiasm they generated would rub off on those older. By 1986 in New York City and Los Angeles, where Swatch awareness was at a maximum, Swatch Watch USA had limited television

EXHIBIT 19

Swatch advertising budget
(000 Swiss francs)

Country	Launch	1983	1984	1985	1986
Switzerland	March 1983	459	620	964	1,107
United Kingdom	March 1983	922	2,398	2,398	2,767
West Germany	September 1983	2,275	4,182	2,706	2,706
United States	September 1983		9,480	32,838	33,404
Austria	January 1984		244	429	472
France	April 1984		2,610	2,423	2,583
Belgium	April 1984		199	295	307
Netherlands	May 1984		148	430	369
South Africa	September 1984		301	133	92
Australia	September 1984		562	883	984
Norway	October 1984			243	246
Sweden	October 1984			571	615
Denmark	March 1985			151	184
Finland	May 1985			236	246
Japan	October 1985			NA	NA
Spain	October 1985			1,230	2,460
Italy	June 1986				3,524

Note: "Advertising" includes production of ads, media spending, in-store programs, etc.

Swatch public relations and special events budget
(000 Swiss francs)

Country	Launch	1983	1984	1985	1986
Central promotion budget			3,690	4,920	6,150
Switzerland	March 1983			258	184
United Kingdom	March 1983			369	633
United States	September 1983			3,978	886
West Germany	September 1983			300	209
Austria	January 1984		29	29	37
France	April 1984		898	1,204	1,291
Belgium	April 1984		139	253	246
Netherlands	May 1984		118	209	260
South Africa	September 1984		18	31	49
Australia	September 1984			86	123
Norway	October 1984			47	80
Sweden	October 1984			77	209
Denmark	March 1985			*	61
Finland	May 1985			*	37
Japan	October 1985			NA	NA
Spain	October 1985			492	1,599
Italy	June 1986				1,458

* Paid for by distributor.

Note: This budget includes music and sports promotions, special events, etc.

Source: Company records (disguised data).

EXHIBIT 19 *(concluded)*

1985 Watch brand media spending in the United States of America

Brand	Share of voice*
A-Watch	1.15
Bulova	0.60
Cartier	0.83
Casio	3.35
Certina	0.13
Citizen	10.33
Ebel	0.97
Gucci	2.16
Guess	0.03
Hamilton	0.32
J. Lassale	7.32
Longines	1.77
Lorus	4.36
Omega	1.02
Piaget	1.56
Pulsar	9.74
Rado	1.87
Rolex	5.05
Seiko	11.17
Swatch	7.05
Timex	15.22
Tissot	0.32
Z-Watch	0.01
Total	86.32
Others	13.68
Total advertisers	100.00

* Share of voice = percentage of total industry media spending.

Source: Compiled from 1985 Broadcast Advertisers Reports, Inc. and Publishers Information Bureau, Inc. figures.

EXHIBIT 20

Selected Swatch TV Commercials in the United States

"Fat Boys" —1985

A *Text:* "Swatch" (opera music) "Oh, Fat Boys, where are you?" "Brrr, Swatch-up, ha ha ha, Swatch-up, tell the hands on the Swatch, oh the sister and the Swatch is water- and shock-resistant. Brrr, Swatch-up, Swatch-up. The new wave in Swiss watches, Swatch!"

"Funwear & Fungear" —1986

B *Text:* "Swatch! Swatch! Funwear and fungear."

"Nefertiti-Sarong" —1986

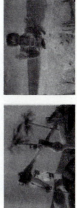

C *Text:* "Swatch! Nefertiti! The enemy is near, put your Swatch guards on. Whoa! Oh, we'll attack from here. Fire! Ha, ha, ha!" Sarong—"La, la, la. Oooh, aaah, oh, my! Aaah. . ." "May I help you?" "Yes, I, aah. . . I like this one!"

EXHIBIT 20 *(continued)*

Selected Swatch print ads in the United States—1986

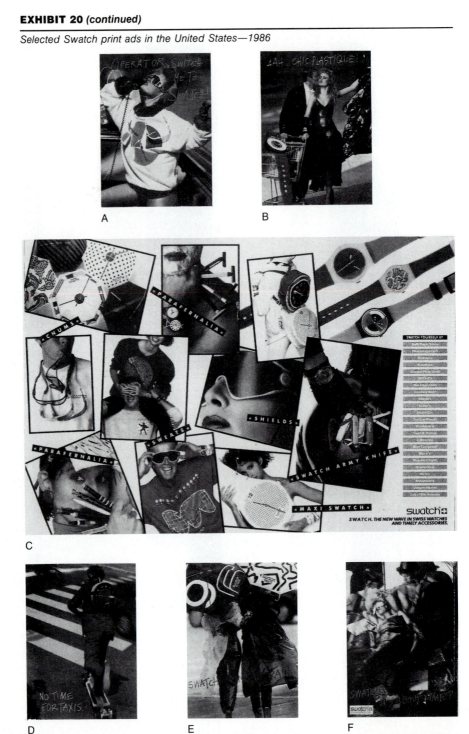

EXHIBIT 20 *(continued)*

Selected Swatch prints ads in the United States

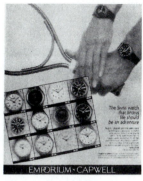

A   Spring 1983

B   Fall 1983

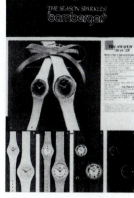

C   Christmas 1984

D   Spring 1985

E   Spring 1985

F   Summer 1986

G   Summer 1986

H   Summer 1986

I   Summer 1986

EXHIBIT 20 *(concluded)*

Selected Swatch print ads in the United States—1986

commercials to MTV[5] to avoid oversaturation. A firm specializing in TV and radio youth audience surveys conducted an analysis for Swatch of American consumers, based on interviews in 15 cities and including reactions to a random sample of eight Swatch ads (Exhibit 21). Scores for recall of Swatch advertising in five countries are presented in Exhibit 22.

Competition

When asked to define the competition, Swatch management's responses varied. Swatch was generally credited with having opened up a new market niche (Exhibit 23). By 1986, however, the market was flooded with Swatch imitations, some bearing similar brand names (e.g., Watch, Watcha, Swiss Watch, Smash, Swatcher, A-Watch, La-Watch, P-Watch, Q-Watch, and Z-Watch), as well as counterfeits using the brand name Swatch. Many Swatch imitations were produced in Hong Kong or Taiwan for distribution in the United States,

---

[5] A music video cable TV station watched primarily by 12–24 year olds.

EXHIBIT 21 A psychographic segmentation of consumers in the United States

Age	Children (6–10)	Teeny boppers (11–15)	Young teen rockers (11–15)	Students (11–15)
Profile/interests	TV: "Jem" rock cartoon, "Nickelodeon." Males: He-man, Transformers, G.I. Joe; females: Care Bears.	Almost 100% female. Middle-middle/upper-class, suburban, clique-oriented, very fashion conscious: trendy, outrageous style, favor So. Calif. over Europe/NYC look. Like partying, dancing, hanging out at malls. Music: breezy pop love songs, New Wave. Main hero: Madonna.	80% male, 20% female. Middle-upper/middle-class, suburban, mall-creatures, macho, heavy-metal look. Hard rock concerts, partying (but isolated, not in cliques). Main heros: Stallone, Schwarzenegger, Iron Maiden ("Madonna is useless".)	50% male, 50% female. Middle-lower/middle-class, very conservative, like professional and participation sports. Music: no allegiance to type of music or artist.
Media	Network TV, MTV*	MTV-crazy, fashion magazines, Top-40 radio.	AOR† radio, critical MTV watchers.	Network TV, AM radio.
Shopping habits	Dependent on parents. Stores: department stores, malls, etc.	Heavy consumers. Stores: dept. stores, record stores, malls.	Not shopping oriented. Stores: record stores, dept. stores, malls.	Consider shopping a function, not an event. Stores: Sears, K mart, chain drugstores.
Reactions to Swatch	42% awareness (of which 76% ownership, 4% interest in teeny bop models). Consider it "cool," something the big kids wear. Parents' interests: durability, price, large face numbers, traditional styles, models that won't become unfashionable.	Very positive—provides a sense of identity—is a lifestyle magnifier but becoming too commonplace, boring. Line extensions: negative. Too expensive, not cool, "Swatch is not a clothing line, but a rock 'n roll time piece."	High awareness due to visibility in schools but strong negative bias: Swatch represents teeny bopper lifestyle, "price too high for a piece of plastic." Only 16% wear watches but 72% desire to purchase Swatch if positioned right (NB: are currently undersymboled).	Price and function outweigh fashionability. Swatch too wild for their lifestyle yet potential interest to "fit in" (80% unawareness of traditional styles).

* MTV = a leading national "basic cable" all music TV station.
† AOR = album oriented rock.

EXHIBIT 21 *(continued)*

	Rockers (16–22)	Preppies (16–22)	Trendies (16–22)
Age			
Profile/interests	60% Male, 40% female. Long hair, clique-oriented, committed to rock groups, *very* frequent concert goers (for music, not as a social event). Like fast cars, comedy and horror movies, 100% American rock 'n roll. Dislike short hair, New Wave, disco. Music: *Pure rock 'n roll* (no synthesizers, drum machines). Hero: ZZ Top.	Career-oriented, traditional views, "controlled" wildness in style (designs more than colors), concerts (more as social event than for music), participation sports. Like dating, movies. Music: "Yuppie" rock/folk/pop. Like songs more than artists.	Movement similar to hippies but smaller scale. Exist only in U.S. art and culture capitals. Avant-garde tastes; outspoken on issues they consider important. Left socially and politically. Go to clubs, not concerts. Music: anti-rock 'n roll, anti-popular groups.
Media	AOR* radio, MTV (77% regular viewers).	Cable TV, some MTV, some fashion magazines, radio (AOR*, CHR*, Light Rock mix) but low station loyalty.	Trendy, artsy magazines and newspapers. Anti-MTV, anti-commercial radio.
Shopping habits	Like all "things American."	Stores: mainstream dept. stores.	
Reaction to Swatch	Aware of wild Swatch styles *only*. Like its disposability, price. Dislike what it stands for: glitzy, hi-tech graphics, New Wave, dancing, slick ads, male model geeks. "A girl's/bopper's watch." Consider multiple Swatch ownership too trendy.	92% awareness—prefer traditional designs, price, fashionability, reliability, practicability. Dislike its young teen image. 73% prefer dressier watches (silver/gold Rolex look) for "special events"; strongly anti-"digital." Line extensions: too expensive, unnecessary.	Consider fashion a vehicle of expression, rejection of anything too popular. 73% wear no watch. Very negative image of Swatch: "a rip-off," "a toy," the corporate world, "fast-food of time pieces."

*AOR = Album oriented rock; CHR = Contemporary hits radio.

EXHIBIT 21 *(continued)*

Age	Transitionaries (22–32)	Older casuals (22–43)	Weekend hippies (33–43)
Profile/interests	Conservative, social climbers. Like wildness (as observers, not participants), competitive sports. Music: "intelligent" rock 'n roll.	The hidden mainstream, ultra-conservative, *very* family-oriented, fast-food patrons, socially inactive, disinterested in fashion. Music: traditional.	Mellowed former hippies. Look like but hate being called Yuppies; still subscribe to basic 1960s principles. Music: mood music, "New Age" movement.
Media	Females: fashion magazines. Males: *Time, Newsweek, Sports Illustrated.* Not MTV (only 16% regular viewers).	Network TV, local newspapers (even National Enquirer-type tabloids).	Cable TV (critical viewers) but no MTV, radio (as background music). Weekend newspaper supplements, traditional magazines (i.e., *Time, Newsweek*, etc).
Shopping habits	Pro-American but respectful of foreign-made goods; appreciate quality/value; balance between fashion and conservatism. Stores: major mainstream dept. stores (91% source of potential Swatch purchase for 76% aware).	Traditional brands (e.g., Timex, Bulova, Casio for watches).	Heavy shoppers, appreciate quality products. Stores: upscale dept. stores (I. Magnin, Saks) for females, mainstream dept. stores for men.
Reactions to Swatch	Positive: consider it a great leisure tool, like its durability, disposability, price, reliability. Line extensions: high awareness but overpriced for females, not really credible for males.	Watches are functional. Awareness: 12% aided, 4% unaided.	High awareness but 43% of those aware have never seen one. Cheap, teen-item image; but like functionality, lightweight, durability. Line extensions: overpriced, not functional, too gaudy. High awareness of competing brands.

Source: Compiled from a Burkhard, Abrams, Douglas, Eliot market study, 1986.

EXHIBIT 21 *(concluded)*

Results

1. Liked by teeny boppers, too "young teeny" for all others. "Camp" humor was appreciated but considered too like "MTV parents." The caption was considered humorous but the visual too unrealistic for adult parents.

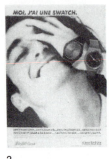

1

2

2. Good idea, poorly executed, not credible. The sports car was positive for males but the model was too unrealistic, too slick. "Race drivers would not wear three watches." The caption was felt to evoke the potential decline of the Swatch trend. The cars were considered too European and sophisticated.

3. Males of all ages except Trendies felt the foreign language caption was counterproductive to the need for Swatch to move away from European "New Wave" clichés.

3

4

4. These items were only of interest to a *very* fashion-conscious minority. The ad tended to reinforce the trendy aspect of the Swatch look, a major concern for potential buyers. Most respondents wouldn't buy a Swatch pen or razor.

5. The Thompson Twins tend to reinforce the young teen image. Use of another group, still appreciated by the teens but more accessible to older, potential and existing Swatch customers (e.g., Transitionaries, Preppies, and Rockers) was advised.

5

6

6. The "collection" concept appealed to most teen females but (*a*). What is it and what does it mean?, (*b*). this concept aroused suspicion mostly among 16–32 age males that it was a ploy to push sales of Swatch non-watch gear.

7. There is limited awareness of Keith Haring outside New York but the ad tested well since most people like animation. Only complaint: "too disco."

7

8

8. 43% of respondents recognized Bruce Jenner but he was considered too "goody-goody," even for young teen female fans.

Europe, or other major markets. These could look strikingly similar to Swatch, some even similar in quality and very price competitive, and the company was involved in a long series of legal proceedings to fight off the competition.

Timex, one of the companies worst hit by the LCD watch glut, had launched a line of colored fashion watches called "Watercolors," priced slightly below Swatch. Timex was also rumored to be preparing a new advertising campaign for its "Big-Bold-Beautiful" fashion watch line for women, introduced in the summer of 1986 and targeted to an older age group than Swatch. According to one industry expert, the Timex range did not seem to have any "winners," at least in Europe. Seiko's Lorus line was expanded in 1984 to include "Swatch-like" fashion models, priced lower than Swatch and doing well when they had special design features. The first solar-powered wristwatch was also launched under the Lorus brand name in 1986. Competitors wondered, however, if Seiko was really committed to competing with Swatch, since nonwatch activities, (e.g., personal computers, printers, and audio and video equipment) were to be increased to 30 percent of worldwide sales by 1989. Don Galliers summarized the challenge in the United States:

> If you want to take a significant market share away from the existing well-established brand, you have to spend three times the amount of advertising that brand spends. To kick us where we hurt worse, in delivery and depth, they'll have to build up $75 million worth of initial inventory, in addition to the $100 million investment in production facilities. That's one hell of an investment!

Citizen apparently did not feel it necessary to launch a Swatch-like product, preferring to focus on its specialization, digitals, and technically sophisticated watches. At first, Casio specialized more specifically in calculators and extremely price-competitive multifunction digital watches and did not jump on the Swatch bandwagon either. In 1986, when the shift from digital to analog watches became apparent, however, Casio launched "Color Burst," a line of quartz analog fashion watches, waterproof to 50 meters, retailing at less than the price of Swatch. Sales were reported to be rather disappointing.

Swatch management claimed that only the very large firms could compete with ETA on price and that smaller firms undercutting Swatch on price were left with virtually no margin to compete with Swatch's intensive communication. Swatch refused to enter into a price war with its competitors. According to Jacques Irniger, ETA marketing manager, Swatch spent more than double the watch industry's average ad spend for a *single* brand: "Competitors can copy our watch but not our media spend. They will also have trouble duplicating some of Swatch's promotional stunts." Examples of "Swatch-like" fashion watches with limited market response were the "Twist" by Accurist and the "American Graffiti" watch by Gillex in the United Kingdom. According to Ernst Thomke, "In an era when superbly accurate quartz watches sell for $10,

EXHIBIT 22   Aided recall of watch advertisements

	United States				Switzerland			
Brand	Total n = 290	Buyers n = 99	Potential buyers n = 140	Non-buyers n = 51	Total n = 212	Buyers n = 90	Potential buyers n = 87	Non-buyers n = 35
Swatch	67*	79	66	47	78	88	70	74
Omega	6	9	6	—	19	22	17	14
Rolex	31	32	25	45	20	29	10	23
Seiko	35	35	36	29	16	22	6	23
Cartier	14	7	16	25	16	22	10	11
Timex	41	37	46	35	4	3	2	11
Gucci	16	17	15	16	—	—	—	—
Citizen	18	17	21	12	5	3	3	11
Pulsar	11	12	14	—	—	—	—	—
Bulova	10	6	12	14	—	—	—	—
Casio	10	14	11	—	6	7	5	6
Longines	11	12	11	12	15	18	9	20
Guess	14	18	12	14	—	—	—	—
Tissot	8	12	7	—	50	50	45	60
A-Watch	10	10	13	—	—	—	—	—
K-Watch	—	—	—	—	—	—	—	—
M-Watch	—	—	—	—	13	18	6	20
Club Med	—	—	—	—	—	—	—	—
Dugena	—	—	—	—	—	—	—	—
Kiplé	—	—	—	—	—	—	—	—
Lorus	4	—	4	—	—	—	—	—
Yéma	—	—	—	—	—	—	—	—

* Percentage of total responses to the question, "Which of the watches on this list have you recently seen or heard advertised recently?" No figure indicates that the brand was not listed on the card.
Source: Compiled from Qualitest A.G. study, Zurich, August 1986.

the key is not technology but image." Exhibit 24 presents Swatch's image in five countries in 1986.

Brands explicitly positioned as fashion accessories varied from one country to another and it was difficult to obtain a global view of the situation as well as market share data to determine the relative threat presented by such brands. Designer watches (e.g., Gucci, Dior, Givency, Nina Ricci, Yves Saint Laurent, Ralph Lauren, Calvin Klein, Guy Laroche, Lanvin, Hermes, Benetton), although often in a different price range from Swatch (i.e., segments C and D— see Exhibit 4), were a growing trend, and the actual concept of "fashion watch" did not appear clear in consumers' minds. Responses to the question "Please tell me all the brands of fashion watches you can think of" included such diverse brands as Timex, Swatch, Bulova, Citizen, and Rolex. Franz Sprecher's definition of a fashion watch was "a watch not only colorful but with accessorizing potential and meaning, a statement of the fashion trends at a specific period of time."

	United Kingdom				France				West Germany		
Total n = 202	Buyers n = 68	Potential buyers n = 83	Non-buyers n = 51	Total n = 200	Buyers n = 66	Potential buyers n = 99	Non-buyers n = 35	Total n = 200	Buyers n = 67	Potential buyers n = 74	Non-buyers n = 59
50	56	53	39	50	62	46	34	67	70	69	61
5	10	—	8	—	—	—	—	19	18	24	14
17	16	22	12	15	17	12	17	34	31	39	31
30	35	28	27	30	32	30	26	31	30	36	25
11	12	13	6	—	—	—	—	—	—	—	—
23	26	19	24	21	23	23	9	22	24	26	15
—	—	—	—	—	—	—	—	—	—	—	—
15	18	18	6	58	64	56	49	—	—	—	—
—	—	—	—	4	3	5	—	6	16	—	—
—	—	—	—	—	—	—	—	—	—	—	—
11	15	11	6	11	11	10	14	—	—	—	—
3	6	4	—	—	—	—	—	13	13	11	14
9	13	10	4	—	—	—	—	—	—	—	—
4	4	6	—	—	—	—	—	12	14	11	10
—	—	—	—	—	—	—	—	—	—	—	—
—	—	—	—	4	6	3	—	—	—	—	—
—	—	—	—	—	—	—	—	—	—	—	—
—	—	—	—	5	6	2	9	—	—	—	—
—	—	—	—	—	—	—	—	15	15	15	15
—	—	—	—	11	12	10	9	—	—	—	—
—	—	—	—	—	—	—	—	—	—	—	—
—	—	—	—	14	17	12	14	—	—	—	—

In Europe, moderate-price fashion watches included Kelton, an inexpensive French watch brand launched by Timex in the early 1960s. After initial rejection by the traditional jewelers' network, Kelton had been very successfully distributed through mass distribution channels. The breakdown of Kelton sales in France was estimated to be 45 percent from "tabacs" (registered tabacconists), 30 percent from supermarkets, and 25 percent from department and variety stores. Kelton was also distributed in the United Kingdom, Portugal, and Italy. Prices ranged from 99 to 320 French francs. K'Watch, Kelton's response to Swatch, launched in June 1984, was priced from 249 to 270 FF. Kelton brand awareness was very high in France and it had a young, inexpensive, active, and fashionable image. Philippe d'Herbomez, Kelton marketing manager, commented:

> When you think about the Swatch strategy you realize that the product was launched on the Kelton concept: "Vous vous changez, changez de Kelton!" (Time to change, change your Kelton!) but the consumer more readily changes his

EXHIBIT 23 A perceptual map of Swatch and other leading brands in West Germany

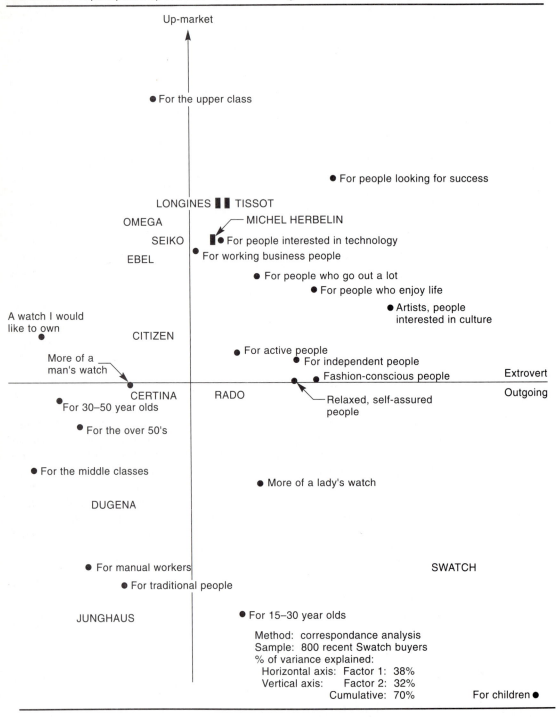

Swatch than his Kelton since with every new Swatch collection the previous ones become virtually obsolete. When Swatch was launched Kelton was no longer very fashionable and had become expensive in comparison with Asian watches. The 1987 Kelton collection is a series of new lower-priced products. Our distribution is wearing thin also so we plan to open up new outlets and invest in communication with emphasis on our well-known, successful slogan.

Other fashion watches had mushroomed in the wake of the Swatch success. The M-Watch, an inexpensive (38 SF) traditional quartz watch containing ETA movements, was launched by Mondaine in Zurich at the same time as Swatch and distributed by the Swiss supermarket chain Migros. In May 1984 the French firm Kiplé launched "Kip'Marine" priced from 210 to 440 FF and distributed through supermarkets, stationers, "tabacs," and variety stores.

In October 1984, Dr. Konstantin Theile, ETA marketing manager during the development of Swatch, left ETA to launch the new brand TIQ (Time Inter Corporation A.G.). This new nonplastic, leather-strapped, silent, and reparable waterproof quartz watch priced at 70 to 150 SF targeted an "optimistic, individualistic, fashion-conscious consumer" ages 25–35 but slightly more conservative than the Swatch consumer. Production costs were three times those of Swatch, and TIQ granted the usual margin to the trade. Distribution was through upmarket department stores, established jewelers, and fashion boutiques. To quote Dr. Theile:

> Not everybody wants to wear a noisy irreparable plastic watch. It is frustrating to become attached to your watch only to find out that your model cannot be repaired and is no longer available.

By early 1985 the French firm Beuchat had introduced a series of metal and plastic strap watches with original and fun faces: a sports line illustrating 27 different sports, a "crazy" line including a face with hands turning counterclockwise, and a "corporations" line illustrating different professions. Distribution was the same as Swatch and prices were slightly higher. Beuchat's plans were to expand into promotional watches, starting with BMW. Under license from Club Méditerranée, the French firm Marckley CDH had launched waterproof metal and plastic quartz watches distributed worldwide through selective channels. Prices were also slightly higher than Swatch. Marckley did not invest in advertising for the "Club Med" watch but point-of-sale promotion included an aquarium display containing a submerged watch.

The American firm Le Jour started testing a $49 kaleidoscope color fashion watch called "Sixty" in 1986. Sales, mainly through department stores, were reportedly encouraging. In the spring of 1986 a Swiss entrepreneur launched "The Clip," a clip-on, waterproof, shock-resistant, silent and reparable quartz watch designed to be worn "anywhere except on the wrist" and sold through the same distribution channels as Swatch. Launched in Switzerland at 40 SF and 50 SF, The Clip was introduced in France, Spain, West Germany, and England in the summer and would roll out to the United States in the fall.

EXHIBIT 24   Image of Swatch, 1986

Swatch	Switzerland				United Kingdom			
	Total $n = 212$	Buyers $n = 90$	Potential Buyers $n = 87$	Non-buyers $n = 35$	Total $n = 202$	Buyers $n = 68$	Potential buyers $n = 83$	Non-buyers $n = 51$
Is Swiss made	39*	43	37	31	15	13	17	14
Is reasonably priced	36	44	34	20	32	32	34	27
Is a sports watch	33	31	39	23	24	28	23	22
Is continuously introducing new models (colors, dials)	32	30	37	26	14	10	23	6
Is a watch for all occasions (business, sports)	30	37	32	9	31	35	25	33
Is a highly fashionable watch	25	27	31	9	37	35	41	31
Is mainly for young people	17	17	18	11	27	25	22	37
Is waterproof	15	16	16	9	10	10	8	14
Is the ideal present	14	17	16	—	11	15	8	10
Has good ads	10	13	7	11	8	6	8	12
Is a trendy watch	8	4	8	17	22	16	30	18
Is a high-quality watch	7	9	6	3	29	32	23	33
Is a quartz watch	6	4	7	9	3	1	6	—
Is shock-proof	5	4	7	—	10	9	5	20
Attracts attention	3	2	3	3	24	25	25	20
I would like to own more than one	1	1	1	—	1	1	—	—

* Percentage of total responses to the question: "Which *three* statements on this card can you think of as the most important ones in describing Swatch?"
Source: Qualitest A.G. study, Zurich, August 1986.

E. A. Day, managing director of Louis Newmark, the Swatch distributor in the United Kingdom, commented:

> It is too early to discuss the future of The Clip. It does appear to sell well when promoted, but once the promotion ends, sales drop back dramatically.

In the summer of 1986, the Swiss firm SAMEL S.A. had introduced "Sweet-zerland," a water-resistant quartz watch with a two-year battery that snapped in and out of interchangable elastic terrycloth wristbands in different colors, priced at $40. Distribution was through jewelry stores, fashion boutiques, accessory and sport shops, perfumeries, and upmarket department stores in France, West Germany, Austria, Benelux, Italy, Spain, and Portugal, as well as the United States through a Californian subsidiary.

Sekonda, an English firm importing watches from the USSR and Hong Kong, launched a new line of fashion watches in 1985, under the brand names "Spangles," "Phantom," and "Nostalgia." Prices ranged from £15 to £20. A mechanical watch named "Hotline," with style variations on the dial and strap,

France				West Germany				United States			
Total $n=200$	Buyers $n=66$	Potential buyers $n=99$	Non-buyers $n=35$	Total $n=200$	Buyers $n=67$	Potential buyers $n=74$	Non-buyers $n=59$	Total $n=290$	Buyers $n=99$	Potential buyers $n=140$	Non-buyers $n=51$
13	12	14	11	21	25	11	29	16	16	16	14
24	30	19	26	16	15	16	15	26	31	24	18
43	52	37	43	44	51	47	31	28	30	26	27
30	29	31	29	50	61	53	32	19	20	20	12
23	18	25	23	18	21	23	8	14	16	16	8
18	15	21	14	33	19	39	41	25	27	24	25
38	23	44	49	40	30	30	63	16	12	13	33
8	15	5	3	8	9	14	—	17	22	16	10
23	26	26	9	12	18	14	2	12	12	14	6
5	8	4	3	16	9	20	19	16	8	21	20
29	21	28	43	10	3	4	24	25	16	27	35
6	9	4	6	6	6	4	8	20	28	16	12
8	5	9	9	8	13	4	7	6	6	7	4
9	12	5	14	5	6	8	—	8	10	7	6
14	11	14	17	15	12	12	22	34	35	35	31
11	15	10	3	1	2	1	—	6	9	5	—

appeared in West Germany and Switzerland in 1986. It was explicitly aimed at preteen age groups and retailed mainly in department stores for 30 DM. Other fashion watches in roughly the same price category as Swatch included Avia, Alfex, Orion, Zeon, Video Clip, and Hip-Hop. Selected advertisements for "fashion watches" in different countries are pictured in Exhibit 25.

The Meeting

Chris Keigel checked the fashionable collection of Swatches on his wrist. It was time to make major decisions for the future of Swatch and the meeting with Thomke, Marquardt, Imgrüth, and Sprecher was approaching fast. He perused the sales figures in Exhibit 26. Keigel knew that Swatch guards and shields, the Parafernalia line, and the Coca-Cola watches yielded profit margins exceeding that of Swatch watches, whereas those of the other items in the U.S. extended product line did not. Apparel profit margins had dropped and sales were lagging behind forecasts. Swatch management knew that the transport and other costs

EXHIBIT 25   Selected Swatch competitors

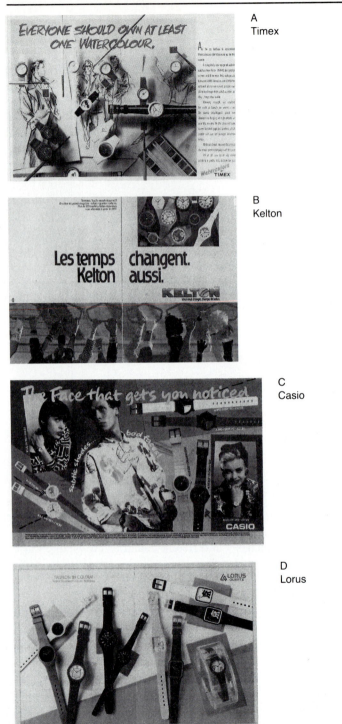

A
Timex

B
Kelton

C
Casio

D
Lorus

EXHIBIT 25 (continued)

A   Sekonda

B   Sixty

C   Beuchat

D   Sweet-zerland

E   Coca-Cola   F   Alfex   G   Club Med

EXHIBIT 25 *(concluded)*

A   Hot Line

B   Le Clip

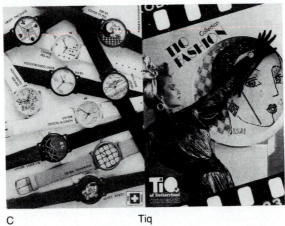

C   Tiq

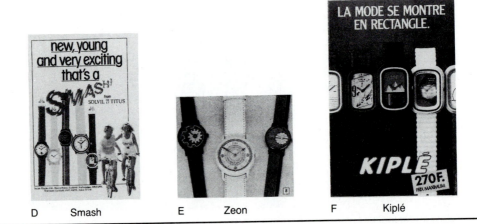

D   Smash   E   Zeon   F   Kiplé

EXHIBIT 26 Swatch sales

Swatch watches (000 units or Swiss francs)

	1983		1984		1985		January–August	1986
Country	Units	SF	Units	SF	Units	SF	Units	SF
World	1,319	27,901	4,496	114,057	10,168	284,832	8,321	209,954
United States	135	NA	1,242	42,475	4,659	167,562	3,817	102,824
Switzerland	NA	NA	1,032	23,451	924	21,707	595	14,585
France			399	8,910	756	17,710	667	14,824
England	NA	NA	455	7,140	762	14,288	524	9,694
West Germany	NA	NA	202	4,514	712	17,152	587	16,837
Japan					141	3,374	18	646

Extended product line (000 units or U.S. dollars)

	1984		1985		January–August 1986	
Item	Units	Dollars	Units	Dollars	Units	Dollars
Swatch guards	7	10	3,617	4,280	2,637	3,721
Chums	13	26	104	226	24	6
Bags			224	2,497	134	1,042
Shields			141	2,418	87	1,381
Knives			263	1,236	4	20
Clocks			4	248	1	77
Umbrellas			181	1,606	109	359
Apparel			620	6,279	1,893	18,877
Parafernalia			387	1,175	440	464
Coca-Cola watches					194	3,392

Source: Company records (disguised data).

involved in importing this line to Europe might put prices out of line, especially since the clothing was designed specifically for the American market. He also knew that Max Imgrüth was pushing for six collection changes per year, but remembered hearing Franz Sprecher advocate a more conservative approach:

> We can't just announce 'Here comes our collection' to the trade. We are an accessory, we are not making fashion. What is more important is what the consumer will think. Are we really enough of a fashion product in the eyes of the consumer to make a planned line extension into fashion wear? If Calvin Klein, Ralph Lauren, or Benetton make a watch, that works because they are established fashion firms, but I have never seen it work the other way around. There is a lot of competition in the department stores, whole floors of T-shirts, so where is our expertise?

Case 38

The Stroh Brewery Company*

In April 1985, the headline in the *Detroit News* asked, "Why Can't Stroh Tap More of the Home Market?" The text went on to explain that while other leading brewers enjoy a generous share of the beer market on their home turf, the Stroh Brewery Company of Detroit, Michigan, had settled into a very distant third place in Detroit and Michigan, behind Budweiser and Miller. (See Exhibit 1 for state of Michigan beer sales.) "It's hard to describe why Stroh is not number one in Detroit," said Don Hill, president of City Marketing, Inc., a Detroit area beer distributor. "If you were to randomly call people and ask them which beer is number one here, they would say Stroh's," Hill said. "If you ask

EXHIBIT 1 State of Michigan beer sales, top 13 brands *(barrels)*

	Brand	Percent total	1984 Sales	1984 Percent change	1983 Sales	1983 Percent change	1982 Sales
1.	Miller	15.9	1,074,375	−9.0	1,180,674	−9.5	1,304,621
2.	Budweiser	14.3	966,310	+12.4	859,993	+10.2	780,408
3.	Miller Lite	13.1	888,407	−1.7	903,405	+4.7	862,603
4.	**Stroh***	**11.5**	**779,712**	**−8.2**	**849,209**	**+3.9**	**817,373**
5.	Pabst	8.2	557,152	−23.0	723,874	−9.3	798,071
6.	**Schlitz†**	**4.5**	**305,520**	**−22.5**	**374,144**	**+13.7**	**328,967**
7.	Michelob	4.1	275,444	+12.8	244,082	−15.5	288,693
8.	Busch	3.2	215,828	+140.8	89,646	−11.2	100,908
9.	Michelob Light	3.2	213,581	−6.9	199,782	−11.3	255,227
10.	Budweiser Light	3.1	212,239	+31.4	162,011	+22.0	132,815
11.	Blatz	2.9	193,242	+24.7	203,727	+26.2	161,454
12.	Altes	1.8	121,488	−15.6	144,028	+22.5	177,566
13.	Colt 45	1.8	119,242	−12.7	136,560	+5.2	129,841

* Includes all Stroh brands.
† Includes all Schlitz brands.
Source: *The Michigan Brewery Record*, Investment Statistics Company, Detroit, 1985.

---

* This case was prepared from public sources by Susan A. Johnstal, under the supervision of Thomas C. Kinnear. Copyright © 1987 Thomas C. Kinnear.

them what they drink, they'll name something else." During 1984, the Stroh brewery's total sales by volume declined 8.2 percent in the state of Michigan.

Along the East and West Coasts, Stroh's beer, the flagship brand of the Stroh brewery, had a ritzy appeal similar to imported beers because of its unique fire-brewing process. It has been said that a case of Stroh's could be traded for any two cases of anything else in the East. In the Midwest, however, Stroh's was not a new name, and the hometown brew enjoyed no such mystique. In the Michigan home base, Stroh's was just another blue-collar thirst quencher. Bolstering the Midwest image of Stroh's and increasing share in its home market were priorities to Stroh management, as was the successful expansion of the flagship brand across the country.

However, the status of Stroh's national expansion was also a question. Stroh began to break out of its traditional Midwest distribution area by taking its flagship labels, Stroh's and Stroh Light, to a national level in 1984. Stroh advertised the two brands heavily with television commercials and outdoor billboards, further developed its wholesaler network, installed on-premise taps in bars and taverns, and sponsored local charity events. As a result, the Stroh geographic distribution area grew. By the end of 1984, Stroh officials were pleased with the preliminary results of the expansion effort. But Stroh's brand, as well as the entire list of Stroh brands, faced a faltering demand for beer in the United States (down .6 percent in 1984), and Stroh's nationwide 1984 beer sales by volume declined 1.6 percent. (See Exhibit 2 for Stroh production by brand.)

EXHIBIT 2 Stroh production by brand (millions of barrels)

	1982	1983	1984
Old Milwaukee (popular priced)	6.0	7.6	7.1
Stroh (premium)	5.4	5.5	5.3
Schaefer (popular priced)	2.5	3.0	4.0
Schlitz Malt (malt liquor)	2.6	2.6	2.1
Schlitz (premium)	4.1	3.2	1.7
Old Milwaukee Light (popular light)	0.8	1.0	1.5
Stroh Light (premium light)	0.6	0.7	0.8
Goebel (popular priced)	0.3	0.3	0.6
Schlitz Light (premium light)	0.4	0.3	0.1
Erlanger (super premium)	0.1	—	—
Other	0.1	0.1	0.7
Schaefer L.A. (popular LA)			
Schaefer Light (popular light)			
Signature (super premium)			
Piels (premium)			
Piels Light (premium)			
Silver Thunder (malt liquor)			
Primo (premium)			
Total	22.9	24.3	23.9

Note: Capacity total = 29.5 million barrels.
Source: *Beverage Industry,* January 1985.

In addition to falling sales, management was concerned about several industry changes expected during the rest of the century. Consumer tastes were changing in the types of beer they preferred; imports and light beers were gaining sales volume at the expense of premium beers. Consumers' changing lifestyles included more often choosing wines and bottled water over beer. Demographic trends, including an aging society, threatened the popularity of beer as the number of people in the 18-to-35-year-old age bracket decreased. Increased consciousness of alcohol abuse brought about proposed legislation on banning beer advertising on television and radio. Within the beer industry, traditional beer wholesaler policies of exclusive territories were in question because of their anticompetitive nature. Finally, the efficiencies of national marketing and distribution were dictating that regional-only breweries could no longer compete as effectively against well-financed national brands, while consolidation of smaller brewers continued. These industry changes and Stroh's weakening position in its home market and lack of solid penetration in its new markets threatened to unseat Stroh from its 1985 number three spot on the list of largest national beer brewers.

History and Past Marketing Strategy

The Stroh family started brewing beer in the United States over 130 years ago. Bernhard Stroh, a German immigrant, opened his first successful brewery in 1865 in Detroit, Michigan. He brewed the beer in copper kettles over direct fire, a process that originated in Europe, while other brewers in America brewed over steam. The company grew in the Detroit area as a family business by delivering the brew to residents and local taverns. During Prohibition, the company survived by producing ice cream, malt extract, near beer, soft drinks, and ice. At the end of Prohibition, Stroh became a successful Midwestern beer brewer. Roger Fridholm, president of the Stroh brewery, attributes this success to quality, consumer service, packaging, and advertising. Also contributing to growing beer sales was the postwar baby boom, which produced 28 million additional Americans in beer brewers' prime age bracket, 18 to 35 years old. Stroh, as well as the entire beer-producing industry, could not help but grow as total beer consumption doubled in the next two decades.

In the 1960s, Stroh's was a popular-priced beer with a reputation for quality and taste generated by its fire brewing. Consumers were loyal to Stroh's because they believed, for the most part, that they were getting a premium beer at popular prices. Until 1979, Stroh had one brewery and essentially one brand: Stroh's (Bohemian style beer).

But during the 1970s, as the national brewers—Anheuser-Busch of St. Louis, Missouri, and the Miller Brewing Company of Milwaukee, Wisconsin—began to dominate the beer industry with tremendous advertising budgets, consolidation of smaller brewers sliced the number of beer producers in the country from approximately 171 to 45. In 1973, Stroh began raising the prices of Stroh's brand in hopes of repositioning it as a premium beer to compete directly with Budweiser and Miller. In the early 1980s, Anheuser-Busch (A-B) and Miller continued to grow without the aid of acquisition and forced many smaller brewers out of business. The Stroh brewery was forced to take on a defensive marketing strategy at that time. Stroh struggled to hold onto its existing Midwestern market and tried to offset the lack of sales growth by expanding into other beer segments and by producing new beer products. Stroh Light was introduced in 1979 as the first internally developed new product in the company's history, but serious production growth was severely hampered by the limits of Stroh's sole brewing plant.

"We woke up in the late 1970s to what was going on around us," says Chairman Peter Stroh, and that is when the brewery began its very aggressive expansion campaign. In 1979, Stroh acquired the F&M Schaefer Corporation, of Allentown, Pennsylvania, the eleventh largest brewer at the time. "We didn't buy a brand, we bought a brewery," explains Hunter Hastings, vice president of brand management. Although Stroh did not abandon the Schaefer brand, Stroh invested over $35 million to convert Schaefer's plant to fire brewing so that it could increase production of Stroh's brands. The Schaefer acquisition became Stroh's first move to dramatically expand the company.

In the summer of 1982, after a bitter battle, the Stroh Brewery Company, the seventh largest brewer in the nation, jumped to number three almost overnight when it acquired the Jos. Schlitz Brewing Company of Milwaukee, Wisconsin. Stroh borrowed $336 million to acquire the third largest brewer, thereby tripling its number of brewing plants to better compete at the national level. Stroh gained 1,250 wholesalers, 7,000 employees, and two very strong brand names: Old Milwaukee and Schlitz Malt Liquor.

Newspapers at the time quoted Peter Stroh's admiration for the Schlitz management. "I've been very impressed by their progress in overcoming the problems they inherited," exclaimed Peter. He was referring to the fact that during the five years before the merger, Schlitz's annual volume slid 35 percent, primarily because of quicker production techniques that noticeably cheapened the beer's quality. Peter Stroh believed his future as an independent brewer was in jeopardy, and the Schlitz failing position made it a prime candidate for takeover. With expansion for the Stroh brewery in mind, management concluded that acquisition was much cheaper than building new facilities. Building a brand new plant would have cost Stroh approximately $60 to $80 per barrel of plant capacity. Purchasing Schlitz cost only $25 per barrel. Schlitz's strategically located plants (see Exhibit 3 for a list of Stroh breweries) and its national, well-established distribution channels, including on-premise accounts in bars, off-premise network of retail stores, and wholesalers and distributors, were a few of the major reasons for Stroh's interest in Schlitz.

Stroh used the additional Schlitz plants nationwide to take advantage of economies of scale in production, distribution, and, probably most important, in advertising. Prior to 1982, as a regional brewer, Stroh had to pay a 50 percent premium on spot television to get the same results as A-B and Miller, who

EXHIBIT 3 Stroh's breweries

Location	Capacity (million barrels)
Detroit, Michigan*	7.25
Allentown, Pennsylvania†	3.5
Longview, Texas‡	3.8
Van Nuys, California‡	2.95
Memphis, Tennessee‡	5.5
Winston-Salem, North Carolina‡	5.0
St. Paul, Minnesota§	1.5
Total	29.5

* Closed June 1985.
† Original Schaefer brewery.
‡ Original Schlitz brewery.
§ Exchanged with Pabst after Schlitz acquisition.

advertised nationally. "Every time we are forced to buy prime time regional spots, we take it on the chin," explained John Bissell, group vice president of marketing. To make up for this inefficiency prior to the Schlitz acquisition, Stroh and the Adolph Coors Company, a regional brewer out of Golden, Colorado, cleverly bought television air time together in the 1970s and split it down the Mississippi River; Stroh commercials aired in the East, and Coors commercials aired in the West. After the Schlitz acquisition, as a national competitor Stroh could get even better representation on network television.

The Stroh brewery management proved its commitment to the growth of the company through its bold takeover of Schlitz. In reference to building the company as a national competitor, corporate Planning and Development Vice President Christopher W. Lole said, "You'd have to give credit to Peter. He's the visionary." But the fact remains that sales of Stroh products, both nationally and at home, have been falling, and Stroh management must further develop its marketing strategy to ensure the future of this independent family business.

Industry Environment

The Competition

The U.S. beer industry is highly competitive. In 1985, there were about 45 national, regional, and local brewers. Beer is an extremely mature product in the product life cycle, and as the industry shakeout continues, national brands are growing only at the expense of the smaller brewers.

Anheuser-Busch has traditionally dominated the beer industry through its sheer size and financial muscle. "The King of Beers" has been the largest brewer for over 25 years, and in 1984, A-B captured approximately 35.9 percent of the beer market, up from 33.6 percent the previous year. (See Exhibit 4 for brewers' estimated market shares.) A-B is the only domestic brewer to

EXHIBIT 4 Brewers' estimated market shares

	1979	1981	1983	1984E
Anheuser-Busch	26.8%	30.0%	33.6%	35.9%
Miller	20.8	22.2	20.8	21.3
Stroh	**15.3**	**12.9**	**13.5**	**13.4**
Heileman	6.6	7.7	9.7	8.6
Coors	7.5	7.3	7.6	7.5
Pabst	12.3	10.5	7.1	6.6
Genesee	2.0	2.0	1.8	1.7
Schmidt	2.2	1.6	1.7	1.6
Pittsburgh	0.4	0.5	0.6	0.5
Others†	6.1	5.3	3.6	1.9
Total	100.0%	100.0%	100.0%	100.0%

* Includes Schlitz and Schaefer totals for all years.
† Includes imports and excludes tax-free sales.
Source: *Beverage Industry,* January 1985.

have meaningful growth in 1984: 6 percent growth in a total domestic market that declined 1.1 percent (or .6 percent, including imports). A-B's flagship brand, Budweiser, topped the most popular beer brands list in 1984 with 24.2 percent of the total beer sales, up from 22.8 percent in 1983. (See Exhibit 5 for the 1984 top 10 beer brands.) Also on the top 10 list was Michelob, the dominant super premium beer brand. New in 1984, Budweiser LA (without periods after the initials; LA is a logo protected by a trademark after Stroh unsuccessfully tried to use it for the Schaefer brand) is a low-alcohol brand with full-scale marketing support in the A-B lineup, with spending equivalent to all other A-B brands except Budweiser.

EXHIBIT 5 1984 Top 10 beer brands

Rank	Brand (brewer)	Market share	1984 Brand growth	Production (million barrels)
1	Budweiser (A-B)	24.2%	+3.7%	44.3
2	Miller Lite (Miller)	9.9	+.1	18.0
3	Miller High Life (Miller)	7.9	−14.7	14.5
4	Coors (Coors)	4.8	−10.0	8.7
5	**Old Milwaukee (Stroh)**	**3.9**	**−6.6**	**7.1**
6	Michelob (A-B)	3.7	−4.3	6.7
7	Pabst (Pabst)	3.6	−12.2	6.5
8	**Stroh (Stroh)**	**2.9**	**−3.6**	**5.3**
9	Old Style (Heileman)	2.8	−12.1	5.1
10	Coors Light (Coors)	2.5	+31.2	4.5

Source: *Beverage Industry,* January 1985.

The Miller Brewing Company, a subsidiary of Philip Morris, was in a strong number two position. Miller's clever advertising and timely product development of Miller Lite, the first successful low-calorie beer, gave Miller almost 21.3 percent of the total beer market in 1984. The trend-setting Miller Lite brand beat its older brother, Miller High Life, for second position on the

1984 top 10 list of beer brands. Overall, Miller had a volume increase, up 1.3 percent in 1984, thanks to Miller Lite and Miller's new popular priced brands, Meisterbrau and Milwaukee's Best. Miller's flagship brand, Miller High Life, experienced declining sales, however, dropping from 17 million barrels in 1983 to 14.5 million in 1984. Problems with this brand have been widely speculated on. Some beer experts believe Miller used the "It's Miller Time" campaign long after its effectiveness had peaked, barely altering it for 10 years. Miller also raised the price of Miller High Life in 1980 in a slumping economy. Although Budweiser eventually followed, the higher price may have permanently driven countless High Life drinkers to Budweiser. In 1985, Miller reviewed several ad agencies in an attempt to pump life back into the brand's sagging sales. J. Walter Thompson USA won the six-month-long competition, and began promoting Miller with a "Made the American Way" campaign.

Although Miller had reported operating profits since being acquired by Philip Morris, according to *Fortune* (March 3, 1985) these profits have been so paltry that they have covered only the interest on the roughly $1 billion Philip Morris borrowed to build breweries and bottling plants in the 1970s. Miller had a $450 million brewery that it had never used as of 1985, and there was widespread speculation on Wall Street that Philip Morris would sell Miller. Yet, many brewing analysts believed The Miller Brewing Company was still the only serious competition A-B had in terms of market share and financial backing.

While A-B and Miller had faced little real competition in previous years, they had to contend in the 1980s with a trio of second-tier companies who were breaking out of their traditional regional boundaries in order to avoid losing market share. These brewers included Stroh, G. Heileman Brewing Company of La Crosse, Wisconsin, and the Adolph Coors Company. Like Stroh, Heileman and Coors were becoming more adept at competing with the leaders.

During the past decade, Heileman jumped from 15th place to 4th in the beer industry. The company has built its empire chiefly by acquiring and successfully revitalizing regional brands, including Old Style, its lead brand among the 24 brands it had. A strong brand identity was important for Old Style, which sought new markets as a means of improving brand share and becoming a national brand. Heileman had nine breweries and a mammoth wholesaler network. Overall, Heileman's marketing strategy, based on brand acquisitions and heightened price competition, added up to a rough year in 1984: Heileman sales declined over 11 percent.

Heileman also tried to merge with Schlitz in 1982, but the move was blocked by the Justice Department on antitrust grounds. In 1984 and 1985, Heileman attempted to acquire the ailing Pabst Brewing Company, the sixth largest brewer. This move was blocked by federal injunction after Stroh and the Christian Schmidt Brewing Company of Philadelphia, the number nine brewer, began a lawsuit alleging unfair competition.

Despite shrinkage of sales in its western base, Coors expanded outside of its traditional market into the Southeast in the 1980s. With a renewed financial position (Coors traditionally has no debt) after a disastrous labor strike in 1977,

Coors established itself in a strong number five position among national beer brewers. Coors benefited from very strong brand identification for its premium Coors and Coors Light labels. These brews are unpasteurized and always shipped in refrigerated compartments, which contribute both to the brands' quality image and to customer confusion. Consumers were hesitant about buying Coors from unrefrigerated retail displays during large holiday promotions. As a result, in the summer of 1985, Coors advertised that while refrigeration certainly was desirable, it was not necessary to ensure the purity of Coors's taste.

1984 marked the first year that Coors had its two major brands in the list of top 10 most popular beer brands. Coors has not competed significantly in other beer segments. It seems the major limitation to Coors's expansion is that the company produces beer at a lone brewery in Golden, Colorado.

Beer Segmentation and the Consumer

For the first time in almost three decades, beer consumption in the United States declined in 1984. Consumption was 182.7 million barrels, down from 1983's 183.8 million barrels. Most industry researchers attribute this decline to changing lifestyles and social pressures. As brewing analysts predicted overall growth in domestic beer consumption to continue at 1 percent annually or less for the rest of the century, beer brewers sought to gain a larger portion of a steady-size pie through segment proliferation. Since many experts feel there really is no significant perceived difference among beer brands, especially after the first taste, brewers attempted to appeal to all different consumer backgrounds and introduced a brand image for almost every lifestyle, income, and taste.

1984 was a good year for light beer (for the more health-conscious consumer), popular priced beer (code term meaning inexpensive), and imported beers. Light beer sales increased its total industry share by 8 percent, moving up to 36.4 million barrels, or 19.9 percent of the total. Popular priced brands, the second most important segment, moved up to 42 million barrels, or 23 percent of the total. Imports accounted for 3.9 percent of total consumption, or 7.1 million barrels. (See Exhibit 6 for industry beer sales by market segment.)

EXHIBIT 6   1984 Industry beer sales by market segment

	Barrels (millions)	Percent
Light beer	36.4	9.9%
Popular priced	42.0	23.0
Imports	7.1	3.9
Premium priced	82.3	45.0
Super premiums	9.1	5.0
Other (Malts, LA)	5.8	3.0
Total	182.7	100.0

Source: *Beverage Industry*, January 1985.

However, the gains in these segments did not make up for the losses in the super premium segment (expensive beers of perceived higher quality), the premium segment (generally a brewer's flagship brand), and the malt liquor segment (beers with high alcohol content). Premium priced products, by far the largest beer segment, accounted for 82.3 million barrels sold, or 45 percent of the total in 1984. Super premiums, generally priced higher on a par with imports, were down 1.3 million barrels, accounting for 9.1 million barrels in sales, or 5 percent of the total market. Stroh had representation in every beer segment and was committed to continuing this strategy.

The majority (83 percent) of the nation's beer drinkers are males. They are usually between the ages of 18 and 34, with per capita consumption declining rather steadily with age (see Exhibit 7). Demographic trends were less than favorable for beer producers in the 1980s as the postwar baby boom generation moved beyond the prime beer drinking age. The 18-to-34 age group was predicted to decline by 4 million people before 1990. Stroh reacted to this unfortunate trend by seeking national market penetration.

EXHIBIT 7 Consumer characteristics

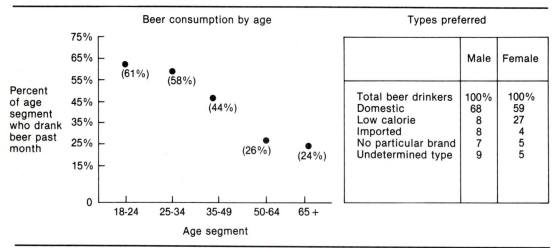

Source: *Advertising Age*, January 16, 1984, p. M-10.

Changes in eating and drinking habits also impeded growth in beer sales. The most prevalent change centered around our society's health concerns. Light beers have been very successful in addressing consumer demands for low-calorie foods since Miller introduced Miller Lite in the mid-1970s. During the 10 years following Miller Lite's introduction, light beer sales grew to account for over 20 percent of total beer sales and two thirds of the total growth in beer consumption for the period. Stroh markets almost one third of its brands with light labels, including Stroh Light, Old Milwaukee Light, Schlitz Light, Schaefer Light, and Piels Light.

A large threat to increasing beer sales in this country in the 1980s was increased concern over alcohol abuse. Various community groups, especially Mothers Against Drunk Driving (MADD), opposed brewers for allegedly glamorizing drinking in their advertising. Peter Stroh said the drinking/driving problem was probably the single most important issue he faced in 1984. While many states raised the drinking age from 18 to 21, lawmakers also stiffened the penalty for driving while drunk. ''This is an issue the beer industry cannot back away from. It is in the brewers' best interest to assist in educational efforts aimed against alcohol abuse,'' says Peter Stroh. Stroh has been very closely associated with efforts at Johns Hopkins and other leading universities to study health-related alcohol abuse effects.

On a related issue, consumer groups like SMART (Stop Marketing Alcohol on Radio and TV) were attempting to ban all alcoholic beverage advertising from TV and radio. Coalitions formed on both sides of the issue, and at Stroh, management felt brewers should work to shape any serious activity in this critical area rather than leaving the future of advertising laws only to the politicians. Stroh certainly did not want to see higher excise taxes to fund the fight against alcohol abuse, cigarette-type warning labels, or taglines on beer commercials warning consumers about the damage of abusing alcoholic beverages. Brewers traditionally imposed their own advertising standards, such as having actors in their ads who were over 25 years of age and never actually drank the beer on camera. Brewers claimed that there has been no credible scientific evidence to show that advertising encourages alcohol abuse and that the Supreme Court has previously ruled that truthful advertising has Constitutional protection. On the other hand, many legal scholars profess that a ban on advertising beer and wine on radio and television will withstand Constitutional law, and they point out the cigarette ruling as an example.

A-B addressed the alcohol-related issues by introducing a low-alcohol brand beer in 1984. Stroh quickly followed with Schaefer L. A. but was only distributing it on a limited basis until October 1985. In mid-1985, although A-B declined to give sales numbers for its low-alcohol beer, A-B called its LA ''the bar call of the 80s'' and did say that off-premise sales had been stronger than anticipated. Since exact sales figures on low-alcohol brands are not readily available, experts can only estimate that low-alcohol beers had only a negligible share of the beer market in their first year after introduction. Many analysts predict low-alcohol beers will not become a major market segment.

Advertising

''The Big Two,'' A-B and Miller, have capitalized on their high volumes with economies of scale in both production and distribution. This has allowed them to increase advertising expenditures well beyond what others can afford. (See Exhibit 8 for some national advertising expenditures by brand.) In an industry where savvy marketing is a key success factor, A-B and Miller secured the major live-action sports telecasts in the early 1980s with exclusive network

EXHIBIT 8 Some national advertising expenditures by brand ($000s)

Brand	Medium	1982	1983	1984
Budweiser and Bud Light (A-B)	Magazines	$ 2,560	$ 5,208	$ 2,907
	Newspapers	1,929	2,242	2,246
	Network TV	50,479	68,165	93,421
	Spot TV	21,905	30,094	29,087
	Network radio	4,572	4,052	2,179
	Spot radio	20,261	19,804	17,660
	Outdoor	3,191	2,217	2,123
Total		$104,897	$131,782	$149,623
Miller High Life and Miller Lite (Miller)	Magazines	$ 1,555	$ 1,352	$ 1,870
	Newspapers	490	1,556	1,279
	Network TV	74,651	84,082	104,930
	Spot TV	19,868	22,374	18,514
	Network radio	—	—	—
	Spot radio	16,051	5,194	17,449
	Outdoor	661	470	657
Total		$113,276	$125,028	$144,699
Michelob and Michelob Light (A-B)	Magazines	$ 13,993	$ 6,371	$ 2,040
	Newspapers	11,657	980	812
	Network TV	22,355	19,760	49,566
	Spot TV	14,653	2,209	6,643
	Network radio	—	503	2,017
	Spot radio	1,867	7,746	3,445
	Outdoor	74	30	252
Total		$ 64,599	$ 37,602	$ 64,775
Coors and Coors Light (Coors)	Magazines	$ 56	$ 29	$ 46
	Newspapers	1,153	1,016	657
	Network TV	7,069	9,746	11,218
	Spot TV	11,367	18,658	24,398
	Network radio	—	—	—
	Spot radio	8,081	21,209	18,528
	Outdoor	451	547	517
Total		$ 28,179	$ 51,205	$ 55,364
Stroh's and Stroh Light (Stroh)	**Magazines**	**$ 260**	**$ 255**	**$ 1,988**
	Newspapers	**113**	**242**	**450**
	Network TV	**3,578**	**24,962**	**27,780**
	Spot TV	**7,649**	**7,014**	**5,936**
	Network radio	**—**	**—**	**—**
	Spot radio	**1,842**	**3,472**	**6,141**
	Outdoor	**610**	**951**	**2,642**
Total		**$14,052**	**$36,896**	**$44,937**
Heineken (Van Munching)	Magazines	n/a	$ 4,708	$ 5,006
	Newspapers		15	150
	Network TV		2,895	3,004
	Spot TV		5,532	7,143
	Network radio		1,645	548
	Spot radio		7,659	12,983
	Outdoor		—	—
Total			$ 22,454	$ 28,834

EXHIBIT 8 *(concluded)*

Brand	Medium	1982	1983	1984
LA (A-B)	Magazines			$ 742
	Newspapers			1,618
	Network TV			19,218
	Spot TV			783
	Network radio			2,036
	Spot radio			558
	Outdoor			872
Total				$ 25,827
Lowenbrau (Miller)	Magazines	$ 111	$ 130	$ 454
	Newspapers	131	81	18
	Network TV	16,096	15,918	12,387
	Spot TV	6,412	4,748	5,762
	Network radio	—	—	—
	Spot radio	1,359	4,020	3,045
	Outdoor	6	18	14
Total		$ 24,115	$ 24,915	$ 21,680
Meister Brau (Miller)	Magazines		—	—
	Newspapers		$ 1,028	$ 41
	Network TV		8,300	18,336
	Spot TV		2,887	2,906
	Network radio		—	—
	Spot radio		—	—
	Outdoor		9	25
Total			$ 12,224	$ 21,308

Source: *Marketing and Media Decisions,* 14th Annual Report, "The Top 200 Brands."

advertising contracts that prohibited other beer competitors from airing their ads. The audience that watches live-action sports is the audience beer makers everywhere strive to attract: males aged 18 to 35. Stroh believed that network exclusive pacts hurt company business. "We have all the tools to compete, except for access to these sporting events. We have made offers to purchase time based on the terms and conditions customary to the television industry," explained Christopher Lole. The inability to reach a target audience through major network sports programs has critical trade implications also. Not having a presence on major sporting events makes it harder for local wholesalers to compete against those wholesalers whose product gets plenty of national exposure, and therefore it is more difficult to get ample shelf space from retailers.

After persistent efforts by Stroh management, including Peter Stroh himself, lengthy negotiations with the networks, and an investigation by the Department of Justice, the networks changed their policies on ad exclusivity in 1984. While no lawsuits were actually filed, Stroh made it clear that it would sue the networks on a restraint of trade basis if the two sides could not come to an agreement. Stroh was able to buy enough network time in 1984 to put off litigation over the matter. In fact, the networks actually offered Stroh more time than it could afford, according to Hunter Hastings, vice president of brand management. Stroh contracted to sponsor ABC's "Monday Night Baseball" on a nonexclusive basis for 1984. In addition, Stroh bought time on two NBC boxing matches and a CBS auto racing series.

In June 1985, the Stroh brewery introduced the "Stroh's Circle of Sports." For two hours every weekend for 13 weeks, Stroh's pursued a strategy of "going where the big guys ain't" on the USA cable network and a broadcast TV syndicate. The show featured interviews, analyses, opinions, historical flashbacks, and an "event of the week" shown from the perspective of a sports participant. The "Stroh's Circle of Sports" signaled that the brewer would look for advertising niches instead of always going head-on against A-B and Miller. This also represented the first example of Stroh's efforts to target audiences at a lower cost by creating its own programming. Stroh spent an estimated $200 million for advertising and sales promotions in 1985, but still could not match the spending of A-B and Miller.

Domestic beer brewers spent an estimated $575 million on advertising their products in 1984, which does not include the costs of promotion and distribution. Beer has gone from emphasizing traditional taste and quality claims to heavy consumer imagery. Certainly quality is an important factor in selling beer (as Schlitz found out only too late), but advertising, especially on TV, is the strategy of choice for the big beer makers.

Promotion

Brewers' promotional tactics came in many forms. Sporting events around the country throughout the year were usually the events of choice for national brewers—again, as a way of attracting young beer drinkers to their brands. Stroh sponsored the "Stroh Thunderfest," a hydroplane race in Detroit in which *Miss Budweiser* was often the boat favored to win. Other sponsorships by major brewers included bowling teams, auto races, rodeos, and track-and-field events. Budweiser was the official beer of the 1984 Olympics.

Many brewers sponsored special events such as rock concerts or symphonies to associate their beers with the lifestyles of those who participated in the events. Signature was the official beer of the 1982 World's Fair in Knoxville, Tennessee. Many brewers also sponsored charity events, including raising money for the renovation of the Statue of Liberty and making local donations to children's hospitals.

Brewers, in cooperation with local distributors, were very aggressive in providing quality point-of-purchase displays in retail outlets. Brewers attracted consumers in liquor and party stores with permanent and temporary illuminated prestige signs, nonilluminated plaques, and neon signs. Decorated mirrors with company logos were universally found in taverns and bars.

Stroh's very successful retail merchandising programs included the 10-year-old "Stroh a Party" campaign, which Stroh implemented to build sales of Stroh's and Stroh Light during the high-volume, peak summer selling season. The "Strohman"—a large plastic, stand-alone snowman—gave retailers a high-visibility display for Stroh's and Stroh Light during the winter holiday season. The "Strohman" program included not only the familiar snowman but also six-pack toppers, price cards, and cooler stickers for use in every display setting.

Super premium beers and malt liquors generally did not discount their prices to wholesalers in order to protect their upscale image. However, premium beers and popular priced brands often discounted their prices to wholesalers who in turn passed the savings on to retailers who, hopefully, sold the beers at sale prices during promotional campaigns. One of the wholesaler's jobs was to keep tabs on retail prices. Old Milwaukee offered periodic cents-off coupons, mail-in refund offers, and sweepstakes. These promotions were offered through newspapers, point of purchase, and direct mail.

Distribution and Pricing

Stroh brands, like all beers, were distributed through a three-tiered distribution system:

1. The brewery sold to wholesalers, who were independent, local businesspeople.
2. Wholesalers sold to retailers (bars and stores).
3. Retailers sold to consumers.

A brewery could not legally sell to retailers or to consumers.

Stroh officials, as described in a company document, believed the three-tiered system worked well because wholesalers agreed to provide service to all accounts, from mom-and-pop stores to high-volume chain stores. The wholesalers must maintain Stroh's strict standards of product quality by never selling beer over 90 days old and by keeping the product in temperature-controlled warehouses. In return, Stroh signed territorial agreements with wholesalers, giving them exclusive rights to sell Stroh products in their territories. From the brewery's point of view, this meant that the company did not have to pit wholesalers against one another. This industrywide practice was controversial because of its anticompetitive aspects.

Brewers set their prices of low-margin, popular priced beers to wholesalers based on a cost plus profit method. Brewers set prices of super premium beers, on the other hand, on a more consumer-oriented approach. Wholesalers and retailers were free to set their own prices based on their usual markups, but brewers hit certain price points by establishing a price to the wholesalers that, when marked up by the wholesalers and retailers, would match the desired retail price. (See Exhibit 9 for 1985 typical domestic retail beer brand prices.)

Laws governing promotional pricing varied widely from state to state. When a brand offered a lower promotional price, some states required it to stick with that price for as long as 120 days. For regular retail prices, most brands followed the segment leader's pricing strategy in any particular geographical market.

EXHIBIT 9 1985 Typical retail beer brand prices (six-pack of 12-ounce bottles or cans)*

Brand	Brewer	Price
Popular priced		
Blatz	Heileman	$2.50
Busch	Anheuser-Busch	2.49
Carling Black Label	Heileman	2.50
Goebel	**Stroh**	**2.25**
Meisterbrau	Miller	2.49
Natural Light	Anheuser-Busch	2.49
Old Milwaukee	**Stroh**	**2.39**
Old Milwaukee Light	**Stroh**	**2.39**
Premium		
Budweiser	Anheuser-Busch	$2.98
Bud Light	Anheuser-Busch	2.98
Miller High Life	Miller	2.98
Miller Lite	Miller	2.98
Old Style	Heileman	2.98
Pabst	Pabst	2.98
Schlitz	**Stroh**	**2.98**
Schlitz Light	**Stroh**	**2.98**
Stroh	**Stroh**	**2.98**
Stroh Light	**Stroh**	**2.98**
Super premium		
Erlanger	**Stroh**	**$3.39**
Lowenbrau	Miller	3.49
Michelob	Anheuser-Busch	3.39
Signature	**Stroh**	**3.39**
Malt Liquor		
Colt 45	Heileman	$2.98
Schlitz Malt Liquor	**Stroh**	**2.98**

* Price does not include sales tax or bottle deposit.

Current Marketing Strategy and Brand Management at Stroh

The Stroh Brewery Company's objective in 1985 was to keep a strong and growing number three position in the beer industry, with the ultimate goal of unseating the second largest industry leader, Miller. Industry experts predicted that consolidation of brewers in the next few decades would leave only four or five major beer producers. Although the company policy in 1985 did not include long-term planning of five years or more, Stroh was determined to be one of those few.

With the purchase of Schaefer, Stroh became a company in transition. Hunter Hastings said the company had to "make the switch from being a production company to a marketing company." In 1985, the entire marketing department was only six years old. The company recruited many young marketing MBAs, but most of the senior marketing executives came from other marketing-oriented firms. J. Wayne Jones, formerly with Coca-Cola, accepted the newly created position of executive vice president of sales and marketing in 1984, and John Bissell, group vice president of marketing, came from General Mills. Before the mid-1970s, Stroh did not bring outside talents into the company.

A-B and Miller relied on the ''block buster brand'' approach to the beer market for many years with their hugely successful Budweiser and Miller brands, respectively. Stroh, on the other hand, used the portfolio theory of brands after gaining so many different brands from acquisitions, and focused on the many segments in the beer market. Stroh had a brand of beer for all popular beer segments in the 1980s: popular priced, premium, malt liquor, etc. Stroh also concentrated on special niches, including demographics (African-Americans and Hispanics) and geographics (targeting different states and cities with unique campaigns).

In 1984, Stroh concentrated its energy on taking its flagship brands— Stroh's and Stroh Light—nationwide. Stroh planned to market Schaefer nationwide in 1985 and have Signature not far behind. Other brands, such as Schlitz Malt Liquor and Old Milwaukee, already made Stroh a national firm through the Schlitz acquisition. But in 1984, Roger Fridholm hoped Stroh's brand penetration nationwide would broaden its 13.4 percent market share to 15 percent. Fridholm did not, however, pin down a time frame for this objective.

The Stroh marketing strategy contained six priorities for the company:

1. Maintain and grow Stroh's and Stroh Light as national competitors.
2. Maintain Old Milwaukee as the market leader in the popular priced segment.
3. Maintain and grow Schlitz Malt Liquor as the clear leader in the malt liquor segment.
4. Maintain leadership as the only beer company to specifically target the needs of Blacks and Hispanics.
5. Establish a super premium beer brand.
6. Continue the company's effort in new product development.

To support these six priorities, Stroh devoted almost 75 percent of its financial budget to 6 of its 15 brands: Stroh's, Stroh Light, Old Milwaukee, Old Milwaukee Light, Schlitz Malt Liquor, and Signature.

Stroh's and Stroh Light

For the best possible financial efficiencies, Stroh's and Stroh Light came under the same brand manager, had the same budgets, and were advertised in the same advertising campaigns (a strategy that had worked well with Old Milwaukee and Old Milwaukee Light). Stroh gave these flagship brands the same consumer positioning as the heavyweights in the premium beer category, Budweiser and Miller High Life. But Stroh wanted this image to carry a few discerning characteristics. Stroh's and Stroh Light were brewed with Stroh's unique fire-brewing process, which the company believed gave these beers the finest taste. In the 1980s, Stroh's and Stroh Light targeted what the company called the "type A" beer drinker. This was someone who drank at least a case of beer per week: the heavy user. Therefore, Stroh was careful to package the Stroh's brands in colorful, bright cartons and cans to attract this young, fun-loving consumer. Beginning in 1969, Stroh's used the advertising theme "From One Beer Lover to Another, Stroh's." In 1984, Stroh's was extremely successful with its clever "Alex the Dog" television advertising campaign (see Exhibit 10 for a copy of Stroh's television photoboard). Stroh believed humor makes these brands more memorable. Budweiser and Miller High Life did not use humor to advertise in this premium segment. Budweiser long used its familiar tagline, "For all you do, this Bud's for you!" and Miller began using a new theme song for its television commercials in 1985; "Miller's made the American Way, born and brewed in the USA, just as proud as the people who are drinking it today, Miller's made the American Way!"

In May 1984, Stroh's and Stroh Light became nationally distributed in Stroh's big push to become a national brewer. 1984 consumption of Stroh's and Stroh Light was 6.1 million barrels, which captured 7.4 percent of the national premium market. The two beers became available in all 50 states, but total sales for these two brands were down over 1 percent nationally in 1984, and sales in Michigan were off 8.2 percent for the same year.

Taking Stroh's and Stroh Light national had an advantage in that it allowed the company to address the key Hispanic populations in the West like no one else had before. Stroh appointed a new national manager of Hispanic market development in 1984 and spent over $4 million in the ethnic market with heavy advertising in radio, outdoor displays, and newspapers. Other brewers also attempted to capture the Hispanic market in the West and Southwest, but Stroh was emerging with the first major effort to court the Hispanic market. Stroh's success in this area is yet to be evaluated.

Old Milwaukee and Old Milwaukee Light

Old Milwaukee (OM) and Old Milwaukee Light (OM Light) was the best-selling duet of Stroh brands at 8.6 million barrels in 1984. The goal for these two original Schlitz brands was to continue to dominate the popular priced beer brands with a national image that says OM and OM Light have everything premium but the price. Stroh spent heavily to create this image and has attracted drinkers from other competitors. In a stagnant industry, OM's brands grew 16.9 percent in 1983. OM was the fifth most popular brand in 1984, climbing from number seven the previous year. OM and OM Light's large volumes were very important for assuring the utilization of full plant capacities, but at their popular prices, OM and OM Light did not provide very large profit margins.

Stroh emphasized image and taste rather than price when advertising OM on radio and television. Stroh believed Miller was making a mistake when it

EXHIBIT 10

Stroh's

CLIENT: Stroh Brewery Co.
TITLE: Alex the dog

COMMERCIAL NUMBER: OUSB 3301
LENGTH: 30 seconds

POKER PLAYER: I'd sure like another Stroh's.
HOST: No, wait. Alex!

DOG: ARF

HOST: Two cold Stroh's.

DOG: ARF
HOST: Wait till you see this.

(SFX REFRIGERATOR DOOR OPENING)
He just opened the refrigerator.

(SFX BOTTLE OPENING)

He just opened one bottle.
(SFX BOTTLE OPENING)
He just opened the other.

(SFX STROH'S BEING POURED INTO GLASS)
Now he's pouring yours.

(SFX OTHER STROH'S BEING POURED)
Now he's pouring mine.
(SFX DOG DRINKING)

Alex, you better be drinking your water.

MUSIC

From one beer lover to another.

mentioned low prices in the advertising of its new popular priced Meisterbrau, OM's chief competition from Miller. Meisterbrau ended its television commercials in the early 1980s by claiming Meisterbrau "Tastes as good as Budweiser, at a better price!" Stroh believed advertising low prices did not reflect the proper image for quality.

OM and OM Light came in premium packages: tall bottles with colorful cartons and cases. (For pictures of OM and OM Light containers as well as of the rest of the Stroh line, see Exhibit 11.) They were carefully merchandised with premium point-of-purchase signs and premium print advertising. In television ads, Stroh differentiated OM through a "hard play/reward" theme rather than the "hard work/reward" style of Meisterbrau. The characters in those OM television commercials were younger, vibrant types who enjoyed stone crab fishing in the Gulf of Mexico or bar-hopping in New Orleans, just the type of

EXHIBIT 11   Stroh bottles and cans

Source: Stroh media pamphlet.

events that are capped off with Old Milwaukee. At the end of each commercial, the characters observed, "It doesn't get any better than this!" (See Exhibit 12.)

OM used many techniques to promote the beer. Charles Powell, brand manager for OM and OM Light, explained that "While a lot of beer is consumed by men, it's actually bought [off premise] by women. So we try to provide incentives for women to buy our beer." OM capitalized on the gatekeeper effect by stressing refunds and product discounts. OM set trends with coupons on a more extensive basis than had been seen before. OM sponsored five in-store promotions each year, including sweepstakes and give-aways. OM ran ads on all three networks in prime time slots during big league sporting events. OM also constantly tried to get retail trade attention through heavy advertising in trade publications.

Schlitz Malt Liquor

Schlitz Malt Liquor (SML) was clearly the brand leader in the malt liquor segment with a 40 percent market share in 1984 and 2.1 million barrels sold. Schlitz achieved this position with a superior product, and Stroh maintained it with ongoing taste tests to achieve the best flavor in this segment. Stroh stressed specific consumer targeting techniques for SML. Blacks consume almost 75 percent of this specialty product, so Stroh featured top Black pop groups like Kool and the Gang in television commercials. Malt liquors contain more alcohol and have a fuller, more robust flavor. For many years Schlitz used the strength of a bull crashing through a brick wall to create this imagery. All of SML's advertising copy showed celebration and times when people want more alcohol. (See Exhibit 13 for a sample Schlitz Malt Liquor television photoboard.) Because it produced the dominant product in malt liquors, Stroh used leadership pricing techniques and never resorted to discounts. However, SML sales were down .5 percent in 1984 as were sales of the entire malt liquor segment.

Signature

Signature was introduced in 1982 as the second new internally developed product in Stroh's history. Only in limited distribution in 1985, Stroh planned to expand this super premium product on a national level in the near future. The objective was to gain a significant share of the super premium segment. This segment, however, has traditionally been completely dominated by A-B's very popular Michelob brand, which sold almost 74 percent of the beer in this segment in 1984. Miller's Lowenbrau sold another 13 percent.

Signature, brewed from 100 percent European hops through the Stroh fire-brewing process, closely targeted the high-priced super premium segment with what the company believed was a fine-tasting product (200 recipes were rejected before Signature was personally chosen by Peter Stroh) that combined drinkability with a definite, distinctive flavor that was smoother and less bitter

EXHIBIT 12

BBDO

Batten, Barton, Durstine & Osborn, Inc.

Client: **STROH BREWERY**		Time: **30 SECONDS**
Product: **OLD MILWAUKEE DUAL BRAND**	Title: **"SUMMER SKIING"**	Comml. No.: **SZDB 4053**

VO: Mount Hood, Oregon and Old Milwaukee

both mean something great to these guys.

Mount Hood means the best summer skiing

in America.

And Old Milwaukee means a great beer.

Cold, crisp Old Milwaukee beer.

And smooth, golden

Old Milwaukee Light.

SONG: OLD MILWAUKEE

VO: And Old Milwaukee Light.

SONG: TASTE AS GREAT AS THEIR NAME.

GUY: Man, it doesn't get any better than this.

EXHIBIT 13

BENTON & BOWLES
909 THIRD AVENUE
NEW YORK, N Y
(212) 758-6200

CLIENT: SCHLITZ
PRODUCT: MALT LIQUOR
TITLE: "BACHELOR PARTY/FP"
COMM'L NO.: SZML 0108
LENGTH: 30 SECONDS

(MUSIC UNDER)
FOUR TOPS SING: Tonight you're still a
bachelor, tomorrow's almost here.

So while you're still a free man, let's
bring on the beer. . .

KOOL AND THE GANG: Bull!

FOUR TOPS: Bull???

KOOL AND THE GANG SING: On this
night to remember, it's so clear.

You deserve to celebrate with more taste
than beer.

The bull's got a taste so big, so bold,
so smooth.

Let's all party with the Schlitz Malt
Liquor Bull.
ALL SING: Don't say beer, say Bull.

BACHELOR: Hey Gang how about
another Bull?

(SFX: CRASH)

(SFX: CRASH)

ALL SING: No one does it like the Bull!

673

than other premiums. Signature tried to be distinctive not only in flavor but on other levels as well. Although Signature was on a parity pricing schedule with Michelob, Signature really focused on packaging, and Stroh proclaimed that Signature had a better shelf life than Michelob. Signature came in a uniquely shaped, old-fashioned-type bottle with gold foil around the top and elegant gold-trimmed labels. This package won Signature the coveted Clio award for packaging.

Signature bears the signature of former Chairman John W. Stroh, and the Stroh family history told through print ads (see Exhibit 14) conveyed to consumers why they should pay more for this product.

Michelob specifically targeted the yuppie crowd (young, urban professionals). This was quite evident in Michelob television advertising, which professed, "There's a style in your life, no one can ever deny. You're on your way to the top, and along the way you've always known just who you are. Where you're going, it's Michelob!"

Signature concentrated on the same young, financially stable age group in a somewhat different fashion with television commercials that featured independent, bearded role models who left corporate America to become entrepreneurs in such exciting fields as scuba diving and car racing. (See Exhibit 15 for a sample of Signature television advertising.) John Bissell, group vice president of Stroh marketing, described the target audience for Signature as "carefree, independent, self-confident, well-educated, and successful young men and women—the people who tend to dress differently than others, go into business for themselves, and, while viewed as responsible individuals, are definitely free-thinkers."

All the Rest

The Stroh Brewery Company had 11 other brands in 1985: Goebel, Schaefer, Schaefer Light, Schaefer L.A., Piels Beer, Piels Light, Schlitz, Schlitz Light, Erlanger, Silver Thunder, and Primo. These brands combined received only 25 percent of all the financial support of the company. Most of the brands competed on price, especially Goebel.

Stroh was repositioning its super premium beer, Erlanger (a label originated by Schlitz), for the 1980s as a specialty beer parity priced with imported beers. Erlanger management planned to make its brew available on a limited basis in upscale retail and on-premise accounts. Erlanger planned for three new labels on a rotating schedule and a new bottle in order to take advantage of high gross margins in this segment, although total industry sales in this segment declined in 1984.

Stroh took advantage of regional tastes, making Piels brands available in the East, Primo in Hawaii, and Goebel in the Midwest. As of the summer of 1985, Stroh intended to expand the popular priced Schaefer brands' distribution area, breaking them out of their original distribution area in 14 eastern states.

EXHIBIT 14

There's a lot of Stroh behind the great taste of Stroh Signature.

This exceptional premium beer is a product of over 200 years of Stroh family brewing experience.

Our family began brewing in Kirn, Germany in 1775. Three quarters of a century later, Bernhard Stroh introduced Stroh's Beer to America. Through the years, Stroh has come to represent the highest standards of the brewer's art.

We believe that Stroh Signature is as fine a beer as can be produced. It contains none but the choicest ingredients, including 100% imported European hops.

I personally hope you enjoy it.

© 1985, Stroh Brewery, Detroit, Michigan

John W. Stroh
Chairman

EXHIBIT 15

STROH SIGNATURE

"CAR BUILDER"

MAN: (VO) I gave up a great job with an auto company

to do what I always wanted--design and build race cars.

(MUSIC)
SINGERS: WHEN A MAN HAS SOMETHING EXTRA DEEP INSIDE HIS SOUL. . .

IT SHINES LIKE A DIAMOND

AND IT'S WORTH MORE THAN GOLD.

MAN: (VO) This is the way to make a living.

SINGERS: SO HERE'S TO THE MAN

WHO LOOKS DEEP INSIDE.

AND HERE'S TO THE MAN

WHO FINDS SOMETHING EXTRA.

ANNCR: (VO) Stroh Signature is something extra.

You have our name on that.

MCA ADVERTISING, LTD.

The Schlitz Problem

One of Stroh's biggest challenges after the Schlitz acquisition was to develop a new marketing program to breathe life into the ailing Schlitz brands, which sold only 1.8 million barrels in 1984. Stroh management monitored Schlitz sales, which slumped 26 percent in 1982, the first year under Stroh. Christopher Lole noted that "the first step to revitalizing the brand is to slow the erosion." Analysts say "The Beer That Made Milwaukee Famous" lost over one million faithful Schlitz drinkers after the company reformulated the Schlitz brewing process, which made the brew taste "funny." Schlitz again revised the brew's formula and claimed that it was even better than the original Schlitz product. However, despite Schlitz's extensive advertising efforts, the old crop of regular Schlitz drinkers did not return.

Stroh began the new Schlitz campaign with a makeover of the Schlitz packaging. The new Schlitz brand marketing team replaced the "government-issue" yellow packing cartons with a more colorful design and also redesigned the Schlitz logo and bottle configuration. "The major change was just brightening it up so it didn't look like it was only available for people over the age of 60," said Marketing Vice President John Bissell. "I don't think we spent more than $25,000 on the research, because we needed to move fast."

Apparently, Stroh did not pump big money into Schlitz until revitalization signs warranted more financial backing. Stroh did, however, continue to support promotional efforts in Schlitz's 28 strongest southern states, especially in Texas. Although many analysts thought Stroh was merely milking Schlitz, management insisted in 1984 that it would not drop the Schlitz name. "Any brand that can generate some reasonable sales and profits determines its own viability," said Bissell.

Special Products Division

The Stroh Brewery Company instituted a new special products division at corporate headquarters in 1985. Although Stroh had continually marketed Stroh's ice cream since Prohibition, Stroh was definitely less diversified than the other major brewers, who owned everything from a major league baseball team (Anheuser-Busch owned the St. Louis Cardinals as well as many other nonbeer ventures) to cigarette companies (Miller, for example, was a subsidiary of Philip Morris, the tobacco company that also owned 7UP). Stroh was very busy developing a nonbeer beverage in early 1985: White Mountain Cooler. It is a flavored malt beverage similar to a wine cooler, targeted especially at women and nonbeer drinkers. Stroh was also investigating an all-natural flavored water beverage and the possibility of producing baked goods or snack foods since these products all require essentially the same ingredients Stroh already used in beer and could be distributed through some of the same retail beer channels.

Position in Home Market

The lag in home market sales was a puzzle for Stroh officials. In 1984, all Stroh brands captured approximately 16 percent of the Michigan market, down 10 percent from 1983. This compares unfavorably with a 28.91 percent Michigan market share for the Miller Brewing Company and 28.9 percent for Anheuser-Busch. Meanwhile, A-B commanded a 51 percent share of the market in its native Missouri in 1984. In Wisconsin, Miller beat another local brewer, G. Heileman Brewing Company, for the top slot, gaining 28.6 percent of the market to Heileman's 27.8 percent: a total of 56.4 percent for the home team.

Stroh closed its original brewery in Detroit in June 1985, which greatly disappointed many Stroh loyalists, although Stroh had long been a conscientious corporate citizen and involved in Michigan special events. Previous to the brewery's closing, Stroh had not been a firm that sought headlines. Detroit newspaper writers attributed this to the low profile Chairman Peter Stroh traditionally took because he didn't want to pat himself on the back. But during

EXHIBIT 16

We Are Still Here

Dear Michigan Consumers and Retailers,

The Stroh Brewery Company was founded in Detroit in 1950. Since then, the names "Stroh" and "Detroit" have become linked in the minds of people throughout the United States and, in fact, throughout the world.

Our difficult decision to close the least-efficient plant in our seven-brewery system was not a severance of that link. It was a decision made to ensure our future in a highly competitive industry. That future will show that the Stroh Brewery Company's commitments to Detroit and to Michigan remain as strong, if not stronger, than before.

Possibly the most visible sign of our sustaining commitment is our River Place corporate headquarters, a major development along the Detroit waterfront that will be a long-term asset to this city and its people. When the offices, shops, restaurants, and residences open at River Place, our 750 corporate employees will be joined by thousands of Detroiters sharing in the beauty and excitement River Place offers.

Other Stroh commitments are seen in our support of civic and cultural events. If you enjoy the Detroit-Montreux Jazz Festival or the Signature concerts at Meadowbrook; if you're in the stands for the hydroplane "Thunderfest" or the Detroit Formula One Grand Prix; if you watch "Late Night America" or "Michigan Outdoors;" if you attend the Detroit Symphony, or visit the Detroit Institute of Arts; then you are touched by the Stroh commitment to our home.

These are but a few of our commitments to Detroit and to Michigan. There is one more, which is perhaps the most important of all. That is our commitment to you that the brewing of fine beers will continue to be our top priority. Our Michigan distributors will continue to provide this state with the finest, and we intend to share it with the people of Michigan regardless of where you may live.

Sincerely,

Peter W. Stroh
Chairman
The Stroh Brewery Company

the summer the local brewery closed, Stroh published full-page ads in the Detroit area enumerating Stroh's community activities, apparently responding to Michigan consumers' anger. (See Exhibit 16 for a reprint of those advertisements.)

As the Stroh Brewery Company pondered the current state of the beer industry, both at home and nationally, management knew that it could institute long-range and risky plans without worrying about impressing any shareholders since the company was privately owned. The corporate management style was open and aggressive. But as the company grows, in Peter Stroh's words, "The thing to keep our eyes on is not so much our size, but the size of the guys we're up against."

It was against this background that the management at the Stroh Brewery Company developed its strategy to slow the erosion of sales in the home market. At the same time, meaningful penetration of the Stroh and Schaefer brands in the national market was certainly one of Stroh's top objectives, and further refinement of its implementation techniques was appropriate. Stroh's market planners knew where they wanted their expansion strategy to take them: closer to the top of the list of national competitors. However, while analyzing the effectiveness of the national expansion efforts thus far (see Exhibit 17), Stroh did not have the financial strength to take on all potential successful projects at once. Stroh had to establish which alternatives claimed the highest priorities, while balancing them against a declining beer market and powerful competition.

EXHIBIT 17
THE STROH BREWING COMPANY
Selected Financial Data*
Year Ended March 31
(amounts in $000s)

	1983	1982	1981
Barrels of beer sold	22,900	9,100	8,900
Brewery capacity	29,550	12,250	11,000
Sales	$1,535,126	$593,444	$561,578
Sales net of excise taxes	1,317,986	499,124	467,292
Earnings (loss) from operations	1,228	(6,172)	2,973
Discontinued operations	—	—	4,863
Change in accounting principles	—	11,774	—
Net earnings	1,228	5,602	7,836
Pro forma net earnings (loss)	1,288	(6,172)	10,716
Depreciation	39,868	19,724	15,918
Working capital	45,666	14,369	22,891
Year-end working capital	(46,502)	(19,370)	25,946
Property, plant, equipment	456,876	168,210	139,882
Total assets	721,142	263,433	231,588
Long-term debt†	321,328	72,996	69,648

* Includes operations for Schlitz from 1982 and Schaefer from 1980.
† Includes redeemable preferred shares of Schaefer.
Source: The Stroh Brewery Company 1983 Form 10-K.

Case 39

Quaker State*

OIL CITY, PA   In the ultracompetitive motor-oil market, cutthroat discounting has become a way of life. So when Quaker State decided a year ago to stop slashing prices and emphasize quality, it was a big gamble.

The early results are in, and they aren't pretty. The company's nine-month revenue fell 9 percent, and fourth-quarter earnings are expected to show a big decline from a year earlier. The stock isn't far from its 52-week low. Wall Street is disenchanted.

The Wall Street Journal, Heard on the Street column, January 8, 1990

It has been three years since the devastating loss of 1987, and the Quaker State marketing strategy has been reworked again and again. With greater competition and new entrants, it appears Quaker State's future for the 1990s is in jeopardy. The relatively small independent oil company in Oil City has been repeatedly rumored as a takeover candidate. Management at Quaker State realize they need to regain past levels of profitability and market share to maintain their independence. There is no more room to gamble with the company's future and lose. The marketing strategy for the next year, 1991, and subsequent years, needs to identify and meet consumer needs.

The Passenger-Car Motor-Oil Market

The passenger-car motor-oil (PCMO) market can be characterized as a very competitive mature market with very little growth. Subsequently, the market is very price sensitive, and new product developments are closely watched by all competitors. The market is made up of the motor-oil specialist companies who produce and market strictly motor oil and the gasoline companies who primarily market gasoline. Traditionally, the motor-oil specialists have been the market share leaders based on their distribution networks and their product innovation.

* This case was written by Craig F. Ehrnst under the supervision of Thomas C. Kinnear. The authors wish to thank the people at Quaker State without whose assistance this case would not have been possible. Copyright © 1990 by Thomas C. Kinnear.

However, during recent years the gasoline companies have increased their efforts to capture market share through mass merchandisers and other distribution channels formerly dominated by the motor-oil specialists.

Influenced by the automotive manufacturers, motor-oil quality has been increased to meet the performance needs of engines built in recent years. The higher quality standards have required increased research among motor-oil industry producers. These standards have been met with new additive packages to further prevent rust, corrosion, and sludge buildup. Most motor oil producers reformulated their products to meet the new industry standards during the mid-1980s. However, due to the nature of the competitive market, the full costs associated with the new additive packages have not been passed on to consumers. The reformulated products offered to consumers provide a higher-quality product to consumers and a lower margin for producers.

After reformulating their products, motor-oil producers took very aggressive positions to reintroduce their products. Advertising expenditures have essentially doubled, from estimates of $50 million in 1984 to well over $100 million in 1988 (see Exhibit 1). Promotional expenditures have also increased at a similar rate. The heavy advertising and promotional expenditures have been

EXHIBIT 1 Advertising and promotion expenditures

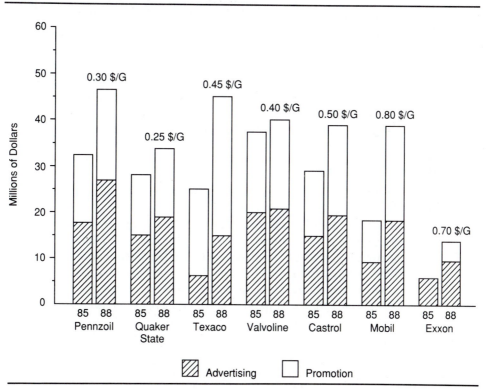

led by the motor-oil specialists. Their dependence on brand awareness is essential to pull their products through the distribution chain of mass merchandisers and auto parts stores.

Motor Oil Classifications

The consumer is quality conscious but is probably unaware of measures to distinguish real quality from perceived quality motor oil. Fortunately, classification systems have been developed to measure motor-oil viscosity and engine service requirements (see Appendix A). First, the motor-oil viscosity standards, developed by the Society of Automotive Engineers (SAE), provide a guide for users to select motor oil according to the climate conditions of their automobiles. For example, a multigrade motor oil 5W–30 would perform better in subzero temperatures than a multigrade motor oil grade of 10W–30. Next, the engine service classification system, developed by motor-oil industry specialists, defines characteristics of a motor oil to help the consumer with the selection of appropriate products. Motor oil manufacturers label their product with a letter classification system according to recommended engine service requirements. For example, the motor oil with the letter designation "SG" is the recommended motor oil with the highest standards acceptable for 1989 gasoline engine warranty maintenance service. There are several other lower grades of motor oil, but the "SG" grade would be preferred because of its superior quality and because it can be substituted for other grades of motor oil.[1]

Both systems can provide the consumer with useful information, but typical consumers are probably not aware of the systems and they are most likely confused by the mix of numbers and letters used in the classification systems. Consumers will often rely on friends, their mechanics, or a salesperson when deciding which brand of motor oil to purchase. Appendix A provides a detailed overview of the two classification systems.

The Consumer Markets

The PCMO market is segmented by consumer usage into two principal areas—the do-it-yourselfer (DIYer) or the installed segments. Exhibit 2 illustrates the breakdown between the two primary market segments and their respective subsegments. The DIYers prefer to purchase their motor oil and install it themselves (or with the assistance of friends). There has been a decline in the DIYer market, from 70 percent in 1985 to 66 percent in 1988. In contrast, the installed segment has shown continued signs of growth, as service and convenience have influenced the buying perspectives of consumers.

---

[1] Quaker State, "Oil and Lubricants Vital to Your Vehicle's Survival," May 1, 1989, pp. 6–9.

EXHIBIT 2 Distribution channel structure

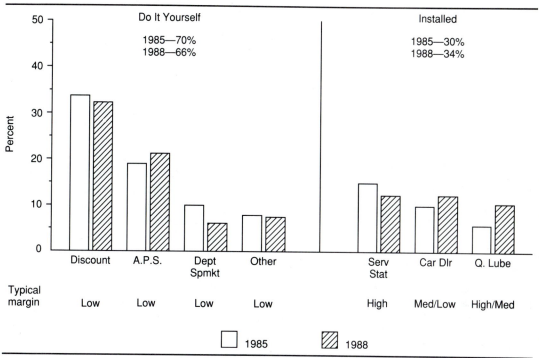

| Typical margin | Low | Low | Low | Low | High | Med/Low | High/Med |

The Do-It-Yourself Market

The DIYer has been the single largest market for two primary reasons: First, the DIYer wants to ensure that the oil change is done correctly. An individual's investment in an automobile is typically a substantial part of his or her income. Therefore, it is worthwhile to protect their investments with the necessary motor oil changes. In addition, the DIYers are generally very proud of their cars and they don't mind changing their motor oil, but they don't particularly like it either. Rather, they change their own oil so they can be sure that it's done right. Second, the DIYers prefer changing their motor oil because they are price sensitive. Promotional discounts have been a common tradition in recent years, and thus the DIYers have become accustomed to discounted product prices.

Past industry surveys indicate that half of the DIYers are brand loyal for a variety of reasons. Perceived product quality and reliability are two reasons for maintaining this loyalty, but there is also a mixing problem that forces brand loyalty. The brand-loyal DIYer will purchase motor oil by the case, particularly if the brand is on sale. As the case empties, all of the single quart bottles may not be used up prior to the next oil change. The brand-loyal DIYer will consider the potential negative impacts of mixing two different brands of motor oil and thus, remain brand loyal to the last remaining quart of motor oil, rather than discarding it.

Approximately half of the DIYers are switchers who either switch and stick or switch less on the basis of quality and more based on price. The switch and stick DIYers switch brands of motor oil because of concerns with product quality or because they purchased a new car. Most automobile manufacturers have extended the life of engine warranties and are now more inclined to recommend specific brands of motor oil. With the combination of a new car purchase and the extended engine service warranties, it has become increasingly more important to maintain a single brand of motor oil throughout the ownership of the auto. The switch and stick DIYers are willing to try other motor oils perceived to better preserve and protect their automotive investment. The price-driven switchers see no problem in switching brands because they perceive no difference in the various brands of motor oil. The lowest price motor oil will virtually guarantee their next purchase decision.

DIYers can be characterized as either brand loyal or switchers. They install their own motor oil not because they enjoy the task, but rather because they want to make sure that it is done right. DIYers are generally very price sensitive and more likely to become switchers when their preferred brand is not on sale. This market segment continues to be the larger of the two consumer markets, but the DIYer market has been declining and future growth is considered unlikely.

The "Installed" Market

The installed market consists of those consumers who have their cars' motor oil changed at service stations, car dealerships, or at quick-lube centers. Exhibit 2 shows the 4 percent growth in recent years of the installed market, as well as the rapid growth of the quick-lube centers, primarily at the expense of service stations. Price has not been as great a factor as convenience to these buyers. Based on consumer research, the installed market prefers a high-quality brand of motor oil that is expeditiously installed. Convenience to the consumer has become increasingly more important, as demographic trends indicate that more and more dual-income families have less free time available to do such things as changing their own motor oil.

The quick-lube centers have been one of the newest developments in the motor-oil industry. The rapid growth of quick-lube centers, which specialize in fast motor-oil changes (10 minutes or less), could be attributed to their convenience and expertise based on volume. The traditional quick-lube service center performs only motor oil changes in a three- to four-bay building. These buildings are frequently located near high-traffic centers, and some are converted service stations. The quick-lube service's bay doors are located in the front and back of the building in order for customers to drive in and out easily. The quick-lube centers also have a pit below the automobile service bay area for technicians to perform service without raising the car on a service platform, typical of most service stations. The pit reduces service time and provides added customer convenience since customers do not have to leave their cars.

Roughly half of the quick-lube centers are independently owned and they have been one of the fastest-growing businesses of the automotive service sector. Motor-oil specialist companies have been very aggressive in acquiring and building quick-lube centers. However, several major gasoline companies have been experimenting with building their own quick-lube centers, as well as modifying existing service stations.

Service stations have historically had the largest market share of the installed market, but they have lost market share to the quick-lube centers. Most service stations have not been regarded as very convenient to customers, nor have they been particularly price competitive. It is difficult for service stations to justify having a highly paid mechanic perform motor oil changes. Other service and preventive maintenance performed at service stations are preferred because of their higher profit margins. In addition, traditional service stations have been designed without pits because service platforms used to raise and lower cars are more desirable for other forms of maintenance. The service platforms are particularly advantageous because mechanics can obtain easier access to perform tire, brake, transmission, and other undercarriage repairs. The choice of a pit or a service platform is mutually exclusive. The pit requires a basement below the garage floor, while the service platform base is typically embedded in the garage floor.

Some industry analysts feel that the car dealerships offer another area of potential market growth. Extended engine service warranties are valid only with performed preventive maintenance, including frequent motor oil changes. The car dealerships have access to a large customer base, and they perform the majority of the manufacturers' service guarantees.

Growth in the installed market has also been fueled by environmental concerns about used motor oil and proposed legislation. Legislators have become increasingly concerned with the means of disposal of used motor oil, particularly by the typical DIYer. Currently, there is little incentive for a DIYer to return used motor oil to a community collection point, nor is there an incentive to create a collection point. While it is advantageous to recycle used motor oil, it is difficult to distinguish used motor oils from other more hazardous oils. There are significant health risks associated with unknowingly handling contaminated motor oil that may be a more harmful hazardous waste. Greater environmental awareness could lead to direct legislation affecting the DIYer and the future handling of used motor oil.

The installed market consumer prefers a high-quality motor oil conveniently installed. The recent growth in market share of quick-lube centers, and the frequency of discussed environmental legislation, make the installed market an attractive market for future growth.

Distribution

Motor-oil products are distributed from the blending plants to both mass merchandisers and motor-oil distributors. The mass merchandisers include discount and department stores such as K mart, Montgomery Wards, Wal-Mart, Zayres, and others. The distributors handle distribution to smaller accounts such as individual quick-lube centers, service stations, grocery stores, drug stores, and hardware stores. Depending on the purchase volume, the accounts of auto parts stores could be handled as either mass merchandisers or distributors.

Generally, mass merchandisers purchase directly from the manufacturer and sell the motor oil by offering discounted prices to consumers. It is not uncommon for mass merchandisers to have their own private-label brands priced slightly less than the name-brand motor oils. The private-label brand is usually produced and packaged by a major oil company. The mass merchandiser's consumers are DIYers who are very price sensitive. Therefore, the mass merchandisers negotiate larger discounted volume purchases to resell name-brand motor oils at discounted prices across the country.

The distributors resell either a single company's products (as exclusive distributors) or they handle several different brands of motor-oil products for resale. This depends on the distributors' relationship with their suppliers. Some distributors are independently owned, while others are managed by motor oil companies. The relationship with the motor oil supplier may provide preference on whether the distributor handles more than one brand of motor oil. The distributors' consumer markets include both the DIYer and installed consumer. Pricing is extremely important to the independent distributors, as they are often in direct competition with the mass merchandisers for business.

Pricing

As a result of the cutthroat competition in the motor-oil industry, pricing has left most firms remaining in the industry with very small margins. The product pricing decisions are driven by competition for additional motor-oil market share. Although raw material cost may vary significantly from month to month, these price fluctuations are not passed on to consumers. There are a variety of reasons for current industry pricing practices, including factors affecting distribution channels, market share, and product image.

Mass merchandisers and large discounters have been particularly skillful in obtaining large volume discounts from most motor-oil producers. However, discounted volume sales to mass merchandisers can alienate the independent distributors. The independent distributors supply motor oil to both the installed and the DIYer consumer markets, while the mass merchandisers supply motor oil primarily to the DIYers. The pricing dilemma for motor-oil producers is extremely difficult. Independent distributors are very astute about product prices, and they sell motor oil to hundreds of service operations daily. Discounted motor oil offered at the mass merchandisers directly undercuts the distributors' price and is considered a threat to future business. As a result, motor-oil producers often deal with negotiated product pricing issues on a daily basis.

Market share is also an important factor in product pricing. The firms with large market shares—typically the motor oil specialists—have followed a more consistent pricing strategy ranging well within 50 cents per gallon of each other (see Exhibits 3 and 4). The gasoline companies, generally with lower market shares, have a larger variance in price range, as noted in Exhibit 4. Gasoline companies have virtually perfected instant price changes at the fuel pump, and they have not been afraid to frequently change the prices of their motor oil. Some firms with low market share have discounted their product price to tempt DIYers to switch brands. Havoline, owned by Texaco, has been particularly successful in gaining market share with this strategy, but it has been very costly. Depending on the firm's market share, pricing can influence the frequency of price changes and the price level.

Product image and positioning also significantly influence motor-oil pricing decisions. The motor-oil specialists have been the most successful in developing premium-brand images. The premium image commands a higher price and typically a higher demand. However, some gasoline companies have

EXHIBIT 3 PCMO market share

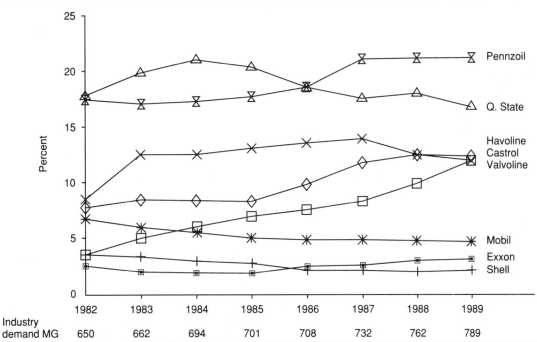

EXHIBIT 4 Retail pricing trends—Do it yourself

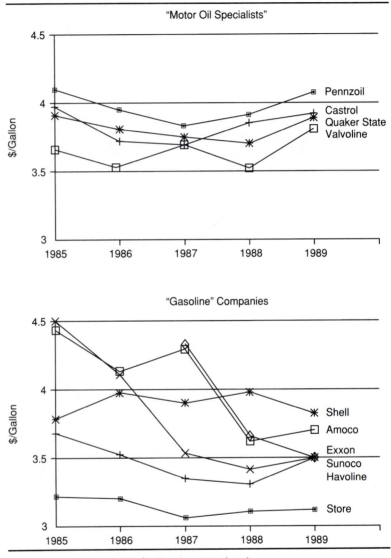

+ Market leader averaging 0.80 $/gallon above store brand.

followed premium price strategies even though their product was not perceived to be a premium product.

Product pricing has been further complicated by product discounts offered to consumers and distributors. In the mid-1980s the motor-oil industry quickly caught onto the concept of offering product coupon discounts to consumers. Rebates were readily available to most consumers by virtually all motor-oil producers in an effort to protect or capture market share. This rebating reduced margins and increased the intensity of competition among the key players. Overall, product pricing decisions must carefully weigh the trade-offs within distribution channels and brand-quality perceptions.

The PCMO Competitors

The competitors in the PCMO industry have each carefully positioned their products to meet specific market niches or to address future growth potential. Pennzoil and Quaker State have been successful in maintaining market leadership, but others such as Castrol and Havoline have successfully increased their respective market shares. A brief summary of all the key PCMO players follows.

Pennzoil

Pennzoil displaced Quaker State in 1986 as the market-share leader by capturing 21 percent of the PCMO market (see Exhibit 3). Their marketing strategy has been to remain as market leader by pushing their product hard into the quick-lube services. Pennzoil has approached the quick-lube market by franchising their name and flooding the quick-lube markets with their products. In 1988, Pennzoil claimed to have supplied about two-thirds of the motor oil sold in the booming U.S. quick-lube business. Pennzoil also has a long-term commitment with Jiffy Lube, the largest U.S. quick-lube franchise. The Pennzoil-Jiffy Lube relationship developed partly out of necessity, since Pennzoil was one of their largest creditors and Jiffy Lube had overbuilt their operations too quickly. Pennzoil stepped in with much needed cash, and over the following years Pennzoil has gained a greater controlling interest in Jiffy Lube.

Pennzoil has emphasized quality and brand loyalty to maintain their premium price level. As a result, Pennzoil users are brand loyal and less likely to become switchers. The 1988 annual report summarized part of their market approach:

> While motor oil sales were healthy in 1988, they failed to match the record levels of 1987. One major reason was deep discounting on the part of competitors, a tactic that tends to make motor oil a commodity. Pennzoil avoided this trap, unlike some of its competitors, and managed to hold market share, thanks to strong brand loyalty on the part of Pennzoil consumers. It finished the year comfortably ahead of its nearest competitor by a margin of several points.[2]

The motor oil and automotive products segment of Pennzoil had revenues of $1,312.2 million and an operating income of $110.8 million (excluding a $122 million write-down of assets) in 1988. Pennzoil earned a profit of $115.9 million and $168.7 million in 1987 and 1986.

---

[2] Pennzoil, 1988 Annual Report, p. 14.

Pennzoil's advertising and promotion has been directed at building their installed market position, while maintaining their DIYer position. Their advertising theme has stressed the multidimensional aspect of their motor oil to handle thermal breakdown, lubrication, and reduced friction; that is, "world-class protection." Given Pennzoil's strong cash position and their market leadership, Pennzoil will adamantly defend their market share against competitor's threats.

Castrol

Castrol has been one of the most successful marketers of PCMO in recent years. This is evidenced by their rise in market share from 5 percent in 1983 to almost 10 percent in 1988. Castrol has focused their product on the small car users, emphasizing their product as a high-performance motor oil developed for small-car engine needs. Their users are considered younger and more upscale and tend to drive cars with four-cylinder engines. Castrol users are in a class by themselves, with high brand loyalty and a specific market.

Castrol developed their market by focusing on the small-car DIYer and aggressively marketing the car dealers. Castrol has not directed any investment at the quick-lube business. Castrol has established their market niche as "an oil for small engine protection" tied to the advertising theme "engineered for smaller cars."

Havoline

Havoline has progressively increased its market share on a consistent basis. First, Havoline successfully dropped its name association with Texaco in the mid-1980s. Gasoline company motor oils in general are perceived negatively compared to their rivals, the motor-oil specialist. Second, Havoline has maintained a clear low-price strategy to obtain market share. While this strategy has been costly—a $25 million estimated loss in 1988 alone—market share has increased almost 2 percent for each of the last three years.

The Havoline users tend to be switchers who perceive their motor oil as a second choice, not as good as Pennzoil or Castrol, but effective. Havoline seems to be used because of price and product availability. Their advertising message has emphasized the formulation's ability to reduce sludge with the theme "more protection than you'll ever need."

Valvoline

Valvoline has had significant trouble in recent years, resulting in estimated break-even performance. Valvoline, owned by Ashland Oil, has been the price leader, but they have lost market share primarily due to the aggression of Texaco. Valvoline consumers are not as brand loyal as Pennzoil or Castrol consumers. When prices began to decline in the mid-1980s, Valvoline consumers departed.

Valvoline obtained brand awareness in the 1970s with their advertising theme using "Val the chimp" to make Valvoline a household name.[3] Television commercials and print advertising showing Val performing an oil change with Valvoline made it look easy. Clearly targeted at the DIYer, it was a creative advertisement that caught the public's attention. Today, Valvoline has switched its emphasis to the motor oil's product quality and brand image. The current advertising utilizes aggressive comparison advertising aimed specifically at the market leaders, such as Quaker State. Valvoline advertises that their motor oil is the highest-quality oil recommended by car manufacturers, with the theme "People who know, use Valvoline."

Others

The gasoline companies, Mobil, Exxon, Shell, and others, round out the rest of the PCMO business with break-even profits at best. Only Mobil has successfully utilized the gasoline company name with its name brand motor oil, particularly Mobil 1. Exxon has made some efforts recently to revitalize their brand, SUPERFLO, with heavy advertising and the building of experimental quick-lubes. Shell has introduced a reformulated motor oil specifically aimed at the rapidly expanding small truck market. The product, called Truckguard, offers the protection needed for small trucks, but there are no preliminary results to indicate success or failure of this product.

The PCMO industry remains a very competitive industry, and throughout the next few years margins are expected to remain low. The threat of new entrants is highly unlikely; however, there are clear opportunities for consolidations or external acquisitions in order to capture market share. Niche market segments have been successfully developed at the DIYer level to foster and maintain brand loyalty.

Finally, another factor to consider is the potential for a revolutionary development in the PCMO market. Environmental concerns about the illegal disposal of used motor oil have been increasingly brought to the attention of legislators. Legislation may be created to address this concern, possibly leading to the development of an engine sealed for life, with no oil added after the purchase of the car. Another possibility to consider is the usage of alternative fuels, such as methanol, requiring different lubrication needs. Any significant investment in this competitive industry should consider external factors which may affect the product life cycle of PCMO.

Quaker State—Background

Established in 1931, Quaker State has always been known as a leader in product innovation and in establishing motor oil standards. The founders of Quaker

---

[3] "Val the Chimp Made Valvoline a Household Name," *The Oil Daily,* April 20, 1988, p. B–9.

State pioneered one of the first brands of motor oil which was the oil of choice in the early days of the automobile. However, the PCMO environment has changed, and today Quaker State has lost both market share and past profit performance. In 1987, the company reported its first loss ever, $1.82 a share, and surrendered its number one market position to Pennzoil (See Exhibit 5).

EXHIBIT 5 Quaker State stock price

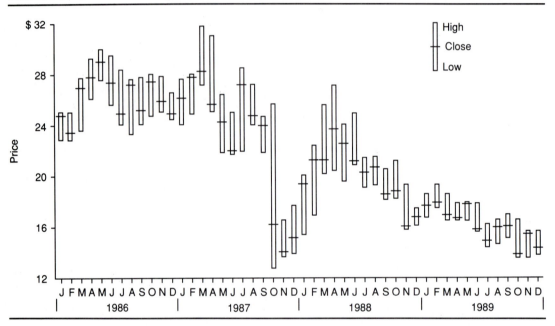

Overall, operating margins collapsed from 12.9 percent to 6.0 percent, reflecting deep product discounting. Quaker State's net income has fallen from profits of $50.3 million in 1986 to $14.9 million in 1988. The 1989 profits have fallen even further to $11.8 million on declining sales of $734.7 million. Within a 15-month period, the company switched chief executives three times.[4] These results have been disturbing for Quaker State and the marketing issues have not been resolved to restore past market share and operating profit performance.

Similar to other oil companies, Quaker State used the benefits of their abundant cash flow over the years to diversify their business away from the volatile motor oil business. Through various acquisitions, the firm is divided into five separate business units:

---

[4] Kerry Hannon, "Run over by the Competition," *Forbes*, September 5, 1988, p. 80.

	Percent		
1989 Data	*Sales*	*Profit*	*Assets*
1. Motor oil/auto	59%	41%	31%
2. Coal operations	13	22*	11
3. Insurance group	11	17	32
4. Truck-lite	7	20	6
5. Minit-lube, Inc.	10	0	20

* Includes +29 percent unusual item less −7 percent from operations.

The petroleum operations still provide the majority of sales, profits, and proportionate assets. In order for Quaker State to have a successful recovery, the core motor oil business needs to be turned around.

Quaker State's roots go back to the oil fields of Pennsylvania, first discovered at the turn of the century. The superior Pennsylvania, crude oil enabled Quaker State to offer a premium-quality product, with refineries located near the producing fields in Pennsylvania. Today, the Pennsylvania fields are not nearly as productive as in prior years, and now Quaker State must obtain most of their raw materials from other sources.

Manufacturing

Motor oil is produced from a refined barrel of crude oil into a specialty product called a lube basestock. Typically refinery production of lube basestock is less than 30 percent of all refinery output. The remaining 70 percent of the output is made up of gasoline, kerosene, and fuel oil, which can be sold to other consumer markets. The lube basestock is then blended with Quaker State's unique additive package and filled in the appropriate containers for consumer usage.

Quaker State's manufacturing facilities were designed to maximize motor-oil production, but overall this method of production is considered extremely inefficient. Essentially 70 percent of their output is resold as undesirable products with a break-even margin, at best. The major gasoline companies, on the other hand, maximize output streams by separating these streams and further refining the outputs into more valuable products.

Quaker State's cost structure on motor oil production has increased. The production inefficiencies have become more apparent as the availability of Pennsylvania-based crude oil has decreased and their outside purchases have increased. Recently it has been more efficient for Quaker State to purchase their lube basestock needs from the major gasoline companies and blend the motor oil at Quaker State packaging facilities. As a result, the future need of Quaker State's three refineries is extremely questionable. The 1987 loss included a $30 million write-down of assets related to the closure of the Ohio Valley Refinery.

Their other refineries and some related plants have also been rumored to be on the auction block. Currently, it appears Quaker State's future will primarily be directed at blending and packaging their motor oil and marketing the product to consumers. Without raw material advantages, it is expected that this will increase their cost basis. However, it is probably the most attractive opportunity given the alternative—inefficiently producing motor oil with higher raw material costs and transportation costs.

Quaker State Marketing Strategies

In 1987, Quaker State realized the early results of a disastrous marketing strategy when it lost its number one market share to Pennzoil. With the assistance of the outside consulting firm, McKinsey & Co., management tried to force their distribution subsidiaries to carry Quaker State products exclusively, and to increase sales to mass merchandisers.[5] The company's profits plunged as its distributors lost business to competitors with a larger variety of brands. In addition, distributors became increasingly upset with the company as the firm offered deep discounts to the mass merchandisers. The relationship between the motor oil distributors and Quaker State was significantly weakened in 1986.

Distribution

Jack W. Corn, a former distributor of the company's products, was brought in to turn the company around, as the new president of Quaker State. He increased the company's investment in the firm's Minit-Lube shops, and he has attempted to patch up relations with the distributors. As noted in the 1988 annual report, Jack Corn stated:

> The first move we made was to change our program direction so that selling Quaker State would be attractive and profitable to independent distributors. In my opinion, that is the part of our business that has built consumer brand image and demand over the years. The independent distributors create the demand for the big mass merchandisers. And future demand depends on having a strong independent marketing force in as many markets as we can possibly have.[6]

In 1986, the company had 223 independent distributors handling their product. By 1988, the number of distributors dropped to 202. The firm appealed to their distributors by reversing past discount pricing strategies offered to the mass merchandisers. However, it is difficult to assess the extent of the damage done to the company's distribution network.

---

[5] Michael Schroeder, "Quaker State Switches into a Quick-Change Artist," *Business Week,* October 16, 1989, p. 126.

[6] Jack W. Corn, Quaker State, 1988 Annual Report, p. 15.

Pricing

In an effort to smooth the problems with the independent distributors, pricing policy became a critical issue. While pricing problems have always been a thorn in Quaker State's side, they became a larger problem. After discounting the company's products in 1986–87 and having several different price schedules for different consumers, Quaker State moved toward a uniform pricing policy. This meant that all customers, mass merchandisers and distributors, would pay comparable prices for the Quaker State products. However, in order to appease each of the distribution channels, Quaker State has priced their product in the low end of the motor oil price range (see Exhibit 4).

Products

The Quaker State product mix is illustrated in Appendix D. The product strategy for Quaker State has been to be a leader in product quality across all of their products. In 1988, the firm completed upgrading all of their motor oils to the highest standards.[7] In 1989, Quaker State's 5W–30 and 10W–30 grades completed tests confirming that they qualify as "Energy Conserving II." This certified that these grades allowed motorists to achieve at least 2.7 percent greater mileage than a standard motor oil.[8]

Quaker State continues to improve product quality on a regular basis, and they anticipate matching any new product innovations that appear in the motor-oil market.

Packaging

Quaker State was one of the first major motor oils to change their product package from the can to the plastic bottle. In 1985, Quaker State also came up with an astute marketing innovation—a new easy-pour container. But its plastic can was round and hard to stack on store shelves. Pennzoil, 18 months later, produced a square container that fit more product on a tight shelf space. Quaker State was pushed aside, as it was less convenient to stack and reshelf.[9]

Minit-Lube Operations

Quaker State chose to expand its efforts in the quick-lube market with the additional acquisitions of quick-lube service centers. As of year-end 1989, the firm had over 450 Minit-Lube outlets either franchised or company owned. Mr. Corn has indicated that they would like to maintain a 60/40 percent owner/franchisee relationship.

---

[7] Quaker State, 1988 Annual Report, p. 6.
[8] Quaker State, 1989 Annual Report, p. 6.
[9] Hannon, "Run over by the Competition," p. 80.

The Minit-Lube outlets have focused their efforts on increasing the quality of service provided to customers. Quaker State is planning on a premium service worth a premium price. Quaker State has increased the prices at Minit-Lube operations to meet the high costs of the physical facilities.

Promotion

The promotion strategy for Quaker State has a focus for both the DIYer market and the installed market. First, the company continues to sponsor a racing program to demonstrate the high-quality attributes of the motor oil at major race events. Quaker State feels that the DIY user of motor oil is a "car-caring person who is intensely interested in auto racing."[10] The racing program has sponsored a number of racing events in NASCAR competition and international road races. The racing program emphasizes to DIYers the quality of Quaker State motor oil which can work for professionals, and therefore, "it can work for you, too."

Second, the company moved to enhance its position in the installed market by offering a lubrication limited warranty, available for new cars and good for 250,000 miles or 10 years (whichever comes first to the original owner)—see Appendix B. The warranty provides for repair or replacement of lubricated engine parts, provided certain rules are followed. The primary rule requires the owners to have their motor oil changed over 4,000 miles or four months by a professional installer who uses Quaker State.

Advertising

The emphasis on quality has been reduced in the 1990 print and commercial advertisements to stress Quaker State is "One Tough Motor Oil." This is supported with several different television advertisements emphasizing the 250,000-mile guarantee, NASCAR racing, and company testing of the product—sample advertisements are in Appendix B.

Appendix A SAE Classifications

Over the years, the Society of Automotive Engineers (SAE) developed a classification system (Crankcase Oil Viscosity Classification—SAE J300–JUN 86) based on viscosity measurements. Thick, slow-flowing oils are assigned high numbers; thinner oils that flow more freely receive low numbers. Modified several times, the system establishes distinct motor oil viscosity grades: SAE 0W, SAE 5W, SAE 10W, SAE 15W, SAE 20W, SAE 25W, SAE 20, SAE 30, SAE 40, and SAE 50.

---

[10] Quaker State, 1988 Annual Report, p. 12.

Viscosity: A measure of how much a fluid resists flowing. Motor oil is more viscous than water.

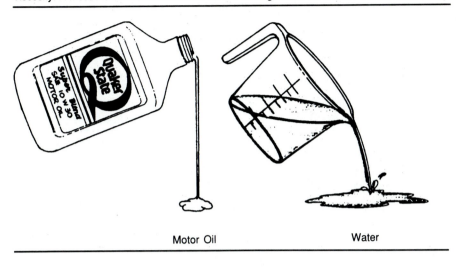

Motor Oil　　　　　　　　Water

SAE: Society of Automotive Engineers

The "W" in the SAE grades stands for winter. Viscosity grades with the W classification are based on their maximum viscosity and borderline pumping temperatures at specific low temperatures. The W grades also are based on the minimum viscosity at $+100°C$. These oils are tested to ensure that they have proper flow characteristics and are suitable for use in cold seasons and climates. Oils without the W classification, on the other hand, are tested to ensure the proper viscosity at $+100°C$ only. Although SAE 20 and SAE 20W oils are separate classifications, each will generally meet the viscosity requirements of the other. Those that do meet the requirements are classified SAE 20W–20. This simple form of multigrading is one of the few possible without adding a viscosity index improver.

The viscosity index is an arbitrary scale in which oil from Pennsylvania crude is typically 100 and oils from naphthenic crudes are placed in the 0 to 70 range. These numbers are not related to the actual viscosity of the oil or its SAE number. Viscosity index numbers measure the change in viscosity as the operating temperatures change; the higher the number, the smaller the change. Motor oils used in a wide range of operating temperatures may have viscous polymers or polymeric compounds added to decrease this rate. Called "viscosity index improvers" because they raise the index number, these additives make possible the multigrade or "all-season" oils that have been marketed by U.S. oil companies for more than four decades.

Because the multigrades, such as SAE 5W–30, 10W–30, and 10W–40, are light enough to crank easily at low temperatures and heavy enough to perform well at high temperatures, they are among the most widely used motor oils.

Table 1 shows single and multigrade oils and the lowest temperatures at which they can be expected to perform satisfactorily.

TABLE 1 SAE grades of motor oil*

Lowest temperature	Singlegrade oils	Multigrade oils
32°F/0°C	20, 20W, 30	10W-30, 10W-40, 10W-50, 15W-40, 20W-40, 30W-50
0°F/−18°C	10W	10W-30, 10W-40
Below 0°F/−18°C	5W	5W-20, 5W-30, 5W-40

* "Motor Oil Guide," American Petroleum Institute, Washington D.C., 1982.

These grades refer to viscosity only and provide no information about the type or quality of an oil or its intended purpose. For this reason, another system was needed to take other factors into account. An early classification system developed by the American Petroleum Institute (API) classified engine oils as regular, premium, and heavy duty. A later API effort, in conjunction with the Society of Automotive Engineers (SAE) and the American Society for Testing and Materials (ASTM), described and classified the various service/engine-operating conditions as a basis for selecting the proper crankcase oil.

Engine Service Classifications

The changing requirements of the automobile industry, along with the need for more effective communication among engine manufacturers, the oil industry, and the consumer, led to a new API Engine Service Classification System. This system, developed by API, ASTM, and SAE, allows engine oils to be defined on the basis of performance characteristics and their intended types of service (see Table 2). Together, the API and SAE systems define the characteristics of a

TABLE 2 Service classification

Letter Designation	API Engine Service Description
SG	1989 gasoline engine warranty maintenance service. For passenger cars, vans, and light trucks beginning with the 1989 model year operating under manufacturer's recommended maintenance procedures. These oils provide improved control of engine deposits, oil oxidation, and engine wear relative to oils developed for previous categories. These oils also provide protection against rust and corrosion; they can be used where SF, SE, SF/CC, or SE/CC are recommended.
SF	1980 gasoline engine warranty maintenance service. For passenger cars and some trucks, beginning with 1980 models operating under engine manufacturers' warranties. These oils provide increased oxidation stability and better antiwear performance than the oils that meet the minimum requirements for the SE classification.

TABLE 2 (concluded)

Letter Designation	API Engine Service Description
SE	1972 gasoline engine warranty maintenance service. For passenger cars and some trucks, beginning with 1972 (and some 1971 models) operating under engine manufacturers' warranties. These oils provide better protection than SC- and SD-classified oils.
SD	1968 gasoline engine warranty maintenance service. For passenger cars and some truck models operating under engine manufacturers' warranties in effect for model years 1968 through 1970, plus some 1971 or later models. These oils provide better protection than SC-classified oils.
SC	1964 gasoline engine warranty service. For passenger cars and some truck models operating under engine manufacturers' warranties in effect for model years 1964 through 1967.
SB	Minimum duty gasoline engine service. For engines operating under conditions mild enough to require only minimum protection through compounding.
SA	Formerly for utility gasoline and diesel engine service. For engines operated under conditions so mild that they do not need the protection of compounded oils; there are no performance requirements.
CE	Service typical of turbocharged or supercharged heavy-duty diesel engines manufactured since 1983 and operated under both low-speed, high-load and high-speed, high-load conditions. Oils designed for this service may also be used when previous API engine service categories for diesel engines are recommended.
CD-II	Service typical of two-stroke cycle diesel engines requiring highly effective control over wear and deposits. Oils designed for this service also meet all performance requirements of API Service Category CD.
CD-Diesel	Severe duty diesel engine service. For certain naturally aspirated, turbocharged, or supercharged diesel engines in which effective control of wear and deposits is essential or when fuels ranging widely in quality (including high-sulfur content) are used. These oils provide protection from bearing corrosion and high-temperature deposits.
CC-Diesel	Moderate-duty diesel and gasoline engine service. For certain naturally aspirated, turbocharged, or supercharged diesel engines in moderate- to severe-duty service; also used for some heavy-duty gasoline engines.
CB-Diesel	Moderate-duty diesel engine service. For light- to moderate-duty diesel engines operating with lower-quality fuels that require greater protection against wear and deposits; occasionally used for light-duty gasoline engines.
CA-Diesel	Light-duty diesel engine service. For light- to moderate-duty diesel engines using high-quality fuels; sometimes used for gasoline engines in mild service.

motor oil to help consumer selection of appropriate products. Table 3 shows the API classifications and SAE grades of Quaker State motor oils.

Oil manufacturers are responsible for ensuring that a given motor oil has the performance characteristics essential for the recommended service classification(s). Engine manufacturers, on the other hand, are responsible for evaluating the class of service applicable to the engine's design and intended use and

TABLE 3 Quaker State motor oils: SAE grades and API classifications

Product	SAE Grade	API Classification
Sterling	10W-30	SG–SF/CC–CD
Deluxe	10W-40	
Deluxe Performance	5W–30, 20W–50	
Super Blend	10W–30, 20W–40	SG–SF/CC–CD
HD	10W, 20W–20, 30, 40	
Turbo	10W–30	SG–SF/CC–CD
Regular	30	
Motorcycle Motor Oil (4-cycle)	20W–50	
HDX Universal Fleet	10W, 20W–20, 30, 40, 50 15W–40	CE, CD II, CD/SG–SF

recommending the appropriate classification of oil for the engine. The consumer's responsibility lies in being aware of the engine manufacturer's recommendation and purchasing the proper oil.

Appendix B Quaker State advertising

EXHIBIT B-1

ONE TOUGH MOTOR OIL ANNOUNCES ONE TOUGH GUARANTEE...

250,000

TWO HUNDRED FIFTY THOUSAND MILES OR TEN YEARS.

Use Quaker State exclusively in your new car, and our limited guarantee will cover lubricated engine parts for 250,000 miles or ten years, whichever comes first.

How tough is today's Quaker State?

Tough enough to make this promise: Use only Quaker State in your new car's engine, and if any lubricated engine part not covered by the manufacturer's warranty or extended-service contract suffers an oil-related breakdown during its first 250,000 miles or ten years, Quaker State will pay for the repair.

We'll guarantee lubricated parts in engines of all sizes—domestic or imported.

Quaker State's limited guarantee covers lubricated parts in engines of every single imported and domestic car or light truck sold in the United States. It even covers the deductible on any extended warranty you might have purchased from your new-car dealer. Enrollment is absolutely free.

See a copy of lubrication limited warranty and enrollment details at participating service centers.

Complete details and enrollment forms for the Quaker State 250,000-mile or ten-year guarantee are available at

participating Quaker State service centers. These include many new-car dealers, automotive service centers and fast lubes nationwide.

To participate in the guarantee program, enroll your new car at a participating service center within six months or 6,000 miles of purchase. Use only Quaker State Motor Oil, and have your oil and filter changed at a service center according to manufacturer's instructions for severe driving conditions but not to exceed 4,000 miles or four months between changes. Save your receipts.

How can Quaker State make a guarantee this tough?

Today's Quaker State has proven its toughness over and over again in the most rigorous tests that the world's auto makers have thrown at it. The result: Quaker State actually exceeds lubrication specifications for every single car sold in the United States. It takes a tough oil to offer a guarantee this tough. But Quaker State is One Tough Motor Oil.

The Big Q is One Tough Motor Oil.

© 1990 Quaker State Corporation DON'T POLLUTE. PLEASE DISPOSE OF USED MOTOR OIL PROPERLY.

EXHIBIT B–2

QUAKER STATE---
ONE TOUGH MOTOR OIL
BRINGS YOU A TOUGH NEW
ADVERTISING CAMPAIGN!

EXHIBIT B-3

QUAKER STATE ONE TOUGH MOTOR OIL PRESENTS A TOUGH ADVERTISING CAMPAIGN.

LEADERSHIP LEVELS OF QUAKER STATE
IMAGE ADVERTISING BEHIND OUR
"ONE TOUGH MOTOR OIL" THEME

- We will <u>dominate</u> television auto racing with our
  year round motor oil exclusivity on ESPN <u>and</u>
  major network races.

- We will <u>dominate</u> consumer magazines –
  automotive enthusiast, do-it-yourselfer,
  and outdoor publications.

- We will <u>dominate</u> broadcast advertising in
  major ADI's covering the U.S.

QUAKER STATE'S MEDIA SPENDING WILL BE UP +63% VERSUS 1989!

EXHIBIT B–4

"GUARANTEE"

LENGTH: 30 SECONDS

COMM'L NO.: QOAZ 0133

ANNCR: One tough motor oil announces one tough guarantee.

The Quaker State

250,000 mile or 10 year guarantee.

Register your new car at a participating service center.

Then use only Quaker State.

Have oil and filter changed as directed at a service center

and if any lubricated engine part suffers an oil related break down

within 250,000 miles

or 10 years

you're covered. Quaker State guarantees it in writing.

The Big Q

is one tough motor oil.

EXHIBIT B-5

"TESTED TOUGH"

LENGTH: 30 SECONDS

COMM'L NO.: QOAZ 0063

ANNCR: It's one of the most technologically advanced, most rigorously tested fluids on earth.

Relentlessly measured for maximum protection against the friction...(SFX)

the wear

and tear...(SFX)

the heat and stress of today's engines.

It is today's Quaker State.

In Europe, in Japan, in America

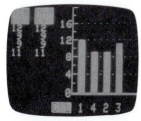

Quaker State quality has passed the most demanding tests

auto makers can throw at it.

At Quaker State we don't just say we're tough, we're tested tough.

The Big Q

is one tough motor oil.

EXHIBIT B-6

"TOUGH ENGINES"

LENGTH: 30 SECONDS

COMM'L NO.: QOAZ 0043

ANNCR: What makes a Quaker State engine so tough? One tough motor oil.

And being tough takes more than just talking tough.

There's a brand that says it's been engineered for smaller engines.

Well, Quaker State

has been tested tough for small engines

in Japan, in Europe and in America.

In fact, Quaker State has toughed out the most demanding specs

for every size engine in every size car sold in the U.S.

What makes any size Quaker State engine so tough?

Quality engineered Quaker State.

The Big Q

is one tough motor oil.

EXHIBIT B-7

"NASCAR"

LENGTH: 30 SECONDS

COMM'L NO.: QOAZ 0083

ANNCR: They got the green flag at Daytona.

Roared through Talladaga.

Left Darlington in the dust.

And which car piled up the most tough NASCAR miles in '89?

The Quaker State King Racing Buick.

Its engine getting maximum protection

from one tough motor oil. The same Quaker State you buy right off the shelf.

Only one car was tough enough to stack up NASCAR's highest mileage total.

Only one oil was tough enough to tough it out every single one of those miles.

Quaker State.

The Big Q

is one tough motor oil.

EXHIBIT B-8

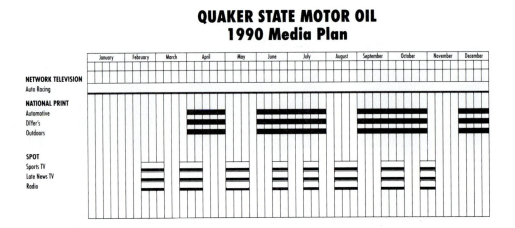

QUAKER STATE MOTOR OIL
1990 Media Plan

Ordering of Co-op Advertising Materials

To order materials call Customer Service at 1-800-759-2525 and give them the appropriate advertising material code number.

The following co-op advertising materials are available at no charge for use by case goods or bulk retailers:

Lube Warranty	Order Code Number
20 Second Television	3000559
45 Second Radio	3000560
30 Second Radio	3000561
16 1/2" x 11 1/4" Black & White Newspaper Ad	3000562
8 1/4" x 11 1/4" Black & White Newspaper Ad (Available 4/15)	3000563
Tested Tough (Beaker)	
20 Second Television	3000564
45 Second Radio	3000565
30 Second Radio	3000566
Tough Engines (Tested for all size engines)	
15 Second Television	3000568
45 Second Radio	3000569
30 Second Radio	3000570
Reprints of this Storyboard Handout	3000571
Copy of 1990 Ad Campaign Videotape	3000572

Retailers will have to produce their remaining portion of the co-op ad; plus buy and place the media. **All tags for these ads still must receive copy approval by Quaker State Marketing.** Please refer to the 1990 Retailer Merchandising Program for more information and details.

IT TAKES A TOUGH OIL TO OFFER
AN ADVERTISING CAMPAIGN
THIS TOUGH.

BUT QUAKER STATE IS
ONE TOUGH MOTOR OIL.

Appendix C

Annual income statement ($ millions)

	Dec. 1988	Dec. 1987	Dec. 1986	Dec. 1985	Dec. 1984
Sales	$869.104	$847.952	$899.065	$974.251	$924.630
Cost of goods sold	626.390	611.501	642.930	731.336	721.022
Gross profit	242.714	236.451	256.135	242.915	203.608
Selling, general, and administrative expense	190.977	183.958	139.716	132.037	114.780
Operating income before depreciation	51.737	52.493	116.419	110.878	88.828
Depreciation, depletion, and amortization	39.201	39.467	35.675	36.416	34.777
Operating profit	12.536	13.026	80.744	74.462	54.051
Interest expense	9.048	6.977	8.926	13.509	12.922
Non-operating income/expense	8.341	11.744	18.070	18.752	10.322
Special items	5.804	−122.000	.000	1.887	−24.695
Pretax income	17.633	−104.207	89.888	81.592	26.756
Total income taxes	2.700	−56.150	39.600	35.700	9.000
Minority interest	.000	.000	.000	.000	.000
Income before extraordinary items and discontinued operations	14.933	−48.057	50.288	45.892	17.756
Extraordinary items	.000	.000	.000	.000	.000
Discontinued operations	.000	.000	.000	.000	.000
Net income	14.933	−48.057	50.288	45.892	17.756
Preferred dividends	.000	.000	.000	.000	.000
Available for common	14.933	−48.057	50.288	45.892	17.756
Savings due to common stock equivalents	.000	.000	.000	.000	.000
Adjusted available for common	$ 14.933	$ −48.057	$ 50.288	$ 45.892	$ 17.756

EXHIBIT D-1

Case 40 _____

L.A. Gear*

September 13, 1989 The Los Angeles Palladium is packed with reporters waiting for L.A. Gear CEO, Robert Y. Greenberg, to formally introduce their new spokesperson, singer/entertainer Michael Jackson.

Taunted by rumors, the press wants to confirm the two-year, $20 million plus stock option contract Jackson is reputed to have signed in exchange for starring in new commercials, wearing L.A. Gear footwear in his music videos, and designing a new line of apparel and shoes under their new 1990 campaign, UNSTOPPABLE.

Once the star appeared, however, he merely read a prepared statement about the alliance, blew a kiss to the crowd and left the stage, allowing no questions. Industry analyst, Steven Levitt of Market Evaluations, immediately cast doubts on the arrangement, predicting that Jackson would be valuable to L.A. Gear only if he sang in the commercials and if the target were narrowed to 6- to 11-year-old girls.

Thus, without direct confirmation on L.A. Gear's dealings, the press and the public were left to speculate on L.A. Gear's future marketing focus and strategy for the 90s for the $9 billion retail athletic footwear market, and its ability to achieve Greenberg's goal of "building the biggest brand name in the world."

Although Greenberg predicts that L.A. Gear will surpass both Reebok and Nike for sales within the next five years, there is still doubt within the industry that the upstart company will be able to successfully disseminate its trendy styles and its California moniker throughout the world.

Athletic Footwear Industry

The athletic footwear industry, expected to reach $5.4 billion in 1990, has seen rapid growth over the past 15 years, particularly during the past 5 years.

---

* This case was written from public sources and from interviews with people knowledgeable about this industry by Joanne E. Novak, under the supervision of Thomas C. Kinnear. Copyright © 1990 by Thomas C. Kinnear.

Averaging 21 percent growth wholesale and 23 percent growth retail between 1985 and 1990, the forces that have been driving the growth can be identified as:

- *Late 1970s*—The popularity of running.
- *Early 1980s*—The aerobics craze.
- *Early 1980s*—The emphasis on overall health and fitness.

    —The introduction of specialty shoes for each sport (basketball to boardsailing) or all sports (cross-training).

    —The emergence of technological innovations in material and design.

- *Late 1980s, early 1990s*—

    —The use of multimillion-dollar media campaigns and star-studded spokespeople.

From these trends, two distinct market segments have emerged—performance and fashion. There used to be classic, all-purpose, $15 sneakers—such as Converse ''Chuck Taylor'' All Stars, P.F. Flyers, and Keds—that could easily be replaced once they had worn out and that *never* would label their wearers as slaves to fashion. In the 90s, however, with numerous styles and new players vying for a piece of the market, athletic footwear can cost as much as $170 per pair and new styles appear every 8 to 10 months as manufacturers have decreased their new product introduction cycle. Today, athletic footwear is worn to make a statement.

Emergence of Fashion Segment

The development of the fashion segment began with ''the runner's look.'' Running had become a popular sport, dominated by men, during the early 1970s. After American Frank Shorter won the gold medal for the marathon during the 1976 Olympics, however, many more Americans were inspired to run or jog for exercise. This boom created a demand for runners' apparel and running shoes—supplying growth to the athletic shoe industry from 1977 to 1983. The popularity of the sport eventually reached nonrunners who liked the image of the runner. This image spurred the purchase of running shoes for casual use and reflected the beginning of a nationwide trend toward a more casual lifestyle.[1]

The advent of aerobics in 1983 created a new fashion/fitness trend as women who aerobicized wanted apparel and footwear specific to the sport. They preferred stylish gear that was more comfortable, more colorful, and had more variety than traditional exercise outfits.

---

[1] Angela Hinton et al., ''Reebok and Nike: The Athletic Shoe Industry,'' University of Michigan Research Report for Prof. S. Hariharan, April 18, 1989.

EXHIBIT 1 Males/females purchases of athletic footwear (000s)

	Bought in last 12 months	Bought 1 pair	Bought 2 pairs	Bought >3 pairs
Males				
Total male population = 84,066				
Percent of total male population	20.80%	10.80%	6.00%	4.00%
Total buyers	17,467	9,105	5,027	3,336
Age 18–24	3,915	2,147	1,040	728
25–34	5,910	2,810	2,000	1,099
35–44	3,441	1,668	1,049	724
45–54	2,121	1,259	424	437
55–64	1,155	635	293	227
65+	925	584	220	122
Total shoes	>29,197	9,105	10,054	>10,008
Age 18–24	6,411	2,147	2,080	2,184
25–34	10,107	2,810	4,000	3,297
35–44	5,938	1,668	2,098	2,172
45–54	3,418	1,259	848	1,311
55–64	1,902	635	586	681
65+	1,390	584	440	366
Regions of Buying				
Northeast	4,346	2,258	1,279	809
Midwest	4,757	2,367	1,388	1,002
South	5,276	3,070	1,239	968
West	3,088	1,410	1,121	557
Females				
Total female population = 92,184				
Percent of total female population	28.20%	10.50%	6.30%	11.50%
Total buyers	26,033	9,636	5,827	10,571
Age 18–24	4,263	1,753	677	1,833
25–34	7,874	3,030	1,972	2,872
35–44	6,625	2,325	1,348	2,952
45–54	3,300	1,008	778	1,514
55–64	2,129	775	553	801
65+	1,841	745	498	559
Total shoes	>52,730	9,636	11,654	31,713
Age 18–24	8,606	1,753	1,354	5,499
25–34	15,590	3,030	3,944	8,616
35–44	13,877	2,325	2,696	8,856
45–54	7,106	1,008	1,556	4,542
55–64	4,284	775	1,106	2,403
65+	3,418	745	996	1,677
Regions of buying				
Northeast	6,809	2,449	947	3,413
Midwest	6,986	2,882	1,469	2,634
South	7,718	2,773	1,970	2,975
West	4,520	1,531	1,441	1,548

Source: Simmons, 1988.

EXHIBIT 2 Male/female spending patterns (000s)

Total male population = 84,066

Spending	Buyers	Percent who bought in last 12 months	Percent of total buyers
If men buy athletic footwear			
Spend < $15	4,032	23%	4.80%
Spend $15–$29	6,426	37	7.60
Spend ≥ $30	7,010	40	8.30
Total female population = 92,184			
If women buy athletic footwear			
Spend < $15	9,636	37%	10.50%
Spend $15–$29	5,827	22	6.30
Spend ≥ $30	10,571	41	11.50

77% of men who buy spend over $15.
63.5% of women who buy spend over $15.
Source: Simmons, 1988.

Thus, fashion was brought to the forefront and, for the first time, women were driving the market. By 1987, women bought sneakers more often than men and they bought more of them (Exhibits 1 and 2). The average woman in 1989 owned 2.6 pairs of sneakers compared with 2.5 pairs owned by the average man.

By the end of the decade, athletic footwear manufacturers were facing yet a different market. Inner-city kids began to define territories by brands of sneakers (i.e., on Boston's Intervale Street they would be seen only in Adidas sneakers, whereas Nike streets were Hamilton and Crawford); teenage girls developed sneaker etiquette, shunning boys donning sneakers incompatible with their own; and young urban professionals and teenagers bought several pairs of sneakers to match their wardrobes and their moods. They needed all-night dancing shoes, "impressing the ladies" shoes, and Saturday-at-the-park shoes to let their peers know they had style. As one teen simply said, "If I wear black, I wear black sneakers. If I wear red, I wear red sneakers. If I wear purple, I wear white sneakers."[2]

> Ten years ago, people had an average of 1.2 pairs of athletic shoes in their closets. In 1987, Reebok customers owned an average of 4.5 pairs. By the mid-90s, those same customers will own six to six and a half different pairs of sneakers apiece. Footwear will no longer be an accessory, it will be the main course.[3]
>
> Paul Fireman, CEO, Reebok

---

[2] "Much Ado About Rubber," CBS's *Sunday Today*, March 25, 1990.
[3] E. M. Swift, "Farewell My Lovely," *Sports Illustrated*, February 19, 1990, p. 80.

These wearers were shifting 40 percent of the athletic shoe demand (30 percent direct demand, 10 percent influential demand) to the 15- to 22-year-old age group and defining athletic footwear as *the* fashion statement.[4]

Acquisitions

Growth in the industry has been the result of not only these trends but also savvy marketing and new product design. Strength abroad and acquisitions of other footwear manufacturers has helped to grow market share (Exhibit 3). Reebok has brought several footwear manufacturers into its corporation: Rockport, 1985; Avia, 1987 (who previously bought Donnor, a hiking/walking shoe company, in 1986); Ellesse, 1987; Frye (boots), 1987; and Metaphors (women's casual shoes), 1987.

EXHIBIT 3   U.S. share of footwear market

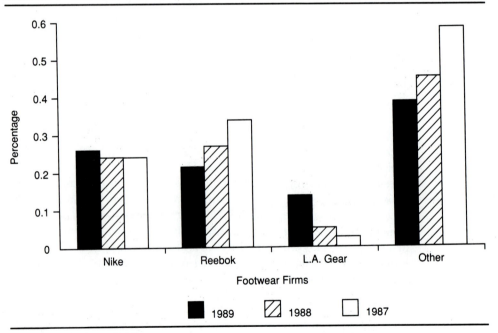

Assumes total market = $9 billion.

Interco, owner of the Florsheim brand, purchased Converse in 1986 and Yarsel Investment Corp. bought Pony (Exhibit 4).

---

[4] Joseph Pereira, "The Well-Heeled," *The Wall Street Journal,* December 1, 1988, p. 1.

EXHIBIT 4 Ownership of athletic footwear brands

Brand	Ownership
Adidas	Private
Autry	Private
Etonic	Private
Fila	Private
K–Swiss	Private
Kaepa	Private
Kangaroos	Private
Lotto	Private
New Balance	Private
Pony	Private
Spalding	Private
Tretorn	Private
Turntec	Private
Hyde	Public
L.A. Gear	Public
Nike	Public
Reebok	Public
Foot-Joy	Public, a division of American Brands
Converse	Public, a division of Interco
Avia	Public, a division of Reebok
Ellesse	Public, a division of Reebok
Keds	Public, a division of Stride-Rite
Brooks	Public, a division of Wolverine
Puma	Public, Germany
Asics Tigers	Public, Japan

Source: Drexel Burnham Lambert Industry Report, December 1987.

Buyers

As the 1990s approach, the athletic shoe manufacturers are forced to address the fashion issue. With their current penetration into the market at only 20 to 30 percent, footwear firms have a great potential to attract new buyers and penetrate the market further.

Buyers are not only serious athletes but also working women, casual or weekend athletes, and casual fashion wearers in search of comfortable, attractive shoes. Within each buyer segment, there are different priorities—performance, fashion, comfort, and price sensitivity—and for each buyer the priorities differ. Currently, 80 percent of all athletic shoe purchases are for casual use.[5]

Additionally, more segments or subsegments have emerged within each segment: male/female; single sport user/multisport user; infant/toddler; young/old. Each of these subsegments has specific needs that they want addressed.

The market also can be segmented according to psychographic profiles. A recent Harvard Business School case study identified segments by athletic

[5] Ellen Paris, "Rhinestone Hightops, Anyone?" *Forbes,* March 7, 1988, p. 78.

lifestyles: serious athletes, weekend warriors, and casual athletes. The case identified the serious athletes as the opinion leaders, prompting the manufacturers to cater to them. By satisfying this segment, it is assumed that other types of buyers would follow their lead.

Capabilities

The competition for these buyers has intensified. Nike and Reebok, the number one and number two U.S. market share holders, respectively, are fighting for more share in the media and the stores. They have invested millions of dollars on highly produced, star-studded media campaigns (Exhibit 5) and new product introductions that include air, color, and new materials (Exhibit 6). Reebok and Nike have been focused on performance with technological attributes in the lead for product differentiation.

This competition has forced a change to the product development and product life cycle for athletic footwear. The average product development cycle has been trimmed to 6 to 10 months while the product life cycle has been shortened to 8 to 10 months. Nike is using CAD/CAM technologies to shorten their development time for the introduction of new products.

New styles appear with new technologies, materials, colors, or endorsers capitalizing on or creating the latest trends. For the buyer, there is more choice and more confusion about a brand and an athletic shoe's attributes. Also, with the possible eight-month turnaround for new styles—prices can conceivably rise every eight months. The largest retail hike in 1989 has been with basketball pump models retailing between $170 and $180. (Nike's Air Pressure, $175; Reebok's Pump, $170.)

EXHIBIT 5 Advertising and promotional expenditures (in $ millions)

	1986	1987	1988	1989	1990*
L.A. Gear	$ 2.6	$ 5.4	$12.6	$25	$ 50
Reebok		12	35	60	70
Nike	62.5	65.9	85.3	50	100

* Estimated for 1990.

For L.A. Gear, dollars include trade shows, trade and consumer publications (.12), merchandise, TV (.50), and specialty billboards. International advertising of $3 million is not included.

For Reebok, the $70 million is divided between $40 million domestic and $30 million in promotions. International advertising of $20 million is not included. Ten percent of expenditures in 1989 were for children's footwear.

For Nike, $25–$30 million will be spent on promotions in 1990.

Sources: Linda Williams, "On the Right Foot," *Los Angeles Times*, September 31, 1989, s. 4, p. 1.

"Reebok," *Adweek*, February 5, 1990, p. 12.

E. W. Swift, "Farewell My Lovely," *Sports Illustrated*, February 19, 1990, p. 80.

Nike 10–K 1988.

Reebok 10–K 1988.

David Jefferson, "Fashion Victim? L.A. Gear, Highflier in Sneakers, Discovers Perils of Shifting Fads," *The Wall Street Journal*, December 8, 1989, p. A16.

EXHIBIT 6   Reebok energy return system

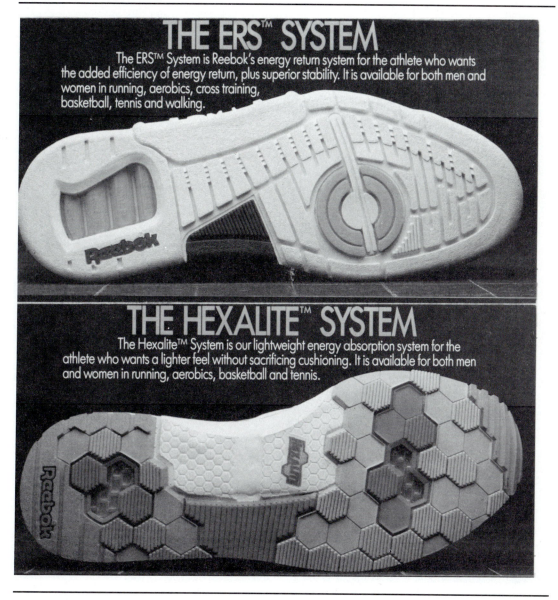

EXHIBIT 6 *(concluded)*

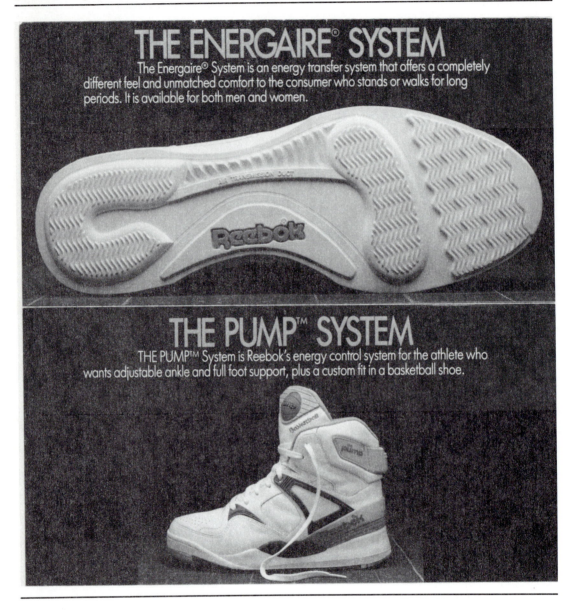

Considering that the top three manufacturers use low-cost production facilities in South Korea and Taiwan and that it costs only $15 to $20 to manufacture a pair of sneakers that will retail at $60 to $100, in addition to manufacturing, the revenues from these athletic shoes support R&D, advertising and promotion, and company profits.

L.A. Gear, third in retail sales in the U.S. market, replacing Converse in 1989, is growing with the fashion segment (Exhibit 7). As the market expands to new users, however, old competitors (Keds, Converse, Adidas, and designers) are trying to capitalize on the industry's growth to recapture market share.

EXHIBIT 7   U.S. sales of athletic footwear

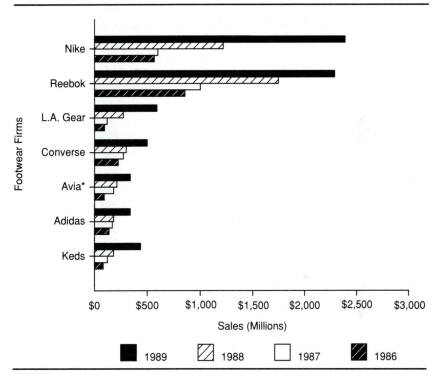

* Avia was purchased by Reebok in 1988.

With buyers willing to purchase several pairs of shoes for different uses, the market for performance shoes overlaps with the fashion shoe market. Thus, the two dimensions—fashion and performance—will not stay separated in the 90s. Manufacturers are faced with positioning themselves effectively in these markets to maintain, grow, or recapture market share.

Driving the 90s

Shoe design—with a technological or fashion emphasis—and advertising become two driving forces in the industry to support manufacturers' positioning. While technological innovations lead to a better-made shoe that has state-of-the-art fit and performance, heavy advertising and promotional activity serves to decrease brand blur and support manufacturers' unique images. The strength of a firm's R&D and image advertising is heavily correlated with leading market share and/or high sales growth.

L.A. Gear's performance over the past four years demonstrates how positioning and strategy can change the perceptions and performance of a company (Exhibit 8).

Net sales increased 217 percent from 1987 to 1988 due to not only higher wholesale prices but also the number of shoes that were purchased—4.4 million units to 10.1 million units (Exhibit 9). Internationally, sales increased from $2.3 million to $20.5 million—a 791 percent gain.

By 1990, sales forecasts for L.A. Gear are projected to exceed $1 billion (Exhibit 10). First quarter 1990 results for revenue already show L.A. Gear

EXHIBIT 8 Statement of operations (in thousands)

	Year ended November 30				
	1988	*1987*	*1986*	*1985*	*1984*
Net sales	$223,713	$70,575	$36,299	$10,687	$9,007
Cost of sales	129,103	41,569	20,880	7,294	6,116
Gross profit	94,610	29,006	15,419	3,393	2,891
General and administrative expenses	54,024	20,559	10,263	2,722	2,685
Interest/factoring expenses	4,102	1,110	686	526	368
Provision for loss from litigation	0	0	2,295	0	0
Royalty income	−856	−604	−1,210	−285	−65
Earnings (loss) before income taxes, discontinued operations, and extraordinary item	37,340	7,941	3,385	430	−97
Income tax benefit (expense)	−15,310	−3,570	−1,634	−199	45
Earnings (loss) before discontinued operations and extraordinary item	22,030	4,371	1,751	231	−52
(Loss) from discontinued operations, net of income carryforward	0	0	−6	−31	−392
Earnings (loss) before extraordinary item	$ 22,030	$ 4,371	$ 1,745	$ 200	($444)
Extraordinary item—use of net operating loss carryforward	0	0	0	133	0
Net earnings (loss)	$ 22,030	$ 4,371	$ 1,745	$ 333	($444)

EXHIBIT 8 (*continued*) Consolidated balance sheet data L.A. Gear, Inc. and subsidiaries (in thousands)

	November 30	
	1988	1987
Assets		
Cash	$ 4,205	$ 3,245
Accounts receivable	49,526	15,148
Inventory	66,556	15,813
Prepaid expenses and other current assets	3,383	951
Total current assets	$123,670	$35,157
Property, equipment, net	3,110	
accumulated depreciation		1,010
Deferred tax charges	1,034	14
Other assets	1,019	613
Total assets	128,833	36,794
Liabilities and Shareholders' Equity		
Current liabilities:		
Line of credit	$ 57,230	$ 7,126
Accounts payable	7,748	3,886
Accrued expenses and other liabilities	10,029	585
Accrued loss from litigation	2,373	2,341
Accrued compensation	5,927	414
Income tax payable	4,217	323
Total current liabilities	87,524	14,675
Shareholders' equity		
Common stock	n/a	n/a
Preferred stock	n/a	n/a
Additional paid-in capital	13,008	15,848
Retained earnings	28,301	6,271
Total Shareholders' Equity	41,309	22,119
Total liabilities and shareholders' equity	$128,833	$36,794

EXHIBIT 8 (*concluded*) L.A Gear, Inc. and subsidiaries' consolidated statement of income and retained earnings (thousands)

	Three months ended February 28	
	1990	1989
Net sales	$187,281	$66,070
Cost of sales	113,605	37,486
Gross profit	73,676	28,584
Selling, general, and administrative expenses	46,498	17,419
Operating income	27,178	11,165
Interest expense, net	4,013	2,118
Income before income taxes	23,165	9,047
Income tax expense	9,266	3,689
Net income	$ 13,899	$ 5,358
Weighted average shares	20,022	17,311
Earnings per share	$0.69	$0.31

Source: L.A. Gear press release, February 1990.

EXHIBIT 9   U.S. sales of footwear market

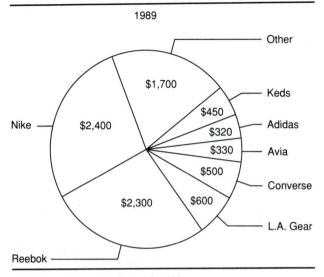

1989

Other — $1,700

Nike — $2,400

Keds — $450

Adidas — $320

Avia — $330

Converse — $500

L.A. Gear — $600

Reebok — $2,300

* Avia was purchased by Reebok in 1988.

EXHIBIT 10   L.A Gear sales

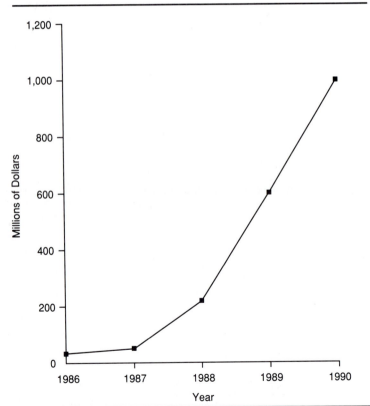

Note: Figure for 1990 was an estimate.

724

exceeding industry analysts' forecasts of $160 million to $165 million. Their revenue grew 257 percent—from $66.1 million to $170 million.[6]

Greenberg notes, however,

> To achieve increased market penetration and to ensure that we meet the large customer demand for our products, we sold certain styles in the first quarter [1990] at gross profit margins lower than the Company's historic norms.
>
> This decision had its intended effect, increasing market share and retail shelf space for new styles . . . sales during the quarter were substantially in excess of analysts' expectations and the Company's gross and net profit margin percentages decreased somewhat during the period.[7]

By increasing their advertising and trade show presence during the late 1980s and increasing their marketing efforts in large department stores, L.A. Gear developed a stronger push strategy to help increase primary demand for their athletic and athletic-styled leisure footwear.

L.A. Gear's success has been reflected in its stock price (Exhibit 11). Previously considered only a trendy valley girl shoe company, L.A. Gear had the best performing stock in 1989, showing an increase of 185 percent total return to investors.

EXHIBIT 11 L.A. Gear common stock sale prices

	Sales prices	
	Low	High
1987		
First quarter	$ 1.63	$ 3.07
Second quarter	2.32	3.28
Third quarter	2.16	3.16
Fourth quarter	1.72	3.47
1988		
First quarter	$ 1.85	$ 4.47
Second quarter	3.91	6.97
Third quarter	5.82	9.88
Fourth quarter	8.38	11.38
1989		
First quarter	$10.00	$17.56
Second quarter	15.07	26.32
Third quarter	25.75	33.75
Fourth quarter	29.94	45.75

Note: Prices adjusted for an August 1988 and September stock split.
Source: L.A Gear 10–K Report, February 28, 1990.

---

[6] "Nike, L.A. Gear, Reebok are Expected to Post Increaesd 1st Quarter Earnings", *The Wall Street Journal,* March 29, 1990, p. A4.

[7] L.A. Gear Press Release: L.A. Gear Inc., Reports Significant Increases in Revenue and Net Income for First Quarter, 1990.

L.A. Gear

L.A. Gear found a niche in the fashion segment of the 1986 $5 billion athletic footwear industry and exploited it. Known as Good Times Industries until 1985, the company initially designed and sold roller skate shoes and owned roller palaces. In 1983, the company introduced a canvas tie-on shoe with a flat rubber bottom from South Korea and called it The Street Walker. By 1985, the company—now L.A. Gear—had $10.7 million in sales of women's aerobic shoes and leather athletic-styled leisure shoes.

Greenberg says, "I was watching the popularity of athletic shoes as casual shoes."[8] As athletic shoes ceased to be worn for running and jumping, L.A. Gear provided shoes for wearers who chose athletic shoes as their casual shoe of choice. L.A. Gear now has an extensive product line (Exhibit 12).

An entrepreneur by nature, Greenberg began his retailing career in the 1960s selling wigs to beauty shops in Boston. He moved on to selling Wild Oats jeans to department stores in the 1970s, and in 1979 licensed Steven Spielberg's *E.T.* for use on kids' shoelaces. That venture reaped $3 million in 90 days.

Greenberg prides himself on being able to spot trends in his market and continues to introduce products that will appeal to his current customers. He readily acknowledges that designing for trends that take hold of young women can be risky, but he believes that if L.A. Gear stays in close touch with its shoe buyers, the company will only grow. Greenberg himself meets with his customers regularly—when he occasionally poses as a shoe salesman in a nearby mall.

Greenberg hopes to make L.A. Gear "America's No. 1 family brand" and has helped to generate enthusiasm for his goal—beginning with his executive officers (Exhibit 13). He has preprinted tee shirts and caps that say "L.A. Gear 1 in '91" for his executives.

Jonathan Ziegler, industry analyst with Sutro and Company, attributes L.A. Gear's success to good advertising and merchandising in Southern California. By placing their advertisements on MTV and cable stations, he says, L.A. Gear played to their target—the young female who would wear skirts and athletic shoes.[9]

> They identified a niche—the valley girl niche. . . . It's sort of like women in Reeboks and business suits. L.A. Gear hit the juniors with casual clothes and sneakers. It's not a technical shoe that would impress Michael Jordan [Chicago Bulls basketball star], but a fashion shoe that's got more look than technology.[10]
> John Horan—Publisher, *Sports Goods Management News*

As of 1988, L.A. Gear had 4.7 percent market share and currently has a 13 percent share. "There's no doubt that it was the name that caught on," says

---

[8] Linda Williams, "L. A. Gear Posts Huge Increases in Second Quarter Earnings," *Los Angeles Times*, June 29, 1988, s. 4, p. 1.

[9] Ibid.

[10] Ibid.

EXHIBIT 12 L.A Gear, Inc. product mix

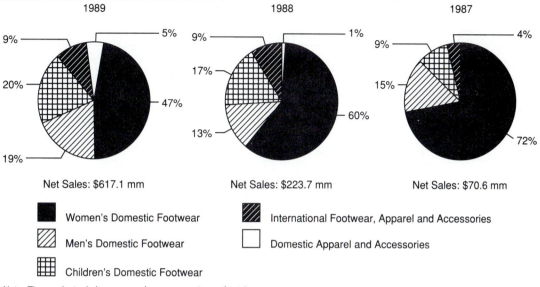

1989   1988   1987

9% — 5%   9% — 1%   9% — 4%
20%   17%   15%
19%   13%   72%
47%   60%

Net Sales: $617.1 mm   Net Sales: $223.7 mm   Net Sales: $70.6 mm

■ Women's Domestic Footwear   ▨ International Footwear, Apparel and Accessories

▨ Men's Domestic Footwear   □ Domestic Apparel and Accessories

▦ Children's Domestic Footwear

Note: The product mix is expressed as a percentage of total revenues.

L.A. Gear Product Split—1988

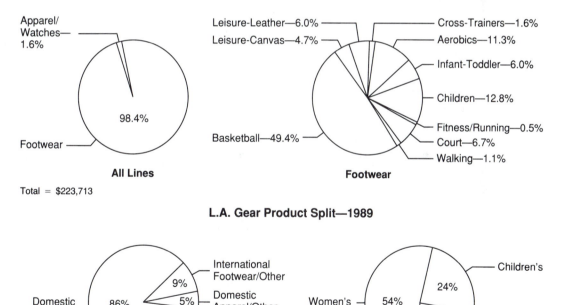

Apparel/
Watches—
1.6%

98.4%

Footwear —

All Lines

Total = $223,713

Leisure-Leather—6.0% ——— Cross-Trainers—1.6%
Leisure-Canvas—4.7% ——— Aerobics—11.3%
                          Infant-Toddler—6.0%
                          Children—12.8%
                          Fitness/Running—0.5%
Basketball—49.4% ——   Court—6.7%
                          Walking—1.1%

Footwear

L.A. Gear Product Split—1989

International
Footwear/Other
9%
Domestic   5%   Domestic
Footwear   86%   Apparel/Other

All Lines

Total = $617,080

Women's   54%   Children's
                24%
                22%
                Men's

Domestic Footwear

Source: L.A. Gear press release, February 1990.

EXHIBIT 13 Corporate personnel (as of February 1989)

Full-time employees	431
Corporate management	42
Administration	38
Advertising and promotion	13
R & D	16
Sales, customer service	39
Jeanswear	3
Watches	1
International operations	13
Overseas offices	36
Technical reps	4
Warehousing	226
Directors and Executive Officers	*Age*
Allan E. Dalshaug, director	56
Robert Y. Greenberg, chairman of the board, president and director	48
Elliot J. Horowitz, executive vice president, chief financial officer and director	42
Sandy Saeman, executive vice president, secretary and director	41
Richard W. Schubert, director	37
Gil N. Schwartzberg, executive vice president and chief administrative officer	46
Stephen Williams, executive vice president	52
Donald B. Wasley, vice president—promotions	41
Larry Clark, vice president—product sourcing	31
Sudeepto Killick Datta, vice president—international operations and licensing	29
Ralph Hulit, vice president—marketing	45
Angelo Maccano, vice president—research and development	41
Ralph W. Polce, vice president—sales	50

Gilbert Schwartzberg, executive vice president, L.A. Gear. "It has a magic to it . . . we are trying to capture that magic."[11]

Their tactic was to target their products to women, mainly teenagers, and stress the style of California. In its design studio, dozens of artists between age 20 and 30 churn out prototypes with potential fads for the future. Their shoes are splashed with color, multiple laces, inlaid rhinestones, fringes, colored cutouts, neon trim, marbilized leather, vibrant lace colors, silver buckles, and leather lattices.

They exuded the Southern California lifestyle of "fun, colorful, fresh, and young," according to former L.A. Gear CFO Elliot Horowitz. By making themselves popular with trend-seeking women from coast to coast, L.A. Gear has developed a stronghold in the fashion segment.

L.A. Gear attributes their success to their ability to identify and respond promptly to changes in consumer preferences. Sales have skyrocketed from $9 million in 1984 to $223 million in 1988 to $600 million in 1989.

L.A. Gear believes their initial toehold into the market was due to Reebok's initial success in developing the demand for athletic shoes for women. With their soft-leather Freestyle aerobic shoes, they developed a strong niche.

---

[11] Carl Lazzareschi, "A Great Leap Forward for L. A. Gear," *Los Angeles Times,* April 30, 1989, s.4, p. B26.

In 1986, however, when a fire devastated their Korean contract manufacturing plant, they had a shortage of inventory, and L.A. Gear stepped in with its soft-leather fashion shoe. Thus, L.A. Gear entered the industry in the fashion segment and positioned themselves to challenge Reebok on the fashion front.

Manufacturing

L.A. Gear manufactures their shoes using independent producers in Pusan, South Korea, and Taichung, Taiwan. The producers contract the manufacturing on a purchase order basis from L.A. Gear's Korean and Taiwan offices. Specifications for the shoes are predetermined in Los Angeles by management and a production design staff. The 32-member Korean staff and 4-member Taiwan staff only inspect the finished goods prior to shipment and arrange for the shipments.

L.A. Gear does not have a master manufacturing agreement with its producers, and they compete with other shoe companies, such as Reebok and Nike, for production capability. (Adidas, however, is unique and directly manufactures more than 6 percent of its products.) In fiscal 1988, L.A. Gear used 21 producers in Korea and 4 in Taiwan, 6 of which accounted for 57 percent of their total production.[12]

Distribution

L.A. Gear distributes its products in department stores, shoe stores, specialty stores, and sporting goods stores. Unlike its key competitors, Nike and Reebok, who rely on sporting goods outlets for 80 percent of their sales, L.A. Gear does not rely on any customer for more than 10 percent of total sales.[13]

L.A. Gear uses heavy promotions to create brand image and pull the buyers into the stores. Greenberg hopes to export that image and license it, predicting a Japanese opportunity of 500,000 pairs of sneakers sold to young women and teens. Greenberg says, "I want the distributor to set the course for the brand name to grow. If it's in lots of shoe store windows, then people will knock on our door asking to make L.A. Gear products—the name can go on anything."[14] In 1987, seven U.S. licensees put L.A. Gear's name on everything from doll clothes to sunglasses.

Sales

Domestic. L.A. Gear divides their sales into four divisions: (1) department stores and women's shoe stores, (2) sporting goods stores and athletic footwear stores, (3) men's stores, and (4) children's shoe stores. They use 102

[12] L. A. Gear 10–K Report, p. 8.
[13] L. A. Gear 10–K Report, p. 7.
[14] Ellen Paris, "Rhinestone Hightops, Anyone?" p. 78.

independent, regional individual sales representatives divided among those divisions and employ their own national sales manager plus three to six regional sales managers per division. L.A. Gear employees sell L.A. Gear merchandise exclusively. This sales force calls on the trade and offers to assist in training their salespeople.

Additionally, L.A. Gear employs five national account managers and 14 technical representatives who assist in marketing. They are responsible for improved product displays and point-of-purchase advertisements.

Since Reebok and Nike are offering the same services, the trade can be overwhelmed with the manufacturers' persistent sales and marketing forces. As the number of styles and shoes increase, their relationship with the trade becomes crucial since they control the limited shelf space. Many small retail outlets cannot stock all of the different footwear categories and hundreds of styles (Exhibit 14).

EXHIBIT 14 L.A. Gear product categories (as of first quarter 1989)

Type	Introduction date	Retail price range for selected styles	
Basketball	Apr. 1986	Shooter	$39.90
		B–424	77.90
Children's	Jun. 1985	Workout	19.90
		B–527	55.90
Aerobic	Feb. 1985	L.A. Impact	43.90
		CMR Trainer	55.90
Leisure	Feb. 1985	Canvas—Workout	21.90
		Surf Cat	37.90
		Leather—Westwood	29.90
		High Beach	53.90
Court (tennis, squash, racketball)	Sep. 1985		39.90
		T Slammer	61.90
		L.A. PRO	
Infant/toddler	Jun. 1986	Gidget	17.00
		Kids Rawhide	47.90
Walking	Dec. 1986	Streetwalker	23.90
		Imperial	59.90
Fitness/running	Aug. 1985 (men)	Skateboard	23.90
	Nov. 1986 (women)	Bandett 2	49.90
Apparel (312 combinations)	Oct. 1987 (men, jr. women)		
	Feb. 1989	Tees	
		Tank Tops	
		Sweatshirts	
		Sweatpants	
		Sweatshorts	
Jeanswear	Aug. 1988 (jr. women)	Pants	
		Jackets	
	Feb. 1989	Shorts	
		Skirts	
Watches (7 styles) (25 combinations of styles and colors)	Nov. 1988 (teen, jrs.)	Quartz/analog	$36–$38

Source: L.A. Gear 10–K, February 28, 1989.

L.A. Gear has only recently been able to penetrate the specialty store. They believe this penetration has been facilitated by their "open stock" system. This system lets retailers order as few as four pairs of shoes in any size, style, or color. According to Schwartzberg, they fill the order from their own inventory instead of reordering from the factory and are able to meet their customers' needs quickly.[15]

L.A. Gear has begun to diversify by entering the men's and children's market in 1986; the apparel market with sweatshirts, T-shirts, and shorts in 1987; and the watch and jean market in 1988.

Their watches are sold through six independent, regional sales representatives and some footwear sales representatives. Apparel is sold through 20 individual, regional sales representatives and some footwear sales representatives. Eight of these independent, regional representatives also sell Jeanswear. L.A. Gear employees sell watches, apparel, and Jeanswear, exclusively.

International. L.A. Gear only began selling overseas to Japan, Switzerland, and Germany in 1987. They now have agreements with 43 distributors in 77 countries for distribution of footwear and apparel. By 1991, they intend to be selling in 100 countries including the Soviet Union. They sell domestic designs in most foreign markets but have occasionally modified their product design in consideration of cultural norms.

After they had put a significant emphasis on international operations in early 1989, net sales from international operations increased from $2.3 million (3.3 percent of net sales) in fiscal 1987 to $20.5 million (9.2 percent of net sales) in fiscal 1988 to $52 million (8.67 percent of sales) in 1989. Killick Datta, vice president in charge of international operations and licensing, expects 1990 sales to reach $110 million. In five years, he predicts sales of $500 million. For 1988, approximately 61 percent of sales were in Canada, Japan, Italy, and England.

In early 1990, L.A. Gear signed a letter of intent with the Asics corporation of Japan for the marketing of L.A. Gear products in Japan. Greenberg indicated that Asics's strong distribution channel, their resources, and their selling experience in Japan would complement L.A. Gear's marketing skills and would help to get L.A. Gear products into the market quickly.

Distributors are given exclusive rights to distribute L.A. Gear to retailers in their specific geographic areas, but to maintain consistency in advertising and promotions, all materials they use must be approved in Los Angeles. Distributors, under the L.A. Gear contract, agree to spend 5 percent of their sales on advertising; they actually spend closer to 10 percent.

Datta believes L.A. Gear's utilization of distributors rather than an international sales force is not a deficiency in their strategy. He believes their distributors know the market "as well as you do or better."[16]

---

[15] L. A. Gear Press Release: Strategies for Continued Growth, 1990.

[16] Rose Horowitz, "Sports Shoe Makers in U.S. Lace Up for Global Race," *Journal of Commerce,* November 27, 1989, p. 5A.

Although L.A. Gear considers their relationships abroad to be strong, they realize Reebok, Nike, and Adidas [industry leader worldwide] are more established in international markets and have greater financial resources at their disposal.

Marketing

L.A. Gear conducts extensive marketing research—product testing, focus groups, store and consumer interviews, and surveys—to help determine designs and technological attributes consumers want and to evaluate the feasibility of expanding existing product lines. Besides point-of-purchase promotions, L.A. Gear channels their research findings into new product designs and image-oriented advertising.

They have developed the 12- to 25-year-old-market with their rhinestone-studded, pink and white basketball shoes, and they continue to make styles incorporating different gadgetry. "Technical is another word for gadgetry," says Greenberg, "and we have gadgets in our products."[17] Further, he says, "whether they're technically fashionable or fashionably fashionable, it's all the same thing. . . . Everyone is playing the same game. I just say it."

In 1990, L.A. Gear will spend $50 million on footwear advertising with a heavy concentration on television. The remainder of their dollars will go to trade shows, consumer publications, merchandising, and specialty billboards (Exhibit 5).

L.A. Gear has built a 28,000-square-foot trade show booth with over 50 areas where they can show customers their products and write orders. The booth includes replicas of famous Los Angeles landmarks—the Beverly Hills and Bonaventure hotels, the Forum, the Coliseum, Santa Monica Pier, and City Hall—and illustrates L.A. Gear's commitment to the trade and various shows to spotlight their products.

Reebok and Nike have the resources to outspend L.A. Gear, but in the past, L.A. Gear has been able to effectively target a segment with their fashion message and build product image and brand awareness. As Elliot Horowitz, former CFO of L.A. Gear, says, "You get to a point where you can spend enough money on advertising and promotion that retailers will have to carry the brand. L.A. Gear has passed the critical mark where they are here to stay."[18]

For smaller players, the advertising war means more lost dollars in sales. Gary Jacobson, analyst for Kidder Peabody estimates that the big three—Nike, Reebok, and L.A. Gear—will take another $250 million from the smaller makers. He adds, "If I were a small company, I'd be shaking in my shoes. No small company has the marketing dollars to compete nor the research and development dollars to thrive in a business built on the next big gimmick."[19]

---

[17] Ellen Benoit, "Lost Use," *Financial World,* September 20, 1988, pp. 28–31.

[18] Linda Williams, "On the Right Foot," *Los Angeles Times,* September 31, 1989, s. 4, p. 1.

[19] "Nike, L. A. Gear, Reebok are Expected to Post Increased 1st Quarter Earnings," p. A4.

As a solid player in the fashion segment, getting 75 percent of their sales from 15- to 25-year-old women, however, industry analysts caution that if L.A. Gear intends to go beyond $600 million in sales, they will need to be a major player in the men's market. In 1988, 10 percent of their market was sold to men and 15 percent to children. Industry analysts ask: "How long will women want to wear basketball shoes?"

"I may still have some reservations that they can just go in and penetrate that men's market," says James Hines, vice president and corporate director of marketing for footwear at Oshman's sporting goods chains. "It's pretty hard to

EXHIBIT 15 Reebok product split—1988

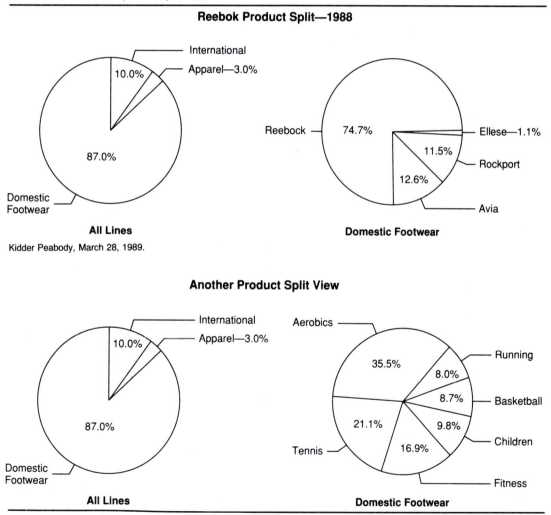

Reebok Product Split—1988

Kidder Peabody, March 28, 1989.

Reebok, 1989 Annual Report.

go in from a dead start and compete.'' Greenberg sees it another way: ''We are predators. Predators look at someone who has a nice big market share, go after it, and take it.''[20]

For 1989, 23 percent of their sales were made to men, up from 10 percent in 1988. That is a small percentage attributable to men compared to their competitors with a 70 percent share. For 1990, analysts predict 40 percent of L.A. Gear's sales will be made up of men's footwear. 15 percent of L.A. Gear's sales are for children's shoes, and most of their buyers (men and women) have been leisure, nonathletic wearers. Competitors' product splits are shown in Exhibits 15 and 16.

EXHIBIT 16 Nike product split—1988

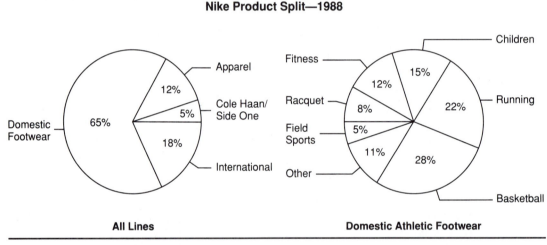

Kidder Peabody, March 28, 1989; Nike, 1989 Annual Report.

Advertising

Greenberg had begun to follow the leaders with high-performance athletes as endorsers in late 1988 when he signed L.A. Lakers Kareem Abdul-Jabbar as spokesman. ''We could have gone out and got some hot shot, but we wanted the Ambassador of Basketball,'' says Sandy Saeman, executive vice president, L.A. Gear. ''Until someone else comes along who has played for 21 years, Kareem will be the ambassador.''[21]

Featured in advertisements for Court Fire, Abdul-Jabbar continues to appear as their performance ambassador in the 1990 UNSTOPPABLE campaign (Exhibit 17). Industry analysts believe, however, ''Jabbar will not be able

---

[20] Jobeth Daniel, ''L. A. Gear Tries Full Court Press,'' *New York Times,* September 16, 1989, s. 3, p. F4.

[21] ''Even without Layups Kareem Is a Shoo In,'' *Los Angeles Times,* January 17, 1989, s. 4, p. 20.

EXHIBIT 17 L.A. Gear advertising

EXHIBIT 17 *(concluded)*

to persuade serious athletes to wear L.A. Gear. Their male market is the boyfriends of the women buying hot shot—the men more concerned about making a fashion statement.''

Additionally, L.A. Gear has enlisted L.A. Laker, Mychal Thompson; Houston Rocket, Akeen Olajuwon; Utah Jazz, Karl Malone; and San Francisco 49er/Super Bowl MVP, Joe Montana, for their performance image. Montana, signed in 1990, will be marketing their Muscle High cross-training shoes.

Other members of their all star team include: Gary Grant, L.A. Clippers; Winston Garland, Golden State Warriors; Craig Hodges, Chicago Bulls; Scott Hastings, Detroit Pistons; Kenny ''Sky'' Walker, New York Knicks; Paul Pressey, Milwaukee Bucks; Purvis Short, New York Nets; Jedric Toney, Atlanta Hawks; Byron Nix, Indiana Pacers; and ESPN's ''Body in Motion'' star, Gil Janklowicz. L.A. Gear also utilizes noncelebrity advertising for 1990 (Exhibit 17).

Even though some industry analysts doubt Abdul-Jabbar's credibility as a performance spokesperson and see L.A. Gear's investment in celebrities as promoting a fashion image, with the signing of athletes L.A. Gear signals a clear indication of its step into the performance arena.

Fashion, however, will continue to be the main thrust of the company, and more ads will appear featuring children (Exhibit 18). Celebrities used to promote the fashion image are Heather Locklear, Priscilla Presley, and Michael Jackson. Greenberg does not see an identity blur for its customers. ''This company is not a sporting goods company like Nike and Reebok. It's a fashion company. It's about looking pretty for women and looking good for men.'' He disagrees with industry analysts who claim the signing of Michael Jackson draws a clear line to teenagers and will clash with the image they are trying to create with Abdul-Jabbar.

For the spring of 1990, L.A. Gear has produced a black and white hightop similar to the space boot worn by Michael Jackson in his movie *Captain Eo* with L.A. Gear embossed on the shoe in five places. More Jackson apparel and footwear under the MJ line will be incorporated throughout the next two years. Jackson's first commercial is scheduled for August 1990.

L.A. Gear produces their advertising in-house under the direction of Saeman, except for Hispanic and international business. Saeman indicated that Michael Jackson made the agreement with L.A. Gear since their creative process is tightly controlled.

Dissatisfaction in early March 1990 prompted Saeman to dismiss their agency with their Hispanic business and to contemplate hiring another agency or also bringing that business in-house.

Competitors

Others with strong positions in the performance arena are Nike, Adidas, and Converse. Nike's million dollar advertising campaigns in the past, Revolution

EXHIBIT 18 L.A. Gear advertising

EXHIBIT 18 *(continued)*

EXHIBIT 18 (*continued*)

EXHIBIT 18   *(concluded)*

in Motion (1988) and Just Do It (1989, 1990) have become the epitome of strong performance positioning.

Nike. Nike contracted with Chicago Bull's Michael Jordan for another seven-year contract ($19 million) to market their Air line, enlisted baseball/football athlete Bo Jackson to promote their cross-training shoes, and signed Joan Benoit Samuelson to advertise their running shoes. Their past campaigns have stressed their state-of-the-art technology in a superior performance shoe.

Nike CEO Philip Knight, age 52, a University of Oregon graduate, started Blue Ribbon Sports in 1964 with Bill Bowerman, 78, his former track coach, to give the public these state-of-the-art performance shoes. They imported and distributed Japanese-made Tiger brand track shoes, and in 1972 designed and introduced their own line. His goal was to finely tune shoes to human motion and physiology, and he began with a waffle iron sole.

Their sales have grown from $270 million in 1980 to $920 million in 1984 to $2,400 million in 1989. Knight saw his market share sink below Reebok's in 1987 and 1988, prompting him to decentralize decision making to encourage innovation. Realizing that marketing and sales were taking precedence over R&D, he selected a group of his innovators, advance product engineers (APEs), and gave them the mission to create more aggressive designs.

Working in a design shop apart from the main one, they created Nike's Air Pressure by reviving an old idea of incorporating several features of ski boots, basketball shoes, and hockey skates. Also, they created cross-trainers. "What Nike produces depends on whether the consumers will accept innovation in the marketplace," says Dr. Martyn Shorter, Nike sports research lab biomechanic.

Product strategy. Nike changed its outlook in the 80s from risk averse to adventuresome, prompted by the entrance of Reebok into their market. They became more innovative with new products and big technological changes instead of incremental improvements. "It was healthy for the company to get hit between the eyes," says C. Joseph LaBonte, now former president of Reebok, about Nike. "Nike got hot. God bless 'em."

Nike also changed their strategy. In 1987, Knight said, "For Nike to be a solid company in the long run, we have to concentrate on making the best-quality, best-performing shoe we can. The fashion business is just too hard to manage year in and year out."

In 1988, however, Nike purchased Cole Haan, a dress shoe marketer, and in early 1989 they introduced a new brand of shoes, Side One. These shoes were aimed at junior girls who wore fashion athletic shoes. Nike entered the fashion market—through the side door.

"Now more than ever, we know what the Nike name stands for and how far it can be stretched—and it can't be stretched that far," says Elizabeth Dolan, spokeswoman for Nike. She indicates that Nike has not compromised its name for the fashion segment, but they have entered the market. Side One competes directly with L.A. Gear and Reebok.

In late 1989, Nike had introduced its first non-Nike named brand—i.e., a line of women's casual footwear. For 1990, they plan to add a similar men's casual footwear line in a joint development project with Cole Haan. Keri Christenfeld, an analyst with Needham and Co., indicates both the performance and fashion dimensions are needed for athletic footwear manufacturers to gain market share.

She says that the strategy is a good one and the timing is good, especially as the boundaries blur between athletic and regular street shoes. The manufacturer that is able to capture the sales growth in the blurred area will most effectively be positioned for the growing industry.

Advertising Strategy. For 1990, Nike has continued to use Just Do It in their television and print executions with Jordan and Jackson depicting hardcore performance and promoting their new technologies. They have expanded that slogan to address the market with a more personal health and personal winning strategy.

In their running and walking print advertisements, they tout exercise as physical therapy and stress management (Exhibit 19). Their Air line of print ads show how the hardcore athlete's driven to perform, but they have developed the runner's drive within a serene context: the busy city runner, the late night loner, and the rural adventurer. The scene is vivid with one serious runner; his or her shoes are not visible (Exhibit 20).

Consumers learn about new technologies from other players, too. Adidas and Converse introduced Torsion and Energy Wave, respectively, which give the consumer new attributes and materials to consider.

The new addition to Nike's 1990 campaigns is a series of Spike and Mike commercials—directed by and starring Spike Lee as a character named Mars Blackmon. Blackmon is a character from Lee's 1986 movie *She's Gotta Have It*. Lee's co-star in the commercials is Michael Jordan.

''We want to show something that conveys the excitement of sports, but still brings our athletes across as human beings,'' says Dolan. She believes the Spike and Mike advertisements are particularly successful at conveying this with the awestruck fan and the athletic great. ''That's kind of how we imagine people are responding to all our ads.''[22]

Reebok. Unlike the successful performance campaigns, Reebok has not been successful with delivering a clear performance message to consumers: Life is not a spectator sport (performance); Let U.B.U. (fashion); Physics behind the Physiques (performance), and Legends (performance) have occurred since the 1983 Freestyle aerobic campaign. In 1988, their lack of success is reflected in

---

[22] Gene Seymour, ''Spike and Nike: The Making of a Sneaky Sneaker Commercial,'' *Entertainment*, March 30, 1990, p. 29.

EXHIBIT 19   Nike Advertising

EXHIBIT 20   Nike advertising

EXHIBIT 20 *(concluded)*

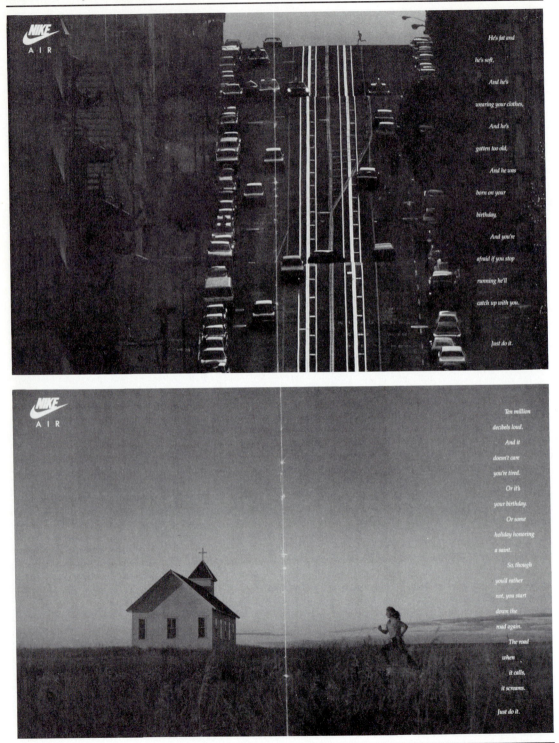

Reebok's first ever decline in earnings. Their campaigns have tried to produce both a performance image and a fashion image but have served to clutter the market rather than draw brand distinction.

In particular, their surrealistic, $10.6 million U.B.U. campaign—with such slogans as, "If U. ain't U., U. ain't nobody"—lasted only six months and was the object of competitors' mockery more than consumer's remembrances. "U. Gotta B. Kidding. Why pay for high performance shoes if U. just want to bang around in sneakers?"(Keds).

With the numerous athletic footwear ads in the media, brand blur occurs where consumers may remember the ads but not the make of the shoe being promoted.

Paul Fireman, CEO of Reebok, acknowledges the problem with UBU. He says, "We had put together a campaign that would bring us awareness, bring us controversy. And that's what 'UBU' came from."[23] He believes Reebok's problem with the campaign was not knowing when to stop it. During its initial phase, in tests compared to Nike's Just Do It, Fireman indicates that consumers had a higher recall of UBU. "The unfortunate thing is that we didn't make a transition. . . . We probably should have shifted to a more normal approach. . . . We did not follow it through into the performance business."

Fireman has built Reebok through knowing when to make changes. His management style includes frequent personnel changes, internal reorganizations, and acquisitions to strengthen their market share. Reebok has had a cash surplus for the past 15 months, and Fireman confirms that if the right acquisition candidate came along, he would continue to build Reebok. "In a perfect world, we'd be in the $300 million-to-$400 million range (for an acquisition) . . . the company could deal with a $1 billion acquisition if we found the right one."[24]

He adds, for 1990, Reebok's most important focus is the international marketplace. He believes the international market has "the opportunity to be as big if not bigger than Reebok USA." He says that they are targeting their wholesale level to be $1 billion by the mid-1990s.[25]

Product Strategy.   Until 1989, Reebok had been known and had thought of itself as a "maker of stylish sneakers that give the wearer an edge in social competition."[26] But, in early 1989, while not forsaking the "image drive shoe," Reebok announced its intentions to get a larger piece of the performance driven market. The growth in the market, they believed, was coming from the performance segment.

According to management consultant Heidi Steinberg, "They're defining their strategic outlook . . . And they're now defining themselves as a lei-

---

[23] Pat Sloan, "Reebok Chief Looks Beyond Nike," *Advertising Age*, January 29, 1990, p. 16.

[24] Ibid.

[25] Ibid.

[26] Douglas McGill, "Reebok's New Models, Fully Loaded," *New York Times*, February 14, 1989, p. D1.

sure/lifestyle company. They're not defining themselves as an athletic footwear company any longer."[27]

Advertising Strategy. For early 1990, Reebok is showing product specific advertisements (Exhibit 21):

- "If it's not one thing it's another" (cross-training).
- "Pump it up" (basketball).
- "Because its never the same game twice" (Energy System—all shoes).
- "Millions of girls want to be in her shoes, but she wants to be in ours" (dance).
- "Wear emblems, not labels" (fashion).
- "It's hard to improve a classic" (aerobics).
- "Go ahead, stick out your tongue" (fashion).
- "Training wheels for the feet" (children).
- "The Pump from Reebok. It Fits a Little Better Than Your Ordinary Athletic Shoe." (performance).

They continue to use Michael Chang, youngest champion of the French Open, as spokesman, and they have added singer/choreographer Paula Abdul to appeal to the younger consumers of their fast-growing competitor, L.A. Gear.

1990 Issues/Competitors' Actions—Reactions

Reebok

January 22, 1990 Reebok announced a split in its U.S. operations. To help keep pace with competitors in both fashion and performance markets, they are splitting into two units so they can focus their actions on performance and fashion, separately.

Citing that the structure will "enable us to move even more quickly to respond to consumer needs," Reebok claims it will shorten its product development cycle to three to six months for its lifestyle footwear. "Fashion is a very quick-moving phenomenon. To be competitive, we have to be able to do this."[28]

Some industry analysts believe the division of function will be a good move since marketing performance shoes is very different from marketing lifestyle shoes. Others, however, disagree saying that with a split personality, Reebok has potential to further confuse the customer, disseminate uncoordi-

---

[27] Pat Sloan, "Reebok May Slip Back into Fashion," *Advertising Age,* September 4, 1989, p. 27.

[28] Joseph Pereira, "Reebok Sets Up Separate Units for Shoe Business," *The Wall Street Journal,* January 22, 1990.

EXHIBIT 21 Reebok advertising

Pump it up.

Introducing The Pump™ by Reebok. It's the
first shoe with a built-in pump that inflates to
give you a personalized fit you control with
your fingertips. You pump up by squeezing the
ball on the tongue, and release air with the
valve on back. You've never seen or felt a shoe
like this before. Check it out.

Reebok Basketball

EXHIBIT 21   *(continued)*

While it may appear that we are stretching the truth, surprisingly it's a fact.

Every time your foot strikes the ground, the impact of three times your bodyweight is sent shuddering up your legs.

Armed with this and years of research, Reebok has developed the Sole Trainer™ 5000.

With the impact of three times your bodyweight in every stride, your lightweight shoe better be cushioned.

At only 10 ounces it's a lightweight shoe, but more importantly, it's exceptionally well-cushioned.

The secret lies in the midsole. It's comprised of Hexalite,™ a unique honeycomb of highly resilient yet light thermo plastic.

(Basically, the honeycomb, one of nature's lightest yet strongest designs, absorbs and spreads shock waves over a much larger area than EVA or polyurethane.)

The bottom line is that the Reebok Sole Trainer 5000 lets you run in a durable, lightweight shoe without sacrificing cushioning or comfort.

Now that should take a load off your mind.

Reebok

EXHIBIT 21 *(continued)*

Training wheels for the feet.™

The revolutionary Agility™ shoes by Weebok® are designed to help beginning walkers the way training wheels help beginning riders – by giving them the extra balance and support they need.

The heart of the Agility system is a series of 10 strategically located pods on the sole. These pods follow the natural weight shift of the child's foot, while a snug-fitting heel cup helps

to prevent unnecessary movement inside the shoe. At the same time, Agility shoes provide greater flexibility and breathability for your child's growing feet. Visit your local children's shoe store. Compare Agility™ with other shoes. We think you'll agree that all this comfort and technology is a terrific value.

Agility. It's one of the most important advances in children's footwear in 50 years.

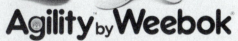

Agility by Weebok®

Weebok® shoes are carefully fitted at select children's specialty and department stores. For more information, call 1-800-843-4444.

EXHIBIT 21 *(concluded)*

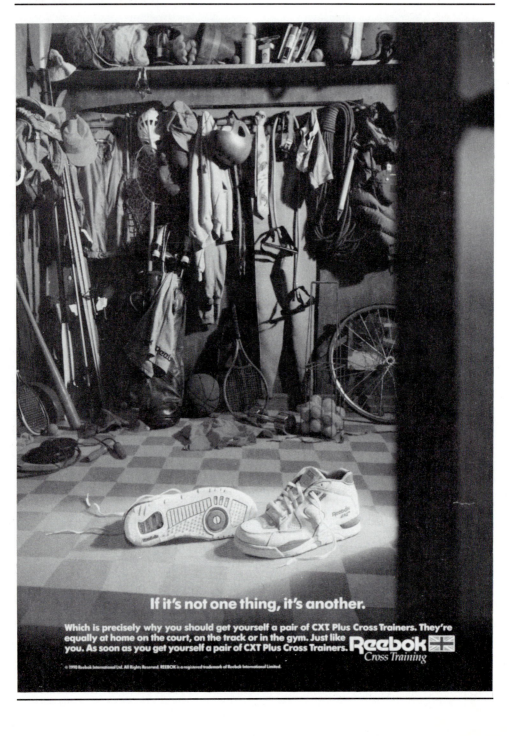

nated messages and develop a false belief that they can be all things to all people.

To complement the new structural change, the domestic and international advertising accounts are out to bid. There is speculation that two agencies may be assigned to the account, one for fashion and one for performance. Frank O'Connell, Reebok's U.S. division president, says, "We will choose the best creative in terms of advertising. We want spectacular advertising."[29] The company is looking for an umbrella campaign and hopes to have a new domestic agency by May 1, 1990.

February 19, 1990 There is speculation that Reebok's old agency now will be invited to bid for the business from which they were just dismissed. The speculation arose with the appointment of John Duerden as president of Reebok's new global marketing unit.

Duerden, the former international president, replaces Frank O'Connell. O'Connell's departure was due to Reebok's recent consolidation of U.S. and international business into one worldwide unit. This departure follows last December's resignation of C. Joseph LaBonte, Reebok international's president, and Mark Goldston, marketing chief.

March 26, 1990 Reebok's recent Pump advertisement touting the shoe's superior fit has been pulled after airing in only four spots. Reebok pulled the ad in response to customer concerns that people might imitate the bungee jumping sport shown in the commercial.

Once again, Reebok's advertising has been deemed controversial. While Reebok's premise for the ad is fit, for the first time, the company shows a competitor's shoe in the ad. In the ad, two jumpers, one wearing Reeboks, the other Nikes, leap from a Seattle bridge with bungee cords wrapped around their ankles. The elastic cord which is supposed to prevent them from hitting bottom after their thrilling free-fall ultimately works only for the wearer of the Reeboks. The audience sees the Reebok jumper hanging safely upside down while the Nike shoes float—empty—dangling in the wind.

Nike

February 16, 1990 Nike filed a lawsuit accusing L.A. Gear of misappropriating their (Nike's) intellectual property by mimicking Air Jordan's (basketball shoes). The suit cites:

- Trade dress infringement.
- (L.A. Gear style MVP-1:) Mimicking of eight to nine attributes that give Air Jordan's their distinctive recognition.
- Creation of confusion in the minds of consumers.

---

[29] Pat Sloan and Jon Lafayette, "A Race for Reebok," *Advertising Age*, January 29, 1990, p. 3.

Nike representatives state, "While imitation is a form of flattery, we think they (L.A. Gear) cross the line. . . . It's not one or two, but a bundle of them."[30]

L.A. Gear's MVP–1 style was introduced in 1989 and has produced $5 million in sales. Nike is asking for a restraining order and as of March 1990 no decision has been reached.

Analysts

Industry analysts believe the high-tech emphasis coming from shoe manufacturers is not significant in creating consumer demand. "What matters," says Samuel Krause of Durham's Athleisure of Drayton Plains, Michigan, "is that the customer tries it and makes his own decision. It gives the customer a reason to buy the product."[31]

Analysts continue to speculate how successful footwear firms will be in the 1990s. With more players, the need for more resources and effective advertising and promotions and distribution expertise, they are uncertain as to which firm will take the number one position. Already retailers from a random survey have had their thoughts published in *Sporting Goods Business*'s March 1990 issue:

- 88.3 percent—Nike
- 29.1 percent—L.A. Gear
- 28.1 percent—Reebok

With the results showing retailer's perceptions making L.A. Gear number 1 over Reebok, analysts point to L.A. Gear, in particular, trying to access their performance in the 80s and to project their success in the 90s.

They speculate whether L.A. Gear will have the products that will effectively meet their customers' constantly changing preferences, and if they will be able to keep a strong image in the consumers' minds as advertising wars escalate between the top athletic footwear players and the new entrants that may find a niche with a fad.

Clearly, the effectiveness of their product, marketing, and advertising strategies for the 1990s in developing consumer perceptions and preferences will be their major challenge.

---

[30] Ken Wells, "Is the Air Jordan Intellectual Property or Just Athletic?," *The Wall Street Journal*, February 16, 1990, p. B4.

[31] Douglas McGill, "Reebok's New Models, Fully Loaded," p. D6.